Robin Lane Fox's study of Alexander is the fullest available and has already won the Duff Cooper prize, the James Tait Black memorial prize and the W. H. Heinemann award from the Royal Society of Literature. The famous victories are discussed on their terrain, much of which the author has visited. The clues to Alexander's personality are traced from his own publicity, and the important background of his Macedonian Kingdom and the Persian Empire is seen through the many new discoveries of recent archaeology.

It is the achievement of this book to bring a colossal figure to life through his own age, not the centuries of subsequent dispute and legend.

Robin Lane Fox was born in 1946 and educated at Eton and at Magdalen College, Oxford. He teaches classics at Worcester College, Oxford and is gardening correspondent of the *Financial Times*.

Robin Lane Fox

Alexander the Great

Futura Publications Limited

An Omega Book

First published in Great Britain in 1973
by Allen Lane
A Division of Penguin Books Ltd

First Omega edition published in 1975
by Futura Publications Limited,
49 Poland Street, London, W1A 2LG

ISBN 0 8600 77071
Printed in Great Britain by
Hazell Watson & Viney Ltd
Aylesbury, Bucks

Futura Publications Limited
49 Poland Street,
London W1A 2LG

CONTENTS

TO LOUISA

ἄτλητα τλᾶσα

LIST OF MAPS

PREFACE

I first met Homer and Alexander fourteen years ago and for different reasons I have been intrigued by them ever since; if any one reader puts down this book with a wish to read Homer or with a sense of what it might have been like to have followed Alexander, I will not have written to no purpose. I have not aimed at any particular class of reader, because I do not believe that such classes exist; I have written self-indulgently, as I myself like to read about the past. I do not like the proper names of non-entities, numbered dates of unknown years or refutations of other men's views. The past, like the present, is made up of seasons and of faces, feelings, disappointments and things seen. I am bored by institutions and I do not believe in structures. Others may disagree.

This is not a biography nor does it pretend to certainty in Alexander's name. More than twenty contemporaries wrote books on Alexander and not one of them survives. They are known by quotations from later authors, not one of whom preserved the original wording: these later authors are themselves only known from the manuscripts of even later copyists and in the four main sources these manuscripts are not complete. The most detailed history goes back to only one manuscript, whose text cannot be checked; another, much used, has often been copied illegibly. Alexander left no informal letter which is genuine beyond dispute and the two known extracts from his formal documents both concern points of politics. On the enemy side his name survives in a Lycian grave-inscription, in Babylonian tablets on building work and astronomy and in Egyptian captions to temple dedications. It is a naive belief that the distant past can be recovered from written texts, but even the written evidence for Alexander is scarce and often peculiar. Nonetheless, 1,472 books and articles are known to me on the subject in the past century and a half, many of which adopt a confident tone and can be dismissed for that alone. Augustine, Cicero and perhaps the emperor Julian are the only figures from antiquity whose biography can be attempted. and Alexander is not among them. This book is a search, not a story, and any reader who takes it as a full picture of Alexander's life has begun with the wrong suppositions.

I have many debts, none more lasting than the generous support and complete freedom from duties which I have enjoyed first as an under-graduate, then as a Fellow at Magdalen College, Oxford. During my time there, Mr C. E. Stevens first showed me that history did not have to be dull to be true. Mr G. E. M. de Sainte Croix revived my interest in Alexander and fed it with many intriguing insights into the classical past. Dr J. K. Davies has been a constant source of suggestion and shrewd comment. Dr A. D. H. Bivar directed me to Iranian problems which have since become a primary enticement. The lectures of the late Stefan Weinstock on Roman religion raised much that I wanted to ask of Alexander and his remarkable book on Caesar would have raised even more if I had been able to take it into full account. But at a time when so much of ancient history is a desert, I have gained most from the lectures and writings of Mr Peter Brown; it is my great regret that there is not the evidence to begin to treat Alexander's age as he has treated late antiquity.

I am grateful to The Hogarth Press and Harcourt Brace Jovanovich, New York, for permission to reproduce the poem 'In the Year 200 B.C.' from *The Complete Poems of C. P. Cavafy* translated by Rae Dalven and to Faber & Faber Ltd and Random House Inc., New York, for permission to quote from W. H. Auden's poem *The Shield of Achilles*.

Other debts are more personal. Like Alexander's treasurer, I have been helped through solitary years by a garden and a lady, and in both respects I have been more fortunate. The garden has grown more obligingly and the lady, though not a goddess, is at least my wife.

When Alexander's sarcophagus was brought from its shrine, Augustus gazed at the body, then laid a crown of gold on its glass case and scattered some flowers to pay his respects. When they asked if he would like to see Ptolemy too, 'I wished to see a king,' he replied, 'I did not wish to see corpses.'

Suetonius, Life of Augustus, 18.1

As for the exact thoughts in Alexander's mind, I am neither able nor concerned to guess them, but this I think I can state, that nothing common or mean would have been his intention; he would not have remained content with any of his conquests, not even if he had added the British Isles to Europe; he would always have searched beyond for something unknown, and if there had been no other competition, he would have competed against himself.

Arrian (c. A.D. 150), Alexander's Expedition, 7.1

ONE

FLUELLEN

I think it is in Macedon where Alexander is porn. I tell you, captain, if you look in the maps of the 'orld, I warrant you shall find, in the comparisons between Macedon and Monmouth, that the situations, look you, is both alike. There is a river in Macedon, and there is also moreover a river at Monmouth: it is called Wye at Monmouth; but it is out of my prains what is the name of the other river; but 'tis all one, 'tis alike as my fingers is to my fingers, and there is salmons in both.

Henry V, IV, vii

CHAPTER ONE

Two thousand three hundred years ago, in the summer of 336 B.C., the king of the Macedonians was celebrating another royal wedding. For King Philip marriage was nothing new, as he had already lived with at least seven wives of varying rank, but he had never been father of the bride before; he was giving away his daughter to the young client king of Epirus who lived beyond the western border of his kingdom. There was no romance about their marriage: the bridegroom was the bride's own uncle. But the Greeks, correctly, saw neither danger nor distaste in a liaison with a niece, and for Philip, who had mostly combined his passions with sound politics, it was a convenient moment to settle a daughter within his own court circle and bind the neighbouring king to a close and approved relationship.

The occasion was planned for magnificence, and the guests were meant to find it to their liking. The Macedonian kings had long claimed to be of Greek descent, but Greeks had seldom been convinced by these northerners' insistence and only to flatterers was Philip anything better than a foreign outsider. Two years before, he had conquered the last of his Greek opponents and become the first foreign king to control the cities of mainland Greece; these cities, he had arranged, were to be his allies, allies who shared in a common peace and acknowledged him as Leader, a novel title which confirmed that his conquest was incidental to a grander ambition. As a Leader of Greek allies, Philip did not mean to stay and oppress the cities he occupied, but to march with Greeks against an enemy abroad. In the spring before the wedding he had lived up to his title and sent an advance army eastwards to fight with the Persian Empire in Asia. Now, in high summer, the full invasion awaited him, his allied Greek council had elected him to its supreme command, and his daughter's wedding was his chance for a splendid farewell. Foreign friends had been invited from conquests which stretched from the Black Sea to the coast of the Adriatic, from the Danube to the southern tip of Greece: Greek guests were coming north to see inside the Macedonian kingdom, and this wedding of niece and uncle might help to persuade them that their Macedonian Leader was less of a tyrant than they had so far protested.

But Greeks and Greek opinion were not Philip's only concern. Uneasy memories stirred nearer home, recalling his own last wedding in Macedonia more than a year ago and how it had split the royal family by its sudden implications. On the verge of middle age, Philip had fallen in love with Eurydice, a girl from a noble Macedonian family, and had decided to marry her, perhaps because she was found to be bearing his child, perhaps, too, because her relations were powerful in the court and army. His five other wives had watched the affair with indifference, but his queen Olympias could not dismiss it as another triviality among the many of the past. As mother of Alexander, Philip's only competent son, and as princess of neighbouring Epirus, she had deserved her recognition as queen of Macedonia for the past twenty years. But Eurydice was a Macedonian, and an affair of the heart; children from a Macedonian girl, not a foreign Epirote princess, could upset Olympias's plans for her own son's succession, and as soon as the two wives' families had met for the wedding banquet, that very suggestion had been voiced by Eurydice's uncle. A brawl had begun, and Alexander had drawn his sword on Philip; he and Olympias had fled the court, and although he had soon returned, she had gone to her native Epirus, and stayed there. Eurydice, meanwhile, had borne a daughter whom Philip had given the name of Europe; in the autumn, she had conceived again. Now, days before Philip's farewell for Asia, she had delivered him a son, and as Philip's foreign guests arrived for his wedding celebrations, the court and royal family were alive to a shift in the balance of favour. The baby had capped it all: it seemed impossible now for Olympias to return to her old authority.

Even in her absence Olympias had retained two claims on Philip's respect; her son Alexander and her kinship with neighbouring Epirus. One, her son, was no longer unique, and the other, her Epirote kinship, was about to be confounded by Philip's farewell wedding. It was a neat but complicated matter. Olympias was mother of the bride and elder sister to the bridegroom, but their marriage went flatly against her interests; that was why Philip had promoted it. Her brother, the bridegroom, was also the king of Epirus to whom she had fled for revenge on Philip's remarriage; she found no help, for he had spent his youth at the Macedonian court, where gossip suggested that Philip had once been his lover, and he owed his kingdom to Philip's intrigues only five years before. By agreeing to marry his niece and become Philip's son-in-law, he had compounded Olympias's injury. Political custom required that Philip should be linked by marriage to his neighbouring subjects in Epirus and Olympias had met this need for the past twenty years as an Epirote princess. But if her brother, the King of Epirus, were to marry into Philip's family

she would not be required for Philip's politics or private life. At the celebrations in Macedonia's old royal capital, the wedding guests were to
witness more than their Leader's farewell. They were assisting at the last
rejection of his queen Olympias, planned to settle his home kingdom and
its borders before he left for Asia.

They had come to Aigai, the oldest palace in Macedon and a site which
has long eluded its modern searchers. The palace, in fact, has long been
discovered and only the name has been misapplied. Aigai is not to be
found on the steep green hillside of modern Edessa beside the mountain
ranges of Bermion and Barnous, where the waterfalls plunge far into the
orchards below and where no archaeologist has found any more proof
than a city wall of the Aigai placed there by modern Greek maps; it is the
long-known palace of Vergina away to the south, where the Macedonian
tombs begin a thousand years before Philip and the northern foothills of
mount Olympus still turn back the clouds from the brown plain of lower
Macedonia, a trick of the weather which a Greek visitor to Philip's Aigai
observed as a local peculiarity. Vergina's palace now shows the mosaics and
ground plan of later kings, but Philip's ancestral palace must have lain
beside it, easily reached from the Greek frontier to which his wedding
guests had travelled by boat and horse; a brief ride inland would have
brought them to the edge of Macedonia's first flat plain, and they would
have seen no further into this land which they knew for its silver-fir forests,
free-ranging horses and kings who broke their word and never died a
peaceful death.

The wedding that brought them was planned, they found, in their own
Greek style. There were banquets and athletic games, prizes for artists
of all kinds and recitations by famous Athenian actors who had long
been favoured as guests and envoys at Philip's court. For several days the
Macedonians' strong red wine flowed freely, and golden crowns were
paid to Philip by allied Greek cities who knew where their advantage
lay. They were rewarded with happy news from home and abroad. In
Greece, the Delphic oracle had long pressed Philip's cause and its prophecy
for his invasion seemed all the more favourable in the light of eastern
despatches. His expeditionary force had been welcomed by the Persians'
Greek subjects far down the coast of Asia Minor; there were native
upheavals in Egypt, and it was rumoured that away in the Persians'
palace of Susa, a royal eunuch had poisoned the former king of the Persians, whereupon he had offered the throne first to a prince, whom he
also poisoned, and then to a lesser courtier, now acknowledged as King
Darius III. The ending of the old royal line by a double poisoning would
not encourage Persian governors to defend their empire's western fringes,

and further success in Asia was likely. It was a pleasing prospect, and when the wedding ceremony was over, Philip, Leader of the Greeks, announced a show of his own; tomorrow, in Aigai's theatre, the games would begin with a solemn procession, and seats must be taken by sunrise.

At dawn the images of the twelve Greek gods of Olympus, worked by the finest Greek craftsmen, would be escorted before the audience; in the city life of the classical world, few occasions would prove more lasting than the long slow procession in honour of the gods, and it was only natural that Philip remained true to this deep tradition. But he had added a less familiar feature, for a statue of himself was to be enthroned among those of the immortals: it was a bold comparison, and it would not have seemed odious to his chosen guests. Greeks had received honours equal to those of the gods before and already in Greek cities there were hints that Philip would be worshipped in his lifetime for his powers of benefaction. Grateful subjects believed him to be specially protected by Zeus, ancestor of the Macedonian kings, and it was easy to liken his black-bearded portrait to that of the king of the gods or to display it prominently in local temples. The sacred enthronement of his statute may have been Philip's own innovation, but his explicit aim was to please his Greek guests, not to shock them by any impiety. He succeeded, for his example at Aigai became a custom, passing to the Macedonian kings who were later worshipped in Greek Asia, from them to Julius Caesar and so to the emperors of Rome.

As the images were carried into the arena, Philip ordered his bodyguards to leave him, for it would not be proper to appear in public among armed men, the mark of a tyrant, not an allied leader. Only two young princes were to accompany him, Alexander his son by Olympias and Alexander king of Epirus, whose wedding had just been celebrated: between his son and son-in-law, King Philip began to walk forwards, settling his white cloak about a body which showed the many wounds of twenty years' fighting, one-eyed, black-bearded, a man whom Greek visitors had praised for his beauty scarcely ten years before.

He was never to reach his audience. By the theatre entrance, a young bodyguard had disobeyed his orders and lingered, unnoticed, behind his fellow officers; as Philip approached, the man moved to seize him, stabbing him and driving a short Celtic dagger into his ribs. Then he ran, using the start which utter surprise had given him; those royal bodyguards who did not race in pursuit hurried to where Philip lay. But there was no hope, for Philip was dead and Pausanias the bodyguard from the westerly hill kingdom of Orestis had taken his revenge.

At the town gates, horses and helpers were waiting by arrangement, and Pausanias seemed certain to escape. Only a few strides more and he would have been among them, but he overreached in his haste to jump astride; tripping, he fell, for his boot had caught in the trailing stem of a vine. At once three of his pursuers were on him, all of them highland nobles, one from his own kingdom. But familiarity meant nothing and they killed him, some said, then and there; others claimed more plausibly that they dragged him back to the theatre where he could be questioned for accomplices and then condemned to death. By a usual Greek punishment for robbers and murderers, five iron clamps were fixed to a wooden board round his neck, arms and legs and he was left to starve in public before his corpse was taken down for burial.

'Wreathed is the bull; the end is near, the sacrificer is at hand': Philip's sudden murder seemed a mystery to his guests and in mysteries the Delphic oracle was believed once more to have told the only truth. The oracle, men later said, had given this response to Philip in the spring before his murder; the bull, he thought, meant the Persian king, the sacrificer himself, and the oracle's verse confirmed that his invasion of Asia would succeed. To Apollo, god of the oracle, the bull was Philip, wreathed for his daughter's wedding, and the sacrificer was Pausanias; the response came true, but an oracle is not an explanation, and in history, especially the history of a murder, it is not only important to know what will happen. It is also important to know why.

Amid much gossip and confusion, only one contemporary account survives of Pausanias's motives. Philip's murder, wrote Aristotle the philosopher, was a personal affair, and as Aristotle had lived at the Macedonian court where he tutored the royal family, his judgement deserves to be considered: Pausanias killed the king 'because he had been abused by the followers of Attalus', uncle of Philip's new wife Eurydice and therefore high in Philip's esteem. Others knew the story more fully, and some fifty years later, it had grown and gained implausibilities: Pausanias, they said, had been Philip's lover, until jealousy involved him in a quarrel with Attalus, not a nobleman to be affronted lightly. Attalus invited Pausanias to dinner, made him hopelessly drunk and gave him to his gamekeepers to assault according to their fancy: Pausanias had sought revenge from Philip, but Philip was not to be turned against his new bride's uncle, so he ignored the complaints. Soon afterwards, Attalus had been sent to command the advance invasion of Asia, and Pausanias was said to have turned against the only target who remained in Macedonia: in a fit of irresponsible revenge, he had killed the king who had let him down.

Pausanias's grievance may perhaps be true, but the story which Aristotle sponsored is not a full or sufficient explanation. He mentions it in passing, in a philosophical book where Philip's murder is only one of a series of contemporary events which he can otherwise be shown to have judged too shallowly for history; he knew Macedonia well, though only as a court official, and in the matter of Pausanias it is not hard to criticize his judgement. Even if Pausanias was as unbalanced as most assassins, it was strange that he should have picked on Philip when avenging a sexual outrage allegedly sustained many weeks before from another man; too many crimes have been wrongly explained by Greek gossip as due to homosexuality for one more example to carry much conviction. There was cause, perhaps, for the story's origin; within weeks of Philip's death, Attalus would be murdered in Asia on the orders of Alexander, Philip's heir and Aristotle's former pupil. Possibly the new king's friends had blamed Pausanias's crime on the arrogance of an enemy who could no longer answer back; officially, they may have put it about that Attalus had raped Pausanias, and Aristotle believed them, involving Attalus in a murder for which he was not responsible; other enemies of the king can be proved to have been similarly defamed, and there was no name more hateful to Alexander's friends than that of Attalus.

A different approach is possible, taken from the murder's timing and its beneficiaries, both of them broad arguments but backed by facts in Pausanias's background which owe nothing to Attalus or tales of unrequited love. Pausanias was a nobleman from the far western marches of Macedonia whose tribes had only been added to the kingdom during Philip's reign; he was not a true Macedonian at all, for his tribesmen had previously paid allegiance to Epirus beyond the border and called themselves by an Epirote name. But Epirus was Olympias's home and place of refuge: she could claim past kinship with Pausanias's people, accessible even in her exile, and she might not have found it hard to work on a nobleman whom Philip had recruited away from his local friendships. The puzzle was the timing of the murder, for a Macedonian seeking revenge would not naturally wait to kill Philip at a family wedding festival, in full view of a foreign public; Pausanias, some said, was one of the seven Royal Bodyguards, and if so, he would have had many chances of a murder in private. But for Olympias, the murder had been timed and planned ideally; Philip was killed at the wedding designed to discard her, within days of the birth of Eurydice's son and within hours of the family marriage which had made her Epirote ancestry irrelevant. No sooner was Philip dead than her own son Alexander could take the kingdom from rivals and restore her to her former influence. Officially, Pausanias's outburst could be laid to Attalus's charge; Olympias, perhaps, may have known that it had begun from more desperate instigation.

Of the murder's convenience Olympias is said to have allowed no doubt:

On the same night that she returned to Macedonia, she placed a golden crown on Pausanias's head, though he was still hanging on his murderer's stake: a few days later, she took down his body and burnt it over the remains of her dead husband. She built a mound there for Pausanias and saw that the people offered yearly sacrifices at it, having drummed them full of superstition. Under her maiden name, she dedicated to Apollo the sword with which Philip had been stabbed: all this was done so openly that she seemed to be afraid that the crime might not be agreed to have been her work.

This may be exaggerated, but there is no reason to dismiss all its detail as false or as malicious rumour; its source cannot be checked independently, but Olympias was a woman of wild emotion, who would later show no scruple in murdering family rivals who threatened her. Gratitude alone cannot incriminate her but it is one more generality that involved her in what Aristotle, perhaps on purpose, failed to explain.

These generalities can be extended. Pausanias had evidently been assisted, not least by the men who waited with his other horses, and if Olympias had been his adviser, she could not have rested content with the mere fact of the crime. She was plotting for her return, and only her son, Philip's probable heir, could have guaranteed it. If she had reason to turn to Pausanias, she had reason to turn to her son Alexander, and though no remotely reliable evidence was ever cited against him, it is proper to consider his position too.

A year before, when Philip had married Eurydice, Alexander had quarrelled sharply with his father and followed his mother into retreat; he had soon been reconciled and restored to favour, as his presence at Philip's side on the day of the murder confirms, but he had not lived securely through the months since his return. Despite his age, ability still marked him out as Philip's probable successor, but he was living under the disgrace of Olympias's dismissal; too anxious for his own inheritance, he had recently caused his closest friends to be exiled, and when Eurydice bore a son his fears can only have gained in urgency. It had already been said by Attalus that Eurydice's son would be more legitimate than those by other wives and though the boy was only an infant, he had powerful relations to help him to a throne which had never passed on principle to the eldest son. He was a threat, though perhaps not an immediate one, but when Philip was murdered, Attalus was conveniently far away in Asia and the boy was only a few weeks old. No sooner was Alexander king than the baby was killed and Attalus assassinated as a traitor too far from court to rally his friends.

Fears for the succession had twice divided Alexander from Philip, but it is one thing to profit as a father's heir, quite another to kill him for the sake of his inheritance. At most Alexander was later suspected by Greek gossip; there was no evidence whatsoever against him, and theories about his presumed ruthlessness can hardly fill such a gap. A ruthless parricide would have done better to encourage a secret coup, so much safer and neater for the seizure of a throne which nearly proved elusive. A wedding festival for foreign guests was an absurdly clumsy moment for Philip's aspiring heir to stage his murder, as its witnesses would quickly spread the news and inflame the many foreign subjects he would have to retain. Alexander's first year as king showed what dangers this could mean. Whether Alexander could ever have brought himself to connive at Philip's murder is a question which only faith or prejudice can pretend to answer; they had quarrelled, certainly, but Alexander had also saved his father's life on a previous occasion, and there is no evidence to prove that he hated Philip's memory, let alone that he claimed credit for his death. Arguments from timing and benefit make Olympias's guilt a probability, Alexander's only a speculation; it is more relevant, as Alexander himself was aware, that they could be applied no less forcefully elsewhere.

'The Persians say that nobody yet has killed his own father or mother, but that whenever such a crime seems to have happened, then it is inevitable that inquiry will prove that the so-called son was either adopted or illegitimate. For they say it is unthinkable that a true parent should ever be killed by his true son.' To the Persians, as seen by a Greek observer, Alexander's complicity would have been unthinkable on a point of human principle; to Alexander it was excluded on stronger grounds. The Persians, he said, had designed the murder themselves. 'My father died from conspirators whom you and your people have organized, as you have boasted in your letters to one and all': so Alexander would write in a published despatch to the Persian king four years later, and the reference to public letters proves that the Persians' boast, at least, was a fact of history. If benefit alone is a proof of guilt, then the Persians had as much reason to murder Philip as did any outraged wife or son, for their empire, an easy eleven days' march from Macedonia, had just been invaded, and if Philip could be killed, his army could be expected to fall apart in the usual family quarrels. Persian boasts, however, are no guarantee of the truth, especially when they could have been made to attract allies against Philip's heir. Of the murder's beneficiaries, at

24

home and abroad, it is Olympias who remains most suspect; her guilt will never be proved, and the role of her son should not be guessed, but it is all too plausible that Philip was murdered by the wife he had tried to discard.

If the murder can be questioned, it is wrong to imply it can ever be solved, for even to contemporaries it remained a famous mystery. Not so its likely effects, for Philip was dead, the 'man whose like had never been seen in Europe', and there was no reason to suppose that his twenty-year-old son would ever claim his inheritance from the feuds of brother against brother, father against son which a change of king had always inspired. But within five years, that same boy would have left his father's extra-ordinary achievements far behind; he could look back on Philip, fairly, as a lesser man: he had overthrown an empire which had stood for two hundred years; he had become a thousand times richer than any man in the world, and he was ready for a march which seemed superhuman to those who freely worshipped him as a god. History has often seemed the study of facts beyond our control. With Alexander it would come to depend on the whims and choices of a twenty-five-year-old man, who ended by ruling some two million square miles.

If his effects, necessarily, were swift, their consequences would prove more lasting. 'We sit round our sea,' Socrates the philosopher had told his friends, 'like frogs around a frog-pond.' Greek art had already reached to Paris; Greeks had worked as craftsmen near modern Munich or lived in the lagoons of the Adriatic south of Venice, but no Greek from the mainland had ever been east of Susa or visited the steppes of central Asia, and the frog-pond remained the Mediterranean sea. As a result of Alexander, Greek athletics would come to be performed in the burning heat of the Persian gulf; the tale of the Trojan horse would be told on the Oxus and among the natives of the Punjab; far from the frog-pond, Greeks would practise as Buddhists and Homer would be translated into an Indian language; when a north-west Indian city came to be excavated, the love story of Cupid and Psyche was found to have been carved on ivory and left beside the elephant-goads of a local Indian mahout. Alexander's story does not end with warfare or with the problems of his personality; had he chosen differently, the ground would never have been cleared for a whole new strand in Asia to grow from his army's reaping.

Personally, his fascination was more immediate, and least of all did it die with him. His tent, his ring, his cups, his horse or his corpse remained the ambition of successors who even imitated the way he had held his head. One example can serve for them all, for once, on the eve of battle he appeared in a dream to Pyrrhus, boldest of Greek generals, and when Pyrrhus asked what help a ghost could promise, 'I lend you', he answered, 'my name.' True to the story, it was the name which retained a living fascination for two thousand years. It attracted the youthful Pompey, who aspired to it even in his dress; it was toyed with by the young Augustus, and it was used against the emperor Trajan; among poets, Petrarch attacked it, Shakespeare saw through it; Christians resented it, pagans maintained it, but to a Victorian bishop it seemed the most admirable name in the world. Grandeur could not resist it; Louis XIV, when young, danced as Alexander in a ballet; Michelangelo laid out the square on Rome's Capitol in the design of Alexander's shield; Napoleon kept Alexander's history as bedside reading, though it is only a legend that he dressed every morning before a painting of Alexander's grandest vistory. As a name, it had the spell of youth and glory: it was Julius Caesar who once looked up from a history of Alexander, thought for a while and then burst into tears 'because Alexander had died at the age of thirty-two, king of so many peoples, and he himself had not yet achieved any brilliant success'.

Alexander, then, is that rare and complex figure, a hero, and in his own lifetime, he wished to be seen as the rival of his society's heroic ideal. Through the continual interest of the educated West in the Greek past and through the spread, mostly in Oriental languages, of a legendary romance of Alexander's exploits, his fame reached from Iceland to China; the Well of Immortality, submarines, the Valley of Diamonds and the invention of a flying machine are only a few of the fictitious adventures which became linked with his name in a process which each age continued according to its preoccupations; when the Three Kings of the Orient came to pay homage to Jesus, Melchior's gold, said Jewish legend, was in fact an offering from Alexander's treasure. Nor has he been forgotten by ordinary men at either end of his empire. Because of the spread of the *Romance of Alexander*,* there are Afghan chieftains who still claim to be descended from his blood. Seventy years ago they would go to war with the red flag they believed to be his banner, while on stormy nights in the Aegean, the island fishermen of Lesbos still shout down the sea with their question, 'Where is Alexander the Great?', and on giving their calming answer, 'Alexander the Great lives and is King', they rest assured that the waves will subside.

'But where is Alexander, the soldier Alexander?' Neither fame nor legend has helped his history, and the young man who first took power from a murder at Aigai has been lost among varying stories and an array

* This legendary narrative took shape in Egypt, mostly some five centuries after Alexander's death. Earlier elements and a few facts survive among its wild fiction.

of half-reported histories. More than twenty contemporaries wrote of his career, but not one of their books survives in its original and only one extract from a letter of Alexander is genuine beyond dispute. Four hundred years or more after his death, two historians and two abbreviators interwove or cut down his original histories and it is from their long narratives that his life must mostly be recovered. Writing under the Roman empire, they did not understand Alexander's age, and it is as if the history of Tudor England could only be recovered from Macaulay's essays and the histories of Hume the philosopher. And yet by minute comparison, their originals' outline can mostly be mapped out and art and inscriptions can help to discount their prejudices; they yield a picture and by building a frame from each of the societies in which Alexander moved, this picture can often be set in a convincing perspective. Alexander is the subject for a search, not a story, for such was the style and content of his first written histories that any confident narrative can only be disreputable. Still less is he a lesson or a moral warning. To study the past for human folly or popular superstition is only to be patronizing about our own same hopes and fears, expressed in a different society. The merit of ancient Greek history is not as a moral sermon, but as a study that reaches back through a vast passage of time; it is still possible to share what men, even Alexander, experienced at such a distance, and after two thousand years, the search, though never easy, is often vivid, always worthwhile.

CHAPTER TWO

The search for Alexander begins darkly but dramatically. When Philip was murdered, the Macedonian court could only expect another of the family struggles which had weakened their kingdom for the past hundred years; such struggles are seldom reported in detail, but clues can be found, often in the most unlikely places, and together they suggest a pattern, misleading perhaps by its thinness but consistent with the way in which Macedonian kings had always had to behave. First, the pattern needs a background.

Set between northern Greece and Europe's tribesmen, Philip's Macedonia was a broad patchwork of kingdoms, stitched together by conquest, marriage and the bribes and attractions of his rising fortune. At the time of Alexander's birth, it would have seemed a land of impossible contrasts, and thirteen years of Philip's energy had not altogether removed the differences of interest which had troubled previous kings. It was still a land of lowlands and highlands, which Philip and his ancestors ruled from the south-east plains, a fenland of the four great rivers which water the crops and the winter pasturage on their rich light loam. Marshy and densely forested, these fens and their bordering hills were a land for pioneers and Philip and his ancestors had attacked them with the necessary spirit. Drainage had channelled the flooding rivers for irrigation; roads had been cut through the dense pine-forests and pitch had been boiled from their logs by a native technique and sold to Greek shipbuilders in the timberless south; old gold mines had been seized on Philip's eastern border and forced to yield a thousandfold by a mass of new slave labour and Greeks skills of extraction; wild oxen, bears and lions were hunted on horseback for sport and food; Macedonians near the coast had mastered the art of fly-fishing for trout on their rivers and had introduced the fig and olive to lands where they fruited twice yearly. 'Lovely Emathia' Homer had called these rolling plains, a fit home for herds of cattle; an old Macedonian dance mimed the life of the cattle-rustler, clearly the trade of many local farmers. Cattle had never abounded in Greece where meat was seldom tasted outside religious sacrifices; Macedon's more frequent diet of meat may not be irrelevant to her toughness on the battlefield.

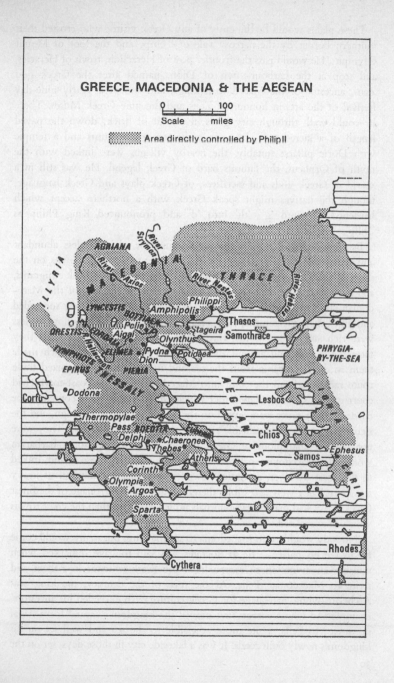

GREECE, MACEDONIA & THE AEGEAN

0 _____ 100
Scale   miles

░░░ Area directly controlled by Philip II

River Strymon

AGRIANA

ILLYRIA

MACEDONIA

River Axios

THRACE

River Nestos

River Hebros

LYNCESTIS

BOTTIAEA

Philippi

Amphipolis

Pella

Aigai

Stageira

Thasos

Samothrace

ORESTIS

EORDAEA

Olynthus

ELIMEA

Pydna

Potidaea

PHRYGIA-BY-THE-SEA

Hellespontis

STYMPHIOTIS

Dion

PIERIA

EPIRUS

THESSALY

Dodona

Corfu

AEGEAN SEA

Lesbos

Thermopylae Pass

BOEOTIA

Chios

Delphi

Chaeronea

Thebes

Athens

Ephesus

CARIA

Samos

Corinth

Olympia

Argos

Sparta

Rhodes

Cythera

These plains would be the envy of any Greek visitor who crossed their southern border by the narrow vale of Tempe and the foot of Mount Olympus. He would pass the frontier post of Heraclion, town of Heracles, and stop at the harbour-town of Dion, named after the Greek god Zeus, ancestor of the Macedonian kings, and site of a yearly nine-day festival of the arts in honour of Zeus and the nine Greek Muses. There he could walk through city gates in a wall of brick, down the paved length of a sacred way, between a theatre, gymnasiums and a temple with Doric pillars; suitably, the nearby villages were linked with the myth of Orpheus, the famous bard of Greek legend. He was still in a world of Greek gods and sacrifices, of Greek plays and Greek language, though the natives might speak Greek with a northern accent which hardened 'ch' into 'g', 'th' into 'd' and pronounced King Philip as 'Bilip'.

Bearing on up the coast, he would find the plain no less abundant and the towns more defiantly Greek. The next two coast-towns on the shore of the Thermaic gulf had originally been settled by Greek emigrants, and ever since they had watched for a chance to cut free of the Macedonian court which had grown to control them. At times they succeeded and amid their vicissitudes, they remained towns of spirit, whose leaders were rich and whose middle class could equip themselves for war; they farmed the lush land around them, and the extra revenues which made them so desirable came from the sea and its traders. A recognized trade route ran west from the coast into Macedonia, and the coast-towns had courts with a system of law under which Greek traders were content to be tried; harbour-taxes were levied on the trade that passed through, and the rich would corner the valuable right to their yearly collection. They were not the last champions of Greek culture on the fringe of a barbarian world: the Macedonian palaces of Pella and Aigai lay close inland, linked to the coast by river, antiquity's swiftest and cheapest method of heavy transport. They were accessible, therefore, and their patronage of the finest Greek artists had made their externals no less civilized than the coast towns which they coveted.

'Nobody would go to Macedonia to see the king, but many would come far to see his palace . . .'; so Socrates was said to have remarked when refusing an invitation to escape from the death-sentence in Athens and retire to Macedonian Pella. At the turn of the century, the king was Archelaus whose patronage for Greek culture even exceeded his ancestors' example and whose energy first moved the kingdom's capital from Aigai north-east to Pella, a site more accessible to the sea and well set on his kingdom's newly built roads. It was a lakeside city in those days, set on the

River Loudias and equipped with a natural harbour where the river spread out into a muddy sheet of water. By the 380s, Pella was acknowledged as the largest town in Macedonia; Philip, of course, improved it, and within twenty years of Alexander's death it would become a boom town on the profits of world-conquest, boasting temples and palaces over a hundred yards long with two or three grand courtyards each, whose colonnades of Greek pillars supported richly-painted friezes and mud-brick walls above marble thresholds and floors of pebble-patterned mosaic. It was a place where a man could banquet in surroundings that befitted the richest Greek taste; the large town houses were built round a central courtyard off which the reception-rooms opened, while a second storey housed bedrooms on the north side and cast a welcome shade in summer. These palatial houses are now well known from recent archaeology, and they probably belong soon after Alexander's death. Alexander had been brought up in Archelaus's older palace on the more westerly of Pella's two hills, and its heavy marble pillars were as fashionably Greek as those of the later houses of the lower town. It was a cultured home, probably in the style of the palaces that succeeded it; one of their later mosaic floors probably took its design of centaurs from a painting which Archelaus had commissioned from a Greek master. These famous pebble-mosaics, also the work of Greek artists, were probably laid out soon after Alexander's life at Pella, for one shows a hunting-scene from his career, another the god Dionysus, ancestor of the kings, another a lion-griffin attacking a stag, perhaps the royal seal of the kingdom or at least the emblem of Antipater whom Alexander left as his general in Macedonia. Though much admired, they come close to vulgarity; Archelaus's older palace may well have had mosaics too, for the earliest known mosaics on the Greek mainland are to be found in the northern Greek city of Olynthus which had come within the influence of Macedonia's palace, and their designs were developed from the schools of Greek painters whom Archelaus is known to have patronized. Except for a love of gardens, there is no finer test of a civilized man than his taste for paintings: in Alexander's Macedonia, too often remembered for conquest, the pillared tombs of his nobility bear the first known *trompe-l'oeil* paintings in art history on their architectural façades, and in Aigai's palace, the central courtyard may well have been laid out as a secret garden. In the new town of Philippi Philip's Macedonian settlers, the 'dregs of the kingdom' as critics called them, had planted wild roses to soften the bleakness of a home on the distant Thracian coast.

Beyond these civilized plains of the coast and lowland where the Garden of Midas turned all to green, if not to gold, lay the ridges of

Mounts Barnous and Bermion barred with snow and behind, to the west and north-west, a highland world of timbered glens and mountainous lakes which was far removed from the luxuries of coast and palace. Here men had always lived in tribes, not in towns, and their lakeside villages were often built on wooden stilts with only a dry-walled fort on a nearby waterless hilltop for refuge in case of invasion. Among Alexander's officers and among later Macedonians, the distinction remained in the tribal titles by which they identified their homes; the highlanders were tribesmen, with none of the towns to which lowlanders claimed to belong. Each of their kingdoms was sealed like a capsule by the landscape and behind their cliffs' defences, the tribal government of village chieftains survived for centuries, long outliving the dynasty of the lowland kings and their attempts to build frontier towns. Their timber, minerals, fisheries and upland grazing supported a dense population whose royal families each claimed descent from a different Greek hero. In the far south-west, adjoining Greek Thessaly, the Tymphiot tribesmen worshipped their own primitive form of Zeus, and until Philip won them over, they had no more belonged among Macedonians than the nearby Orestids who honoured their founder Orestes and had formerly joined with the western tribes of Epirus. Further north, round the lakes of Prespa and Kastoria and astride the main corridor-road from Europe, lived the rich and rebellious kings of Lyncestis who traced their origin to the notorious Bacchiad kings of Greek Corinth, as tight a family clique as any in seventh-century Greek history. These Bacchiads had been expelled from Corinth and fled north to Corfu from where, like the Corinthian trade goods which then appear in north-west Macedonia, they may indeed have found a home in mainland Lyncestis on the edge of Europe's Illyrian kingdoms. Their self-styled descendants had not disgraced them. Like other highlanders the Lyncestians dressed in the drab woollen cloak of the modern Vlach shepherd and spoke a primitive Greek dialect which southerners could no longer follow. They worked their land with ox-drawn carts and the help of their womenfolk and it is perhaps no coincidence that in the lists of the confiscated property of rich Athenians in the late fifth century far the highest price for a slave was paid for a Macedonian woman. Philip's mother had been a Lyncestian noblewoman, and she had not learnt to read or write until middle age; her kinsman Leonnatus is one of Alexander's only two known friends of Lyncestian family, and he was remembered for his bellicosity and such a taste for wrestling that he was said to have taken trainers and camel-loads of sand wherever he went in Asia.

For at least a hundred years most of these highland tribes had been formally known as Upper Macedonia, but their sympathies with lowland kings were superficial and nowhere ancient. Lyncestis, for example, was harder pressed by her Illyrian neighbours to the north than by Philip's ancestors in the plain, and her chieftains had often preferred Illyrian interests to those of the court at Aigai. A balance, though, could be worked out. The lowlanders needed the highlands' loyalties, for their tribes controlled the passes and river beds down which the European barbarians of the north and north-west had tried to invade the plains by the sea. The highlanders also needed the lowlands for the more mundane reason of their sheep. Flocks of sheep were the lasting bond of the inland landscapes of antiquity. In summer the highlanders grazed them on their glens and spurs, but in winter they drove them down to the plains for pasture, and so the moving life of the herdsman was also a life of ceaseless dispute. In spring his sheep were trampling the plainsman's crops and in summer he was herding them through the mountains, caring little for the property of this temporary home; from Orestis there has come an inscription ordering the rights of farmers against the summer grazers and setting limits on summer shepherds' cutting of wood. Probably to help his lowland farmers Philip had tried to discourage the herding of sheep and to spread the settled crop-growing which suited the plains. If he succeeded, he would have broken the one natural bond between highland and plain; he had therefore tried more official means to unite the two worlds round him.

Where possible, his lowland ancestors had driven out hill tribes altogether, from Pieria around Dion, or from Eordaia, for example, 'walled in on east, west and north by cliffs like the keep of a castle'. Elsewhere they had taken political wives, from nowhere more often than from Elimea to the south-west where noblemen were rich and tribesmen hardy in battle. Philip too had kept an Elimiot mistress, and he had also founded towns on his highland frontiers and forcibly moved a lowland population to guard them. He needed this new strength on the borders, for at the same time he was drawing the old power of the highland nobility and their young sons down to his court at Pella, where he bribed them to settle on lush estates from his conquests of grassland to the east and southeast. Highland chieftains had thus been tied more closely to a court and a king whom they served as feudal lords on conquered estates; Alexander's first months are a study in a new Macedonian society which had been slowly torn from its old ties of kinship and local territory to be grouped more tightly round its king. Part of their interest is to watch how far these old traditions still worked on a man's allegiance.

This breaking of old roots had long been a necessity for the survival of the lowland kings. Among Illyrians beyond the northern border, as in modern Albania, nobles would still go to war with their cliques of retainers and relations, but in the army which Philip inherited, the highlanders had already been brigaded by the loose geography of tribes, not the narrow allegiance of clans. Local barons and royalty still led these tribal brigades, but they had already been weaned from their private retinues and gathered over the past two hundred years as a retinue to the king himself, whom they served as honoured Companions, or even, in eight or so esteemed cases, as Bodyguards about his person. So, at his accession, Alexander was facing more than sixty Companion nobles, some of them elderly, all of them inheriting their rank from his father's reign: they were there, nominally, to assist and advise him, but if it was perhaps coincidental that the Macedonian word for a counsellor could also be derived from the word for a grey-haired man, it was certainly relevant that the kings had long extended their titles of royal honour to the thousands of lesser dependants whom they wished to befriend. The name of King's Bodyguard now also applied to 3000 lesser Shield Bearers, new king's men; the name of Companion extended to the units of small farmers who served as the royal cavalry. Once there had been a special Royal Squadron of horse, but just as the King's Own regiments in the British army grew to be recruited from Scotsmen, so all the cavalry were now called the King's Own and even the highland infantry of tribesmen were known as the King's Foot Companions in order to bind new friends to the crown. Only the former Companion nobles had lost by this spreading of their title, because the spreading had been aimed against them. As these new circles of king's men warned, it was among the nobles that Alexander's enemies were most to be feared.

Because power in Macedonia was personal, the nobles had wielded it through the tentacular links of their families. Their justice, presumably, had been the system of the blood feud which set family against family. The old kingdoms knew no courts or written law code; they relied on vengeance, tempered by a fixed price for blood. To a nobility concerned with this family power and property, marriage was not romantic but an expression of goodwill between the households of two great families. Neither the age of the brides nor their degree of affinity was any more of an obstacle than among other upper classes in Greece; the Bacchiad kings, from whom the nobles of Lyncestis claimed descent, had been famously intermarried and an element of inbreeding should be allowed for among Philip's highland Companions. This maze of marriages and blood relationships could impose rigid duties of help and revenge, as it still does among the shepherds of north-west Greece, and these duties are not always obvious to outsiders. Alexander was heir to a bevy of barons to whom the mood of a

Mafia member would seem more natural than that of a moralist.

Again, the lowland kings had long tried to replace these local loyalties by their own central authority. For crimes which could cost a suspect his life, their justice was not a blood feud but a public hearing before the people. Only if the audience agreed would the king and his agents punish. Their methods, of course, were still rough, killing both a suspect and his kinsmen. Urgent murders were still conducted privately, and even a public hearing was not democratic. The audience expressed their will by clashing their spears, not raising their hands for their votes to be counted. It was the king who decided for which verdict they had clashed the louder. As for marriage, he could take wives himself from rival families and marry loyalists to women of the wide family household which he headed. He could also promote marriages between his courtiers and if he seemed to offer a strong future, his suggested wives were not likely to be refused. It was the king's business to stand as a rival centre of power, outside the links of tribe and family. Philip and his ancestors had weakened these links until they could no longer dictate a man's behaviour; at Alexander's accession they were pressed by a broader issue, the promise, quite simply, of Alexander himself.

Alexander's royal blood commanded respect but he was not the only prince to enjoy it. In practice the throne had not always passed to the eldest son and the custom that the king should be of royal blood was a hollow one, for barons could hail a royal infant and then rule through him, while many barons could themselves claim the blood of their local royalty. Philip's baby son by Eurydice was one such danger, for barons like his great-uncle Attalus would hope to rule in his name. Although a regency was possible, it was unlikely while other princes of suitable age were alive. Here Alexander's main rival was his cousin Amyntas who had actually been a child heir to the kingdom twenty-three years before. His uncle Philip had been appointed regent and continued to rule as king when he proved his extraordinary powers of conquest and diplomacy, but Amyntas had survived, a man of twenty-five or so when Philip died, and as a sign of continuing favour, he had been married recently to Philip's daughter by an Illyrian mistress. Against Alexander, he had the vital advantage of age and, in so far as rights mattered, a claim to return to the kingship which he had once been too young to inherit. Besides Amyntas there were the highland princes who might lead their tribes to independence; there was, in the last resort, Arrhidaeus, Philip's son by a mistress from Thessaly whom gossip described as a dancing-girl. Clearly, his mother was not royal, and her low birth would diminish his status: he was also half-witted, and yet it is a fine proof of Alexander's nervousness that several months before Philip's death he feared displacement by this last resort.

As a prelude to his Asian invasion Philip had been approached by the native ruler of Caria, a country far south on the western coast of the Persian empire and invaluable to an invader with a fleet as weak as Philip's. Diplomacy, as usual, was to be sealed by marriage, and Philip had decided to offer his Arrhidaeus to the Carian's daughter: it was as delicate a bargain as all his others, for a half-witted son was a light price for such an alliance, but without Alexander, it would have worked. Just back from his months in voluntary exile, Alexander had not adjusted to the fact of Olympias's divorce. Seeing Arrhidaeus's honour as another threat to his inheritance, he had drawn his own friends around him and despatched his friend Thettalus, the famous Greek actor, to plead his cause at the Carian's court; he was no illegitimate idiot, he was a rightful son and heir, so the Carian should accept him in marriage instead. The man had been delighted beyond what he had dared to hope, but news of the offer had reached Philip first, and he had marched into Alexander's quarters, accused him of meddling and exiled the friends who had helped his interference; sensing trouble, the Carian ruler at once took fright and gave his daughter to a Persian aristocrat. A brilliant coup was ruined, because Alexander was nervous and could not understand that his father would never have wasted his heir on a passing Oriental marriage.

The Carian affair showed up Alexander's youth and sounded the first note for the grim discordance that would follow Philip's murder. The sequence of events was familiar enough. Philip and every other Macedonian king had begun their reigns with a family purge of rivals, a customary necessity in any ancient monarchy, whether Persian, Greek, Roman or Egyptian, and one which Alexander would certainly not neglect. Once these palace affairs began to seem settled, the heir would appeal to such commoners and soldiers as were near him; their support was usually a matter of course, and could be used to round off the purging of rivals. No Macedonian king was ever created by the lone fact of his commoners' support; it was worth having, but family and nobles counted for far more. They were never easily won by a younger man.

At the age of twenty, with his young friends in exile, Alexander had shown how he needed more practised support for his inheritance, and at once in the theatre at Aigai it had become clear where it might be found. As his father lay dead, first to declare for him was his namesake Alexander, a prince of highland Lyncestis, who put on his breastplate and followed his chosen king into the palace: here was more than the first sign of highland loyalty, for this Alexander was son-in-law of the elderly Antipater, one of Philip's two most respected officers and enough of a baron to create the new king. Such immediate homage was itself suspicious, and the Lyncestian's link by marriage foundered on other doubts; the sequence of events cannot be dated, but soon after Alexander had been welcomed his two brothers were killed on a charge of sharing in Philip's murder.

Round Lyncestian Alexander, not for the last time, the ties of two Macedonian families seem to have conflicted, until he had to choose between his brothers and his marriage; possibly, his homage was swift because he knew of his brothers' plottings, and yet his link with Antipater's family sufficed to keep him straight. All three brothers were sons of a man with the Lyncestian name of Aeropus, and nearly two years earlier an Aeropus is known to have clashed with Philip and been sent into exile for the trivial offence, it was said, of dallying with a flute-girl instead of appearing on parade. Possibly, two of his sons had sworn revenge for their father but failed to enlist a brother who had married away from them. Instead they may have joined in Pausanias's plot where they perhaps were the men who had waited with his horses: perhaps, but enemies' accusations are never proof of guilt, and the two Lyncestian brothers may have been rivals rather than murderers. To Alexander's supporters the distinction was hardly important; a faint trail of friends and relations suggests that their arrests were as justified as past Macedonian history made them seem.

When Philip died, wrote a biographer four hundred years after the event, 'Macedonia was scarred and looking to the sons of Aeropus together with Amyntas', and Amyntas's past suggests this informed guess may be correct. Amyntas, former child-heir to the kingdom, had recently been married by Philip to a wife who was half Illyrian. This may have helped to link him with the north-western tribe of Lyncestians and like Alexander he could point to a grandmother of Lyncestian blood. Only two more facts can be ascribed to him, both of them tantalizing; at some date, possibly in his early youth, he had probably travelled in central Greece and visited the famous cave of Trophonius, where he would have gone through an elaborate ceremonial before braving the descent to question its oracle and offering a gift, as an inscription suggests, on his own behalf. Remarkably, he was recorded as 'king of the Macedonians', possibly because he had retained his title when Philip supplanted him, possibly because his visit had occurred when Philip was still his regent. He reappears as Macedonian representative for a disputed frontier town, also in Boeotia; this honour was shared by another Macedonian who defected to Persia at Alexander's accession. This coincidence is probably irrelevant to their loyalties in 336 as their joint honour was granted at least two, maybe ten, years earlier. But another dedication from the shrine of the

37

same frontier town names a Greek contemporary, most probably a general from Thessaly who is known to have fought in Philip's advance force before he too defected to Persia. It is unsound to use these local inscriptions to link the two defectors with 'king' Amyntas. Maybe his friends were the two Lyncestian brothers who championed him, perhaps, as a king more suited to their tribe. But the defectors may have been dislodged differently, perhaps by the next coup, directed against the advance force in which one, maybe two, served. However, another Lyncestian defected too, perhaps the son of one of the suspect brothers. The links, therefore, between Amyntas, the Lyncestians and defection remain unclear, though these Macedonians' willingness to fight against their countrymen is proof of the affair's gravity.

Against Amyntas, Alexander took the traditional action, but it is not known exactly when he took it; Philip's death cannot be dated to any one summer month, although July is a sound guess, and Alexander's accession is only known to have been settled before October. Throughout those three months his baronial enemies may well have been turbulent; as quickly as possible he had the two Lyncestians executed; and, presumably soon afterwards, he had his rival Amyntas killed too, although his death cannot be dated more closely than within ten months of Philip's murder. There may have been a chase, there must have been drama, and these three deaths were only one side to the story.

Even without this 'king' Amyntas, Alexander was still exposed on two different fronts and required to appeal to three separate groups; the army and commoners in Macedonia, the palace nobles, and the advance force of some ten thousand men away in Asia. The main lines of opposition all now met in the three high commanders cut off in Asia, a convenience if Alexander acted swiftly in their absence. One was the baron Attalus, whose interest in palace intrigue was directed through his niece Eurydice and her infant son. Another was also an Amyntas, probably son of one of the offending Lyncestians; the third was Parmenion, over sixty years old and the most respected general in the kingdom. 'The Athenians elect ten generals every year,' Philip was once rumoured to have said, 'but I have only ever found one: Parmenion.' With Antipater already on his side, Alexander only needed one of the other two marshals, and as there could be no dealings with Attalus, committed to the family of Philip's second wife and loathed for his past remarks that Alexander was no longer a proper heir, he would have to turn hopefully to Parmenion. But two family ties were pulling the elderly general away from Alexander's ambitions; his daughter was married to Attalus, and his son Philotas was known for his friendship with 'king' Amyntas, one reason perhaps why he

38

had stood at the edge, not the centre, of Alexander's young circle of friends.

Alexander had one advantage, and he used it decisively: unlike his main enemies, he was at home in Macedonia with the court and the troops. Before Attalus could upset him, he gave orders for the execution of his stepbrother, Eurydice's infant son; he spared the women and the half-witted Arrhidaeus, because nobody would ever rule through them, and thereupon he presented himself to the army as the one determined heir. The government, he told them, was changing only in name and Philip's example would remain in all things; there would, however, be a brief cut in taxation, and so his father's army accepted him despite their doubts. He was secure at home, and could organize Philip's funeral to please Philip's men. Philip would lie in state behind the bronze studded doors and pillared façade of a Macedonian mausoleum near the ancient palace of Aigai, home of the royal dynasty. By tradition, his funeral games would include armed duels among warriors and perhaps the killing of the nobles accused as his murderers; then, the army would be purified by ancient ritual, being led by Alexander between two halves of a dog's corpse. The ritual would bind them to him, and if 'king' Amyntas had not yet been seized it was becoming plain that his hopes were unfounded. One of Philip's most practised diplomats was also put to death, perhaps for their sake; the army were indifferent to the family murders which marked the start of every reign.

From Asia, the outlook seemed far less fair than before. Attalus had lost his niece's baby, the only prince in his family; the elder statesmen were in peril, Olympias was returning and the troops had been wooed away by Alexander's promises. Attalus was popular with his own men, and cut off in Asia, he could only wait. It is uncertain how many months he waited, but soon, said his enemies, he received a letter from Athens, suggesting a common rebellion; he turned the letter in to Alexander, too glib a proof of his innocence, and Alexander seized his chance. Persuading a party of his newly won soldiery that Attalus was dangerous, he gave them a Greek friend as leader and ordered them to go east and arrest him, or kill him if he struggled. This Greek, Hecataeus, was a crucial supporter; later a friend of Antipater, he may have been the elderly marshal's first contribution to Alexander's reign. He led the way to the Hellespont where he ruled as local tyrant, crossed into Asia, and when Attalus struggled, put him to death. The one man who still mattered watched the coup with most welcome indifference; Parmenion allowed his son-in-law Attalus to go to his death, preferring the cause of his own three sons who were trapped at a court secured against him. Others fled to the Persian high command, but a Greek, a Lyncestian and a senior Macedonian were no loss beside the gain of Parmenion.

With the death of Attalus, the first phase of Alexander's accession ended. His mother and his close friends could return, and with the highland tribes, he could compromise through his new clique of courtiers; the Lyncestians saw their Alexander favoured: the Orestids could look to a link with Epirote Olympias and the honour of three Orestid nobles as Alexander's intimate Companions; from Eordaea came two boyhood friends and future bodyguards; Elimea saw her nobility rise with Attalus's fall and an Elimiot, perhaps, favoured as one of Alexander's returning friends: the elderly king of the Tymphiots pledged support, helped by young Tymphiot nobles whom Parmenion would soon befriend. Each hill kingdom had its representative for the future, and over them all Parmenion and Antipater were wielding the same influence as before. And yet, on considering their king, there were those in the army who doubted him.

It is hard not to form a picture of Alexander; Alexander marching through the Libyan desert to put his mysterious questions to the oracle at Siwah, Alexander receiving the captive Persian queen and her daughters, or Alexander drunk, spearing an insolent Companion in a moment of blind passion. It is harder to be certain what he looked like, for the only descriptions are posthumous, and either designed to suit a view of his character or else derived from his many statues and portraits. Officially, Alexander liked to control these, and as an adult he would only sit to be painted by Apelles, sculpted by Lysippus or carved on gems by Pyrgoteles; some originals survive, and others can be recovered from copies, but all are stylized when they are not official, and as Napoleon once remarked 'certes, Alexandre n'a jamais posé devant Apelles'. There is none which shows him warts and all.

There are features, however, which are either too unusual or too commonplace to be artists' fictions. His skin was white on his body, a weathered red on his face; unlike his father and all previous Macedonian kings, he kept his beard clean-shaven, a fashion which enemies called effeminate but which was common among Philip's courtiers and became a precedent for all Alexander's successors. His hair stood up off his brow and fell into a central parting; it framed his face, and grew long and low on his neck, a style which was in sharp contrast to the close-cropped haircut of athletes and soldiers and was already insulted in antiquity as a sign of moral laxity. In Pella's mosaic of a lion hunt he is shown with fair hair and dark eyes and in an early copy of a contemporary painting made for a Roman owner, his dark brown eyes are suitably Latin, while his dark brown hair shows a lighter streak which was more true to life. There is nothing to challenge their evidence although legend later claimed that his left eye was black, his right one blue-green, a double colouring which was meant to suggest a magical power of bewitchment. The liquid intensity of his gaze was famous and undisputed, not least because he believed in it himself; Lysippus the sculptor caught it best, and his Successors would imitate it, not only in their own bearing but also in their portraits of Alexander which exaggerated the eyes and showed them gazing upwards to suggest his acknowledged divinity; with this famous gaze went the turning of the neck and head to one side, stressed in art but also in life, and again, an example for his Successors; it is wrong to explain this as due to a wound, for official artists would not then have emphasized it. As for his body, a pupil of Aristotle said that he was particularly sweet-smelling, so much so that his clothes were scented; this may be a compliment to his divinity, for sweet scent was the mark of a god, but more probably, the comment referred to his suspect liking for ointments and sweet spices.

Like his father, he was a very handsome young man. His nose, as statues and paintings stress, was straight; his forehead was prominent and his chin short but jutting; his mouth revealed emotion, and the lips were often shown curling. But art could not convey his general manner, and for his subjects that was more important. He walked and spoke fast, and so therefore, did his Successors; by contemporaries, he was believed to be lion-like in appearance and often in temper, and for a young man of streaming hair and penetrating gaze the comparison was apt, the more so as he had been born under the sign of Leo and was best known from the portraits on his coins, which showed him in the lionskin cap of his ancestor Heracles, a headdress he may have worn in everyday life. Later, the comparison was overdone, and his hair would be said to be tawny and even his teeth to be sharp like a lion cub's.

The problem, however, is his height, for no painting betrays it, any more than a Van Dyck reveals the smallness of Charles I. Certainly, he was smaller than Hephaistion, the man he loved, and he may well have been smaller than almost anyone else; when he sat on the throne of the Persian king, he required a table, not a stool, for his feet, and although the throne was designed to be high, this suggests a definite shortness of leg. His only measurement is given in the fictitious *Romance of Alexander*, where he is said to have been three cubits, or four feet six inches high; this surely cannot be correct, nor can it confirm his historical smallness, although legend liked to play on the theme that the world's great conqueror was reduced to a mere three cubits of earth. Only in German myth was Alexander remembered as king of the dwarfs, and it would perhaps be rash to explain his ambition on the assumption that he was unusually small. Physically, however, Alexander had inherited all of his father's toughness against wounds and climate.

To his Macedonians this new king would have seemed, above all else, young. His long hair, fresh clean-shaven skin and nervous energy belonged to the very essence of youth, and there was little enough in his past to imply that audacity would now be tempered with discretion. Two years before, he had galloped at the head of the cavalry charge which had defeated the army of Philip's Greek enemies, and after the battle he had gone as one of three envoys to Athens, the city which so affected his later politics in Greece. He had served with his father on a march to the Danube and two years before that, at the age of sixteen, he had held the seal of the kingdom while his father was away at Byzantium. Most notably, he had led an army to victory against a turbulent Thracian tribe and founded his first city, Alexandropolis, to commemorate this dashing success. There was decided promise in such behaviour, but more than promise was needed if Philip's inheritance was to be held together.

The tribes of Illyria threatened to north and west; to the east, Philip's many new cities could hardly suffice to hold down Thrace along the banks of the Danube and the shore of the distant Black Sea. The advance army, split by a quarrel, had begun to be hard pressed in Asia; to the south, there were few Greek states who did not see the death of their allied leader as the start of a new independence. Troubles within Macedonia had been settled with such speed and ruthlessness that the highlands had not, after all, deserted and Philip's two most respected generals had ignored their families to pledge support. But Olympias was back, and never peaceable. It may be significant that Alexander's two most trusted Macedonians, Perdiccas and Craterus, came from Orestis, the hill kingdom once closest, politically, to Olympias's own. There is reason to suppose that his intimate friend and future historian, Ptolemy, was born in Orestis too. If so, Alexander's personal clique may have drawn heavily on friendships derived from his mother, and after his mother's possible role in Philip's murder, these allegiances might not be to every courtier's taste. The deeper question of the new king's abilities remained, and an answer could only be gleaned from memories of his earlier years; men would be looking backwards, and in search of Alexander, it is time to turn in that direction too.

CHAPTER THREE

Born in an age when biography had not developed, Alexander is fortunate in the lack of detail for his early years. If children find childhood a time of boredom, the same is seldom true of their biographers, for nowadays, childhood is seen as a source of so much that follows and there may be lasting significance in the experiences of youth. In antiquity there was no psychological theory, and not until Augustine would a man write memoirs which treated the child as father of the man. Life's perspective was reversed, and youth was mostly described through a series of anecdotes which falsely mirrored the feats of the adult future; proven kings or bishops were remembered as kings or bishops when young, and so it was said of the boy Alexander, future conqueror of Persia, that he had once astonished Persian ambassadors to his father's court by precocious questions about their roads and resources. Such stories are no less suspect for being fashionable. At least three of Alexander's historians had grown up with him, and one wrote a book on his upbringing; another may have been connected with his first literary teacher, but none of their works survives, and Alexander's youth is left mostly to romance and fancy, to three famous figures, his mother, his horse and his tutor who have inspired a world of legend of their own.

Alexander was born son of Philip and Olympias in 356 B.C., at a time when his father's expansion to north, south and east was already proving diplomatic and extremely profitable. Three different dates are given for the day of his birth; accurate records for birthdays are a modern addition to history, and indeed it had once seemed strange to the Greeks that the Persians should celebrate their birthdays at all, but in Alexander's case, the disagreement was not only due to ignorance. Of the three dates mid-July, on or near 20 July, is the most plausible; one of his officers later vouched for a date in October, but this may be a confusion with his official birthday, which came to be celebrated, as in Persia, on the date of his accession. The third date, 6 July, reflects a different fashion, for the day was sacred to Artemis, goddess of childbirth and hence especially auspicious. In the same spirit, it could be said that Alexander's birth concided with the fire that destroyed the goddess's great temple at Ephesus, because she was away supervising Alexander's arrival and had left her

43

temple to chance, a fact which caused her Oriental priests to prophesy the birth of disaster for Asia's peoples.

There was also dispute about his parents. Much of this was posthumous legend; the Persians later fitted Alexander into their own line of kings by a story that Olympias had visited the Persian court, where the king made love to her and then sent her back to Macedonia because her breath smelt appallingly bad. There was more to the argument than nationalist romance. Olympias, it was said, probably by Alexander's own court historian, spread wild stories about the manner of Alexander's birth and referred his origins to a god: this will raise acute problems later in his life, but for the moment it is enough to remember that Olympias was a divorced woman who might well disown the husband who betrayed her. Her past behaviour and her character, itself a problem, make this only too plausible.

Olympias was an orphan under her uncle's guardianship when Philip first met her; they caught each other's eye, so the story went, while they were being initiated into a mystery religion of underworld demons on the island of Samothrace; falling in love, they promptly married. There could be few more dramatic settings for romance than a night-time ceremony by torchlight in the huge triple-doored hall of Samothrace, and certainly, the mystery cult was later favoured conspicuously by Macedonians and their kings, a fashion which Philip himself may have started. Problems of age and dating confuse the story; perhaps Philip and Olympias first saw each other on Samothrace, but others maintained more plausibly that they did not marry until the year before Alexander's birth, when Philip had already stretched his power to the south and north-west of Macedonia and would have welcomed a political marriage with Epirus's princess. But the story of her Samothracian love-affair fitted the popular views of her person, and these are more difficult to judge.

Olympias's royal ancestry traced back to the hero Achilles, and the blood of Helen of Troy was believed to run on her father's side; there is no contemporary portrait of her, but stories of her wild behaviour multiplied beyond the point of verification. They turned, mostly, on religion. Worship of Dionysus, Greek god of nature's vital forces, had long been established in Macedonia, and the processions which led to the slaughter of a goat and the drinking of its blood, or even in extreme cases to a human sacrifice, were nothing new to the women of the country. To the Greeks, Olympias was known as a devoted Bacchant, or reveller in the god's honour, and there must be truth in their exaggerations; she would head the processions herself, and on Philip's Macedonian coins, as never before, the portrait of Heracles, ancestor of the kings, is often combined with the grapes and cups of Dionysus, a deity honoured in Macedonia but surely also a reference to the religious preferences of the queen. 'During his rites', it was said, 'Olympias would drag out long tame snakes for the worshippers to handle; they would lie concealed in the ivy and ceremonial baskets, rear their heads and coil themselves around the wands and garlands of the women, so as to terrify the men.' Again, there is truth in this, for according to Cicero, Olympias kept her own pet snake, and snake-handling is a known practice in the wilder sorts of Greek religion; when Olympias's childhood home at Dodona was excavated, archaeologists were much impressed by repeated signs of its people's fondness for snakes.

'Whereas others sacrifice tens and hundreds of animals,' wrote Aristotle's most intelligent pupil, 'Olympias sacrifices them by the thousand or ten thousand.' Theophrastus would have known Olympias personally, and although he had cause to slander her his remark confirms her strong attachment to religious ritual which letters and stories of doubtful authorship suggest. On Alexander this example would not be wasted. His mother's wild mysticism was also combined with a quarrelsome temper and a reputation, at least partly deserved, for atrocity; certainly, she quarrelled with royal officials and other women of the family, and whatever the truth of Philip's murder, she showed herself as capable as any other Macedonian of killing family rivals who threatened her. The methods and number of these murders were enlarged upon by Greek gossip. whereas in Macedonia they were not inexplicable, but here too gossip was founded on truth. When Alexander heard how his mother was quarrelling with Antipater in his absence, he is said to have complained that she was asking a high price of his patience in return for the nine months she had taken to bear him. There can be no doubt that Alexander's mother was both violent and headstrong. She was seldom, however, without provocation.

The influence of this highly emotional character on Alexander's development can be guessed but never demonstrated. For the last eleven years of his life, he never saw her; she still cared for him, and so, for example, she would send a dedication to the goddess of Health at Athens when she heard that he had recovered from a serious Asian illness; although they wrote letters to each other, no original survives of any significance. As a baby, she handed him over to a well-born Macedonian nurse, but she still took a mother's interest in his education; his early life can hardly be traced beyond his various tutors, but it was Olympias who began the choosing of them. From her own family, she chose Leonidas, and from north-west Greece, an area close to her home but not known for learning, came Lysimachus, a man of middle age; their welcomes made an amusing contrast. Lysimachus was much loved by Alexander and later followed him into Asia, where his pupil one day risked his life to save him. Leonidas was stern, petty and prying. He believed in hard exercise and, it was said, he would rummage through Alexander's trunks of clothing to satisfy himself that nothing luxurious or excessive had been smuggled inside; he reproached his pupil for being too lavish with his sacrificial offerings. At the age of twenty-three Alexander was able to retort. He had already routed the Persian king, and from the Lebanon he sent Leonidas a gigantic load of precious incense, pointing his present with a message: 'We have sent you frankincense and myrrh in abundance, to stop you being mean to the gods'; there is nothing worse than an old man's meanness, and Alexander used humour and generosity to show it up.

Of his other Greek teachers nothing certain is known, and not until the age of ten does Alexander appear for the first time in contemporary history. This appearance is itself unusual, and a proof that teachers had been busy with their job: it is to be found in the public speech of an Athenian politician. In the spring of 346 Philip's court had been thronged with ambassadors from all over Greece, none more prominent than those from Athens with whom, after much negotiation, he was preparing to swear an agreement of peace and alliance; they dined with him, and after dinner they saw Alexander for the first time. 'He came in,' said Aeschines the ambassador, 'to play the lyre, and he also recited and debated with another boy'; the memory was only revived back in Athens a year later, when the ambassadors had begun to disagree among themselves, for accusations flew in public that one or other Athenian had secretly flirted in Macedonia with the boyish Alexander. In these slanders his after-dinner performance before the ambassadors was used as a sexual *double entendre*; such bland charges of homosexuality are an interesting comment on their society, and ten years later, when a grown-up Alexander marched on Athens and demanded the surrender of her leading politicians, they must have seemed a very distant irony.

Poetry and music continued to hold Alexander's attention throughout his life; his musical and literary competitions were famous all across Asia, and his favour for actors, musicians and friendly authors needs no illustration. In music, especially, his interest was perhaps more popular than informed. He enjoyed the rousing pieces of Timotheus, a poet and composer who had once visited Macedonia, and his own learning of an instrument is nicely put in a story, well found if not original: when Alexander asked his music-teacher why it mattered if he played one string rather than another, the teacher told him it did not matter at all for a future king, but it did for one who wanted to be a musician. For Macedonians, music was one of life's luxuries, and when Alexander next comes into view, at the age of eleven or so, it is in a more Macedonian manner.

'Every man who has loved hunting', the Greek general Xenophon had recently written, 'has been a good man.' No Macedonian at Philip's court would have quarrelled with his judgement, for hunting was the focal point of a Macedonian's life. Bears and lions still roamed the highlands, and elsewhere there were deer in abundance, for whose sport Macedonians grouped themselves in hunting societies with the hero Heracles as their patron, honoured under a suitable title of the chase. Alexander remained true to his native pastime. If he had a favourite interest, it was hunting, and every day, if possible, he liked to hunt birds and foxes; he was always keen to be shown fine dogs, and he was so fond of an Indian one of his own that he commemorated it by giving its name to one of his new towns. He also needed a horse both for war and relaxation. By the age of twelve, he had found one, for it was at this early age that he first met his black horse Bucephalas, with whom he would one day ride to India and far on into legend and distant memory, Bucephalas the first unicorn in western civilization, Bucephalas the man-eater whose master would conquer the world, Bucephalas born of the same seed as his master and whinnying and fawning with his front legs at the sight of the only man he trusted.

The tale of his arrival is irresistible, and it was probably told by Alexander's future master of ceremonies, a man inclined to romance but none-the less present at royal dinner-parties where he would often have heard the story. Demaratus the Corinthian, most valued of Philip's Greek friends, had bought the horse from his Thessalian breeder for a price said to be as high as thirteen talents, more than three times higher than any paid for other known horses in antiquity, and having bought it, he gave it as a present to Philip; Bucephalas must have been youthful to be so expensive, and the date of the gift is a nice point. Later, Alexander's officers believed Bucephalas to have been born in the same year as his master, but by then the horse was ageing and their dates can only have been a guess; it is an important fact that the Greeks never knew how to tell an adult horse's age from its teeth. Bucephalas's arrival can be dated better from the giver than the horse, for when Alexander was twelve, Demaratus had sailed to Sicily as a general, where he stayed to fight for some four or five years; probably, he had given Bucephalas before he left, and so Alexander was still a boy, a probability which makes the story more remarkable.

On arrival in Macedonia, Bucephalas was led out into the plain for Philip's inspection, but he bucked and reared and refused to heed any word of command, and Philip ordered him to be taken away. Alexander had seen differently. Promising to master the animal, he ran towards him, took him by the halter and turned him towards the sun; by a plausible trick of horsemanship, he had noticed that Bucephalas was shying at his own shadow, so he patted, stroked and soothed, leapt astride and finally cantered round to shouts of applause from the courtiers and tears of joy from Philip, who is said to have predicted that Macedonia would never contain such a prince. Bucephalas was Alexander's for the keeping, and he loved the horse for the next twenty years; he even taught him to kneel in full harness before him, so that he could mount him more easily in armour, a trick which the Greeks first learnt from the Persians.

Already a horseman and a musician, Alexander passed his early years at Pella, and the contrasts in Macedonian life were all the sharper for being met at Pella's court. The Macedonian kings, who maintained that their Greek ancestry traced back to Zeus, had long given homes and patronage to Greece's most distinguished artists; Pindar and Bacchylides the two lyric poets, Hippocrates the father of medicine, Timotheus composer of choral verse and music. Zeuxis the painter, Choerilus the epic poet, Agathon the dramatist had all written or worked for Macedonian kings of the previous century. Most memorable of all, there had been Euripides the playwright who had left his Athens on the verge of old age and come to live at King Archelaus's Pella, where he was made an honorary Companion; he died, it was said, from a pack of wild dogs, owned by a Lyncestian nobleman. 'Loudias', he wrote of Pella's main river, 'generous giver and father of men's prosperity, whose lovely waters wash a land so rich in horses.' Alexander could quote Euripides's plays by heart and would send for his plays, together with those of Sophocles and his greater predecessor Aeschylus, as his leisure reading in outer Iran. It was Macedonia, perhaps, which left the deeper mark on its visitor, for it was probably there that Euripides wrote his Bacchae, the most disturbing and powerful play in Greek literature; its theme was the worship of Dionysus, and the Macedonians' wild cult of the god, which Olympias later upheld, may have worked on his imagination no less than the lush green landscape, which moved him to some of the few lines in Greek poetry with a romantic feeling for nature.

The entertainment of these artists was only part of a wider encouragement of Greek settlers. The kings had given homes to many Greek refugees, once to a whole Greek town; they had welcomed exiled politicians from cities like Athens who could be usefully bribed with lowland farms.

At the end of the fifth century Macedonian noblemen had fled for refuge to Athens. Some thirty years before Alexander's birth Pella was over-run by Greek neighbours, and in Philip's youth more than fifty Companions went as hostages to Thebes. These interludes among Greek culture must each have left their mark, even if other contacts were less of an enhancement: 'While we were in Macedonia,' the Athenian Demosthenes told his audience, back from his embassy to Philip's Pella, 'we were invited to another party, at the house of Xenophron, son of Phaidimus who had been one of the Thirty: naturally, I did not attend.' The orator was playing on every prejudice in his democratic public; Macedonia, a party, and worse, a son of the Thirty, for the Thirty were the toughest junta in Athenian history, having briefly tyrannized Athens at the turn of the century. 'He brought in a captive lady from Greek Olynthus, attractive, but free-born and modest, as events proved. At first, they forced her to drink quietly, but when they warmed up – or so Iatrocles told me the next morning – they made her lie down and sing them a song'; the wine took hold, butlers raced to fetch whips, the lady lost her dress, and ended up with a lashing. 'The affair was the talk of all Thessaly, and of Arcadia too.' Demosthenes had made his point; the Pella at which Alexander grew up was a congenial home for a junta member, and the court which patronized Greek art also received Persian aristocrats in exile and invited the philosopher Socrates, although under sentence in democratic Athens because of his excessively right-wing circle of gentlemen pupils.

Men who have to import all their art never lose a streak of brashness. 'They gamble, drink and squander money', wrote one visiting pamphleteer about Philip's Companions, 'more savage than the half-bestial Centaurs, they are not restrained from buggery by the fact that they have beards.' Theopompus, the author, was a man who wrote slander, not history, and his judgement is certainly exaggerated. Philip he called 'the man without precedent in Europe', a comment that referred more to his alleged vices than to his energy and diplomatic skills. But he had a certain truth, for Macedonians, especially highlanders, were indeed a rough company, as barbarous as the crude styles of their native pottery which persisted, of no artistic merit, long after Alexander's conquests. Young Alexander would have to fend for himself among them, but friends and stories show that the Greek civility at court already attracted him more. His reign and patronage saw a golden age of Greek painting, many of whose masters were drawn from cities governed by his friends, and from an early age, there are stories to show that he knew how to treat them. Once, when he arranged for his favourite painter Apelles to sketch a nude of his first Greek mistress

Campaspe, Apelles fell in love, so he found, with the girl whom he was painting. So Alexander gave him Campaspe as a present, the most generous gift of any patron and one which would remain a model for patronage and painters on through the Renaissance and so to the Venice of Tiepolo.

As Philip's fortunes rose, the court at Pella became increasingly cosmopolitan, a change that goes far to explain his son's sudden success. From the newly conquered gold mines on his eastern border, there was a sudden flood of gold to attract Greek artists, secretaries, doctors of the Hippocratic school, philosophers, musicians and engineers in the best tradition of the Macedonian monarchy. They came from all over the Aegean world, a secretary from the Hellespont, painters from Asia Minor, a prophet, even, from distant Lycia, who wrote a book on the proper interpretation of omens; there were also, as befitted him, the court fools, those 'necessary adjuncts of absolute monarchy', and the flatterers who wrote for pay. As Alexander grew up, he could talk with a man who had lived in Egypt or with a sophist and a secretary from Greek towns on the Dardanelles: in the late 350s, the exiled Persian satrap Artabazus brought his family to Pella from Hellespontine Asia and here Alexander would have met his beautiful daughter Barsine for the first time. Some ten years older than Alexander she could never have guessed that after two marriages to Greek brothers in Persian service, she would return to this boy among the spoils of a Persian victory and be honoured as his mistress, while her father Artabazus would later surrender near the Caspian Sea and be rewarded with Iranian satrapies in Alexander's empire. Barsine's visit had started a very strange trail for the future. No contact was more useful than this bilingual family of Persian generals whom Alexander finally took back on to his staff in Asia.

Among Greeks at Pella, Alexander made friends for a lifetime with Nearchus the Cretan, well versed in the ways of the sea, and with Laomedon from Lesbos, who could speak an Oriental language, while from the western end of the Greek world the old family friend Demaratus returned from Sicily with stories of the Greeks' recent fight for freedom. Six of the fourteen Greeks known as Alexander's Companions first came to Macedonia in Philip's reign, and there were others, less talented in war, with whom he retained a lasting friendship. Aristonicus, for example, his father's flute-player who later died in Afghanistan 'fighting not as a musician might, but as a brave man' and whose statue Alexander set up at Delphi, or Thettalus the tragic actor, whose playing of Oedipus had won him prizes at Athens and who remained a close friend from boyhood to death.

This Greek class of king's friends were chosen for merit; the Macedonian aristocracy of King's Companions were assured by birth, and the growing pressure of Greek outsiders was one of the uneasier currents at the court of Philip and Alexander. Under Alexander, Macedonians defined themselves sharply as a distinct class against the Greeks, not in terms of race, for the Macedonians claimed to be of Greek ancestry and immigrant Greeks like Nearchus the Cretan or Androsthenes, son of an exiled Athenian politician, became recognized as Macedonians when they received estates near the lowland coast. The distinction was one of status and all the sharper for being so; Eumenes the secretary, Critobulus the doctor, Medeius the cavalryman remained mere Greeks against whom a mood of Macedonian superiority was never far from the surface. So Alexander was growing up a Macedonian in a rough Macedonian world, the more so as his father had brought the life of Macedonia's highlands directly into his daily circle: he had decreed that the sons of highland nobles should serve and be educated as pages at Pella. The plan was greatly to Philip's advantage, for the pages were a valuable hostage for the conduct of their baronial fathers, and as they grew up, they were given new estates and revenues from newly conquered farms in the lowlands to endear them to their second home. Alexander profited too; men of two worlds, the pages became officers more likely to be loyal, for they arrived in the lowlands at the age of fourteen and naturally, they turned to a prince of their own age for friendship. In four known cases, sons of the highland nobility rehoused at Pella are future members of Alexander's bodyguard, that intimate clique of seven or eight of his most trusted friends. This bridging of Macedonia's contrasts was of the greatest consequence for the age that followed.

As royal pages, they were educated and set at the centre of affairs. They dined and listened at the king's dinner table, guarded his bedroom, helped him astride his horse and accompanied him out hunting or in war; in return, only the king was allowed to flog them. Their life was still rough and uninhibited, but there was a new side to it: Even in the towns which Philip was building in the highlands there were none of the signs of cultured life, but at Pella the sons of Upper Macedonia could take the plot of a Greek play in their stride, learn a Greek poem, listen to Greek orators, move among Greek paintings and sculptures, discuss modern strategy and know of its history and theory, attend a Greek doctor and watch Greek engineers at work. Like the warlords of Heian Japan who absorbed all their skills from China, the Macedonian barons owed their broader horizons to Greece. There had been highlanders of note before, a diplomat, for example, or a vigorous leader of cavalry, and against the long tradition of Greek culture. Macedonians of another age had already distinguished themselves; Antipater, Alexander's elderly viceroy, wrote a military history and edited his own correspondence, and Philip himself was a fluent public speaker. But Alexander's age-group grew to a new variety. Ptolemy, like Nearchus the Cretan, wrote an artful history, more notable for its attitude to Alexander than its rough literary style and Marsyas, brother of Antigonus the one-eyed, produced three books on Macedonian affairs. To Hephaistion, Alexander's favourite, two Greek philosophers dedicated volumes of letters, while Lysimachus listened attentively to a Brahmin guru in India and took an interest in botany and trees. Whereas Philip's mother had not learnt to read or write until middle age, Peucestas learnt to speak Persian and showed a marked favour for the customs and dress of the Persians he came to govern. As befitted the new generation that planned to invade Persia, Herodotus's great history of the Persian wars was read and enjoyed by Alexander's friends; one of Philip's Greek visitors had produced a shortened version, perhaps at Philip's request, and Alexander knew it enough to quote and follow its stories; both Ptolemy and Nearchus were influenced by Herodotus's way of seeing the foreign tribes of the north and east, although they could not aspire to his style. Whereas their highland fathers had owned rough pottery, primitive bone bracelets and archaic swords with gold-plated handles, this new generation had the money and taste for paintings and mosaic floors; their mothers had worn gold jewellery in rough and primitive styles and joined in battles against barbarians, but Alexander's friends maintained Athenian mistresses and introduced their women to bracelets and necklaces of oriental elegance and their artists to Iranian carpets whose patterns they copied in painted friezes. The tough life of drinking, hunting and war persisted, but there was more to Alexander's officers than is usually credited; out in Babylonia, Harpalus would help to supervise the largest treasury in the world and see to new plants for an oriental garden, while one of Antipater's sons became a drop-out and founded a community on Mount Athos with an alphabet of its own. Nothing could be further from the highland customs of his father's contemporaries; again Alexander escaped a purely Macedonian life.

Alexander, therefore, was finding his feet among adventurous friends in a widening world. His father Philip could do little more than guide the process, for in the years while he marched between the Dardanelles and the Dalmatian coast, fighting, founding towns and always negotiating for control in the Greek cities to the south, he could only appoint the most suitable Greek tutor for a son who had already outgrown his boyhood attendants. The post was enviable, and the candidates who hoped for it were a measure of Philip's new influence. He had long had close links with Plato's pupils, both as a boy and as a politician, and in Athens the most famous teacher and speaker of the age had been his continual correspondent and might expect, in return for his flattering letters, that the tutor's job should go to one of his many former students. Candidates were canvassed from far Aegean islands and Ionian cities of Asia with the usual academic warring, but while praises of Philip were being sounded by the hopeful the king made up his mind; from the island of Lesbos, he sent for Plato's most brilliant pupil, Aristotle son of Nicomachus, 'thin legged and small-eyed' and as yet unknown for his philosophical publications.

'He taught him writing, Greek, Hebrew, Babylonian and Latin. He taught him the nature of the sea and the winds; he explained the course of the stars, the revolutions of the firmament and the life-span of the world. He showed him justice and rhetoric: he warned him against the looser sorts of women.' That, however, is only the opinion of a medieval French poet, for in his surviving works, Aristotle never mentions Alexander nor alludes directly to his stay in Macedonia. According to Bertrand Russell, Alexander 'would have been bored by the prosy old pedant', but that, too, is only a fellow philosopher's guess.

Personal connections would have drawn Aristotle to Macedonia, for his father had been a doctor at the court of King Amyntas III; Philip had also been friendly with his former patron Hermeias, who maintained an impressive local tyranny on the western coast of Asia and had married his daughter to the philosopher. Later, men said that he had taken the job to persuade Philip to rebuild his ruined home town Stageira, now annexed to Macedonia's eastern borders, but the story was told of too many philosophers at court to be especially convincing, and the ruin of Stageira was probably an error of legend; the motive may have gained favour as an answer to those who had protested, probably unfairly, that Aristotle had grown to ignore his fellow citizens. Privately, Aristotle did receive a handsome fee for his services, and so as his will proves, he died a rich man: according to rumour, Philip and Alexander also patronized his researches into natural history by giving him gamekeepers to tag Macedonia's wild animals. As the observations for his astonishing works on zoology can be shown to have been made almost exclusively on the island of Lesbos, this rumour is untrue.

'In Aristotle's opinion,' said the most reliable of his biographers, 'the wise man should fall in love, take part in politics and live with a king.' The remark, if authentic, suggests that the Macedonian visit should have made a happy memory. Critics complained that Aristotle had gone to live in a 'home of mud and slime', an allusion to Pella's lakeside site, but before long Alexander and his friends were sent to the lowland town of Mieza where they could learn in a peaceful retreat of grottoes and shaded walks, believed to be sacred in the nymphs; traces of their school surroundings have recently been found near modern Naoussa, but how long this interlude lasted and how continuously the boys were taught is far from certain. After two years, Alexander became involved in government business, and although Aristotle is known to have been in Macedonia the following summer, it may no longer have been as a tutor.

Whether briefly or not, Alexander spent these school hours with one of the most tireless and wide-ranging minds which has ever lived. Nowadays Aristotle is remembered as a philosopher, but apart from his philosophical works he also wrote books on the constitutions of 158 different states, edited a list of the victors in the games at Delphi, discussed music and medicine, astronomy, magnets and optics, made notes on Homer, analysed rhetoric, outlined the forms of poetry, considered the irrational sides of man's nature, set zoology on a properly experimental course in a compendious series of masterpieces whose facts become art through the love of a rare observer of nature; he was intrigued by bees and he began the study of embryology, although the dissection of human corpses was forbidden and his only opportunity was to procure and examine an aborted foetus. The contact between Greece's greatest brain and her greatest conqueror is irresistible, and their mutual influence has occupied the imagination ever since.

'The young man', Aristotle wrote, 'is not a proper audience for political science; he has no experience of life, and because he still follows his emotions, he will only listen to no purpose, uselessly.' There speaks, surely, a man who had tried philosophy on Alexander and failed, for there is little evidence that Aristotle influenced Alexander either in his political aims or his methods. He did, however, write pamphlets for him, perhaps on request, although none survives to be dated: their titles, *On Kingship*, *In Praise of Colonies*, and possibly, too, *Alexander's Assembly* and *The Glories of Riches*, seem valid themes for a man who would become the richest king and the most prolific city-founder in the world, but Aristotle had already shown himself well able to flatter his patrons, and these works may have complimented Alexander's achievements rather than advised him to new ideas. Much has been made of Aristotle's supposed advice to 'treat the barbarians as plants and animals', but the advice may be fictitious. Although he did take the common view of his Greek contemporaries that Greek culture was superior to the ways of the barbarian east, he cannot be condemned as a thoroughgoing racist; he was interested in Oriental

54

religion and he praised very highly the constitution by which the Carthaginians were governed. When Alexander appointed Orientals to high positions in his empire, it is often said that practice had shown him the narrowness of his tutor's views on foreigners; their differences are not so very marked. Aristotle's political thought was formed from life in a Greek city, and it was these same Greek cities that his pupil planted from the Nile to the slopes of the Himalayas, where they lasted and mattered far longer than any age of kingship whose supposed importance Aristotle is often criticized for failing to anticipate. Not only through his cities, Alexander remained a Greek by culture in the world of the east, and although politics and friendship caused him to include Orientals in his Empire, he never took to Persian religion and may never have learnt an eastern language fluently.

Though politics were not at issue, a boy could not help learning curiosity from Aristotle, and to fourteen-year-old Alexander, he would seem less the abstract philosopher than the man who knew the ways of a cuttlefish, who could tell why wrynecks had a tongue or how hedgehogs would mate standing up, who had practised vivisection on a tortoise and had described the life cycle of an Aegean mosquito. Medicine, animals, the lie of the land and the shape of the seas; these were interests which Aristotle could communicate and Philip had already instanced, and each was a part of adult Alexander. He prescribed cures for snakebite to his friends, he suggested that a new strain of cattle should be shipped from India to Macedonia: he shared his father's interest in drainage and irrigation and the reclaiming of waste land; his surveyors paced out the roads in Asia, and his fleet was detailed to explore the Caspian Sea and the Indian ocean; his treasurer experimented with European plants in a Babylonian garden, and thanks to the expedition's findings, Aristotle's most intelligent pupil could include the banyan, the cinnamon and a bush of myrrh in books which mark the beginnings of botany. Alexander was more than a man of ambition and toughness; he had the wide armoury of interests of a man of curiosity, and in the days at Mieza there had been matter enough to arouse them. 'The only philosopher', a friend referred to him politely, 'whom I have ever seen in arms.'

To Aristotle the meeting may have seemed more irksome. The young, he wrote.

are at the mercy of their changeable desires. They are passionate and quick tempered, they follow their impulses: they are ruled by their emotions. They strive for honour, especially for victory, and desire them both much more than money. They are simple-natured and trusting, because they have not seen otherwise. Their hopes fly as high as a drunkard's, their memories are short.

They are brave but conventional and therefore easily abashed. Unchastened by life, they prefer the noble to the useful: their errors are on the grand scale, born of excess. They like laughter, they pity a man because they always believe the best of him ... unlike the old, they think they know it all already.

Behind such a confident analysis, there must be memories of Alexander and his fellow pupils. 'A child must be punished ...': 'the young do not keep quiet of their own accord', wrote Aristotle, 'but education serves as a rattle to distract the older children,' Discipline, it seems, was none too easy at Mieza.

Alexander was not his only Macedonian pupil. Aristotle began a friendship with Antipater, a man whose varied intelligence is easily forgotten, and Antipater's sons would have come for lessons at Mieza; so would the royal pages, and perhaps also Hephaistion, son of Amyntor to whom Aristotle dedicated a volume of letters. Hephaistion was the man whom Alexander loved, and for the rest of their lives their relationship remained as intimate as it is now irrecoverable: Alexander was only defeated once, the Cynic philosophers said long after his death, and that was by Hephaistion's thighs. There is only one statue that has claims to be of him; short-haired and long-nosed, he does not look unduly impressive, but looks may not have been his attraction. Philip had been away on too many campaigns to devote much time in person to his son and it is not always fanciful to explain the homosexuality of Greek young men as a son's need to replace an absent or indifferent father with an older lover. Hephaistion's age is not known and its discovery could put their relationship in an unexpected light: he may even have been the older of the two, like the Homeric hero with whom contemporaries compared him, an older Patroclus to Alexander's Achilles.

In ancient Greece moderate homosexuality was an accepted companion of sex with wives and prostitutes. It was a fashion, not a perversion, and the Persians were openly said by Herodotus to have learnt it from the Greeks, just as émigré Englishmen have made it fashionable in smart Australian society. Extreme homosexuality and male prostitution were as absurd or abhorrent as they often seem nowadays, but between two young men or a young and an older man affairs were not unusual; homosexuality, so Xenophon had recently written, was also a part of education, whereby a young man learnt from an older lover. Such affairs could be expensive, but if they could be romanticized, they were unobjectionable.

The Macedonian nobility may have been more extreme: there was a belief among Greeks that homosexuality had been introduced by the Dorian invaders who were thought to have swept down from Europe around 1000 B.C. and settled the states of Crete and Sparta. It is irrelevant that this belief was probably false. Educated Greeks accepted it because of what they saw around them and they acted according to what they believed; descendants of the Dorians were considered and even expected to be openly homosexual, especially among their ruling class, and the Macedonian kings had long insisted on their pure Dorian ancestry. They were credited with the usual boy-lovers by Greek gossip, and king Archelaus was said to have kissed the poet Euripidts. When Theopompus the Greek pamphleteer returned from a visit to Philip's court, he enlarged most virulently on the homosexuality of its noblemen, dismissing them as *hetairai* not *hetairoi*, prostitutes not companions. He was mistrusted for his wild abuse but he is more likely to have overstated his case than invented it entirely; if so, Alexander may have grown up in a court where the conventions of age were less respected and homosexuality was practised with the added determination of men of Dorian ancestry. At the age of thirty Alexander was still Hephaistion's lover although most young Greeks would usually have grown out of the fashion by then and an older man would have given up or turned to a young attraction. Their affair was a strong one; Hephaistion grew to lead Alexander's cavalry most ably and to become his Vizier before dying a divine hero, worthy of posthumous worship.

'Sex and sleep,' Alexander is said to have remarked, 'alone make me conscious that I am mortal'; his impatience with sleep was shared by his tutor, and many stories came to be told to illustrate his continence and his consideration for women, Alexander losing his temper with a man who offered to procure him small boys, Alexander punishing Companions for rape or agreeing to help a soldier's courtship provided it was pressed by means appropriate to a free-born woman. The theme may be near the truth, but philosophers liked to spread it, and no more can be said with certainty than that Alexander respected women rather than abused them. He was neither chaste nor prudish. According to Theophrastus, pupil of Aristotle, Philip and Olympias had once been worried by their son's lack of interest in sex, so they hired an expensive whore from Thessaly and told her to liven him up, but Alexander refused her advances in a mulish way, as if he were impotent. If his parents had tried to force a girl on him, he could hardly be blamed for refusing her; however, Theophrastus is known to have been thoroughly prejudiced against Alexander and Olympias, and his charge of impotence is a slander, not least because of Alexander's fathering of three or four children. Other stories are more to the point; when Alexander heard that his sister was having an affair, he is said to have commented that he did not see why she should not enjoy herself just because she was a princess. From a man who was to sleep with at least one man, four mistresses, three wives, a eunuch and, so gossip believed, an Amazon, the comment was honest enough.

Not that the years of Aristotle's stay were only memorable for first loves and physical pleasure. There is a curious sidelight on Alexander's progress, a letter to him from the elderly Athenian Isocrates, who had corresponded with Philip and had hoped that the tutorship would be given to one of his pupils. 'I hear everybody saying', he wrote soon after Aristotle's arrival, 'that you are fond of your fellow men, of Athens and of philosophy, in a sensible, not a thoughtless, sort of way', and he followed these politenesses with the sound advice to eschew academic quibbling and devote the time to the art of practical argument. The advice was a sly insult against Aristotle, whose school of philosophy gave time to such dry debating, but the politenesses which introduced it had a certain relevance; the widening of interests which is so noticeable among Alexander's friends was itself a widening through Greek culture, and here Aristotle stands as symbol of a process which bore Alexander the most valuable fruit. Again, the sons of highland nobles had come into contact with a civilized world of thought which had been denied to their fathers; Ptolemy, a nobleman from Eordaea, was said to blush if he was asked the name of his grandmother, but he died the pharaoh of Egypt, presiding over a bureaucratic kingdom and a system of state monopolies which needed skills that owed nothing to highland tribal life. The same could be said of Perdiccas, Seleucus and the other giants of the Age of the Successors; the young nobility were learning a little of what it meant to adapt; and in explaining Alexander's extraordinary successes, a high place must go to his officers, the widening of whose early days can only have broadened their contribution to Alexander's career. Alexander's own generation grew to share and support his ambitions with a new self-confidence which could be alarming and an intelligence which often went further than mere war. Aptly, the one Macedonian who adjusted to a Persian way of life was also a man from Mieza.

But if Aristotle stands as a symbol of new horizons, he has added more to legend than to the facts of Alexander's life; to the east, especially the Arab east, the pair of them were a fascination, and their exploits as endless as the world itself, Aristotle and the Valley of Diamonds, the Wonder Stone or the Well of Immortality, Aristotle as Alexander's Vizier or as his magician, who gave him a box of wax models of his enemies and so ensured his success. In his own writings, he has left nothing to bring Alexander within reach, while the details of Pella and Olympias, Hephaistion and Bucephalas are a study in themselves but too disjointed to frame his personality. It seems as if a search for the young Alexander is bound to fail, and yet this personal issue cannot be avoided, for Alexander's personality is probably his most unusual contribution to history. As a conqueror he came less to change than to inherit and restore; but as a man he inspired and demanded what few leaders since have dared to consider possible. From his childhood there are only stories, of Alexander complaining that Philip would leave him nothing glorious to achieve, of Alexander snubbing an impossibly general question from Aristotle with a sensibly practical answer, or of Alexander refusing to compete in races unless his opponents were all of them kings; these stories are colourful, but they are mostly invented and the problem of his personality owes nothing to their perspective.

Among the scattered ruins that survive from his childhood, a personal search might well seem an impossibility, and indeed it has often been said that personal judgements on Alexander owe more to their judge's psychology than to his own. There is, however, one delicate thread to explore. It begins among the stories of his youth and it leads, through his own publicity and popular image, to the way in which he wished himself to be seen; in the search for Alexander it is wrong to suggest that the man must be disentangled from the myth, for the myth is sometimes of his own making, and then it is the most direct clue to his mind. In this case contemporary hints support it and flattery helps to give it body; there are reasons, many of them within Macedonia, for assuming that Alexander meant its pattern to be taken seriously. It is on any view unusual, for it turns, not on power or profit, but on the poet Homer.

' "Take this son of mine away." ' King Philip is made to say to Aristotle in the fictitious *Romance of Alexander*, ' "and teach him the poems of Homer", and sure enough, that son of his went away and studied all day, so that he read through the whole of Homer's *Iliad* in a single sitting.' In spirit, this charming fiction comes near to life, for the theme of Homer's *Iliad*, and especially of its hero Achilles, is the link which spans the figures and stories of Alexander's youth. Through his mother Olympias he was a descendant of Achilles; his first tutor Lysimachus owed part of his life-long favour to giving his pupil the nickname of Achilles; his beloved Hephaistion was compared by contemporaries with Patroclus, the intimate companion of Homer's hero; Aristotle taught him Homer's poems and at his pupil's request, helped to prepare a special text of the *Iliad* which Alexander valued above all his possessions; he used to sleep, said one of his officers, with a dagger and this private *Iliad* beneath his head, calling it his journey-book of excellence in war. In the second year of his march, when the Persian king had been routed, 'a casket was brought to him, which seemed to be the most precious of Darius's treasure-chests, and he asked his friends what they thought was so particularly valuable that it should be stored inside. Many opinions were expressed, but Alexander himself said he would put the *Iliad* there and keep it safe.' But the *Iliad* was among the oldest Greek poems, at least three hundred years older than Alexander and seemingly as distant as Shakespeare from a modern king.

In deciding how he meant this, there is a danger of taking publicity too seriously or of following a theme of flattery too far. Nicknames from Homer were popular in Greece, Nestor for a wise man, Achilles for a brave one, and the mood of the *Iliad* was not an irrelevant revival for Philip's heir. Homer's poems were widely known in Macedonia. One of Antipater's sons could quote Homer fluently, as could subsequent kings; even in Philip's highland Macedonia, pottery has been found painted with scenes of the sack of Troy. Philip had already been compared with King Agamemnon, leader of the Greek allies who fought for ten years round Troy, and the style of his infantry was likened to Agamemnon's; the Trojan War had been cited by Herodotus as the first cause of the ancient enmity between Greece and Asia's monarchies and Philip's pamphleteers continued to draw the parallel between a new Greek invasion of Asia and the expedition described by Homer. Past history bore witness that Agamemnon and the Trojan war were worthwhile themes for a Greek invader of Asia to evoke and imitate. But Alexander was stressing his link with Achilles, a younger and more passionate hero, and hardly a symbol of kingly leadership. There were public overtones here too, for Achilles was a hero of Thessaly, and Philip's heir was ruler of the Thessalians, a people essential for his army and control of southern Greece. Achilles was also a stirring Greek hero, useful for a Macedonian king whose Greek ancestry did not stop Greeks from calling him barbarian; in a similar vein, the great Kolokotronis, hero of Greek freedom, would dress and parade as the new Achilles when ridding Greece of the Turks in the 1820s. But, it was said, 'Alexander was emulous of Achilles, with whom he had had a rivalry since his earliest youth'; publicity and politics do not determine a young boy's heroes, and if Achilles can be proved to belong to Alexander's youth, and not to have been read back into it, then the man himself may still be within reach.

The proof is difficult, but again not impossible: it depends on a famous Athenian joke. In the year after Philip's murder, Alexander was fighting near the Danube, and back in Athens, his political enemy Demosthenes ridiculed him as a mere Margites; this obscure insult reappears in the history book of a Macedonian courtier, and it must have been apt to be remembered and repeated. Now Margites was one of the more extreme figures in Greek poetry. He was the anti-hero of a parody of Homer's *Iliad*, wrongly believed to be by Homer himself, and he was known as a famous simpleton who could not count further than ten and who was so ignorant of the facts of life that among much else he was only persuaded to make love to a woman when he was told it would cure a wound in her private parts. By calling Alexander the new Margites, Demosthenes meant that so far from being an Achilles, he was nothing but a Homeric buffoon; they had met in Macedonia when Alexander was a boy, and the joke was pointless unless Alexander's Homeric pretensions were known before he ever invaded Asia.

There is every sign, moreover, that others took them seriously, not least Alexander himself. He began his Asian expedition with a pilgrimage to Troy to honour Achilles's grave, and he took sacred armour from Troy's temple to accompany him to India and back again; his own court historian, who wrote to please him, picked up this theme and stressed parallels with Homer's poems in reports of his progress down the Asian coast; in art, the effects were more subtle, for if Alexander's appearance deliberately matched that of a youthful Greek hero, his features also came to influence portraits of Achilles until the two heroes could hardly be distinguished out of their context; the court sculptor Lysippus portrayed Alexander holding a Homeric spear and on the coins of the small Thessalian town which claimed to be Achilles's birthplace the pictures of the young Achilles grew to look like Alexander's own. The comparison mattered, and was known to matter: when the people of Athens wished to plead for the release of Alexander's Athenian prisoners they sent as their ambassador the only man by the name of Achilles known in fourth-century Athens; previous embassies had failed, but one Achilles pleased another, and this time, the Athenian prisoners were released. It is the smallest details which are always most revealing.

The rivalry, then, existed and was thought important, but it is a different question how it was meant to be taken. Whether written, sung or dictated, Homer's poems were at least three hundred years older than Alexander, and their heroic code of conduct, when men strove for personal glory and knew no greater sanction than public shame and disgrace, had probably belonged to a society at least six hundred years older than that. In this world of heroes, whose ultimate ancestors are the ruined palaces of Troy and Mycenae, no figure is more compelling than Alexander's chosen Achilles; like Alexander, Achilles is young and lordly, a man of passion as much as action with a heart which, though often merciless, can still respond to another's evident nobility. In war, he knows no equal, and even when he sulks in his tent, black anger filling his heart, his reputation overshadows the battle he refuses to join. Like his fellow-heroes, he fights in the name of personal glory, whose first ideal is prowess and whose betrayal is shame and dishonour, but success and status are not his only inspirations: respect for an ageing father, blind love for a favourite Companion, and for a mistress removed by his overlord, a regret which is not just the self-pity of a hero deprived of his prize, Homer's Achilles, of all poetic figures, is a man of intelligible emotion. Above all, he is tragic, for as he has been told by his goddess-mother Thetis, who knows his unhappiness long before he tells her and yet has the sense to ask for it to be retold, 'Two fates bear him towards death's end . . .; if he stays and fights around the city of the Trojans, Gone are his hopes of return, but his fame will be everlasting. But if he goes home to his own dear land, Gone is his fair fame, but his life will be long. And the end of death will not be swift to find him.' Firmly, Achilles chose fame against return; like Alexander, he died a young man.

Such was Alexander's hero, and if he indeed took this rivalry literally, aspiring to what he had read, then his ambitions and character can still be brought to life. At first sight it seems so implausible, the emulation of a poem which looked back to an age of kings and prowess a thousand years before. But rivalry with Homer's world was not irrelevant romance; Homer's poems were still regarded by many Greeks as a source of ethical teaching, and from what is known of political life in Alexander's Athens, the combative code of the *Iliad* had in no way been outgrown. It was a fiercely self-assertive society and what was still implicit in democratic Athens was written larger in the north. In aristocratic Thessaly, on the borders of the Macedonian kings, the bodies of murderers would still be dragged behind a chariot round their victim's tomb, just as Homer's Achilles had once dragged the dead Hector through the dust in memory of his victim Patroclus. But Homer's ethic belongs in an even longer tradition. For Homer's heroes, life was not so much a stage as a competition, and the word for this outward striving for honour, *to philotimo*, is still fundamental to the modern Greeks' way of life; it is an extrovert ideal, not a moral one, and it owes more to emotions and quarrels than to reason and punishment; it belongs with an open-air style of living where fame is the surest way to immortality; it is an attitude that has deep roots in Greece, and it is this word '*philotimo*' which was used to describe Alexander's Homeric ambitions. Homer's Achilles sums up the doubts and conflicts of *to philotimo*, a hero's emulous struggle for glory; the ideal is a lasting one, and against the perspective of Macedonia it would have made living sense.

Through Aristotle and the fine Greek art at Pella, it is easy to overstress one side of the contrast in Alexander's Macedonian background. Pella was also a palace society, and kings and palaces had vanished for some three hundred years from the Greek world; it was the centre of a tribal aristocracy, to which the highland chieftains had come down from their townless world, and on both accounts, it was more archaic than its patronage of Greek art and intellect suggested. 'Idomeneus,' Homer's Agamemnon had said, judging a hero in terms of the old heroic age, 'I honour you above all the swift-horsed Greeks, whether in war or any other work or at the feast when the heroes mix the gleaming wine.' Horses and hunting, feasts and fighting, these were a hero's fields of prowess, but in Macedonia kings and barons continued them each in their distinctive way. Once, according to an old Macedonian custom, a Macedonian could not have worn a proper belt until he had killed a man in battle, and in Alexander's day single combat not only belonged to the ceremony of a royal funeral but was the recurrent business of his officers, who wrestled, jousted and speared in duels worthy of any Homeric hero. Hunting promised similar glory, and was given free rein by Alexander from the Lebanon to the hills of Afghanistan; according to custom, a Macedonian could not recline at dinner until he had killed a wild boar, another link with the world of Homer's poems, for only in Homer's society, not in contemporary Greece, did Greeks ever dine without reclining.

At dinners, the king entertained his nobles and personal guest friends in a ceremonial style which recalled the great banquets of Homeric life. Gossip maintained that Macedonians would be drunk before they reached the first course, but such drinking was more a challenge than an indiscriminate debauch. Successes in battle were toasted formally and one noble pledged another to a cup which had to be equalled on pain of honour. These royal feasts were a vital part of the loose weave of the kingdom. They brought king and nobles together in a formal relationship, just as feasts in the palace halls had daily confronted Homer's kings with their counsellors and neighbouring aristocrats. It was a personal relationship, governed by favour and friendship; the old Homeric traditions of kingly presents, of generosity and pious respect for ancestral friends still lived on in Alexander, who always respected past ties with the Macedonian kings, whether of long-dead Greek poets, an Athenian general or kinsmen of his mythical ancestors, even after an interval of more than a hundred years.

This honour for guest friends had been central to the personal links which patterned the life of Homer's kings; others, the links of family and blood feuds, also found their parallel in Alexander's Macedonian home. But the nobles themselves shared a different and no less evocative honour, for at the court of their lowland king they served as his Companions, and to any lover of Homer, Companions are an unforgettable part of heroic life. Loosely, Companions may be partners in any common enterprise, fellow-oarsmen rowing with Odysseus or kings fighting with Agamemnon before Troy, but they also serve in a stricter sense. In Homer's *Iliad*, each king or hero has his own personal group of Companions, bound by respect, not kinship. Busy and steadfast, they dine in his tent or listen as he plays the lyre; they tend his bronze-rimmed chariot and drive his hoofed horses into battle, they fight by his side, hand him his spear and carry him, wounded, back to their camp. They are the men a hero loves and grieves to lose, Patroclus to the brooding Achilles or Polydamas to Hector rampant. With the collapse of kings and heroes, it is as if the Companions withdraw to the north, surviving only in Macedonia on the fringe of Europe. Driven thence when Alexander's conquests bring the Macedonians up to date, they retreat still further from a changing world and dodge into the swamps and forests of the Germans, only to reappear as the squires of early German kings and the retinues of counts in the tough beginnings of knighthood and chivalry.

In Alexander's Macedonia, selected Companions still attended the king in battle, but their ranks had been expanded to include the nobles of highland and lowland, while foreign friends from Greece and elsewhere had increased their number to almost a hundred. Not every Companion was the king's friend; they dined with him and advised him, and they had lost none of their aristocratic pride; a festival was held yearly in their honour, and when they died they were buried in vaulted underground tombs behind a façade of tapering Greek columns and double doors studded with bronze. It was a grand style, and they took it with them to the East. Its roots were older and more in keeping with the Companions' name, for the vaulted tombs of Macedonia recall the mounded burials of royal Mycenae, ancestor of Homer's heroic world.

It was among these Companions, turbulent and nobly born, that the Macedonian king had to force respect for his will, and his methods again picked up the style of Homeric kingship. Custom and tradition supported what no law existed to define, and as in Homer's poems, superlative prowess could justify a man in going beyond convention: the kings began with the asset of noble birth, and like Homer's kings, they could claim descent from Zeus, a point of the first importance both for Alexander and his father. Noble birth needed to be buttressed by solid achievement. No rights or constitution protected the king; his government was personal, his authority as absolute as he could make it; he issued his own coins, bound his people to his treaties, led their charges into battle, dispensed the plunder and attended to suitable sacrifices and yearly rituals of purification, hoping to 'rule by might', in a favourite Homeric phrase, and meet his duties with the proper energy of a king among lesser kings. It was a demanding position, and if age or achievement was against him, he was deposed or murdered. None of Alexander's ancestors had died in their beds. The common people, most of them wild tribesmen, respected his birth and were consulted, mostly, as a counter to turbulent nobles: if their will was displeasing, a strong king would defy it. Like Homer's King Agamemnon, Alexander twice ignored the opinions of his assembled soldiers. Agamemnon's reward was a nine days' plague from heaven; once, Alexander failed, but once he scared his men into agreement within three days.

In this king's world of custom and prowess, where all power was personal and government still took place among Companions, success and achievement were the means to authority, and the restless ideal of a Homeric hero was a very real claim to them both. Throughout the letters of Greek academics to Philip, the theme of personal glory in battle or contest recurs deliberately; such glory is godlike, worthy of royal ancestry and the fit reward of a Macedonian king, and like a new King Agamemnon, Philip should lead the Greeks to plunder and revenge among the barbarians of the east. Such glory had been the mainspring of Homer's kings, but where Philip had been urged to follow Agamemnon, Alexander marked out Achilles for himself, more glorious, more individual, and less of a king and leader. Among his Macedonians, this combative ideal made sense, but Alexander grew to govern more men than his Macedonians; part, therefore, of his career is the story of an Achilles who tried, not always happily, to face the problems of an Agamemnon.

From a new Achilles it would be a mistake to look for peace or a new philosophy. His rivalry was a response to the values of his own society. Fear, profit and glory had been singled out as three basic motives of man by his most percipient Greek observer, and it was to the last of the three that a hero's life was given over; glory won by achievement was agreed to be the straightest path to heaven, and so Alexander's Homeric rivalry led, through prowess, to his free worship by contemporaries as a living god. It was an old ideal, which Aristotle too had shared, but it also had its weaknesses. A hero rules more by reputation than by inherited majesty and cannot allow his prowess to be challenged often or excelled. If he fails, he often shifts a part of the blame on to others or on to causes outside himself, for a loss of face is loss of the title by which he lives and governs. It is a bold attendant who persists in praising another man's courage above his master's. Alexander's generosity was often commended, but it stressed the matchless excellence of his own riches and position; the slander of rivals and a taste for mocking others' failures are the hero's natural reverse to this open-handed display. Alexander's own historian belittled Parmenion's prowess, probably after his death; singers entertained the younger officers by belittling the generals who died commanding the one grave defeat of Alexander's career; Alexander himself is said to have added touches to a comic satire against a close friend, put on to amuse the court soon after he had deserted to Athens. These flatteries and slanders are not a proof that truth and a despot can never rule together. They belong more subtly to a hero's necessary ethic. 'Ever to be best and stand far above all others'; this was agreed to be one of Alexander's favourite lines in Homer. Personal excellence and the shifting of the blame for failure on to others have remained lasting principles of all political life, but they were most pronounced in a society ruled by a heroic ideal.

It is through Homer that Alexander still comes to life: only one of his dreams is recorded, and it could hardly be more appropriate. In Egypt, as he laid out his new Alexandria, a venerable old man with a look of Homer himself is said to have appeared in his sleep and recited lines from the Odyssey which advised him where to site his city. Even in his dreams, Alexander was later believed to be living out the poems he loved, and to any lover of Homer, his ideal is not, after all, such a strange one. For of all poems, Homer's *Iliad* is still the most immediate, a world whose reality never falters, not only as seen through the new dimension of its similes, where kings banquet beneath their oak trees, children build castles of sand, mothers keep flies away from their sleeping babies and old women watch from their porches as the wedding processions dance by, but also through the leisurely progress of a narrative rich in ritual and repeated phrases, deceptively simple but infinitely true, where heroes strive for glory, knowing that death is inescapable, where a white-armed lady laughs through her tears and returns to heat the bath-water for a husband who she knows will never return from the battle, where gods and goddesses are no more remote for being powerful, one raining tears of blood for the death of a favourite hero, another making toys, another bribing Sleep with the promise of one of the younger Graces and then making love with Zeus her husband on a carpet of crocus and hyacinth. Homer's only magic is his own, and if he still speaks directly to the heart how much more must his poems have come home to Alexander, who saw their ideals around him and chose to live them, not as a distant reader but more in the spirit of a marcher baron living out the ballads which mirrored his own home world.

Once, men said, when a messenger arrived with news and could barely conceal his delight, Alexander stopped him with a smile: 'What can you possibly tell me that deserves such excitement,' he asked, 'except perhaps that Homer has come back to life?' Alexander could not revive his favourite poet, but there is one last twist to his Homeric rivalry, more extraordinary, perhaps, than he ever knew. In his cavalry, served a regiment of lowlanders, whom his ancestors had annexed on their eastern borders; they had migrated, said Aristotle, many hundreds of years ago from ancient Crete. In the same lowlands, there also lived Greek refugees to whom his ancestors had offered a home: they had come, on the ruin of their home town, from the ancient village of Mycenae. But the palace societies of Crete and Mycenae were the giants of the heroic age which Homer, centuries later, had used as the theme for his poem; their only descendants were living, by chance, in Macedonia, and at the call of a new Achilles they would prepare for Greece's last Homeric emulation, for a march as far as the Oxus and the Punjab, in search of the personal prowess which had once made their kings such a famous subject of song.

CHAPTER FOUR

Inside Macedonia Alexander had already shown a speed worthy of his Homeric hero. In mid-autumn it was time to extend his authority abroad, for Philip had left a foreign legacy which stretched from the Danube and the Dalmatian coast to the southern capes of Greece and the islands of the Aegean. The Macedonian throne was secure and it was Greece which first required his heir's attention.

When Alexander was asked how he managed to control the Greeks, he would answer 'by putting off nothing that ought to be done today until tomorrow'. No sooner were palace affairs settling in his favour than he put this stern but admirable philosophy into practice. Leading the Macedonian soldiers whom he had befriended, he marched south from Aigai to the abutting foothills of mount Olympus, and so towards the border with Greek Thessaly, where his father had long been recognized as ruler. The vale of Tempe was entered by a pass five miles long and so narrow that cavalry could only ride it in single file; local Thessalian tribesmen were guarding it, and if the history of Greek warfare had one lesson to teach, it was that mountain passes were impenetrable for cavalry and infantry in formation and were not to be undertaken confidently even by the fashionable units of light-armed peltasts. Alexander improvised a bold alternative: he ordered steps to be cut in the cliff-face of nearby mount Ossa and he led his Macedonians over its peaks by the methods of a mountaineer. The pass was turned, the nobles of Thessaly welcomed the man they had failed to stop, and Alexander did not forget a stratagem which could serve him again in his career.

Like his father Philip, he was promptly recognized as ruler of the Thessalians, a remarkable honour for an outsider and crucial for the financial dues and disciplined cavalry to which it entitled him. In return, he reminded his subjects of their kinship with him through the hero Heracles, ancestor of the Macedonian kings, and through Achilles, to whom his mother's family traced their descent. Achilles's kingdom had lain in Thessaly, and as a personal tribute Alexander now dedicated the district to his hero. His father's diplomacy had bequeathed him his broad inheritance, but he had interpreted it in his own heroic way; the pattern ran deep in Alexander's early years.

If he was ruler of Thessaly, he was also by hereditary right the leader of the Greek allies, for Philip had exacted an oath from the Greeks that his newly created office of Leader should pass to his descendants. But his death had started disturbances in every allied city with a grievance, and only by a frighteningly fast march could Alexander win his rightful acknowledgement. Storming through Thermopylae, the narrow Gates of Greece, he carried the central Greek tribes, summoned the Delphic council, a body of more prestige than power, and made them ratify his Leadership, because he controlled them; there had been dissidence in Thebes and Athens, where news of Philip's murder had arrived very quickly from northern agents and caused the people to vote Pausanias the honour of a shrine, but Alexander careered southwards to their borders, scaring Thebes into surrender, Athens into herding her livestock and farmers inside her walls for fear of invasion. Fulsome honours were voted to him, including Athenian citizenship; he accepted them, and passed south to Cornith on the isthmus to summon the allied Greek council of which he was now leader both by example and by right. Not for the last time, he had shown his troops the value of speed, and yet this was the man whom Athenian politicians had predicted would never leave Pella.

War was the natural state of every Greek city. In theory, they were considered to be at war with each other, except for particular cases where they had sworn a temporary alliance and theory was usually born out in practice. The Greece which Philip had outmanoeuvred and Alexander had overawed was a society obsessed with instability and poisoned with revolution. It was not a decadent society, which had somehow betrayed the ideals of a so-called golden age under Pericles's Athens a hundred years before; it was a more level world, both in the balance of power between its states and in the openness of office to men outside its traditional ruling classes. Being more level, it was also more varied. But it was also living proof that for all their variety, the Greeks had failed to produce any political or economic form which could hold a community together or offer to the majority of their citizens a life which was any comfort in a desperately poor landscape with a negligible stock of technology to surmount it. For the past twenty-five years the balance of power in Greece had declined, through feuds between states and upheavals between classes, into an uneasy balance of weakness. Philip had exploited this as an unattached outsider, and his final result, of a common peace among 'free and independent' Greek allies, was intended to stop dissension both between and inside the Greek cities by means to his own advantage. He had already set up friendly governments where necessary, and in the name of stability, Alexander froze them into power by an absolute ban on revolutionary

69

disturbance; in the name of independence, like the Spartans fifty years before him, he broke up the local empires of the larger states on which so much of their mutual aggression had been based, and this measure won him popularity among their many smaller neighbours. Elaborate provisions were made for disputes between cities to be arbitrated, but the detailed clauses of this common peace among allies cannot now be recovered; even if they could they would be as dull as any other dead constitution from the past. The only point which mattered was that Philip and his Macedonians kept control despite their slogan of Greek freedom and that they did not mean to squeeze Greece for tribute or for any cooperation beyond a sullen acquiescence in their aims in Asia.

'Covenants without the sword are but words, and of no strength to secure a man at all'; so Thomas Hobbes wrote in seventeenth-century England, and like Plato and Aristotle, he was mapping out his political philosophy in a real world of revolution and little stability. All three saw the need for authority around them, and Philip and Alexander, no less than Cromwell, appreciated the truth which was written large in the political philosophies of their time. In four key states Macedonian garrisons held the Greeks to their convenants, and if one was removed by Alexander to appease natives who had already rebelled to throw it out, a second was maintained at Thebes, despite similar protest by the Theban people. Events were soon to prove him right; meanwhile, a meeting of his father's allied council confirmed him as supreme general of the Asian expedition, and the last link in the chains of Philip's Greek inheritance had safely been forged for him: 'By his authority he hath the use of so much power and strength conferred on him that by terror thereof, he is enabled to form the wills of them all to peace at home and to mutual aid against their enemies abroad.' More than any clause of Philip's Greek alliance, it is Hobbes's ideal sovereign who sums up the Macedonian leadership of the Greeks.

Only one Greek state stood out against his authority: the Spartans sent Alexander a message saying that it was not their fathers' practice to follow others but to lead them. This splendidly stubborn comment was not as unwelcome as they might have hoped. By their past history in southern Greece, the Spartans had earned the anxious detestation of their smaller neighbours who remembered how Spartan calls to freedom or independence had persistently led to their subjection. Spartan power had been broken for thirty-five years, but it was showing unwelcome signs of a revival, and Philip had played astutely on small neighbours' fears of another Spartan tyranny. Although there were those in more powerful states who called Philip and Alexander the tyrants of Greece, their small and vulnerable neighbours did not see the rise of Macedonia as the death of Greek freedom. Such a concept begged too many questions. Several enemies of Sparta in southern Greece had shown unease at the death of their protector Philip, but Sparta's continued opposition to Alexander reminded them that their best hope of protection lay with a Macedonian leader.

So it suited Alexander to leave Sparta alone, and instead he had words with a Greek philosopher whom he happened to find in Corinth's suburbs. Diogenes, founder of the Cynic school, was visiting Corinth and as a believer in the vanity of wordly riches, he was living in a wooden tub: passing by, Alexander saw him and asked if there was anything this abject figure wanted. Yes, replied Diogenes, stand aside a little, for you are blocking the sun. One of his pupils later joined Alexander as an admiral and wrote a colourful history, including the story of this meeting, but it was probably his fiction that Alexander went on to comment: 'If I had not been Alexander, I would like to have been Diogenes.' And yet both of them shared, for different ends, an extraordinary power of physical endurance.

As winter began, Alexander left Corinth and returned northwards, stopping to make a dedication at the Delphic oracle. His visit was the start of a new and persistent theme. The priesthood had always repaid Philip's favours, but Alexander, it was said, was refused an oracle because he had come on an unfavourable day. He man-handled the priestess and dragged her to the shrine, and during the struggle she acknowledged him as invincible. These 'unfavourable days' are not known until Roman times and the story of the struggle and refusal is likely to be a Roman slander, belittling Alexander's invincibility against that of their own emperors. But the theme is rich in consequences. The troops would believe that the Delphic oracle had somehow guaranteed it, probably because Alexander encouraged the story at Delphi himself. When he was later proposed for divine honours at Athens as an invincible god, the title must have been known to be his favourite. No man, and only one hero, had been called invincible before him, and then only by a poet, but the hero was Heracles, ancestor of the Macedonian kings. Alexander emphasized the theme of Victory on his coins, in his dedications and the names of his cities, and as a result of his exploits, a newer and mightier Heracles the Invincible entered into Greek and Roman religion. In Iran, his Successors continued the titles he had begun, and the idea of Invincibility passed from the Greek East to Caesar and finally to the Sun whose worship grew to rival Christ's. When Alexander began to stress this powerful link with Victory and the hero Heracles, whose assistance he constantly recognized, a new concept was born for divine kingship. It was the first, and not the least, of his legacies to religion and it also caught his confident mood; on returning to Macedonia, he called out his father's army for training and drill, and on this army, more than any claim to victory, his invincibility always depended. To modern field-marshals the Macedonian army has seemed the most enviable force in history. Its design is intriguing and leads straight to Philip, the most immediate reason why Alexander ever became great.

For twenty-three years Philip had welded his growing Macedonia for war. Toughness was obligatory, and reflected in numerous anecdotes: Philip stationing his horsemen behind the lines to cut down any deserters, Philip refusing to allow women into camp, Philip berating a Macedonian for washing in warm water because in Macedonia only a woman who had just given birth was allowed to bath in comfort. Discipline was backed by plunder, foreign tithes, new farmland and the old gold mines which were seized on Macedonia's eastern borders and transformed to yield a solid supply of gold coin; a standing army could thus be supported, a luxury which only Sparta among the Greeks had braced herself to afford, and at once Philip began to teach it how to march. Whereas the infantrymen of Greek citizen armies would take one servant each to war with them, Philip allowed only one attendant to every ten soldiers; he banned carriages for his officers and forced them to march for thirty miles at a time in high summer with thirty days' supplies on their backs. They were to rely on as few oxdrawn carts and mules for transport as possible. Stone handmills were taken to grind the corn in camp, and a regulation diet of bread and olives was only supplemented by plundered livestock, although Macedonia was also rich in fish and fruit, especially figs, whose high sugar content was thought suitable for soldiers. The army learnt to live off the land whatever the season, even if they had to scratch a living from native storepits in the grip of a Bulgarian winter. For the first time, distance had ceased to matter in Balkan warfare.

This trained army was balanced by Philip's tactics, but great tactics are born less of originality than of a shrewd use of contemporary fashion, and Philip's army did not, like the goddess Athena, spring fully armed from its parent's brain. Greek society had seldom analysed its skills in technical pamphlets, but warfare had been better served than arts as basic as mining or forestry, and the writings of such men as the general Xenophon were an accessible source of ideas both for oriental hazards and for the equipment of the horses which he so enjoyed. Infantry tactics were best learnt from example and discussion, and increasingly they had passed in the last sixty years from Greece's landed aristocrats to a new breed of common professionals, sons of a cobbler or a tradesman, who hired out their services abroad and spent most of their life in an army camp. Macedonia lay close to their operations, and in assessing Philip's army, the influences of Greek theory and professionals are central; Philip had inherited a siege train from his predecessor, but he hired his own Greek engineer, Polyeidus of Thessaly, and sponsored his inventions. 'A good deal of circumstantial evidence suggests that the principle of torsion was invented under the auspices of Philip II', who first applied spring of sinew or horsehair to the recently discovered arrow-catapult, doubling its range and power. Polyeidus also designed a system of toothed city walls and a siege tower 120 feet high, and he taught the pupils who devised ever stronger machinery for Alexander's siege-craft section. No Macedonian could have done it for himself.

On the battlefield, cavalry and infantry were Philip's two staple units, and he balanced them into a coherent line. On the right wing, the cavalry delivered the hammer blow, and in the centre, the infantry followed up like a heavy press; this was his standard tactic and Alexander's too, and it was held together by links of differing armour. Already it gave them an advantage. Because Greek infantry drifted to their right, or shielded side, generals usually placed their strongest units on their respective lefts, with the result that they never met in combat. The Macedonian right and left were equally balanced to upset their enemy's formation and their infantry never drifted from the centre; Philip may have learnt his line from the Theban general Pammenes who had entertained him in his youth at Thebes. As the punch force, the cavalry had the distinction of deciding the pitched battle, usually at the gallop; this method is spectacular, but many have failed to control it, for cavalry units are an unruly group of young bloods and gentlemen who only respond to a dashing example. This dash Alexander provided even more than his father, and his leadership turned the Companions into the finest unit of cavalry in history, Genghis Khan's included. For this, they had needed a proper home.

In southern Greece sparse summer grazing and a lack of men rich enough to own horses had mostly stopped cavalry from developing decisive style or numbers. But the feudal nobility of Macedonia were men born to ride and their European climate of glen and plain had given them watered pasturage. The highlands too had always grazed good horses, and by conquering the lush grass beyond his eastern borders in the first ten years of his reign Philip had won a broad acreage on which to settle nobles and a new class of landowners on new horse-pastures, until eight hundred Companion cavalrymen could be said to enjoy estates as vast as the total lands of the ten thousand richest men in Greece. Fertile estates meant more horses and revenues for a wider group of riders, and the number of Companion cavalrymen had risen from some six hundred or more at Philip's accession to some four thousand by the end of his reign. As for the horses, they were increased and varied by plundered mares from the barbarian north, a crossing which may have helped their speed. The horses of antiquity are coarse and heavy to an eye accustomed to Arab blood, and pictures on coins and paintings imply that Macedonian breeds had become heavier in the hundred years before Alexander. No stud books were kept of their lines, so improvement could not be planned; gelding was practised on most Greek warhorses and the technique of binding two wooden blocks to the testicles was as modern and effective as would be expected in a world well supplied with eunuchs.

The Companion rider was modestly defended. In art, he is never shown carrying a shield, though his attendant groom might. He wore the usual breastplates of leather or metal in various designs, fitted with armpieces for close combat when he took to using his sword or curved hunting scimitar. He had no stirrups and he sat on a saddlecloth which was strapped round the horse's neck and sometimes padded to protect his knees. Over his belted tunic he sported a flowing Macedonian cloak and a fringed skirt of leather or metal to protect his private parts; his shoes were characteristically Macedonian and opened at the foot like sandals, with no defences. His helmet resembled a fluted sou'wester of metal and was sometimes worn with a metal neck guard; Xenophon had recommended these items in his books on cavalry, and the distinctive helmet, which he had singled out for wide vision, was invented in Greek Boeotia where Philip had spent early years as a hostage. But of Xenophon's suggested metal leg shields and horse armour, the Companions copied nothing.

Techniques of skirmishing and wheeling had been developed by aristocrats and tribesmen, in the open plains of Sicily and the barbarian north, and these fluid manœuvres were causing a favour in Greek tactics for lighter armour, javelins and a more distanced use of cavalry. Philip made no concessions to this. On the few occasions when the corseleted horsemen of Macedonia had been seen by Greek armies in the past hundred years, they had always astonished them by the plain shock of their charges, Philip did not discard this dramatic form of attack. Stirrups had not been invented, so a rider's legs could not be braced against impact and his lance could neither be stout nor supported under his arm. Nonetheless, the Companions surged into their enemy and lanced them. Their lances were

74

fitted with a metal blade and cut from the cornel wood whose toughness Xenophon praised; they were so slender that they vibrated at the gallop and often broke on contact. Their use was mostly as a menace to scatter the line, whereupon men hacked and jostled against an enemy whom their bravado had unsettled. All Alexander's wounds from cavalry came from daggers and swords, not lances. However, the enemy too had no stirrups and experiment shows that a passing blow will topple a man without them, especially if he is heavily armoured.

Riders were expected to steady themselves by holding on to the mane, but even this aid was no more essential than stirrups to an effective charge; Philip had recruited a force of Mounted Scouts who rode most usefully on reconnaissance and returned to charge in the front line with a lance so long that both hands were needed to hold it. They guided their horses by the pressure of their knees, like any expert modern horseman and far from being an idle experiment, their two-handed technique survived not only among Russian cavalrymen in Africa but also among the Scythian nomads of the south Russian steppes. What writing has done to the memory, stirrups have done to riding; without them, men simply had to grip harder and ride better than they mostly do nowadays.

There was, however, one technicality which helped the Companions to victory. Their basic unit was not a block but a wedge, shaped like a triangle, apex first. Cavalry have never been able to charge down a solid line of heavy infantry by a frontal attack, so the Companions first shattered or drew off the cavalry on the enemy's wing, then changed direction to cut diagonally into the flanks of the moving infantry in the centre. The wedge formation was pointed, and therefore more piercing, and it was adapted to diagonal changes of course 'because all the members fix their eyes on the squadron-leader at their point, like a flock of cranes which are flying in formation', and so took their cue from one conspicuous drill-master. Controlled turns were not easy even in a wedge. The Companions' reins and bridles were modern in appearance, but they could not be adjusted quickly to suit their circumstances, as the buckle did not exist; there were no curb-chains, so bits, especially the spiked 'hedgehog' variety, were very severe. The horses' mouths were hardened, therefore, and there were no martingales to keep their heads down when the bits were being pulled too hard. But Alexander still managed to lead with his Companions on the right wing, feint to the far right and pierce back into the centre in every pitched battle. The reason, surely, was the fluid wedge formation, which had been discovered by the brilliant horsemen of the barbarian Scyths and Thracians, and copied by Philip, who had repeatedly campaigned in the north against it.

The Companions punched and pierced on the right; the Foot Companions, in the centre, were designed for a solid follow-up. Some 9,000 in number, they were packed shoulder to shoulder in six brigades, the centre files of which seem to have been known as the Citizen Companions, a title whose purpose is obscure. They were armed, memorably, to cause mass terror. They carried the Macedonian pike, or sarissa, a most extraordinary weapon; its longest variety was eighteen feet long, tipped at the point by a foot-long blade of iron and at the butt by the usual metal butt-spike which helped to balance it and allowed it to be rammed into the ground for a rest or for a guard against an enemy's frontal charge. It had to be held with both hands and like the cavalry lance, it was made of cornel wood, cousin of the dogwoods from which spits and skewers have often been cut for their hard grain. The cornel tree grows abundantly in several forms, not only on Macedonia's hillsides but also in Greece and the western hills of Asia which Philip planned to conquer; its most common form, Cornus mas, has deceptively slender branches of a wide-spreading and is nowadays admired by knowing gardeners for its primrose-yellow spring flowers. Probably Macedonian foresters pruned it so that it threw up stocky stems. They made up each sarissa's full length by joining two selected branches into a central tube of bronze which helped to balance the centre of gravity.

Because of the sarissa's length, the metal points of the first five ranks projected, perhaps in a graded series, beyond the Foot Companions' front line. It is uncertain whether the centre ranks also held sarissas or whether they were only included to give weight to the formation; they might be asked to fan out and broaden the front, so they probably did have sarissas too. If so, they could keep them vertical in deep formations and break the flight of enemy missiles, while the rear ranks could face about and drop their spears to the horizontal to make up a bristling rectangle. Drill had to be perfect, for the Foot Companions were a liability if they split, and the few known drill commands belie their years of complicated training. They could march in columns, rectangles or wedges, broaden their front by thinning their depth to a basic eight files or pack and narrow them to sixteen, thirty-two or even, in a crisis, a hundred and twenty. The file leaders were the most highly paid and seasoned troops in the unit. By marking time, they could wheel and advance at an angle, and by raising their sarissas vertically, countermarching or drilling round, then lowering them to the horizontal, they could face about. Against an enemy charge they would ram their sarissas into the earth and dress together to less than three feet between each man, so that the small shields strapped on their shoulders were contiguous. But they were never finer than when powering their way into infantry whom their cavalry had routed. Nobody who faced them ever forgot the sight; they kept time to their roaring of the Greeks' ancient war cry, *Alalalalai*; their scarlet cloaks billowed, and the measured swishing of their sarissas, up and down, left and right, seemed to frightened observers like the quills of a metal porcupine.

The button-shaped shield of the Foot Companions became the national emblem of Macedonians, and yet their unit may not have been wholly a Macedonian creation. Foot Companions had fought in files of ten before Philip's reign, and although it was he who introduced their sarissas and packed their formation in multiples of eight, it is very relevant that he had spent his youth as a hostage at the Greek city of Thebes, where the two boldest generals of the age, Epaminondas and Pelopidas, were already experimenting with the deep lines and slanting battlefronts which Philip and Alexander later favoured. As for the long pikes, they were compared with those of Homer's infantry, but a truer parallel lies in Egypt where the natives had always fought with long spears and wickerwork shields. In the past forty years, professional Athenian captains had been advising the pharaohs on their army, and one of them had doubled the length of his Greeks' spears as a result; another, Iphicrates, had done likewise for the open plains of Asia, and he was a well-known friend of the Macedonian royal family, especially of Philip's mother, whom he had served, probably soon after the Foot Companions were first recruited. Another Athenian professional, Charidemus, had often campaigned on Macedonia's borders, and it was from him that Philip is said to have learnt the tight shield-to-shield formation which the Foot Companions used on the defensive. But the city of Thebes was to be destroyed by its former visitor's army and Charidemus was exiled to Asia on Alexander's orders, where he advised the Persians against the troops whom he had once helped to teach.

Infantry armed with sarissas were every Greek state's ambition in the age that followed, and the Foot Companions became the most famous unit in Macedonia. But their formation was beset with difficulties, and those who saw them with Alexander knew it. In each of his big pitched battles, the Foot Companions either played little part or else split out of line on uneven ground, and before they invaded India, they gave up the sarissa altogether; they were a battle-winning force only if the cavalry shocked the enemy first, but they could not keep in step when the cavalry began to gallop, and once their wall of sarissas parted, through rough terrain or incompetence, the men inside were extremely vulnerable. Probably they had always worn metal greaves on their legs and breast-plates of leather or metal, an expensive but necessary defence against missiles, at least for the file-leaders; their helmets were made of metal too, and because both hands were busied with the sarissa their shields had to be small, some eighteen inches in diameter, and were slung by a strap across the left shoulder and upper arm. Often of bronze, they were convex in shape like a button, studded and painted with geometrical patterns; against heavy infantry they were a poor protection when the line had broken. Sarissas, of course, were almost useless in close combat, and the short daggers which Foot Companions wore on their hips were very much a last resort.

Both Companions and Foot Companions were troops for open ground and weather. The Companions' horses, like all ancient cavalry, had no nailed horseshoes, and the leather boots which were slipped over their feet in icy conditions soon wore as thin as the hoof itself. But rough ground abounded in Greece, Thrace and Asia, and Philip was too varied a planner not to have taken lameness, broken ranks and the impossibility of charges into account; from three different units he developed a skirmishing force who could also fight in the front line. No troops worked harder or more often. From an early date, he hired archers from Crete, the celebrated home of Greek archery; slingers from Rhodes were added to them, and their sling-stones have been found in the ruins of one of Philip's sacked cities inscribed with suitably rude messages. The crack troops were the 3,000 infantry whom Philip had developed as king's men and given the name of Royal Shield-bearers, formerly confined to the king's grooms and bodyguards. The finest foot force in antiquity, they deserve the credit which is given too often to the men with the sarissas.

The Shield Bearers were troops with two functions. Because the Foot Companions wore their small shields on their left shoulders, their right flank would have been exposed if the Shield-bearer had not been stationed on it and ordered to guard it tightly with the broad circular shields from which they took their name. They served, then, as part of the Foot Companion's block, linking them to the wing of horsemen. From carvings, it seems that as front line troops they wore crested helmets, metal greaves and breastplates and fought with swords and, presumably, spears. But they also served as shock troops on night raids, hill climbs and forced marches of more than thirty miles a day, and the clear evidence of the histories confirms that they were lighter and faster than the Foot Companions; they had no sarissas, of course, and they probably left their heavy shields and body armour behind when detailed to do the work of commandos. As dual-purpose troops, their fitness was amazing. When many of them were over sixty years old, they could still cover thirty miles through desert in one summer's day; they were first up the ladders into besieged cities, or mountain forts in the Hindu Kush, first to savage the elephants and ruin the Persians' scythed chariots. After Alexander's death, they returned from the road to retirement and decided his Successors' grandest battles by showing improvised Foot Companions how their lines could be hacked apart by men old enough to be their grandfathers; they were drilled for war and nothing else, and they loved it.

Archers and slingers for long-range provocation; arrow-shooting catapults for cover and the clearing of city walls; Companions for piercing charges; Foot Companions for routing broken infantry; Shield Bearers for tough missions and for locking the sarissas and cavalry into a solid and well-flanked battle front; Philip had trained the first balanced standing army in the Balkans, and he could add to it his foreign subjects, whether the heavy Thessalian cavalry in their diamond-shaped formations, the light-armed horsemen and javelin-throwers of the Thracian tribes, or the hired Greek infantry who served against their fellow-Greeks without any show of reluctance. But balance was pointless without the freedom to campaign on demand, and here was the last, though not the least, of Philip's innovations.

In the Greek states armies were mostly conscripted from citizens as and when they were needed, and because the citizens were also farmers the army could not go to war in the months of the harvest. Only in Sparta, where a thousand aristocrats had ended by tyrannizing a massive body of Greek serfs, was there enough farm labour to back a standing army; by conquest and plunder, Philip had raised Macedonia to the situation of a Sparta. Too much has been made of the apparent leap in Macedonia's birth rate between Philip's accession and Alexander's death. The figures are misleading and are also influenced by the kingdom's widening boundaries and the recruitment, perhaps, of new tribes and classes; the raw imports of prisoners are far more relevant, as all prisoners who were not sold were enslaved as usual and in an agricultural and unmechanized world where leisure was otherwise impossible Greece's talent for literature, direct democracy and citizen-warfare had always depended on the exploitation of slave labour. Philip had dragged home slaves by the 10,000 to work his mines and farm his feudal nobility's estates. Some, as Athenian visitors to Pella noticed, were given away in droves as presents; others, fellow-Athenians even, were despatched to Philip's own vineyards. Their general effect had been to free Macedonian soldiery from the bonds of the farmers' and foresters' calendar.

'He does not distinguish,' complained one of Philip's enemies, 'between summer and winter; he sets no time of the year aside for inactivity.' Philip's army was not only balanced, it was also backed by enough slaves to make it mobile. In late autumn, Alexander had hurried it through Greece; the following spring, in the month of the harvest, he would direct it up to the Danube, across to Illyria, south again for vengeance in Greece on a march as brisk and varied as any of his father's. The army had only lacked one element, a leader of natural genius; at the age of twenty-one, Alexander would show that his invincibility might, after all, be a theme of substance.

CHAPTER FIVE

If Greece seemed submissive, there were still old scores to be settled in Philip's legacy among the barbarian kingdoms of the European north. Philip had played one Thracian king against another beyond Macedonia's north-east borders and settled an impressive network of new towns through modern Bulgaria as far north as the river Danube and the Black Sea. He had controlled most of the huge rough hinterland of his road to Asia and enjoyed the rich rewards of its royal tithes. It had been the most brilliant of his conquests, but it was not complete: three autumns before his death, Philip had been returning from a conquest on the banks of the Danube with a rich plunder of cattle, girls, small boys and brood mares when the free-spirited tribe of Triballians in Thrace raided his lines, removed all the spoils and wounded him badly in the thigh. The losses were especially annoying as Philip's finances were under strain and his troops were wanting pay; Alexander had served on the march, and he now set out in spring 335 to avenge his father and protect the flanks of the road between Macedonia and the Asian invasion. He knew how lines of communication mattered. Any recovered plunder would be welcomed by the treasury.

For the first time he was very much on his own. Antipater was left in Macedonia and Parmenion was probably in Asia with other proven generals. Alexander had twice had experience of Thracian tribes and landscape; he would now overcome them by an expert use of varied weaponry, the main principle of his military success. All Philip's units were brought into use, except for the Mounted Scouts with their two-handed lances, for they were already in Asia, where the open plains suited them. Only one unit was added as Alexander's own, and though small, it was very significant. During Philip's lifetime, he had privately befriended the King of the Agrianians, a mountain tribe on the upper Strymon river near Macedonia's northern border; a thousand or so of their javelin-throwers now came with their king to join Alexander's skirmishing-troops, and as a foil to Philip's Shield Bearers, they would show most admirable ferocity. The Ghurkhas of Alexander's army, they are the one point at which he already excelled his father's balanced armoury.

The march was planned on the model of Philip's expedition four years earlier, and its aims were the Danube and the Triballians, Philip's enemies. Orders were sent for the small fleet of long warships to row from Byzantium, where they were guarding the Dardanelles. They were to hug the shore of the Black Sea northwards to the mouth of the Danube, and then come up river to meet the land army. Only Philip, among Greece's generals, had ever reached the Danube, but Alexander had watched him do it; in emulation of his father, he was already thinking ambitiously, and while attending to the sacrifices which were the business of every general, he chanced on support for his thoughts. While he offered meat to Dionysus in the famous sanctuary of Crestonia in eastern Macedonia beside his road, the flame flared up unusually high, a peculiarity of the shrine, and his prophets were quick to recognize the traditional omen of a victorious king. It was not long before the omen of flame was confirmed on the battlefield.

In appallingly rugged country his road ran through a narrow defile, perhaps the modern Shipka pass, whose tribesmen had bivouacked behind a defending line of carts. First, as in Thessaly, Alexander looked for a way round them; he failed, so he assessed the chances of forcing them directly. The carts seemed a defence, but he quickly realized they could also be rolled downhill into his packed ranks; his men were told to advance, and those with room to manœuvre were ordered to spread out if the carts began rolling, those with proper shields were to lie flat on the ground and use them as cover. Down came the carts, and some ranks opened, others dropped down as ordered, and the carts either rumbled through the gaps or else bounced over the wall of shields, 'and not one of the Macedonians was killed', implied Alexander's friend Ptolemy* in his history of the incident. When Alexander faced Persian chariots four years later, he defeated them as he defeated these Thracian carts; great generals remember ruses which have worked before, and soon he would show that he memorized as much from reading as from experience.

Thrace's wooded landscape was more of an obstacle than its unarmoured tribesmen, so much so that Philip had once used a pack of hounds to flush his enemy from the thickets. Alexander balanced his weapons nicely. His father's slingers and archers provoked the barbarians out of the woods, then his infantry pitched into them, uphill if necessary, and his cavalry either jostled or punched in from the flanks wherever there were clearings. Before long he had routed the Triballians so thoroughly that their king retreated with a few loyalists to an island in the Danube itself, where he

* I do not, of course, imply that Ptolemy's entire history or precise words have ever survived; see the General Note on Sources at the end of this book for this point and for the identity of our main historians.

was watched from the far bank by its nomadic tribesmen. Alexander despatched his booty back to Macedonia, for he remembered his father's unhappy losses, and advanced to Europe's great river to round off his first foreign campaign.

His ships met him as requested, but they were too few and feeble to storm the Triballian island, so Alexander abandoned the sea power which, like Napoleon, he never mastered, and decided to float his troops across the Danube for a show of terror on the far bank. Fishing canoes were commandeered, and orders were given for the troops to fill their leather tent-skins with chaff and sew them together to make rafts; on these makeshift transports they crossed the river under cover of night, their horses swimming beside them. They landed cunningly near the cover of a tall cornfield, and were led through the crops by the Foot Companions who smoothed a way with the flat blades of their sarissas. On open ground, they loosed a classic charge, punching forwards with the Companions on the right wing, backing up with sarissas in square formation in the centre. The tribesmen fled first to a fort, then retreated on horseback into the steppes. Alexander knew better than to follow a retreating enemy into barren steppeland, and so returned to count the plunder and sacrifice to 'Zeus the Saviour, Heracles and the river Danube for allowing him to cross it'.

The manner of his crossing was not just a matter of the river's goodwill. Nomad relations of the Danube tribesmen were known to stuff their horses' skins with chaff when they died, but there is no evidence that Alexander's straw-stuffed rafts were a native custom; they belonged, rather, to the East, to the Euphrates and the Oxus, and the rivers of the Punjab where stuffed skins able to carry some two hundred pounds still serve as *kilik* rafts for the natives. No Macedonian had ever seen so far into Asia, and only one Greek general had described it; Xenophon the Athenian, who led the Ten Thousand Greeks through Mesopotamia at the turn of the century, and recorded his march in his memoirs. Faced with the Euphrates he had been shown how to cross it on rafts of stuffed skins; at the Danube, Alexander evidently turned to a trick he had read in a military history.

After the bold example of the first Balkan troops ever to cross the Danube, tribes along the river sent presents of friendship, and the Triballians surrendered on their island; later, more than 2,000 joined Alexander in Asia. Even the so-called Celts of western Europe who lived far up river near the Adriatic coast, sent envoys to plead for alliance. Alexander asked them, wrote his friend Ptolemy, 'what they feared most in the world, hoping they would say himself, but they replied that they were most afraid that the sky would fall on to their heads', an old Celtic belief which had already been described by Herodotus; not for the last time, a Macedonian described an unknown tribe through Herodotean eyes. But the Celts' presence was more pleasing than their stubbornness, for Macedonia was serving history in a way that her Greek subjects could not recognize at the time; bestriding the Balkans, she acted as a barrier against the pressure of Europe's restless tribesmen, and a strong Macedonia guaranteed the safety of the Greeks' city life in the south. Not for another fifty years would hordes of Gauls pour into Greece from Europe and threaten her civilization, and then only at a time of feeble confusion in the Macedonian royal family. The European conquests of Philip and Alexander belonged to a wider perspective, essential to the safety, if not the freedom, of Greece. But there was another corridor to Europe, and no sooner had Alexander received the Celts than he heard that it too was giving trouble.

West and north-west of Macedonia's highlands lived the tribes of Illyrians whose villages controlled the main road of invaders from Europe into Greece and whose kings were dangerous in their own right. When Philip took the kingdom, they had overrun much of Macedonia, killing the king and claiming heavy tribute. Philip fought them back, and pierced far up the Adriatic Coast at all seasons to harass them; he had peopled his north-west frontier with new garrison towns, uprooting his subjects 'like a shepherd who moves his flocks from winter to summer pastures', but he had never ensured their security and the Illyrians had been one of the failures of his reign. The king he had learnt to respect was Bardylis, who had twice exacted tribute from Macedonia and was known as an extraordinarily rich man; he had recently died aged ninety, and it was his son who threatened Alexander with frontier war.

Within weeks, the Danube had been forgotten and Alexander was deep in Illyrian marshes and borderlands. Penning Bardylis's son into a stronghold in late summer he had settled down to besiege him in a narrow glen, only to find that a neighbouring king appeared in force along the passes that blocked his escape. This was a very unpleasant situation. He was short of food and his foraging-parties had to be rescued from harassment; he could not retreat unchallenged, for Bardylis's son would sortie from his fort and launch into his rear with troops who had already shown proof of their taste for human sacrifices. The escape route was a narrow wooded valley between the foot of a sheer mountain and a river beneath, and it was only broad enough for four men abreast. Trapped, Alexander resorted to an impudent bluff.

On his patch of open ground, he narrowed his infantry into a line 120 ranks deep and placed a few cavalry on either wing. Sarissas were to be held erect and on command, the first five ranks were to lower them for the charge and swish them in perfect time from left to right; all troops would advance, swinging from one wing to the other to match the front sarissa bearers, and they would form into a wedge on the left and charge towards the enemy. Shields were to be clashed and the war-cry of *Alalalalai* was to be echoed down the glen. On the first rapid strides forward, the main enemy fled in panic from the hill-tops, scared by the disciplined drill and the sound of the war-cry.

The next task was to secure the lower slopes of the mountain from the few remaining guards. A troop of Companions galloped up to dismount and do battle, but the guards fled again at their onset and the hill passed to Alexander and his skirmishing force of Agrianians, archers and Shield Bearers. While they held the slopes against the enemy higher up the mountain, the rest of the army forded the river on one side of the narrows, continuing the war-cry and forming swiftly up on the far bank to deter attackers; Alexander held their rear with his trusted skirmishers and only joined them when it seemed safe. More shouting and firm drill from the infantry scared off the worst of the danger, and when Alexander was finally forced to ford the river himself, he arranged for arrow-shooting catapults on the far bank to give him cover across the water. Holding off with his skirmishers, covering with his artillery, and menacing with his heavier troops, he escaped disaster by an intelligently balanced with-drawal. Three days later he slipped back by night across the river and launched two brigades of Foot Companions and his invaluable archers and Agrianians into an enemy who were casually encamped and not expecting to see him again. Many were slaughtered, more captured and the Illyrian kings fled northwards, discredited.

But unwelcome news prevented any further pursuit. It was already mid-September and by circling round his northern frontiers, Alexander had presumed on the obedience of the Greeks and the continuing safety of Philip's advance force in Asia. On both points he was mistaken. In Asia, Attalus had been murdered, and it was perhaps on news of this that Olympias had taken vengeance into her own hands in Macedonia and murdered Eurydice, niece of Attalus and the girl who had supplanted her in Philip's affections; for completeness, she had murdered her baby daughter Europe too. But in Asia, perhaps because of Attalus's removal, the advance force had faltered and been driven back by the vigour of the Persian king's generals; as part of a coherent strategy, 300 talents were said to have been sent to Demosthenes, most hostile of Athenian politi-cians, and there were hopes that the Greeks would rebel against their leaders. Rebellion had indeed come, but it owed nothing to Persia or to Athenian politicians.

Three years before Philip had punished the city of Thebes in central Greece harshly for her opposition on the battlefield; she had been his ally, then changed sides as her hopes were disappointed; after the Greeks' defeat, she had seen her prisoners sold as slaves and her dead buried only after she had paid for the privilege. In the city prominent Thebans were killed or exiled and their property was confiscated; a Macedonian garrison invested Thebes's fortress and a council of three hundred Thebans, many of whom had already been exiled by their fellow citizens, were set in authority over men who loathed them for their debt to Macedonia. Worst of all, in the name of independence Philip had promised to restore the smaller cities in surrounding Boeotia; these cities Thebes had persistently tried to tyrannize for the sake of more land and power, and nearly two hundred years of Theban history could be written round her domination of small and reluctant neighbours. Now they were to be independent, by order of a Macedonian.

It was not, then, Alexander who was to blame for Thebes's latest upheaval. Philip's severity was working itself out in Alexander's name, and the cause was the secret return of Thebans whom Philip had banished three years before. They talked of freedom and they alleged that Alexander had been killed in battle near the Danube. This sounded too convincing to resist, and when they described the misbehaviour of the Macedonian garrison, whom the Thebans had been too slow to eject the previous autumn, two of its leaders were seized and assassinated. It was open rebellion, now, but their talk of freedom was hardly disinterested: among the returned exiles, there were former officials of the league through which Thebes had dominated her neighbours, and if they were protesting against Macedonia's tyranny, they were also indignant that their own sweet days of local empire had ended.

Alexander treated the news with the speed and gravity which it deserved. He did not waste time in returning to Macedonia, but in a tremendous forced march he stormed down Macedonia's western border, across the brown plains near Trikkala, and was over all hills and mountain passes and up before Thebes within fourteen days. Thebes had been hoping for Athenian troops and for citizen armies from southern Greek cities, but only the Arcadians were stirring to join her, and other states seemed dangerously likely to stay neutral or even to help the Macedonian leader to whom they were sworn allies. When a Macedonian army, more than 30,000 strong, was reported from the city walls, the Thebans could not bring themselves to believe it: 'Alexander', they assumed, must be Antipater, or perhaps Alexander of Lyncestis who had been set in command of Thrace. But to their cost, Alexander it was, and within a week he had begun the 'swiftest and greatest disaster', it could be said, which had ever befallen a Greek city.

Alexander's movements were decisive and much deplored, and the dispute, as often, left its mark in the delicacies of his various histories. Ptolemy, his friend and officer, stressed his reluctance to attack the city, his repeated delay in the hope that Thebes would send ambassadors, the division, no doubt true, between Thebans who wished to talk and between instigators who would have none of it; others agreed on the fact of Alexander's delay, but when Alexander asked for the surrender of the rebel leaders, the Thebans, they said, answered him by shouting from a high tower for help in freeing the Greeks from their tyrant, and Alexander thereupon launched irrevocably into plans for attack. Three days later he opened battle with the Theban army outside the walls and was very hard pressed indeed, for the Thebans had been training in their city gymnasium; not until Antipater led his reserve line into action did his Macedonians begin to recover ground. As they rallied Alexander noticed a postern-gate in the city wall which the Thebans had left unguarded, and this turned the battle. He hurried Perdiccas and his regiment to take it, and once the city had been entered behind the Thebans' backs, their defence was vain; the looting was helped by the Macedonian garrison who had hitherto been blockaded inside their fortress, and it knew no bounds.

Ptolemy put it more cunningly: so far from attacking intentionally, Alexander had continued to delay, and it was only when Perdiccas acted without orders and took it into his head to attack the Thebans' stockade that battle was joined at all. For Perdiccas tried an unofficial raid and was 'wounded badly', and 'almost stranded'; only when the Thebans drove his men back into Alexander's camp did Alexander feel obliged to charge to the rescue. As if by accident, some of the Macedonians followed up so fast that they were trapped inside the city itself; they were almost unopposed, and with the garrison's help, the city fell to them, more by accident than savage design. This sly apology is very interesting. Writing after Alexander's death Ptolemy had strong reason to slander his rival and enemy Perdiccas, and so he explained away Thebes's capture as due to his insubordination and the chance reprisals of his master Alexander. He also posed as a protector of Greek freedom and had reason to conceal Greek opposition to the Macedonians.

And yet one fact was agreed, and of great significance. In the brutal sack of the city, Alexander's Greek allies from Thebes's neighbouring cities distinguished themselves by looting worthy of any Thracian, and given their past history, their enthusiasm was wholly forgivable. In Greece Philip had repeatedly supported the smaller cities against their bigger neighbours; now, when Alexander dismantled the power of Thebes, it was these small cities who joined him wholeheartedly as allies. The sack of Thebes cannot be dismissed as one more outrage to the freedom of the Greeks, for Thebes herself had infringed that freedom by her local empire, and fellow Greeks had avidly repaid in Alexander's name all that they had suffered from Thebes in the past. Alexander shrewdly entrusted the fate of the city to the decision of these allied Greek assistants, probably at a meeting on the spot rather than at a full council of his 'allies' in all Greece. They voted for Thebes's utter destruction, as he knew they would. So the city was destroyed, all private ground was given to the allies to farm as a reward, and 30,000 Thebans are said to have been enslaved, women and children included; they were sold at a reasonable price for such a sudden glut on the local market. Priests were exempted, as were the known opponents of the rebellion and all friends and representatives of the Macedonians' interests, down to the descendants of the poet Pindar, who had written poems to the Macedonian king a hundred and fifty years before. His house, conspicuously, was bidden to be spared.

In the name of his Greek allies, Alexander thus destroyed one of the three great powers in Greece that had threatened him. Men remembered, it was said, how Thebes had once abetted Persia in the distant days of the Persian invasion, and the memory was a cunning one to revive at a moment when Alexander was about to invade the Persian empire as if to avenge their ancient insults against the Greeks. If his allied council did not vote at once for Thebes's ruin, they would naturally have decreed their approval of an act which they were too frightened to condemn; only the Arcadians had moved to help Thebes, but they promptly sentenced their own leaders to death, relieved that their troops had not crossed the isthmus. Others did likewise, but there remained the power centre of Athens, and here Alexander intervened.

Despite rumours, witnesses even, of Alexander's 'death' on the Danube, Athens had not sent troops to the Thebans' cause. Alexander still controlled the ports of the Dardanelles through his fleet and his advance force, and possibly his ships were already detaining the corn fleet from the Black Sea, on which Athens depended for her food supply. Open assistance to Thebes would have been repaid by more rigorous blocking of this lifeline, so she had stayed neutral, even if Demosthenes had sent money and weapons from the presents given him by the Persian king. Besides, Athenians had hated Thebes for almost two hundred years and their rapprochement was only a thing of the past four years, whereas Thebes herself had voted to destroy a helpless Athens only seventy years before, a memory which had not died easily. At the time of the sack the city was celebrating a religious festival and no Greek army would disrupt honours to the gods for the sake of a march to war. Fresh from his Theban terrorism, Alexander was nonetheless keen to teach Athens a lesson. He could not easily risk a siege of her long walls and he was unwilling to outrage a city whose fleet and reputation he needed to use against Persia, so he merely ordered the surrender of the generals and politicians most patently opposed to him. The list of his victims was disputed, but a pleading embassy from Athens persuaded him to moderate his terms and he was content that Charidemus alone should leave Athens. This revision was perhaps true to legal propriety, for alone of his enemies Charidemus had not been born an Athenian and may not have been made a full honorary citizen, so he could be forced into exile without infringing the city's laws. In practice it was a bad mistake, for Athens's most seasoned general thus fled into service with the Persian king, and two other of Alexander's suspects, both of them citizens, followed of their own accord. He should have seized them, citizens or not, while he could; a year later, they were rousing Asian resistance, and their escape, more than any ruin of Thebes, must have seemed regrettable to the Macedonian camp.

On this high note of terror, Alexander returned to Macedonia in late October, secure on all four frontiers and able to plan for a full-scale invasion of Asia. Like his father, he prefaced his march with pomp. The annual festival of Zeus and the Muses was due to be celebrated in the border town of Dion, and this year he invited friends, officers and even ambassadors from his allied Greek cities to share it. An enormous tent was put up to hold a hundred sofas, and for nine days the court caroused and enjoyed the arts, properly careless of a treasury whose monetary debt had almost been paid off by booty from Thebes and the Danube. The entire army were given presents and animals for sacrifice, which they ate after they had offered a part to the gods. The officers received presents according to their influence and more estates as a bribe for their loyalties.

It was also a time for marriages between the noble families of highland and lowland. Both Parmenion and Antipater had eligible daughters, and they suggested to Alexander that he too should marry and father a son and heir before invading Asia; Alexander refused, perhaps because he was wary of his father's matrimonial muddle, perhaps because he did not wish to risk an heir through whom his elderly generals might try and rule. Antipater's daughter he gave to one of his Bodyguards, Parmenion's to an Elimiot baron whose brothers mattered in his army commands. A host of other marriages followed, some to heal old wounds, others to produce the officer-class of the future, but Parmenion and Antipater did not go unrewarded.

Antipater, nearing sixty, was to stay as general over the Balkans and Europe; Parmenion, already sixty-five years old, was to be deputy-commander of the army with authority over the whole left wing in the line of battle. One of his sons, Philotas, was to command the Companion Cavalry, another son the Shield Bearers; a nephew, or cousin, led half of the Mounted Scouts, and the leader of the Elimiot foot-brigade was now his son-in-law. Three other infantry officers and a prominent cavalry colonel may already have been his close friends, and yet there is nothing to prove that Alexander had been compelled to promote Parmenion's friends and family against his own wishes. The high command reflected Parmenion's influence, but it was hardly in his grip, and nothing suggests that king and deputy were already at odds with each other.

If anything, the opposite was true. There were many among the Companion nobles who opposed an Asian invasion, but Parmenion alone urged Alexander on, perhaps because he had already seen the country for himself. There was, however, an alternative, far away in the west; Alexander answered it by making plans for war on two fronts at once. While his main army crossed the Dardanelles into Asia, a transport fleet and twelve warships were to sail with cavalry and infantry to southern Italy under the command of his brother-in-law King Alexander of Epirus, brother of Olympias, who thus left his wife with a baby daughter and a son after only two years of marriage. Through Greek Companions, Alexander knew the political balance of the Greek west; the Greek colony of Tarentum had invited his help against the neighbouring tribesmen and he had ordered his brother-in-law to intervene in the interests of Greek settlements in Italy. The problems of piracy in the Adriatic had already attracted his attention, and he had corresponded with Rome on the clearing of the seas; within three years, Rome, which Aristotle's pupils described as a Greek city, would have sworn an alliance with his brother-in-law's invasion and the Macedonian cause in Italy seemed to be established.

It was a brave moment, the spreading of Macedonia's armies through the Greek cities and against barbarians at either edge of the Mediterranean world, and of course there were courtiers who mistrusted it. As Alexander completed his gifts of land and money to friends, his faithful Perdiccas, leader of one of the two Orestid brigades, felt bound to question him: 'And for yourself, my lord,' he is said to have asked, 'what are you leaving?' 'My hopes,' replied Alexander. It is worth considering how those hopes deserved to be rated.

CHAPTER SIX

As an idea, a Greek campaign against Persia was nothing new. For more than sixty years it had featured as a theme for professional orators and pamphleteers and it had been repeatedly urged on Philip and other outsiders by the eloquent letters of the ageing Athenian Isocrates, who on his own admission wrote for display and was not taken seriously. These paper expeditions ignored the balance of power in a divided Greece, and they did not reconcile the claims and rewards of an outside leader with the hopes of Greek allies who were bound to be fighting as subordinates; their advice was academic, and as Catherine the Great once told Diderot, the advice of academics 'existe seulement sur le papier qui souffre tout'. Reality would prove very different; the Greeks would have recognized it only too clearly as Alexander prepared to set out.

Ten years before Philip's reign, it had been boasted that Asia was easier to conquer than Greece, that depended on where Asia was thought to end. but the subjection of Greece was indeed the first and most awkward essential for any invader who crossed the Aegean. As heir to his father's Greek council, Alexander was dictator to Greece in all but name. There are three recognized aids to a dictatorship: police, a myth and an army, and on leaving for Asia, he arranged Greek politics with the help of all three.

His mother Olympias was to act as Macedonia's queen, her daughter Cleopatra as queen of Epirus; Antipater was appointed general over Greece and Europe with 12,000 Macedonian infantry and 1800 cavalry and the power to recruit more in times of crisis both from Macedonia and from her Greek allies. Personally, Antipater and Olympias would never settle down, but in Greece there were Philip's methods of policing to simplify their task; at least three strategic cities were being garrisoned, and elsewhere there were the favourable governments which had been frozen into power by Philip's treaties. A 'common peace' had been agreed among the Greek cities, whose presiding council forbade domestic revolution and the return of exiled undesirables in any member state. 'Supervisors of the common stability' had been set up to see that none of the three traditional means of social upheaval, redistribution of land, freeing of slaves and abolition of debt, took place inside an allied city's constitution. Externally, the political balance was suitably feeble; Thebes was now broken, Sparta was detested by neighbours who feared her for her past history, and only Athens remained of the major Greek powers. Alexander's brush with her had been indecisive, but as long as he held the Dardanelles and their cities, 'the corn-table of the Piraeus', he controlled the grain route from the Black Sea on which she depended for food and so was her ultimate master. It was an uneasy relationship. Although the allied Greek council had guaranteed stability for Greek cities, the Athenians were so afraid that Philip and Alexander might interfere with their city's laws that they had already approved a commission to recommend protections for their democracy. But Philip and Alexander still saw this strongly walled city as central to their plans, and their moves on her behalf were very revealing, for it was with Athens in mind that they had turned to the use of myth.

Already, on his gold coinage, Alexander was displaying on one side the goddess Athena, on the other the figure of Victory holding a naval symbol and shown in the style of the statue of Victory on the Acropolis in Athens. Very possibly, in the first autumn of his reign, he had helped to restore two such bronze statues on the Acropolis, and this conscious publicity fitted with his theme of Victory and Invincibility and with his hopes for Athens in the Asian invasion. Victory, his coins implied, would be forthcoming, won by a fleet with Athenian connections; Macedonia owned the finest ship-timber in the Balkans, but only through her Greek harbour towns did she have any ships of her own, whereas Athens's dockyards housed more than 350 warships, too expensive for the city to man in force but still more powerful than any fleet docked in the Aegean and a dreadful danger if they fell into Persia's rich hands. The myth of naval victory was meant to woo them, and although events refuted it, the Athenian fleet did at least remain neutral to overtures from Spartan kings and Persian admirals during the next four years. 'Athens, would you ever believe what dangers I endure to win your commendation?'; so Alexander's vice-admiral recorded him as saying, and the myth of Victory was part of this calculated policy. It was supported, moreover, by the slogan of the whole invasion.

War, Philip had announced, 'was being declared against the Persians on behalf of the Greeks, to punish the barbarians for their lawless treatment of the old Greek temples': he was fighting as the Greeks' crusader, and had chosen his slogan for its many subtle overtones. Historically, it referred back to the dark days of 480, when the Persian King Xerxes had invaded Greece and left a trail of sacrilege which only ended with his sensational defeats at Salamis and Plataea: it was not, however, an idle echo of the past, for a Greek crusade brilliantly disguised a Macedonian venture led by Macedonians, and it flattered, above all, the interests of Athens. In 480, it was the temples on the Athenian Acropolis which Xerxes had burnt, and for more than thirty years they had been left unrestored as a war reminder to her allies; these allies she had led in a protective league which had fast degenerated into her empire, but its slogan, too, had been a crusade of revenge against Persian sacrilege, By reviving this old political theme, Philip appealed directly to Athens's lively memories of her imperial past, and the tone of contemporary speeches and decrees confirms that her past glory and her 'Dunkirk spirit' in 480 were still worth invoking; since her defeat by Philip, Athens's horizons had been narrowing in space and turning back in time, and her political mood combined sentiment with bitter bursts of incrimination. A Greek crusade against Persia's 'barbarians' implied justice and religion and promised plenty of the plunder on which Greek warfare depended; it coloured the way in which Greek allies saw their Macedonians' task, and this colouring worked into the bones of the expedition. The small Greek town of Thespiae had delightedly helped in the ruin of her dominant neighbour, Thebes, and so she sent a squadron of cavalry to join Alexander's army; when those cavalrymen returned rich and victorious from Hamadan, they made a dedication from their spoils, not as Greeks who had served Alexander's Macedonian interests, but as avengers of their ancestors' virtue against the insults of Asian barbarians. The Greek crusade was a myth, for the Macedonians fought it with the barbarian help of Thracians and Illyrians and the Greeks featured mostly as Alexander's hostages and Persia's allies; only seven hundred Athenians accompanied the land army, a mere seventh of which was drawn from Greeks. But the myth was not outdated or without a real effect.

To its Macedonian leaders it had other attractions than glamour. Thorough crusades should begin their revenge at home, so the slogan licensed the use of Greek allies against troublesome pockets of Greek resistance, whether 'treacherous' Greeks in Persian service or rebellious Thebans whose help to Xerxes's Persians in 480 had not been forgotten; it went unsaid, of course, that the Macedonians and their Thessalian allies had also aided Persia when it mattered most. The myth was more than a flexible call to arms; it created a mood which its leaders could share, and one of the reasons why Philip had chosen Corinth as the centre for his Greek council was surely that Corinth had been the only Greek city to have recently repulsed barbarians from the Greek world. In Sicily, as Philip's friends had told him, Corinth had supported her own Timoleon in a triumphant liberation of the Greek cities from the threat of Carthage, a mirror in the west of Philip's declared aims in the east. So too, with

Alexander's attitude; the interests of the Greek allies of course remained secondary to his own, but a mood of Greek revenge and religious retribution did influence his actions, and it was not inconsistent with Greek ideas of such an expedition that he soon took Persian nobles into his court in return for surrender and that he appointed 'barbarians' to commands where they knew the countryside and language. It was still possible to punish the Persians by ruling through them, and revenge for Greece's past did not exclude an ambition to be Asia's king of the future. Part of Alexander's fascination is to watch how this second aim would grow to be dominant, but it is wrong to dismiss the theme of the crusade as mere publicity, cynically adopted and always disbelieved. The stress on the role of Greek allies was a polite formality, but the call to revenge of past sacrilege was only upheld because it was taken seriously.

Through Alexander, too, this mood was sponsored and written carefully into his history, for the leader of the Greeks' war of revenge needed his own historian, and with Aristotle's help, the man for this lucrative job had been forthcoming. Callisthenes, cousin of Aristotle, was already known among educated Greeks for his book on *Greek Affairs from the King's Peace to the Sacred War*. He had worked with Aristotle and learnt from him, and they were jointly engaged on the compilation of a list of the victors in the Pythian Games at Delphi, a labour of chronological love which contrasted with their flighty disregard for historical fact in other more familiar writings. Callisthenes was a man with an academic turn of mind; he was interested in the origins of place names and had theories on the date of the fall of Troy; like his mentor Aristotle, he used early Greek poems as evidence for history; he had a knowledge of botany and geography and perhaps of astronomy too; he argued for the influence of the sea on earthquakes, and he supported his argument not only by his own observations but by the fact that Homer had called the sea-god 'shaker of the earth'. He knew his Herodotus well, as befitted an author who had to describe a march through Asia and he was through and through a man of Greek culture; in the lively controversy over the origins of the Egyptian Pharaohs of the Nile Delta, he sided with those who argued, absurdly, that their ancestor was an Athenian. Academic interests went, as often, with a decided streak of silliness, mostly in keeping with attitudes shared by Aristotle and his pupils: he explained away the outbreak of the Crisaean war by the absurdly personal cause of an heiress's abduction; he admired the repressive constitution of Sparta, a common opinion among Greek intellectuals who did not have to live there; he agreed with Aristotle in the myth that the philosopher Socrates had kept two wives; worse, he maintained that Aeschylus, greatest of Greek dramatists, had written his plays when drunk. When he wanted he could be perverse, but it never perturbed his conscience that his home town of Olynthus on the eastern borders of Macedonia had been ruined by the Philip whose son he now flattered. Through Aristotle, presumably, he had first come to court, and Alexander commissioned him to write up his exploits in a suitably heroic manner; he had already shown, like Aristotle, that he knew how to compose a panegyric, and he made himself welcome by helping to prepare Alexander's treasured copy of the *Iliad*.

'Alexander's fame,' Callisthenes is said, very plausibly, to have remarked, 'depends on me and my history,' This is true, and one of the difficulties in the search for Alexander is that this history only survives in some ten informative quotations by other authors. The literary models for such a work were more panegyric than historical and Callisthenes wrote in a rounded rhetorical style. The tone of his book was extremely favourable, for it was written to please Alexander, who was presented as the glorious equal of the gods, expressed in terms of the Greek culture which dominated Callisthenes's outlook. His starting point and end are unknown and he does not seem to have sent back his work in instalments to keep the Greeks informed. The theme of the Greek crusade was presumably stressed, although no surviving extract mentions it, and it was no doubt pleasing to Alexander that Callisthenes was thoroughly familiar with Homer's poems and well able to cap his feats of glory with quotations from the *Iliad*. 'A man who is trying to write properly,' Callisthenes remarked, 'must not miss the character he is describing, but must try to fit his words to the man and his actions'; through his efforts Alexander can still be seen as he wished to be seen, and the wish is the nearest route to his personality. Other historians, whether officers or literary artists, would read Callisthenes to add to their factual outline, but they were not dominated by him; from facts which are common to them all, his history appears to have been a detailed and flattering report of Alexander's route and prowess, and not only personalities but also such statistics as enemy numbers and losses were wildly distorted to set off the achievements of the new Homer crusader. Callisthenes, in short, was the sponsor of Alexander's personal myth, and the search for Alexander is also a search for Aristotle's academic cousin.

For men faced with the invasion of Asia, these touches of heroic exaggeration were not altogether out of place. To Greeks who only knew the western coast of Asia Minor, the Lebanon and coastal Egypt, the conquest of Asia might indeed seem easier than that of Greece. In Persia's strictly graded society, even a minor nobleman could be called the 'slave' of his superiors, the king or the barons of the Seven Families. '*Mana bandaka*, my slaves' so the Great King addressed his satraps, but his empire had never been the slavish kingdom of an all-powerful master. Centralized rule is the victim of time and distance and in an empire where a royal letter could take three months to go from Phrygia to the Persian Gulf, power had had to be local to avoid dilution by mountains and slow roads. The Greeks had watched the satrapies of western Asia become the privileged duchies of recognized families or the subject kingdoms of native rulers who knew the language, the local villagers and tribal chieftains of the ever-present mountains. It suited the Great King to allow the empire to pass to these local governors, each of whom bore no love for his neighbouring equals; it also seemed to suit an invader, who could play one interest off against another and travel through the empire on its own in-coordination. But for an invader who meant to control his conquests, it was not so easy. When no one foundation supports the whole edifice of empire, the defeat of the centre is never final and freedom still flourishes in unrelated fringes.

To Persians the world seemed increasingly hostile the farther a man moved away from the circles of Parsa, his home province. As their court travelled ceaselessly from palace to palace in attendance on their itinerant king, they needed no reminder of the wearying presence of the empire's independent fringes. 'Taking a dry and hardened sheet of ox-hide he laid it on the ground and trod on one edge of it', men said of a Hindu philosopher who talked in India with Alexander's officers, 'and as it bunched together its other parts rose off the ground. Then he walked round the rest of it, pressing hard on each corner to show how it had the same result, until he stood in the middle and the whole of the skin subsided. This was his way of proving that Alexander should press hardest on the centre of his empire and never stray far beyond it.' The Great King knew that the centre mattered most, but he was not prepared to give up his fringes without a fight. He had never recognized Egypt as an independent kingdom, although she had only submitted to the empire for the past seventy years. The Suez canal, creation of the Pharaohs, had become unusable and the seafaring kings of Cyprus and Phoenicia had a respectable history of recent rebellion; twice in Philip's lifetime the satraps and local dynasts of western Asia had threatened to desert the empire and once, even, to march down the Euphrates and take Babylon. Against each of these western dangers royal generals had been despatched to raise armies of varying enormity: after repeated, and sometimes spectacular, attempts, they had trampled the empire's fringes back into place. If the memory of revolt remained to help Alexander, western Asia had at least returned to its allegiance to the king.

The Persian concern for the west is not easily explained, except by the wish to retain an ancestral empire. As the middle kingdom between China and the Mediterranean, Iran does not have a natural interest in the Mediterranean sea; by Aegean observers, reared on memories of Persia's invasions of Greece, it was easily forgotten that the empire existed for its Iranians and they wanted three things of it. They wanted protection for their estates and country castles against the tribes of the mountains and forests and safety from the fearsome nomads of central Asia whom drought and the need for grazing might force across the Oxus or south from the Caspian Sea; they wanted a court with ceremonial which would mark out the unique majesty of their king and set him above his aristocratic circle of Honoured Equals. These ideals of security and ceremonial depended on food and precious metals, without which there could be no garrisons, no court honours; hence the high value of Babylon's Fertile Crescent from whose artificially watered farmlands a third of the court's yearly food and a mass of its raw silver were drained east to the Persians' palaces and to courtiers from the harsher world of the Iranian plateau. Even among the Greeks, who knew little of the Persians' eastern empire, there were those who thought the Euphrates or the rivers bounding Asia Minor to be the natural frontier of Persian rule. But the Persians had gone to great expense and trouble to disagree; the kings who had mounted huge expeditions against the west had allowed their former conquests in the Punjab to return to local rajahs, the lands beyond the Oxus to be governed by allied barons from forts of unassailable rock and all memories of Persian rule to fade on the lower course of the river Indus. But as long as Babylon's farmland was safe, Egypt, the fleets of the Levant and the cities of Greek Asia ought to have been irrelevant to the needs of an Iranian court.

Geography may help to explain the Great King's priorities, for Iran and the 'upper satrapies' east of the river Tigris were a land of two main landscapes, neither of them suited to the passage of great armies. There was the boundless prospect of the desert steppes in the centre and the north of the empire where men strayed no faster than their flocks and the only rapid movement was the post haste of the courier and the king's work-parties down the stageposts of the rough Royal Road. Food was confined to a few oases of the water which Iranians always worshipped. If a man strayed into the desert he would not go far without the help of the Bactrian camel, hardy in mountain winters no less than in summer heat. 'When a desert wind is brewing, only the old camels have advance knowledge', wrote a Chinese traveller who had seen them, 'at once they stand in a group and snarl and bury their mouths in the sand. The men too cover their noses and mouths in felt and though the wind moves

97

swiftly past, they would meet their deaths if they did not take this precaution.' The desert was not an enviable field for close administration, but it was at least more accessible than the mountains which ringed it round.

To the west, the Zagros mountains, to the east the Hindu Kush, to the north the impenetrable forests of Gurgan and the Elburz range, to the south the fastnesses of Persia itself, a province which Artaxerxes III, contemporary of Philip, had never visited during his reign: these ranges were the lair of cave dwellers and mountain shepherds, forest tribes and nomads where an army had to cut a path if it was to progress at all and where snow and mud kept its season unusually short. On the outskirts of the Persian palaces a traveller would meet with nomads whom the king, left alone in return for a safe passage through their routes of migration older and more basic than any centralized empire. The hill tribes too were left free and now had less of a grievance against their rulers; the Persians' empire spread like a ground mist through the plains and valleys and when it came up against a mountain it could only halt and state its own powers all the more firmly at the mountain's foot. It was not the least of the powerful claims of Persepolis, ritual centre of the empire, that it stood in a plain ringed round with chains of mountains which the king could never have controlled.

For this empire's survival, the kings relied on such bold and uncompromising statements of their power: they were far more easily made in the western empire. The Royal Road was smoother and faster; there was no Hindu Kush or unavoidable desert blocking authority's few routes. Politically, the difference was summed up in the different systems of water, the heart of Asian life. In upper Iran, the ingenious 'water-mines', or underground qanats fed local villages and rested in the local nobility's control. Power, like the water, was dispersed through these aristocracies, and the King's grasp was loose. But in the west, in Babylonia, water was centralized in the long royal canals. Officials held the centre, and multiplied: judges and inquisitors were attached to provincial garrisons and satraps' courts in order to enforce the King's Law in public disputes, taking priority over the law codes of their subjects. The King's bureaucracy worked in written languages which illiterate Iranians could not read; evidence of its detail is still being recovered and although its documents do not extend within seventy years of Alexander's march, it can no longer be underestimated. The precise taxing of the king's colonists, the hearing of appeals in the satrap's court, the uniform system of weights and measures, the elaborate documents for travellers on the Royal Road who deserved daily rations from its regular points of supply, these hints of an intricate government raise questions of interpreters, scribes and civil servants which only new clay tablets and Egyptian papyri will allow to be filled in. In the absence of detailed evidence it would be wrong to write off a bureaucracy which on a point of principle sent half as many rations to mothers of a new born daughter in their king's work-forces as to mothers of a new born son and which balanced the number of women in each local task force exactly to the number of men.

Despite the scribes and law codes, power at the Persian court was personal, depending on access to the king. The politics of Persia were the politics of the palace gate and usher, the cup bearer, eunuch and brides of the royal harem: just as the king received his power by the grace of the good god Ahura Mazda, so the courtier received his rank from the hand of the king, being set apart by the honour of a purple cloak, a golden brooch or necklace or the right to kiss the king on the cheek or see him face to face. In Persia too, the old court titles had been widened to new faces; the Honoured Equals had become a whole squadron in the army and few Royal Relations still had a claim to kinship with the king; there were the same banquets as at Pella, whose expense was minutely observed and whose occasions brought the king and his advisers into daily contact. 'And the king made a feast unto all the people that were present in Shushan, the palace, both unto great and small, seven days in the court of the garden of the king's palace, where there were white, green and blue hangings, fastened with cords of fine linen and purple to silver rings and pillars of marble; the beds were of gold and silver upon a pavement of red and blue, and white and black marble.' There is no surer insight into the workings of the Persian court than the politics of the Bible's Book of Esther.

At this court the king was a figure of superhuman majesty, of a sanctity which derived from his position and did not depend on the force of his achievements. Little is known of Alexander's opponent Darius III, but it is suggestive. His father and mother were brother and sister, and Darius too married his sister as a second wife. This incest may have become a necessary symbol for the Persian royal family, emphasising their superiority to an ordinary family's taboos. Its mental effects are still uncertain. Darius was handsome, at least, and was brave by repute, for he was said to have distinguished himself in single combat against the most seditious tribe in central Iran. Naturally, there were Greeks who slandered this inbred king as the son of a slave, or as a former courier on the Royal Road; in fact, his uncle was descended from a branch of the royal family and he had made his name as satrap of mountainous Armenia. Perhaps it was during this office that he married his first wife from neighbouring Cappadocia; it is

99

noticeable how this wild tribal kingdom, so often rebellious, would fight for his cause repeatedly and become the refuge for noble Iranian refugees during Alexander's conquests and the age of the Successors. From this little regarded satrapy, Darius had progressed through poisonings to the throne. His friend the Vizier Bagoas had the influence and the severity to make or destroy a king, and it was with his help that Darius had removed his family rivals and taken the kingdom in default of other royal adults. The young son of the great Artaxerxes III was still alive, and there may have been Persians who would have preferred him to a Darius of such distant royal blood. No judgement can be passed on Darius's abilities, because there is no solid evidence; it is likely, however, that the manner of his accession had helped to scatter the court and weaken the loyalties of several provincial governors. It was not for nothing that Alexander proclaimed him publicly a mere usurper.

Recent rebellion in western Asia and this royal intrigue at the Persian court could not detract from the massive power which the king should be able to mobilize. Alexander's fleet totalled a mere 160 ships, a negligible number for a Greek expedition when Athens alone controlled 400; from Cyprus and Phoenicia, the Persian king could man more than 300 warships with trained native crews and techniques more powerful than any known in Greece. Alexander's money expenses already equalled his father's money income, and a separate debt of 800 talents had accrued for the invasion; the Persian kings received more than 10,000 talents of precious metal as yearly tribute, probably after deduction of the provinces' expenses, and their palaces housed reserves of metal worth 235,000 talents, some in coin, most in the bar ingots which probably served as currency east of Babylon and north to the river Oxus. Alexander's army numbered some 50,000 troops about 6,000 of whom were cavalry; Asia's population numbered millions and only terrain and the problem of supplies limited the Great King's armies. Some 120,000 men or more could be deployed for a decisive battle, 30,000 of whom could be cavalry from tribal nomads and the king's feudal colonists; as for horses, there were ponies to pull chariots, famous studs in north-west Asia and Media, tribes of horsemen in Armenia, Cappadocia and outer Iran, while the lucerne pastures of the Nisaean fields near Hamadan alone pastured 200,000 of the heavy warhorses. In his youth every Persian nobleman had learnt to ride, tell the truth, and shoot a bow; Alexander had a mere thousand archers and slingers and a thousand javelin throwers, whereas the home province of Persia could provide 30,000 trained slingers and archers whose composite bow could kill at a range of 200 yards.

Only in infantry was the Great King at a disadvantage. He had his trained palace foot-guards, 10,000 in all, but the hot climate, the lack of a class of small farmers and the traditions of archery and riding among his colonists meant that the empire had no heavy infantry apart from the Honoured Equals of its court. Greek infantry had served in the armies of Egypt's Pharaohs for the past three hundred years, and the Persian kings had taken to hiring them too; 50,000 Greeks, as many as Alexander's entire army, are said, with only slight exaggeration, to have fought against Alexander's crusade, most of them hired for the occasion, few of them retained as garrisons and none on permanent duty east of the Euphrates. There is no more vivid reminder of the facts of life in ancient Greece. Fifty years of Greek revolutions and domestic wars had swelled the hordes of exiles which Philip's diplomacy had anyway encouraged. Continuous and savage poverty in Greece had always made salaried service in Asia the landless man's most plausible means of survival and social betterment, a means far more certain than the hazardous gambles of sea trade or the temporary life of hired labouring in a world well stocked with slaves. The imaginative became pirates, the rest were mercenaries; sons with no inheritance, bored or incompetent farmers, failed merchants, bastards, all could look for a new start, their keep, and an adventure if they took to fighting in Asia. Some were desperate through famine, others through exile; some had fled to fight the Macedonians whom they hated, others simply liked soldiering, or had stayed on as veterans of recent campaigns in Egypt and the Levant. Most had been unable to settle, some did not wish to; their ruthless roaming had long been the horror of landed Greek gentlemen, and among conservative Greek opinion there would be no regrets that Alexander the Greek Leader was invading the barbarians to do battle, on foot, with Greeks who threatened the security of every gentleman's estate.

To every Persian statistic, there were to be reservations, but there was one figure which could not be gainsaid; the Persians ruled an empire of vast horizons, too vast for the Greeks to know their extent. To Aristotle the world's edge came beyond the Hindu Kush mountains in Afghanistan, and although he knew that the Caspian Sea was not an ocean, the depth of Asia from the Black Sea to the Persian Gulf was narrowed in his mind beyond all recognition. Yet under one and the same allegiance, tall Persian towers surveyed the fox-fur traders of the upper Oxus and the spice-bearing caravans from the Arab sheikhs of the Hadramut; the teak woods of the Punjab, the tiger forests of Gurgan, the cedar woods of Lebanon and the pitch-pine slopes of Mount Ida acknowledged the King of Kings' wishes at a range of 5,000 miles; salts were sent to his table by the priesthood of the Libyan desert; lapis lazuli adorned his palace from the blue mines of Badakshan; for two hundred years, the Persian Empire had kept an open road for the cultures of the East, bringing iron through invasion to the Negroes of the Sudan, Greek bridge-builders from the Aegean to the Euphrates, peaches, peacocks and the water-goddess of Iranian nomads to the temples and villages of Greek Asia Minor. All the while, the Persian kings had shifted their court from winter to summer palace at their empire's centre, as much as three months' journey from the Aegean coast and yet still in close touch with emergencies through their Royal Road and their enviably swift system of fire signals, by whose beacons and bonfires news could travel from Sardis to Susa in less than a week. Beyond them, mountain pressed on broad grass prairie, desert was broken by mirrorlike fields of green rice; language was as varied as the Empire's many landscapes, and for uniformity, among themselves, the Persians' governors ruled in an official tongue which they could not speak or write grammatically. Without maps and ready interpreters, it was through this variety that Alexander was meaning to find both a living and a way.

It is, therefore, the scale of his organization which impresses and puzzles most. He is known to have taken Greek surveyors, men trained as long distance runners who paced out the roads of Asia and recorded their distances; one of them, a Cretan, had already distinguished himself with a famous run across southern Greece, bearing news from city to city of Alexander's sacking of Thebes. Greek doctors of the Hippocratic school gave their services for the sick and wounded, and Greek prospectors were to search out minerals, whether the rubies of India or the red gold of Kirman, for Alexander had his father's keen eye for mineral resources. Of the cooks, the grooms and the leather workers history has left no word; Greek and Phoenician engineers are known, but the soldier carpenters who planed the planks for the ship timbers and maintained the army's wagons are never mentioned, though they must have numbered thousands. As servants were limited, the unsung heroes of the expedition are to be found, as always, among the supplies. Even if money was paid for each individual to buy what he could, then cook it himself, there were formidable tasks of organization. Bread, fruit and cheese were the staple diet of the soldiery, and although handmills were taken with the army for grinding grain on the march, the grain itself had to be bought in a market arranged with free enterprise, the satraps or the local towns. Invaders can hardly delay to reap their enemy's corn for themselves, but in their first four years, the army is never known to have starved. Transport was essential for such efficiency and, except by water, it was slow and costly; the fleet could ship the army's food along coasts and rivers, but inland, a week's supplies for 50,000 troops could rarely be transported, and the interminable train of oxdrawn carts or mules and panniers would have been impossible except on the level surface of a road. Of all Alexander's friends in Asia, the Royal Road which ran between post-houses from Sardis to Susa was far the most precious; by this one road which they inherited and improved, the Persians had bared their empire to invasion, for Alexander had no more accurate directions through Asia than Herodotus's history, Xenophon's memoirs of his march and the stray advice of local friends and guides. But he had only to follow the Royal Road and its daily staging posts and he would one day reach a palace; it is more true to say that Alexander conquered Asia's main roads than that he conquered Asia.

The campaign, which he accepted from his father, was proclaimed as a march against barbarians, and yet of all its untruths, this, as he found, was to prove the worst. It was more than two hundred years since the Persians had turned from nomads into a ruling court and the Great King's audience-tent and his ritual accession still recalled those old nomadic days of the self-sufficient life of moving flocks. But since leaving the proudest way of life in history, they had turned into a society which many have envied as civilization, rich in the rural life of landed gentlemen where men have the time to plant trees and tend their game parks, hunt and keep ornamental birds. In the courts and castles of a satrap, men could lay out an intimate garden and set off their loggias with quincunxes and canals; 'wherever the Persian king stays, his concern is to create stupendous gardens, called paradeisoi, filled with the choicest fruits and flowers of that land ... how fine and even the trees are, how straight their rows, how exactly arranged at right angles, how heady the scent of the flowers!' Greek gardens of vegetables and herbs never rose to such a high art and the flowerpots let into the surrounds of one of Athens's temples were in the worst municipal taste. Similarly, no Greek ever wrote a prose work worth reading as fiction until the influence of Persian romances and love stories had worked into their imaginations. The Persian kings, wrote Aristotle's pupils, had promised rewards to inventors of new pleasures, and so hastened defeat by their sensuality; there were harems, certainly, but there were also purple dyes and beautifully patterned carpets, spices, cosmetics, haute cuisine, fantastic dances, furs of ermine and snow leopard, golden and ivory harness and gem-set rings of carnelian and lapis lazuli; it was remembered how when a satrap had visited Greeks, he had brought Persian servants as the only men who knew how to make up a comfortable bed. The society which Greeks called slavish was also expressive and spiritual; nudity was a disgrace, justice severe and women respected with courtesy, and as an obedient community, content to follow their nobles, it was not surprising that the Iranians should have worshipped and spread the worship of Anahita, the most appealing goddess before the virgin Mary, who moved west from her home as water goddess of the Oxus and grew to dominate the huntress Artemis, goddess of Greeks in Asia. It is more remarkable, though disputed, how the philosophic wisdom of their prophet Zoroaster may have influenced the most admired intellectuals of the Greeks themselves.

'We are not living normal, human lives,' an Athenian politician wrote during Alexander's conquests, 'but we have been born to be a lesson in paradox to future ages. For the Persian king, who dared to write that he was master of all men from the rising to the setting sun, is struggling now, not for lordship over others but for his own life.' To the ordinary man in Greece, Alexander's crusade coincided with a starker fact. For seven consecutive years, the crops would fail in a series of summer droughts in the Mediterranean world, and pirate-ridden seas, politics and new centres of demand did not incline other corn-producing areas to help the desperate search for food. For most Greeks of the time Alexander was only a name amid hunger and grim survival, the constant struggle which conditioned any glory which fell to Greece. But the 'age of paradox' was true, and felt to be true, among Persians whose past made it all the more painful.

When a Persian stood in his great fire-temple, watching the flame dart up from a platform of logs arranged like the Great King's throne, he felt that the eternal *fravashi* or spirit of the king was present in the fire's every movement, quivering and never dying away. As he watched, he felt safe in an empire destined to last for ever; in a normal season the price of food for his royal labourers never wavered from levels known in Iran right through to the Middle Ages and the coinage of his local governors never fell from the value the kings first fixed. It was as stable a world as the weather and baronry allowed, and away in Babylon a Persian might even lease out one of his country houses for as long as sixty years. To his ancestors, Macedonians were only known as '*yona takabara*', the 'Greeks who wear shields on their heads', an allusion to their broad-brimmed hats; they had first met them some 170 years ago, when the Macedonian king had promised Darius I the tokens of submission, the earth and water, or *tin min*, as they were known in the empire's bureaucratic language. On the tomb of Darius I these Macedonians were carved beneath the seat of the Great King's throne, helping to hold it in a posture of submission; on the tomb of King Artaxerxes III who died nearly two centuries later in the year of Philip's victory over the Greeks, the ancient carvings were repeated indiscriminately, among them the *yona takabara* who had long been lost to the empire. 'If you now shall ask', ran the inscription beneath their carvings, 'how many are the lands which Darius the King has seized, then look at those who bear this throne; then you shall know, then shall it be known to you: the spear of the Persians has gone forth far.' Within four years the spear of the *yona takabara* would have gone far further into the heart of Persia's empire. It was to be the last, but not the least, of Persia's boasts.

TWO

She looked over his shoulder
　　For ritual pieties,
White flower-garlanded heifers,
　　Libation and sacrifice,
But there on the shining metal
　　Where the altar should have been,
She saw by his flickering forge-light
　　Quite another scene.

W. H. Auden, 'The Shield of Achilles'

CHAPTER SEVEN

In early May 334 Alexander set out for Asia. A brisk land march eastwards along the coastal roads to Thrace brought him safely across its four great rivers and so, within twenty days, to the Dardanelles, where the remnants of his father's advance army were encamped and alerted. He had been encouraged on his way by Olympias who had 'revealed to him the secret of his birth', as she believed it, and 'bidden him to think and act worthily of his parentage'; on this note of personal mystery, mother and son had parted, never to see each other again.

At Sestos, on the straits between Europe and Asia, Alexander was met by the 160 warships of his Greek allied fleet. Before him lay three miles of sea, known for their lively spring current; his horses and siege machinery would have to be shipped in flat-bottomed craft, and if Persia's far stronger fleet were to threaten in mid-ocean, the crossing might well have been vulnerable. Alexander appeared to give the danger no thought. While Parmenion saw to the transport he turned away on an adventure of his own, and only rejoined his main army on the farther shore; the crossing, so it happened, would go unchallenged, and luck, not Alexander, has often been given the credit. But there is a background which goes deeper and helps to explain that more than mere fortune was involved.

In war there are always two sides to the story, and in Asia one must be drawn from Alexander's enemy, the Persian empire, whose inner workings were mostly ignored by the historians on his staff. The Persians are elusive witnesses, for they never wrote their history, and mostly, like their Great King, they were unable to read or write at all; except for their art, their royal inscriptions and such business documents as were written on clay, papyrus or leather, it is seldom possible to see behind the enemy lines. But at the Dardanelles, the darkness can be penetrated and the enemy can be seen to have had problems of their own: Egypt had detained them, the running sore of their empire, and Egypt is a province whose history can begin to be recovered from papyrus.

'The south', wrote a native chronicler, 'was not in order; the north was in revolt.' Two years before, Khabash the rebel, possibly an Ethiopian, had stormed the capital city of Memphis and ousted its Persian governor; his slingstones have been found among the ruined palace's foundations.

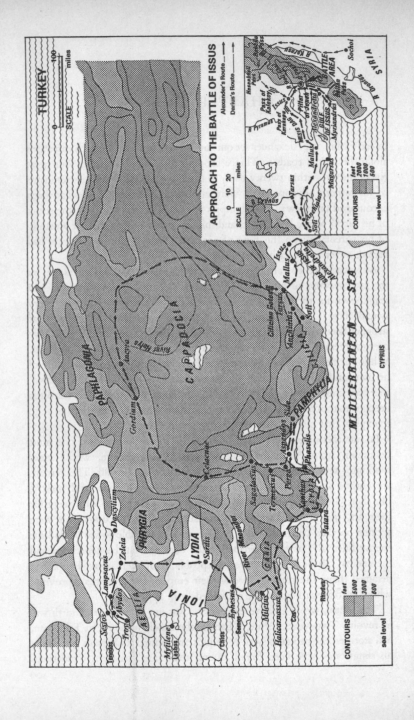

TURKEY

SCALE

0   100
miles

APPROACH TO THE BATTLE OF ISSUS

→ Alexander's Route
→ Darius's Route

SCALE
0   10   20
miles

CONTOURS
feet
2000
1000
500
sea level

BATTLE AREA

SYRIA

Sochoi

Hasanbeyli Pass

Pass of Jonah

Pass of Kurkkungu

Issus

Alexandria

GULF OF ISSUS

Myriandrus

Bahçe Pass

R Pyramus

Issus

Mallus

Magarsus

Mopsuestia

Tarsus

Adana

Soli

Soft Cilicians

R Cydnus

R O U G H   S Y R I A

PAPHLAGONIA

Ancyra

River Halys

CAPPADOCIA

Gordium

Cilician Gates

Tarsus

Mazaca (?)

Soft

Issus

Mallus

GULF OF ISSUS

Alexandretta

PHRYGIA

Dascylium

Zeleia

Sardis

LYDIA

River Maeander

Gordium

PAMPHYLIA

Celaenae

Sagalassus

Aspendus

Termessus

Perge

Side

Phaselis

CARIA

Xanthus
Patara

Telmessus

IONIA

AEOLIA

Troy (Abydos)

Lampsacus

Assos
Chios
Ephesus
Samos
Miletus
Cos
Halicarnassus

Lesbos
Mytilene

Tenedos

Nagos

Rhodes

Patara

MEDITERRANEAN   SEA

CYPRUS

GULF OF ISSUS

Issus

Mallus

Soli

Alexandretta

CONTOURS
feet
5000
3000
600
sea level

Fearing reprisals, he had then inspected the Nile delta and the local marsh-lands, but after a year's grace the Persian navy had sailed to put him down, entering the river in autumn when it was no longer impassably flooded. By January 335 the rebel king of Upper and Lower Egypt, ever-living, likeness of the god Tenen, chosen of Ptah, son of Ra, had come to grief. The Persian ships would remain to restore the peace until the weather at sea improved, but in early May of the following year, Alexander had already reached the Dardanelles and the empire's forces, as often, could not be diverted against this second danger. His crossing was neither rash nor fortunate; at least one official from Egypt had been living at Pella and Alexander would certainly have heard that the native revolt had given him an opportunity.

Safe from the sea he was nonetheless to behave remarkably. From Sestos he began with a visit to a well-known landmark, the tomb of Protesilaus, first of the Greek heroes to set foot on Asian soil in the distant days of the Trojan war; this prowess, as prophesied, had cost the hero his life, so Alexander paid him sacrifice in the hope that his own first landing would turn out more auspiciously. Already, therefore, like Protesilaus Alexander had decided to be the first man ashore in Asia; he was matching, too, his own invasion with the grandest episode of the Greek epic past, when Greek allies like his own had last marched into Asia to besiege Troy. Already the careful ritual, the essence of Greek epic, was setting the mood for the sequel. While Parmenion and the main army planned their passage from Sestos, Alexander put out to sea from Protesilaus's tomb; for the first and only time in his life, he had turned in the opposite direction to that which tactics required, but his destination was much too compelling to be missed.

Sixty warships were with him on the open waters of the Dardanelles, but Alexander insisted on taking the helm of the royal trireme himself. In mid-journey, as the trees round the tomb disappeared from view, he paused to placate the ocean, slaughtering a bull in honour of the sea-god Poseidon and pouring libations from a golden cup to the Nereids, nymphs of the sea. The cup he chose was linked with the cult of heroes. Then, as the long low coast of Asia drew near, he dressed in his full suit of armour and moved to the bows; when the boat grounded, he hurled his spear into the soil of the Persian empire to claim it thenceforward as his own, received from the gods and won by right of conquest. Again his gesture had come down from the heroic past. Like Protesilaus, he leapt on to Asian soil, the first of the Macedonians to touch the beach still known as the harbour of the Achaeans.

The landscape around him could hardly have been more evocative. At the harbour of the Achaeans, he could see the beach where the ships of the Greek heroes' fleet were believed to have lain when they came, the sons of the Achaeans, to recover fair-haired Helen and sack the citadel of Troy: beyond the beach stretched the dunes and hillocks where Homer's heroes were thought to have been buried and inland lay Troy itself, still set in its windswept plain. Alexander had aimed his landing at the country of his favourite *Iliad*; with his chosen companions, the new Achilles could go in search of the Homeric world and begin his crusade with nothing less than a pilgrimage.

By the time of his visit, Troy had long decayed to the status of a village, best known for its temple and priests of Athena. Homer's 'holy city of Ilion', Troy VIIA when Schliemann found it, lay buried under the debris of some eight hundred years, and if Troy still mattered to the Greeks whom Alexander led, it was more as the centre of a murderous game of hide-and-seek than as a memorial of the heroic past. The story was a strange one. Because the Thessalian hero Ajax had murdered the prophetess Cassandra at the end of the Trojan war, oracles had ordered the nobles of the Hundred Families of Locri in Thessaly to send two virgins yearly to the Dardanelles and leave them to make their own way through to Troy. By tradition, the natives would come out to catch and kill them, armed with axes and stones, and only if the virgins escaped would they enter Athena's temple by a secret passage and live there in safety, dressed in a slave's robe and shorn of their hair until a replacement managed to relieve them. The rite was to last for a thousand years, but at some point in Alexander's life, it is known to have been interrupted. As ruler of the Thessalians, it was perhaps Alexander who first dispensed his subjects from their duties.

Virgins apart, at every point on his road Alexander attended respectfully to ceremony. Among the Greeks it was commonly believed that if one member of an enterprise were to offend or neglect the appropriate gods, his fellows were all liable for the consequences; as king, allied leader and general Alexander always observed religious custom carefully and suited his sacrifice to his situation. So on his way up to Troy he continued his link with the first Greek invasion in the Homeric past; he paid heroic sacrifice at the graves of Ajax and Achilles and honoured them as worthy predecessors, for on first invading Asia it was the favour of the divine Greek heroes of the Trojan war which he thought most relevant to his campaign.

At Troy itself the citizens were uncertain how to receive him. A king called Alexander, they heard, was approaching, and no doubt, they guessed, he would wish to see the relics of his namesake, Homer's Alexander, better known as Paris of Troy. But when they offered to show him Paris's lyre, 'for that lyre', he is said to have answered, 'I care little, but I have come for the lyre of Achilles with which, as Homer says, he would sing of the prowess and glories of brave men.' Homer's Alexander, keener on women than war, was not to the taste of his Macedonian namesake; Achilles was the hero with whom this Alexander was identified, but unlike Achilles, he had no Homer to immortalize his name. All the more need, therefore, to make his own view of himself explicit, and down to the smallest detail, the visit to Troy was to leave no doubt of his personal preference.

On entering the village, Alexander was crowned with a golden crown by his helmsman, as a tribute, presumably, to his control of the steering in mid-sea. However, the helmsman's name meant more than his crown: he was called Menoitios, and after Troy he never appeared in history again, but from Homer's *Iliad*, Menoitios was well known as the father of Patroclus, Achilles's closest friend; the man had been chosen, once, for the sake of a name which suited the moment, and after more crowns of gold had been offered by local Greek dignitaries to pledge their submission, Alexander began to show them how deeply he felt for such Homeric niceties.

Anointing himself with oil, he ran naked among his companions to the tombstone of Achilles and honoured it with a garland, while Hephaistion did likewise for the tomb of Patroclus. It was a remarkable tribute, uniquely paid, and it is also Hephaistion's first mention in Alexander's career. Already the two were intimate, Patroclus and Achilles even to those around them; the comparison would remain to the end of their days and is proof of their life as lovers, for by Alexander's time, Achilles and Patroclus were agreed to have enjoyed the relationship which Homer himself had never directly mentioned. Then, at an altar of Zeus, the theme of the new Achilles was stressed again. Alexander sacrificed and prayed to Priam, legendary king of Troy, begging him to stay his anger from this new descendant of his murderer, for Achilles's son had killed old Priam at just such an altar of Zeus.

It remained to honour Athena's temple, and again Alexander's pious rivalry did not desert him. He sacrificed and dedicated his own suit of armour to the goddess; in return, he took from the priests the finest relics of heroic times, a shield and a set of weapons which were thought to date from the days of the Trojan war. No gesture could speak more clearly of his personal ideals. Homer's Achilles, too, had received divine armour of his own before going out to battle, none more famous than his shield 'well worked on every side, edged with a triple rim of gleaming metal and held by a strap of silver; five layers in all, their face worked with many wonders'. Alexander had now equalled his hero, and such was his favour for the Trojan shield and armour that they would accompany him to war as far as India and back, carried before him by his bodyguard-at-arms. The shield's design must have been extremely impressive, and posterity would spend much ingenuity in guessing its probable emblems: dressed in his hallowed armour, Alexander would live out the splendour of another age.

With the receipt of the sacred shield and armour, the Trojan visit came to an end. In all Alexander's career, there is no behaviour more memorable, none more eloquent of his personal ideals. Only in the fictitious *Romance* of his exploits is he made to voice disappointment in what he saw: the river Scamander, he was made to say, was so small that he could jump across it, and Ajax's 'sevenfold ox-skin shield' was scarcely more remarkable. Contemporaries had no reservations about their king's keen interest. Troy, in return, was granted handsome privileges, not least a new democracy, and later a pupil of Aristotle, a man, 'with a most inquiring mind', would write a pamphlet entitled *The Sacrifice at Ilion*. Unfortunately it has not survived, for the title implies he had realized the visit's importance.

Throughout, Alexander's purpose was written large in his detailed behaviour. It is true that the Persian king Xerxes, for whose wrongs Alexander was taking revenge, had visited Troy 150 years earlier and also paid sacrifice before launching out on the Dardanelles, but Xerxes's offerings had been differently planned and arranged and nothing shows that Alexander had had his enemy's precedent in mind: no Persian king had steered his ship in person or run naked round his hero's tomb. Alexander's visit was Greek and spontaneous; it turned on a link with the Trojan war and, above all, in its every tribute it had evoked the hero Achilles, his fellow seeker for fame and glory. Publicly Achilles had his relevance, not least for the Thessalian troops. Thessalian horsemen, it was later said, had ridden in mock battle round Achilles's tomb and invoked his chariot's horses by their names, calling them to their side for the coming war. But to Alexander, lover of Homer and rival of Achilles, the visit surely appealed more to his personality than his politics. The new Achilles, facing his sternest test, had come first to honour the old, not for motives of power or idle glamour, but because Homer's hero had fired his imagination, and as a Macedonian king he lived by ideals which came close to the old Homeric world. The visit to Troy befitted a true romantic, and the romance was a part of how Alexander wished himself to be seen. The lesson, moreover, would not be forgotten.

Nearly 550 years later the Roman emperor Caracalla would choose Alexander as the hero for an emulation of his own. Marching through Thrace, he dressed and armed himself like Alexander and recruited elephants and a Macedonian phalanx of 16,000 men. He crossed the Hellespont, less deftly than his hero as his ship capsized, went up to Troy, sacrificed to Achilles and ran, not naked but fully armed, around Achilles's tomb. The visit had a sequel whose story is even more irresistible. Seven years later, Alexander rode again, as a stranger arose from the Danube and frolicked his way through Thrace, attended by four hundred Bacchic revellers who waved their wands in a gay procession, as if triumphant behind Alexander himself. Every day, the impostor announced his route in advance and enjoyed both food and housing at the public expense, as no official dared to challenge his credentials. But on reaching Byzantium, he crossed into Asia, built his last laugh, a hollow 'Trojan horse' of wood, and disappeared. Obviously he had passed himself off as Caracalla, back for a second journey in Alexander's style, and thus danced his way on the strength of his emperor's own pretentions. There could be no more extraordinary tribute to Alexander's memory; Alexander, it was said, had envied Achilles for having a Homer to spread his fame, but even without such a poet, his trip to Troy remained a lasting inspiration.

It was long perspective, then, that Alexander left behind him as he returned eastwards from Troy to rejoin Parmenion. There was no escaping the heroic past, for the road he travelled was as old as Homer, being expressly mentioned in his favourite poem. His personal myth was with him; ahead, his army was waiting. Gods and heroes had been summoned to his side, but the time for romance and ceremony was over.

CHAPTER EIGHT

The main army had crossed the Dardanelles by a more conventional route, and when Alexander joined their commander Parmenion, all hopes were for a rapid meeting with the enemy. Thirty days' food, it was said, had been brought with the army, a quota for which the Macedonians had been trained by Philip; half had already been eaten, so they must either conquer or arrange for the usual market supplies with enough Greek cities to sustain them. The Persians' most probable base was their satrap's castle some eighty miles to the east; before setting out in its general direction, Alexander reviewed and counted his united troops.

With him he had brought some 32,000 infantry, 9,000 of whom were the six brigades of the Macedonian Foot Companions, 3,000 the Shield Bearers, 1,000 the foreign skirmishers and a mere 7,000 his allied Greeks. Seven thousand barbarian infantry from Thrace and Illyria, probably armed lightly, lent a note of valuable savagery; the Thracians, in particular, were troops to whom common decency meant little, and 'interesting parallels are to be found in the use of Red Indians by the British, French and Americans in the late eighteenth century'.* The victories of the previous summer had persuaded their chieftains to join the expedition, Triballians included; their numbers increased with reinforcements, and until they were abandoned as garrisons in India, they are a reminder that every atrocity should not be blamed on Alexander and his Macedonians.

Apart from a few allied Greeks, lightly armoured Thracians and the trained horsemen of Paeonia from Macedonia's northern border, the power of the cavalry lay with the 1,800 Companions and 1,800 heavily equipped Thessalians, less than half the horse-power of the one Greek state with the nobility and plainland to match Macedonia's riders. Together with the advance force, which had contained most of the Macedonian Mounted Scouts, the cavalry totalled about 6,000; the advance infantry had contained Macedonians and many hired Greeks, and so raised the total foot force to some 43,000. There were 5,000 hired Greeks in Alexander's main wave too, probably armed for light work rather than the front-line

* A. Andrewes and K. J. Dover, *Historical Commentary on Thucydides* (1970), p. 410.

service against Persians in open plains, for which they were unsuited. Pay as well as food would soon become pressing unless there were a quick victory.

When the two armies joined, all but a few small towns on the empire's north-western coastline had been lost again to Persia; only one loyal ally was still significant, and she mattered most from a Persian viewpoint. Away to the west the island city of Cyzicus continued to favour the new invasion: the Persians had tried to capture it, even disguising their troops in broad Macedonian hats, but Cyzicus had held out, and this resistance cost the Persians dearly. Most remarkably, the Persian satraps of the Hellespont province were the only governors in western Asia never to have minted coins of their own; the province's tribute had to be sent to the king each year in money, and to meet this need they can only have used a local substitute, none more probable than the abundant coinage of Cyzicus, one of the most widely known currencies in the Greek world. But the city did not belong to the Persian king, as it was not a part of mainland Asia; it was free to close its gates, and by closing them in favour of Macedonia it inconvenienced the Persians' army most of whom were hired for the moment and looked to regular payments of money for food and wages. Their commander had made a name for paying maintenance money promptly, but without Cyzicus this might not continue so easily.

Elsewhere, Alexander could only trust to his father's policy of freeing the Asian Greek cities. But liberation is always a dubious promise and his advance force had already been seen to betray it; Alexander did not go far before meeting with native distrust of what freedom might mean this time, for the first three days of his march took him north-eastwards along the Asian coast, where his goal was evidently Lampsacus, a prosperous Greek city beside the sea. But Lampsacus was most reluctant to admit him. Persian satraps had been minting coins in the city and their generals had drawn on her funds, perhaps because Cyzicus was closed: assistants of Persia would make no move for Alexander, and so the first Greek city he had come to free merely turned him away unwanted. Later, when victory had given his promise of freedom more meaning, envoys pleaded for Lampsacus to be pardoned, but until Alexander had shown his strength he could neither subvert nor assure the leaders of Greek cities, who had heard and suffered too often the offer of 'freedom' from invaders.

So he delayed his liberation and turned south-east towards the local satrap's castle, hoping for battle along the road. Villages of no importance were received in surrender wherever friendly, but hard though his horsemen scouted the hills, the enemy was nowhere to be found. The ground opened out into a generous plain, and scouts again went forwards towards the nearby sea; there was nothing there to report, except for a welcome from one more village. And yet all the while to the south, only twenty miles distant, the Persian troops had been massing, still unseen.

On receiving news of the invasion, the Persian high command had left their lakeside fortress of Dascylium and moved through its thickly treed parks and forests to a steeper hill range in the west. Here in the small Greek town of Zeleia the local tyrant had made them at home, and they were discussing their possible tactics. There were two alternatives: either confront Alexander directly or else burn the crops in his path and hope to repel him through lack of food. The second plan was Memnon's, a Greek from the island of Rhodes who had followed his brother into Persian service, survived the changes of fifteen years and shone as a general against the Macedonian advance force. With the help of hired Greek infantry, he had driven the enemy back from their early gains; proof of his generalship can perhaps be seen in a unique series of Persian coins, on whose backs are stamped what appear to be maps of the country-side round Ephesus, scene of Memnon's campaign; when he paid his hired troops it seems that he gave them handy reminders of local geography on the back of their wages. Deviser of the first field maps to be used in Greek warfare, he was not a general to be despised; some ten years before, he had also lived as an exile in Macedonia and he had seen the style of Philip's army for himself.

His plan was sensible, and when adopted a year later it nearly proved successful. But although Memnon had married a Persian wife he was a Greek advising Persians how to fight Greeks, and there were deep ob-jections to his policy. He was asking the satraps to burn a land which was highly productive; besides, they and their fellow Iranians had taken the best for their own estates. Around Zeleia, for example, where they were arguing, stretched the woods and parks of the former Lydian kings which the Persians now kept for their favourite sport of hunting; on marble reliefs from the site of their satrap's castle, they can still be seen enjoying the chase on horseback, while the castle looked out over lakes and game parks whose trees and animals were a revelation to Greek eyes, and the region is still renowned for its rare birds. The Persians farmed as well as hunted. Down by the coast, Persian nobles lived at the centre of farms which were worked by many hundreds of local serfs; their tall private castles served as spacious granaries, so much so that a local official could have supplied a sizeable army with corn for almost a year. When estates were on such a scale, it was all very well for Memnon to propose a devastation, but he was a foreigner talking of others' home coverts. He owned a large estate himself, but it was a recent present; others had seen their old homes burnt before, and the memory was most unpleasant. It was doubtful, too, whether their subjects would help by burning their own crops.

Bravely but wrongly the Persian command overruled him and ordered the all-out attack which Alexander had wanted. Down from Zeleia, the town, Homer had said, 'which lies at the foot of mount Ida, where men are rich and drink of the dark waters of the Aisopus', the Persian army descended westwards into the plain, while some thirty miles away in the mid-May morning, Alexander was still marching unawares, his infantry in double order, his cavalry on either wing and the baggage train tucked in behind for safety. A day passed before his Mounted Scouts came galloping back through the scrub of the open fields: the Persian army, they told him at last, was waiting for battle on the far bank of the Granicus river.

After the nervous searching of his past six days, Alexander must have greeted the news with relief. But some of his officers were not so confident; they would not reach the river until afternoon, and the month, they pointed out, was the Macedonian month of Daisios in which their kings had never made a practice of going to war. Their scruples, however, were irrelevant, for the ban had probably arisen from the need to gather the harvest in that month, and Macedonia now had slaves and workers enough to do the job without the army's help. Alexander refuted them, characteristically, by ordering the calendar to be altered and a second month of Artemisius to be inserted in Daisios's place. He would go ahead regardless, and by early afternoon he had reached the river Granicus, where he could inspect the enemy, a sight which justified his evasion of the date.

Rumour later exaggerated their numbers farcically, but there is no doubt that at the Granicus, the Persians' army was markedly smaller than Alexander's, perhaps some 35,000 to his 50,000. Except for Memnon, their commanders were Iranian aristocrats, most of them satraps or governors of the tribes of western Asia, some of them relations real or honorific of the Persian king. However, no unit from Persia, ruling province of the Empire, was present, and the cavalry, their customary strength, was either drawn from the royal military colonists who had long been settled in return for service on the rich plains near the Asian coast away from their homes by the Caspian Sea or the Oxus, or else from the mountain tribes of Cappadocia and Paphlagonia, whose horses were famous but whose governors had raised rebellion against the Persians' loosely held empire less than thirty years before. Some of these were heavily armoured with the metal protections which Xenophon had noticed and which Persian sculptures confirm; the flanks of the horses and the legs of some riders were guarded with large metal sheets, while metal leg-guards projected like flaps from others' saddles to guard them against blows from a sword. The head pieces and breastplates of the horses were also of metal, while rich riders wore metal-plated armour and an encasing metal helmet, ancestors of the chain-mailed cataphracts of Sassanid Persia whom the Roman army nicknamed 'boiler-boys' because of the heat and metal of their armour. Such horsemen are far from mobile, but on the edge of a river bank where a jostle was more likely than a joust, heavy body-armour was more useful than mobility; it was a point, however, in Alexander's favour that their fellow-cavalrymen were armed with throwing-javelins, while his Companions carried tougher thrusting-lances of cornel-wood. But this was only favourable if he could give himself space to charge, and a riverbed did not seem to allow this.

On foot, the Persians had summoned no archers but had hired nearly 20,000 Greeks from the usual sources of recruitment. At the moment they were positioned behind the line, but Memnon was a skilled commander of mercenaries, and if battle was joined immediately they would no doubt be advanced; the Companions would find it hard to break their solid formation unless they could take them in the flank, and not until they were broken could the Foot Companions charge with their sarissas. It promised to be a heavy fight.

One element ruled out hopes of a fair trial of strength: the river which ran between the two armies. Lining its far bank, the Persian troops held a splendid defensive position; for part of its course the river Granicus flows fast and low between sheer banks of the muddy clay which Alexander's histories expressly mention as a hazard; its width is some sixty feet, and its sheer-banked section beneath the foothills of Mount Ida allows little freedom of movement for troops climbing down, through or up it. The Macedonian army had marched perhaps as much as ten miles in the day, and they needed time to spread out into battle order, especially as their commands were mostly passed down the line by word of mouth. The afternoon would be far advanced by the time they were ready for Alexander's strategy. As he rode along the river bank on his second horse, for Bucephalas was either lame or too precious to be risked, he cut a prominent figure in his helmet with the two white plumes. But it is very disputable which kind of strategy he was about to choose.

According to one of his officers, writing after Alexander's death, there was no doubt about it. The elderly Parmenion came forward to give his advice: it would be wisest, he was reported as saying, to camp for the night on the river bank, for the enemy were outnumbered in infantry and would not dare to bivouac nearby. At dawn, the Macedonians could cross the river before the Persians had formed into line, but for the moment a battle should not be risked as it would be impossible to lead troops through such deep water and up such steep and clifflike banks. 'To fail with the first attack would be dangerous for the battle in hand and harmful for the outcome of the whole campaign.'

Alexander rejected the advice: he retorted, wrote his officer, that 'he knew this to be the case, but was ashamed if, after crossing the Hellespont with ease, the petty stream of the Granicus should deter him from crossing there and then. He did not consider that delay was worthy of his Macedonians' glory or his sharpness in the face of dangers. Besides, it would encourage the Persians to think they were a fair match for his men if they did not suffer the immediate attack which they feared.' Parmenion was sent to command the left wing, while he himself moved down to the right; there was a long pause, and then to prove his point he launched the Mounted Scouts, followed by the Companions, against enemy cavalry who lined the far bank; by a display of personal heroics against the Persian generals which lost him his lance and nearly cost him his life, he cleared a crossing for the Foot Companions and a path to an afternoon victory.

This conversation with Parmenion is probably fiction, for Parmenion appears suspiciously often as Alexander's 'adviser', not only in his officers' histories but also in legend, whether Greek or Jewish, where he is usually refuted and so serves to set off his master's daring and intelligence. It is more relevant that within four years of the battle, Parmenion was killed, on Alexander's orders, for his son's conspiracy. From the few surviving scraps of Callisthenes's official history, Parmenion's part in the great pitched battle of Gaugamela can be seen to have been criticized strongly and probably unfairly, and a story which was used at Gaugamela could easly have been applied at the Granicus too, perhaps again by Callisthenes, or by one or both of the later historians, Alexander's friend Ptolemy and his elderly apologist Aristobulus. If Callisthenes began it, then this 'refutation' of Parmenion must have been to Alexander's liking, perhaps because it was written after Parmenion had been killed and his memory was thought fit to be blackened. But it was not only a device to set off Alexander's boldness; it was also dishonest, for others described a battle fought exactly as Parmenion suggested, and for various reasons they were probably correct.

Alexander, wrote a historian who owed him nothing, did encamp for the night on the Granicus banks. There was no dialogue with Parmenion, but at dawn Alexander crossed the river unopposed, probably because the Persians had indeed bivouacked on a hill a mile or two back; it was not a Persian practice to begin a march before sunrise, and their universal habit of camping casually at a distance and even hobbling their horses in front of camp had already been emphasized by Xenophon as a fine chance for attackers. Having stolen a march by stealth at dawn, Alexander fanned out his battle line and clashed with a headlong charge of the Persian cavalry, who had leapt astride on news of the surprise crossing and galloped ahead of the infantry. Against them, Alexander showed a heroism worthy of any Achilles, unhorsing several satraps and receiving a mass of weapons on his Trojan shield, but on the left, Parmenion and the Thessalian cavalry ran his gallantry a close second, a fact which the officers had failed to mention. After a prolonged jostle and much use of the scimitar, the Persian cavalry fled, having lost several satraps and generals; as dawn broke, Alexander's battle line poured into the enemy camp, surrounding the Persians' hired Greek infantry, who tried to make a stand. Outnumbered, they did manage to wound Alexander's horse, but most of them were killed and a mere 2,000 were taken prisoner. Alexander could not afford to hire them himself, so he decided to make an example of them to all other Greek rebels; by his officer's figures, this meant a massacre of more than 15,000 men.

The battle was fought and won in exactly the style which Parmenion, according to Alexander's officers, had wrongly advised. Cunning at dawn, perhaps, seemed less dashing in retrospect and so less worthy of a hero; thus they invented an afternoon charge to replace it, and blamed the real battle on Parmenion's excessive caution. In the search for Alexander the various myths and memoirs of his friends must be tested against the narrative of a literary artist, written within fifteen years of Alexander's death from what he had heard and read from participants, and the Granicus battle is the first warning that the artist, though romantic and given to exaggeration, has kept truths which the officers distorted to set off the bold planning and invincibility of their king. Personal bias in matters of military glory should not surprise connoisseurs of history, but the weaving of a myth round a famous leader and his murdered general makes the lesson of the search no less immediate for being grounded in the distant past.

Of the sequel to the victory there is no room for doubt and little for complaint. As a leader of men, Alexander cast a spell which was firmly based on effort, and events on the Granicus showed its notable beginnings. Memnon and several satraps escaped, but Alexander buried the Persian leaders, a Greek gesture of piety which would have distressed its recipients, as many Persians did not believe in burial for religious reasons. In happier style, he 'showed much concern for the wounded, visiting each of them in turn, looking at their wounds and asking how they got them', and, human to the last, 'he gave them a chance to tell and boast of what they had done in the battle'. Twenty-five of the Companion cavalry had been killed in the charge he led, so on the morrow, he ordered them to be buried gloriously, and decreed that their parents and children should be exempt from taxes, duties of service and capital levies; bronze statues of each of them were commissioned from his official sculptor Lysippus to be set up in Macedonia's border town of Dion. As for the hired Greeks in Persian service, thousands of the dead were to be buried, but the prisoners were bound in fetters and sent to hard labour in Macedonia, 'because they had fought as Greeks against Greeks, on behalf of barbarians, contrary to the common decrees of the Greek allies'. Under cover of his father's myth, Macedonia gained a work force, and on a legal pretext an example was made to deter any future Greek recruits from joining the enemy's cause.

The spoils were treated with similar glamour and astuteness. Their surplus was sent to Olympias as queen of Macedonia, but three hundred suits of Persian armour were singled out for dedication at Athens to the city's goddess Athena, and the following inscription was ordered to be attached to them: 'Alexander son of Philip and the Greeks, except the Spartans, from the barbarians who live in Asia.' With this simple wording Alexander must be given credit for one of the most brilliantly diplomatic slogans in ancient history; Alexander, he called himself, not King Alexander nor leader nor general, but merely the son of Philip, in impeccably humble style; from the Greeks, he wrote, not the Macedonians not the Agrianians nor the tribes of Europe who had won a battle in which Greeks had only featured prominently on the enemy side; from barbarians, whose outrages he was avenging, but whose leaders he had none the less buried; from a victory, above all, of the Greeks 'except the Spartans', three words which summoned up emotions from all Greek history of the past two hundred years. On the one hand, no Spartans present, none of Greece's best-trained soldiers, none of the Spartans who had turned back Xerxes long ago at Thermopylae, caring nothing for arrows which darkened the sun, because 'Sparta did not consider it to be her fathers' practice to follow, but to lead'; but also none of the Spartans whom the smaller cities of southern Greece still feared and detested, whose unpopularity had been shrewdly exploited by Philip, whose shadow had darkened the history of democracies not only at Athens but also throughout the Greek world, Spartans who had come to free the Greeks of Asia seventy years before and cynically signed them away to the Persian king; it was a message of clear meaning, and it tells much that it went to Athens, the city whose culture Alexander and his father had respected, but whose misconduct they had fought and feared for two decades.

A thousand years, said the historians, divided the victory at the Granicus from the fall of Troy, which Callisthenes had calculated to occur in the same month as Alexander's invasion; a thousand years, therefore, between one Achilles and the coming of his rival to the plains of Nemesis, goddess of revenge, as Callisthenes described the site of the battlefield. It was indeed the start of a new age, though none of those who turned away from the site could ever have realized how; not in a new philosophy or science, but in the geographical width of conquest and the incidental spread of a people's way of life.

We can very easily imagine
how utterly indifferent they were in Sparta
to this inscription, 'except the Lacedaemonians.'*
But it was natural. The Spartans were not
of those who would let themselves be led and ordered about
like highly paid servants. Besides,
a panhellenic campaign without
a Spartan king as commander in chief
would not have appeared very important.
O' most assuredly, 'except the Lacedaemonians.'

That too is a stand. It is understood.

So, except the Lacedaemonians, at Granicus;
and then at Issus; and in the decisive battle
where the formidable army that the Persians
had amassed at Arbela was swept away,
that had set out from Arbela for victory and was swept away.

And out of the remarkable panhellenic campaign,
victorious, brilliant in every way,
celebrated far and wide, glorious
as no other had ever been glorified,
the incomparable: we were born;
a vast new Greek world, a great new Greek world.

We, the Alexandrians, the Antiocheans,
the Seleucians, the innumerable
rest of the Greeks of Egypt and of Syria,
and of Media, and Persia, and the many others.

With our extensive empire,
with the varied action of our thoughtful adaptations,
and our common Greek, our Spoken Language,
we carried it into the heart of Bactria, to the Indians.

Are we going to talk of Lacedaemonians now!†

* Lacedaemonians is the usual
Greek word for Spartans.
† C. P. Cavafy, 'In the year 200 B.C.'

CHAPTER NINE

'My sharpness in the face of dangers . . .', in the weeks which followed his victory at the Granicus, Alexander deserved the motto which historians later put into his mouth. Tactically, his problem was plain. He had to follow up his advantage before the Persians could regain their balance and defy him at any of the strong strategic centres down the coast. Distance never inhibited him, and the western coast of Asia had never been heavily occupied by the king's garrisons and feudal colonists, but he was moving into a world of complicated interests, each of which would have to be consulted in order to hasten his progress.

In the administrative jargon of the Persian empire, the coast of Asia Minor was divided into the country and the cities; the agreed owner of the country was the king, who received its fixed taxes and distributed farms as he pleased to colonists, administrators or Persian and Greek nobles with a claim to royal favour. The interposing buttresses of hills and the more remote parts of the interior were left to wild native tribes who were as independent as they could make themselves; the coastline, however, was thickly settled with Greek cities, and their status had long been argued between mainland Greek powers, who wanted to dominate them, and the Persian king, who wanted to tax them. For the past fifty years, these cities had been agreed by a treaty of peace to belong to the king; by his father's slogan, Alexander was now committed to the familiar ideal of freeing them.

In finance and religion, the Persians had been neither meddlesome nor extortionate masters; their scale of tribute was fixed, most cities were rich from their land, especially those with an active temple bank, and just as some of the numerous magi in Asia Minor had found a home in Ephesus, so the Persian king respected the rights of the nearby precincts of the Greek gods Apollo and Artemis, whom he identified with gods of his own. But politically, like the Romans or the British, the Persians had found it most convenient to strike a bargain with the cliques of the rich and powerful. Local tyrannies flourished in the smaller and less accessible Greek cities, knowing that their narrow power had the support of the Persian administration. In the larger cities, Persian hyparchs, generals, judges and garrison commanders lived on contented terms with the local grandees, establishing friendships which in several cases bridged the differences of east and west with commendable warmth. As the cities were surrounded by the country, richer citizens were men with a double allegiance, for as country landowners they owed taxes to the Persian king but as citizens, they retained their eligibility for office within the city walls. Inevitably, the two allegiances tended to merge into one and usually it was the freedom of fellow-citizens which suffered, for the rich and powerful would follow their Persian sympathies and set up a political tyranny. Where rule by the rich was in the nature of Persian control and was often promoted by Persian intervention, city feelings clashed bitterly, and men lived in one of the most revolutionary situations in the ancient world. Rich were divided against poor, class, therefore, against class, and democrat loathed oligarch with an intensity which even the odious divisions of Greece could not equal, free from the provocation of a foreign empire. 'The cities', wrote Lucian, an Asian Greek sophist, when the Romans were playing the part of the Persians, 'are like beehives: each man has his sting and uses it to sting his neighbour.' His metaphor fitted Alexander's age even more aptly for then, stings were as virulent and cities, like true hives, were actively divided on class lines.

Into this tangle of civic strife and class hatred, Alexander was heading with need for a quick solution. His father's campaign was committed only to punishing the Persians on behalf of the Greeks; there had also been talk of freeing the Asian Greek cities, but punishment and freedom might mean little more than the riddance of Persian masters. The allied Greek leader was also a Macedonian conqueror: it would not be hard to stop his two positions from conflicting.

Immediately after the Granicus, he made three revealing moves. He issued orders that his army should not plunder the native land; he meant to own it, therefore, like a Persian king, and so he appointed the Macedonian leader of his advance invasion as satrap of Hellespontine Phrygia, a continuation of an enemy title which complimented Persian government, though it may have surprised his Macedonians. As for the natives who came down from the hills to surrender, he sent them back as disinterestedly as any of his Persian predecessors. Throughout the province tribute was to be paid at the same rate as to Darius. Troy was declared free and granted a democracy, a hint of where Alexander's liberation might lead him, though as yet, no general provision was made for the Greek cities; the men of Zeleia, the Persians' headquarters, were 'excused from blame as they had been forced to take the Persian side'. Their tyrant, presumably, was to be deposed, if he had not already fled.

Parmenion was despatched from the battlefield to take the satrapal castle of Dascylium; as its guards had deserted, that presented no problem.

Meanwhile Alexander took the ancient route south-west across the plain to Sardis, seat of the satrap of the Lydians, whose empire had been seized by the Persians more than two hundred years ago after a defeat of their renowned king, Croesus. Quick to strike, Alexander was not the only man in a hurry. Some seven miles outside the city walls, he was met by Mithrines, commander of the Persian fortress, and the most powerful men of Sardis, who offered him their city, their fortress and its moneys. Alexander took Mithrines on to his staff as an honoured friend and allowed Sardis and the rest of Lydia 'to use the ancient laws of the Lydians and to be free'. As nothing is known of Persian government inside Sardis, except that the Lydians had been garrisoned and disarmed, it is impossible to decide what privileges this grant was meant to restore, but the Persians were famous for their provincial judges, and documents from Babylon and Egypt show how widely the 'king's law' was invoked against their subjects. In spirit, Alexander made a gesture to the Lydians' sensitivities, though his Greek crusade owed them nothing as they were not Greeks. Climbing the heights of the acropolis which still towers split in half above the tombs of the old Lydian kings in the plain below, Alexander marvelled at the strength of the Persian fortress and admired its triple wall and marble portico. Momentarily, he considered building a temple to Olympian Zeus on its summit, but thunderclaps broke from the summer sky and rain streamed down over the former palace of the Lydian kings: 'Alexander considered that this was a sign from god as to where his temple to Zeus should be built and he issued orders accordingly.' At this omen from Zeus the Thunderer, thoughts of a temple on the site of former domination gave way to a generous recognition of the Lydian kings, suppressed by the Persians for the past two hundred years, and diplomatically Alexander had more reason to choose the latter than obedience to a shower of rain.

As a conqueror, he meant to govern. A Companion was left to command the Persian fortress; one of Parmenion's brothers became satrap of Lydia and Ionia with a suitable force to support him. This splitting of the commands was partly in keeping with the Persians' practice and it divided the burden of work in an area that was not yet secure; as the Romans later realized, one officer could watch the other's behaviour and report it to the king. A Greek, moreover, was charged with collection of the 'tribute, contributions and offerings'. As a free city Sardis presumably paid the 'contribution', rather than imperial tribute, and the provision of a garrison of Argive Greeks was not necessarily a breach of her freedom, as enemy retaliations were likely and the city might need defence. But though Sardis profited, the rest of Lydia had only changed one master for another.

There was no point in wasting time on further rearrangements. The fortress treasure was a very valuable addition to army funds. The next goal was Ephesus, some fifty miles south-west by Royal Road. This powerful city had welcomed Philip's advance force two years earlier, and there was every hope that it would prove friendly again. First, however, Alexander despatched all his allied Greek forces northwards to 'Memnon's country' behind him, and if this was the general Memnon's estate, he may have been hoping to catch his enemy in person. These forces were to rejoin him afterwards, as their help was valuable.

On hearing the news of the Granicus, the hired garrison at Ephesus had fled. 'On the fourth day' Alexander reached the city, restored any exiles who had been banished on his account and set up a democracy in place of an oligarchy. This, his first contact with a Greek city since his victory, was an important moment, particularly as Ephesus illustrated civil strife in full. Two years earlier, it had been held by a pro-Persian junta; then, Philip's advance force had expelled the junta and restored democracy; a year later, the junta were back, exiling the democrats of the year before; now Alexander had tipped the balance and restored democracy decisively. Revelling in their return, the people ran riot and began to stone the families who had ruled through Persian support, fine proof of the bitterness they felt for tyrants. Alexander was man of the world enough to realize that one class is always as vindictive as its rival, and he forbade further inquisition and revenge, knowing that innocent lives would be taken in the name of democratic retribution. 'It was by what he did at Ephesus, more than anywhere else, that Alexander earned a good name at that time.'

The news soon spread and as a result, it brought Alexander power. Two nearby cities offered their surrender, perhaps on democratic terms. and Parmenion was sent by road with enough troops to hold them to their word. Alexander was beginning to feel more confident as his influence spread, so he despatched one of his most practised Macedonian diplomats 'to the cities of Aeolia behind him and as many of the cities of Ionia as were still under barbarian rule'. His orders were justly famous: he was to 'break up the oligarchies everywhere and set up democracies instead: men were to be given their own laws and exempted from the tribute which they paid to the barbarians'. Alexander, too often remembered solely as a conqueror, was staging a careful coup.

At a stroke, he had resolved the contradictions in his own position. Democracies did ample justice to his slogan of freedom, and by reversing the Persian's support for tyrants and gentlemen, he had released class hatred and the fervour of suppressed democrats to conquer the cities of

Aeolia and Ionia; he had not committed himself to similar treatment of the Greek cities further south, but he had ensured the thanks and loyalty of his new Greek governments behind and around him. There were sound precedents for his method. At Ephesus, at least, Philip's advance force had set up a democracy; in the more distant past, the Persian king Darius I had recognized the force of the Asian Greek cities' hatred for their tyrants and given them democracies after their rebellion of protest. So far from improvising, Alexander was exploiting the oldest political current in Greek Asia, and indeed the lasting ambition of most ordinary Greeks wherever they lived; only five years before, at the other end of the Greek world, the Greek cities in Sicily had been won by the Corinthian adventurer Timoleon and his similar promise of freedom through democracy, a precedent which may not have been lost on the Macedonians. Philip's valued Companion, Demaratus of Corinth, had fought for Sicily's liberation and as he had accompanied Alexander to Asia, he could have told him what democratic loyalties meant in a Greek city abroad; Alexander himself is implied to have preferred the rule of aristocrats. The coup may have been obvious, but others had ignored it, not least the Spartan invaders sixty years before, who had cynically domineered or deserted the Asian Greek cities whom they had come to free.

'There is no greater blessing for Greeks', proclaimed the Greek city of Priene fifty years after Alexander, 'than the blessing of freedom.' Such an attitude cared nothing for Asian natives, many of whom were serfs for the Greeks and their cities, but it was one which Alexander had turned most neatly to his own advantage. His announcement marked the end of an era, and was treated accordingly. Among those whom he restored, the mood was one of that jubilance peculiar to politicians who return to power beyond their expectations; many Ionian cities began to date their official calendars by a new age altogether, and thereafter, freedom would become identified with democratic rule, as if the two centuries of Persian tyrannies had been an illogical interlude. The vocabulary of politics changed, and in return, it is probable that the new governments paid Alexander, now or later in his lifetime, honours otherwise reserved for gods. This first sounding of a theme that loomed large in later years cannot yet be dated precisely. At Ephesus, perhaps soon after his visit, when Alexander asked that the rebuilt temple of Artemis should be dedicated in his own name, the citizens refused him 'because it did not befit one god to do honour to another', proof, if true, that men were already paying him worship. Again for the temple at Ephesus, the court artist Apelles painted a portrait of Alexander holding the thunderbolt of Zeus; this too suggests that Alexander had been deified as a new Zeus, but the date of the painting is uncertain. Lysippus, the court sculptor, is said to have protested that a hero's spear would have been more appropriate than Zeus's thunderbolt; he was, however, Apelles's rival and prided himself on his statue of Alexander holding just such a spear. He was not a humble Ephesian, outlawed for his belief in democracy and now miraculously returned to his home town by courtesy of a twenty-two-year-old king. Alexander was not the first Greek to be honoured as a god for political favour; even his father's brief liberation of several Asian Greek cities had been repaid by high religious honours that almost amounted to worship; the exultation of the moment made it thoroughly natural, but it is proof of the cities' profound gratitude that their worship of Alexander as a god was no temporary and forced reaction. It was to persist spontaneously for more than four centuries, complete with temples, priesthood and sacred games; the rich came to value its various offices, but few oligarchs of the time would have viewed its beginnings with anything better than disgust and resentment.

Besides guaranteeing democracy, Alexander had abolished the payment of tribute by his Greek cities, a most generous privilege which no other master had ever granted them. But like modern governments, he had enough political sense to rename the tax which he claimed to have abolished; instead of tribute, some, if not all, Greek cities were to pay a 'contribution', probably a temporary payment until he could finance his fleet, army and garrisons entirely from plunder. At Ephesus the tribute was to continue; it was to be paid to the city's goddess Artemis, whom Iranians had long identified with their water-goddess Anahita, and the revenues would presumably be used for the cost of rebuilding her splendid temple; an Iranian official was confirmed in charge of the temple funds and administration, a responsible job for which the oriental nature of the cult suited him, and in the goddess's honour, Alexander held a procession of his army in full battle order. He then left the city for Miletus, an Ionian city on the coast whose governor had promised surrender in a letter. Once over the first hills, his road wound through level hayfields, down which he moved his lighter baggage in wagons, while the machinery and heavy gear were shipped along the coast by the transport vessels in his fleet. On the way Parmenion and his troops rejoined him, and they made their way through the river valley of the Meander, receiving the surrender of small cities where they could set up democracies and ask for contributions.

At Miletus, an Ionian city, their hopes were to be disappointed: the city was set on a jutting headland, and as soon as its garrison commander heard that help from the Persian navy was on its way, he had changed his mind about surrender. This was disturbing news as naval support could keep this powerful position open indefinitely; as so often before, Alexander's solution lay in his speed. He captured the outer city, installed his allied Greek fleet in the harbours to block anchorage by the Persians, and settled down to wall off the rest of the city and besiege it into submission by slow but traditional means. Three days later, the Persians' fleet appeared in force from Egypt 400 ships strong in the opinion of Alexander's officers. For the first time in Asia Alexander was outnumbered. As he now held the strong defensive position, he need only have continued to block the city's harbour from attack and go about his siege as usual; however, the sight of Persian ships, it is said, moved Parmenion once more to offer his advice; after their dialogue at the Granicus, suspicion stirs uneasily.

Parmenion advised Alexander to attack both because he expected that the Greek fleet would win and because he was convinced by an omen from heaven: an eagle had been sitting on the shore by the stern of Alexander's ships. If they won, it would be a great help for the war as a whole: if they lost, it would not be a grave disaster as the Persians were already masters of the sea. He would go on board in person and take his share of the danger.

Alexander, however, considered that

Parmenion's judgement was wrong and his interpretation of the omen was improbable. It made no sense to fight with a few ships against many more, especially as the Cypriots and Phoenicians on the enemy side were a practised unit, whereas his own fleet was not fully trained: in an insecure position, he did not wish to surrender the experience and daring of his Macedonians to the barbarians. Defeat at sea would be a serious blow to the initial glory of the war, the more so as the Greeks would revolt if encouraged by news of a naval disaster.

As for the omen, 'the eagle was indeed in his favour, but because it had been seen sitting on dry land, in his opinion it meant that by land, he would overcome the Persian fleet'.

This refusal to fight at sea was tactically sound. It would have been foolhardy to risk a naval battle against so many ships. some of which were technically superior to Alexander's Greek fleet. They were an expert force, even if their crews were drawn from Cyprus and Phoenicia, areas where Greek culture had made its mark and revolt against Persia had been recent. It is most unlikely that the experienced Parmenion ever proposed such an indiscretion except in the pages of court history, where first Callisthenes, then Alexander's friend Ptolemy could work up his 'proposal' as a foil to their myth of Alexander. Events soon explain why they invented such a discussion; as for the eagle, bird of Zeus, it was a suitable omen for a king whom Zeus protected and it was also the symbol on the first gold coins which Alexander issued in Asia.

At first, Miletus tried to beg neutrality, but Alexander rightly refused it, and battered his way into the streets with the help of his siege engines. Many Milesian citizens 'fell in front of Alexander and implored him as suppliants, delivering themselves and their city into his hands'; these no doubt, were ordinary men who yearned for a return to democracy. But a few Milesians fought bitterly beside the hired Greek garrison until they were forced to launch into the sea and swim or paddle their way to an offshore island for safety; these, no doubt, were the richer citizens who had domineered the city with Persian support. Even on their island, they prepared to resist heroically, until Alexander intervened and offered to spare them, 'being seized with pity for the men because they seemed to him to be noble and true'. He enrolled all 300 of them in his army, no longer branding them as traitors; unlike the hordes he had punished at the Granicus, he had made them a promise in return for their surrender, and so lived up to it, not least because a mere 300 soldiers would not be a strain on his army treasury.

Mercenaries apart, a signal victory was being won out to sea. Like all warships in the ancient world, the Persians' men-of-war were like 'glorified racing-eights' and had so little room on board in which to store provisions that they were forced to remain in daily touch with a land base. Meals could not be cooked on the move and fresh water had to be collected by putting into a nearby river-mouth. Sharp as ever, Alexander had anticipated them and sent several units by land to beat them off. Thwarted and thirsty, the Persian crews sailed away to the island of Samos where they stocked with stores, perhaps with the help of its resident Athenians. On their return to Miletus, they still fared no better for water, and so gave up the struggle in the interests of their stomachs, and sailed away southwards. Having won his victory from dry land, as prophesied, Alexander took the decision which was to determine his route for the next two years; except for twenty Athenian ships who could carry his siege equipment along the coast and serve as hostages for their fellow citizens' obedience, he disbanded his entire fleet.

Even in antiquity, the merits of this bold order were vigorously disputed and at an early date, historians who had served with Alexander felt bound to defend their king's sound sense. Hence, at the beginning of the siege, they inserted a naval dialogue with Parmenion as a preface to the fleet's dismissal. Just as on the banks of the Granicus, Parmenion had been introduced into the story in order to stress Alexander's daring and play down the cautious truth, so at Miletus he was used in reverse, stressing Alexander's safe logic and smoothing over the very real risk which he was soon to take by disbanding his allied navy.

'He considered', wrote his officers, 'that as he now held Asia with his infantry, he no longer needed a fleet.' This does so little justice to Alexander's foresight that it can only be pious publicity; so far from not needing a fleet, let alone a Greek fleet, seven months later Alexander was forced to order his allied ships to reassemble in the face of the Persian counterattack which he must always have feared. His allied Greek fleet employed at least 32,000 men at the gigantic cost of some 160 talents a month and despite the treasures of Sardis and the hopes of tribute and contributions, he was seriously worried about his finances; his Greek allies were presumably not obliged to pay for their crews' upkeep, an imposition which was only tried later in a special case. The following spring, he could send 600 talents home to Antipater and a further 500 to finance the recruitment of his second allied navy, but this surplus may not have been ready at Miletus and anyway, tactics, as much as money, were at the root of the dismissal. Outnumbered, and unable to risk a head-on engagement against superior crews, 'Alexander thought that by capturing the coastal cities he would break up the Persian fleet, leaving them nowhere to recruit crews or use as a seaport in Asia'. In view of an ancient warship's dependence on its land base for daily supplies, Alexander had calculated this strategy shrewdly. On a lesser scale, it had worked already at Miletus and reapplied, it would eventually force the Cypriot and Phoenician ships to surrender and join his side. Friends later passed off the strategy as safe and free of risk, but it needed two years' faith and patience to succeed. During this time the Persian fleet threatened the entire Aegean, regained the use of many harbours which Alexander thought he had closed, and might, with more luck, have forced him to return to the Asian coast. It was a strategy shot through with short-term danger. Nevertheless finance and numbers made it the one sound option. Alexander, at least, had the foresight and daring to pursue it to its hazardous end.

Land bound, therefore, like his eagle, he prepared to leave Miletus and follow the coast south. As an Ionian city, Miletus was given a democracy, 'freedom' and exemption from tribute, but all foreign prisoners, as was the custom, were enslaved and sold. Out of gratitude, the restored democrats agreed that Alexander should be the city's honorary magistrate for the first year of their new epoch; he did not, however, delay, for the first hills of the satrapy of Caria rose beyond him and it was here that he could expect Memnon to rally Persians from the Granicus and their un-scathed fleet. Since his victory, Persians had hardly been in evidence at all; it was probably during the past weeks that a fugitive son of Darius had tried to enlist Alexander's help, only to be assassinated on Darius's orders. Such treacheries in the royal family were very much to be hoped for, but in Caria a more solid rally seemed inevitable, while Memnon was alive to supervise it.

As in Ionia, Greek cities still lined Caria's increasingly jagged coastline, but their citizens were secondary to the natives of the pine forests and patches of plain inland. In the past two decades, many of these natives had been introduced to the ways of hellenized city life by their local dynasts who had also ruled as Persian satraps. This voluntary patronage of Greek culture had become a political issue, for it had encouraged Caria's ruling family to bid for independence when the Persian Empire seemed weak. Even in the remote interior, pillared temples had been built in honour of Greek gods, and in the four main cities, decrees were passed in keeping with Greek protocol. Greek names and Greek language had al-ready gained control in the more accessible areas and Alexander was not yet confronted by serious barriers of language; the barriers, rather, were political. Many villages had been merged some twenty years ago into the rebuilt town of Halicarnassus, a hellenized capital of Greek origins, and hellenism always fostered independence from Asia; however, Caria did not share Greek culture enough to be won over by another promise of democracy and the slogan of Greek revenge. There was no class hatred to exploit in Caria and Alexander needed a line of attack which would appeal to native politics without involving him in long-drawn effort. On crossing the border, he found precisely what he wanted: he was met by a noble lady in distress.

Ada, former Queen of Caria, could look back on a life seldom in-dependent, repeatedly sad. Born into a ruling family where women retained certain rights of succession, she had watched her remarkable brother Mausolus civilize and extend her home kingdom in the 350s until she had bowed to the pressures of family politics and married his only son, resigning herself to a husband some twenty years her junior who was unlikely to respond with passion to the advances of his elderly aunt. Though childless, the couple had remained true, until first Ada's brother, then her nephew-husband had died and Ada had found herself a widow, heiress to a kingdom which was not an alluring inheritance for a woman in her middle age. Meanwhile her youngest brother Pixodarus was alive and scheming. He had banished Ada into retirement, taken the title of satrap and plunged into foreign politics with the proper energy of a man.

It was Pixodarus who had exchanged envoys with King Philip three years before to discuss a marriage between his daughter and one of King Philip's sons, the very plan which Alexander had frustrated by his over-anxiety. Instead, Pixodarus had married his daughter to an Iranian administrator; shortly afterwards, Pixodarus too had died and for the first time for fifty-seven years, the satrapy of Caria had been inherited by an Iranian, that son-in-law Orontobates who owed his marriage and position to a bungling act of Alexander's youth. Ageing in the confinement of a single fortress, Queen Ada had reason to reflect on the sorrows of her past.

Now from the maze of her family history, hope had strangely reappeared. That same Alexander was approaching, no longer a nervous boy of nine-teen. Ada left her citadel at Alinda and came to meet him at the border, keen to retain at least the little she still controlled. She knew the con-ventions of her family, knew also that she was royal and childless, that the years were slipping by. She came, therefore, with a tentative suggestion: she would surrender her fort in the hope of reinstatement, but she also requested that Alexander might become her adopted son.

Alexander was quick to recognize a windfall, however unusual, and received her with respect. Through Ada, he could appear to the Carians as protector of their weaker local interests against Persia; support for a member of their hellenizing dynasty would fit with his liberation of the resident Greeks. His adoption was popular. Within days, nearby cities of Caria had sent him golden crowns; he 'entrusted Ada with her fortesss of Alinda and did not disdain the name of son': his new mother hurried home delighted, and 'kept sending him meats and delicacies every day, finally offering him such cooks and bakers as were thought to be masters of their craft'. Alexander demurred politely: 'he said that he needed none of them; for his breakfast, his preparation was a night march; for his lunch, a sparing breakfast'; it was a tactful evasion of Asian hospitality, and his mother countered by renaming her Carian fortress as an Alexandria, in honour of her lately adopted son.

Culinary matters were not Ada's only concern. She confirmed the ominous news that Memnon and Persian fugitives from the Granicus had rallied again at Halicarnassus, the coastal capital of Caria; Memnon had been promoted by order of royal letter to the 'leadership of lower Asia and the fleet' and as a pledge of his loyalty, he had sent his children inland to Darius's court. With ships, imperial soldiers and a strong hired garrison, he had blockaded Halicarnassus, trusting in the circling line of walls and the satrapal citadel which had been built by Ada's eldest brother; Alexan-der, therefore, should expect a serious siege. The necessary equipment was carried by ship to the nearest open harbour and the king and his army marched south to meet it by the inland road.

The siege of Halicarnassus is a prelude to one of the major themes of Alexander's achievement as a general. Nowadays, he is remembered for his pitched battles and for the extreme length of his march, but on his contemporaries, perhaps, it was as a stormer of walled cities that he left his most vigorous impression. Both before him and after him, the art was never mastered with such success. Philip had been persistent in siegecraft without being victorious and it is the plainest statement of the different qualities of father and son that whereas Philip failed doggedly, Alexander's record as a besieger was unique in the ancient world. Though a siege involves men and machines, a complex interaction which soon comes to the fore in Alexander's methods, it is also the severest test of a general's personality. Alexander was imaginative, supremely undaunted and hence more likely to be lucky. At Halicarnassus, he did not rely on technical weaponry of any novelty and his stone-throwers, the one new feature, were used to repel enemy sallies rather than to breach the walls, probably because they had not yet been fitted with torsion springs of sinew. He was challenged by the strongest fortified city then known in Asia Minor, rising 'like a theatre' in semicircular tiers from its sheltered harbour, with an arsenal to provide its weapons and a jutting castle to shelter its governor. As the Persians held the seaward side with their fleet, Alexander was forced to attack from the north-east or the west where the outer walls, though solid stone, descended to a tolerably level stretch of ground. The challenge was unpromising, especially as the enemy were masters of the sea, and it is not easy to decide why he succeeded, even after doing justice to his personal flair.

Two descriptions of the siege survive and they match each other most interestingly; the one, written by Alexander's officers, again minimizes his difficulties, confirmation of the way in which the myth of his invincibility was later developed by contemporaries; the other, probably based on soldiers' reminiscences and Callisthenes's published flatteries, rightly stresses the city's resistance and notes that the defenders were led by two Athenian generals with the stirringly democratic names of Thrasybulus and Ephialtes, whose surrender Alexander had demanded in the previous autumn; though spared, they had crossed to Asia to resist the man who was supposed to be avenging their city's past injustices. A third leader, it was agreed, was a Macedonian deserter, probably the son of one of the Lyncestians who had been killed at the accession; they made a strong team, but neither of the histories makes it plain that their main defence was to last for two months, including the heat of August.

At first, Alexander skirmished lightly, probably because his siege engines had not yet laboured their slow way by road from the harbour some six miles to the rear, the one port unoccupied by the Persians' fleet. He encamped on level ground half a mile from the north-east sector of the wall and busied his men first with an unsuccessful night attempt to capture a sea-port some twelve miles west of the city which had falsely offered surrender, then with the filling of the ditch, 45 feet wide and 22 feet deep, which had made the north-east wall of Halicarnassus inaccessible to his wheeled siege towers. Diggers and fillers were sheltered by makeshift sheds until their ditch was levelled out and the siege-towers, newly arrived by road, could roll across it into position; thereupon catapults cleared the defenders, rams were lowered from the siege towers on to the walls, and soon two buttresses and an appreciable length of fortifications had been flattened. Undaunted, the defence sallied forth by night, led by the renegade Lyncestian; torches were hurled into the wooden siege engines and the Macedonian guards were unpleasantly surprised in the darkness before they had time to put on their body-armour. Having made their point, the defenders retired to repair the hole in their outer wall and build a semi-circular blockade of brick on hilly ground. They also finished a sky-high tower of their own which bristled with arrow-catapults.

The next incident is unanimously ascribed to the heartening effect of drink. One night, two or more soldiers in Perdiccas's battalion, flown with insolence and wine, urged on their fellows to a show of strength against the new semicircular wall. The ground was unfavourable, the defenders alert and amid a flurry of catapults, Memnon led such a counterattack that Alexander himself was forced to the rescue of his disorderly regiment. But though the defenders retired, they did so as they pleased: Alexander had to admit defeat and ask for the return of the Macedonian dead, the accepted sign that a battle had been lost. In his history, King Ptolemy recorded the start of this drunken sortie, knowing that it discredited Perdiccas, the rival with whom he had fought after Alexander's death, but he suppressed the defeat which followed, unwilling to reveal a failure by his friend Alexander; it thus went unsaid that within the city, the Athenian exile Ephialtes had urged his fellow defenders not to return the enemy bodies, so fervent was his hatred of the Macedonians.

Anxious at this setback, Alexander battered and catapulted as furiously as ever. Again the Persians sallied, and again, covered by their fellows from higher ground, they came off well. That was only a prelude. A few days later, they planned their most cunning sortie, dividing themselves into three separate waves at Ephialtes's bidding. The first wave was to hurl torches into Alexander's siege-towers in the north-east sector; the second was to race out from a more westerly gate and take the Macedonian guards in the flank, while the third was to wait in reserve with Memnon and overwhelm the battle when a suitable number of opponents had been lured forward. According to the officers, these sorties were repelled 'without difficulty' at the west and north-east gates; in fact, the first two waves did their job splendidly and Alexander himself was compelled to bear the brunt of their onslaught. The entry of the third wave into the battle startled even Alexander, and only a famous shield-to-shield rally by a battalion of Philip's most experienced veterans prevented the younger Macedonians from flinching and heading for camp. However, Ephialtes was killed, fighting gloriously at the head of his hired Greeks, and because the defenders shut their gates prematurely, many of his men were trapped outside at the mercy of the Macedonians. 'The city came near to capture,' wrote the officers, 'had not Alexander recalled his army, still wishing to save Halicarnassus if its citizens would show a gesture of friendliness.' Night had fallen and presumably Alexander's men were in some disorder; if he had thought he could attack successfully, citizens or no citizens, as at Miletus, he would have done so.

That night the Persian leaders decided to abandon the outer city: the wall was broken, Ephialtes was dead, their losses were heavy and now that their garrison had dwindled, perhaps they feared betrayal by a party within the city. 'In the second watch of the night', about ten o'clock, they set fire to their siege-tower, their arsenals and all houses near to the walls, leaving the wind to do its worst. The satrap Orontobates decided to hold the two promontories at the entrance to the harbour, trusting in their walls and his mastery of the sea.

When the news reached Alexander's camp, he hurred into the city, giving orders, said his officers, that any incendiaries should be killed, but that Halicarnassian citizens in their homes should be spared. When dawn showed him the extent of the damage, he 'razed the city to the ground', a detail recorded in both versions but evidently exaggerated as the city's famous monuments remained unscathed. Probably, Alexander only cleared a space from which to besiege Orontobates's two remaining strongholds, for some 3,000 troops were ordered to continue the siege and garrison the city. As Halicarnassus had been stubborn, there was no reason to give her a democracy or call her free. She was a Greek city, but she was not Ionian or Aeolian and had been promised nothing; her promontories were to hold out for another whole year and serve the Persian fleet as a base of supply. But Caria, at least, had fallen; mother Ada was named its satrap and given troops under a Macedonian commander to do any work.

that might prove too strenuous for an elderly woman. Thus, under a female eye, Alexander's principle of a province split between a native satrap and a Macedonian general was introduced for the first time.

The siege of Halicarnassus leaves a mixed impression. Alexander had persevered, and personally he had fought with his usual courage, but his victory, and that only within its limits, was not due to bold ingenuity or mechanical subtlety so much as to outnumbering an enemy who had sallied repeatedly. None the less, an important point of supply for an Aegean fleet had been breached, if not wholly broken, and as autumn was far advanced, most generals could have been forgiven for relaxing. Typically, Alexander did nothing of the sort.

Before advancing, he gave orders that all Macedonians who had married 'shortly before his Asian campaign' should be sent back home to Macedonia to spend the coming winter with their wives. 'Of all his actions, this earned Alexander popularity amongst his Macedonians', besides helping their homeland's birthrate and encouraging more reinforcements. Led by the husband of one of Parmenion's daughters, the bridegrooms bustled homewards, and Alexander thinned out his forces, detailing Parmenion to take the supply wagons, the Greek allies and two squadrons of cavalry back by road to Sardis and thence to await him further east on the Royal Road. The siege equipment was despatched to Tralles, and ever inexhaustible, Alexander announced that he would head south to the coast of Lycia and Pamphylia 'to hold the seaboard and render the enemy useless'.

Putting his dry-land tactics into action, he thus turned his back for ever on the Asian Greek cities whom he had come to free. Their freedom, of course, depended on him and only extended as far as he wanted; that, often, might be far enough, while he also showed them the favour of plans for new buildings, here a causeway, there a new street-plan, and at the Ionian city of Priene, centre of the Pan-Ionian festival, he dedicated the city's new temple to Athena, probably contributing to its funds. Just as he had honoured Zeus at Sardis or Artemis at Ephesus he favoured the local gods of the Greek cities down to the smallest details of cult and decoration. Like his plans to rebuild Troy, several of his building schemes were delayed or only carried out by local decision, but nonetheless in Greek Asia, if anywhere, the Greek crusade became a holy war of revenge and restoration. Its fervour must not be played down.

Other schemes had a longer and more calculated future. An ingenious policy seems to have begun with Alexander, whereby royal favourites who were rewarded with country estates were now forced to attach them to the 'free' territory of a Greek city and become its honorary citizens. The

140

result was a system of local patronage. Under the Persians, such land grants had been made without restrictions and created a provincial baronry free from the king, or a class of absentee landlords, free from their locality. Alexander and his Successors arranged that their favourites should be local citizens, able to report and maintain their king's interests in city affairs, while the Greek cities gained a rich local benefactor and an added acreage of land. By tying country estates to city life, a balance of interest was struck, and it lasted. Typically, it was city life which Alexander put first in his empire.

Country life, as always, saw less change. The colonial villages of the Persian kings' provincial soldiery remained on their old sites. The same baronial towers, perhaps now in Macedonian hands, surveyed the landscape from Pisidia to the Cyzicene plain and their name still survives in the common Turkish place-name Burgaz; their land was still farmed by serfs whom nobody freed, although many of them lived in some comfort in their own houses. But through this continuity, a new current had begun to flow. In the Caicus valley, for example, the colonists from distant Hyrcania, who had fought with their satrap at the Granicus, lived on in the land called the Hyrcanian Plain, where Cyrus had settled them two centuries earlier but over the years their villages would be merged into a town and mixed with Macedonians. Their traditional fire-worship continued, but when they appear in Roman history, it is as citizens dressed and armed in the style of Macedonian westerners.

After Alexander the force of Greek culture came to be guaranteed in western Asia; the cities' recognition of a new age was more than a detail of their calendars, for many felt that Alexander was what he said: a saviour of the Greeks from Persian slavery and an avenger of Persian sacrilege in the name of Greek freedom. It was thus among Iranians of the former empire that this mood of Alexander's passing made itself most felt. Repeatedly in the next hundred years, Iranians who lived on in Asia Minor are known to have joined the councils and magistracies of the Greek cities whose future Alexander had underwritten, a life of civic duty which contrasted with the baronial isolation of their past. Only their religion remained as a solid landmark in a changed world. The worship of the water goddess Anahita was continued by the magi who met to read their sacred texts among assemblies of the Iranian faithful in the hinterland of Greek Asia. An Iranian could no longer be sure of his country tower, but he could still find a place in his goddess's worship; an Iranian eunuch was left to run the temple affairs of Artemis at Ephesus, and in a small Carian town in Alexander's lifetime two Iranians became honorary citizens in order to serve as priests of Anahita, whom the Greeks saw as Artemis, a job for which their background suited them and which they passed from father to son for another three generations. These priesthoods were to prove their one safe haven in a world of civic duty, the rest of which bore little likeness to their past. But as Alexander turned south to Lycia, leaving his Greek cities to an unchallenged Persian fleet, it was still far from certain that an Iranian's days of satrapal politics had been more than momentarily interrupted.

CHAPTER TEN

While Parmenion arranged haulage for the siege equipment and led most of the cavalry and the wheeled supply wagons back to Sardis, Alexander advanced to Lycia and Pamphylia further south. The daily range of a warship was about thirty miles from its base, and Alexander meant to cut off the bases which the Persian fleet had used when sailing from the Aegean to Syria and the Levant. In the tough winter campaign which followed, little known beyond the disputed details of its route, he gave the first hint of his most precious quality of leadership: his refusal to be bound by any awkwardness of season and landscape. Even nowadays, the southern crook of the modern Turkish coast, the most glorious stretch of country which can still boast Greek ruins, is a challenge to the traveller. The highlands north of Xanthus, the twisting coast roads of Lycia, the citadels of the longlived Lycian league or the Pamphylian river plains, all these sites can still be visited, unspoilt and imposing in early summer but extremely daunting in the winter months. Though there are tracks and passes which remain open throughout the snows, they are enough to deceive the resident shepherds, whereas Alexander had no maps, no supply train, no fleet to support his coastal advance; his treasure was too heavy to accompany his travels and hence he relied for army pay and presents on whatever moneys he could exact from the towns on his way. Throughout he must have been very short of food.

Travelling light, he had to be selective, never risking a long siege and only stopping for willing allies or the more important harbours. Usually, the ground was too rough for horses, and citadels which were too strongly sited were left alone; at Termessus he bluffed his way through the natural defences of the defile but left the towering town alone, while at Aspendus, where moderate terms had been agreed only to be rejected as soon as his back was turned, he scared the inhabitants into severer submission by reappearing and showing off his strength. At the mercy of local knowledge, he seldom strayed far from the path of friends and native allies; his prophet Aristander and perhaps, too, his Cretan friend Nearchus had connections in several cities, but Lycia, like Ionia, was a tangle of hostile factions with no love lost between one city and its neighbour, one wild tribe and its marauding rival. If Alexander's army wanted local knowledge of the ground, they had to pay by being directed to the route which suited the locals' own disputes. Hence, no doubt, the hesitant loops and retreats in the Macedonian army's advance.

Iranian colonists had lived in Lycia, but the tribes and mountains had never been properly tamed or given their own satrap, and Alexander made swift progress, demanding help against the Persian fleet and showing favours to coastal cities with a slender claim to be considered Greek. However, his thoughts were with Parmenion, now in the north and only accessible by roads which the enemy could cut, and on reaching the city of Xanthus, where Lycia's coastline bent southwards, he hesitated and wondered whether to turn back. But, said his officers, 'a local spring was seen to upheave itself and cast up a bronze tablet from its depths, imprinted with archaic letters which proved that the Persian Empire would be destroyed by the Greeks'. The omen, a sign that Alexander was in two minds, justified the king's decision to press on eastwards down the curving coast. Wherever possible he saved his men's energies, only loosing them on a brief campaign in the frozen Lycian highlands which was probably meant to clear a path to the main road and the plains of the interior. On no account could he risk being cut off from Parmenion and the units wintering up in Phrygia, and this concern for his lines of the north was soon to cause an intrigue within his high command. The story was peculiar.

Alexander came to rest at Phaselis, a coastal city which was later renowned for the possession of Achilles's original spear. The citizens were friendly, golden crowns of submission were offered and native guides were promised to lead the army eastwards along the seaboard. In such genial company, Alexander relaxed, finding time for an after-dinner revel in the course of which he threw garlands on to a statue of Theodectas, a citizen who had been well known in his lifetime as an orator in Greece and whose writings were familiar to at least one officer on Alexander's staff. Flushed with wine, the king joked and remarked that he owed Theodectas a gesture of honour 'as they both had associated with Aristotle and philosophy in their time'. More serious business, however, was soon forthcoming. From Parmenion's base in Phrygia, there arrived an Oriental called Sisines, bearing information of extreme urgency. The king took council with his Companion nobles; as a result, a trusted Orestid officer was disguised in native dress and despatched northwards with a verbal message for Parmenion's benefit. Local guides were to see him through the mountains: 'it was not thought fit to commit anything to writing in such a matter.' It is a separate question just what this matter was.

According to Alexander's friend Ptolemy, Sisines the Oriental had been sent by Darius to make contact with Alexander of Lyncestis, brother of the two highland princes who had been involved in the killing of King Philip. Hitherto, this other Alexander had prospered in the Macedonian army, holding one high command after another until he had been appointed general of the Thessalian cavalry, an esteemed position. Sisines had set out 'on a pretence of visiting the satrap of Phrygia', whereas 'in fact', he was under orders to meet the Lyncestian in Parmenion's camp, offer him 1,000 talents of gold and the kingship of Macedonia, and persuade him to murder his namesake the king. Letters, it was believed, had already passed from Lyncestian Alexander to a Lyncestian relation who had deserted to the Persian side. Sisines had fallen into Parmenion's hands and revealed the true purpose of his mission, and Parmenion had hurried him southwards through enemy territory so that the king could hear the truth for himself. Alexander, supported by his Companions, sent back orders that the suspect Lyncestian should be arrested; only a few weeks before, at Halicarnassus, a swallow had been seen twittering above the king's head, and the prophets had taken it as a warning against treachery by a close friend. Through the Lyncestian the omen had come true.

That was only Ptolemy's opinion, and it bristles with unlikelihood for anyone who is prepared to doubt the word of Alexander's friend; Ptolemy liked to include good omens in his history, but the sign of the swallow is perhaps too subtle not to rouse suspicion. Why had Parmenion risked sending such a valuable captive as Sisines through miles of enemy territory? Alexander's own precautions in reply, the native guides, the disguise, the verbal message, show the journey could not be undertaken lightly even without a prisoner and his guard in tow. Why was the official arrest of the Lyncestian so important that it could not be entrusted to writing for fear of enemy interception? Even if the enemy captured such written news, how could they exploit it? Parmenion had heard Sisines's story and was surely shrewd enough to keep a serious suspect under arrest until his king, some 200 miles and a frozen mountain barrier distant, could come to a decision. Why did Sisines ever reveal the 'true cause' of his mission rather than the 'pretext' that he was visiting his satrap in Phrygia, a plausible story which Parmenion could hardly have disbelieved? It is all most implausible, and it deserves to be suspected, for Alexander the Lyncestian was an officer of considerable mystery and embarrassment.

It was not just that his brothers had been killed on a charge of murdering Philip; in Seistan, four years later, he was to be brought out of close arrest and accused before the soldiery at a time of purge and crisis in the high command. Denounced as guilty, he was promptly speared to death, an awkward fact which Alexander's officers omitted from their histories. Ptolemy, it seems, never mentioned the Lyncestian again, content with his story of the arrest for treachery; Aristobulus, who wrote in his eighties and elaborately defended Alexander, seems to have taken an even more extreme stand. Most probably, he implied that the Lyncestian had been killed by an enemy before he ever reached Asia. During the siege of Thebes, he wrote, a Macedonian called Alexander who was leading a squadron of Thracians broke into a noble lady's house and demanded her money. He was a 'stupid and insolent man, of the same name as the King but in no way like him', and, proud daughter of a Greek general, she showed him to a well in the garden and pushed him down it, dropping boulders in afterwards to make sure that she killed him. For this act of defiance, Alexander spared her from slavery, a pardon which illustrated his chivalry. However, Alexander the Lyncestian was the commanding general of Thrace at the time and known to be present with an army of Thracians at Thebes; it is most unlikely that there were two Macedonians called Alexander in command of Thracians at the same time, and indeed the tone of Aristobulus's story suggests that he was disposing of the Lyncestian, whose true fate he omitted, as an unprincipled plunderer who went to a deserving death. As a contemporary and an eye-witness, Aristobulus has been used as an authority for Alexander's history, but on the subject of an officer, well known as a cavalry commander in Asia and as a victim of Seistan's purge, he could construct a monstrously apologetic falsehood. His history does not seem to be notable for accurate detail or for lists of high officers, except those reported already by Callisthenes who would anyway omit the Lyncestian's arrest from his panegyric. It is as if Aristobulus felt bound to conceal the truth, and he does not deserve to be trusted elsewhere.

Against Alexander's friends, there is once again a rival story, written up from soldiers' reminiscences, but its view of Sisines and the Lyncestian is very different. Sisines, it alleged, was an Oriental who had fled from Egypt to Philip's court and followed Alexander in a position of trust; during the winter in Lycia, he cannot, therefore, have been arrested as a spy from the Persian army. Not until the following autumn is anything said of his fate, for shortly before the battle of Issus, when Persians were threatening everywhere, he was suspected of receiving a letter from the Persian Vizier asking him to kill Alexander, but was himself killed by the Cretan archers 'doubtless on Alexander's orders'. The suspicion may have been true, his murder may only have been a security precaution but the fact that he was one of Alexander's own courtiers puts Ptolemy's story of the Lycian affair in a very different light. If Sisines was a friend and a courtier, at once the implausibilities disappear. Some two hundred miles north of Phaselis, Parmenion must have been anxious about communications with his king; anxious, moreover, with good reason as Alexander himself had skirmished in the Lycian highlands to clear the one main road to his absent generals. Perhaps Parmenion wanted to check the plans and timing: perhaps news of a Persian threat had suddenly been intercepted. One, and only one, officer could be sure of passing unnoticed down a road flanked by the enemy and through a satrapy still in the Persians' hands: Sisines, the loyal Oriental, inconspicuous master of the necessary languages. Sisines, then, slipped southwards with a secret message; Alexander sent back one of his friends in native disguise, as a sign that the trusted messenger had fulfilled his mission and the accompanying orders were genuine. It was a dramatic piece of intelligence work, but it concerned strategy; it had nothing to do with the Lyncestian, let alone with his treachery, and here too an alternative story survived.

Nine or ten months later, at the time of Sisines's murder, the Lyncestian was said to have been arrested for a very different reason. Shortly before the battle of Issus, letters arrived from Olympias with warnings against the Lyncestian, and Alexander, it was said, put him into chains. Possibly, Olympias had had private evidence, for it was a time of mystery and upheaval in Greece, but sheer jealousy against the Lyncestian might also have been a motive; he was married to Antipater's daughter, and the fierce quarrels between Antipater the general and Olympias the queen regent were soon to become a serious difficulty. By a strange chance, the story can be shown to have been timed so plausibly that it must be believed. A few weeks after receiving Sisines and leaving Phaselis, Alexander entered battle, having put the entire left wing of his army under the command of a man who was probably the offending Lyncestian's nephew; such trust would have been an impossible folly if the Lyncestian had just been caught in a conspiracy. However, the battle was the nephew's final appearance in history, and ten months later he had been deposed for ever from the high command. He was a young man and there had been no fighting meanwhile to cost him his life; his fall, surely, had been due to his uncle's arrest, not through Sisines's visit, which he survived unharmed, but through letters from Olympias which cost him his job in the following autumn.

In the search for Alexander, this intrigue is illuminating. It is of some

147

interest that shortly before his battle of Issus, Alexander deposed the last of his Lyncestian commanders, even though he had been indebted to them at the time of his accession; it is far more telling that his friend Ptolemy and his officer Aristobulus could pass off the arrests by an intricate trail of deception. Possibly they had no clear memory of the high commanders in the invasion's early days; possibly, but it is far more plausible that they were concealing the brute truth of the Lyncestian's execution in the Seistan purge which they underplayed. They never mentioned it again, for Aristobulus pleaded that the man had been killed by a Theban woman five years earlier, Ptolemy that he had been a proven traitor; for Ptolemy, perhaps, there were grounds for the false suggestion. Sisines and the Lyncestian were killed and arrested in one and the same month, each for different reasons; in Seistan, one fact about the Lyncestian's death caused comment, that when denounced, he faltered and found nothing to say in his defence. Perhaps the name of Sisines was used against him, an obscure Oriental who had died at the time of the Lyncestian's earlier arrest on a charge of treason, but of whom he knew nothing at all. Ptolemy may have heard the charge and connected it, falsely, with Sisines's only other exploit on the expedition. As at Thebes or Halicarnassus, the Granicus no less than the dismissal of the fleet, Alexander's story cannot be written exclusively from histories based on his friends and officers; their literary rival, like every other historian of the expedition, was no less admiring of Alexander and his achievements, but he also retained a disarming honesty, and when officers fell, or were denounced on spurious charges, such honesty, it seems, was very easy to lose.

Leaving Phaselis, with the Lyncestians still in honour, Alexander continued briefly and briskly on his coastal campaign, only doubling back to scare his dissident subject city Aspendos. Near Mount Climax, he rode down to the shore to take a short cut across the bay and save himself a six-hour ride through the hills behind. As he rounded the promontory the southerly wind stopped blowing and opened a way through the waves for his horsemen, a lucky chance which he described as 'not without the help of heaven', and which Callisthenes developed into a formal bowing of the sea before its new master. At Termessus and Sagalassus, he repulsed the tribesmen and cleared his road to the north without capturing their fortresses. There were no more harbour-towns nearby, so in early spring he at last turned northwards to join Parmenion, having done what he could to close the Lycian ports. His efforts would not, however, stop the Persian fleet from sailing between Syria and the Aegean islands the following summer. He had half-closed a coastline, but he had not cut off a sea route of any importance, and longer marches were needed before his dry-land policy could begin to work.

It was a beginning, at least, but after a rigorous winter's exploits, he would be pleased to find the landscape of the Phrygian satrapy stretching northwards before him, bare of cover for an enemy, its pebbled plough-land broken only by the occasional belt of poplars. Its flatness was hearten-ing to an army wearied of winter highlands, so much so that within five days they had reached the centre of Phrygia and encamped before the satrap's citadel at Celaenae. As soon as its foreign garrison realized that no Persian forces would rescue them in later winter, perhaps because Par-menion had moved to cut them off, they surrendered their sumptuous palaces and parks to their new masters; elderly Antigonus, one-eyed and prominent among Philip's veteran officers, received a satrapy so important for keeping the roads of communication clear of enemy attack. After sending another officer westwards to raise more troops from southern Greece, Alexander rode on northwards over richer lands to Gordium, his agreed point of meeting. There, behind the city's Persian battlements, he awaited Parmenion's arrival.

Gordium lay on the Royal Road, and as reinforcements were expected from Macedonia, it had been chosen as the convenient meeting-point with Parmenion's army and their fresh draft of troops from the Balkans. Parmenion soon appeared, but the reinforcements were slow to arrive. They could not sail the sea, as there was no fleet to protect them, and they had to march the five hundred miles from Pella to Gordium by road. Spring broke, and they still had not set out; May was already well begun and as disturbing news came of a Persian sea-offensive, the reinforcements had still not arrived, perhaps because they were detained at the Dardanelles. Gordium, an ancient capital city, had few excitements to offer; the troops fretted and idled, and Alexander needed a diversion to keep up morale.

Word reached him of a local curiosity, a chariot in the palace of the former kings of Phrygia which was linked by legend to King Midas's accession at Gordium four hundred years before. It had been dedicated to a Phrygian god whom the officers identified with Zeus the King, Alex-ander's royal ancestor and guardian, and it was bound to its yoke by a knot of cornel-bark which no man had ever been able to undo; that in itself was a challenge, and the story had a topical appeal. King Midas was connected through legend with Macedonia where the lowlands' Gardens of Midas still bore his name, and Phrygian tribes were rightly believed to have once lived in Macedonia, in memory of the early migration during which they had ruled the country and mined their wealth, according to Callisthenes, from the Bermion mountains. Alexander's prophet Aristander, a man whose 'prophecies he always liked to support', also had an interest in the chariot, for Midas's father was said to have consulted Aristander's own people about it, the Telmissians of Lycia, who were famed for their powers of divination. Several themes converged on the chariot, and Alexander reserved it for the largest possible audience.

It was late May before the reinforcements arrived, some 3,000 Macedonians and 1,000 or so Greeks and allies, together with the host of Macedonian bridegrooms who had returned to winter with their wives. With them, came ambassadors from Athens to beg the release of Athenian prisoners taken at the Granicus, but Alexander refused them 'for he did not think it was right, while the Persian war was in progress, to relax any terror for Greeks who did not refuse to fight against Greece on behalf of the barbarians. They should approach him again later.' It went unsaid that at Sardis, letters had been found to prove that Persian generals had sent money to Demosthenes the Athenian to stir up rebellion in the first year of his reign; sheltering behind his father's myth of a Greek expedition, Alexander kept up his hold on the one Greek city where it was most needed.

It was also time to encourage his myth in a new direction. On the day before leaving Gordium he went up to the acropolis meaning to try the chariot which he had saved for his farewell; friends gathered round to watch him, but hard though he pulled, the knot round the yoke remained stubbornly tight. When no end could be found, Alexander began to lose patience, for failure would not go down well with his men. Drawing his sword, he slashed the knot in half, producing the necessary end and correctly claiming that the knot was loosed, if not untied. The aged Aristobulus, perhaps reluctant to believe in his king's petulance, later claimed that Alexander had pulled a pin out of the chariot-link and drawn the yoke out sideways through the knot, but the sword-cut has the weight of authority behind it and is preferable to an eighty-year-old historian's apology; either way, Alexander outmanœuvred, rather than unravelled, his problem. He also managed to arouse an interest in what he had done. 'There were thunderclaps and flashes of lightning that very night', conveniently signifying that Zeus approved, so Alexander offered sacrifice to the 'gods who had sent the signs and ratified his loosing of the knot'. As a king under Zeus's protection, he then encouraged gossip and flattery to elaborate on his efforts.

As usual, they spread apace. Perhaps, according to local legend, the loosing of the knot had been connected with a claim to rule the Phrygian natives; certainly, in every account of the matter that survives, it now became proof that Alexander was destined to rule Asia, and the theme must have begun with his own historian Callisthenes. The inevitability of victory keeps recurring in the histories of the campaign, and on the next day as the army took their leave of Gordium, troubled by news that the Persians' fleet was mounting a serious counterattack at sea, there were many worse rumours for Callisthenes to encourage throughout the camp. 'Rule over Asia' was spiriting talk but it was also purposefully vague. For where did the rule of Asia end? In Asia Minor, perhaps; perhaps even over the river Tigris and down in the palaces of the Persian King; when Asia had been conquered, Alexander had recently announced, he would return all the Greeks to their homes. But as the reinforcements mustered and the bridegrooms resumed their places, nobody, least of all Alexander, would have dared to claim that within eight years, Asia would mean the Oxus, the crossing of the Hindu-Kush and a fight with the elephants of a north-west Indian rajah.

CHAPTER ELEVEN

'According to the Magi of the East', wrote Aristotle, who had not spent his early life in Asia Minor for nothing, 'there are two first principles in the world, a good spirit and an evil spirit; the name of the one is Zeus or Ahura Mazda, of the other Hades or Ahriman.' As King Darius sat listening to the news of Alexander's past twelve months, there could be little doubt on which side of this heavenly division he would have placed his opponent. Lion-like, dressed in the lionskin cap of his ancestor Heracles, Alexander was the very symbol of lion-embodied Ahriman. 'For three thousand years, say the Magi, one spirit will rule the other: for another three thousand, they will fight and do battle until one overcomes the other and finally Ahriman passes away.' In the meantime, some of the king's fellow-Persians would sacrifice to Ahriman and privately acknowledge his regrettable abilities, but for Darius III, chosen by the great god Ahura Mazda, there could be no such dalliance with the powers of darkness. In the name of the Good Spirit, who 'created earth, who created man, who created peace for men', he must repulse the advancing force of Lies, Unrighteousness and Evil, and from Susa, strike a blow for the development of the world of time.

Hope, however, was still lively, and it turned on the trusted Memnon, whom the Great King now raised to the supreme command. From his base on the island of Cos, he could sweep the Aegean with 300 warships of the empire's fleet, manned with Levantine crews and as many Greek mercenaries as remained to be hired after the mass surrender on the Granicus and the loss of recruiting grounds in Greek Asia; it was an expensive form of war, but the fleet could sail wherever it could set up supply bases, and Alexander had no ships with which to retort. Communications across the Dardanelles could be cut and Alexander's reinforcements from the Balkans could be prevented; merchant shipping could be sunk or commandeered, and interference with the autumn sailing of the corn fleet from the Black Sea kingdoms could put extreme pressure on Athens to join a rebellion even though Alexander was holding twenty of her citizen crews as hostages. Bribes and secret negotiations with Sparta and other open allies might well lead to an uprising against Antipater in Greece and to a mutiny among Macedonians in Asia who saw their home country threatened. Alexander would be forced to return to the Balkans, and to this end Darius had no need to summon a grand army and challenge him first inside the empire; better to lure him far on into Asia and burn the crops in his path, while cutting his lines behind him. Alexander had been reinforced and did not depend on supplies from his rear, as he lived off the land: it was conceivable that he himself might dare to continue inland, even if the Aegean and the Balkans were lost to him, but his soldiers would certainly refuse.

In spring 333 Memnon set out on his new commission. He began with Chios and the main cities of Lesbos, all sworn members of Alexander's Greek alliance, where he overthrew such democratic governments as dated from the end of Philip's reign and replaced them with tyrants and garrisons, those omnious signs for the common islander that Persian repression, like their exiled men of property, was due to return. Except for Mitylene on Lesbos, which had received troops from Alexander, the cities of both islands gave up their democracies and obeyed with reluctance.

Waiting at Gordium for his reinforcements, Alexander had heard the news which he ought to have expected. Perturbed, he sent 500 talents home to Antipater and gave another 600 to the leader of the Mounted Scouts and Amphoterus brother of Craterus the Orestid, ordering them to raise a new allied Greek fleet 'according to the terms of his alliance'; the new year's tribute and the treasures captured at Sardis allowed the fleet's dismissal to be revoked so soon, but even 600 talents would only finance a fleet as large as Memnon's for a mere two months at sea. The two chosen officers are not known to have had experience of naval work, and their return to Greece with the burden of money would be hazardous by sea, slow by land. Memnon had several clear months ahead of him, and Alexander could only reflect on his prospects. Memnon, after all, had not set himself an easy ambition. Antipater had an army and garrisons; Athenians were being held hostage; many Greeks mistrusted Sparta and the promises of Persians whose past brutality could not be forgotten, all these would help to stop any general Greek uprising, and anything less would be troublesome rather than dangerous. If Alexander had not believed that he could trust some of his Greek allies to fight Persia, he would never have asked them for a second fleet; there was also an enemy problem of money. Memnon had funds from the king, but Asia Minor's tribute had been lost and as no other area paid in coined currency, its loss might restrict the Persians' plan for a mercenaries' war at sea. Memnon had already resorted to plundering and piracy, and neither would endear him to Greeks with an interest in sea trade. He might succeed locally, but Greece needed sterner tactics; there was nothing more to be done in defence except wait helplessly for the second fleet, so in June Alexander left Gordium and prepared to follow the Royal Road east, then south to the coastal towns of Cilicia to continue to capture Persian harbours.

Memnon's chances were to remain untested, for in June, while blockading the city of Mitylene, 'he fell ill and died, and this, if anything, harmed the King's affairs at that time'. It was a marvellous stroke of luck for Alexander, as there was no other Greek general with a knowledge of Macedonia, a long career in Persian service and a way with the hired Greeks under his command. Persia was soon to recognize it. The news of Memnon's death took some time to travel to Susa; the ponderous machinery of the Persian Empire was not to be lightly turned in a new direction, but such was the Great King's dismay at the loss of this one commander that as soon as he heard it in late June or July, he planned to alter the entire strategy of the war. Memnon could wish for no more telling epitaph than this change, but while the new plans were put into effect, events were to drift until late July giving Alexander scope for good fortune and Persia less chance of a quick recovery of face.

It is not certain when Alexander learnt of Memnon's death, but it could only have confirmed him in his business inland. Swinging eastwards along the Royal Road, he welcomed the token surrender of stray mountain tribes north of Ancyra whom the Persians had never troubled and whom Callisthenes could have identified by pleasing quotations and his comments on Homeric verse. Paphlagonia made its peace and was added to a western satrapy; then, the 50,000 troops followed their king along the edge of the salt desert, across the river Halys and on down the Royal Road, the smoothest surface for their supply wagons. Cappadocia is a desolate area, as grey and parched as some dead elephant's hide, and so Alexander put it under the control of an Oriental, probably a native; the North had been divided off by the Persians as an untamed kingdom, and although the centre and south fringed the Royal Road, Alexander did not waste time on securing it. The mountains remained more or less independent, a refuge for fugitive Persians, and thereafter an untamed pocket in the wars of Alexander's successors. Though populous, they were not particularly important.

Two weeks or so after crossing the river Halys, Alexander reached the south-east border of Phrygia, where he would have hit upon the camp site used by Xenophon's soldiers in 401 B.C. From his readings of Xenophon's works, he could reason that he would shortly be faced by the defile of the Cilician Gates, 'impassable if obstructed by the enemy'. There are ways over the surrounding shoulders of the Golek-Boghaz hills which do avoid the extreme narrows of the pass, but Alexander decided to force it. Either he had made no reconnaissance, in the absence of native guides, or he reckoned that like Xenophon, he could scare the defenders into withdrawal. In this he was justified; the lightly armed units of archers, Shield Bearers and Agrianians were ordered to muster after dark, Alexander led them in person and by a night attack he so unnerved the local pass-guards that their satrap retreated, burning the crops behind him as he headed southwards to his capital at Tarsus. Relieved, Alexander marched the rest of his army through in safety.

On the far side of the pass, Alexander 'examined the position and is said to have marvelled at his own good fortune: he admitted that he could have been overwhelmed by boulders if there had been any defenders to roll them down on to his men. The road was barely wide enough for four abreast.' Happy in his entry into Cilicia, probably in late June, he descended into the 'large and well-watered plain beyond, full of various trees and vines' as Xenophon had found it, 'and abounding with sesame, millet, wheat and barley'. Enough would survive to satisfy the hungry troops as king and army hurried over the sixty odd miles to Tarsus, Callisthenes pointing out the sites of old Homeric cities in the neighbourhood which, no doubt to Alexander's excitement, had once been sacked by the spear of swift-footed Achilles.

Whatever Alexander himself may have said, the forcing of the Cilician Gates was not entirely due to his good fortune. Part of the reason lay, for once, where he could not see it: at the enemy court of the Persian king. In the royal palace at Susa there had been nothing smooth or Homeric about the progress of the months of June and July. They had begun with hopes that Memnon's good news would continue, that Alexander would be lured far into Asia and a confrontation would be avoided, while the land would be ravaged along his path, as Memnon had first suggested at the Granicus. This is exactly what the satrap at the Cilician gates had continued to do. In late June Alexander had entered Cilicia while Memnon's strategy was still in force, but by a cruel stroke, as his army passed unopposed through the defile, Memnon's death had become known at Susa and with it, the Great King had decided on more positive plans. By then, the narrows of the Cilician Gates had been wasted; Alexander had been invited through them for the sake of a policy which was now to be abandoned.

In late June or July, on hearing of Memnon's death, King Darius anxiously summoned a council of noble advisers. As Alexander bore down on distant Tarsus, word went round the court that tactics were under review. Honoured Friends and Royal Relatives, some honorific, others indeed descended from the imperial harem, satraps and staff-bearers, Table Companions, Vitaxas, Benefactors of the King, Wearers of the Royal Purple, Chiliarchs of the Immortals, Orosangs and all the lesser Hazarapats foregathered in anxiety, knowing that at Susa their future was to be settled. In the council chamber, the assembled company paid obeisance to the superior presence of their king; opinions were expressed, points of strategy were mooted, but Darius's conviction that without Memnon he could no longer rely on war being shipped to the Balkans was generally agreed to be correct. A new move must be made against Alexander himself. The question for discussion was where a move would be most effective. The Athenian general Charidemus had joined the Persians after being exiled by Alexander and here he is said to have proposed that he himself should take 100,000 men, including 30,000 Greek mercenaries, and oppose Alexander alone. But Darius was unwilling to divide his army and was annoyed at the insolent remarks which Charidemus had added; he therefore 'seized him by the girdle according to the Persian custom and handed him over to his attendants for execution'. The story may have been dramatized by a patriotic Greek, but the central fact of their disagreement is probably true. Darius's reaction was to insist on summoning the fullest force and going to war in person. No renegade Athenian would dissuade him from his opinions; stewards, therefore, passed the word, scribes translated the details into Aramaic, couriers rode forth with their sealed letters; hyparchs and eparchs read, resigned themselves to the worst and left their district headquarters. Eyes and Ears of the king prowled round in search of stragglers, while the royal wives and imperial concubines dressed themselves for their customary attendance on a moving army and awaited their chariots and camels.

In the oppressive heat of July, Darius moved westwards to Babylon, a sweltering city with a low-lying palace which his ancestors had always tried to avoid in the height of summer. Sun and sand burnt alike but the Great King knew he had to hurry uncomfortably; already news would have arrived that Alexander had entered Cilicia, and within six weeks, he could be menacing Babylon's massive walls. There was too little time to call out the troops of the upper satrapies east and north-east of Hamadan to meet the emergency, but there was power enough within range. The two main horse-breeding grounds of the empire were still accessible, the Nisaean fields of the Medes with their famous acreage of lucerne, and the equally productive pastures of Armenia, reputed to send 20,000 horses each year as tribute. Armed riders could be summoned from the king's colonists and local nobility; the problem was their supporting infantry, for the only trained natives, apart from slingers and archers, were the famous palace guard of the 10,000 Immortals. They needed heavier allies, and there was no alternative but to weaken the sea-campaign in the Aegean by summoning most of the hired Greeks from the fleet.

On his deathbed, Memnon had appointed his Persian nephew and his deputy as temporary admirals and the pair of them had been fighting on boldly. By August, they had finally forced Mytilene to surrender, 'urging the Mytilenaeans to become allies of Darius according to the peace of Antalcidas made with Darius', an extraordinarily crooked settlement, as this peace of Antalcidas, which had been sworn fifty-three years before to King Artaxerxes II, had left the Aegean islands free and in no way obliged to Persia. The treaty had perhaps been infringed often enough to be forgotten by a new generation of islanders; if so, Mytilene was rewarded for its poor sense of history with a garrison, a foreign commander, the return of rich exiles to half their property, a tyrant, and a punitive fine. The capture of Lesbos opened the fleet's path to the Dardanelles, but before the two admirals could pursue this, orders arrived for the delivery of most of their hired Greek troops. So, perhaps in mid-August, nearly two hundred ships were diverted east along their open supply points at Cos and Halicarnassus to Tripolis on the coast of Syria where they could hand over their mercenaries to another nephew of Memnon. The ships were to be beached there, and the mercenaries were to march inland to Darius, '30,000 Greeks' according to Alexander's staff, a number which should be reduced or even halved.

The Persian admirals rejoined forces in the Aegean to continue their war with a mere 3,000 mercenaries and a hundred warships. Their prospects were much reduced, but Darius had not disturbed them unnecessarily, for he needed all possible infantry on land. From court, he had sent for the raw trainees of the Persians' youth-corps, boys who were conscripted in plenty for tree-cutting, hunting and wrestling as a preparation for army service. In the crisis, they were pitched into grown-up life, regardless of age or inexperience. Every ablebodied man within range was summoned, and from the land round the royal headquarters at Babylon the effects of such urgency can still be detected. By lifting the curtain on the Persians' empire, it is possible to lay bare the local problems of a call-up and see straight to the heart of an imperial soldier's life.

When the Persians had first conquered Babylon two hundred years before, they had divided its gloriously fertile land to suit their own interests. Much of it had been allotted to their servants and soldiers as a means of maintenance; the Persians faced the need for expensive and complex weaponry and as only land grants could finance this in a rural society without cash or coinage, they had introduced a feudal system which, like much that was sophisticated in the language and methods of Persian government, can be shown to trace back to their imperial predecessors, the Medes. As in the plains of Lydia, so in the plains of Mesopotamia families of foreign troopers from far afield had been settled on land grants, some seventy acres in the few cases where their extent is known, and arranged according to cantons of class or nationality, whether Arabs, Jews, Egyptians, Syrians or Indians, each supervised by district officers who were responsible for collecting the annual taxes due from the grant-holders to their king. Unlike the foreign colonists in Lydia and elsewhere, those in Babylonia recorded their business dealings on clay tablets in the dead Akkadian language and as baked clay can survive the ages, a hoard of their tablets has been found intact near the city of Nippur. Their information relates to the activities of a sharp firm of native entrepreneurs called the Murasu, which means, appropriately, a 'wild cat', and from their detailed evidence an important pattern can be extracted.

Three main types of land grant had been issued, horse land, bow land and chariot land; the very names are an insight into the Persian army, for the owners served as feudal archers, heavy cavalry and charioteers, complete with chariot and horse. All were liable for annual taxes, 'flour for the king', 'a soldier for the king' and 'taxes for the royal household', which were paid in weights of unminted silver. No family could sell any part of its land grant, and as many preferred to idle rather than to farm, increasingly they would strike a bargain with natives like the Murasu bank who were prepared to take a lease of their land grant, meet the yearly taxes from the proceeds and farm it for their own business profit. Unlike the colonists, the bankers were helped by a massive backing of men, silver, oxen, seeds, water rights and chain pumps. But though the taxes and the land could be leased to a wild cat entrepreneur, colonists in some, if not all, of the cantons were also liable for military service. The duty of military service was personal and had to be met from the owner's family; it could not be leased out with the land, and as the Murasu records show so neatly, ninety years before Alexander, complications were already at work within the system. They are unlikely to have changed by the time that Alexander invaded, for the system was still surviving under his Successors.

In one remarkable document, the problems are set out in detail. In 422 King Artaxerxes had summoned his colonists to attack the city of Uruk, but the summons had caught the Jewish owner of a land grant off his guard. Probably because of financial embarrassment, the Jew's father had been forced to adopt a member of the Murasu bank as his son, so that the banker could inherit a share in the family allotment, and as the land grant could only be owned by a member of the family, adoption was the one means of evading the king's law and endowing an outsider. When the father died, the adopted banker held one part of the farm, the true male heirs the rest. In 422 they were presented with the king's demand for silver, weaponry and the personal service of one family member as a fully equipped cavalryman, complete with horse. Fortunate in his banking 'brother', the Jew had struck an advantageous bargain; the wild cat bankers would not fancy fighting and so their adopted agent would finance the armour, silver tax, horse and, very probably, the groom, while the Jew would ride out at the risk of his life.

In the joy of his heart, Gadal-Iama the Jew has spoken thus to the son of the Murasu: the planted and ploughed fields, the horse land of my father, you now hold because my father once adopted your father. So give me a horse with a groom and harness, a caparison of iron, a helmet, a leather breastplate, a buckler, 120 arrows of two sorts, an iron attachment for my buckler, two iron spears and a mina of silver for provisions and I will fulfil the service-duties which weigh on our lands.

As the horseman owned no bow, the arrows were presumably to be handed in to the cashier and then distributed to owners of bow and chariot land.

But in summer 333, not every colonist would be sharing his land with a rich wild cat banker who could pay for his army outfit; the adoption of the banker is itself a sign, like the increasing number of leases and mortgages in the Murasu documents, that the colonists had found life more strenuous or awkward as the years went by. The annual tax was fixed, making no allowance for a bad harvest, and worse, the allotments remained the same size, though they had to pass to all male members of the family; even by 420, colonists were living on thirds, quarters, eighths or even fifteenths of their original grant. Their obligations remained the same, one fully turned-out soldier from the whole farm, but the number of family mouths to be fed from the land had risen sharply. Private Indians or Syrians could not meet the increase by intensive farming on the scale of the Murasu entrepreneurs, so the colonists' yearly surplus grew smaller as their home demand grew larger. They might fall into debt or adopt a banker as son; either way, they were no longer so capable of arming themselves to their king's expensive requirements. Horses and chariots need maintenance and an allotment split into fifteen parts is hardly a home for either; too much must not be built on the documents of one small area, especially as Babylonia was more urbanized than other satrapies, but it does seem that one reason why the Great King had relied on hired Greek troops in the fourth century was the declining abilities of his own overcrowded colonists.

Thus, as Darius awaited his feudal archers and horsemen he might be excused for the dreams which Greek historians attributed to him, the visions of the Macedonian camp aglow and of Alexander dressed in the Persian royal robe and vanishing into a Babylonian temple. Distressed feudal horsemen and a royal youth corps were hardly the ideal match for the Macedonian infantry and the Companion cavalry, but in the plains near the city, the Great King took refuge in numbers and consoled himself with counting his summoned troops. A circular enclosure was fenced off, able to hold some 10,000 men at a time. This was filled and emptied until the army had all passed through and the tens of thousands had been counted. Medes, Armenians, Hyrcanians, North Africans and Persians themselves: 'from dawn till dusk', in the exaggerated view of historians, 400,000 of these peoples filed through the stockade. Their true numbers cannot be estimated, nor do they matter for the sequel; but early one morning in late August or September, they decamped in their thousands and lumbered their way westwards among the canals of the well supplied Assyrian land.

To the sound of the trumpet, the Sacred Fire was hoisted forwards on its silver altars: priestly Magi followed chanting their traditional hymn; 365 young Wearers of the Purple strode behind them, 'equal to the number of days in the Persian year'. White horses from the Median fields tossed and stamped before the Chariot of Ahura-Mazda, their drivers dressed in white with matching whips of gold; the largest horse of all prepared to draw the Holy Chariot of the Sun. Immortal Guards, so called by the Greeks because their numbers never fell below 10,000, marched close behind in solemn order, as Royal Relations and Spear Bearers cleared the way for the chariot of the King. Gold beyond telling gleamed on its coachwork, the yoke was aflame with varied gems; on either side rose pictures of the gods, among whom an eagle of gold, symbol of Ahura-Mazda, benevolently stretched its painted wings. Inside stood the bearded King Darius, thin-faced and dressed in a purple-edged tunic of white: from his shoulders streamed an embroidered cloak 'on which golden hawks were fighting with their curved beaks'; from his golden belt, hung a scimitar whose scabbard was made of a single gem; round his head, ran the fluted crown of the King of Kings, bound with a ribbon of blue and white cloth. Cavalry and footmen paraded in attendance, protecting the chariots of the Queen and the Queen Mother who followed behind them; farther back fifteen mule-drawn wagons bore the eunuchs, the governesses and the royal children in their charge; 365 King's Concubines kept their distance, dressed for the occasion, while 600 mules and 300 camels edged them forwards, laden with a selection of the imperial treasures.

Back in the Macedonian camp, in the two months while Darius's army mustered, events had taken an unfortunate turn. After forcing the Cilician Gates in July, Alexander had hurried to seize Tarsus, rescuing it from burning by the Persians. He had marched fast in the heat, descending some 3,000 feet into an airless plain, and when he arrived in the city, he was understandably tired and dusty. Through Tarsus, run the yellowish waters of the Cydnus, a broad river which was said to be cool; Alexander, said Aristobulus, was already feverish. Others said that he swam, as yet in good health. But the local waters have a bad record; in 1189, the Calycadnus chilled Frederick Barbarossa, also rash enough to swim in the course of a Crusade. Within hours, Alexander developed a chill, hastened on by the cold water. His attendants laid him sleepless and shivering in his royal tent, but as he grew increasingly cramped, the doctors despaired of their treatment, until Philip the Greek stood forward, a man 'very much trusted in medical matters and not inconspicuous in the army'. He had attended Alexander as a boy and knowing his temperament, he proposed a purge with a strong medicine. Alexander was desperate to recover and gave his agreement.

While Philip assembled the necessary drugs, a letter was said to have been handed to Alexander from Parmenion; some say, implausibly, that it had arrived two days before and that Alexander had concealed it under his pillow. According to Parmenion, Philip the doctor had been bribed by Darius to kill his royal patient, but when Philip reappeared, Alexander disregarded any such warning. Handing Philip the letter, he took his glass of medicine and drank it down at the same time as Philip read the message. At once, Philip 'made it quite clear that nothing was wrong with his medicine: he was not in the least disturbed by the letter but simply ordered Alexander to obey any other instructions he might give him. If he did so, he would recover.' The purge eventually worked and Alexander's fever eased: 'Alexander then gave proof to Philip that he trusted him, convincing his other attendants that he was loyal to his friends in defiance of suspicion and that he was brave when faced by death.' Aristobulus may have agreed, though denying the swim.

The story of this letter has been disbelieved largely because it seems too dramatic. But history is not only true when dull and though inter-ventions by Parmenion are not to be trusted lightly, there is no outside evidence with which to challenge this telling scene. In legend, certainly, Parmenion is later made into a personal enemy of the doctor, or even into a cunning poisoner, hoping to kill Alexander and clear himself of guilt by his letter of warning beforehand. But these legendary embellishments do not prove that the story first arose to discredit him. Trust and daring are virtues to be expected in any great general and even if Alexander was not so indiscriminate in his loyalties as flattery implied, he was sharp to distinguish between true friends and false, prizing the former and purging the latter. It is much in favour of the story of doctor and letter that it brings this feature to the fore.

Alexander's sickness at Tarsus was a more serious delay than any of his historians made plain. Through the long weeks of July and August and on into mid-September, the king lay abed, apparently unaware that Darius's army had been summoned, let alone numbered and led out westwards from Babylon. Tactics, for Alexander, still centred on the coastline, and as he slowly recovered, there was enough to worry about at sea. Even without their Greek mercenaries, Memnon's successors were making themselves felt; they had sailed north to Tenedos, an island base for merchant shipping just off the Dardanelles, and they had taken it, again with a false reference to a peace of the past. Ten ships had been detached to the islands of the Cyclades off southern Greece, where they were to await overtures from Spartans and other disgruntled Greeks; Antipater was alarmed for the safety of Greece's coastline and had called out what warships he could, placing them under a Macedonian, probably the nephew of Alexander's nurse. A raid captured eight of the Persians' advance fleet and scared off the rest, but it could not be long before all hundred of the enemy ships came south. The two recruiting officers of Alexander's allied fleet were finding their business slow and difficult, perhaps because most Greeks preferred to stay neutral. Alexander could only press on with capture of Asian land bases, that desultory process which was bringing him nearer the ports of Syria and Phoenicia, although island harbours and the port at Halicarnassus were still open to the enemy behind him.

From now on, he was without detailed maps or local contacts, and for knowledge of what lay ahead he would surely consult the narrative of Xenophon's march, neatly detailed into marching-hours and distances. From it, he could deduce that the next enemy stronghold on the coast was the pass of the Pillar of Jonah from Cilicia into Syria some seventy miles distant, and on the basis of his reading he sent Parmenion at a leisurely pace round the coast to take it in advance, hoping that its complex of double turret walls and intervening river would not be too heavily guarded. Personally, he would march westwards in the opposite direction as soon as he felt fit.

How ironically these careful plans now read. All the while, Darius was approaching the plains of Syria, where he would encamp and wait to attack as soon as Alexander came out through the Amanus mountains into the plains. Meantime Alexander marched and countermarched, surely ignorant of the Great King's whereabouts, let alone of his change of plans; otherwise, he would not have dared to divide his troops. To the Macedonians this routine work was to seem like one more stage in the laborious capture of the coast; they delayed till their king felt better, they watched Parmenion disappear eastwards with the cavalry, and in late September, when Alexander had finally recovered, they retraced their path towards the decaying city of Anchialus, unaware of the risk they would soon have to run. In the centre of that high-walled city stood the tomb of its founder Assurbanipal, King of Assyria in the mid-seventh century B.C., with a carving of the king clapping his hands above his head and an inscription beneath him in Assyrian script. Intrigued, Alexander made the Assyrian settlers translate it for his benefit: 'Sardanapalus son of Anakyndaraxes', it ran 'built Anchialus and Tarsus in a single day; stranger, eat, drink and make love, as other human things are not worth this', 'this' being a clap of the king's hands. The historian Aristobulus, writing his book in his eighties, took such exception to this blunt reference to sex that he rephrased the advice as 'eat, drink and be merry'; Calisthenes's history noted the exact impropriety for Alexander's pleasure, who then marched forwards, a living denial of any such drop-out philosophy.

The next ten days were proof of the king's return to health. Wild tribesmen were routed in a seven-day campaign, a pro-Persian city was fined and the very welcome news arrived that the remaining strongholds of Halicarnassus and its coast, including Cos, had fallen at last to the Macedonians. Alexander was keen to celebrate this first success in the naval campaign, so he offered sacrifice to the Greek god of Healing as thanks for his own recovery, and held a torch race, athletic games and literary competitions. The success, had he known, was shortlived, as Cos and Halicarnassus were soon to be threatened and lost again. Nonetheless, Alexander moved south-east to Mallus, where he stopped its civil strife and abolished its payment of tribute, pleased by its alleged link with his legendary Greek ancestors; generous and moving freely in the world of myth, the king was plainly back into his stride. October was now far advanced, when all of a sudden a message arrived from the distant Parmenion on the borders of Syria and Cilicia: Darius had been seen encamped with a large army only two marching days from the Syrian Gates and the Pillar of Jonah.

It must have been hard to keep calm on receipt of this information. For the past month, Alexander had been lingering along the southern coast of Turkey with his forces widely divided and winter all but upon him; his thoughts had been on the Persian fleet and their dangerously free manœuvres towards Greece, and he must have hoped for rough autumn weather to close the sailing season early. There were troubles too both within and beyond his high command.

Recently he had received letters from Olympias warning him finally against Alexander the Lyncestian, and it was now, not a year earlier, that he took the step of arresting him in his cavalry command. At the same time, his close friend Harpalus, lame and unsoldierly, had left for Greece across a thoroughly hostile sea to make contacts in the southern Greek harbour town of Megara, presumably to ward off the approaching Persian fleet. Another envoy had gone with him on a still more daring sea journey, across from Greece to south Italy to talk to Olympias's brother King Alexander of Epirus, again no doubt about possible help for Greece by sea. It was a worrying time on all fronts, and now it had been joined by the threat of a Persian grand army.

Never happier than when challenged, Alexander 'assembled his Companion nobles and told them the news; they ordered him to lead them straight ahead exactly as they were. Praising them he broke up the meeting, and on the next day he led them east against Darius and the Persians.' By comparing notes with Xenophon's history, Alexander could calculate that at a reasonable pace, the army would reach the borders of Syria in three days or some twenty-five regular hours on the road. It was not, however, a time for being reasonable and the army was thinned by Parmenion's absence; let the men march at the double and cover the seventy-odd miles within forty-eight hours. The coast road east was level and inviting, and fertile farms lay on either side; where the shore of the Mediterranean bends sharply southwards to Syria, the road hooked round and continued to follow it, with the sea still on Alexander's right and the shadowing Amanid mountains on his left. At the very edge of Cilicia lay the town of Issus, pointing the way to the satrapy of Syria and the south; there Alexander abandoned all stragglers and invalids for whom the march was proving too fast. Meanwhile, Parmenion had come back from reconnaissance to meet him, and together king and general hurried on to the fortified Gates of Syria, the modern Pillar of Jonah, which the advance force had already captured. A few miles south of this frontier-post they called a halt at Myriandrus, knowing that at last they were within range of the Beilan pass. From here they could cross the edge of the Amanid range and hurry east into Assyria and so, they hoped, into King Darius's encampment before he knew of their approach. By now the evening of the second day was drawing on and the march had stretched the infantry to their utmost; it was a mercy when during the night 'a heavy storm broke and rain fell from heaven in a violent wind. This kept Alexander in his camp.' The implication is that otherwise he would have been back on the road before dawn.

He could not know what a heaven-sent blessing this late autumn gale was to prove. At least four days had passed since Parmenion's spies had last observed Darius to the east in the plains near Sochoi, and the Great King's tactics deserve a closer consideration than any of the Macedonians had given them. He had reached Sochoi, perhaps, in late September and as advised by his officers, he had waited in its open spaces to deploy his full force against Alexander emerging from the coastal hills over the Beilan pass. But he had become impatient. He had detached his baggage-train south-west to Damascus, a curiously distant choice of site but perhaps intended to ease the burden on the food supplies of the Sochoi plain and to put the camp-followers nearer the mercenaries' transport ships which were beached at the nearby harbour of Tripolis; perhaps too, the choice would be more understandable if the ancient city of Sochoi could be located with any accuracy. Having shed his baggage, Darius had begun to move northwards to look for Alexander himself, against the strong advice of the Macedonian deserter Amyntas.

His advance intelligence can only be guessed. Probably he had heard a rumour of Alexander's illness; possibly, scouts or fugitives had already warned of Parmenion's approach down the coast to the Pillar of Jonah. If so, it seemed that Alexander was detained far away in Cilicia and had split his forces most unwisely. The moment seemed ripe to march north-wards, on the inland side of the Amanid mountains, and penetrate the Hasenbeyli pass at a height of some 4,000 feet, and then to bring the army southwards and back on to the main road, down the Kalekoy pass into Issus. If Darius already knew of Parmenion's advance, he may also have known that these passes had been left undefended; if he did not, luck was to see him safely through them.

He must have begun this northward march very shortly after Parmenion's scouts had retired with news of his whereabouts. In some four or five days, he would have reached the Hasenbeyli pass, still expecting to swing round on to the main road and occupy Issus. He would either wait there to fight Alexander as he came east down the road over the Kara Kapu pass from Tarsus, or else he would move westwards to Tarsus and hope to catch him on his sick bed. He cannot have known that as he marched north on the inland side of the Amanid range, Alexander was marching south down its coastal side, still less that Alexander was marching at a pace that has seemed incredible to those who have never tried a forced march. During one night, Alexander careered down one side of the coast road, while Darius was either encamped or marching on the other; there are few stranger tributes to the lack of proper reconnaissance in the history of ancient warfare. On the same night that Darius came through the Kalekoy pass into Issus, expecting to meet Alexander marching east, Alexander crossed the Pillar of Jonah, expecting to meet Darius encamped to the east at Sochoi. Neither knew the other's whereabouts.

When Darius descended into Issus, he found the Macedonian invalids whom Alexander had already abandoned. He was now some fifteen miles north of Alexander, facing into his rear, and yet it was only the exceptional speed of Alexander's advance which had given him this enviable position. At most Darius may have hoped to separate Alexander from Parmenion; he can take no credit for arriving in the rear of them both. As if to celebrate, he cut off the hands of the Macedonian sick whom he found at Issus, a pointless atrocity which was to cost him dear, for others escaped by boat and warned Alexander that the King of Kings was actually encamped in his rear. At Myriandrus on the sea, Alexander was unable to credit what they told him. But he sent several Companions in a thirty-oared skiff up the coastline to test the facts for themselves, and on rowing into the Gulf of Alexandretta, they sighted the campfires of the Persian army and realized that the worst had happened. At last Alexander's legendary luck appeared to have deserted him.

Footsore from his forced march and soaked by the past day's rain, Alexander was given little chance by natives who were freely assisting Darius's army. There was one hope of escape from the trap into which his headlong advance had thrown him. Darius, presumably, would march south down the coastal narrows, and expect to fall on Alexander's rear once he had emerged into the open beyond the Beilan pass. What if Alexander faced about and met the king in the Cilician narrows first?

With a wet and weary army that is a difficult order to give, but, as Amyntas the Macedonian deserter had told Darius, advising him never to leave the plains; 'Alexander was sure to come wherever he heard Darius to be.' Within hours, sarissas had been shouldered, horses had been wheeled about, and a fight was to be made on Alexander's terms; Alexander was indeed coming, coming to where he had heard of Darius. Darius, however, had not yet heard of Alexander's return, and for the battle on the morrow surprise would not be the least of the Great King's disadvantages.

CHAPTER TWELVE

At Myriandrus, on turning back to face Darius, Alexander's first move was to harangue his troops. To each unit he is said to have made a different point, advising them that the gods were on their side. 'He also recalled their past successes as a team and mentioned any individual feats of daring which were especially brilliant or conspicuous, naming the man and his action in each case. In the most unexceptionable way, he described his own unsparing part in the battles.' He is also said to have added historical encouragement, reminding his men of Xenophon's long safe march through the Persian Empire seventy years before; in reply, said his Macedonian historians, possibly exaggerating the case, 'his men crowded round and clasped their King's hand, bidding him lead them forwards then and there'. First, Alexander ordered them to eat their dinner, while advance troops returned in the winter evening to hold the Syrian Gates through which they had passed the night before.

After dark the rest of the army turned about and headed for the Syrian–Cilician border which they duly reached at midnight. Pickets guarded the camp, with the Mediterranean seashore below them to their left, and the troops took a cold but well-earned rest on the hillside around the Gates. By the light of torches, Alexander is said to have conducted certain sacrifices and in one late narrative history, of which only a few short sentences survive on papyrus, these sacrifices are specified: 'In great anxiety. Alexander resorted to prayers, calling on Thetis, Nereus and the Nereids, nymphs of the sea and invoking Poseidon the sea-god, for whom he ordered a four-horsed chariot to be cast into the waves; he also sacrificed to Night.' This scrap of information cannot be checked, but it would have been most appropriate if the new Achilles did indeed offer prayers to his hero's mother, to Thetis of the silver feet in her cave beneath the waves, consoler of Homer's Achilles at similar moments of crisis.

As dawn broke at half past five in the morning, on or about 1 November 333, the trumpet announced the beginning of the all-important march. In columns, the troops strode down the road of the narrow rocky pass by the Pillar of Jonah, with the sea on their left and hills encroaching on their right. Some four miles from Darius's reported position, the ground

168

opened slightly and the infantry found room to fan out into line formation, while the cavalry trotted behind in traditional order. Where the mountains receded from the seashore, curving inwards to leave a sinuous plain between their foot and the beach, Alexander spread his infantry still wider, arranging them in their classic battle-order, Shield Bearers on the right, protecting the vulnerable flank of the infantry, Foot Companions in the centre, and foreign mercenaries adjoining on the left. As the mountain buttresses gave way and the plain spread out still further, Alexander passed the word for his formations to broaden again, thinning their depth from sixteen to a mere eight men, unless this thinness has been exaggerated by his flatterers, while the cavalry moved up from the rear, allied brigades to the far left, Companions, Thessalians and Lancers to the far right. The line now stretched from foothills to seashore, Alexander commanding the right, Parmenion commanding the left, and battle was expected on an advantageously narrow front. By midday Darius's army would be in full view.

At this point, geography intervenes. As at the Granicus, the Persian army had taken up a defensive position behind a river south of the town of Issus but this time, the river has not been identified beyond doubt, though immense industry has been devoted to the problem, culminating in 690 unpublished pages by a French Commandant, based on a false premise. There are three main rivers and five intervening streams for consideration, and this range of choice is most awkward for those who claim to have found the solution. But before consulting the ground, a more important decision must be taken; parts of the battle narrative of Callisthenes have survived but can the details of Alexander's own historian be trusted?

Even in antiquity, Callisthenes's battle narrative was criticized, and although the criticism is illogical, it gives the only hint of what he wrote: three of his measurements are specified and he describes the riverbanks of the battle as 'sheer and difficult to cross'. The many experts who have placed the battle on the most northerly river available, the Deli Chai, have defied the indications which Callisthenes has given them. Their excuses are none too cogent. It is possible, as they point out, that Callisthenes exaggerated the roughness of the riverbanks in order to glorify his king's victory and that the two of his measurements which are given in round numbers are only estimates; that does not make them wholly untrue, and his third measurement, the most important for what follows, cannot be avoided so easily. The battle site, he claimed, was fourteen stades wide and though the exact length of his stade can be disputed to two places of decimals, this amounts to some one and a half miles. A flatterer would surely have broadened rather than narrowed the battlefield, as the narrows were the one stroke of unforeseen luck in Alexander's favour; an observer would not have given such a confident figure as fourteen stades if he were only guessing it by eye from a hill behind the lines. As Alexander paid professional Greek surveyors to pace out accurate distances of any length in Asia, it is very possible that their fellow-courtier Callisthenes would have used their results in his history and thus arrived at the figure of fourteen. Even if not, it is bad method to reject the only precise evidence of an eyewitness in order to save the theories of German generals who have rationalized the battle and lost its haphazard excitement by placing it too far north.

Acceptance of Callisthenes means farewell to the broader banks of the Deli and support for the southerly Payas. Alexander and Darius must have fought on a very narrow front, even narrower than most of their critics believe, and as the Macedonians were probably only arranged eight deep, their effective numbers are likely to have been low, nearer 25,000 than 35,000. On the day of the engagement, their march from camp to battle would have been shorter but they would have faced a rougher and steeper river than the northerly Deli. As for Darius, his tactics too need a new stress, though Alexander's historians ignored them. Two evenings before the battle he had emerged from the mountains north-east of Issus into Alexander's rear, doubtless expecting in his ignorance to move on westwards through Cilicia and find his enemy still lingering or divided on the southern coast of modern Turkey, perhaps in the neighbourhood of Tarsus. As soon as the natives surprised him with news that Alexander had already passed south on the day before, heading for Syria, he must have blessed his luck and followed rapidly, the open plains of Assyria his target, a fully deployed attack from the rear his purpose. By the morning of the day of battle, his army would easily be as far south from Issus as the narrow Payas river, expecting to fall on Alexander in the open on the following day; he would not have bargained with his enemy's about turn, and so Alexander's sudden reappearance, marching boldly back on his tracks from Myriandrus, must have been much more of a shock to the Great King than is usually admitted. If Issus was the battle which on paper Alexander should have lost, it was also the battle which was fought earlier than Darius expected. When Darius heard the unexpected news of the Macedonian about turn, he preferred to stay put on the banks of the Payas rather than retreat northwards to a slightly wider point of the plain nearer the town of Issus. His army could fan out where they encamped, while an advance guard would hold the river until he was ready. Wisely, he ordered a palisade to be set at level points on the river banks

170

in order to hinder an enemy charge. 'It was at this point', wrote a Macedonian historian, 'that those around Alexander realized quite clearly that Darius was slavish in his ways of thought.' Trapped in a Cilician pass where his numbers, larger than Alexander's but not nearly so large as his enemy pretended, were now of no avail, the Great King can be forgiven for his extra defence.

The distinguishing features of the battlefield, wherever its site, are undisputed. By marching northwards for some ten miles from his camp of the night before, Alexander had come down through hill country into what little plain the Mediterranean coast and the inland Amanid mountains leave between them. Persians and Macedonians were now divided by a river which ran straight across Alexander's path of advance, flowing from the foot of the mountains into the sea and forming a natural rampart which favoured Darius as its defender. The narrowness of the plain was greatly to Alexander's advantage, as a frontage of fourteen stades would stop Darius making any use of his superior numbers. But though cramped, the Great King at once planned competently. He had to use the two natural boundaries of the battlefield, on Alexander's right the curving foothills of the mountain chain, on Alexander's left the level beach of the Mediterranean. There he could distribute his weight of men as effectively as possible and hope to break through his enemy's flanks and encircle him. All the while, there was the intervening river to hamper the Macedonian infantry.

Before Alexander could think of the idea for himself, Darius had sent troops up into the mountains so that they could circle unseen behind Alexander's right and descend to attack him from behind. This tactic could have been decisive, had not Alexander ordered his Agrianians and archers to drop back and stop them. By pinning down Darius's troops in the foothills, they soon forced them to retire. If the ruse on the right failed, that on the left was more promising. Alexander had stationed surprisingly few cavalry on the far left wing where the river levelled out to run into the sea, though the seashore was the one obvious point for an enemy charge. Noticing the weakness, Darius massed his own horsemen to exploit it; again Alexander realized his mistake in time and transferred his Thessalian horsemen unseen behind the lines in order to stiffen the defences. As their removal weakened his right, where the longer frontage of the Persians outstretched Alexander's line, two units of Companion cavalry were shuffled rightwards, also in secrecy behind the lines, and the Agrianians and archers returned to join them now that their work in the foothills was finished. Most interestingly, these additions were enough to give Alexander a longer battle frontage than his enemy's, despite Darius's alleged large numbers. But both armies were hemmed in by sea and hills, and Darius, especially, had kept much infantry in reserve.

After these furtive moves in the game of military chess, Alexander had to assess his new position. He would be thankful that his swift return on the night before had trapped Darius in the narrows, but he had worries enough of his own. His left might still veer away from the beach, allowing the Persians to outflank them and gallop round his rear, and he could only trust to Parmenion to prevent this. More urgently, his centre and his right were confronted by a river with rough banks and waters swollen from the recent gale. This time, he was confined by the mountains and could not move upstream and repeat the turning manœuvre which had worked for him at the Granicus. His cavalry might manage the slippery ground without losing impetus against the Persian archers and light infantry, but his Foot Companions were bound to find the going most troublesome. Their formation always tended to split apart on broken ground and, if the enemy could hack their way inside, short daggers and small shields would be no protection against their onslaught; the most sensible plan was to allow for this weakness and leave the main charge to Alexander's cavalry, who would ford the river ferociously, hoping to scatter the enemy on the wing opposite. If they succeeded, they would circle round and divert the hired Greek troopers in Darius's centre from harassing the floundering Foot Companions whom as, a symbol of Macedonian tyranny, they so detested. All depended, then, on the horsemen, and with horsemen morale and leadership are fundamental. They would look to their king for a lead: in a real sense, the battle of Issus was to turn on Alexander's personality.

Plans and rearrangements take more time than historians often allow, especially in an army where messages can only be passed from one wing to the other by word of mouth, and it must have been the middle of the November afternoon before Alexander could shout his final exhortation, reminding the men in each unit of their individual past glories and calling on the commanders by name and title. 'From all sides there came the answering cry: delay no longer but charge into the foe.' At first the troops stepped slowly forwards, their *alalalalai* reechoing down the mountain-fringed plain, then, at a sign from their king, the cavalry on the right kicked at their horses and dashed towards the river, Alexander at their head and the Persian archers in their mind's eye. On both flanks, however, Darius's cavalry had begun to move first into a charge; the two sides collided and the battle that followed is as obscure to posterity as it no doubt was to its participants, splashing manfully through mud and spray; detailed reconstructions of an ancient battle are always a matter of faith, but four vital facts cannot be gainsaid and for once it is unlikely that Alexander's role has been overstressed by his historians. He was to matter very much indeed.

On the right, at the foot of the mountains, Alexander's meeting with Darius's cavalry was bold, and entirely successful. The enemy archers, light infantry and heavy cavalry gave way at the first shock; there was much jostling, whereupon the Companions, pulling hard on their bits, managed to swing their horses round to the left and strike into the Persian centre where, according to royal custom, Darius had stationed his chariot. Their virtuosity was well-timed; back in the Macedonian centre, the phalanx was faltering on the brink of the river and beginning to come adrift as it tried to match the speed of the king and cavalry: ranks were breaking, the wall of sarissas was parting and Darius's hired Greeks had hurled themselves across the river into the gaps, 'challenging the phalanx's widespread reputation for invincibility'. Fighting was fierce and the Macedonian losses would have been severer had not Alexander's horsemen, wheeling into the Persian centre, cut off the hired Greeks from behind and forced them to look back to their encircled rear.

On the seashore to the left Parmenion's brigades had held firm in the face of oriental slingers and heavy cavalry. Far from piercing a gap beside the sea, Darius's horsemen found themselves thrown back to join their centre, while the Thessalians ripped past them down the left wing, meaning to circle round and join with Alexander in the pursuit. As the winter darkness came on and cavalry fought their way towards him on both sides, the Great King realized his danger and decided to turn his chariot and flee, leaving his brother Oxathres to fend heroically for himself among the advancing Macedonian horsemen. For one vivid moment, caught in an ancient mosaic of the battle, probably based on an original painting by a contemporary, king met the eye of king, Darius urging his tossing horses to swing about. Alexander pushing through the press, intent on spearing his rival to death. This contest, at least, Darius was to win; his brother Oxathres and other Persian nobles came to brave terms with the Macedonians, and behind the protection of his Royal Relations Darius was free to rattle over the hilly ground in his chariot until the streams and gullies impeded his advance and he was forced to take to his horse. His shield and his Persian robe he abandoned in his empty chariot for Alexander to find behind him; as he made the most of his start, night's onset stayed the Macedonians and Thessalians from more pressing pursuit.

In the battle 110,000 Persians were killed, said the historians, whereas the Macedonian dead totalled 302; their general agreement suggests that

173

these farcical figures were derived from Callisthenes, writing up the triumph for his king's enjoyment. Ptolemy, who shared in the pursuit, even overstepped Callisthenes's limit and claimed that he had ridden across a ravine on the bodies of the Persian dead which filled it. Despite the official figures, the Macedonian infantry, split and unprotected, would surely have suffered heavily from the opposing Greeks and it is perhaps relevant that among these glamourous fibs a figure of 4,000 Macedonian wounded is also recorded, possibly nearer the painful truth. For the battle of Issus had exposed the recurrent limitations of the Foot Companions forced to march on rough terrain; victory, as never before in Greek warfare and seldom afterwards even in modern times, had been won wholly by the merits of the cavalry, outnumbered and seriously hampered by the lie of the land, yet still able to meet the Persians' right, swing lefthanded and pierce the flanks of its centre. Such horsemanship would not be seen again until the Carthaginians' double charge at Cannae, when the ground was level and their Roman opponents were neither so skilled nor so heavily armoured as Darius's Orientals. Alexander's victory cannot be attributed to any notable superiority of weapons, although some if not all, of the Persian horses and riders were heavily armoured, so much so that their weight slowed their final retreat. They were beaten because they were bowled over by a charge, and then jostled off balance at close quarters; this bowling over was the result of that training, dash and high morale which make the Companions the finest cavalry in history, and for this, their commander Alexander must be held directly responsible.

From the battlefield the Persian forces scattered to all four points of the compass, many following Darius eastwards to the safe heart of the empire, many risking the northerly route through Cilicia into the fastnesses of the Taurus mountains, others heading westwards for the Asia Minor coast and others, some 4,000 soldiers of fortune, rallying to Amyntas the Macedonian deserter and circling southwards to try their hand in that richest of Asian prizes, the satrapy of Egypt. For some twenty miles those with Darius were dogged by Alexander and his Companions, hoping for the prey which would turn their victory into a triumph. But with half a mile's start through unfamiliar country, the Great King had time to escape eastwards through the Amanid mountains, and eventually Alexander gave up the chase, arriving back in his camp on the verge of midnight. His failure was a grave disappointment but back on the field of victory there were prizes enough to make up for the loss of Darius's person.

Even in his army camp, Darius had encumbered himself with riches and paraphernalia, though these were only a foretaste of what lay abandoned

174

at his base in Damascus. The Macedonians had plundered all that was to hand, reserving the royal tent for the man who now deserved it, so that when Alexander returned at midnight, bloodstained and muddied, expressing a wish to wash off his sweat in Darius's bath, they could lead him forwards to his rightful prize, a Companion reminding him that Darius's bath was in future to be known as Alexander's. On the threshold of the royal tent, Alexander stood surprised, struck by a sight which no young man from Pella could ever have imagined to be true:

When he saw the bowls, pitchers, tubs and caskets, all of gold, most exquisitely worked and set in a chamber which breathed a marvellous scent of incense and spices, when he passed through into a tent whose size and height were no less remarkable, whose sofas and tables were even laid for his dinner, then he looked long and hard at his Companions and remarked: 'This, it would seem, is to be a King.'

But there is more to kingship than its treasures. Alexander was tired; he wanted his bath and dinner; he was limping from a dagger-wound in his thigh which court gossip attributed to a thrust from King Darius himself. And yet he was perturbed by the sound of ladies wailing close to where he stood, and on asking what ladies could possibly be responsible he was told that these were Darius's wife, mother and children, weeping for the king whom they believed to be dead. Promptly, Alexander sent a Companion, Leonnatus, to reassure them and to tell them, perhaps in Persian, that Darius lived, though his cloak and weapons had been captured in his chariot: Alexander would grant them royal state and the continuing rank of Queen, as it was Darius, not his family, upon whom he was making war.

The following morning, Alexander summoned Hephaistion and went to visit his royal captives. When they entered her tent, it was said, the Queen Mother did obeisance to Hephaistion, mistaking him for Alexander as he seemed so plainly the taller of the two. Hephaistion recoiled and an attendant corrected her; she stood back, flustered at her mistake. Alexander, as with his Carian mother Ada, had the tact to cope with a lady's embarrassment: 'No mistake,' he replied, 'for he too is an Alexander.' Then, he complimented Darius's wife on her six-year-old son and confirmed the ladies' privileges, presenting them with dresses and jewellery and giving them leave to bury any of their Persian dead; they were to live unmolested in quarters of their own, honour being paid to their beauty. Once more, Alexander had shown himself able to respect feminine nobility; his captives could have been valuable hostages, but he never used them for political bargaining, and not for nine years did he marry Darius's daughter.

Respect for captive royalty had a long history in the ancient East, and Alexander was not the man to betray it; the Persian Queen Mother, especially, came to recognize his kindness.

As at the Granicus, his army were shown this quality in his own inimitable way.

Despite his wound, he went round all the other wounded and talked to them; he collected the dead and buried them magnificently with all his army arrayed in their full battle-finery; he had a word of congratulation for all whom he himself had seen distinguishing themselves particularly bravely or whose valour he heard from agreed reports: with extra presents of money, he honoured them all according to their deserts.

That is the way to lead one's men.

The royal tent and the royal family were not the sum of Alexander's reward. Parmenion was sent to Damascus with orders to capture the treasures; the guards surrendered him 2,600 talents of coin and 500 pounds of silver, unminted as was the Great King's practice. The coin alone equalled one year's revenue from Philip's Macedonia. and sufficed for all debts of army pay and six months' wages; 7,000 valuable pack-animals heaved it back to the main camp. Parmenion further reported that '329 female musicians, 306 different cooks, 13 pastry chefs, 70 wine waiters and 40 scent makers' had been captured. With them came two more personal prizes, the first being the precious casket in which Alexander, after much debate, decided to store his copy of the *Iliad*, the second the Persian lady Barsine, some thirty years old, with an attractive family history. She had been married first to Memnon's brother, then to Memnon himself, and was thus brought up to a Greek way of life. She was the daughter of the respected Persian satrap Artabazus, who was of royal blood on his mother's side, and she had taken refuge at Philip's Pella some twenty years earlier when her father was exiled from Asia Minor. Barsine met Alexander when he was a boy. 'On Parmenion's advice', wrote Aristobulus, 'Alexander attached himself to this well-mannered and beautiful noblewoman.' It was a fitting climax to what may have been a childhood friendship, and Alexander retained his first bilingual mistress for the next five years.

This favour for Barsine was understandable, but she was only one among several women of status and varied upbringing. At Damascus, Parmenion had captured the wife and three daughters of the previous Persian king, the wife and son of Artabazus, Memnon's two other nieces, who were half Greek by birth, and Memnon's son. These bilingual families would one day stand at the centre of Alexander's plans for marriage among his commanders, but they mattered for the moment as a pull on their husband's loyalties, not least on Memnon's nephew and Artabazus's son, brother of Barsine, who were sharing the command of Persia's Aegean fleet.

This collection of Persian wives and interrelated children was the first faint sign of where Alexander's future might one day lie. 'In Cilicia,' a polite Greek correspondent later wrote to him, 'men died for the sake of your kingship and for the freedom of the Greeks.' It is as well to be reminded that flatterers could still refer to Greek freedom, but the kingship was beginning to loom the larger of the two. On the banks of the Payas river, Alexander dedicated altars to Zeus, Athena and Heracles; he also ordered the first of his many commemorative cities, Alexandria-by-Issus, on the coastal site of the modern Alexandretta. The example of new cities had already been set by his father Philip, and these cities of Cilicia were to be organized as royal mints and ordered to strike Alexander's own silver coins. Their weight was to conform to the standard spread by Athens and already favoured in the area. Philip had used it too, so Macedon, the Aegean and Asia were linked for trade and army payments. Gradually, the king was moving towards a permanent empire, and an Emperor could not be content with a Greek campaign of revenge.

CHAPTER THIRTEEN

On land the victory at Issus was inconclusive, not least because of Darius's escape, but at sea its effects were far more definite. The king's Greek fugitives had commandeered or burnt the hundred or so ships which had been beached for them at Tripolis, and neither ships nor Greeks would be seen in Persia's service again: the fall of western Asia and the capture of the baggage at Damascus made further shipments of coined money to the Persian admirals impossible, as only western Asia paid tribute to the king in coin and there was no route left open for Darius to despatch coined reserves to the Aegean. Above all, Alexander's Greek allies were less hesitant in providing another fleet now that he had proved himself in a battle they had expected him to lose. The Persian admirals could only look to a difficult spring ahead of them, in which they must improvise men, ships and money: their overtures to Agis, King of Sparta were poor reassurance, and his plan to recruit the fugitives from Issus had a decided air of desperation.

For Alexander victory had opened the way to the coastal cities of Phoenicia, where his policy of defeating the fleet by land could at last show results. These cities and nearby Cyprus provided the crews for the Persian fleet, but they were not a world on which he had no grip, for they had already shown a spontaneous favour for Greek culture and language among their kings and merchants, while Cypriots spoke Greek and mostly strove to be Greeks themselves; better still, it was only twelve years since both Cyprus and the leading naval city of Sidon had rebelled vigorously against their Persian masters. This memory, like several of its participants, was still alive, and without it Alexander's strategy might well have failed him. The local kings and their sailors were away in the Aegean, but Alexander could bargain with their sons and elders and once again use local hatreds in the name of liberation.

He began with Arad, a stronghold on its own island with thirty-foot walls of stone, a small land empire and an ingenious water system in case of siege. Its king was at sea, and his son offered Alexander a golden crown of submission, the first move in a long history of favour from Macedonians. Thereupon, couriers arrived with a diplomatic letter from Darius. He was

178

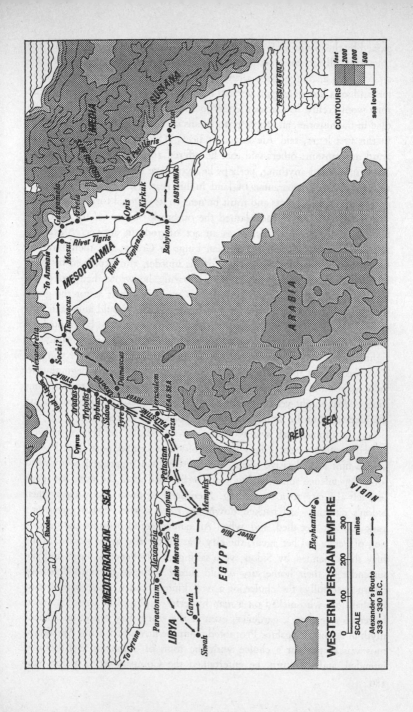

WESTERN PERSIAN EMPIRE

SCALE

0   100   200   300
              miles

Alexander's Route ⟶
333 – 330 B.C.

CONTOURS

feet
2000
1000
500
sea level

pained by the loss of his family and wrote as one king to another, to ask for friendship, alliance and their return. Darius was not yet in a mood for concessions, but a strange story survives that Alexander forged one of his letters and set a more arrogant version before his Companions to be sure that they would refuse it. Darius's letters to Alexander was disputed and muddled in the histories, and there is no means of verifying this unlikely story. In this first letter, said Alexander's officers, Darius promised neither reward nor ransom; others said that he offered 10,000 talents, and if Alexander suppressed anything, perhaps he may have suppressed this mention of ransom and a guarantee of land in his rear. His reported answer is agreed in its main points and must be near to its original form.

In his letter, Darius had blamed the outbreak of war on the Macedonians and dismissed his defeat as an act of god; in answer, Alexander invoked the sacrileges of the Persian kings in Greece and their hostility to Philip, including Darius's plans for his murder, and explained his own invasion as a campaign of vengeance. Darius, he wrote, had seized the Persian throne by crime and bribed the Greeks to rebel; as for the gods, they were with his own army and in future, Darius should approach him as King of Asia. Only as suppliant before a King would he be granted his family. 'If you dispute your right to the kingdom, stand your ground and fight for it; do not run away, for I will come after you, wherever you go.' This was a blunt manifesto, and Greek revenge was already beginning to fade against the wider perspective of Asia's kingship. But the aspiring king of Asia might yet be confined to the western coast of the continent; that depended on his strategy in the sea-ports, and he knew it.

For the moment, all was working out splendidly. At Byblos he welcomed another absent king's son; at Sidon, a crucial port, past history helped him to a decisive coup. The Persians had suppressed Sidon's bid for independence some twelve years earlier and after the usual savagery had left the city to a tame king. Memories of those heady days when Sidon's citizenry had hacked down the trees in the Persian governor's park had not yet died, and when Alexander could promise the deposition of Persia and her agent, the city was his to treat as he pleased. Some fifty ships manned by Sidon were sailing in the Persians' fleet, and the surrender of their home city would surely persuade them to defect or return peacefully; the choice of a new king is said to have been left to Hephaistion, who picked on a man hitherto employed in a garden. Who better to rule than a gardener, even if the story may reflect an ancient myth in Semitic kingship? Promoted from the flowerbed, King Abdalonymus was as popular a choice with the mass of Sidonians as Alexander intended, and in return, he entertained the Companions to a lion-hunt in his nearby royal game park; scenes from the hunt were carved on his sarcophagus when he died, a Companion himself.

However, friendship with Sidon meant likely trouble at the ancient harbour city of Tyre, for while Sidon had recently suffered from Persia, her rival Tyre had flourished and so lay powerful and forbidding on Alexander's coast route southwards. When Alexander approached, he was met by the city's elders and the son of their absent king with gifts and a golden crown, promising to do whatever Alexander might command. Alexander replied that he wished to pay sacrifice to Melkarth, a Tyrian god whom he identified with his ancestor Heracles: this had been advised by an oracle. He had once watched his father use the same pretext for an unavoidable war and it was shrewdly calculated, for it exposed the Tyrians' offer and revealed that at heart, they wanted to remain neutral. If Alexander wished to sacrifice, there was an adequate temple to Heracles at Old Tyre on the mainland; he was not to enter their new island city. This retort made Alexander angry and within days he had begun to demolish Old Tyre in order to use its stone and timber for an assault on New Tyre's offshore position.

Anger was not his principal motive. Tyre, like Sidon, was one of the home ports for the crews in the Persian fleet and as Alexander had already decided to head south into Egypt, he could not leave it unsubdued on his main route of communication, especially as many of Tyre's warships had remained in the city. On a wider front, the Tyrians had been holding a grand festival in honour of Melkarth, to which representatives had come from Carthage, a city once founded by Tyre; these Carthaginians promised help in the event of a siege. Alexander may not have known of their promises but he would be aware of Carthage's link with Tyre and the possibility of naval help once his back was turned. It might be important to scare off this new threat from the west.

The process was bound to be laborious. New Tyre stood on a walled island two and three-quarter miles in circumference, cut off from the coast by half a mile of sea, shallow at first but soon dropping to a depth of some 600 feet. The city was fitted with two harbours, one on the north and another on the south-east outside the walls, and the wall itself rose as much as 150 feet, at least in the opinion of the besiegers. Though a king of Cyprus had once taken Tyre by force forty years before – a remarkable success about which regrettably little is known – he would have been supported by his strong fleet; in early January, a month of rough seas, Alexander was proposing to assault an island city and its remaining fleet when he had no ships of his own. In the early sixth century, Tyre had withstood siege by Nebuchadnezzar, King of Babylon, for thirteen consecutive years, and against a landbound Alexander it must have reckoned that its chances of survival were equally high. Evidently the Macedonian soldiery had their reservations; Alexander was forced to tell them that he had seen Heracles in a dream, extending his right hand and inviting him inside the city, while his favourite prophet Aristander announced cheering interpretations of such omens as blood-dripping rations of bread. In the background there were more solid reasons for confidence, though the historians never explained them.

In antiquity the assault of a walled city already required the combination of men and machines. It is naive to exalt the inventions above men's moods and opinions; Greeks in Alexandria would later discover steam-power but only use it to propel toy engines, and Buddhists were content if their newfound water power would peacefully revolve their prayer-wheels. But on the battlefield, inventions are more readily applied and there they can help to conquer the most soldierly courage. Like men, the inventions have fought a to-and-fro battle of their own. That primitive weapon for smashing, the mace, was first defeated by the helmet; to the helmet, the axe made cutting reply, only to be kept at bay by the new-found bow and arrow. Arrows brought on body armour, body armour diminished the earlier man-sized shield, smaller shields left a hand free for the thrusting-spear, and the discovery of the long-range composite bow in Mesopotamia in the seventeenth century B.C., backed by the mobile platform of the chariot, had been an innovation on the scale of powder and musket. So too with the race between siege technique and city walls. Axes, poles and ladders had menaced third millennium walls of brick and mud, but in the second millennium, walls had improved and regained the upper hand. Battering rams and siege-towers reached their peak in seventh-century Assyria, whereupon walls, shocked and over-topped, grew sloping banks at their base, bastions and recesses in their outlines and often changed their water-soluble bricks to massive thick-nesses of stone. Since the heyday of Assyria, siege technique in the east had been exported to the Mediterranean, but until recently, it had not been advanced; city walls had had things more their own way, and there was no uniformity of stone materials or defences among the Greek cities. In 332 Alexander, like King Tiglath-Pileser III of Assyria and his lightly built battering ram, was one step ahead in the battle of weapons; he was patron of a stone-throwing catapult, fitted with washers and powered by springs of twisted sinew.

It is ironic that the walls of Tyre were to be the first fortication to feel the force of boulders from Greek engines. Compared with the kingdoms of the east, the Greeks had been slow to develop advanced siege equipment, drawing their knowledge of siege-towers and rams in the course of the fifth century from their contact with the Orient; probably the techniques had passed from Assyria to Tyre, from Tyre to Carthage, from Carthage to the battlefields of Sicily, where the resident Greeks could have learnt from their Carthaginian enemies. Tyre, then, had been a vital link in the roundabout passage of siegecraft to the Greeks. But the route had also worked in reverse. At the turn of the century. Dionysius I, ruler of Syracuse, had first sponsored an elementary form of arrow-shooting artillery which he then turned against the startled Carthaginians: Carthage no doubt had reported her new wounds to Tyre and hence in 332 the Tyrian engineers had copied Dionysius's idea, and evolved arrow-catapults of their own. But they had not bargained with Philip and the intervening rise of Macedonia. By 340 Greek engineers under Philip's patronage had disovered the powers of a torsion spring; at first they fitted it to the old Sicilian brand of catapult, but soon pupils of Philip's head engineer, Polyeidus the Thessalian, had gone on to experiment with torsion-powered stone-throwers for Alexander's benefit. The old Syracusan catapult, presumably still used at Tyre, was repeat-firing without a torsion spring; whereas its range was some two hundred yards and its weapon a metal-tipped bolt, Alexander's new stone-throwers, improved since their first appearance at Halicarnassus, could rip through the ranks of defenders at 400 yards, and at 150 yards they could damage a city wall. To judge from several stories, the accuracy of ancient artillery was most impressive; when the Spartan king Archidamus was shown an arrow-shooting catapult for the first time, 'By Heracles', he remarked, 'man's courage is now a thing of the past.'

Alexander's technicians had not stopped at stone-throwers; stronger and taller siege-towers than ever before were waiting to be assembled, leaving space for archers and battering rams on as many as twenty different levels, up to a height of 180 feet; they were an extraordinary feat of carpentry, for their axles were made of oak, their planking of fir and their wooden towers were coated with lime and hung with sheepskins to keep off enemy missiles. There were improved grappling irons, though Alexander's head engineer disputed their merits; there was also a borer on wheels whose long iron-tipped pole was poked into mud-brick walling by a newly improved method. Wide drawbridges fell from each storey of the towers, down which more troops could pour than on usual designs; rams were mounted on a superior form of 'tortoise' 48 feet square, beneath which they were worked by ropes and a roller, while animal skins and a three-storey tower protected them, its top level carrying catapults, the bottom two holding buckets of water to put out any flames. But without exceptional leadership no number of new machines would bring Tyre down. Men as well as mules would have to heave these gigantic towers into position, and encouragement rested with Alexander, cut off by half a mile of water from the point at which conventional siegecraft could begin. 'Genius,' Napoleon once remarked, 'is the inexplicable measure of a great commander.' Before Tyre, Alexander's generalship had been good rather than great; with a characteristic leap forward to meet a challenge, he was now to show for the first time that genius which singles him out in military history. Before settling down to besiege, he sent heralds to offer Tyre peace in return for surrender. The Tyrians seized and killed them, hurling their bodies off the city walls in full view of the enemy. 'A truce must not be broken or a herald killed; a man who has surrendered to a superior must not be abused': the Tyrians had flouted an unwritten law of Greek warfare.

In reply, Alexander's first plan was bold. If he could not sail to Tyre, he would build a mole across the waves and walk there. For the mole, he had a successful precedent. In 398 Dionysius I had taken the city of Motya in north-west Sicily after rebuilding its sunken causeway across a whole mile of sea. Tyre was only half that distance away and though no previous earthwork survived as a foundation, most of the sea channel was so shallow that its mud could be used to bind the stonework together. It would be interesting to know how, if at all, Alexander had estimated the depth of the sea, as a hundred yards or so short of the island the water deepens suddenly. But even at that distance, Alexander's causeway would have served its purpose; his siege-towers would still overtop the wall, allowing his archers to shoot down on to the defenders, while his new stone throwers could batter the fortifications. Fortunately the forests of the Lebanon were a nearby source of timber, whereas Old Tyre, fast being demolished, provided the necessary stone; any further transport of building materials would have been impossibly slow, especially in the absence of the fleet. Ancient Greece knew no efficient carthorse collar and had never even devised a wheelbarrow.

Through the shallows the work proceeded apace, watched by Alexander who, said his officers, 'explained each step in person, encouraging some with a kind word, lightening the labours of others who had worked conspicuously well with a gift of money'. The people of Tyre were sceptical, harassing the builders from their warships and jeering at Alexander for daring to rival the God of the Sea. But the mole drew nearer, Poseidon notwithstanding, and the Tyrians soon took to pelting it with arrows from their arrow-catapults: in reply, Alexander hung up leather hides to protect his men and ordered two tall siege-towers to be erected to that he could shoot back. The Tyrians, themselves engineers with a respectable history, replied with a show of technical cunning.

In the secrecy of the city harbour they built up a transport ship to hold as much dry timber, shavings and torchwood as possible, adding pitch, sulphur and other inflammable material. The idea of a fireship was not new, but to each of its two masts near the prow they lashed two beams and hung up cauldrons filled with fuel; when the beams burnt, the cauldrons would tip and fan the fire, like the famous firepots which Rhodes would popularize over a century later. After ballasting the stern so that the prow was well clear of the water the crews waited for a favourable wind and then arranged for triremes to tow them towards the mole. Within range, they set light to the cargo, dived for safety and left the ship to blow straight into Alexander's siege-towers. The triremes bombarded any Macedonian defenders, and skiffs put in to the mole elsewhere and destroyed all available catapults. Victim of a most intelligent manœuvre, Alexander ordered new machinery to be built and the mole to be widened to some 200 feet in order to hold more siege-towers. Personally, he departed to Sidon on the happy news that the Phoenician fleet was at last returning home from Persian service; they might well be compelled to join him now that they had heard how their bases had surrendered, and as his hewers of wood in the Lebanon cedar forests were being harassed by natives, the Shield Bearers and Agrianians came too, prepared for a short sharp exercise.

On reaching Sidon, Alexander was more than compensated for the slow and disastrous progress of his mole. The kings of Byblos and Arad had returned to put in his power the ships with which they had deserted from the Persian admirals. Sidon did likewise, pleased by her change of king, and Rhodes sent nine warships, a precious gesture from an island whose entrepreneurial skills were becoming indispensable to the trade of the south-east Mediterranean. A hundred warships in all had joined him, enough to cripple the Persians' fleet at the start of their sailing season and to vindicate his long-term policy of taking the sea-ports one by one. It did not seem too disturbing when a fifty-oared pinnace arrived from Antipater with an urgent message in its captain's keeping; across enemy seas and against a March wind, the journey must have been dramatic and it would not have been undertaken for a triviality. As the captain had been the hero of the surprise of the ten Persian triremes in the Cyclades the previous autumn, his message probably concerned the evident attempts of the Spartan king Agis to rebel with Persian naval and monetary support. Alexander was already aware of Spartan discontent and none too worried that the Greek allies would abet it; the Persian ships were now a dying threat, so he left Sidon for ten days and menaced the tribesmen of the Lebanon cedar forests in order to safeguard his timber-cutters, sparing himself nothing in the process, as is plain from a delightful incident.

Lysimachus, Alexander's favourite boyhood tutor, had insisted on joining the march to the woods but as darkness fell, cold and unfamiliar in the mountains, he was lagging far behind the professional soldiers. Rather than abandon him to the enemy, Alexander fell back by his side and together, pupil and tutor soon found themselves cut off from all but a few of their troops. The night was growing chilly and they had no supplies to light a fire; in the distance, Alexander saw the enemy camp fires and 'trusting in his own agility – for, as always, he consoled his Macedonians by sharing their hardships in person', he set off to fetch his men a light. Reaching the camp fire, he surprised and stabbed two enemy guards with his dagger, snatched a torch from the embers and brought it back to warm his followers. Having scared off enemy reprisals, tutor, pupil and friends spent the night by their own blazing fire. In the search for Alexander's personality, this story must not be discounted; Chares its teller was Alexander's Master of Ceremonies, who would hear it told at dinners by his king, and any exaggerations may come not from his own imagination but from fellow-guests at table. Serious concern for his soldiers, a personal daring which in a lesser man would be a foolish waste of life: it was only proper that the new Achilles should have risked himself in the manner of his hero for the tutor who had first given him his Homeric nickname.

On returning to Sidon, he must have thought that his good news would never end. A hundred and twenty Cypriot ships and three prominent kings of Cypriot cities had left the Persians to pledge him their services; he now had a fleet nearly three times as large as Tyre's and he could call on that most modern invention in sea power, the quinquireme. Cypriots and Phoenicians used this expertly, for it meant manning their normal three-banked warship with two men to each oar on the two bottom layers, one to each oar on the top layer; this doubled manpower on the lower levels had increased the speed and ramming-power over the usual trireme. The Cypriot kings kept this prestige ship as their privilege; in the age after Alexander the quinquireme would touch off an arms race of the usual royal pomposity, one king competing with another until the definitive futility of a thirty-banker had laboured on to the Aegean. No king more merited a quinquireme than the elderly Pnytagoras of Salamis, a man whose past may have decided the fate of the Cypriot fleet; his grandfather had been bold Euagoras, who had fought for independence from Persia's empire. Twelve years earlier, this grandson Pnytagoras had been raised to Salamis's throne to throw off Persian control at a time of revolt in Egypt and Phoenicia. Eventually he had secured himself by changing sides for a bargain with Persia, but his independence was a recent memory and when he looked to Alexander, he was not altogether disappointed. Alone of the Cypriot kings, Pnytagoras ruled a city with no minerals, so Alexander granted him a nearby copper-mine on Cyprus. Like the kings of the Phoenician cities, the Cypriot kings were restored and acknowledged as allies, and although they were to strike coins with Alexander's name and type, strict uniformity was not enforced, and money in their own name continued to appear in small quantities.

Besides the Cypriots, one final blessing arrived in Sidon: 4,000 hired Greek reinforcements who had been summoned the previous spring from southern Greece. If they had marched by land they may have brought news more welcome than their numbers, for during the winter, Alexander had been unaware of a desperate danger to Asia Minor and the Royal Road behind him. Persian troops had fled northwards from Issus into the desolate wilds of Cappadocia which he had scarcely troubled to subdue that very autumn, and in the winter months they had streamed west with the help of the native tribes and cavalry in an effort to break out to the coast and link up with the Persian admirals. Three pitched battles of much moment had been fought, and Philip's veteran officer, the one-eyed Antigonus, had covered himself in glory from his neighbouring satrapy in Phrygia. Each time the Persian fugitives had been routed, perhaps with the fresh help of these reinforcements, again, in Darius's absence, the enemy's plan was notable for its vigorous sense of the possible, but it had been frustrated even before Alexander had heard of it. Antigonus had won the day, and Iranians only survived in Anatolian hideouts where their numbers had been too reduced to be a disturbance. It had been a winter of extreme danger and ferocity and the victories which saved it deserve as much credit as most of the pitched battles in the front line.

Returning to Tyre, Alexander found that the mole had been severely damaged by a spring gale in his absence. However, his new sea power made up for the loss and his next step was to challenge the outnumbered Tyrian warships with his own. But the Tyrians had blocked their harbour and they could safely refuse battle, restricting their losses to three rammed ships; short of a decisive new strategy, Tyre seemed certain to stand, at least until a thorough blockade, no easy business, could starve her to surrender. But behind the lines brains were being brought to bear in one of the many international meetings of Alexander's career. As well as sailors, engineers had joined Alexander from Cyprus and Phoenicia and then were now enjoying an exchange of ideas with their Greek equivalents.

Their first suggestion was valuable enough to be imitated by several subsequent kings: two large ships were to be lashed prow to prow and a battering ram was to be suspended above their decks so that their crews could row it up to the island's walls. They would anchor directly beneath doubtless protected by roofs of hide, and thus work the rams against the stonework as if they were still on dry land.

Though these battering-ships lessened the need for a full-length mole, Alexander was much too efficient a besieger to limit his assault to one area; the combination of varied troops and weaponry was his military stock-in-trade, and the mole, therefore, was rebuilt at an angle to the prevailing wind, the tallest siege-towers ever known were commissioned for its tip, complete with drawbridges, and all the while, stone-throwing catapults were to keep up a barrage against the wall from both ship and mole. The Tyrians were every bit as energetic; they repaired their breaches and put into practice the schemes of their own engineers.

To cushion the arrows and boulders, they hung long leather skins stuffed with seaweed along their battlements and set up large wheels of marble which they revolved with an unspecified mechanism; their whirring spokes were enough to break the missiles' course. They dropped rocks into the sea against the battering ships, which were already foundering in rough water, and hoped to prevent the crews from anchoring within range; by a master stroke, Alexander's men replied by hauling up the rocks on rope lassoes, loading them into their stone-throwers and hurling them far out of harm's way. Undaunted, the Tyrians sent armoured ships to cut the Macedonians' anchor cables and when these were beaten off by guards, they resorted to underwater divers, a familiar force in Greek warfare, who cut through the ropes until the Macedonians changed their anchor cables to solid chain. Patience was running out and a blockade had not brought Tyre any nearer to surrender.

When the battering-ships did manage to anchor at the foot of the walls they fared little better. The Tyrians used sharp poles to slice through the ropes by which the rams were swung and followed this up with sheets of flame from their flame-throwers. Against the siege towers on the mole they fitted tridents to long ropes and harpooned the enemy on their various levels, dragging them like speared fishes into the sea. Those who ventured on to the tower's drawbridges were trapped in large fishing nets and flung down on to the rocks. Workers at the foot of the wall were showered with sand which had been heated in upturned shields. Red hot, it poured inside their body armour and drove them to a frenzy.

This gallant resistance to naval blockading and battering continued from April until early July and against it the stone-throwing catapults could make little headway. Now that the Phoenician fleets had surrendered there was more to be said for swearing a truce with Tyre and moving south to Egypt, but Alexander refused to leave an enemy city behind him as long as Persian admirals were at large in the Aegean and southern Greece was unsettled by Sparta. Only one of his Companions is said to have backed his opinion in council.

A tempting alternative was not hard to find. While Tyre still stood Darius sent a second communication, offering a large ransom, his daughter's hand in marriage, friendship and alliance and all the lands up to the river Euphrates, later to be the furthest eastern boundary of the Roman Empire. It came at a very opportune moment, and when Alexander put it to his friends, he may well have thought first of the judicious forgery which was mentioned in connection with one of Darius's letters. But its reception was agreed, presumably because it was recorded by Callisthenes, writing up the court's personalities to please his patron. 'If I were Alexander,' Parmenion is said to have commented, at least in the official myth of his king, 'I would accept the truce and end the war without further risk.' 'So would I,' answered Alexander, irrefutably, 'if I were Parmenion.'

On this defiant note, a refusal was sent to Darius who also heard, through a eunuch escaped from camp, that his wife had died in childbirth and that Alexander had given her a magnificent funeral, a tribute which he had no political need to pay. The news of her death and Alexander's refusal of the peace offer finally determined Darius to muster a truly grand army from the Punjab to the Persian Gulf, a task which would take a whole year; it was evident that the Aegean offensive would now fail, as the Levantine fleets had surrendered, although his admirals still put up a resourceful struggle with the help of that scourge of Greek sailors and sea trade, the pirate. The coast of western Asia had been thoroughly harassed by land and sea in the past nine months, despite the attempted closure of its ports. Cos had been retaken and fifty pirate long-boats had helped raid even the apparent stronghold of Miletus, restoring a Persian governor and exacting badly-needed money. Ephesus's new democracy may have been similarly disturbed, and as if by design, the wild mountain tribes of three satrapies in Asia Minor had drawn off Alexander's generals in punitive expeditions. These were their last signal successes, for Alexander's second Greek fleet had finally put to sea. It at once cleared the Hellespont, then freed its islands and pursued the Persians southwards. Their henchmen were rooted out with them, not least the Athenian soldier of fortune, Chares, who had set himself up in Mitylene less than three years after he had crowned Alexander at Troy: he throve on chaos and disorder, but not for the first time he had changed sides too late and was expelled by the Macedonian admirals.

Back at Tyre, the next incident selected by the historians was centred on Alexander himself. One July morning, after careful preparation behind screens of hide, the Tyrians sailed out in their thirteen smartest warships, meaning to surprise Alexander's Cypriot fleet which had been beached in the north harbour while its crews had left as usual for lunch. Their adventure began auspiciously. They approached in hushed silence, then raised their cox's call, plashed their oars and rammed three royal Cypriot quinqueremes to pieces before the crews could return. Alexander was lunching in the southern harbour but had not returned to his royal tent as usual; he hurried to his quinquereme on hearing of the sortie, and sped round the city with ships to the rescue, urging his crews to ram and sink the Tyrian attackers. His own role was conspicuous, its results important, for his surprise retaliation deprived Tyre of her swiftest ships. Their sortie was said to have been prompted by a festive bout of drinking, but it was more likely to have been inspired by hunger, as Alexander had long been mounting a blockade on both harbours. Without their best warships the Tyrians were now more hemmed in than ever. Even Carthage had withdrawn her offers of help.

After two days' rest, the Macedonians were able to follow up their naval victory. In keeping with Alexander's methods, the final blow was to be delivered by varied weapons at various places. Battering-ships were to breach given points in the wall, machine-bearing ships would give cover and two more shiploads of infantry were to emerge down newly devised drawbridges and storm a way through any breaches. Meanwhile the fleet was to attack both harbours, north and south; archers and catapults were to be carried round the island in a flotilla of warships in order to create an unpleasant diversion. Such a mixture of concentrated and diversionary tactics is the mark of a great general, able to see his decisive chance and seize it. As planned, walls were rammed until they tottered, artillery rounded off the damage, warships and archers drew off the defenders, drawbridges dropped downwards and the Shield Bearers poured into the breach, led by their captain Admetus, with Alexander heading the second wave. Admetus, first to mount the wall, died a hero's death. Alexander was quickly astride the battlements to fill his place. Conspicuous both in armour and performance, he speared some, stabbed others and hurled Tyrians down into the sea. As the infantry followed his lead Tyre fast fell to Macedonian hands, no longer having the ships to keep its attackers at bay. A last-ditch stand by the shrine of the city founder was to no avail.

Enraged by Tyrian atrocities and the seven-month length of the siege, Alexander's army killed some 8,000 of the citizens and enslaved a further 30,000 of those who had not already been shipped in safety to Carthage and Sidon; on Alexander's orders, 2,000 more were crucified along the shore. The cruelty was not wholly wanton, for as the army burst upon the city, a truce had been announced for all who might take refuge in shrines or temples. Though most of the Tyrians were now too stubborn to comply, those who did so were spared, including Azemilk, King of Tyre, and the thirty envoys from Carthage whom it would have been unwise to violate. Azemilk was to be restored to his kingship and the city was to be resettled with loyal garrison troops and native survivors; as a sign of the times, it was given a Greek constitution.

On the following day, Alexander paid his overdue sacrifice to Heracles or Melkarth, dedicating the catapult which had first broken the city walls and consecrating the sacred ship of Tyre which he himself had been responsible for sinking. Never can the god have received such a blood-stained sacrice: 'Tyre', said a Macedonian historian, possibly Callisthenes, 'had fallen in the month of July when Aniketos was official magistrate at Athens.' But the magistrate's name is known to have been Nikeratos; the word Aniketos means Invincible and in a forgivable burst of enthusiasm, even the name-date of the year was altered to suit Alexander's invincibility as a besieger.

Encouraging, explaining, 'sharing the hardships in person', whether on the mole or among the cedars of Lebanon, Alexander had deserved his touch of historical glamour. As usual, the histories centre their story round the king, but there is one chance reminder that the new Achilles could no longer sack cities in the manner of his Homeric forbear, 'laying them low by the might of his own spear'. In a work on technical engineering, Diades the Greek from Thessaly, pupil to King Philip's inventor, is later described as the 'man who besieged Tyre with Alexander'. The fall of the city perhaps owed more to the drawing-board than will ever be known.

Once Tyre had fallen, Alexander could continue south through the coastal plains to Egypt, sure of the surrender of lesser cities in Syria and Palestine. Dor, Ashdod and Straton's Tower made terms because they depended on Tyre and Sidon, but a mere hundred miles south he ran into more obstinacy. Gaza, that large and ancient Philistine city, bestrode his route two miles from the sea, and from the Lebanon's trade of frankincense and the Arab's trade in spices, it had long grown very rich. It was garrisoned by hired Arabs, and it was urged to resist by its oriental governor Batis, who went down in history as ugly, fat and a eunuch.

Gaza's most formidable defence was its own mound, for like many cities in biblical lands it was perched on a 'tell' or heap of its earlier layers of habitation, from which it surveyed the open desert. It was well provisioned, and as soon as Alexander ordered the machinery which had been shipped from Tyre to be reassembled his engineers protested that the city was 'too high to take by force'. Undeterred, Alexander 'thought that the more impossible it seemed, the more it must be captured; the feat would be so extraordinary that it would greatly unnerve his enemies, whereas failure would be a disgrace if ever the Greeks or Darius should hear of it'. Gaza, like Tyre, was too strong to be left on Alexander's one route of communication, and this must have weighed as heavily as any attractions of the impossible.

Alexander's solution was characteristic. The citizens of Gaza prided themselves in their steep fort; very well, if the city was too high, then the ground level must be raised to meet it. Orders were given that against the south wall of the city a mound was to be built up, 400 feet wide and 250 feet high according to Macedonian estimates, though these are surely an exaggeration, for the siege only lasted two months and it would have been impossible, even unnecessary, to pile up so much sand in the time available. The method of such a mound was extremely old; it had been used two centuries earlier by Persian generals. Now it was to serve a new purpose: catapults and siege-towers were to be hauled to its top, presumably, on wooden ramps, and the defenders were to be battered from a point which overtopped them. At the same time, sappers were to dig tunnels under the walls to cause them to subside, an effective method against cities set on a 'tell' of earth and one which was standard practice; in 83 B.C., when the Romans were besieging a town in Asia Minor, the defenders even stole out and released a bear and a swarm of wasps down the enemy siege tunnel in order to discomfort their diggers.

Battered by artillery and rammed from the siege-towers, the city walls of Gaza soon subsided into the sappers' tunnel. As the Macedonians poured in, the natives resisted heroically and Alexander himself sustained two wounds. One came from an Arab who knelt as if in surrender, only to stab with a dagger concealed in his left hand, the other, more serious, from an enemy arrow-catapult whose bolt cut through the king's shield and breastplate and embedded itself in his shoulder causing a wound which 'was treated' with difficulty. Nonetheless Alexander saw his purpose fulfilled: at the fourth attempt, the Macedonians managed to mount the 'tell' and scale its shattered walls on movable ladders. Once inside they opened the gates for the entire army, and by late October, despite a vigorous defence, Gaza had fallen.

If only more details were known, the capture of Gaza would surely rank among Alexander's most remarkable exploits. As at Tyre, he had forced through a constructional scheme of admirable daring with an almost outrageous sense of what was possible, for to have prevailed on an army, weary from the trials at Tyre, to heap up a huge sand mound in the heat of late summer is no small tribute to Alexander's inspiration: as for his generalship, once again he had shown that pugnacious sense of style and that readiness to attack by several means at once which single out the great besieger. No other general in ancient history can boast of two siege successes comparable with the fall of Tyre and Gaza in ten consecutive months.

About the treatment of Gaza more is known, and even in antiquity the information aroused warm comment. The male inhabitants were killed to a man, mostly during the capture of the city, whereas all the women and children were enslaved, in keeping both with the customs of the time and with Alexander's habitual treatment of 'rebels'. The city itself was repopulated with native neighbours and used as a fortress for the rest of the war, proof of how Alexander had valued its site. Batis's fate was more discussed: Alexander's officers are not known to have referred to it, but camp gossip said that thongs were passed round his feet and lashed to the back of Alexander's chariot, and the horses then dragged him round the city while Alexander compared his punishment to that of Homer's Hector at the savage bidding of his slayer Achilles. As time passed, the description of the incident grew more lurid, but that is no reason to doubt it; in Thessaly, for example, men still dragged a murderer's body behind their horses round the grave of his victim, and Alexander was accompanied by a large contingent of Thessalian cavalry. They could well have suggested a punishment which appealed to their ruler's Homeric pretensions; at Gaza, Alexander had been wounded twice, and his army always took especially fierce vengeance on cities that gave him a wound.

The fall of Gaza had opened the way through marsh and desert to Egypt, and so after nine months of bloodshed, Alexander could enter unchallenged the most powerful kingdom in Darius's empire. During the past nine months he had introduced Syria and Palestine to the Macedonian weaponry which would sweep to and fro across them for more than a century in wars for their forests, fleet and precious metals; Gaza had been repopulated and Tyre resettled with a Greek form of government, but there can have been few thanks among the families of the thousands who had died for the beginnings of the flood of Greek culture which would overwhelm them with such rich results in the course of the next hundred years.

CHAPTER FOURTEEN

Once, according to a pretty story, Alexander and his elderly historian Aristobulus were sailing in the same boat down the Indian river Jhelum, and to ease the journey, Aristobulus was reading aloud from his history, elaborating the truth, as he thought that he would most please his king by adding fictitious heroics to the story. But Alexander seized the book and flung it into the river, saying: 'And the same, Aristobulus, is what you deserve, fighting these duels on my behalf and spearing all these elephants with a single javelin.' If Alexander had ever been so honest about the months which follow the siege of Gaza, his historians might well be in danger of a similar ducking. In November 332 Alexander crossed the desert into Egypt; by the following April, his myth had taken a new and strange direction. Legend and flattery soon set to work on this shift of tone, but behind them lie the deepest questions about Alexander's personality: whether Alexander was in any sense a mystic, how seriously he regarded the divine honours which were paid him in his lifetime, whether he came to disown his father Philip and if so, what this could have meant to him. This is a far cry from the sarissas and siege machinery of the year before and stands in the sharpest contrast to the carnage at Tyre and Gaza; if part of Alexander's spell has been his youth and part his impetuous curiosity, the most extraordinary part has based itself on the events of the next five months.

The road from Gaza to Egypt was particularly hazardous, as it led first through three days' desert, then through the famous Barathra or Serbonian bog which had brought a Persian army to grief only twelve years earlier. It is not known how Alexander supplied himself with water, perhaps from his fleet, or how he avoided these coastal marshes, but by November he found himself on the easterly arm of the Nile Delta, the prize of Egypt before him and a winter of plentiful food in store for his army. In November the Nile was no longer prohibitively flooded, and winter was the season of leisure for the Egyptian farmer. At Issus, the former satrap of Egypt had died leading his troops, and after the battle Amyntas the renegade Macedonian had led some 4000 fugitives from the Great King's mercenaries by boat to Cyprus, then south to the Nile where they had disembarked to an eager welcome from the natives. Later, when Amyntas's Greeks began to loot Egyptian farms they lost popularity; Amyntas and his troops were killed, possibly on Persian instigation. But his example remained as a spur to the next adventurer; Egypt was waiting, her natives responsive to tact, her army, as always, no serious obstacle.

As a civilization, Egypt was as old as the world and proud of it. Greek philosophy, so her priesthood claimed, had been discovered by an Egyptian, son of the Nile, 48,863 years before Alexander's arrival. It was nearly two hundred years since the Persians had first conquered her Pharaoh and seized a kingdom so rich in men and grain; the Persian king had been recognized as the new Pharaoh and a satrap had ruled as his deputy, supported by military colonists from all areas of the empire, whether ews or nomads from Khwarezm, who lived in garrison enclaves as far. Jsouth as the Nile's first cataract, border of Egypt and independent Nubia Despite legends of Persian atrocity, remembered among the priesthood, Persian rule had not weighed as heavily as it might have done. Persian noblemen enjoyed Egyptian estates which they farmed with native slaves through Egyptian agents; the yearly tribute, at its height, was a mere 700 talents of silver and the payments in kind had not been severe. The move to a state monopoly and a tax on all production would later yield the Ptolemics more than twenty times as much in value, but under Persian rule it was at most partial and in several vital trades and harvests it had not begun at all. Aristocrats of the Delta towns had survived the Persian conquest in the same high office as before; a temple could still own twelve square miles of farmland, and yet their educated classes had never accepted the Persians for long. Rebellion had been persistent and for all but five of the seventy years before Alexander's arrival, Egypt had maintained her independence under various Pharaohs, some of them, probably southerners from Ethiopia, who had set up new dynasties in the Delta. The Persian attempts at reconquest had been repeated and often spectacular. Four times they had invaded and they did not regain the country until the winter of 343. Even then success was brief; within five years of the Delta Pharaohs' fall, Khabash the pretender had again stirred the country to revolt and it was only three years since he had been put down.

Heir to recent and repeated rebellion. Alexander was welcomed enthusiastically by the natives. The Persian satrap met him at the fort of Pelusium and offered him 800 talents and all his furniture in return for a safe pass; Macedonians were sent by boat down the Nile to the capital city of Memphis and Alexander marched to meet them by land. Within a week he had entered the monumental palace of Upper Egypt, home of the Pharaohs for more than a thousand years.

The Egyptian society which greeted him was as rigidly shaped as one of its pyramids; at the base stood the millions of native peasants, the fellahin whom invaders and aristocrats had taxed and dominated because they could not escape; near the top were the family dynasties of the Delta regions, men like Semtutefnakhte or Patesi who made their peace with Alexander and continued without disturbance in the priesthoods and local governorships which their families had held for more than two hundred years; at the peak stood the Pharaoh, and around him the priesthood, whose education and ceremony made them the most articulate class in Egyptian history. 'In Egypt', Plato had written, expressing the priests' own view, 'it is not possible for a king to rule without the art of the priests; if he has forced his way to power from another class, then he must be enlisted into the priestly class before he can rule.' The priests were placed to control a coronation and they judged each wearer of the crown by the terms of their own law, the Ma'at or code of social order which abounded in ritual and complexities; even the brave native Pharaohs of the recent rebellions were denounced as 'sinners' by the priesthood because they had offended their arcane commands for a righteous life. A stern verdict was passed on the two hundred years of Persian 'misrule and neglect' by priests who exaggerated Persian sacrilege beyond all recognition; Artaxerxes III, who had reconquered Egypt eleven years earlier, was known to the priests as the Sword and was accused of killing the sacred bull of the god Apis, eating it roast and substituting that accursed animal the donkey in its place. Under Persian rule the temples may have had their presents and privileges reduced, but these legends of atrocity went far beyond the truth. However, they suited the purpose of Alexander, the acclaimed avenger of Persian impiety.

Inside Memphis, he was not slow to delight his likeliest critics. 'He sacrificed to other gods and especially to Apis.' By this one sacrifice, he reversed all memories of Persian unrighteousness and paid honour to the Egyptian god Apis in the form of his sacred bull, most famous of Egypt's many religious animals, who represented the god at Memphis until an age of some twenty years when he made way for a younger bullock, died and was interred with pomp in a polished sarcophagus. In return, Alexander is said to have been crowned as Pharaoh of Upper and Lower Egypt, an honour only mentioned in the fictitious *Romance of Alexander*; this crowning cannot be dated to any one month, but is supported by the Pharaonic titles which were applied to him in the inscriptions of the country's temples. As Pharaoh, he was the recognized representative of god on earth, worshipped as a living and accessible god by his Egyptian subjects: he was hailed as Horus, divine son of the sun god Ra whose worship had prevailed in Lower Egypt, and as beloved son of Amun, the creator god of the universe, whose worship had flourished in the temples of Upper Egypt and grown to incorporate the worship of the more southerly Ra. This divine sonship fitted him into the dynastic past of the native Pharaohs, for he could be said to share their common father Amun-Ra, who visited the Pharaoh's mother to father each future king; courtiers would have explained the doctrine and addressed him by its titles, but before many months had gone, it would prove to be rich in possibilities.

'Pharaoh, Pharaoh,' an Egyptian priest had written of the Persians' reconquest, 'come do the work which awaits you'; as crowned king of the two lands, 'lord of sedge and bee', Alexander was indeed to fulfil the hopes of the temples and bear out the daily routine of the priestly Ma'at. His crowning had come at a time of confusion. The last Pharaoh, Nectanebo II, had fled south, probably to Ethiopia, to avoid the Persians' reconquest but he was believed by Egyptians to be ready to return and resume his rule: Alexander had replaced him, and it was perhaps more than a rumour that he considered a march into Ethiopia, border home of Nectanebo's possible supporters. Instead, his historian Callisthenes is said to have gone south up the Nile to investigate the causes of the river's summer flooding, a story which may well be correct. The floods had long exercised the ingenuity of Greek authors, some of whom had guessed the answer, but it was left to Aristotle to write that the matter was no longer a problem, now that Greek visitors had seen the truth of Ethiopia's summer rains for themselves. Probably these witnesses were his kinsman Callisthenes and other soldiers in the Macedonian army.

As for Alexander, he took ship from Memphis early in the year of 331 and sailed northwards down the Nile to make his most lasting contribution to civilization. At the river's mouth, he visited the Pharaohs' frontier fort at Rhacotis and explored the other outlets of the Delta. He was much struck by the possibilities of the site at its western edge:

It seemed to him that the place was most beautiful for founding a city and that the city would be greatly favoured; he was seized by enthusiasm for the work and marked out the plan in person, showing where the gathering-place should be built and which gods should have temples where, Greek gods being chosen along with the Egyptian Isis; he arranged where the perimeter wall should be built.

So Alexandria was born, a new centre of gravity in all succeeding Mediterranean history which 'was to stand, like a navel, at the middle of the civilized world'.

Like every other Alexandria it grew round the site of a fortress used by the Persians. Rhacotis became a quarter in the new city and absorbed the herdsmen who had long lived round it in villages: its site had been admirably chosen and its natural harbour may already have been exploited by Egyptians. To Alexander it promised a particularly benign climate, shelter from the island of Pharos and a raised position on the shoreline which would catch the north-west breeze in summer. A site further east on the Delta would soon have been ruined by the silt which the natural current at the river mouth washes down shore from the west.

Apart from fame and the wish for the city to prosper, the motives for founding Alexandria can only be guessed. Its site was not well defended and its position on the fringe of Egypt's administration suggests that access to the Aegean was its prime attraction, perhaps for economic reasons. Greeks had long maintained a trading-post at Naucratis in the Delta and their trade with Egypt is not known to have dwindled before Alexander's arrival, though Persian invasions cannot have helped it. How far commercial relations with Greece and their possible growth weighed in Alexander's decision is most uncertain. The Aegean, when he founded the city, was infested with pirates and too hostile to deserve development; even in its maturity more trade was thought to pass into Alexandria from inland Egypt than from the entire Mediterranean. The inland granaries of Egypt could ship corn quickly into the city by river and canal to feed its large population; this ready supply of food was more important to its founder than the casual trading of its surplus or the harbour taxes taken from trade in the port. In Alexandria, as in other Greek cities, traders were seldom citizens and their organization into official groups was a very slow development. Trade therefore was not a natural force in a city's politics and during the next century Alexandria's commerce spread more through the entrepreneurs of Rhodes than her own citizens; when the city was founded Rhodes was an uncertain friend to Alexander.

The citizen body was exclusive rather than commercial. Macedonian veterans, Greeks and prisoners, perhaps too a contingent of Jews, were detailed as the new citizens, and native Egyptians were mostly added as men of lesser status. The laws and charter of the city are very far from certain; it perhaps had an assembly and council from the start but their qualifications for membership are nowhere mentioned. The architect was a Greek from Rhodes and the building was entrusted to Cleomenes, a Greek from Naucratis with a shrewd head for finance. As the barley-meal was sprinkled to mark out the city in the shape of a Macedonian military cloak, Aristander the prophet is said to have predicted that 'Alexandria would be prosperous in other respects, but especially in the fruits of the earth'; home-grown food was the city's first concern, not balanced trade or the export of Egypt's sail-ropes, drugs and spices and the import of Greece's wine and painted pottery.

As the building work began, Alexander was rewarded by a pleasant surprise. From the Aegean, so early in the season, one of his admirals sailed in to deliver prisoners and report on his campaign; now that the Cypriot, Rhodian and Phoenician fleets had changed sides, the news could only be welcome. The Persian admirals were left with dwindling money, a mere 3,000 Greek mercenaries and only as many boats as they could enlist from Aegean pirates. Their tyrants and oligarchs had been expelled from the cities of Tenedos, Lesbos, Chios and Cos, usually to the delight of the mass of their citizens: pirates and one of the two Persian admirals had been ambushed in Chios's harbour. However, the Persian admiral had since escaped and his fellow was somewhere in hiding; Chares the Athenian, who had seized one of Lesbos's cities, was also ranging free, and by no means the last had been heard of them. For the moment it was more alarming that Aegean shipping was still at the mercy of pirate long-boats. Less serious were reports that Agis King of Sparta, whose negotiations with the Persian admirals had come to nothing, had since transferred 8,000 Greek fugitives from Issus to Crete and won over Crete's towns and fortresses with Persian help. Persian desperadoes would flock there now that the Aegean war was over, but if Agis shipped his bandits back to Greece, they were unlikely to cause uncontrollable revolt. Against Antipater and the allies, their numbers were negligible and their pay would soon start an argument, especially as Sparta used no coinage and had no ready means to finance a hired army. Among the spoils of Issus Alexander had captured Spartan ambassadors to Darius; two more had been sent since then but they were unlikely to meet with any more help from a king whose strategy now centred on Asia.

As leader of the Greek allies. Alexander arranged the punishment of all his Aegean prisoners. The pirates were executed and most of the tyrants were sent back for trial in home cities whose democracies had been restored; there was no comfort in legality, for in one freed town the two pro-Persian terrorists were condemned to death by 883 votes to 7, resounding proof of the hatred with which a democratic court regarded them. The ringleaders from Chios had been so dangerous that Alexander dealt with them personally, sending them in chains to serve in an old Persian garrison on the Nile's first cataract; other Chian offenders were to be tried locally or refused asylum if they fled. Alexander did not await reports of their sentence; in early spring, while the building began in his Alexandria, he marched westwards along the coast of the Mediterranean, leaving his army to speculate about his intentions. With their speculation, the problems of his personality begin.

In the next month, Alexander was to travel westwards with a small group of attendants and then turn south for three hundred miles through an eerie stretch of desert in order to put certain questions to the oracle of Ammon, a ram-headed god who was worshipped in the oasis of Siwah on the remote western border of Egypt and Libya. In his lifetime, Alexander was to reveal neither the questions nor the answers, but clues to their content have been drawn from his own behaviour and from the way his historians have described it. Only once before in Asia had Alexander diverged from the route required by strategy, and then only for his pilgrimage to Troy; this suggests that whatever drove him to Ammon's oasis, it was nothing easily satisfied. In the fullest surviving account of his motives, given by Arrian five hundred years later on the basis of wide and varied reading, he is said to have been seized by a burning desire to go 'because he was already referring part of his parentage to Ammon . . . and he meant either to discover about himself or at least to say that he had done so'.

This challenging remark is an introduction to the strangest strand in Alexander's life and legend. As a result of his visit to the oasis, at several points in his various histories he will be said to have disowned his father Philip and come to claim Ammon as his father. On coins, especially those issued by his Successors, he is shown round-eyed and mystical, adorned with a curling ram's horn, symbol of the god Ammon. In the Alexander romance, he writes letters addressed from Ammon's son; in the Bible's Book of Daniel, he appears in the guise of the ram-horned conqueror. In his legend, from early Moslem Syria to Modern Afghanistan, he is remembered as Iskander Dhulkarnien, Alexander the Two-horned, who is identified with the two-horned prophet in the Koran, who searches for the Springs of Immortality, defies the barbarians beyond Iran and still guards the north-east frontier against Russian 'invasion. Because of this one adventure in the desert, Alexander has exchanged fathers and sprouted horns, but it is a separate question how far these developments are true to his character.

Historically, the visit to Ammon's oasis has long been the victim of hindsight and legend and nowhere is this plainer than in the disputed motives for the expedition. According to Callisthenes, who wrote what Alexander wished to be known, 'it was Alexander's glorious ambition to go up to Ammon because he had heard that Perseus and Heracles had gone there before him'; although this rivalry with two Greek heroes was to Alexander's liking, Callisthenes was writing some twenty months after the event. Both Perseus and Heracles were agreed to be sons of the god Zeus and as Alexander was recognized as a son of Zeus after his visit, it made sense for a flatterer to read back the visit's result into his motives for setting out; Callisthenes 'tried to make a god out of Alexander' and gave him the attributes of Zeus, so he presented the Siwah pilgrimage as the rivalry of one son of Zeus with another from the very start. While it is of the first importance that this motive was later to Alexander's liking, Perseus and Heracles are also an interesting pair. Heracles was ancestor of the Macedonian kings and regularly honoured by Alexander, but Perseus appears nowhere else in his myth. It is not even certain that he was previously believed to have visited Siwah. Perhaps he had other attractions; it is a revealing fact about the Greeks that they would trust the simplest puns or word-plays, especially where place names of foreign peoples were concerned. By a pun, foreign names could be linked with the circles of Greek culture and in this sense, it was seriously believed by the Greeks that the Persians were descended from their own Greek hero Perseus, just as the Medes were descended from Medea. This belief was shared by Xenophon who knew and admired the Persians, also by Plato, and Herodotus, and was even upheld by the Persians themselves while, locally after Alexander, Perseus would recur as a symbol of city myths and coinage at many sites in Asia Minor where Greeks and Persians are known to have been living side by side. In short, Perseus became the hero of integration between East and West and for Alexander, the first king ever to rule both peoples at once, a rivalry with Perseus and Heracles was not irrelevant. In Greek eyes, they were his ancestors as the Persian and the Macedonian king, and when Callisthenes wrote up the visit to Siwah, Alexander had already replaced Darius as king of Asia and come to be heir to both heroes at once. A year and a half before, when he set out for Siwah, the two of them are unlikely to have weighed heavily on his mind.

Others took the theme further. Besides the rivalry with Greek heroes, 'Alexander set out for Ammon with the added intention', wrote the Roman Arrian, possibly taking his cue from Ptolemy's history, 'of learning about himself more accurately or at least of saying that he had so learnt.' This personal problem was connected already with his parentage, 'for he was referring a part of his birth to Ammon', and this belief can be most naturally explained by his new position as Pharaoh, eventually inherited by Ptolemy. For the Pharaoh was the 'begotten son of Amun-Ra, beloved of Amun'; on this view, Alexander went to the Siwah oasis in Libya in order to find out the meaning of the Pharaoh's titles, a motive which seems as confused as the rivalry with heroes of Greek legend. Why should Libyan Ammon know the truths of Egyptian Amun-Ra and why should the remote Siwah oasis have been brought to Alexander's notice as the place to find the truth? Only if Ammon and Siwah are set in context can the motives for the pilgrimage be narrowed to a plausibility; Ptolemy is known to have added miracles to the visit and his account of its motive is unlikely to be impartial.

In the god Ammon, the traditions of three different peoples had long combined. Originally the Siwah oasis had been home of a local Libyan god, who may have been related to Baal Haman of the Carthaginians on his western border; his shrine lay some four weeks' journey from the centre of the Egyptians' kingdom, and it is very possible that for a thousand years, he had never come under the Pharaohs' control. But two hundred years before Alexander, if not earlier, Egypt had mastered Siwah beyond any doubt, and the Pharaoh Amasis is known from hieroglyphics to have built the oracular temple which Alexander was going to visit. The temple's architecture is not distinctively Egyptian, and its carvings show the native Libyan king of the oasis in an independent rank. Egypt, it seems, had merged with Libya, not taken her over completely, and so she was left with a new foreign god to explain. She identified him with her own lord Amun, ram-god and begetter of the universe, married to Mut and father of Khonsu; the ceremonies at Siwah took an Egyptian turn and oracles were given in the Egyptian fashion.

A third people had also intruded. During Amasis's reign, colonists from Greece had been settling in Cyrene, a Libyan town to the west of the Siwah desert, where they intermarried with the native Berbers and heard of the local divinities. Always attracted by an oracle, they had visited Siwah in its Egyptian phase and given its god the Greek name Ammon, which suggested both the Egyptians' own Amun and the Greek word 'ammos' or sand, as befitted a god in the desert. Just as Egypt had already equated Siwah's god with her own pre-eminent ram-god Amun, so too the Greeks explained this highly honoured Ammon as a form of their Olympian Zeus, king of the Greek gods. In Cyrene they were soon to build a splendid Doric temple to Zeus Ammon, and to use his features, distinguished by a ram's horn, on the plentiful coinage of the city. The complex origins of the god were established from Greek, Libyan and Egyptian sources and it only remained for him to spread.

Since 500 B.C. Ammon's expansion had been astonishing. Throughout, it was the Greek city of Cyrene which passed on the god's name to Greece, and it is very striking that Pharaoh Amasis, the first Egyptian known to have taken an interest in Siwah, maintained a Cyrenean mistress. Many of Cyrene's Greek settlers had family links with Sparta on the Greek mainland, so that worship of Ammon soon spread by sea to Sparta's southern harbour town and thence inland; the great shrine of Zeus at Olympia set up a cult of this new Zeus whom Cyrene had discovered, and in the Theban poet Pindar, 130 years before Alexander's visit, Ammon had found his most able publicist. Pindar had visited the King of Cyrene to write a hymn in his honour and had been so impressed with Zeus Ammon that he had set up the god's statue in his home town of Thebes on his return and written him a poem; the priests of Siwah were said to have prayed that Pindar should receive life's greatest blessings, whereupon, in fulfilment, the poet died peacefully. Pindar, moreover, had honoured connections with the Macedonian kings.

Pindar was not the last of Ammon's famous Greek admirers. Presumably through Cyrene, the family of Lysander the Spartan general had connections with Siwah, and Lysander was to use the god during his career in the late fifth century. While besieging a town on the eastern borders of Macedonia he claimed to have seen Ammon in a dream, and he withdrew from the siege on the god's advice, so unexpectedly that the defending city set up a cult of Ammon in gratitude, which Alexander may have known from his nearby home before he ever reached Egypt. Athens, meanwhile, had been equally receptive. In the 460s Cimon the Athenian general had tried to consult the Siwah oracle while his fleet was moored near Cyprus; before invading Sicily, the Athenians had sent envoys to do likewise and at least thirty years before Alexander's visit a temple of Zeus Ammon had been built in the Piraeus port, perhaps by merchants who knew the god through the grain-trade with Cyrene. Gold had been sent from Athens to Siwah; Ammon was a recognized oracle among Athenian poets, which was not surprising as the gods' fame had long spread right through Asia Minor, from Cyzicus on the Sea of Marmara to the Lycian kings in the far south, and had entered the islands of the Greek Aegean. Zeus Ammon had spanned the Greek world for more than a hundred years before Alexander set out in search of him, and this background helps to explain his decision.

As a well-known Greek god, Ammon would have attracted Alexander's attention whether or not he had become Pharaoh at Memphis. Although the ceremonies at Siwah followed an Egyptian pattern, Egypt and the Pharaohs are scarcely known to have troubled the priesthood of the oasis, and no Pharaoh is known to have travelled the 500 miles through desert from Memphis to Siwah, an unnecessary exertion for a man who believed that its semi-Libyan god was a form of his own lord Amun, as Amun had more illustrious temples within reach of a boat trip down the Nile. Nor was the oracle thought to be an Egyptian puppet. When nearby border tribes had wished to know whether or not to support the Pharaoh, it was Ammon to whom they had sent for impartial advice. There is only one exception to the Pharaoh's apparent disinterest. Some ten years before Alexander's arrival, Nectanebo II, the last independent Pharaoh, had dedicated a secondary temple in the Siwah oasis to the Egyptian Amun-Ra, but as Nectanebo may himself have been of Libyan birth his sudden interest in Siwah is of no consequence for Egyptian policy or for Macedonian Alexander. Siwah was not a convenient or obvious place to learn about the mystique of Amun, even if Alexander had set out with this in mind; it was the Delphi of the Greek East and as a Hellene, not as Pharaoh, Alexander would be curious about a god who was known and patronized by Greeks because of his truthfulness. Zeus Ammon at Siwah was the last available oracle of Greek repute before Alexander led his troops inland into Asia, and Alexander wished to consult him for this simple reason alone. Curiosity, it is agreed, was matched by a spirit of adventure, attracted by the hazards of the journey, and it may be relevant that in a work on Thirst, his tutor Aristotle had told the vivid story of an Argive pilgrim who had starved his body to the limit and travelled many weeks through the desert to Siwah without once drinking water on the way. This feat of endurance might have appealed to his emulous pupil, had it ever been told in the schoolroom.

But in Egypt, Aristotle seemed far distant and a nearer reminder of Ammon was needed, which owed nothing to the Pharaoh's titles as son of Amun-Ra. While busied with the site of his new city, Alexander had received envoys from Cyrene who invited him to pay their cities a visit, offering him friendship and alliance, 300 horses and five four-horsed chariots. In Arrian's history, suggesting that Alexander set out for Ammon seized by a sudden desire to inquire about himself, this detail is suppressed, probably because he was following the word of King Ptolemy who was ruler, not ally of Cyrene by the time he wrote his history and might not have relished a reference to the city's pact with his predecessor. But it is an important clue, for it was through Cyrene that the Greek world had first come to think highly of Ammon and it was surely the same city's envoys who first reminded Alexander of the god's existence. Very possibly, they did not mention the oasis until Alexander had taken up their offer, gone to visit their cities and reached the town of Paraetonium, 165 miles west of Alexandria and ten miles beyond a usual turning-off point for pilgrims to Siwah. If so, Alexander would have turned west not to consult the god but to follow his envoys from Cyrene and secure his frontier with Libya, an aim which is in keeping with his methods as a general. Only when strategy was satisfied did he think of a detour to Ammon, a familiar and truthful oracle. He did not march from Alexandria as a mystic with a master plan, and as the theme of his divine father only arose by accident at Siwah, from an unpredictable incident on the temple steps, it cannot have been his motive for setting out from Alexandria into the desert.

From Alexandria, he travelled west along the sea-coast with a small group of friends, following the whitened track to Paraetonium. At Paraetonium, where Antony was one day to bid farewell to Cleopatra, he took his leave of Cyrene's envoys and set out southwards into the sand, his attendants mounted on camels with water for four days' journey. The sequel cannot be shared without a knowledge of its scenery and fortunately, Alexander's route has often been followed and described, the most telling account being that of Mr Bayle St John, if only because like Alexander he lost his way. In September 1847, having read his ancient texts with care, he equipped himself with camels, Bedouin guides and a moderate supply of water, and added the luxury of brandy and cigars; his notes are most helpful for what follows.

Soon after leaving Paraetonium, Alexander found himself in a wide expanse of sand, probably because his guides had led him too far west of the direct route which, as St John and others have remarked, should have run over hills of shale. His error was brought home unpleasantly, as a south wind sprang up and whipped across the desert, blinding the travellers in a sandstorm. For four days they wandered as best they could, exhausting their water and intensifying their thirst; supplies had almost run dry when clouds gathered and a sudden storm broke, 'not without the help of the gods,' so they believed, and this enabled them to refill their leather waterbottles.

On emerging from the sandstorm, they regained the long chain of hills which stretches inland from the sea, rising and falling in valley after valley until the reddish cliffs close in, streaks of white across their grotesque faces, and the final pass winds down a ravine to the sandy plains beyond. For the sake of coolness, Alexander would only move by night, steering by the clearness of the desert stars and trusting in the moon to light him on his way, as close as a man can come to his retreating ideal of silence, all quiet around him except for the faintest desert breeze. Even the ground came alive in the stillness, as the sides and floor of the pass were lined with dried-up shells which attracted the notice of the travellers and, according to St John, reflected the moonbeams till the whole road sparkled, like a mythical valley of Diamonds.

A gorge black as Erebus lies across the path [he writes], and on the right stands a huge pile of rocks, looking like the fortifications of some vast fabulous city such as Martin would choose to paint or Beckford to describe. There were yawning gateways flanked by bastions of tremendous altitude; there were towers and pyramids and crescents and domes and dizzy pinnacles and majestic crenellated heights, all invested with unearthly grandeur by the magic beams of the moon but exhibiting, in wide breaches and indescribable ruin, that they had been battered and undermined by the hurricane, the thunderbolt, the winter torrent and all the mighty artillery of time.

Amid this Gothic grandeur, Alexander once more lost his way.

According to Callisthenes, two crows came to his rescue, cawing to round up the stragglers and flying steadily in front until they had set Alexander back on the proper track. Ptolemy, never a man to be outdone, claimed in his history that two talking snakes had acted as guides not only to Siwah but also the whole way back again. These miracles must not be dismissed, though they are a warning that like Alexander, the truth of the Siwah visit was lost from the very start; the travellers did indeed notice many snakes on the way to the oracle, a fact which can be deduced from Theophrastus, pupil of Aristotle, who mentions their numbers in his book on botany, a work which drew its original information from members of Alexander's expedition. As for Callisthenes's crows, they have been sighted since; St John too went astray in the hills and while waiting for his Bedouin guides, he noticed two crows wheeling in the air away to the south-west. Had he followed them, he would have struck the very road he wanted, so it is perhaps no coincidence that the valley in question is still known to natives as the Pass of the Crow.

From the terrors of the pass, Alexander came down into a plain of sand, too hot for any vegetation, which stretches for some ten miles to the foot of the Milky Mountains. Here, among more cliffsides of the wildest architectural shapes, he followed the road out into the open, passing over a level basin of grey gravel. With a change so typical of the desert, on its far side the gravel falls abruptly into a plain of luxuriant palms, bounded by cliffs on either flank and walled across the middle by isolated rocks of massive shapes and sizes. In this, the oasis of Garah, lay the first cities of the people of Ammon; water, hospitality and shade were at last guaranteed and 'the vivid contrast of barrenness and fertility', writes St John, 'where life and death exert their sway beneath the infinite emblem of immortal serenity, excite mingled emotions of wonder and delight'.

From these preliminary cities of Ammon, one day's travelling was enough to bring Alexander to the second oasis, site of the Siwah oracle. Though rapid, his journey was no easier, for on leaving the palm-groves of Garah, he would have wound his way up yet another series of gorges, finding himself again on a gravel plateau, flayed by the heat. It is a place of no comforts until at its edge it too falls into one last ravine, only ten miles away from Siwah, first across valleys of whitened sand, then across land hardened and broken with lumps of natural salt, a rich deposit which the priests of Ammon would pack in baskets and send to the table of the Persian kings. The landscape dazzles the eye, as the salt-fields and dried up salt lakes have all the glare of snowbound glaciers. Before their whiteness can get the better of the traveller the oasis of Siwah has intervened, sweeping its greenness between the remaining pockets of sterility: palms and fruit-trees crowd round the streams, a home for quail and falcons, pomegranates and meadow-grasses, and for ram-headed Ammon, one of the four most truthful oracles known to the Greek world.

The oasis is insulated by saltfields and marshes into a space some five miles long and three miles broad. Near its eastern edge, Alexander would come directly to his destination, the citadel now known as Aghurmi which protrudes on a cliff of limestone eighty feet above the plain. At the time of his visit, it was divided into three enclosures, the inner one for the palace of the rulers, the next for their family, their harem and the shrine of the god, the outer one for the guards and barracks. Beside the temple stood a sacred spring in which offerings to the god were purified; this is still visible, connected to the inner courts of the temple. About half a mile to the south-east stood a second shrine, also known to the Egyptians but less patronized by Greek pilgrims, though they knew of its fountain and wrongly believed it to be miraculous, thinking that it alternated between hot and cold at different times of the day. The Greeks, however, had no thermometers. Alexander's officers picked up its native name of Well of the Sun and linked it, characteristically, with their own Greek myth of Phaethon, fallen driver of the Sun's chariot.

Both for the visitors and the visited this sudden arrival was momentous. Alexander had been travelling for at least eight days through country of the most fantastic outlines, illusion and miracle around him at every turn. He was lucky to have survived, and his sense of relief on reaching the oasis is not difficult to imagine. The people of Siwah would have been no less excited. Historically, their oasis had long been a backwater, never visited by Pharaohs and sheltered from modern life by its surrounding desert; even in the twentieth century its local customs were still thriving, including homosexuality to the point of all-male marriage. A visit from a Macedonian conqueror would have stirred all the natives from their homes, and no doubt Alexander would have promptly made himself known to the ruling family who, like all Libyans, were identifiable by the single-feather headdress which they wore tied into their hair. Gossip claimed that Alexander also bribed Ammon's priests in order to be sure of receiving the answers he wanted, but any consultant of a Greek oracle would first pay the god honour, and it is unthinkable that Alexander gave advance warning of his questions and desired answers; his whole consultation depends on secrecy and ambiguity.

By a present, then, the temple staff had been forewarned and the natives would have led Alexander through their houses at the foot of the citadel and set him on the steps to the temple, traces of which can still be seen. With his friends, he would have climbed up to the pedimented gate of the outer temple yard; at the entrance, or just inside the first court, the senior priest came forward, greeting the king in full hearing of his followers. He was aware of his visitor's high rank, as he allowed nobody but Alexander to enter the inner courts and did not ask him to change his everyday dress; all the other Macedonians waited outside, probably on the steps of the temple rather than in the inner courtyard, and could only hear the oracle at work through the barriers of two, if not three, stone walls.

'The oracles were not given in spoken words as at Delphi or Miletus,' wrote Callisthenes, repeating what Alexander wished to be known, 'but for the most part they were given by nods and tokens, just as in Homer, "Zeus the son of Cronos spoke and nodded with his dark eyebrows"; the priest would then answer on Zeus's behalf.' This publicity has much to tell. There are four ways to treat foreign gods: fight them, disbelieve them, accept them or identify them with one's own at home. At Siwah Alexander chose identification, just as the Athenians and other Greeks had long paid worship to Ammon by a link with their own Zeus. It is a tribute to Callisthenes's tact, and an insight into his patron's tastes, that for the new Achilles the god's procedure was explained by a reference to Zeus in Homer's *Iliad*.

As for the nods and tokens, they match all that is known about the workings of an Egyptian oracle. Like the Greeks and Romans, the Egyptians imagined their gods in terms of the society in which they lived; just as Christ in the Roman Empire was to be hedged about with the protocol of a Roman emperor, so the lord god Amun was thought to behave in the manner of a Pharaoh of Egypt. He could not be approached in his own apartments, and if any of his people had a problem they could only pose it on high days and holidays when the god, like the ruler, left his court and came out into the streets. Just as the Pharaoh was carried in public on a platform which rested on his attendants' shoulders, so too the image of Amun was placed in a sacred boat, hoisted aloft on a board and borne before the people by his purified bearers; the god, like the Pharaoh, was kept cool on his journey by carriers of feathers and fans. At Siwah, ever since the Egyptians had identified the natives' god with Amun, the same procedure had been observed: the god was treated like a Pharaoh. 'When an oracle is wanted', explained witnesses with Alexander, 'the priests carry the bejewelled symbol of the god in a gilded boat, from whose sides dangle cups of silver; virgins and ladies follow the boat, singing the traditional hymn in honour of the deity.'

This apparatus would have startled Alexander, and its giving of oracles was suitably eccentric. In Egyptian ritual, the questioner might read out his problem to the god, or write it in simple form on a potsherd token, or tell it first to the priest who would then repeat it to the boat. The bearers would heave the sacred vessel on to their shoulders and prepare to move like table-turners in whichever direction they felt it pressing them. If the god meant 'no', he would force the boat-bearers backwards; if he meant 'yes', he would force them forwards; if he lost his temper at the question, he would shake furiously from side to side. The priest would interpret his movements, 'answering on behalf of Zeus'; written questions could also be laid out on the ground in alternative versions of 'yes' and 'no' so that the god could lunge towards whichever answer he fancied. This ritual lasted in Egypt for two thousand years, until the coming of Islam, and it still has a parallel in certain African tribes; just as Sheikhs in their coffins have sometimes weighed heavily on their pall-bearers to stop their body being taken to its funeral, so in the Sudan, worshippers are still driven to and fro by the momentum of a holy image on their shoulders.

At Siwah nods and tokens were only given 'for the most part', and so Alexander also went through the boat's small courtyard and entered the holiest shrine behind, a small room about ten foot wide and twenty foot long which was roofed over with the trunks of palm trees. In this sacred chamber he could put his questions direct to the god, a privilege that was perhaps reserved for Pharaohs and rulers only; he would not be aware that a narrow passage, still visible on the site of the temple, ran behind the righthand wall and was linked to the shrine by a series of small holes. Here, the priest could stand out of sight in a cubby-hole and give answer through the wall to his visitor as if he were Ammon speaking in person. Perhaps Alexander revealed his question inside the shrine to the high priest alone, who then put it to the boat outside and returned to announce the result; perhaps Alexander first consulted the boat and then asked more intimate questions inside the shrine. Whatever the order of events, his friends outside had no idea of the questions which their King was asking. The most they would hear would be songs from the virgins and the tramp of the boat-bearers' feet; the mention of 'tokens' suggests that Alexander may not have spoken but written his questions on a potsherd and sent them out to the boat for an answer. His friends could only have watched with puzzlement.

Alexander never revealed what he had asked, but 'he used to say that he had heard what pleased him'. His questions, however, are not all irrecoverable. Four years later, at the mouth of the river Indus in India, he offered sacrifice to the 'gods whom Ammon had bidden him honour', and did the same on the following day, this time to a different set of gods; evidently he had asked the oracle which gods he should propitiate at particular points on his journey eastwards, a request which had been made at Delphi by Xenophon, the last Greek general to have marched inland into Asia. Ammon advised, among others, Poseidon and the other sea gods, perhaps because Alexander asked specifically whom to honour if he reached the outer Ocean. It is unlikely that this was Alexander's only question, as his secrecy and his lasting honour for Ammon only make sense if he had asked something more personal, probably whether and when he would be victorious. But camp gossip had its own ideas, and within twelve years of Alexander's death, two questions to Ammon had gained favour: Alexander, it was said, had asked the god whether he would rule the whole earth and whether he had punished all his father's murderers, but the priest warned him that Ammon, not Philip, was now his father. These fanciful guesses are most interesting evidence of how his soldiers remembered him. The first picked up the themes of invincibility and mastery of the world, both of which were encouraged by Alexander himself; it is also noticeable that the 'sacrifices according to Ammon's oracle' are first mentioned on the borders of his Indian march, when he had reached what he believed to be the outer Ocean; he also made two distinct sacrifices, as if Ammon's advice had been detailed for that particular moment. The second 'question' showed none of the contempt for Philip which others later attributed to him, and it raised the problem of his own relationship to Ammon. It is this which gives the consultation its peculiar importance.

After the visit to the oasis Alexander took Zeus Ammon closely to heart for the rest of his life. He invoked his name among his close friends and he sacrificed to him throughout his march as one of his usual gods; at a most emotional moment, when his exact words are known for certain, he swore an oath in Ammon's name as proof of his own deep gratitude. Personally, he turned to Zeus Ammon at the most painful crisis of his life, and when his beloved Hephaistion died, he sent envoys from central

Iran to the Siwah oasis to ask whether his dead lover should be worshipped as a god or hero; when he died himself, it was announced that he had asked to be buried at Siwah, and although this request is as dubious as his other alleged last plans, Siwah was evidently felt to be a plausible choice for his Successors to put about among his troops. No Macedonian king nor Alexander himself had ever had any link with Ammon or Siwah before, and this personal attachment can only have sprung from the visit to the oracle. In art, the link was drawn especially close, for on local city coinage Alexander was shown dressed in the symbolic ram's horn of Ammon, probably soon after his visit; within three years of his death, his lifelong friend Ptolemy depicted him with the ram's horn on his earliest coins in Egypt, and Ptolemy had known Alexander as intimately as anyone. Zeus Ammon and Alexander were to become a natural pair for succeeding ages, and it was Alexander who had confirmed their close relationship; he favoured the god of the oasis but from Siwah onwards he also liked it to be known that he was Zeus's begotten son.

This was a startling theme. At Siwah, wrote Callisthenes, 'the priest told Alexander expressly that he was son of Zeus', and on his return to Memphis he was met by envoys from Greek oracles in Asia Minor, one of whom, wrote Callisthenes, had broken its silence of the past hundred and fifty years in order to greet the new avenger of Persian wrongs as Zeus's son. Six months later, wrote Callisthenes, on the verge of his greatest battle Alexander prayed to the gods to help him 'if he were indeed sprung from Zeus'; Callisthenes wrote to please Alexander and he can only have stressed this divine sonship because it was to Alexander's liking. Other contemporaries followed suit and the connection between the visit to Siwah and the sonship of god remained a lively one; Seleucus, Alexander's eventual successor in Asia, actually developed a story thirty years later that he had visited a Greek oracle in his Asian kingdom and been similarly recognized as the begotten son of Apollo. To those who had known Alexander personally, the scene at Siwah had lost none of its credibility.

Later, Alexander's divine sonship was wrongly derived from the answers which he received inside Ammon's shrine, but as he never revealed what he asked or heard, it cannot have been these which first gave the cue to Callisthenes. When he wrote that the 'priest had expressly told Alexander he was son of Zeus', the priest must have done this publicly, where Callisthenes could hear him, presumably therefore in his greeting on the temple steps. Either the priest may have heard that Alexander was the new Pharaoh and greeted him by 'son of Amun', one of the five Egyptian royal titles, which Callisthenes then translated as 'son of Zeus' for his Greek audience. Or, more probably, he intended to address Alexander in Greek as 'my boy' (*o paidion*), but erred and said '*o paidios*' instead, which sounded to the listening Macedonians like the two words '*pai dios*' or 'son of Zeus'. This slip of the tongue was widely believed in antiquity, and as Greeks believed such fortunate errors at a solemn moment to be favourable omens, Alexander would have taken it to be another sign from heaven. Frequent visits from Greek envoys had ensured that many of the temple staff could manage a few words of Greek, but there is no reason to suppose that the high priest's pronunciation was ever perfect.

The priest's precise greeting matters very much less than what Alexander wished to be believed of it; according to his own historian, he was the begotten son of Zeus as a result of his visit, and it is very arguable how and why this belief had arisen. Egyptian kingship, at first sight, seems to promise an explanation; in Upper Egypt, the Pharaoh had always been worshipped as 'son of Amun' and whenever the dynasty of the Pharoahs changed, whether for the usurping Tuthmosis III, the native Saites or the invading Persians, the new line had been fitted into the past by this myth of divine fatherhood. Psamtik I, more than three hundred years before Alexander, had begun a new line, but instead of stressing his earthly mother, perhaps because she was Libyan, he publicized his sonship of Amun 'who has begotten me for himself, to please his heart', because Amun was a father whom he could share with the native Pharaohs before him. Like Psamtik, Alexander was founder of a new and foreign line; his sonship of Amun must have been emphasized by the priesthood to suit the old traditions and Alexander's staff may have picked it up, translating Amun into Zeus, as had always been Greek custom. Alexander's sonship, then, would have been known before he set out for Siwah; when he returned to Memphis, he was met by envoys from Asian Greek oracles with messages to confirm his divine father, and if the 'son of Zeus' was nothing more than the Pharaoh explained in Greek terms they could have been forewarned before he left Alexandria to travel into the desert.

This Egyptian influence may well be a part of the truth: it is not necessarily the whole of it. Alexander's lasting reverence for Zeus Ammon suggests some sort of a revelation had indeed taken place at Siwah, and there is no room for this if his sonship was only a Greek translation of a Pharaoh's title; he was probably Pharaoh by the time he reached Siwah, and whether or not he had been crowned officially in Memphis, he would already be familiar with his new royal titles: he may not have understood them fully, but he had certainly heard them, perhaps from native priests

Egyptians at his court or from the Greeks who had long lived near the site of his new Alexandria. True, a queen of the Ptolemies was later honoured as 'child of Ammon', simply as a loose politeness to match her official link with the Pharaohs' Amun through her husband; the Roman emperor Vespasian was perhaps fêted as 'son of Ammon' when he entered Egypt as Pharaoh. But those mild parallels for future western rulers belong later, when Egypt had been hellenized and when Alexander had made the sonship of Ammon famous. Only in one posthumous Greek statue is Alexander ever shown with the crown and symbols of a Pharaoh; none of his friends or historians is known to have alluded to his kingship in Egypt at any other time, and it did not influence his life, any more than later, when he became king of Persia, did he show any grasp or concern for the equally holy doctrines of the god Ahura Mazda. And yet Siwah and his sonship of Zeus were to remain lively themes until the very last year of his reign when Egypt had been forgotten; it is possible to look for a deeper source and it lies, moreover, near to home.

Among Greeks also, to be 'sprung from Zeus' was a mild and intelligible claim. The first Macedonian, for example, was believed to have been Zeus's son; 'Zeus-born' was a frequent description of Homer's epic kings, and in Alexander's day, the foreign royalty of Cyprus maintained that Zeus stood at the head of their family-tree, while the kings of Sparta could be described as the seed of Zeus. Descent from a god could also be used figuratively: Plato the poet and philosopher was praised as a 'son of Apollo, by his cleverest Athenian pupil, but this may have meant no more than that Plato too had a divine mastery of the arts. But Alexander's descent from Zeus was described by the Greek word *genesis*, and this most naturally meant that he was Zeus's begotten son, not his distant descendant.

Surprisingly, there was a Greek precedent for this claim too. In Homer's poems, several kings and heroes had a god as their acknowledged father, and this bluest of all blue blood was a point of especial honour for their reputations, while in Greek Sicily, some ten years before Alexander was born, this heroic fancy had found a true expression. Dionysius II, ruler of Syracuse, had maintained that he was fathered by Apollo, and had composed a verse inscription for his statue to stress this publicly and unmistakably. Without the influence of Egypt, therefore, a claim to be begotten by a god could be shared and understood by Greeks and it is fair to consider whether Alexander had drawn his new sonship as much from his own Greek background as from a pharaonic title which he scarcely understood.

A close attachment to Zeus was in no way remarkable for him. His father Philip had been acknowledged as specially protected by Zeus, and on coins, Philip's bearded features had shown a clear resemblance to the king of the gods. Macedonian kings numbered Zeus among their ancestors, and they may have worn his symbolic aegis or goat-skin cloak in daily life, just as Alexander was shown wearing it on posthumous statues in Egypt, and his friend Ptolemy was shown with it on coin portraits during his lifetime as Pharaoh. In his sacrifices and dedications, Alexander repeatedly honoured Zeus, who remained the most important god in his life: when, in his last months, he received envoys from Greek temples all over the Mediterranean and admitted them to his presence in order of their importance, the representatives of Olympian Zeus came first, those of Ammon at Siwah second, for he still regarded Ammon as his own Greek Zeus in Libyan form. It is not true that after Siwah, Alexander believed himself to be son of a foreign Libyan god, whom he honoured before all the Greek gods of his childhood until the day he died; rather, at Siwah, a Libyan oracle which spoke for the Greek Zeus had supported the belief that he was the Greek god Zeus's son. He had been familiar with Zeus, if not Ammon, long before he journeyed to Siwah, and it is possible, therefore, that Ammon's oracle had only confirmed a belief which had long been growing on him. A fortunate slip of the priest's tongue, against his mystical role as the new Pharaoh, might have turned suspicion into conviction from Siwah onwards for the rest of his life.

There is evidence, by no means negligible, to support this. During Alexander's early lifetime, an educated Greek recorded that at the moment of conception Olympias's womb had been sealed with the mark of a lion, proving that her son would be lion-like; others said that her womb had been struck by a thunderbolt, emblem of Zeus, and these uncertainties may have been known to Alexander himself. In a letter, which may, however, be a forgery, he is said to have told Olympias that he would reveal the 'secret prophecies' of the Siwah oracle to her as soon as he returned to Macedonia; she died before he returned, but because this promise was made to his mother, it suggests that he had asked a question about his parentage and that this had already been discussed privately between the two of them. Morover, Olympias seems to have held views on the topic herself.

'Alexander's fame', wrote Callisthenes, very probably, 'depends on me and my history, not on the lies which Olympias spread about his parentage.' The lies, then, were a fact, and on setting out for Asia Alexander is said to have been 'told the secret of his birth' by his mother and 'ordered to act worthily of it', a doubtful story had it not been upheld by one of the finest scholars of the generation after Alexander's death, a man, moreover, who was known to be sceptical of all reports of Alexander's divinity: evidently, he was prepared to believe that Olympias had had views of her own on Alexander's parentage, however mistaken he thought them. To these private rumours, the nuances of an Athenian joke may again be relevant. At Alexander's accession, the orator Demosthenes had dismissed him as a mere Margites, but Margites was not only known as a Homeric buffoon: he was a sexual simpleton, who knew neither the facts of life nor the identity of his mother and father. The joke went down in history, perhaps because it was doubly appropriate: while it ridiculed Alexander as the new Achilles, it may also have mocked at a current rumour that his father had not been Philip, but some god in disguise, perhaps even Zeus himself. Alexander, a mere Margites, did not know who his parents were; Demosthenes had visited Pella in Alexander's youth, so there could be no better Greek witness to the gossip of Alexander's early years.

This is perhaps too ingenious to be decisive, but there are links with Sicilian Dionysius which suggest the background may be correct. Dionysius's father had had two sons by his two wives, one a Sicilian from his native Syracuse, the other a south Italian foreigner, and it was generally believed that the two sons had been conceived on one and the same night and the wives married on one and the same day. Now it was Dionysius, son of the foreigner, who succeeded his father, although he was the younger of the two; his rights to the succession were not beyond dispute, and a sincere claim to have been fathered by a god would help to give him the necessary pre-eminence. Perhaps this is why he described himself publicly as 'sprung from the intercourse of Phoebus Apollo'; he was also a poet of more pretension than ability and Apollo in particular may have appealed to him as the god of artists. Twenty years later, Olympias's circumstances had been noticeably similar. Though mother of a promising son, she had been dismissed from court in favour of a noble Macedonian wife and she had seen her son's succession threatened. Like Dionysius's mother, she was a foreigner; she was also a queen of heroic ancestry in her own right. Disappointed in her marriage or keen to assert her superiority over Philip's many other women, she might well have spread a story that her son was special because he owed nothing to Philip and was child of the Greek god Zeus. Sexual knowledge in the ancient world was not enough to refute her, for the role of the female in conception was unknown, as it remained until the nineeenth century, and if mares in Thessaly could be believed to conceive through the agencies of a brisk west wind there was no reason why the queen of Macedonia could not have been visited by Zeus in equivalent disguise. The kings and heroes of myth and of Homer's epic were agreed to be children of Zeus: Alexander, like many, may have come to believe of himself what he had begun by reading of others.

The belief was a Homeric one, entirely in keeping with the rivalry of Achilles which was Alexander's mainspring; if it had been latent when he entered Egypt, the traditions of the Pharaoh's divine sonship and the proceedings at Siwah's oracle could have combined to confirm it and cause its publication through Callisthenes to the Greek world. Perhaps by a fortunate slip of the tongue, perhaps by a private remark inside the oracular shrine as well as by his greeting on the steps, Ammon's priest had confirmed what Alexander may have long suspected from his mother, and the apparent chance of Ammon's confirmation need not discredit Alexander's own sincerity. His favour for Ammon was lasting, as was his new sonship; when his Macedonians mutinied at the end of their marching, they were said to have ridiculed him and told him to 'go and fight alone with his father', meaning Zeus, not Philip. The abuse of mutineers is seldom reported accurately, and as no witness described the mutiny, alternative versions of their insults survived. But the sonship of Zeus Ammon is known, independently, to have remained a topic at court, and discontented men have a way of picking on the insult which they know will be most wounding; Alexander, it seems, had taken his divine father to heart, and his soldiers knew it. But it was because of events at Siwah, not the Pharaoh's titles, that the sonship had first been confirmed.

This favour for Zeus might be thought to have lowered his respect for Philip, the more so if Alexander had been aware of the plans for his father's murder; psychologists, too, would willingly see Alexander's love for Hephaistion as a search for a father-figure, later found in Zeus. 'You pass yourself on to Ammon,' one of Alexander's officers is made to say, drunk and outraged, in a biography four hundred years later, 'and you have denied the claims of Philip', and yet there is no proof that this alleged complaint was ever justified. Four centuries later, a letter could be quoted, written as if from Alexander to the Athenians on the most vexed subject of Athenian politics of the day, in which Alexander is said to have referred to Philip as his 'so-called father'. Among so much fictitious correspondence in Alexander's name this letter cannot be taken as reliable, especially on so emotive a topic, and there are very strong grounds for dismissing it as later Athenian propaganda. It is more revealing that after Alexander's death, his successors promptly persuaded the army that one of his last plans had been to build a gigantic pyramid in Macedonia in Philip's honour. These plans had perhaps been faked by his officers to ensure their rejection, but they still had to seem plausible to the troops; the plan for the pyramid is proof that the two sides to Alexander's view of his father were widely credited by many ordinary men at the end of his life. He could be believed to honour Philip lavishly, for there was no proof that he had disowned him. But he could also be believed to wish to honour him in an Egyptian way, with a pyramid 'as large as that of Cheops the Pharaoh'; in Egypt, men thus were aware, Alexander the Pharaoh had found a truer father who might influence even the honours due to Philip. The plan for the pyramid proves what the troops believed of Alexander, not what Alexander believed of himself. But he was soon to move far beyond Philip's achievements, and the farther he moved, the more the special protection of Zeus Ammon must have appealed to him.

Legend, meanwhile, gathered rapidly round it, until Ammon was said to have visited Olympias in order to father her son; some said he came disguised as the last Pharaoh of Egypt, others as her pet snake, and even these absurdities became a theme of importance for the future. At Rome, for example, a hundred years later, Scipio the conqueror of Carthage was said by contemporaries to have been conceived by a snake because his glory was thought to rival Alexander's, while similar rumours were put about for Aristomenes, a hero of southern Greek freedom against Sparta, and for the future Emperor Augustus after his adoption by Julius Caesar, himself a momentary rival of Alexander. Not for the last time Alexander's royal myth lasted for more than three centuries as a spur and a pattern to ambitious men, but the myth itself looked back to the Homeric world.

It is this ability to inspire such personal themes and ratify them for the future by his own achievements that gives Alexander his strongest appeal. The visit to Siwah had not been calculated for the sake of the result that came of it; it was both secretive and haphazard, but its conclusion is perhaps the most important feature in the search for his personality. 'Zeus,' Alexander was later thought to have said, 'is the common father of men, but he makes the best peculiarly his own'; like many Roman emperors after him, Alexander was coming to believe that he was protected by a god as his own divine 'companion', not as a friend of god, like the notable pagans of late Roman antiquity, not as a slave of god, in the grimmer phrase of the Christians who replaced them, but as son of god, a belief which fitted convincingly with his own Homeric outlook, in whose favourite *Iliad* sons of Zeus still fought and died beneath their heavenly father's eye.

Alexander did not intend the truth of his visit to Siwah to be generally known and for that reason it is impossible to be sure exactly how his published view of himself had found its confirmation. Only the result is certain, and as he left the oracle and headed home to Memphis by a different caravan road through the desert, it would have been wrong to explain his consultation as deception or calculated arrogance. It is too easy to rationalize an age which expresses its human needs in different ways to our own, and as for the arrogance, dwelt on by Romans and elaborated since, it is a charge which can also rebound. The history of Zeus Ammon and Alexander was to be a long one, only brought to a forcible end.

Nearly nine hundred years later, in A.D. 529, the natives of a small oasis near to Siwah were still paying worship to Alexander and Zeus Ammon, although Christianity had been the recognized religion of their empire for the past two hundred years. The Roman emperor Justinian saw fit to intervene and ban their malpractice, putting an end, it might seem, to the history of a young man's impudent boast. But that same myth had driven a Macedonian to India and the eastern edges of the world and then remained firm, where it first became public, as a focus of loyalty for nine successive centuries in a rapidly changing world. When millions, now as then, still pin their faith on a subsequent son of god, it is not for the historian to explain away the belief which helped Alexander onwards. It is salutary, rather, to remember that claims to be the begotten son of god have been made before, upheld by companions and ended, so men said, in boos from angry mutineers.

CHAPTER FIFTEEN

From Ammon to Memphis Alexander followed a direct caravan route eastwards through three hundred miles of desert, a journey which lasted eighteen days or more but involved no notable hazards, apart from the continuing guidance, in Ptolemy's opinion, of two talking snakes. Once back in Memphis, the new son of Zeus relaxed, giving free rein to his generosity and his sense of myth. Sacrifice was offered to Zeus the King, the Greek god whom Alexander believed that he had visited at Siwah in a Libyan form, and in Zeus's honour the army processed, a prelude to iterary festivals and more athletic games. Meanwhile envoys arrived from Greek oracles in Asia Minor to find the army alive with rumours of their king's mysterious pilgrimage. 'At the temple of the Branchidae near Miletus,' wrote Callisthenes, meaning to please his patron,

the sacred spring had begun to flow again, though it had been abandoned by Apollo ever since its shrine had been sacked by the Persian Xerxes, one hundred and fifty years before. Its messengers brought many oracles about Alexander's birth from Zeus and the details of his future victories. The Sibyl at Erythrae, an aged Greek prophetess, had also spoken up about his noble origins.

The end of Persian sacrilege, the prophecies of victory and divine birth; a year and a half later; these were themes which Alexander's historian intertwined. These envoys may have set sail for Egypt before Alexander returned from Siwah, but they need not have been forewarned of his divine sonship. They had reason to visit him anyway after the recent naval war, and at Erythrae, Alexander was also considering a generous building plan. On arrival at Memphis, they could have suited their message to the new theme of the pilgrimage; at Erythrae, Alexander was worshipped as a god, presumably soon after he had freed the city, and it was only natural to please him with the name of Zeus.

Having received nine hundred reinforcements from Antipater, who may already have been fearful for the safety of Thrace and southern Greece, Alexander arranged his Egyptian administration. The list that survives may be incomplete, but it reads most interestingly. As under the Persians and native Pharaohs, the country was divided into two, presumably into Upper and Lower Egypt. No satrap is named, perhaps because the Persian title was offensive, but two nomarchs were chosen and if their title is official, it had many precedents in the native and Persian past. One nomarch, Petisis, bore a renowned Egyptian name and probably belonged to the highest native aristocracy of lower Egypt, from an area whose other well-known noble family had already been reinstated by Alexander; the other, Doloaspis, had an Iranian name and was probably meant to govern Upper or southern Egypt where he had no doubt held office before. Their duties involved local justice as well as administration, but because they were both Orientals a Macedonian general was set beside them in each half of the country, As before, an admiral was left with a small fleet in the Nile Delta; the two city centres of Memphis and Pelusium were garrisoned with mercenaries, a few Companions and various commanders, including an officer from a backward area of Greece who was awarded a secretary, perhaps because he was illiterate. Libya, so far as Alexander had entered it, was given a district governor, as was the land east of Memphis in which Arabs lived. As usual in Alexander's empire, these commands did little to disturb the pattern he had inherited from Persian rule.

Marvelling at the size and strength of the country, Alexander is said to have wished no one man to control it. And yet the native Petisis refused the job of nomarch, perhaps because the military and financial commands were loaded against him; Doloaspis is said to have been left as the only supreme official, while in lower Egypt there was one Greek officer with the brains and power to rule in all but name. Cleomenes the Greek had been living at Naucratis in the Delta, before Alexander had invaded; he was a sharp man, and he was well suited to his new office as Alexander's tax-collector in Egypt and Libya. It was a job of peculiar difficulty. The Egyptian economy had always been run in kind, not coin, and ever since the Pharaohs had lost the Nubian gold-mines, there had been no local source of precious metals for a currency. But the hiring of fleets and mercenary armies had needed ready money, and even before Alexander, the Pharaoh Tachos had entrusted his military finances to an experienced Athenian general, who had taxed bullion from the temple priests and nobles who alone still owned it and turned it into coin to pay troops. Cleomenes was alive to this Greek entrepreneurial tradition; his orders were to collect Egypt's taxes without interfering with the nomarch's powers and as he had to raise coined money for the fleet, the mercenary garrisons and the building of Alexandria, which he supervised, he began to enforce the same sort of taxes as his Athenian predecessor. His financial powers made him sole lord of Egypt, even if he was not named satrap; he struck his own coins and may also have prepared the system of state monopolies with which his successors the Ptolemies at last raised Egypt to a centralized economy. His officials, naturally, were no more philanthropic than any others who governed Egypt in antiquity.

Financial interference was never to the temples' liking, but Alexander had dutifully considered their feelings. One of a virtuous Pharaoh's responsibilities, in the opinion of the priesthood, was to restore and adorn the country's ancient temples, and it was a definite gesture to their wishes when Alexander ordered the building of a new chamber in two ancient temples of the Egyptian god Amun. Each project, moreover, was in honour of Pharaohs who had been dead for a thousand years but were venerated as perfect models of priestly government. These honours were well chosen, but Egypt had to reconcile herself to her foreign Pharaoh in her own way, and she did it, as often, by a myth of the past.

The last native Pharaoh, Nectanebo II, had fled southwards to escape the invading Persians twelve years before Alexander's arrival, but like Harold of England or Frederick Barbarossa he was believed to be due to return as a young man to redeem his wartime failure, which was anyway blamed on magic or the anger of the gods. Alexander's liberation was the cue for his revival; the new Pharaoh, though not Nectanebo himself, was at least young enough to be his son, and in Alexander's lifetime, or very soon after it was said that when Nectanebo had disappeared, he had gone to Pella, where he had persuaded Olympias to make love to him, impressing her with his skill in astrology and, according to a later version, disguising himself in the robes of Ammon so as to seem like Alexander's divine father. If Alexander could be adopted, he could also be belittled. Already, as a reaction to Persian rule the Egyptians had idealized a past Pharaoh called Sesostris and invented a career of conquest in which he copied and exceeded the feats of Persian Darius I. When Alexander set a new standard of success, even Sesostris had to be updated to excel him; he was gentle to those he conquered, he took more prisoners than any other king, and unlike Alexander he was 'more than seven feet tall'. After nine years' marching, like his rival, he too was claimed to have died at the age of thirty-three, not through drink or poison, but killing himself, an end which capped the rumours of Alexander's death.

Before Alexander could violate the holy law of the priesthood, he had left Memphis in early May 331 and bridged the Nile on his way back to Phoenicia. While boating across it, he met with disaster. Parmenion's young son Hector fell overboard and came near to drowning by the weight of his clothing; on struggling to the bank, the boy died, much to the grief of Alexander who ordered him to be buried magnificently. It was left to the Roman Emperor Julian, seven hundred years later, to accuse Alexander of the boy's murder; mischievous guesses to discredit him are not only a modern fashion. It was also said by Ptolemy, perhaps correctly, that Philotas, son of Parmenion, was suspected of conspiracy in Egypt and this 'plot' might have been linked with his brother's drowning. No action was taken against him, and on leaving Memphis he was to give more lasting proof of his methods with rebels.

One reason for his swift depature from Egypt had been the news of a winter revolt to the north in Samaria. During the siege of Gaza, the Persian governor of Samaria had surrendered himself and his troops; shortly afterwards, he had died and a Macedonian had been put in his place, only to be burnt alive by the natives while Alexander was in Egypt. Alexander's retort was curt. He destroyed the main town of Samaria and executed all rebel leaders who were handed over; the rest were tracked down and killed in their desert hideout, where their bodies, seals and documents remained until their recent rediscovery. Alexander's one and only way with rebels was ruthless, and the finds in the Wadi Dalayeh caves are a harsh reminder of what it meant to cross the path of a son of Zeus.

Ruin of the Samaritans meant delight among the Jews, and when Alexander resettled Samaria, it is probably true that he gave part to the Jews as a tax-free present. There had been much commotion in Jerusalem because the Persian governor of Samaria had recently married the high priest's daughter; the two peoples now split apart and the ruin of Samaria may have hastened the establishment of a rival Samaritan temple on nearby Mount Gerizim. Though Alexander would have met the Jewish leaders, the story that he did obeisance before the Jewish high priest is obviously a Jewish legend. Perdiccas was probably ordered to settle Macedonian veterans at Jerash and other nearby sites, first of the many colonists who would later turn the area into a second Macedonia.

From Samaria Alexander made his way north to the remains of Tyre where he was met by his Levantine fleet. It was now mid-May, but Tyre was to detain Alexander until late July; there was sense, however, in this inactivity. Not until Darius had summoned a grand army from all over his eastern provinces would Alexander strike inland; he did not want another Issus, but a decisive conflict which would resolve the mastery of Asia in a total victory over all the troops of the empire. Like the 'conquering' of the Persian fleet by land, this bold strategy was well-conceived. Had Darius refused its challenge, he could have held such cities as Babylon or Hamadan in the centre of his empire and exhausted Alexander in siege after siege, burning the food supplies wherever possible. Alexander may already have heard that Darius was summoning a full imperial army; if not, he had nothing to lose by delay, rightly believing that the Great King would eventually give in to the temptations of a big pitched battle. The one mistake would be to march inland against a vanishing enemy, and Alexander was too intelligent a strategist to make it.

As he waited, danger was mounting behind as well as before him. For the past fifteen months he had been aware of the unrest in southern Greece which had been inspired by Sparta and her tireless King Agis, but as yet he had not taken Agis any more seriously than had the Persian admirals who had bargained with him. Since landing in Asia, Alexander had drawn 11,000 fresh troops from the Balkans and recently ordered another large force, many of whom were to be recruited from southern Greece. It was perhaps the news of this fourth draft which finally encouraged Agis to open revolt; he had returned from his victories in Crete with a small flock of mercenaries; Issus' Greek survivors were with him, and with their usual poor timing, the Spartan assembly had evidently voted for war.

From Tyre Alexander took the necessary measure. He sent a hundred Cypriot and Phoenician ships to Crete to undo Agis's work and to clear the sea of its rash of pirates, while one of his proven admirals was to sail to Greece and 'assist as many of the Greeks in the Peloponnese as could be trusted over the Persian war and were not paying heed to the Spartans'. By this one order, he went straight to the heart of the matter, realizing that many Greeks hated Sparta's past too much to lend her any help. With Issus won and the Persian fleet disbanded, the open rebellion had come a year too late, and far more Greeks would join Antipater than Agis when it came to a pitched battle.

By diplomacy he tightened his hold on the situation. During the naval war the strategic sea bases of Chios and Rhodes had been strengthened with garrisons; now they complained, and the garrisons were ordered to be removed. The loyal Mytilene had defied the Persians' navy longer than any city on Lesbos, and so she was refunded the costs of her resistance and granted neighbouring land. Once again, Athens sent envoys to beg for the release of the Athenian prisoners and this time she added one of her state galleys to the embassy's flotilla as a special proof of her sincerity. It was now, too, that Achilles the Athenian was sent to plead with his namesake's rival. Pleased by a name, Alexander released the prisoners, but tempered his favours with discretion, retaining the crews of the twenty Athenian warships as a hostage and so forcing Athens to turn down Agis's calls for assistance. She still feared for the lives of some

4,000 citizens in Alexander's keeping and believed, rightly, that a Spartan call to free the Greeks would be too mistrusted to succeed.

These favours were repaid as befitted the mood of the moment. At Athens, the second of the two state galleys is known to have changed its name from the *Salaminia* to the *Ammonias* within a year of its partner's successful embassy. There is no precedent for naming a ship so obviously after a god, and although perhaps the ship had been used to take presents from Athens to Ammon, it is far more probable that its new name referred to Alexander's new favour for Ammon, heard in the camp at Tyre. In hope of future favours such small flatteries were worth while, as Mytilene also showed in a more sincere mood of gratitude; on the city coinage, Alexander was soon to be shown wearing a plumed helmet which was adorned with the ram's horn, symbol of Ammon. These coins are fine local evidence of the way that the news of his pilgrimage spread and was known to matter to him; by decree of the city, he was to be honoured with a sacrifice on his birthday, an honour otherwise reserved for gods. Mytilene, understandably, was paying Alexander worship; once again, his 'divinity' had sprung not from his own demands or arrogance, but from a community's civic gratitude for a notable public favour.

Satisfied that no more could be usefully done to Sparta, Alexander continued to while away in Tyre the months of May, June and July. He sacrificed again to Melkarth; he rearranged his financial officials, appointing two tax-collectors for western Asia whose duties have caused much scholarly dispute ever since, because there is no evidence to decide them. To Alexander the patience of his army was a more immediate problem, as it was nearly two years since the Foot Companions had fought in formation or the Companion Cavalry had ridden against an enemy. News came from the camp that the soldiers had divided into two factions, one under a leader they called Alexander, the other under a leader called Darius; they had begun by throwing lumps of earth at each other, then they had taken to fisticuffs, and now they were fighting it out with sticks and stones. It was just what Alexander must have feared, so he parted the two sides and ordered the two leaders to fight a duel while their army sat and watched: he would equip Alexander and Philotas, Parmenion's son, would equip Darius. The Alexander was victorious and was granted in, good humour, the ownership of twelve country villages and the right to wear Persian dress; deftly, a disaster had been turned into an entertainment, and the victor's rewards were the first intimation of the oriental honours which Alexander would take for himself when the real Darius died.

To keep up the amusements, Alexander held processions and arranged for literary festivals and athletic games. Among the kings of Cyprus who had joined his fleet the patronage of Greek culture had long been a lively political issue. Greek music and drama had already found a home elsewhere in Cyprus and the only Cypriot king whom Alexander penalized was ruler of the one Phoenician harbour city on the island where Greek influence had most often been resisted. With a wise grasp of character, Alexander invited his Cypriot kings to finance and sponsor a festival of the arts. With that passionate extravagance which had long distinguished Cypriot history, they competed in the production of the most magnificent plays and recitals; choruses sang Greek dithyrambs; the most renowned Greek actors put on Greek tragedies, and although Alexander was disappointed that his friend Thettalus did not win first prize, he must have been glad of the entertainment for his men. Several Cypriot kings and nobles accompanied him on his march to India, and one of them was to be distinguished as the ablest of his governors in an Iranian province; not for the last time, Cypriots had helped Alexander out. Meantime he would have been turning two dominant problems over in his mind.

The first was his supplies. Balkan reinforcements and the recruitment of natives and prisoners had more or less equalled all losses and the provision of local garrisons; the proportion of cavalry to infantry had risen because foot soldiers were more exposed to wounds and disease, and so some 40,000 infantry and 7,000 cavalry were waiting to march through desert to the Euphrates, a three-week journey for which 2,000 supply-wagons were a fair estimate, given that the army could not live wholly off the land. Native grain stacks may have lain along the road, while beyond the river there was a choice of two routes, both of them famously fertile, and the possibility of the Royal Road again, where post-houses kept enough provisions at least to satisfy the officers. In any case bulk supplies would have to be prepared in advance. The region round Tyre abounded in timber for the wheelwrights, while oxen and camels could be requisitioned from the natives, but it was proof of Alexander's anxieties that before setting out, he had 'dismissed the satrap of Syria for failing to provide his quota of supplies'. But these provisions were linked to a broader problem: when should he march inland and how could he be sure that Darius would be ready for the necessary pitched battle?

The one glaring weakness in Alexander's army was the lack of proper advance intelligence, and the Mounted Scouts were not enough to put it right. Darius's army was based more than seven hundred miles to the east at Babylon, a city which none of Alexander's officers had seen; unless

Darius was to reveal when he was ready for battle, Alexander might well find himself marching inland with no hope of the pitched encounter he wanted. But Darius had reason to announce his plans. Once he had martialled his gigantic army, he would not wish to keep it waiting in the Babylonian plains, richly supplied though they were, for boredom and indiscipline would soon affect it. In the confused accounts of Darius's peace offers, a third and final one is recorded while Alexander delayed at Tyre; this is almost certainly wrong, but it is likely that Darius did send a message, not of peace, but of his readiness for battle, thus influencing its timing to his own advantage. Alexander acted at once and was compelled to leave Tyre at a moment which was not entirely suitable; his latest reinforcements from the Balkans, summoned the previous winter, had not yet reached him, although they had probably set out by road for Asia. Some 15,000 men, they were to be caught between Asia and Europe, unable to help Alexander against Darius or Antipater against the Spartan king Agis in the two pitched battles which were about to occur.

In mid-July, Alexander sent Hephaistion ahead to bridge the broad waters of the Euphrates in two places and prepared to follow when the carpenters and engineers had done their work. For Darius, there could be no surprises, provided he planned competently. Alexander was bound to bridge the Euphrates at the usual point of Thapsacus. Afterwards he had a choice of two different roads: either he could turn right and follow the Euphrates south-east to Babylon in the footsteps of Xenophon, along a valley plentifully supplied but broken by canals which could be dammed against invaders; or he could go north from the Euphrates and then swing right to skirt the hills of Armenia, cross the more distant line of the river Tigris and then turn south to Babylon on the Royal Road. It was unthinkable that he should try and march across the blank desert that filled in the angle between these two routes; he was bound to take one of them, but until Darius knew which, he could not choose his battle-field. The northerly loop to the Tigris was longer and more hazardous as it involved crossing the river's very fast current; the way to force Alexander on to it was to devastate the only alternative. Then there could be no doubt that battle would be joined north of Babylon, conveniently near the main road from the Upper Satrapies. So Darius sent his most experienced satrap Mazaeus to wait on the Euphrates with 3,000 horsemen, many of them hired Greeks, and to burn the south-eastern valley route as Alexander advanced to the river. Seeing the devastation, Alexander was bound to turn north for the sake of his army's stomach, whereupon Mazaeus could return to the main army, having determined the site of the battlefield.

The satrap Mazaeus set out as ordered, a man probably in his late fifties and highly distinguished for his past. For thirty years he had governed a satrapy in the west, first in Cilicia and then as Supreme Satrap of Phoenicia, Cilicia and 'Syria both beyond and inside the Euphrates'; in his new mission this local experience would serve him usefully. Possibly he had family connections at Babylon, possibly he could even speak Greek, as two-thirds of his advance party were Greek mercenaries and his coinage as satrap had long shown Greek influence; certainly, he knew the obvious bridge-point of the river Euphrates, the city of Thapsacus, probably on the river bend at Meskene and before Hephaistion could organize his two artificial bridges for Alexander's crossing, he had taken up his position on the far bank. Satrap and royal favourite thus faced each other for several days, Hephaistion not daring to finish his bridges for fear that Mazaeus would wreck them, Mazaeus waiting to witness Alexander's own approach from Tyre through the desert. When Alexander did arrive, Mazaeus turned back his horsemen and disappeared to burn the valley of the Euphrates as ordered and so to block it against Alexander's advance. He had fulfilled his mission, but there is room for a little imagination. Two thousand Greeks had waited with him on one bank of the river; on the other bank, several thousand more had fretted at the delay he was causing. As they waited, the two troops would shout to each other in their shared language. Hephaistion, perhaps, would offer promises and the two commanders may even have exchanged messages by the time that Alexander arrived. By no means the last had been heard of Mazaeus. He was to command the entire right wing in the coming battle, and no section behaved more inexplicably than the Persian right, who threw away an apparently certain victory and fled from the field which they should have encircled. Mazaeus went with them to Babylon, where a week or so later he was reinstated as governor, retaining the right to issue his silver coins. It is conceivable that the battle of Gaugamela was partly won on the banks of the Euphrates and that Mazaeus's reinstatement was less a sign of magnanimity than of a prearranged reward.

In Mazaeus's absence, Alexander finished the two bridges by lashing rafts together with chains of iron, some of which still survived on the site four hundred years later, rusted but believed to be genuine. Once across the river, he took the only unburnt route, as Darius had intended, 'keeping the Euphrates and the Armenian mountains on his left and marching northwards because everything was more convenient for his army; the horses could find fodder, supplies could be taken from the land and the heat was not so scorching'. He must have had local guides to help him, as no Greek handbook had described his route. At the foot of the Armenian mountains he swung east and followed the well-worn road to the river Tigris, halting whenever more supplies were needed. In Armenia, meanwhile, his Greek prospector had heard of the natives' rich mines of gold.

From the Euphrates to the Tigris, the distance was just under three hundred miles, paced as usual by the Macedonian surveyors, but Alexander lingered for five to seven weeks on a journey which could have been finished in a fortnight. On the road, he captured spies from Darius's army who told him 'that Darius was encamped on the river Tigris, meaning to stop him if he crossed. His army was far larger than that at Issus.' Only then did Alexander hasten forwards. When he arrived at the Tigris Darius was not to be found and the Macedonians were able to cross unopposed, their infantry wading through the headlong current, their cavalry lined on either side of them to break the rushing force of water which came above their waists. On the far bank, Alexander rested his army, leaving them to live off the fertile countryside; on 20 September, the moon eclipsed and Alexander sacrificed to the Sun, Moon and Earth, showing that he understood the natural cause of the portent. It was still possible to believe that these natural causes were themselves the effects of an omen, and the prophets and seers agreed in the prediction that during this very moon, battle would be waged and Persia's own eclipse had been foretold.

Alexander's safe and leisurely crossing of the Tigris seems almost too fortunate to be credible. At the same river seven hundred years later, the Roman Emperor Julian was opposed on the far bank by a full force of Persian cavalry, when the country behind him had been so thoroughly burnt that his army could only retreat at the risk of starving, while the river current before him was flowing so arrow-swift that he had to destroy his many ships, knowing they could never negotiate it. Alexander had crossed at the obvious ford, the modern Abu Dhahir, where the Persians' own Royal Road ran through the river and led south-east to Gaugamela and Arbela, Darius's eventual place of battle. His movements had been predictable from start to finish, for only two routes led to the Tigris and one had already been burnt; spies, even, had warned him of opposition on the Tigris and yet, after a month in which to manœuvre, Darius had left him with food and a free passage.

Timing alone cannot excuse the Great King. Perhaps he had unwisely delayed at headquarters until Mazaeus had galloped back from the Euphrates,

600 miles distant, with the news that Alexander had indeed turned north-wards as expected; perhaps his headquarters were still as far south as Babylon. But even then, in the latter half of August, three weeks or more remained before Alexander would have reached the Tigris, time enough for a large force of cavalry to hurry 400 miles, at most, and occupy the Royal Road's crossing, Alexander's obvious choice of the four possible fords. Horsemen, as Julian was to find, could hold the river with the help of its current, and serious devastation would starve any enemy into retreat. The plan, it seems, had been discussed, for when Darius's scouts had been captured, they warned Alexander of plans for resistance on the Tigris; like true spies, they may only have invented the plan to deceive their captor, but three days later, on the far bank, a small force of cavalry did appear and try to burn the grain stacks. Perhaps Darius had hesitated, then ordered them north to the river too late; quickly applied, the idea could have worked, especially if linked to that burning of crops and scorching of earth which King Shapur II was to use so effectively against Julian's Romans in the same area. Here, at least, there was no excuse; Darius, it seems, had been stupid as well as slow.

Stupidity, however, is easier to detect when the sequel is known. At the time, Darius's apparent folly was a measure of his mood, that imponderable element which history has tended to forget. To a King of Kings, chosen by Ahura Mazda and supported by an army which the victors later assessed at a million strong, Alexander's 47,000 troops were asking to be crushed. At Issus, the ground and the gods had been unfavourable but at the chosen site of Gaugamela, seventy-six miles south east of the Tigris crossing, the battlefield was being smoothed for the Empire's traditional weapons, the cavalry and the scythed chariots which its feudal army system existed to maintain. Hyrcanians from the Caspian, Indians from the Punjab, Medes from the empire's centre and allied Scythians from beyond the Oxus; such tribal cavalry from the Upper Satrapies' villages made up for the diminution of the hired Greek infantry, by losses and desertion, to a mere 4,000 loyalists. When these and many others were waiting, at least five times as numerous as the enemy, what need of devastation or unsettling division of the troops? They might only deter Alexander from advancing into a foe far larger than he knew. But if Alexander had underestimated the numbers of the Persians, Darius had underestimated his opponent's military genius.

On the evening of 21 September, the day after the eclipse, Alexander broke camp and marched beyond the Tigris through country which his guides called Aturia, transcribing its Aramaic name into Greek. His route was the well-defined line of the Royal Road; on his right, flowed the river; on his left rose the Kurdish mountains which bordered the lands of the Medes; before him galloped his mounted scouts searching hard for the enemy. For three whole days they ranged south-east while sixty miles passed without any sign, but at dawn on 25 September they were back in a flurry, reporting that Darius's army had at last been seen on the march. Again, this was a failure in advance intelligence, as on a closer look the 'army' turned out to be a thousand horsemen who had been detailed to burn any local barns of grain. They had arrived too late to hold the Tigris, and before their firebrands caused much damage, they were routed by Alexander and his mounted lancers in a typically brisk charge. Prisoners were taken and these put the reconnaissance to rights, warning Alexander that 'Darius was not far away with a large force'. On the evening of the 25th Alexander ordered a halt to take stock of the situation. A ditch was to be dug, a palisade set around it and a base camp made for his baggage-train and followers.

In this camp, at least seven miles from the enemy, Alexander remained for the next four days, in no way distressed by lack of supplies. It was a time, no doubt, for checking horses' fitness and polishing sarissa wood and blades, but as the night of 29 September came on, he at last arrayed his army in battle order and led them off shortly before midnight, evidently meaning to surprise Darius at daybreak. He had already been observed from the hills ahead, perhaps by Mazaeus and a small advance force, but he was unaware of this. Four miles from Darius's lines, Alexander surmounted the ridge which overlooks the plains to the north of the Jebel Maqlub; he looked down to the village of Gaugamela in the foreground and the Tell Gomel or 'camel's hump' beside it, from which it took its name. Here he halted his line of battle and summoned all his commanders to a sudden council of war; nothing is said to explain this, but at the very last moment the plans for attack had obviously worried him. Most of those present at the council advised him to march straight ahead, but Parmenion urged encampment and the inspection of the enemy's units and the terrain, in case of hidden obstacles such as stakes and ditches. For once, Parmenion's advice is said to have prevailed, perhaps because it was true to life; the men were ordered to encamp, keeping their order of battle.

It is not difficult to find reasons for Alexander's hesitance; it does not follow that those reasons are true. He had hoped, no doubt, to surprise his enemy at daybreak, only to see from his hill-top that they were already forewarned and lined up for battle; possibly he had never realized what overwhelming numbers Darius could put into the field. Without surprise, there was little point now in hurrying, especially as Parmenion's advice of reconnaissance was sound; there was much to occupy another day and by waiting, he could pay back Darius for his forethought by keeping his subjects waiting another day and night under arms. The battle would open with a trial of nerves, and he would have dictated its terms.

For all these reasons a halt was advisable, but nerves were perhaps a double-edged weapon, a threat not only among the waiting Persians but also where the historians were later loth to admit them, inside the Macedonian army itself. The men had marched in the dark towards an enemy many times larger than any they had ever seen before, knowing that their king was risking all on the coming encounter. At one point, they are said to have been struck by such panic that Alexander had to order a halt during which they could lay down their weapons until they had recovered; the occasion was probably the night of 29 September, when Alexander did down arms, and the troops, seeing 100,000 camp fires beyond them, had every reason for terror. On the following evening, Alexander was to offer certain secret sacrifices attended by his prophet Aristander, and for the first and only known time in his life, he killed a victim in honour of Fear. This mysterious gesture may have been his propitiation of a power too much in evidence on the night before.

With a day of valuable reconnaissance, morale had reason to revive. On 30 September Alexander took a group of Companions and galloped in a circle round the battlefield; snares and stakes, they saw, had been driven into the ground to hold up a cavalry charge, while the pitch had elsewhere been levelled for the two hundred scythed chariots. Darius's broad plan of battle could be detected, and for once this was advance intelligence which Alexander could put to use. He returned to camp, and as darkness fell he went with Aristander the prophet to offer the necessary sacrifices. When the offerings were complete, Parmenion and the older Companion nobles came out to join him in the royal tent. To a man, they urged Alexander to attack under cover of night, Parmenion helping to put the case, but the King made memorable reply: 'Alexander,' he answered, 'does not steal his victories.' Whether a true remark or only flattery invented to please the king, this was an answer as outrageous as the moment deserved. A night attack would be a confused risk, better foregone. Alexander, like a true Hellene, had never been above tricks in the interest of his army: had he not set out the night before in order to attack, if not in darkness, at least at the break of dawn? He answered boldly for others to hear or at least to record in his public myth; he then turned about, having ordered a march for the following morning, entered his tent and settled down to a night of plans, sifting all that he had seen and working into the small hours of the morning, while the camp fires burnt low among the enemy host whom he had long sought.

CHAPTER SIXTEEN

Deep in thought, Alexander sat by torchlight, pondering his tactics for the morrow. Outside the royal tent midnight had come and gone, but not until the small hours of the morning was he ready for bed, where he soon fell asleep. Dawn broke on 1 October but still Alexander slept on. The morning sun grew full; the officers, it is said, began to worry, until Parmenion gave the troops their orders and gathered a group of generals to rouse Alexander from his bed. They found him relaxed and calm, ready with an answer to their rebukes: 'How can you sleep,' they are said to have asked, 'as if you had won the battle already?' 'What?' he replied with a smile, 'do you not think that this battle is already won, now that we have been spared from pursuing a Darius who burns his land and fights by retreating?'

This story may be fanciful, but Alexander would indeed have been relieved that as long planned, the mastery of Asia was to depend on a pitched battle. The battle itself was daunting. The enemy's numbers were reported to be immense, at least some quarter of a million men, though they could never have been reckoned accurately. In the open plain, where no natural barriers protected his flanks, Alexander was bound to be encircled by the Great King's cavalry who were drawn in thousands not only from the horse-breeding areas of the empire, from Media, Armenia and even from Cappadocia behind his lines, but also from the tribes of the upper satrapies, Indians, Afghans and others, some of them mounted archers, all of them born to ride, none more so than the allied Scythian nomads from the steppes beyond the Oxus. Against their total, perhaps, of 30,000, Alexander's own cavalry totalled a mere 7,000, and not even weaponry was in his favour. Many enemy riders were heavily armoured, a doubtful advantage if the fighting became open and mobile, but since Issus, Darius had revised their weapons of attack, giving them larger shields, swords and thrusting-spears, not javelins, to bring them into line with Alexander's Companions. As for the mounted sarissa-bearers, even they had met their match: some of the Scythian horsemen could perhaps fight with a lance requiring both hands and it was probably for this reason that Darius had placed them opposite Alexander's right, where he had seen their Macedonian equivalents in action two years before. Only his infantry were conspicuously weak, for though plentiful, they had none of the drill of Alexander's Foot Companions. But Darius did not expect that the engagement would be won on foot.

Within this broad problem of encirclement, specific details were reported by scouts and needed close attention. In the centre of the Persian line, where by tradition a Persian king would take up his own position, Darius had stationed some fifteen Indian elephants whose trumpeting and tusking would scare off any frontal charge by Macedonian horses and riders who had never seen or smelt their like before. Some distance from the Persian front stakes and snags had been hammered into the ground as a further precaution against Alexander's cavalry, while closer to the line the plain had been levelled for a counter charge by the two hundred Persian scythed chariots. Their antique form of attack had been evaded by Greeks with success before, but in the circumstances they posed an added danger. Their target was the phalanx as well as the cavalry, and to avoid them Alexander had best head for bumpy ground away from their level pitch. This bumpy ground, let alone a swing towards it, was likely to upset the massed sarissas of his own phalanx; like chariots these were also most effective on smooth going.

There are few finer tributes to Alexander's intelligence than his plan to anticipate these dangers. The fundamentals of his battle line were those which he and his father had long exploited: the Foot-Companions, some 10,000 strong, held sarissas at the ready in the centre, while their unshielded right flank was protected by the 3,000 Shield Bearers, who in turn linked up with the aggressive right cavalry-wing of Companions, led by Alexander himself and preceded by some 2,000 archers, slingers and Agrianian javelin men for long-range skirmishing. On the left wing, the shielded flank of the Foot Companions joined directly with Parmenion and the Greek horse, who would fight their usual defensive battle as the anchor of the slanted line. The threat of outflanking and encirclement had called for special precautions. At the tip of each wing, Alexander had added mixed units of heavy cavalry and light infantry, concealing the foot soldiers among the horses and inclining the whole at an oblique angle to his already slanting front line, so that they extended backwards like flaps, behind his own forward cavalry and went some way towards guarding the flanks and rear if these forward units began to be encircled. If the encirclement continued, they were under orders to swing back to an even sharper incline, until they stood at right angles to the front line and joined, at their far end, with Alexander's second protection. This lay some distance behind the rear of the Foot Companions' rectangle and consisted of some 20,000 Greek and barbarian infantry arranged in a reserve formation, which would face about if the enemy cavalry escaped the flank guards and appeared at the gallop in the rear. This about-turn by reserves would change Alexander's army into a hollow oblong, bristling with spears to the front, rear and sides, and although there were obvious dangers if the rear units were forced back into their front-guards and robbed of any retreat, the use of reserves and a hollow formation were sophistications unusual, if not unprecedented, in Greek warfare. Designed for an outnumbered defence, it was to set an example which would not be forgotten; specific plans against the elephants, snags and chariots would become clear in the course of the action.

After a sound but not excessive sleep Alexander gave the word for his units to take up these new positions and returned to don his armour in a manner worthy of any Homeric hero:

His shirt had been woven in Sicily, his breastplate was a double thickness of linen, taken as spoil at Issus. His iron helmet gleamed like pure silver, a work of Theophilus, while his neck-piece fitted him closely, likewise of iron, studded with precious stones. His sword was amazingly light and well-tempered, a present from a Cypriot king: he also sported a cloak, more elaborately worked than the rest of his armour. It had been dyed by Helicon, the famous weaver of Cyprus, and given to him by the city of Rhodes.

In this cosmoplitan dress he mounted one of his reserve horses and rode out to review his troops; only when the preliminaries were over would the ageing Bucephalas be led forwards.

Riding up and down the line Alexander exhorted each unit as he thought fit. To the Thessalian horsemen and the other Greeks on the far left under Parmenion's command, he had much to say, 'and when they urged him on, shouting to him to lead them against the barbarians, he shifted his lance from right hand to left and began to call on the gods, praying, so Callisthenes said, that if he were truly sprung from Zeus, they would defend and help to strengthen the Greeks'. This prayer says much for how Alexander wished himself to be seen. So far from being blasphemous or implausible, a reference to his own special descent from Zeus was the fitting climax to his harangue of Greek troops at a moment of high excitement; similarly, on the eve of battle, Julius Caesar would remind his men of his descent from the goddess Venus, whom he claimed as his family protector. Taken loosely, Alexander's words need mean no more than that Zeus was his ancestor, as for all Macedonian kings, and the same phrase could be applied, in this unexceptionable sense, to the kings of Greek Sicily or half-barbarian Cyprus. But this ancestry was undisputed, and neither Alexander nor his court historian would ever have hedged it about with the words 'if it were truly so . . .' This cautious reference implies a deeper meaning, and to an audience who had lived with the rumours and flattery that had gathered since Siwah, the words would surely have been taken as hinting at direct sonship of the god. Even then they were an encouragement, not an impossibility; their guarded phrasing is not a proof that Alexander was sceptical of stories of his own divine origin. Unlike others, he realized that such delicate matters can never be considered certain. Support was given by Aristander, his tame prophet, who accompanied him along the lines, dressed in a white cloak with a crown of gold on his head: he 'pointed out an eagle', symbol of Zeus and of Alexander's own royal coinage, 'which soared above Alexander's head and directed its flight straight against the enemy'. Preparing to fight for their lives, no troops would wish to dispute that the bird in the sky was anything less momentous.

Orders and exhortations take time to be delivered, and it cannot have been long before midday that Alexander finally marched his 47,000 men down into the plain against a foe some six times their numbers, whom they had kept waiting under arms, fretful and sleepless, for the past two days. Much ingenuity has been devoted to what follows, but there were facts in the advance which only serve to discredit such attempts; no general, least of all a rival of Achilles, had remained on a vantage point to describe the overall engagement, and no historian, least of all Callisthenes, was in a position to survey the scene with the naked eye. Such a broad view would clearly be impossible: the enemy were relying on horsemen, who always charge and career in frantic competition, and the plain beneath Tell Gomel is dry and dusty. Every account agreed that the battle would end in a billowing dust-cloud. When orders could only be passed by trumpet or word of mouth to distant commanders whose line-up left them to choose between several alternative positions, this dust is a disruptive fact of the first importance: 'Anyone who has witnessed a cavalry charge in dry weather over an Indian maidan will be able to picture what the dust at Gaugamela was like. On one such occasion, the writer remembers that visibility was reduced to four or five yards.'* In every account of the battle, ancient and modern, the dust is only allowed to intervene when the fighting is almost finished. But if the retreat was obscured by a dust-cloud, so too was the advance over exactly similar ground; like philosophers, historians of Gaugamela would do better first to raise the dust and then complain that they, like Alexander, are unable to see from the start.

The more the historian is removed from the facts, the more he imposes a pattern on their disorder: contemporaries would soon describe a battle

* Major General J. F. C. Fuller, *The Generalship of Alexander the Great* (1958) p. 178.

rich in about-turns and flanking manœuvres, and within twenty years their details had been muddled and elaborated by a literary historian. By a Roman, four hundred years later, these various narratives were clumsily intertwined and now, two thousand years afterwards, men draw maps to reconcile differences which ought to be left to conflict. To participants, a battle is neither tidy nor explicable; the earliest accounts of Gaugamela tell more of the mood of Alexander's court after victory than of events on the field itself. Romance and flattery singled out what suited them; though one coherent document, the Persians' order of battle, was captured among the spoils, even this cannot be believed unreservedly. It may only have been one copy among many, never enacted in practice.

Among the dust and disorder, one crucial movement is agreed, all the more credible for being a habit. On sounding the final advance, a mile, perhaps, from the enemy line which comfortably overlapped him, Alexander advanced obliquely, as his men had long learnt from Philip, thrusting his Companions forward on the right, holding Parmenion and the Greeks behind on the left. But when he came closer, he began to lead the whole line briskly to the right, a sideways movement which was made possible by the wedged shape of his units. Parmenion and the left were now exposed to a still more serious encirclement, but if Alexander could ride out beyond the Persian left, he would have saved his own attacking cavalry wing from being outflanked; to cover him, the Persians would probably shift to the left, and in their hurried surprise a gap might open in their front, which was not neatly ordered in wedge-shaped triangles. On the far right, to which he now headed, the ground was rough and unsuited to scythed chariots, and it was well away from the stakes and snares which had been laid against a conventional head-on charge. The line of advance was a sound one, but it was partly defeated by the Persians' swift adjustments.

Darius, too, could move horsemen quickly to the left, and although this was to cost him control of the battle, it was not long before his furthest cavalry were riding parallel to the units on Alexander's right, outpacing them and once more regaining the outside position. By this mad gallop, Alexander's spurt to the right was halted before he reached the rough ground, and at once, two thousand or so heavy armed Scythian and Bactrian horsemen began their expected charge to outflank and encircle. They had not prepared for an intelligent retort by the Macedonians' mobile flank guards. First, the seven hundred or so leading mercenary cavalry provoked them into a direct attack which diverted them from the rear by the promise of an easy victory; then, when they were engaged beyond recall, the rest of the flank-guards were loosed to repulse them, first, the mounted Paeonians, then the several thousand veteran mercenaries concealed in between. 'If each unit of cavalry were to contain infantrymen,' Xenophon had written in a pamphlet on cavalry command, 'and if these were to be hidden behind the horsemen, then by suddenly appearing and coming to blows I think they would work for victory all the more.' The manœuvre had been used by the Theban generals whom Philip had often copied; Alexander, who had also read his Xenophon, felt likewise, and the Scyths, entangled among what had seemed a simple enemy, were in turn outnumbered and forced to retreat.

As the Scyths recoiled on the extreme flank, the rest of the Persian left poured out to back them up; on the inner wings and centre, the scythed chariots hurtled forwards while the going was still smooth. Again in the manner of Xenophon, they had been anticipated. In front of the Companion cavalry, some two thousand Agrianians and javelin throwers had been placed to shoot them down at long range; their volley was accurate, and such charioteers as continued soon found themselves being hauled off their platforms by the bravest units in Alexander's army, while their horses were hacked with long knives. Those who survived this double assault were received by the Companions behind: ranks had been parted wide, and the chariots bolted harmlessly through into the baggage camp in the rear, where they were given a final mauling by the grooms and royal Squires. To be effective, a chariot must charge in a straight line without interruption: Alexander knew this; first he interrupted them and then, as Xenophon had suggested and he had practised against Thracian wagons four years earlier, he cleared an open path down which their scythed wheels would whirl to no purpose. According to the Macedonian officers, the chariots 'caused no casualties'; others, with a taste for drama, said that 'many arms were cut in half, shields and all; not a few necks were sliced through, as heads fell to the ground with their eyes still open and the expression of the face preserved'. On the centre and the far left, where the greater part of the chariots charged with unknown effect, this may have been true. However, many shins were grazed, the dust must surely have been stirred and the battle must have begun to be obscured.

Round Alexander the decisive manœuvre was remembered and recorded. 'The whole art of war', wrote Napoleon, 'consists in a well-reasoned and circumspect defensive followed by a rapid and audacious attack'; Scyths and chariots had been circumspectly countered, and whatever was happening on the extreme left, which nobody described clearly, the mass attack on the right was being valiantly held by an outnumbered flank-guard, so that speed and audacity could begin to come into play. The hectic movements of the Persian left, first riding to one side to match

Alexander, then racing forwards to outflank him, had opened a gap where the left wing met the left centre; this, the site of Darius's own chariot, invited penetration. 'The second principle of strategy', wrote Clausewitz, master of its theory, 'is to concentrate force at the point where the decisive blows are to be struck, for success at this point will compensate for all defeats at secondary points.' Anticipating both Clausewitz and Napoleon, Alexander formed the Companion cavalry into their customary wedge and showed the nearest foot brigades the way to an offensive against a Persian centre, exposed, disordered and not too heavily his superior in immediate numbers. Like a skilled wing forward on the football field, his first moves had drawn the defence far off to the right; now, he halted, changed direction and plunged back into the centre, heading for the goal of the Great King himself and neatly avoiding the stationary elephants.

The Companions charged, came to rest among spearmen and then shoved and hustled; the Shield Bearers followed up with the three right-hand brigades of the Foot Companions, who marched at the double, 'thick and bristling with sarissas', and raising their cry of *alalalalai*. In fine Homeric style, Alexander is said to have thrown a spear at Darius, missed, and killed the charioteer beside him; certainly, Immortals and Royal Relations were much discomforted by this piercing attack, and as corpse piled upon corpse, Darius reversed his chariot and slipped south-east through the covering dust cloud to the safety of the Royal Road. Some 3,000 Companions and 8,000 infantry had indeed turned the battle by concentrating at a point of weakness. But secondary positions were still in danger, and the main prize, Darius, would not be easily detected or overtaken.

As history centres on Alexander, who is even said to have 'meant to settle the whole issue', all million men of it, 'by his own heroics', events elsewhere in the line are left more or less unexplained. On the right, as Darius fled, a massive force of Iranian cavalry had begun to charge down a flank-guard whom they vastly outnumbered, and yet the entry of the 600 or so mounted sarissa-bearers into the battle is said to have turned them promptly to flight; on the left, Parmenion can only have been exposed to every possible threat of encirclement by the units under Mazaeus, but the only result was an outflanking charge by some 3,000 enemy horsemen who rashly continued into the baggage-camp behind the lines, where they are said to have tried to free the prisoners and the Persian queen mother. 'Not a word fell from her lips; neither her colour nor her expression changed, as she sat immobile, so that onlookers were uncertain which course she preferred.' Before she could make up her mind her rescuers had vanished from the story, perhaps because they heard of Darius's flight, perhaps because the reserves had returned to harass them.

In the centre alone the situation was unmistakable. Alexander's headlong charge towards Darius had carried the righthand units of Foot-Companions with him, but the left three files, struggling to keep up, had let their line go out of step and exposed a wide gap, as at Issus, in their centre, into which Persians and Indians had poured delightedly, following the daylight through the wall of sarissas. Had they turned against the Foot Companions' ill-armed flanks they could have done untold damage, but they too had scented the distant baggage camp, and so they careered into its midst, slaughtering its unarmed attendants in the hope, perhaps as ordered, of recovering the Great King's family. They had not reckoned with Alexander's line of reserves, whose role throughout is hard to understand. Whether or not they had split, like the front, and allowed the Indians through in the first place, they now patched themselves together enough to face about and fall on the plunderers from the rear. Thanks to Alexander's original precautions, the baggage was finally saved from its various attackers, and Darius's family remained under arrest.

As Alexander routed the Persian centre, he cannot have known that the rest of his line was either endangered or able, most fortunately, to rally its several weaknesses. He may have suspected something of the sort, but he could not possibly have seen it. Dust was swirling around him and it was a matter of dodging the scimitars and lunging at half-seen turbans in order to stay alive: his angled charge had cut in behind the elephants, and the braver foot soldiers had now set about them too, allegedly with bronze tridents designed for stabbing. Their skirmish can only have added to the confusion. The one certain target was Darius, and he was known to have retreated, so Alexander abandoned all secondary dangers and dashed with a group of horsemen in pursuit. If this seems as impetuous as the disastrous conduct of Prince Rupert at Edgehill, it is not to be disbelieved as too irresponsible: through dust and struggling Orientals, Alexander could not usefully have returned in time to aid his left or centre, even had he known this to be necessary. If history later had an excuse to be made, it was not that he set off in pursuit but that this pursuit of a vital prize was to prove a failure. A scapegoat was needed, and as so often, the blame was put down to Parmenion: as Alexander set off on his chase, accompanied by 2,000 cavalry, a messenger, it was said, arrived from Parmenion, begging him to help the left.

This messenger was beset with problems. Different histories time him differently, varying his message and Alexander's retort: some said he voiced a fear for the baggage, whereupon Alexander told Parmenion to forget the bags and fight the enemy, others said he asked for reinforcements, so that Alexander gnashed his teeth and felt obliged to return. It is extremely unlikely that any message ever reached Alexander through the press of a full-blooded battle; it was generally agreed among historians, presumably because Callisthenes first said so, that Parmenion had been slow and incompetent in the fight, and the tale of his 'messenger' could thus be put about by flatterers, in order to explain why Alexander had delayed and failed to catch Darius. His second-in-command, it was pleaded, had held him back, and by the time the excuse was published Parmenion had been killed on a fear of treachery. History, once more, could be re-written to please Alexander and slander the general he had put to death.

If the pursuit failed, it was more because of the dust and the retreating masses of Persian cavalry; these were trying to break away and follow Darius at the same time as Alexander was trying to cut a path through their lines, and with pursuit and escape at issue the fighting between the two sides was particularly savage. Sixty Companions around Alexander were wounded, Hephaistion among them, before the Persians were finally cleared away; by then Darius was far distant, having crossed the Lesser Zab river. There he had exchanged his chariot for a horse, and ridden away to the Royal Road near Arbela, thirty miles from the battlefield and site of a choice of routes to the heart of his empire. Alexander followed belatedly. By the time he had reached the Zab's far bank the October darkness was beginning to fall and a swift arrest no longer seemed possible. The horses, therefore, were allowed to rest, as the pace of the pursuit was already too much for them; not until midnight did they continue south-east to Arbela, where they arrived by Royal Road on the following morning. Inquiries revealed that Darius had long since passed through; he had also left the highway which could have brought him south-east to Babylon, and taken a shorter and less familiar hill route to Hamadan, meeting-point of the roads to his upper satrapies. His trail led through the little-known Kurdish mountains, over passes as high as 9,000 feet, and rather than risk being lost among their hostile nomads, Alexander contented himself with Arbela's handsome store of treasure and the prospect of a safe march south to the riches of Babylon. Darius's escape was a grave disappointment, but men nonetheless were calling him the new king of Asia.

Back on the battlefield, the enemy had soon lost their impulse after the flight of their royal commander. On the right, Bactrians and Scyths had ridden away, unnerved by the mounted sarissa-bearers: in the centre, the Foot Companions had repaired themselves, and on the left Parmenion had somehow repulsed an opposing mass of cavalry, despite their overwhelming numbers and positioning. One dissenting voice maintained that he and his Thessalian horsemen had indeed fought brilliantly, whereas others accused him of sloth and incompetence; the brilliance may be true, and news of Darius's retreat may also have helped him, as may the presence of Mazaeus, who could well have remembered his contacts with Hephaistion a mere month before at the Euphrates. Commander of the entire Persian right, he was not slow to ignore Darius and ride away to Babylon, where he surrendered within weeks and gained his reinstatement. He knew, most suspiciously, where his advantage lay.

In the rout, 'nearly 300,000 Persian dead were counted and many more were taken prisoner, including any elephants and chariots left intact; of those around Alexander, about a hundred were killed, but more than a thousand horses died of wounds or exhaustion during his pursuit'. These absurd figures are history's final comment on a battle which is confused where it is not downright flattery. Alexander's sudden charge from right to centre was evidently crucial, and in the best tradition of attacking generalship; at other points in his line the Persians' obsession with the contents of his baggage camp and their curious inability to turn their numbers to the proper advantage were blessings for which he could claim less credit. It is the mark of a great general to make his enemy seem insubstantial, and Alexander's planning, audacity and speed of decision, had far excelled the enemy command's: he had won magnificently, and he would never have to fight for Asia on any such scale again.

As he returned from his failed pursuit his own position did not yet seem so decisive. At Gaugamela Alexander had seized what a Persian would call his western empire: he had still to approach what Iranians called their homelands. East and south-east stretched the provinces of Medes and Persians, Bactrians, Sogdians and mountain tribes, to whom Darius could retire from Hamadan and raise a second line of resistance; until Darius was captured, Alexander was not the king of Asia, and he knew it. In the first flush of victory it was still as the Greek avenger that he wished himself to be seen: he wrote to his Greek allies 'that all tyrannies had been abolished and that men were now governed by their own laws', a claim more true of Asia Minor than of mainland Greece, where juntas still flourished under his alliance. His message extended to details too: to the other end of the Mediterranean, he sent spoils of victory to a south Italian town, home, as those Companions who knew the West could remind him, of a Greek athlete who had come to fight a hundred and fifty years before for Greece against the sacrilegious Persian Xerxes.

Such concern for obscurities is partly a credit to his publicity, but also, surely, a sign that the theme of vengeance was taken seriously.

Not even the landscape was spared his commemorations. Behind the battlefield stood the hill of Tell Gomel, which the natives called 'hump of the camel'. For the site of a glorious victory that would never do: he renamed it Nikatorion, Mountain of Victory in his own Greek language, and long after the details of his battle had been obscured this name alone would survive. A name with old associations in the East, it would be turned into Syriac and live on as *awana Niqator*, the post-house of victory, name of a relay station on the highway whose ancestor had been the Persians' Royal Road. The victory indeed had been memorable, but it was not to be the last: a name, given in a moment of exultation, would persist for six hundred years and set a fashion for Pompey and other victorious Romans, but Darius had escaped, a fact which no alleged message from Parmenion could ever conceal. It would need a longer and far harder march before the new master of Asia could call himself its rightful king.

CHAPTER SEVENTEEN

On 2 October Alexander left Darius's camp at Arbela and marched south, keeping the river Tigris on his right and following the Royal Road, which still determined his route. He had lost all hope of catching Darius in the first flush of pursuit, and as before Gaugamela, he would be wise to wait again and see if the Great King would summon one last army to take a stand in open ground. Meanwhile supplies and the prospect of treasure turned him south to Babylon and the promise of well-earned rewards for his troops. He left the battlefield quickly, a decision which flatterers explained by the stench of the enemy dead, but the area was also renowned for mosquitoes and poisonous vapours of asphalt and before long, he paused to examine them.

At Kirkuk, where the Road branched eastwards, he 'admired a chasm in the ground from which fire streamed continually as if from a spring and he marvelled at the nearby flood of naphtha, prolific enough to form a lake'. To show it off, the natives 'sprinkled the path which led to the royal quarters with a thin covering of the liquid, stood at the top and applied torches to the wet patches: darkness was already beginning to fall. With the speed of thought, the flames shot from one end of the street to the other and kept on burning.' For the first time, the Eternal Fires of Baba Gurgan had been shown to the Greeks, and at the suggestion of an Athenian who attended him in his bath, Alexander allowed a second experiment. At court, there was a boy 'absurdly plain to look at but with a pleasant singing voice'; in order to find out whether naphtha would burn as well as blaze, he volunteered to be soaked in the liquid and set alight. The flames, however, burnt him severely, and could only be dowsed by repeated buckets of water. The boy survived, shocked and scarred, a warning to those who believe that in matters of natural science, the Greeks preferred theory to experiment.

Leaving the Eternal Fires, Alexander sent a courier eastwards to Susa, the next palace on his obvious path, and himself turned off the Royal Road and took the other great highway of history to lead him south to Babylon. Near Tuz-Kharmatu, he noted the local source of bitumen and learnt that it had been used for the building of Babylon's walls; at Opis, he recrossed the Tigris and marched down the canals of its west bank, through farmland so thickly stocked with millet and barley that his army could eat as they pleased. Everywhere, they were greeted by date palms, the glory of Babylon's economy and a source of wood, beer, food and bedding; the Persians had made up a popular song about its uses, all 360 of them, so they said, one for each day of the Babylonian year.

The country he travelled had long served Persia with crops, new estates and a tribute which none of the rest of her empire could rival. It was two hundred years since Babylon had first fallen to the Persian king, and ever since her land had been bled of its marvellous fertility: Iranian tribesmen had left a life in desert and mountain to rob her of acres of farmland, waterways and city housing; only the native business documents can set such a social change in perspective. It was not that Iranians had found Babylonia more congenial than their homes, for the heat was appalling, and five hundred years later a Chinese visitor would still find their successors living in underground houses cooled by ice, a valid comment on what their forebears had suffered. Most had come because they had to; some were more fortunate, living away in the relative cool of the Persian court and running their western estates through native slaves and agents as a tax-free gift from their king, the others were government servants, judges, overseers, collectors of annual taxes, and they had to make homes wherever they worked. Nor were they always Iranians. Among them lived groups of the foreign soldiers whom the king settled on communes of land in return for taxes or military service; Indians, Arabians, Jews and former nomads, they had changed the face of whole areas of Babylon's countryside, until it was through the farms of foreigners and Persian favourites that Alexander was mostly marching on his way to the greatest city in the east.

From the Babylonian plains around him the court and empire had long drawn the surplus on which their proper working depended. East in the heartlands of Iran, farmland is scarce and water has always been revered, but in Babylonia 1,000 talents of silver, 500 eunuchs and a third of the food for the Persians' court had been levied yearly from natives and military colonists: the Great King's ceremonial among his Royal Relations depended on the surplus drained from the mud flats of Babylonia. The local satrap had once been believed to stable 16,800 horses of his own, excluding those for war, and to maintain a pack of hounds from the revenues of four villages allotted for the purpose. Private dignitaries had benefited no less conspicuously from a land with a long tradition of large royal estates; Parysatis, queen of Darius II, had owned Babylonian villages whose taxes paid for her wardrobe, some financing her shoes, others her girdles, while her vast farms near Babylon were worked by gangs of slaves and administered by her own sword-bearers and judges. Outside the city, a Persian eunuch or a Paphlagonian favourite might rise to a well-treed park and a planting of rare date palms, while his neighbours were fellow expatriates who had given their own Iranian names, like country squires, to their new home farms; a Persian prince could lease through his agents 2,380 sheep and goats in a single day in Babylon and own farmland in no less than six separate districts from Egypt to Persia, all administered by local foresters and bailiffs. It was an aristocratic style of life which few Macedonians, and fewer Greeks, had ever been able to savour.

'In Babylonia,' wrote Theophrastus the botanist from the reports of Alexander's soldiers, 'badly tilled ground yields a fifty-fold crop, well-tilled ground a hundred fold. Tilling means letting the water lie on the soil for as long as possible in order to form silt; there is very little rain, but the dews feed the crops instead. On principle, they cut the growing crops down twice,' a practice that would amaze most farmers on Greek soil, 'and they let their flocks in to graze it a third time; in Babylon, unlike Egypt, there are very few weeds and coarse grass.' In Babylon, therefore, the prizes were high, not least for Alexander himself, as the long shadow of the Persian king loomed over so much of the countryside's richest assets. Not only had he endowed his favourites, but like the kings of Assyria before him, he had taken the fine royal farms for himself; in private sales, a buyer would even ask for a guarantee that none of the land in question belonged to the Persian king. To the king, it was nothing to rent out a single farm for 9,000 bushels of grain, an ox and ten rams a year; he owned and leased granaries, chicken farms complete with a keeper of the king's poultry, town houses, stabling and even the right to fish. Often his broad estates lay on the banks of canals where they flourished from the nearby irrigation, a privilege which might cost a native farmer a quarter of his annual date crop. As for the canals, those arteries of Babylonian life, he owned many of these too and leased them to native firms of free enterprise, who charged a toll for transport and watering, sold off the fishing and covered their costs from the profits. The canals, meanwhile, grew silted, stifling the farming on which Babylonian life depended, and nobody had the will or the equipment to put them to rights.

Alexander was heir to the king and Babylon marked the first and most important step in his progress to becoming the richest man in the world; Babylon and its farmland could feed the prodigalities of a King of Asia's court. Besides the country estates, so often in Persian hands, there was the city itself and its treasure, a reward of unimagined value; his meeting with Babylon would be crucial, his first encounter with an Asian city since victory had made him master of Persia's western empire. He could hardly have begun more auspiciously. Several miles north of the city's turreted walls, Mazaeus rode out to greet him, bringing his sons as a pledge of his loyalty, and the man who had led the Persian right wing only seven days earlier now offered to surrender Babylon, perhaps as prearranged.

Alexander was by no means as certain of the sequel as his historians implied. When Babylon's massive brick walls were in sight, he drew up his army as if for battle and ordered a prudent advance, hoping to seem a liberator, not another marauding king. He was bluffing, and he also feared a trap, but he was not to be disappointed in his hopes. As he came close, the gates of Babylon were thrown open and out streamed the city's officials down a road strewn with flowers and garlands and lined with incense-laden altars of silver. The Persian commander of the fortress brought herds of horses and cattle, leopards in cages and tame lions: behind him danced Babylon's priests and prophets, chanting their hymns to the sound of lutes and sackbuts. Less mistrustful, Alexander retained an armed guard and mounted the royal chariot; the natives followed him through the main city gate, and so to the Persians' palace where the ovation continued throughout the night.

Alexander's welcome in Babylon had been overwhelming, as striking a moment in his career as any pitched victory over Darius. Fear and the wish to appease a conqueror explain the Persian governors' meek surrender, but the citizens had forced their hand, and their motives were very much older. It is a mistake to invoke economics and point to the Persians' long dominance of Babylon's land and resources; under Persian rule, the rates of barter or bankers' interest in both Babylon and Egypt can be shown to have quadrupled or more within a hundred years, but in a society which used no coinage and where the vast mass of the population lived off what they could grow or be given by their masters, too much must not be made of a rise in the cost of luxuries or a drop in the value of a silver shekel. Under Persian rule deeds for the sale of slaves also increased noticeably in scale, and one class of serfs belongs only on farms of the Persian king; contracts provide ever more stringently against their attempts at escape. But many may have been foreign prisoners of war and slavery on the estates of an alien king was nothing new to Babylonians. Alexander was not heir to the rising of a long-oppressed proletariat; in a society where religion was strong, discontent would take less crude a form, inspired by the evident flourishing of the unjust or ungodly, rather than by visions of perpetual class war. There was none of the dogma to inspire such a protest. The genius of Babylon had been to compile where the Greeks would go on to compose; facts were collected, not framed by an abstract theory, and hence there was never a doctrine of class revolution to work on a slavery which Babylonians took for granted. For nearly two thousand years Babylon had observed, not explained; a Babylonian had already visited Plato's Academy in Athens, and Callisthenes is said to have copied and sent back to his relation, Aristotle, the records of Babylon's many astronomers, which stretched, according to rumour, for 34,000 years. Only in Greece would these records be used for a general theory of the heavens; there are prompt signs of their effects, for Callippus the astronomer soon calculated a more accurate length for the Greek year from a cycle which he began in July 330. He is said to have used Babylonian records and his dating implies these were Alexander's.

Babylon's surrender is better explained from the gestures which Alexander made in return. Inside the city he gave the priesthood an audience and ordered the restoration of the temples which Xerxes had damaged, especially the famous E-sagila, which 'had been made to shine like the sun with gold and jewels', so its founder Nebuchadnezzar had written, 'while its ceilings were made of gilded Lebanon cedar and the floor of the Holy of Holies inlaid with red gold'. At the priests' suggestion, he paid sacrifice to the city's god Bel-Marduk, presumably clasping the hand of his statue to show that he had received his power like the old Babylonian kings, from a personal encounter with the god. Once again, he had turned Xerxes's past misdeeds to his own advantage: as in Lydia or Caria or Egypt, he had also learnt through friends and interpreters where tact would be most appreciated.

In Babylon this respect for the temple communities had long been a precept of wise and kingly government, even under the brutal Assyrian empire of the eighth century B.C., but the example of history had been betrayed by Persian governors. Round the staff and properties of the temple were grouped the city assemblies, run by a council of priests but drawn from a wider class whose links with the temple were often weak or ancestral. These native assemblies had been forced to pay taxes to the Persian king, providing wine, beer, farm produce and gangs of labourers for the royal herds, buildings and gardens. No Persian king is known to have paid the customary tithe to the temples; as never before, temple slaves had been ordered to cut the king's reeds, bake his bricks and shear his sheep, while royal officials saw that the workers and taxes were sent as he commanded. Within sixty years of her conquest, Babylon had revolted four times against such interference, and in 482 Xerxes had sent his brother-in-law to punish Babylon for ever by breaching her walls, denying her the status of a satrapal capital and dropping her title of honour from his royal protocol. Temple lands had been confiscated, however briefly; the holy buildings of E-sagila and the tall sacred ziggurat of Etemenanki were damaged and the solid gold statue of the god Bel-Marduk was hauled away to be melted down. In the procession to welcome Alexander the priesthood and city officials danced behind the Persian commander, and in view of the past the attitude of these educated men was not surprising. In return, they won favours and as so often, what Alexander granted became a precedent for his successors. The Macedonian kings continued to give money for rebuilding the temples; they would call themselves King of the Lands, an ancient title of honour which referred specifically to Babylonia but had been dropped by the Persian kings since Xerxes; they respected the temple citizenry, allowing them to draw up their documents in their arcane scribal language and to be exempt from certain sales taxes, imposed on all other Greek-speaking citizens by a royal Overseer of Contracts. As privileged communities in a vast expanse of king's land, the Babylonian temple assemblies resembled the free Greek cities of Asia and certain royal favours were common to them both. As in Greek Asia, so in Babylon lands endowed on a royal courtier now had to be registered as part of a nearby temple city's land, a contrast to the random gifts of a Persian king; presumably this privilege too first arose with Alexander.

Yet there were reservations. Alexander had ordered the rebuilding of the city's largest temple of E-sagila, formerly more than 200 feet high, but he had not guaranteed its expenses; the money, it seemed, would be demanded from temple land, but the priesthood had long been enjoying these extra finances, because no temple buildings remained to absorb them. Moreover Xerxes's punisher still meant to rule, and his plans combined tact with firmness. Babylon was restored to its long-lost status as a satrapal capital, but tribute was still to be levied and garrisons kept in the city's fortress: these troops were divided between two officers, both with estates in Philip's Macedonia, one of them brother to a soothsayer who would have much in common with Babylon's many astrologers. The choice of satrap was more debatable: Mazaeus, Darius's renegade viceroy of Syria, was appointed to rule the province he had helped to surrender. This hardened Persian official was to be watched by two generals and a royal tax officer, but publicly he seemed to have lost very little of his dignity; he was once more a satrap, and probably silver coins continued to be minted and marked with his name, a Persian privilege which Alexander later tended to replace with standard designs of his own. This reinstatement was remarkable and perhaps rewarded an agreed betrayal of the city: like King Cyrus, the Persian conqueror of Babylon, Alexander may also have chosen his first governor as a man with native connections, for both of Mazaeus's sons had been named after Bel, the primary god of Babylon. Perhaps he had married a Babylonian.

In similar mood Alexander gave the satrapy of Armenia to Mithrines, the Iranian who had surrendered Sardis three years earlier, and reinstated the Persian fortress commander in Babylon; he thus marked out a future theme in his empire, for Persian satraps who surrendered could now expect to be returned to provinces where they had ruled for Darius, but, as in Egypt or Caria, a Macedonian general would be set beside them to keep the local troops in loyal hands. This bargain would encourage surrender and save unnecessary problems of language and organization; the same Persian servants would be re-employed where possible and in the face of an empire, so much for the slogan of punishment and Greek revenge.

Having made known his arrangements, Alexander relaxed inside Babylon for nearly five weeks. There was much to see in a city whose size had long been exaggerated by the Greeks: the huge double walls of brick and bitumen, twelve miles in circumference, the turreted Ishtar Gate with its enamelled plaques of animals, the sacred Ziggurat, built in seven storeys to a height of 270 feet, these were extraordinary sights and all would figure in the various later lists of the Wonders of the World. Between tall gaunt houses, built without windows for the sake of coolness, the city's main highways ran in near-straight lines, their ground plan broken only by the curving course of the river Euphrates, bridged by a famous viaduct of stone. To a Greek, the city was built on an unimagined scale and its government quarters which rambled between the Ishtar Gate and the river Euphrates were no less astonishing: Alexander took up residence in the more southerly of the two palaces, a maze of some six hundred rooms whose four main reception chambers met in a throne-room and main court, built by Nebuchadnezzar to proportions which would not disgrace a Mantuan duke or Venetian doge. From the palace, he visited the northern fortress where Nebuchadnezzar had once kept his treasures and laid out his works of art as if in a museum, 'for the inspection of all people'; these, perhaps, Alexander saw as Persian property, 'while he admired the treasures and furniture of King Darius'. A vast mass of bullion completed his reward, enough to end all problems of finance in his career; never before had coins been used in Babylon, but a new mint was to help to convert the solid ingots to a form which the troops could use.

Riches were not the only concern. Around the palace buildings lay the

Hanging Gardens, whose artificial terraces were so thickly planted with trees that they seemed to the Greeks, themselves mediocre gardeners, to be a forest suspended in the air; their cedars and spruces, it was said, had been transplanted by Nebuchadnezzar to comfort his Syrian queen for her homesickness in a bare and foreign land. Alexander took an interest in the terraced park and suggested that Greek plants should be introduced among the many Oriental trees; the wish was admirable, if none too fortunate, as only the ivies settled down in their new climate. The army's pleasures, meanwhile, were coarser: while Alexander surveyed his gardens, they made up for three years' dearth of women with the strip-tease artistes of the city brothels. Extremely generous pay from the city treasures encouraged them, a reward which may have been overdue.

Among the pleasures of Babylon it was tempting to forget that Alexander was still engaged in an unfinished war. Darius was still alive and no doubt preparing to rally in the mountains near Hamadan, but nothing was to be gained by pursuing him in winter through such rough and unfamiliar country, and the longer he was left, the more he might expose himself to another open encounter. The empire's palaces lay due east, full of treasure and ready for the taking; their capture would cut Darius off from his many surviving Persian supporters and leave him no choice except to retreat into ever more easterly deserts where his royalty might not go unchallenged. Tactically and financially, it made sound sense to continue to follow the Royal Road, and so in late November, Alexander set out towards it through country well stocked with the supplies which could not be amassed from central Iran in winter. His destination was Susa, administrative centre of the empire, and as he had sent a letter by courier to its satrap he was hoping for another surrender.

He had not gone far from Babylon before he met with a reminder of all that he left behind him. On the Royal Road he was greeted at last by the reinforcements which had been summoned the previous autumn from Greece: Macedonians, Greeks and some 4,000 Thracians known for savagery, they totalled nearly 15,000 and increased his strength by almost a third. In a famously well-stocked countryside, he stopped to arrange them. The infantry were distributed according to nationality, and a seventh brigade of Macedonians was added to the Foot Companions; in the cavalry, the squadrons were subdivided into platoons, and the platoon-commanders were chosen not for their race or their birth but for personal merit. These small units were more mobile and their divided commands were more trustworthy. In the same efficient spirit competitions were held, and the army's method of signalling was changed from a bugle to the Persian method of a bonfire whose smoke would not be lost in the hubbub of a crowd.

These reinforcements' fate had been a strange one; they had been caught between emergencies before and behind them they had missed the battles where they could have been most use. They were too late for Gaugamela, and they had left Greece too soon to help Antipater out of the Spartan revolt which had at last come to a head; in the autumn of Gaugamela, 40,000 Macedonians and allies had marched to the hills near Megalopolis in southern Greece and challenged the Spartans and their mercenaries to a pitched battle, outnumbering them two to one. In fierce fighting, Agis the Spartan king had been killed and his rebels routed, but the credit belonged more to Antipater's allies, Greeks themselves, than to the relatively few Macedonians left under arms; Agis's rebellion had been heroic, but in true Spartan style it had come too late, and more Greeks had helped to suppress it than to join in a fight for freedom which Sparta had so often betrayed. To allies who knew of Sparta's past record, the cause of a Spartan king had had even less to recommend it than Alexander's own.

The reinforcements as yet knew nothing of the rebellion's outcome. They could only tell of danger in southern Greece, and it was an anxious Alexander who reviewed his new troops and continued to wait for a letter or sign from his contacts in Susa. Within days the satrap's son arrived to set his anxieties to rest. He offered to act as guide to the river Kara Su, known to the Greeks as the source of the Persian king's drinking water; there, his father was waiting with twelve Indian elephants and a herd of camels as proof of his friendship. Twenty days after leaving Babylon Alexander thus entered the province and palace of Susa in early December, at the end of the Royal Road which had determined his route for the past three years.

'Susa', wrote one of his fellow-officers, 'is fertile but scorchingly hot. At midday, the snakes and lizards cannot cross the city streets for fear of being burnt alive; when the people want a bath, they stand their water outdoors to heat it: if they leave barley spread out in the sun, it jumps as if it were in an oven.' In early December the worst of the weather was over, but its effects were visible in the city's appearance: 'because of the heat, the houses are roofed with three feet of earth and built large, narrow and long; beams of the right size are scarce, but they use the palm-tree, which has a peculiar property: it is rigid, but when it ages it does not sag. Instead, the weight of the roof curves upwards, so that it gives much better support.' Even Babylon seemed preferable to such a climate.

The palaces lacked no magnificence. 'The city', wrote a Thessalian companion, 'has no walls'; despite what many had believed, 'its circumference is twenty miles, and it lies at the far end of the Kara Su bridge'. It was thought by the Greeks to have been founded by Tithonus, hero of an endless old age, but in fact, it had been built by the first Darius nearly two hundred years before Alexander, and it lay in the land of the Elamites, once masters of an empire but long reduced by the Persians to service as scribes, palace guards and charioteers. Every province of the Great King had helped to build Susa. Sissoo-wood for the pillars had been shipped from India, craftsmen and goldsmiths had come from the cities of Greek Asia; among their carvings and goldwork, enamels, carpets and precious woods, Alexander found himself master of another gigantic treasure of bullion, this time a more personal legacy from the Persian kings. On the city's central platform, each king had built a treasury of his own; in the royal bedrooms, at the head and foot of the king's bed, stood two private treasure-chests, while the bed was guarded by the celebrated golden plane tree, so long a symbol of Persia's riches. No treasure was more impressive than the piles of purple embroidery, 190 years old but still as fresh as new from the honey and olive oil which had been mixed into their dyes. Heir to the most magnificent fortune in his world, Alexander had now entered a new scale of power altogether; it was only a beginning when 3,000 talents, six times the annual income of fourth-century Athens, were ordered to be sent to Antipater to help him with the Spartan revolt, still not known to have ended satisfactorily.

His entry to Susa was an emotional moment, for Greeks were celebrating the fall of a palace whose threats and money had determined so much of their affairs in the past eighty years. The occasion was not lost on Alexander: at Susa, he sacrificed to the Greek gods and held Greek gymnastic games, and on entering the inner palace, he was shown to the tall gold throne of the Persian kings where he took his seat beneath its golden canopy; Demaratus, giver of Bucephalas and most loyal of his Greek companions, 'burst into tears at the sight, as old men like to do, saying that a great pleasure had been missed by those Greeks who had died before they could see Alexander seated on Darius's throne'. But the height of the throne was an embarrassment, for whereas a Persian king would rest his feet on a stool, being too revered for his feet to touch the ground, Alexander needed not a footstool but a table, proof of his small size. A table was rolled to the throne, but the insult to Darius's furniture so upset an onlooking Persian eunuch that he burst into tears; Alexander hesitated, but at the suggestion of Philotas, Parmenion's elder son, he is said to have hardened his heart and left Darius's table under his feet. In that trivial moment of hesitation, his new problem had first been put to him, lightly though he passed it by. A Greek had wept for joy at what a Persian had lamented, and Alexander, the first man to rule both peoples, would soon have to compromise between them.

At Susa his attitude remained unashamedly Greek. As his new bargain required, the district was restored to the Persian satrap who had surrendered it, and a Macedonian general, treasurer, garrison and city commander were left beside him for safety and convenience. Other details were more telling. Inside the palace, statues were found of the two most famous Athenian popular heroes, revered as the slayers of Athens's last tyrant. Xerxes had taken them as loot from Athens in 480; Alexander ordered their return, a reply to those Athenians who called him a tyrant himself. He was not merely the avenger of Xerxes's wrongs. He was posing as a sympathizer with the most democratic cult in the Greek city whom he most feared. His publicity was as well informed as ever, perhaps on Callisthenes's advice. In return he left behind Darius's mother, daughters and the son whom he had captured at Issus, and appointed teachers to teach them the Greek language.

So far, in Susa and Babylon, his view of himself and his expedition had not been tested. At Babylon, he could continue to trade on the revenge for Xerxes which his father had once conceived for the Greeks; at Susa the Persians had first set up their palace 'because, most of all, the town had never achieved anything of importance but seemed to have always been subject to somebody else'. From Susa onwards he would no longer be passing through a long-subjected empire; he would not pursue Darius, rightly, until his flanks and rear were protected and the season allowed him to find supplies near Hamadan. His route now led him due east to the province of Persia, home of the empire's rulers. Here there was nobody to free or avenge; resistance was likely, and it would come from men who were fighting for their homes.

Leaving Susa in mid-December Alexander crossed the river Karun after four days, and received his first warning that the world beyond was different. In the hills above the road lived a large tribe of nomads who had always received dues from the Persian king in return for a safe passage through their grazing; this arrangement was new to Alexander and not to his liking, so in a dawn attack, whose two descriptions bear little resemblance to each other, he routed them and reduced them to pleading for their lands. They appealed to the Persian queen mother Sisygambis, aunt of their leader; Alexander heeded her and granted the nomads continuing use of their lands at the cost of 100 horses, 300 baggage animals and 30,000 sheep, the only coin in which they could pay. The sheep were precious supplies, but in the unchanging balance of the East, where nomad and villager bargain and struggle for their rights against each other, it was no way to solve a problem which was as old as the landscape itself.

Three days' march beyond the nomads, danger took another turn. On the edge of the Persians' own homeland, it was natural to expect trouble, and Alexander recognized the task ahead by dividing his forces: where the road branched south-east Parmenion was to take the baggage and heavy-armed troops through modern Behbehan and Kazarun to Persepolis, ceremonial centre of the Persian empire, while the Companion Cavalry, the Foot Companions and the light-armed units were to follow their king eastwards into the province, up the rough but direct route through the mountains. Any pickets could thus be captured before they could fall back and warn against Parmenion. The sequel has been overshadowed by Gaugamela, but it was hardly the happiest memory of Alexander's career.

The road wound up through a narrow ravine to a height of 7,000 feet; it was flanked by thick oak forests, and a fall of snow had helped to conceal its pot-holes. On the fourth day the native guides pointed out the so-called Gates of Persia, a sheer mountain barrier which Arab geographers later praised as an earthly paradise; it was approached by a particularly narrow gorge and at the far end the rocks seemed to form a wall. Alexander entered it carefully, but no sooner was he committed than the wall was seen to be artificial; Persian catapults were mounted behind it and the heights on either side were swarming with Persians, 'at least 40,000 strong' in the frightened opinion of Alexander's officers.

The pickets began an avalanche by rolling boulders down from the cliffs and the archers and catapults volleyed into an enemy 'trapped like bears in a pit'. Many Macedonians clawed for a hold to climb the rock walls but they only fell back in the attempt: there was nothing for it but to retreat, so Alexander led his survivors three and a half miles west to the clearing now known as Mullah Susan. Although an easier road was known to skirt the gorge in a wide north-easterly loop, he rightly refused to take it; he 'did not wish to leave his dead unburied', the concession of defeat in an ancient battle, and he could not risk a Persian retreat to Persepolis and an ambush of Parmenion and the approaching baggage-train. There seemed no way out until a captive shepherd told of a rough sheep track which led round behind the Persians' wall. Like so many guides and interpreters in history, he only half belonged to the society he now be-trayed; he was half Lycian by birth and knew the mountains as an out-sider. Such information was highly risky, but Alexander had to believe it.

As when besieging a city, he first divided his forces to vary his points of attack. Some 4,000 men were to keep the campfires burning and lull the Persians' suspicions; the rest were to bring supplies for three days and follow him up the shepherd's track to the top of the Bolsoru pass, 7,500 feet high. An east wind drove the snow into their faces through the December darkness, and buffeted them against the thick surrounding of oaks, but after about five miles up a route barely practicable for mules, they reached the summit, where Alexander divided his troops. Four brigades of Foot Companions, too cumbersome for the ambush were to descend into the far plain and prepare a bridge over the river to Persepolis; the rest were made to run uphill for another six miles of broken ground, until they had surprised and slaughtered the three outer groups of Persian pickets. In the early hours of the morning, they fell into the rear of the Persian wall. A blast on the trumpet alerted the army beyond in the base camp: from front and rear, the Persians were slaughtered mercilessly. Only a few escaped toward Persepolis, where the inhabitants knew they were doomed, and turned their help away. Of the rest, many flung themselves from the cliffs in despair; others ran into the units who had been stationed behind the ambush to deal with fugitives. After one of the few disasters of his march, Alexander was free in early January to enter Persia as he pleased.

The manner of his entry was a warning for the future. For the first time Alexander had done battle with Iranians on their home ground; they were not to be freed, avenged or won by diplomatic slogans, yet beyond Persia, the mountainous 'deep south' of Iranian allegiance, lay the loosely grouped empire of Iranian tribes which stretched, all but unknown to the Greeks, as far east as the Punjab and as far north as Samarkand. For the first time, the expedition was moving entirely beyond the myths of revenge and freedom with which it had set out.

In Persia the difference was set without being solved. Alexander was still the Greek avenger of Persian sacrilege who told his troops, it was said, 'that Persepolis was the most hateful city in the world'. On the road there, he met with the families of Greeks who had been deported to Persia by previous kings, and true to his slogan, he honoured them conspicuously, giving them money, five changes of clothing, farm animals, corn, a free passage home, and exemption from taxes and bureaucratic harassments. At the river Pulvar a native village was demolished to make timber for a bridge; beyond, the governor of Persepolis could only send a message of surrender and hope for the same reception as his fellow satraps to the west. On receiving his letter, Alexander hurried across the plain called Marv-i-dasht and saw the pillared palaces in the distance before him, raised on a platform fifty feet high.

'This land Parsa,' wrote Darius I, builder of Persepolis, in the inscription on its south wall.

which Ahura-Mazda has given me, which is beautiful, containing good horses and good men, by the favour of Ahura-Mazda and of me, Darius the king, it has no fear of an enemy. ... By the favour of Ahura-Mazda, this fortress I built, and Ahura-Mazda commanded that this fortress should be built, and so I built it secure and beautiful and fitting, just as I wished to do.

But in early January 330, the ritual centre of the Persian Empire had fallen to a Macedonian invader. Persepolis's fate lay in the balance and there was nothing Ahura Mazda could do to resolve it.

CHAPTER EIGHTEEN

Between the Mountain of Mercy and the river Araxes, on an artificial terrace sixty feet high, stood the palace buildings of Persepolis, ceremonial centre of the Persian empire. They were built to be impressive, a vast statement of royal power at the foot of the mountains where Persian rule could never extend: there were two audience halls and a treasury, king's apartments and gates plated with bronze; there were staircases, rooms for the guards and a royal harem. The mudbrick walls stood 65 feet high and were adorned with gold and glazing; tall columns of wood or marble, fluted and set on bell-shaped bases, supported the roofs of cedar timber. The pillar drums were uneven, their capitals grotesquely shaped as pairs of bulls or monsters kneeling back to back; the doors were cumbrous, the paving crazy and the style of the place too jumbled to be pleasing. Once a year Persepolis was the scene of a grand occasion, when envoys from all the peoples of the empire would come with their presents for the Festival of the Tribute. Up the stone staircases and along the front of the terrace walls, the carved reliefs described the ceremony: rows of Immortal Guards stood to attention, their rounded spear-butts resting on their toes; noble Medes and Persians climbed the stairs, some talking, others holding lotus-flowers or lilies, accompaniments of a royal banquet, and while the envoys from the empire waited in their national dress, soon to be ushered in by courtiers, in his hundred-columned Hall sat the King of Kings, carved on a golden throne, holding his staff and attended by the Royal Fly-swatter. For nearly two hundred years, the power of Persia had met in Persepolis for its annual festival.

Now, in January 330, Alexander approached with his army of some 60,000 men, united after their passage through the mountains; he mounted the long low tread of the north-west staircase towards the Gate of Xerxes and its two monumentally sculpted bulls. It was a steep climb into a world of vast pomposity, hitherto unknown to the Greeks, but the Persian governor was waiting to welcome him. He was shown into the pillared hall of Darius I, 150 feet square and linked to the royal living-quarters by a narrow passage; he walked through the small central chamber into the Hundred-columned Hall of Xerxes, at whose entrance the Persian king was shown stabbing the beasts of evil, the winged lion-griffin and

258

the lion-headed demon, those fateful ancestors of the Devil of the western world. Behind this hall stood the treasury, a building of mudbrick whose red-washed floor and brightly plastered pillars were lit through two small skylights, and here Alexander found his reward, 120,000 talents of un-coined bullion, the largest single fortune in the world.

Already he had encouraged his troops with talk of Persepolis as the most hateful city in Asia and for the past four years they had risked their lives in the hope of plunder; they could not, therefore, be left milling round the terrace, and when their king reappeared he gave them the word for which they had long soldiered. Up the staircases they streamed in an orgy of looting which archaeology has since confirmed. Among the ruins of Persepolis pots and glasses were found shattered, the heads of the carvings had been mutilated and there was evidence of vandalism which cannot be excused as the passage of time. The palace treasure was exempted as Alexander's property; elsewhere, marble statues were dragged away from their bases and their limbs smashed and strewn on the ground; guards and inhabitants were killed indiscriminately and women were strip-ped of their clothes and jewellery until Alexander, it is said, demanded they should be spared. Mad for a share in their limited spoils, the troops then took to fighting among themselves.

Revenge on Persia had been a theme in Greek politics for more than a hundred years, and in this plundering of Persepolis it had at last reached its climax; from an army of Macedonian hill tribes and growing numbers of Thracians, the crusade could have taken no other form. But the climax did nothing for the problems of Alexander's own position, and as often, the peak of enthusiasm already contained the first traces of doubt: one chance story brings this new state of mind to life:

On seeing a huge statue of Xerxes, overturned by the hordes which had forced their way into the palace, he stopped beside it and addressed it as if it were alive. 'Are we to pass you by,' he said, 'and leave you lying on the ground because you campaigned against the Greeks, or are we to set you up again, because of your otherwise high-minded nature?' For a long while, he stood by himself and thought the matter out in silence but finally, he passed on by.

The Greeks' avenger was beginning to have doubts: whether to be scourge or heir of Xerxes, how, if at all, to rule, as king of Asia, these were his besetting problems, and for the moment, he left them, like the statue, lying where they were. Darius was still in retreat near Hamadan, and another pitched battle seemed very likely; he could not have guessed that within six months Darius would be dead and the problem would return, too acute to be turned down.

Though looting Persepolis, he had tempered the sack with his usual concern for security and the proper accumulation of treasure. Troops had been sent east to the nearby Mountain of Mercy and so to Pasargadae, where Cyrus the Great had built a small palace some twenty years earlier than Persepolis; its Persian governor surrendered, and a treasure of 6,000 talents was reported to Alexander who was already considering its centralization. Ten thousand baggage animals and 5,000 camels had been ordered from Susa to help remove all treasure from Persia's home land, for Persepolis was not to continue as a storehouse for the empire. While this baggage-train was awaited the main army could relax. Not so Alexander, who set out into the hills round Persepolis with a picked force of infantry and a thousand horsemen.

His intention was to subdue the rest of the province of Persia, rough, populous and seldom visited by its king. The early spring snow was not congenial to such a mountainous campaign, but wherever the ice seemed too thick for the army Alexander dismounted and began to break it with a mattock, an example which his men felt bound to follow. Again his determination was decisive, for the Persian hill-shepherds had never expected a winter attack and they came to terms as soon as they heard they would be fairly treated; neighbouring nomads, who had been left independent by the Persian kings, were surprised in their caves and received in a surrender which meant little to their way of life. After thirty days of hard exertion, enough had been seen of the tribesmen, and Alexander returned to Persepolis, where he continued to distribute most generous presents 'to his friends and other helpers according to their deserts'. There were banquets, games and sacrifices to the gods, and yet it was all a lull before a second storm.

While the treasure was moved from the palace, arrangements were made as if Persepolis were still a place of importance. Its Persian governor was restored to his rank and one of Alexander's men was appointed to a garrison of 3,000 Macedonians. The province of Persia was more of an embarrassment, as it had naturally never been taxed or subjected while it ruled the empire. Alexander's tact was once more applied to a troublesome victim: as satrap, he named a Persian aristocrat, son of one of the Seven Families, whose father had been killed at the Granicus battle; it was a judicious choice in an area where feeling was bitter. Then, one late spring evening, something happened which seemed to make a mockery of the appointments which had gone before: the palaces of Persepolis went up in flames, and the fire was agreed to have begun with Alexander's approval.

No event in his expedition has caused more dispute and speculation, and only when Persepolis came to be excavated, was the scale of the blaze at last appreciated. In the Hundred-columned Hall of Xerxes, wood ash covered the floor to a depth of as much as three feet, and on analysis it was found to be cedar, the material of the beams in the building's roof. Rafters, then, had come crashing down from a height of sixty feet into a blaze which mudbrick walls and timber pillars could only help to feed; the result was uncontrollable and the Treasury and much of the Audience Room was burnt at the same time. As an act of destruction it ranked with any Thebes or Gaza of Alexander's career. So much for the facts; their explanation is another matter.

According to Alexander's officers, the palace fire was a calculated act of vengeance, and it is to Ptolemy's history that the fullest motive should probably be traced:

Alexander set fire to the Persian palaces, though Parmenion advised him to save them, especially because it was not proper for him to destroy what were now his own possessions: the peoples of Asia would not come over to him if he behaved like that, as if he had decided not to hold sway over Asia, but to pass through it merely as a victor. But Alexander replied that he wished to take revenge on the Persians for invading Greece, for razing Athens and burning her temples.

The burning, therefore, was the culmination of the Greeks' revenge.

After the heavy plundering and the removal of the bullion, it might indeed seem logical to have fired a palace which served no useful purpose. Alexander would have delayed until the precious metals had been hauled on to his pack-animals, and then paid a final gesture to the Greek allies whom he was to dismiss within a month. But Parmenion the unfortunate adviser is a figure in the histories whom repetition has worn thin, especially as the true Alexander would soon behave as the permanent king of Asia, whereas Parmenion would be put to death, partly perhaps because he mistrusted the very conduct which at Persepolis he was alleged to have advised. Moreover, if the burning had been so carefully planned, the prior garrisoning of Persepolis seems an inconsistent order. 'It was agreed', wrote Plutarch, wrongly, 'that Alexander quickly repented and ordered the fire to be put out.' There was, therefore, a rival version in which the burning had been a mistake; it too deserves to be considered.

Unlike Ptolemy its author was not a personal friend of Alexander, but within twenty years of the event, he had published a book which often exaggerated, sometimes erred, and was built partly from stories told him by men from Alexander's army, partly from others' writings and partly, perhaps, from the evidence of his own eyes. On the night of the burning, he wrote, the King and his Companions had held a banquet; women were present, the wine flowed freely and musicians added to the revelry.

> Soothed with the sound, the King grew vain;
>   Fought all his battles o'er again
> And thrice he routed all his foes and thrice he slew the slain.
> The Master saw the madness rise . . .

Among the women sat the lovely Thais, a courtesan from Athens who had followed the army across Asia; when the banquet was far gone, she made a speech, praising Alexander and teasing him, daring him to join her in a revel. It was for the women, she argued, to punish Persia for the sake of Greece, punish her harder than the soldiery, and thus set fire to the hall of Xerxes, sacker of her native Athens. Shouts of applause greeted her words, as the Companions bayed for vengeance on the ruin of Greek temples; Alexander leapt to his feet, a garland on his head, a torch in his hand, and called for a rout to be formed in honour of the god Dionysus.

> The jolly god in triumph comes:
> Sound the trumpets, beat the drums . . .
> Bacchus' blessings are a treasure,
> Drinking is the soldier's pleasure,
>   Rich the treasure,
>   Sweet the pleasure,
> Sweet is pleasure after pain.

As lady pipers and flautists encouraged the singing, the guests seized torches and the giddy procession followed Thais up the terrace. At the head of the staircase, first Alexander, then Thais flung torches on to the floor of the Hundred-columned Hall; those behind them followed suit, and as the flames rose, pillars caught fire and began to smoulder. Sparks flew across the platform; the common troopers came running from camp, fearing an accident; they arrived to see the beams draw flame and the palace roofs come crashing on to the ground. Persepolis had its own water-supply and a system of drains, but there was no hope of bringing such a blaze under control; Alexander had done more damage than he intended, and sobriety was followed by repentance.

Such was the story, adapted from the original by three authors more than three hundred years later, each in their different ways. A Roman stressed the wine and minimized the woman; two Greeks stressed the woman and the frenzy, staying closer to their common source; centuries later, they gave the cue to Dryden, who stressed the power of music and wrote *Alexander's Feast*, one of the finest odes in the English language.

The story they shared set the motive of Greek revenge in the background, but it owed nothing to talks with Parmenion or a planned destruction for political ends. What Ptolemy ascribed to resolution others had ascribed to a woman, wine and song. It is from this deep difference that the search for the truth must begin.

Where stories conflict it is tempting to believe the most dramatic, but the tale of Thais, omitted by Alexander's officers, has often been tried and found wanting: 'of course', it has been said, 'there is no need to believe a word of it', and 'naturally, the tale was eagerly repeated by later writers and even finds credence today'. But there is more to Thais than a pretty legend, for history is always human, and behind the burning of Persepolis there lies a very human complication.

Thais, the Athenian, had not joined the Macedonian army for a passing whim; first, she had made sure of her client, and for once, such a private matter happens to be known. In a book on banqueters' conversation, he is named as none other than Ptolemy, friend of Alexander, historian and future Pharaoh of Egypt; this is a chance reference, but it is confirmed by an inscription which honours a son of Ptolemy and Thais as the winner of a two-horse chariot race in Greece. At once, the mystery takes on a very different aspect, all were agreed that revenge inspired the ruin of Persepolis, but it was Ptolemy who omitted all mention of Thais and explained the affair by a debate between Alexander and Parmenion. Ptolemy, it is known, would alter or suppress history to discredit his personal rivals; what he could do for an enemy, he could surely do so much more for a lady he had loved. After Alexander's death, he married for political reasons, but Thais had already borne him three children and she was not a mistress to be forgotten. She may even, perhaps, have been watching while her lover wrote up the past. 'None but the brave, none but the brave deserve the fair . . .', how could he ever involve the mother of three of his children in an act of vandalism which even Alexander regretted? Better by far to drop her from the story and replace a moment of intoxication with a sober rebuttal of the dead and discredited Parmenion. By his confident answer, Alexander would seem so sure of his actions, and nobody would guess that the historian's mistress had been behind the gesture of revenge.

And yet the gesture's own irrelevance, the prior appointments, the tales of regret and of second thoughts survived to impugn the honesty of his story. Alexander, however tentatively, had begun to doubt his role as Persia's punisher and it is only too plausible that wine and a woman's encouragement were needed for an action which he had all but out-grown:

> The prince, unable to conceal his pain,
>> Gazed on the fair
>> Who caused his care
> And sighed and looked, sighed and looked,
> Sighed and looked and sighed again:
> At length with love and wine at once opprest
> The vanquished victor sunk upon her breast.

At a time of indecision, the palace burnt down because a future Pharaoh kept a mistress, wine flowed, the woman teased, and another king showed off before her; the burning could be explained in the light of past policy, but three months later, when Alexander was the heir, not the punisher, of Xerxes, it was rightly regretted as an ill-considered error.

Only the lady, it might seem, had escaped from blame for the ruin she had brought about. So, perhaps, it seemed, but slowly and deviously justice came to be done to her name. Ptolemy's history was too reticent to be widely read, but the author who told her true story was vivid and more to the taste of a Roman public; through Rome, his story passed to medieval Italy, when Ptolemy's writing had long been ignored. Another Thais, meanwhile, had featured in Roman comedy, as a slave-girl who proved unfaithful to her master; the poet Dante combined the two, and the result deserved a place in Hell. In the Eighth Circle, where the flatterers were scourged by demons, Thais as last found retribution: 'before we leave this place,' said Dante's guide Virgil.

> Lean out a little further, that with full
> And perfect clearness thou mayest see the face
> Of that uncleanly and dishevelled trull
> Scratching with filthy nails, alternately standing
>> upright and crouching in the pool.
> That is the harlot Thais. 'To what degree,'
> Her lover asked, 'have I earned thanks, my love?'
> 'O, to a very miracle,' said she.
> And having seen this we have seen enough.

Behind that question and answer lay a finer irony than Dante appreciated: Ptolemy had indeed earned Thais's thanks, through a delicate silence which had seemed convincing for two thousand years. The Pharaoh repaid his mistress, the firing of Persepolis was removed to the plane of reasoned policy and only through a poet's confusion was justice done to her name; Thais, at last, was condemned, but poetic justice has never been part of the prose of politics and kings.

THREE

CLEITUS:

O let me rot in Macedonian rags
Rather than shine in fashions of the east.
Ay, for the adorations he requires,
Roast my old body in infernal flames
Or let him cage me, like Callisthenes.

Nathaniel Lee, *Rival Queens* (1677), Act 4. I.

CHAPTER NINETEEN

Like many defiant gestures, the burning of Persepolis was soon to seem outdated. During the following summer, Alexander was to break with the past, a change so notable that it came to be explained by a corresponding change in his character; hence the history of the next three years was told both as Alexander's victory against the tribes of Iran and as his defeat by his own growing pride and indiscipline. Of the two battles, that against himself is more intriguing, for though new strains and conflicts grew with the expedition, history would cast Alexander in the role which suited its preconceptions. The probable truth ran deeper, at times no less dark, at others certainly more subtle.

By the middle of May Alexander had left Persepolis and taken the main road northwards for the 450 miles to Hamadan, expecting to fight a pitched battle before he caught Darius. He was met on the way by 6,000 reinforcements which he had summoned the previous November, and which increased his army to more than 50,000, apart from the treasure-train and ever-increasing baggage. This was a cumbrous force if matters came to a pursuit of Darius rather than an open fight. Darius, however, could not make up his mind. Since Gaugamela he had fled by mountain road to Hamadan with some 10,000 loyal supporters, including his hired Greek troopers, and at first he had stayed his ground in the hope of discord in Alexander's camp. But when his pursuers turned north to hunt him down he planned a flight towards Balkh in Afghanistan, distant home of many noble families of the empire; then, finding that Alexander was approaching too fast, he changed course again and decided to retreat from Hamadan and hold the nearby Caspian Gates with a draft of Scyths and Cadusians. A rumour of this reached Alexander, but neither the Scyths nor Cadusians would stir to the rescue; quarrels, therefore, broke out among Darius's followers. Those with homes near Balkh were determined to retreat there, and so they arrested their king in the fertile plain of modern Khavar, meaning to escape east as fast as they could. Darius's besetting fault had been his irresolution. This now was to cost him his life.

Meanwhile Alexander's pursuits had varied with his information. As far as modern Isfahan he advanced steadily, taking the local tribesmen and a Persian palace in his stride; then, learning for the first time of Darius's flight, he hastened to Hamadan, a long week's march behind his prey and arrived there by mid-June, eager to gather supplies and continue northwards. Even in his haste he found time for two far-reaching changes: the proportion of the palace treasures which was being transported from Persia was to be centralized in Hamadan by a temporary guard of 6,000 Macedonians while all the allied Greek troops and Thessalian cavalry were to be released from military service. Able to replace his Greek allies with the recent reinforcements, Alexander thus took his leave of a myth which was becoming outdated; after its giddy climax at Persepolis, the slogan of a Greek revenge was not extended to the pursuit and capture of the Persian king, and in future the war was to be a personal adventure, not a public vendetta. On a private basis allies could enlist as adventurers and share in the excitement. Many did so, tempted by the promise of a bonus three times bigger than the splendid farewell paid to those who declined and received their agreed wages, a gigantic present in cash and an escort home to the sea coast, along with their spoils and souvenirs. Nine thousand talents and much finery were given away in a moment; lesser generals who found their units disbanded were given new commands, and Parmenion was to deposit the treasure with Alexander's friend Harpalus in Hamadan and then march north-west with a large force against the Cadusians on whose help Darius had been depending. Expecting to meet in Gurgan, Alexander and his general took a brief farewell. They were never to see each other again.

By advancing northwards, Alexander was putting his quartermasters under severe strain. Persian documents prove that the main roads out to the Oxus were equipped with post-houses at every stage of the journey so that officials could enjoy regular meals if they had the right credentials. Alexander's generals, then, could be sure of food whatever the landscape, but the men had their wagons and little else, for the traders who followed the army would not find it easy to offer them the customary market in a land of desert tribes and no cities. They were entering months of short rations where the army would survive best if divided, and there was also the problem of pay. The wonderfully lavish donations at Hamadan promised well for the future, but there is nothing to show how Alexander paid his men for the next six years. Some treasure, at least, seems to have accompanied him, and a travelling mint was used by later kings; the gold bullion for a year's army pay would not have been impossibly bulky to transport from Hamadan to India, and a currency of silver ingots, valued by weight, appears to have been used across upper Iran under the Persian kings. The troops could be paid in this raw metal, for the total finds of

Alexander's coinage in upper Iran are not impressive, and the small units of everyday exchange are particularly rare. Plunder and payment in kind must have been extremely important, for they always burden lands who receive an army, and perhaps the men served for a promise of huge rewards on returning home. But the amounts and availability of money can never be calculated, and a crucial side to the king and his soldiers' relationship is an insoluble mystery. At standard rates, which Alexander no doubt improved, the next six years were immensely expensive; the treasury could stand them, but even if the methods of their funding are unknown, and likely to remain so, its intricacies and accounting should not be forgotten.

For eleven days Alexander led a force picked for its mobility northwards at furious speed from Hamadan; as Arab caravans later allowed nine days for the journey, he must have turned off the main road, perhaps hoping to catch Darius down a sidetrack. Disappointed, he returned to the Royal Road and rode into Rhagae where he rested for five days; many soldiers had already dropped out exhausted and several horses had been galloped to death.

It was stragglers once more who revealed what had happened. Two Babylonians, one of them Mazaeus's son, gave news of the arrest of Darius, and with a few picked horsemen Alexander at once raced eastwards to overtake the traitors. After two days' reckless gallop, resting only in the afternoon heat, he had reached Darius's last known camp on the edge of the Dasht-i-Kavir: Darius, he heard, had been stowed in a wagon and hustled as if for Shahroud by murderers who would abandon him in the last resort. Any time saved in the desert could prove decisive, so the fittest light infantry were mounted on horseback and ordered to follow a bold short cut across its fringes. Between dusk and dawn, forty miles of the salt-waste were covered, and at last as the morning heat began to take hold, a convoy of carts was to be seen in the green distance, shambling eastwards down the main road near modern Damghan. For the last time, the horses stumbled into a canter, enough at least to raise a dust and scare their unsuspecting prey. Only sixty men were at Alexander's side as the convoy was halted and the carts stripped for inspection. But search though they might, Darius was nowhere to be found.

Wearily, a Macedonian officer strayed to look for water by the roadside; searching, he came upon a mud-daubed wagon, abandoned by its team. He looked inside, and there lay a corpse, bound in the golden chains which signified a Persian king: like Yazdagird III, last of the Sassanid dynasty, in flight from the Arab invaders a thousand years later, Darius III, last of the Achaemenid kings, had been stabbed and deserted by his own courtiers. Only in legend was he left enough breath to greet his discoverer and command Alexander's nobility. Serving officers insisted, conveniently, that Darius had died before Alexander could see him. The assassins had fled too far to be caught.

Left with his enemy's dead body, Alexander behaved remarkably. He stripped off his own cloak and wrapped it round the corpse. Darius was to be taken to Persepolis for a proper royal burial. The Persian prisoners were interviewed and the nobles were separated for release: the grand-daughter of Darius's royal predecessor was restored to her husband, a local aristocrat, and within days, Darius's own brother was enrolled as a Macedonian Companion. And yet, alive, Darius had been denounced as Alexander's enemy, 'who began their enmity in the first place', who 'would regain his family and his possessions only if he surrendered and pleaded on their behalf': it was a complete change of tone, and the soldiery must have watched it with amazement. Hugely generous gifts from the treasure captured with the convoy were distributed to reassure them.

By the death and capture of Darius, Alexander saw himself made heir to the empire which he had formerly come to punish. But the kingship of Persia was not to be assumed lightly; its roots went deep into history, and like the empire's government it had drawn freely on the background of its subject peoples. Alexander was about to succeed to traditions which he had already affronted. He would never come to terms with them, but it is important to realize what their example meant, and why he could not do them justice.

If Greeks had long denounced the Persian monarchy as slavish, and even explained it in terms of Asia's enfeebling climate, it was nonetheless a commendably versatile government. 'The Persians', Herodotus had written, 'admit foreign customs more readily than any other men', and the more that is known of them the more he is proved right. Two hundred years before Alexander, they had overthrown the empire of the Medes and annexed the ancient civilization of Babylon, but in each case they had availed themselves of their subjects' experience. From the Medes, they had acquired the arts of courtly comfort and secluded kingship, besides a legacy in language and architecture which is only now beginning to be recovered: from Babylon and Assyria, they had borrowed the ancient royal myths, whether the Tree of Life or the slaying of the Winged Lion of evil, which gave such sanctity to Persepolis, while at a humbler level, they had absorbed the law and bureaucracy for which their own illiterate pastoral life had not equipped them. As always, new needs had been met internationally: scribes from Babylon and Susa had kept the king's accounts in a language he could not speak, Greeks had served as his doctors, sculptors, interpreters and dancers, Carians and Phoenicians had manned his navy; the Magi of the Medes had managed his prayers and sacrifices, at least initially, while garrison service in the satrapies had brought Indians to Babylon, men from the Oxus to Egypt, Greek sailors to the Persian Gulf and Bactrians from outer Iran to Asia Minor. But skills and government service were not the end of this exchange.

Moving west to rule in foreign Babylonia, the Persian nobility had freely intermarried with their subjects. Within two generations, the native business documents are rich in mixed Persian and Babylonian names, while even among the nobility, a Persian might marry a Jewess, an Armenian or an Egyptian and have his marriage legally witnessed by Babylonians, Arabs or Hebrews. Under Persian rule Babylonia had become a land of half-castes, while even the Persian king had been known to maintain a Babylonian mistress. In the capitals of the Empire, in Memphis no less than Babylon, there were foreign quarters named after the nationality of their inhabitants, exactly as in the cities of Alexander and the Greek kings which succeeded them, but these segregated areas had not isolated one people from another and Persian Babylon, especially, was an integrated world. This integration did not stop at marriage: at the Persian court it can still be detected in the carvings of Persepolis, an accurate record of the Persian empire's officials. The Royal Guards of the private palace quarters are all of them Persians, distinguished by their gold spear-butts and commanded by Persian Staff Bearers. But immediately outside, in the public halls and along the grand staircases, the staff-bearers are often Medes, while Median spearmen are mixed with subjects from Susa, seat of the old Elamite empire, in the nine other 'thousands' of the Immortal Guards, who serve as the élite troops of the king. With the court police, the pattern is even more impressive. The king employed Whip-bearers who controlled the crowds when he processed in public; besides their whips of office, they carry carpets and the royal chair, proof that they also supervised the king's comfort. And yet, at Persepolis, every one of these high officials is shown by his cape and spherical headdress to be a Mede; just as Medes supervise the king's footstool, so Median grooms arrange for his horses, while Elamites from Susa attend to his chariots. Half the envoys from the empire are ushered in to the king by Persian ushers, half by Medes; before the King, the Steward of the Household makes his report, bowing slightly in audience, and yet he, the highest court official, is a Mede. The Persians had not excluded the peoples whose empires they supplanted: from the natives of Susa, they had recruited scribes and foot-guards, as well as borrowing the style of their pleated robes and mantles, their daggers, bow cases and buttoned shoes. From the Medes, well known for their use of cosmetics, their gaily coloured trousers, earrings and high-heeled boots, they had attracted officials to make their court comfortable and to maintain their king in properly secluded style.

Without this Persian background Alexander's own plans for government have been made to seem unnecessarily radical. Already in summer 330 there were signs that the wisdom of such integration was no more lost on him than on his Persian predecessors: he was reappointing Orientals to the satrapies east of Babylon, where they knew the language and the tribesmen, and even the most conservative Greek pamphleteer had advised such a policy to Philip, fighting the Greeks' crusade; he had maintained Persians as Honoured Friends around him; he now respected the dead Darius, just as Darius's ancestors had once respected the kings they replaced, whether live or dead. To administer his conquests he needed the same expertise as the Persians before him, both locally in Babylonia, where taxes passed through a complex sequence of collectors and canton officials, and also at the seats of government, Susa or Hamadan, where the silent majority of supply officers, treasurers, foremen, land agents and accountants had long served the Persian nobility, entirely ignored by Greek historians. Local documents prove that under Persian rule as many as 1,350 labourers from the treasury could be despatched on a single consignment from Persepolis, while a backlog of work could keep scribes up to six years behind with receipts and registrations. Like the Persians, Alexander would surely reappoint this foreign bureaucracy and workforce of serfs, if only for the sake of his taxes and supplies: what he did for the chancellery, he should now do, logically, for his court, and as the Persians had once treated the Medes, so now he should go on to treat the Persians.

But the sequence was not so smooth as it sounded. On his own side stood the veterans of thirty years' fighting, brought up under Philip and often resentful of Greeks, let alone of Orientals. They had not spent their youth with friends who could speak Persian or with tutors who wrote on the Magi. They wanted power for themselves, treasure and perhaps an end to their marching. They had not expected to share their monarchy, any more than the Greeks had expected their crusader to become the Persian King. Educated Greeks had shown no more fondness for the idea of the barbarian than for that of the lower classes: there were Macedonian officers who might feel likewise, especially if Alexander threatened their status with Orientals.

Their agreement would only be hastened by the features of Persian kingship, for if the Persian court was a mixed society, the king himself was set above it in venerable seclusion. Access to him was controlled by Staff Bearers and Chamberlains, and during an audience the visitor's hands were to be kept strictly inside his cape. It was believed by Greeks that no man could be admitted unless he had first washed and dressed in white raiment; certainly, it was death for a subject to sit on the King's golden throne or walk down the royal carpet. Once admitted, he brought his hands to his lips in a respectful gesture which Greeks reserved for their gods, while suppliants or the very humblest classes also went down on their knees. During the court's official dinners, the king dined behind a veil in the company of his wife, mother and royal brothers: he drank specially boiled water, ate a cake of barley and only took wine from an egg-shaped cup of gold. The court nobility set aside food from their table as an offering to his revered spirit, and even cities in western Asia might decree a sacrifice to his royal fortune. Throughout the king's lifetime, a royal fire was kept alight in his honour and only dowsed when he died: at his funeral, his surviving staff-bearers were killed beside his pyre. Though not worshipped as a living god, he was the chosen and protected favourite of Ahura-Mazda and he dressed to suit his majesty. He rode in an ornate chariot, pulled by white horses; his tunic was striped with white and purple and worn beneath the robe of gold embroidery reputed to be worth 12,000 talents; his necklace and bracelets were gold; he was shaded by a parasol and accompanied by a fly-whisk, while his headdress was smooth and rounded, like a tall but brimless top-hat; his shoes were padded and dyed pale saffron, without buckles or buttons and his girdle was woven of pure gold thread. He moved like a god among men, distant but lonely and often insecure.

However respectful of the dead Darius, Alexander could never compete with this religious aura. His officers would not understand it, and already after Gaugamela, his publicity was flouting it deliberately: his coinage from mints in western Asia showed a lion-griffin, Persian symbol of chaos and evil, but so far from being stabbed, as at Persepolis, by the Persian king, the griffin was itself shown slaying Persians, a direct reversal of their royal myth. When a Persian king took the throne, he attended Pasargadae, site of King Cyrus's tomb, and dressed in a rough leather uniform to eat a ritual meal of figs, sour milk and leaves of terebinth. This ancient ceremony recalled old legends of Cyrus's youth in the once nomadic society of Persia; after his meal, the new king even assumed King Cyrus's cloak. Alexander knew from Greek authors and Persian friends how Cyrus's memory was revered by Persians, and soon he would show a concern for Cyrus in his own publicity. But only in his *Romance* is he said to have issued a proclamation to all Persians as the new King of Asia that he would maintain their traditions as before. He is not known to have learnt to speak Persian fluently and although he soon employed eastern Magi, he never ordered this traditional royal ceremony for himself. He was a foreigner who had burnt Persepolis and he could not understand such old nomadic rituals. But the rituals were to survive long after his achievements had been forgotten.

However, he was also approaching outer Iran where a due measure of tradition would be expected of any claimant to the Persian kingship. In the process Alexander might offend his elderly generals, but it ought to be possible to compromise between Macedonian scruples and Oriental expectations. Had he been feeble or unimaginative, he would never have tried. He was neither, and within weeks his court was alive with gossip and conjecture.

First he made sure of his circumstances. Leaving the site of Darius's murder, he returned to the main body of his troops and after a short rest led them up from the edges of the desert to the passes of the Elburz mountains, heading north for the Caspian Sea through forests of oak and chestnut, hill ravines and the lairs of wolves and tigers. Darius's courtiers and the Greek troops who had served him to the end were known to have fled to these thickets for refuge. Within a week, the former Vizier, one of Darius's murderers, had promised surrender in return for a pardon which was later attributed to the charms of his accompanying eunuch. The pardon belonged to a less self-indulgent policy, whereby those who surrendered should be spared, for Alexander began by caring less for the punishment of Darius's murderers than for the luring of Persian nobles out from the forests on to his staff, where they could help with the problems of language and government. The eunuch was indeed a figure to be respected, for of all the finds in the months near the Caspian, none was to prove more precious or remarkable; with Bagoas the Persian, Alexander began an affair which lasted for life.

The name Bagoas was rich in recent and unpleasant memories; some ten years earlier, a Bagoas, also a eunuch, had made his name as a Persian general in Egypt and then served in western Asia where he had sent Hermeias, Aristotle's first patron to his death. He had then poisoned Darius's predecessor and made Darius king, only to be poisoned himself, some said, by way of thanks; his famous tree park at Babylon had now been bestowed upon Parmenion. But Alexander's Bagoas is said to have been young and extremely handsome, son of a certain Pharnuches, who perhaps had connections with the hellenized coast of Asia, he might have been bilingual and was probably no more than a young court eunuch beloved for his airs and graces. What Hephaistion thought of him can only be imagined, for the high importance of Bagoas was left in decent silence by Alexander's friends. So the most startling of all Alexander's intimates is also the least known, but his role must not be played down; a willing source of Persian information, he was also the bluntest proof that Alexander found Orientals' company congenial, and within weeks, Bagoas could be seen as the earliest sign of new times.

Continuing to lure supporters from the wilds, Alexander offered terms of new employment to the 1,500 Greek mercenaries who had stayed devotedly beside Darius. First, they argued; then they took up the suggested bargain, which still recognized Alexander as allied Leader. Those who had joined Persia before Philip had declared war were to be left free, while those who had fought against the decrees of the Greek allies were to enlist in Alexander's army at the same rate of pay. Rich and unchallenged, Alexander had moved far from the massacre of Greek 'rebels' at the Granicus; he then left briefly to hunt out the surrounding hill tribes; for one glorious moment, they managed to ambush Bucephalas, but a furious threat of devastation from Alexander caused them to surrender and give the horse back. This brusque treatment of the mountain tribesmen could only have impressed his new Persian friends, for their kings' authority had long foundered against such inaccessible peoples.

Reunited, Alexander and his troops marched down the mountain slopes to Zadracarta, Gurgan's capital, close to the southern shore of the Caspian Sea. He had entered the lush jungle of a tropical landscape, abounding in supplies and freshened by the luxury of summer rains: no Greek had seen it before, and his officers were suitably impressed: they noted its silver firs, its sappy oak-trees, and the precipices by the seashore, over which the 'rivers poured, leaving room for the natives to feast and sacrifice in the caves below, basking in the sun-light and looking up at the water passing harmlessly above, while before them, stretched the sea and a shore so damp that it was grassy and alive with flowers'. The sea itself was no less intriguing. By command of the first King Darius, it had been explored two hundred years before by Scylax, a sailor from Caria, whose small boat had reached its northern shores and proved that another landmass lay beyond. The facts were not well known in Greece, though Aristotle could have told them to his former pupil, and as many believed that the Outer Ocean of the world flowed round the northern coast of Asia, Alexander now wondered whether the Caspian was perhaps a gulf of Ocean. For the first time, he had the sensation of standing at a possible edge of the world, and whether or not such excitements mattered to him, at the end of his life he would return to a plan to discover its truth. His followers, meanwhile, had tasted the Caspian's water and noted its extreme sweetness, still manifest today; they were also amused by the number of its small water-snakes. But they left its extent uncertain, and for fifteen days they relaxed at Zadracarta while Alexander sacrificed to his customary gods and held the first athletic games the people of Gurgan had ever witnessed. During that fortnight two events are reported, the one as romantic as the other was momentous.

To the shore of the Caspian, it was said, came the Queen of the Amazons, accompanied by 300 women whom she prudently left outside the Macedonian camp. Single-breasted and trained in war, she told Alexander she wished to bear his child. Bagoas notwithstanding, 'the passion of the woman, being keener than the King's, made him spend thirteen days in satisfying her desires'. But none of Alexander's staff historians was prepared to support this disputed story, not even his chief court usher who might have admitted the queen to his presence, and it must therefore be dismissed as a legend. The Greeks had long located the Amazons near the Black Sea, not without reason as the tribes there were matriarchal and ruled by women. But the Black Sea was hundreds of miles away from the Caspian, and the visit of the Amazon queen was invented by two historians who had first confused this geography. Perhaps a nearby queen did call on the camp; certainly, the Amazons were too famous for romantics to admit that Alexander had not received them.

Though spared an affair with an Amazon, Alexander had not been sitting idle. At Zadracarta, Persian noblemen continued to join him from their refuges in the Elburz foothills: some of them were former satraps; one, Artabazus, was a former guest-friend of Philip's court. Father of Barsine, Alexander's Persian mistress taken at Issus, he brought no less than seven sons, the interpreters and minor officials of the future. The policy of free pardons and the affair with Barsine had usefully added to Alexander's growing stock of Orientals. This same pool of Persian collaborators remained central to his plans for his Empire throughout his life. It was prudent and polite to make this new nobility feel at home, and in conversation, they would have discussed what they had always known in the days of a Persian king. Alexander hesitated no longer; as Darius's heir and Bagoas's admirer, he began to wear certain parts of the Persian royal costume.

It is important to realize exactly how he did it. He refused such Median excesses as the royal trousers or sleeved overcoat and he is never known to have worn the rounded tiara or royal headdress. He contented himself with the purple-and-white striped tunic, the girdle and the head-ribbon or diadem which had formerly been worn by the king and by his Royal

Relations. Now, the diadem was confined to the king alone and either worn round his purple Macedonian hat or on occasions wound round his bare head. His Companions were given similar purple hats and cloaks bordered with purple, like the official Wearers of the Purple at the Persian court; they were invited to adorn their horses with ornate Persian harness and saddlery. Henceforward access to Alexander was controlled, as in Persia, by ushers and Staff Bearers, whose chief officer was the Greek Chares from Lesbos, presumably bilingual, who later wrote colourful memoirs. Darius's concubines are also said to have been reinstated, 'three hundred and sixty-five in all', according to the Greeks, who liked to number Persian habits as equal to the days in the Babylonian year which they followed. The concubines are never mentioned again and they are unlikely to have been at hand in the wilds of the Caspian Sea. But sooner or later, no doubt, Alexander did recruit them.

Such a rearrangement was bound to cause comment. 'It was now', wrote his Roman historian, four hundred years later, 'that Alexander gave public rein to his passions and turned his continence and self-control to haughtiness and dissipation.' This well-worn theme entirely missed the point, for Alexander was not even the first Greek king to have worn the diadem or Persian dress. For the past sixty years, the tyrants of Syracuse in Sicily had successively taken it up, not because of any connection with Persia, but because they believed, wrongly, that the Persian king was thought to be a living god, and they too wished to be seen by their dress to represent the god Zeus on earth. These nuances of religion must not be discounted for the casual Greek observer who now saw Alexander in a diadem and knew already how he emphasized his relationship with Zeus. They were not a part of Alexander's purpose: that was political, but nonetheless modest. He had refused the showiest Persian clothing because his officers would resent it, and he only intended to wear the remainder in the presence of Orientals. But by the diadem alone he set a lasting fashion: it would be worn by his Successors, when each laid claim to his Asian heritage, and 150 years after his death it was still being imitated by the distant Greek kings of Bactria, cut off from the West in outer Iran. He himself is said to have called it 'the spoils of victory', but it was also a concession to his new position: as a king, not the agent of Greek revenge, he was bound for the heartland of Iranian tribes and he had assumed for sparing use a part of the costume to which his subjects were accustomed. After three heavy victories, these few Persian customs may seem an irrelevant gesture. But more were to follow, and even these few mattered: when Julius Caesar planned to invade the Parthian empire in Alexander's footsteps, there were those at Rome who wished him, as a fit precaution, to be attired in the diadem and Persian costume before he even entered Asia.

To Alexander's staff these changes told of new ambitions. Alexander had already talked of conquering Asia, but as heirs of Darius, they now saw that Asia would mean the whole Persian empire and that they could not turn back until this much, at least, had been made their own. It would be a hard march, for Alexander had set his heart on two kingdoms, and a detail from his chancellery made this all too clear. Letters, as always, needed his daily attention, but no longer did he head them with the forms of polite greeting, except when writing to Antipater and to Phocion, a trusted Athenian politician; elsewhere, throughout, he used the royal 'we', the title of an absolute monarch. Letters which were bound for Europe he sealed with his former ring, but those which referred to Asia were stamped with the ancient seal of the Persian kings.

Such ambitions would not have developed unless Alexander had tested his ground. Three weeks before, he had been awaiting the rest of his army after Darius's capture near Damghan; he was tired and he had just received news that his brother-in-law, Alexander, King of Epirus, had died in battle in southern Italy. He rested his men for mourning by the road which led to Khavar; for three days they encamped in a fortress which they renamed Hecatompylos, 'city of a hundred gates', because of its position on the local roads. A century later, the fortress had grown to become the earliest capital of the Parthian empire, and though many had searched for its famous site, it was not until 1966 that the disputed measurements of Alexander's own surveyors helped in its rediscovery. Three miles south of the road to the Caspian Gates stand a group of tall mounds at Shah-i-Qumis, thrown into clifflike prominence by the flatness of their arid plain. To the north and west rise the distant peaks of the Elburz mountains, but on all other sides the landscape is bare to a treeless plateau and the salt waste desert of Dasht-i-Kavir. It was here that Alexander assembled his troops and asked them for silence beneath the July sun. In the Hundred-gated city he told his men of their many past victories, of the need to follow up a conquest, of the ease with which the East would be theirs. They had seen their crusade end, and already Darius's death had started them talking of home. But Alexander made light of such common rumour. He carried his soldiery with him until their exhaustion left them and their ambitions seemed to stretch to the far horizon. Then, having roused their fervour, he paused. There was a hush, the reward of the greatest speeches: like the swell on the sea, came the answering shout of agreement: Lead us; lead us, wherever you will.

CHAPTER TWENTY

By wearing the diadem Alexander had laid claim to the whole of Darius's empire. To earn it, he would have to strike eastwards into the fastnesses of Afghanistan through mountain-passes and steppes of sand. 'In Khorasan', runs the Persian proverb, 'the staging posts of the Royal Road are as endless as the chatter of women,' and ahead lay a world of vast space and slowness where the only bustle was the royal courier on the one Royal Road. There was nothing to be gained from Iran's central basin to the south and south-east of him, as it belonged to the Deserts of Salt and Death and was therefore ignored by roads and settlers. Like every traveller, he would skirt it; so, eastwards from his base in Gurgan he marched across a landscape of infinite flatness, hot, hungry but aware that this was only a preliminary to a world of tribes and barons hitherto unknown to the Greeks.

Short of supplies he had to march fast and it was as well that the army was still slimmed of the sections detailed to Hamadan; after four hundred miles he paused at modern Meshed where his Persian Companions explained to the camp surveyors that they now had a choice of two routes. One, the future Silk Road from China, led north-east through hill and desert past the oasis of Merv to the province of Bactria, where the rebel Bessus, a murderer of Darius, was reported 'to have worn his tiara upright', a symbol of royalty, 'and proclaimed himself King of Asia' with the help of Persian refugees, nomads and the local nobility. The other, also to Bactria, turned due south from Meshed towards the dunes and prairies of Seistan and then crooked north-eastwards up the Helmand valley, into the heart of the Hindu Kush mountains and so by any one of four high passes down into Bessus's new dominions along the banks of the river Oxus. For the moment, Alexander preferred the first of these two alternatives, half as long as the southern detour.

He was encouraged in his choice by a local windfall. Meshed lay on the border of the ancient satrapy of Aria, which the Persians called Hariva, and as its name implied, it was a heartland of Iranian tribesmen who had lived there for at least five hundred years; the title Ariana, whence modern Iran, was already applied to the eastern lands beyond it, even as far as the Punjab borders. Possibly it was from Aria, centred on the oasis Hariva

279

and watered by the Hari-Rud river that the Iranians had first swept westwards in their early tribal wanderings: such a history would have made it an awkward province for Darius's heir to pass through, let alone to control, had not its satrap Satibarzanes come to Meshed and surrendered on the border. Leader of the Arians' cavalry at Gaugamela and then, like Bessus, a murderer of Darius, he was nonetheless restored to his high office and given an advance squadron of mounted javelin-throwers, Iranians like himself, to police the Macedonians as they passed along the edge of his province, only too keen to plunder it for supplies. Favouring one royal assassin, therefore, Alexander prepared to pursue another, but first all excess baggage was piled on to wagons and massed in the centre of the camp; Alexander then set fire to it, his own wagon first, the others only when his own example had been observed. From now on, packanimals would serve as transport on roads too rough for wheels. The army acquiesced in the sudden loss of their luggage, knowing that Alexander had suffered too; at least they were allowed to keep their native concubines.

Satibarzanes left with his guards for the distant capital of his province and from Meshed in mid-August, Alexander continued east towards the Silk Road, still meaning to dislodge the pretender Bessus from his distant base at Balkh. He had not gone far along the edge of the Arians' satrapy when grave news compelled him to hurry south to its heart; Satibarzanes had murdered his guards, raised 2,000 horsemen in revolt and blockaded his capital's fortress. In two days Alexander raced a picked force southeast down the seventy miles to Artacoana, the capital city, where reprisals could only be merciless as trust had been badly betrayed. The rebels took refuge on a steeply wooded hill, but the undergrowth was fired until those who stood their ground were smoked and burned to death; at Artacoana, siege towers breached the city walls and all troublemakers were set aside for death or enslavement. Alexander ordered the rest to be resettled on the site which was to be renamed Alexandria and strengthened by new walls and Macedonian veterans. The result still survives in Herat, its modern successor, but not for the last time in the East, an Alexandria had merely developed the buildings of an ancient Persian citadel and satrapal court. Satibarzanes, meanwhile, was nowhere to be found. On news of Alexander's advance he had escaped up the Hari Rud valley and disappeared into the foothills of the Hindu Kush to collaborate with Bessus. He had been a bad mistake, and he was to prove persistent.

Rather than pursue him Alexander reversed his plans. He would no longer return to the north-eastern Silk Road and approach Bessus's henchmen directly; he would entrust Aria to a Persian, perhaps the son of Artabazus, his most trusted Oriental, and follow the more devious route

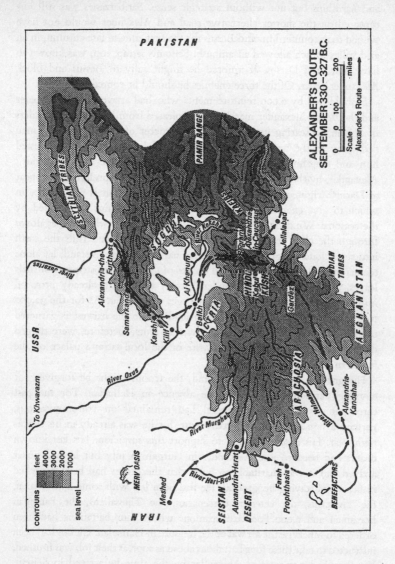

ALEXANDER'S ROUTE
SEPTEMBER 330-327 B.C.

Scale
0   100   200
miles

Alexander's Route ➤

PAKISTAN

PAMIR RANGE

SETTIAN TRIBES

SOGDI...

River Jaxartes

USSR

Alexandria-the-
Furthest

Samarkand

Karshi

Kilif

River Indus

CHITRAL

Alexandria-
in-Caucasus

Jellalabad

HINDU
Kabul KUSH

Balkh

BACTRIA

Garden

INDIAN
TRIBES

AFGHANISTAN

River Oxus

To Khwarazm

MERV OASIS

River Murghab

ARACHOSIA

River Helmand

Alexandria-
Kandahar

CONTOURS

feet
4000
3000
2000
1000

sea level

River Hari-Rud

Alexandria-Herat

Farah
Prophthasia

SEISTAN
DESERT

BENEFACTORS

Meshed

IRAN

due south, to Seistan, the Helmand valley and eventually the passes over the central Hindu Kush. It was a momentous decision, rich in surprises and hardships but not without strategic sense. Satibarzanes was still uncaptured on the shorter alternative road and Alexander would not have wished to encounter him and Bessus for the first time in late autumn, in an arid valley which allowed an ambush. Seistan's satrap, too, was known to have murdered Darius. If ignored he might rally to Bessus and block Alexander's rear. Of the three enemies he should be routed first.

Emboldened by 6,000 reinforcements who had arrived from Antipater and the West, Alexander marched as he pleased from Herat to the borders of Seistan, so scaring its satrap, also a murderer of Darius, that the man fled away to the nearest Indians of the Punjab. But they soon arrested him and sent him back to be executed 'for his crime against Darius'; Alexander, by then, had learnt the perils of mercy and preferred to appear as Darius's righteous avenger. In early autumn, Seistan is not a place in which to give enemies a second chance: its dusty plains are scoured by the seasonal Wind of a Hundred and Twenty Days, which pipes down through the cliffs and sand-dunes of the north-west and rolls the earth into such clouds of greyness that a man has to struggle to stand, let alone to march with a sarissa. Tufts and bushes of greenery are stripped of their leaves, a discomfort for Alexander's horses which had already browsed imprudently among the poisonous spurges near Herat. As for the 32,000 troops, they were short of food in a land where the harvest is garnered early in order to escape the cutting winds: tents, therefore, were tugged down for nine days' rest at Farah, site of the local satrap's palace on the northern edge of modern Seistan.

Hungry and buffeted by the wind, the troops might be forgiven for envying Parmenion his opportune absence in Hamadan. For the past three months the elderly general had remained on communications, perhaps a sign of impending retirement, for he was already in his seventieth year. His absence tended to support this suspicion. His last known orders had been to join Alexander in Gurgan in July but he had never arrived and it was charitable to guess that the orders had been cancelled in favour of staying his ground. He had been left with some 25,000 men, the Thracians, the veteran mercenaries, the Thessalians, the Paeonian horsemen and 6,000 Foot Companions whose four battalions had been ordered to supervise the arrival of the treasure in Hamadan. Cleitus had been instructed to take these four battalions ahead as soon as their job was finished, but they had not reached Alexander by the time he arrived in Seistan. Even if they were already on the road from Hamadan, Parmenion retained a sizeable force. He still controlled nearly twenty thousand troops at a time when Alexander had little more than thirty thousand in his own camp. The balance of forces happened to be nearly equal between king and general; at Farah the general was to spring for the last time into memorable prominence: 'Safe from outside, Alexander was suddenly attacked from within his household.' It was a most mysterious affair. Those who might have known the truth said little about it: others elaborated, guessing freely on the basis of rumour and hearsay.

According to Ptolemy, a plot was revealed to Philotas, Parmenion's son, who failed to pass the report to Alexander even though he visited the king's tent twice every day. A second version fills in the details, and in the absence of anything more convincing it has to be believed. The affair was said to have begun when a Macedonian called Dimnus told his boy-lover that a plot was afoot to kill the king. He gave the names of the conspirators and he revealed in extreme secrecy that their attempt was to be made in three days' time. But his lover was young and indiscreet. He told the secret to his brother Cebalinus and like all young men who give away secrets, asked him to do what he had not: keep the plot to himself. But Cebalinus lost his nerve. He was shocked and he did not wish to be an accessary to murder, so he went to the highest officer he knew and told him all his brother had let slip. The officer was Philotas, son of Parmenion.

Twice daily, Philotas would go to Alexander's tent but for two days he put off Cebalinus's inquiries, saying that the king had been busy and there had been no chance to raise the matter in his presence. Cebalinus became suspicious. Time was running short, so he turned to one of the royal pages whom he found on guard in the armoury. The page had intimate access to the king and at once he made for the royal bathroom where he found Alexander having his bath. The plot was reported and those concerned were ordered to be arrested. Cebalinus told his story, excusing himself as a loyal informer; Dimnus was summoned as the source of the evidence, but killed himself, probably before he could be questioned. The king had lost his prime witness and was left with a garbled list of names, passed by Dimnus to his boyfriend and by the boyfriend to his brother. Only one clear fact had emerged: Philotas had been told of a plot, but had suppressed the news for the past two days. That needed rapid investigation.

It is here, probably wrongly, that the drama is made to gather pace by its Roman historian, elaborating the original histories four hundred years after the event. First, Alexander is said to have received Philotas alone and when Philotas begged forgiveness, Alexander gave him his right hand as a sign that his negligence was not to be punished. Philotas left the tent and Alexander promptly called his closest friends to ask for their opinions. They had no fondness for Philotas, and were led by the loyal Craterus to take the opportunity and turn the king against him. It was this encouragement which proved decisive.

That evening Philotas was due to dine in the royal tent. He arrived punctually, was received without comment by friends who hated him and took his place near Alexander. No change of mood was betrayed. As one course followed another, the guests talked of their orders for the morrow; the army was to leave the camp at daybreak and in expectation of a hard day's march the party broke up at a reasonable hour. Philotas retired to his tent, but at midnight he awoke to the tramp of the royal Shield Bearers: they had come to put him in chains. All the roads out of camp had already been blocked against his escape.

This setting, though vivid, is more than likely to have been invented for a Roman readership, well used to such dissimulation from their emperors. Alexander could afford to act bluntly, and Ptolemy, the only eyewitness, says no more than that Philotas was arrested and brought before the Macedonians where Alexander accused him 'vigorously'; Philotas defended himself, but 'the informers came forward and convicted him and his associates on several obvious charges', conspiracy no doubt among them, 'and especially for the fact that Philotas himself had learnt of a plot, as he admitted, but had suppressed any mention of it'. Philotas and 'those who helped him conspire' were speared by the Macedonians. Others said, probably wrongly, that after his trial Philotas was tortured until he confessed, and only then put to death by stoning. His confession, if true, would say more for the torture than for his guilt: Ptolemy, it seems, added no such 'proof' of the victim's complicity, nor even the stoning which suggested Philotas's guilt. It is the one death penalty which is communal, involving a crowd who must therefore believe in their victim's crime.

Not satisfied with seven culprits, Alexander extended his inquiry. Among his officers, there were four brothers of highland Tymphiot family and dangerous because of their friendships with Philotas. One of them had long ranked high as leader of a phalanx battalion; another had fled as soon as Philotas was known to be arrested and his flight was so suspicious that the other three were hauled before the soldiery and tried for their lives. But their defence was spirited and they managed to acquit themselves; at once they asked leave to fetch their other brother back, a request which seemed to guarantee their innocence, and so with a clear name, they retained their positions of trust. Amyntas died from an arrow wound two months later; Attalus took over his dead brother's brigade

1. Alexander wearing the diadem and horn of Zeus Ammon. The idealized features suggest his divinity. Silver coin of his successor Lysimachus, c. 290 BC.

2. Gold coin of Philip's reign, showing the god Apollo; the features strongly suggest Alexander's own. Comparisons with the god were frequently used afterwards for young and talented princes.

3. Pebble mosaic from Pella c. 300 BC. Alexander, on the left, is being rescued from a lion by Craterus in their famous lion hunt at Sidon in 333.

4. The 'Alexander Sarcophagus', probably made for Alexander's host, the King of Sidon, c.. 320 BC. Alexander, wearing the lion's head helmet of Heracles, attacks Persian horsemen at Issus. The style is very exact, even showing the harness of Bucephalas.

5. Door relief from the Hundred Columned Hall at Persepolis. At the top is the symbol of the protecting god Ahura Mazda, bordered by royal lions. Below sits Darius I (522-486) attended by the Royal Fly-swatter, an ancient and enduring minister of oriental kings. The enlarged throne which frames the lower panel is supported by subject peoples of the empire, among them the Macedonians. Its design of lion's paw feet is seen on the right above characteristic bell capitals used in Persian palaces, and remained a dominant style for thrones in Iran even after Alexander's conquest.

6. Relief from Persepolis of Indian envoy bringing tribute to the Persian New Year Festival. He wears the turban, sandals and cotton robe of his people and leads a wild ass. The baskets before him may carry pearls or perhaps gold dust, tribute of the province.

7. Road to Herat followed by Alexander. Such heavy laden mules would have served as his main baggage train in increasingly rough country where wheeled transport was impossible.

8. Remains near Kandahar of Alexandria-in-Arachosia, founded by Alexander. The name Kandahar is more likely to be derived from Gandahara, the old Persian name for the district, than from Alexandria.

9. Village at the foot of the Khaiwak Pass, by which Alexander probably crossed the Hindu Kush. The village is a later one but the style of the houses with a dome on a square base was noted in the area by Alexander's officers.

10. A Mede, probably steward of the entire Royal Household, bows in audience before Darius I, seated to the left out of the picture. The Mede's hand has finished paying **proskynesis.** Some have thought he is shielding his breath from the sacred fire, but the objects in front of him are plainly incense burners.

11. The inner section of a silver plate from Greek Bactria, possibly late third century BC, to be worn on a bridle. The howdah's towers match possible Greek city walls in the area and may have been a Greek invention. The mahout's goad, the elephant's bell and the griffin on his saddle were all used in the East before Alexander. A similar plate was found in the eighteenth century in the Channel Islands: the widest known spread of a Hellenistic elephant and as yet unexplained.

12. Wooden coffin still used by the Kafirs in Nuristan, alone among Afghan tribesmen. The coffins mistaken by Alexander's men for firewood in this area were presumably the ancestors of this distinctive style. Greek influence, perhaps from later Greek kingdoms in Bactria, has also been noted in the carved pillars of Kafir buildings.

13. Modern raft of goat skin for use near the Oxus. These rafts are sewn and stuffed with chaff, one of Asia's oldest skills. The Assyrian armies used them in the seventh century BC; Alexander crossed the Danube and Oxus by the same method; Roman armies kept a unit of 'bladder bearers' for the purpose. A man can float on one skin only, but this large raft could carry up to 400 lbs.

14. View of the Swat highlands entered by Alexander in the autumn of 327.

15. Tomb of Cyrus the Great at Pasargadae built c. 530.

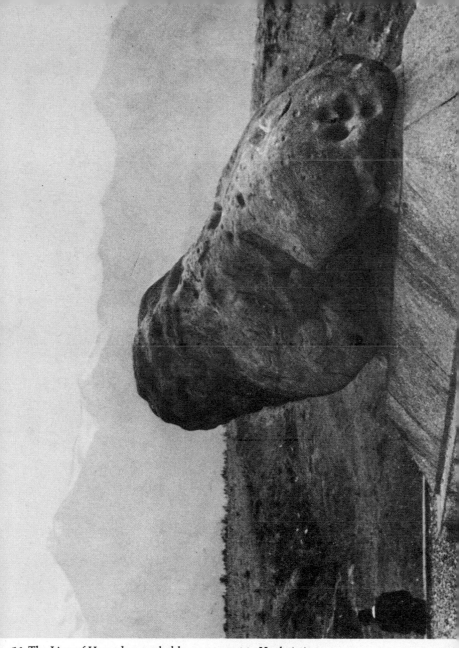

16. The Lion of Hamadan, probable monument to Hephaistion.

17. The funeral chariot to take Alexander's body from Babylon. The detailed
ancient description is the basis for this outline reconstruction by G. Niemann.

and eventually married a daughter of Perdiccas, a well-judged alliance; Polemon made progress from his brother's marriage and reappeared after Alexander's death as an admiral in Perdiccas's fleet. They are a rare example of a family who survived a crisis and backed a rising star.

Once again, there was more to the story than Ptolemy implied. It was three years since Alexander of Lyncestis had been put in custody as a possible traitor, and in the meantime he had been kept with the king as a prisoner too dangerous to be abandoned. Now was the moment to remove him in public; perhaps he had been involved in the plot, perhaps he was no more than a plausible suspect, but Alexander arranged that the leader of the Shield Bearers should begin the prosecution before an army who were ready to expect treason from any quarter. Alexander of Lyncestis heard the case, faltered and found nothing to say in reply, perhaps because the charges went beyond the truth, perhaps because he was involved with the plot of an obscure Oriental called Sisines of whom he remembered nothing. Bystanders speared him to death; the incident was too unsavoury for the histories of Ptolemy and Aristobulus, a sign of the feelings it could have aroused.

The sequel was too infamous to be suppressed. In a crisis Alexander turned his thoughts to the most dangerous suspect of them all. Philotas was son of Parmenion; Parmenion was miles away in Hamadan, commanding the treasuries, the crossroads of the empire and up to 20,000 troops. There was also the danger of Cleitus and the 6,000 Macedonians; they had not yet rejoined the army and at best they were a few miles down the road from Hamadan. Parmenion could recall them and tip the balance between the two halves of the army if it came to an open fight. It was a month's march back to Hamadan down a road still threatened by Satibarzanes.

As usual, Alexander knew the means and the man for the job. He sent for Polydamas a friend of Parmenion, who arrived in trepidation, fearing that his friendship was now to cost him his life. Alexander played on his anxieties and only told him as much as was good for him to know; when Polydamas heard what was required, he obeyed, thankful that the past was not to be held against him. He was to take letters to Parmenion, one from Alexander, one signed with Philotas's seal; he was to give written orders to the generals under Parmenion's command. The journey was urgent, the main road was neither direct nor secure; he was to dress like a native and travel by racing camel directly through the intervening Dasht-i-lut desert. Two guides would show him the way, while his younger brothers were detained as hostages.

Polydamas hurried about his innocent business. The camels were made ready; the desert caused them no distress. On the eleventh day they reached Hamadan, having reduced the journey by three weeks and shown that remarkable speed over waste land which was later to make them the spearhead of Arab armies. Parmenion's generals were sought out, as ordered, and given their written message; their leader, a Macedonian noble, said that Parmenion would best be approached on the following morning. The generals conferred while the messenger retired.

Soon after dawn, Parmenion was ready to receive his visitor. He was taking a walk, it was said, in the palace gardens of Hamadan with the generals at his side; his friend's appearance pleased him and after an embrace, he began to undo his letters. First, a note from Alexander with news of a further expedition; then, the communication sealed as if from his son Philotas. He began to read it 'with an expression of evident pleasure', when his generals drew their daggers and stabbed him repeatedly. Only then would Polydamas realize the horror of his mission; he had been sent, not with a tactical message but with orders for the murder of his friend. Being well known to Parmenion, he had not aroused his suspicions.'

The news caused a commotion in Hamadan. The soldiers threatened to mutiny unless the murderers surrendered, and they were not pacified until Alexander's letters had been read aloud, explaining that Parmenion and Philotas had conspired disgracefully against the king's life. That was enough to satisfy humble men, and within five weeks, some of them had joined Alexander's main troops in Seistan. But what was good enough for the army is not good enough for history. The deaths of Philotas and Parmenion were moments of high crisis whose effects were felt throughout the high command. They need a delicate investigation.

There can be no doubt that a plot had indeed been formed against the king. Dimnus, the first to reveal this information, had killed himself when summoned; such a prompt suicide can only have been due to a guilty conscience, for he knew he was certain to die and he did not intend to talk first. As for the names he had already revealed to his lover, all are otherwise unknown, though men of a certain rank, and they contain no clue to a motive. But their ambitions are less arguable. They were a group of six and they must have discussed the future before they acted. They were proposing to kill the most remarkable king and general in all ancient history and leave the army divided and leaderless in the wastes of Seistan with a rebel raising troops beyond them and the lands behind them far from peaceful. One man, slighted personally, might have struck irresponsibly to satisfy a passion. But a group of six would have had plans for a replacement, especially in the face of Alexander's intimate bodyguards, not the men to sit idle after a murder. It is here that Philotas, son of Parmenion, comes into question.

Philotas, though powerful, had long been the subject of gossip and suspicion. He had served the king as a friend since boyhood, but the past suggests they had never been very close. When Alexander's young circle of friends had been exiled by Philip seven years before, Philotas had stood on the edge of the group, perhaps as informant against others. Then, in the intrigues of Alexander's first months, he had nearly chosen the wrong side; he had been a friend of Amyntas, the former king whom Philip had supplanted and Alexander put to death, and he had married his sister to Attalus, Alexander's bitterest enemy. But unlike others, he had put his misjudgements behind him: within months, he had been invited to command the Companion Cavalry, a remarkable honour for a young man and no doubt due to his father's influence. It was a demanding job and in all the pitched battles, he had fought under Alexander's own command. Presumably they would argue about their respective heroics. Neither was the man to belittle his own abilities, and soon their relationship had come under strain.

Among the spoils taken after Issus, Parmenion had found a noble Macedonian lady called Antigone, whom the Persian fleet had captured during the summer before the battle. She had been sailing from home to take part in the mystery religion on the Aegean island of Samothrace. Philotas had fancied her and taken her on as his mistress; in bed of an evening, they would tease and tell tall stories with all the silliness of perfect intimacy. Philotas would drink and brag of his own incomparable prowess: he and Parmenion, to be quite honest, had done all the work, while Alexander was only a little boy who ruled in their name. Antigone thought him bold and amusing, and she told her friends. The friends told one another until word came to Craterus, the king's devoted general. Antigone was summoned and bidden to continue her affair. But all such boasting and scraps of insolence were now to be passed to Alexander.

It was a year later, in Egypt, said Ptolemy, that Philotas was first reported for plotting, but Alexander had disbelieved the rumour 'because of their long friendship and his own esteem for Parmenion'. It is hard to know how to treat this. Possibly the rumour was invented to make the eventual conspiracy seem more plausible; possibly, but Philotas's youngest brother had recently been drowned in the river Nile, an accident which may have embittered the family and caused Philotas to voice his annoyance again to his mistress. And yet, since Egypt, these vague suspicions had not brought him down. He was boastful and rich; his hunting nets were rumoured to stretch for more than twelve miles, and even Parmenion had warned him 'to be less of a person'. But the advice was painful when the family's power was beginning to ebb away.

When Seistan was reached, Parmenion was past seventy and Philotas his only son left alive. A month before, his second son, who commanded the Shield Bearers, had died in Aria's desert and Alexander had been too short of supplies to stop and honour him. Philotas had been left to attend to his funeral and, as in Egypt, he may have reflected with distaste on a family bereavement. Two other associates had recently died or been sent away to the provinces and Parmenion himself was far removed in Hamadan, where he might soon be retired. Briefly, he controlled the roads, the treasure and 20,000 foreign troops, enough to be dangerous, even under four independent commanders; there were also Cleitus's 6,000 veterans, out of Alexander's reach for the first and last time. Alexander had at most 32,000 men with him, but in another two months, the main army might be reunited with Cleitus and the others and Parmenion might be dead. It was a last chance. If Alexander was removed, father and son could combine to create a new king, none more plausible than Alexander of Lyncestis, son-in-law of the viceroy Antipater and himself of princely blood. Returning from his brother's funeral, Philotas would have the chance to plan and involve the six accomplices who finally let him down.

The conspirators still had to be persuaded, and here there were principles which might be invoked. Only six weeks before, Alexander had worn Persian dress for the first time, having ended his Greek expedition and dismissed the Greek allies who had fought so often under Parmenion. The new dress and court life were a symbol of new ambitions which would not be satisfied until all Asia had been overrun; meanwhile, the Persians would be respected rather than punished, perhaps to the disgust of that same Philotas who at Susa had urged Alexander to use the Persian king's table as a mere footstool beneath his feet. In the course of the trial a detail is said to have been mentioned, too unusual perhaps to be only a history's fiction; Alexander denounced Philotas for speaking in Greek and disdaining the Macedonian dialect of the listening soldiery. Alexander may have seized on a charge which could otherwise have been turned against himself. If any soldier thought that his Persian customs betrayed Macedonian traditions, let him first consider the case of Philotas, too haughty even to use the native dialect. The king's prosecution may have been more than vigorous, for it may have played on the prejudice of ordinary men. But similar prejudice may first have encouraged the conspirators; they may have wanted a Macedonian monarchy, no dalliance with the diadem and, after plunder, a return to western Asia. Conspiracy followed fast on the change in Alexander's myth: 'Alexander was right', wrote Napoleon, in retirement on St Helena, 'to have Parmenion and his son killed, because they were blockheads who considered it wrong to abandon the customs of the Greeks.' When two events are so close in time, it is indeed attractive to link them as cause and effect.

This background of principles and personalities makes Philotas's guilt very plausible, but it is not enough to prove it. For in Philotas's case, so far as it is known, there were few solid truths which the informers could have adduced. They cannot have known him to be involved in the conspiracy, for they chose him as the fit man to expose it to Alexander; there were further accomplices of whom they were unaware at the time, but their ignorance about Philotas cannot have lent support to their other evidence. Had Philotas indeed been plotting, he would have welcomed the informer's approaches as a stroke of extraordinary luck; he could have arranged for them to be silenced or at least acted swiftly before they turned to anyone else. But he had done neither: he had simply suppressed their rumour, and although this negligence was held against him it strongly suggests that he had no part in the conspiracy. He did not take it seriously, because he did not care: that, perhaps, was criminal in its own right, especially to Alexander's friends who hated him anyway. In Seistan influence ran strongest among the bodyguards and baronial leaders of the phalanx, Craterus again most prominent among them. But Philotas was a cavalryman, whose platoons had been subdivided a year ago between minions chosen for merit, not nobles distinguished by birth. He was vulnerable, therefore, and unpopular: enemies led by Craterus, may have seized their chance to bring him down.

Even so the affair is more of a mystery than a scandal. A letter is said to have been cited, written by Parmenion to his two sons, at least a month before: 'First, take care for yourselves, for in that way, we shall bring off our plans.' Even if genuine, it was most ambiguous: it helped little that Philotas, as a last resort, blamed the design on a certain Hegelochus, as Hegelochus was recently dead. Nobody believed that Philotas was innocent and it is absurd to idealize him as a martyr to Alexander's ruthlessness simply because the histories explain so little. Neither the timing nor the method of his death suggest the affair was a ruthless purge. Had Alexander wished to kill an innocent man, he could have poisoned him, exposed him in battle or quietly lost him on the next mountain march; he had no need to prosecute him clumsily in a public trial, where other suspects contrived to acquit themselves despite his prosecution. Above all, the moment was far from ripe for sly murder. A ruthless intriguer would first have detached Parmenion from his resources, waited for Cleitus and the 6,000 veterans and then pounced secretly: the man who staged an inopportune trial in Seistan must surely have believed that right, and a grievance, were suddenly on his side. Numbers, certainly, were not.

Whatever its precise justice, condemnation of Philotas made Parmenion's murder inevitable. It was a grave risk but it had to be taken, for Parmenion was the most powerful figure in the entire army, well up to the art of judicial murder himself and he could not possibly have been left alive to use his resources and supporters for a rebellion based on Hamadan. A fight against Cleitus's veterans and 20,000 troops was not to be relished, especially when they held the money and could find more food. Parmenion, powerful father to a condemned son, was a threat quite unprecedented since Alexander's accession, and it is not in the least surprising that in self-defence Alexander arranged his assassination. It is irrelevant to complain that he might have mistaken his general's ambitions; among Macedonians, the king who waited in a crisis in order to be certain would find himself dead first. There was no law to protect and limit the monarchy: custom could be ignored by a strong character, and self-preservation went just as far as the people would condone. It was said, perhaps correctly, that the soldiery in Seistan had approved Parmenion's murder before it was ordered: certainly, most of them cared little when they heard of it, and even the troops in Hamadan were pacified. Alexander had friends there, among them Harpalus the treasurer, and they had seen him through; doubtless by royal request, it was now that Parmenion's memory would be blackened in court histories. The victory on the Granicus, the burning of Persepolis were probably rewritten against a murdered general.

Among the officers there was consternation. The noblemen in the cavalry panicked and began to fly to the desert, fearing their past friendships in the light of what had happened. Alexander was forced to announce that relations of the conspirators would not now be punished, although his rapid treatment of Philotas's father had implied exactly the opposite. In an emergency nothing breaks quicker than a clique of family and friends: Philotas, for example, had been accused most vigorously by his own brother-in-law, while Parmenion had been murdered by this same turncoat's brother in Hamadan. Such men were scared of their former connections, and they betrayed them decisively. Others, absent from camp, could not be so bold; Asander, perhaps the brother or nephew of Parmenion, was away in the west raising reinforcements, but he is not known to have received another job when he arrived in camp a year and a half later. Possibly he died of sickness or a wound, but more probably Parmenion's name was held against him.

With the plot only half-uncovered, Alexander could not afford to be too magnanimous. For some months the army's letters home had been opened and censored in secret: now Parmenion's few known sympathizers were separated into a unit known as the Disorderlies, along with any who had complained in their letters of military service. Their discipline was to be stern, but 'no group was ever keener for war: they were all the braver for being disgraced, both because they wished to redeem themselves and because courage was more conspicuous in a small unit': any who malingered could always be abandoned in the next Alexandria.

There remained the Companion cavalry. They had been led by Philotas 'but it was not thought safe to entrust them now to any one man'. Hephaistion took half the command as an officer above suspicion and known to sympathize with Alexander's Persian customs; the other half was left open until the missing 6,000 Macedonians arrived from Hamadan. Their loyalty, or their ignorance, had helped to decide Parmenion's fate. Many were veterans, Philip's men, and they arrived to find a court much changed from the one they had left at Hamadan; their king had his eunuchs, ushers and diadem. Their loyalty had to be repaid and reassured; they had been led to camp by Cleitus, also a veteran and the most experienced leader of cavalry. Cleitus was named as the second Hipparch, beside Hephaistion who had never led horsemen. His promotion would steady a shaken high command, but it was a reward not altogether of Alexander's choosing.

The last and only certain word went to Alexander himself. Before he left Farah he decided to rename it Prophthasia, a puzzle only until the name is translated. For Prophthasia is the Greek for Anticipation: here, then, is how Alexander saw himself, not as a judge with certain evidence, but as a king who had struck others before they could strike him first. The justice or injustice of Philotas's plot will never be known precisely, any more than Alexander had waited to know it precisely himself. But for the first time in history a conspiracy had been put on the map; its survivor had acted fast and as the Wind of Seistan at last began to drop, it was time for him to consider how best to advance his anticipation elsewhere.

CHAPTER TWENTY-ONE

Within days of his anticipation, Alexander set out on a march of exemplary daring. His aim was to capture Bessus and his Bactrian province, not to humble any latent mutineers: to this end, he abandoned the Iranian provinces behind him, though Satibarzanes was still uncaptured, and prepared for such cold and starvation as could never have been risked unless the men and the officers were believed to be trustworthy. Common morale and personal example would alone bring them through: neither army nor leader disappointed.

In late September 330, he left Farah and followed the regular desert road eastwards towards Kandahar and the outlying hills of the Hindu Kush range; Cleitus's 6,000 men joined him within a month, so he was leading more than 40,000 men into country where supplies could not be moved by wagon, where pack animals would find the going treacherous and where the oncoming winter would hinder him from living off the land. For the past two months, his army had been short of food and thus it was no surprise when Alexander favoured a tribe on the borders of Seistan, 'personally observing that they did not govern themselves like other barbarians in the area but claimed to use justice like the Greeks'. These fair-minded people were the Arimaspoi or Benefactors who had rescued Cyrus and his Persian army from starvation two hundred years earlier: by origin, they had been nomadic Scythians who perhaps had wrecked the early city-culture of Seistan, but on their second appearance in history, food as much as political theory caused Cyrus's self-styled heir to give them money and whatever lands they wanted. They were to be governed by Darius's former secretary.

Nearer to Kandahar, the desert landscape breaks into comparative lushness round the middle course of the Helmand river. The province, called Arachosia, was known to the Persians as the well-watered land, a name which Alexander's staff transcribed into Greek: besides its fertility it also commands the narrow corridor between the peaks which stretch north-east to inner Afghanistan. Persian history had long shown the importance of its satrap, and for the first time since Gaugamela Alexander removed a province entirely from Oriental hands, appointing an experienced Macedonian, perhaps to sole command; perhaps, too, the change reflected protests in the recent conspiracy. Troops were left to keep the communications open and the satrap was ordered to settle in modern Kandahar, now to be expanded with 4,000 troops and renamed Alexandria. In late November Alexander left the warmth of this low-lying land and began the severer route up country: he would cross the mountains of the Hindu Kush and search the surrounds of Balkh for Bessus. The march was tactical but nonetheless remarkable. The Hindu-Kush runs north and south like a dragon's backbone between India and Iran; it first earned its modern name, meaning Hindu-killer, from the heavy death-rate of the Indian slavewomen who were herded into Iran through its passes by mediaeval entrepreneurs. Among ancient mountaineers, it is Hannibal who nowadays holds pride of place for his crossing of the Alps. But Alexander's army was larger than the Carthaginian's and his road was no less spectacular. Unlike Hannibal, he had the sense to leave elephants out of an uncongenial adventure; any present in his army could have been loosed in the elephant parks to the west of Kandahar, known to the Persians and still patronized by the Ghasnavid kings some 1500 years later. There they could wallow in swamps of warm mud, happy in the winter comforts which they needed.

The men and their pack-animals were less fortunate. News arrived, unpleasantly, that Satibarzanes had indeed returned to the tribesmen round Herat and begun to raise another revolt among the Iranians of Parthia and Aria. Alexander must have regretted his initial trust in him, as he was now threatened in his rear by a valuable source of support for Bessus, who had given the rebel help and horsemen from his base at Balkh. Short of troops, he could only detach a mere 6,000 troops to protect Herat's garrison; the main army of at most 32,000 were ordered to continue their long hard course up the Helmand valley, menaced by winter, famine and rebellions ahead and behind them. Their numbers had hardly sunk so low before. They are unlikely to have followed the line of the modern road from Kandahar to Kabul, the 320-mile stretch which was to be made so famous to Victorian Englishmen of the 1880s by the relief march of General Roberts; native guides and the old Persian road kept them on the rougher and more mountainous ground to the east and must have brought them up by the long-used road through Gardez, later a Greek city, and so briefly on to the shoulders which descend on their eastern slope to the valleys of the Punjab. It was here that they met with a tribe which the Persians knew as Indians, a loose description of an outlying people from the plains of West Pakistan, but as food was very scarce there was no time to waste on these first indications of a world beyond. The winter skies hung morosely over thick-lying snow and the more the soldiers climbed the more they were distressed by the thinness of the atmosphere. Stragglers were soon lost in the murky light and left to frost-bite and a certain death; others blundered into snowdrifts which were indistinguishable from the level whiteness of the ridges. Shelter was sought wherever possible, but it needed sharp eyes to pick out the native huts of mudbrick whose roofs, as nowadays, were rounded into a dome above the deepening snows. Once found, the natives were amenable and brought as many supplies as they could spare: 'Food,' wrote the officers, 'was found in plenty, except', nostalgically, 'for olive oil'. But there is no means of huddling 32,000 men away from the winter in the gorges which led towards Begram and Kabul; the army's one hope of relief was to keep on moving, while Alexander did what he could to keep up morale: he helped along those who were stumbling and he lifted up any who had fallen. Self-denial had long been a principle of his leadership.

But the march was not a wanton struggle against nature. By moving in winter, Alexander had surprised the mountain tribes and as British armies were to discover, snow and ice were far preferable to ambush by natives who knew and cared for the surrounding hills. There was also the likeli-hood of catching Bessus unawares. Safe beyond the Hindu Kush, he might expect to be left alone or at least not invaded until late summer; meanwhile, when the snow had melted, he could ride due west to Herat through the passes he had closed and join Satibarzanes in the revolt which had even spread to Parthia, a grave threat. Then if Alexander came down into Bactria his communications with the west could be cut and he could be isolated in the hot nomadic satrapies along the river Oxus. Foolishly, but understandably, Bessus made no attempt to block the Hindu Kush's northern passes so early in the year. He did not believe that his enemy would brave them, but with Alexander, nothing was safely incredible: his anticipation was not confined to members of Parmenion's family, and so as soon as possible he attempted the mountain-barrier.

East of modern Kabul, the army returned to the valleys along the modern main road into India and relaxed in smoother ground. They were still ringed round by mountains, but with the worst of the journey before them, they were allowed a three-month winter camp at the Persians' satrapal capital of Kapisa. Again, Alexander was moved to refound a Persian fort, settling it as a Greek city with 7,000 natives and with veterans and such hired troops as he could spare from his dwindling army. The result, known as Alexandria-in-the-Caucasus, has never been found on the ground, though brief French excavations at Borj-i-Abdulla south of modern Begram have uncovered traces of Greek towers and the wall of a city which succeeded Alexandria 150 years later. On the gentle slopes of these foothills, the most abundant basin in the area, the city was surely intended to guard the ancient routes through the Hindu Kush, for in the valleys of Begram and Kabul no less than three main roads converge, while the citadel overlooked the confluence of two main rivers, the Persian's favourite site for such a fort. For the past two hundred years since Cyrus, the Persians had maintained a garrison town on the same strategic site; Alexander, as so often in the far east, had taken the cue for an Alexandria from his Persian predecessors. The new town's style of life, if not its site, was entirely different: there had never been a theatre in a Persian outpost, but 150 years after Alexander, Alexandria-in-the-Caucasus still contained carvings of Greek comic actors, dressed for the stage which had flourished inside its walls. Even by a road-post for veterans the banner of Greek culture was defiantly raised in an Afghan valley.

Not until May, a seven-month delay, would Alexander have 'sacrificed to the usual gods'. the most easterly sacrifice that had yet been wafted to the Olympians, and exhorted his army to the climax of their march. Like Tamurlane after him, he was to climb the northern buttress of the Hindu Kush by the Khaiwak pass, which rises to a height of 11,000 feet before dropping down to the plains of Bactria and further Asia beyond. The south and nearer face, which rears to the sky beyond Begram, was not attempted until the snows began to melt. Hunger, not cold, was the problem. The march to the summit took a week, and supplies throughout were desperately scarce except for the plants of terebinth and asa fœtida, savoury but insubstantial herbs. Though the histories hurry over the experience a background of landscape can still be restored. There is an intensity of sunrise and sunset in these Afghan mountains which even the hill-farmers of upper Macedonia cannot have watched unmoved. The light throws patches of blue and violet on to the melting snow, striking the pink mountain rock and the grey clumps of prickly thrift, a plant as sharp as a hedgehog which carpets the slopes and discomforts the unwary traveller. 'A thin purple veil', a German explorer has written, travelling, like Alexander, through the Hindu Kush in the early season, 'very subdued and as misty as a breeze was daily drawn across the eastern sky. As I gazed, the clouds turned to flame and blood-red; the snowy peaks were glowing while a deep and inexpressible yearning filled me through and through.' That same sense of yearning was seen in Alexander by his fairest Roman historian, perhaps correctly; it was an emotion which drove him in search of myth or places of mystery; it was proper to a king living out the Homeric past. In the Hindu Kush myth and landscape combined as if to bring it into play.

'In the middle of the mountains, there was a rock half a mile high in which the cave of Prometheus was pointed out by the natives, along with the nest of the mythical eagle and the marks of his chains.' In Greek legend, the hero Prometheus was punished for his inventive intelligence and imprisoned by Zeus on an eastern rock where an eagle would gnaw at his liver; here in the Hindu Kush, the site of his punishment seemed at last to have been discovered. But this greatest of all myths had always been placed in the Caucasus, miles away to the north-west; in order to reconcile myth and geography, Alexander's staff maintained that the Hindu Kush was attached to the Caucasus as an easterly continuation. Ever since, scholars ancient and modern have treated their mistake unkindly, dismissing it as a flattery which deliberately brought Alexander into contact with the distant Caucasus mountains, an area which he never reached. But that is to misunderstand a very human error. The Greek name for the Hindu Kush, the Paropamisus, was derived from the Persian word 'uparisena', meaning 'peak over which the eagle cannot fly'. The eagle was part of local knowledge, and as with Prometheus it was a symbol with a history of its own; in local Iranian myth, the eagle Sena had saved the hero Dastan, son of Sam, from cruel imprisonment. Alexander's staff were evidently told the story by the natives and at once equated the details with their own Prometheus; if these mountains confined the mythical eagle, they must be the Caucasus whatever the geography, for that was where Prometheus and his eagle were known to lie. The marks of the chains were easily detected in the jaggedness of a Hindu Kush rockface: to Alexander's officers, geography was only accurate if first it fitted myth, and although the Hindu Kush is grander than Greek mountains and as weathered a brown as its natives' bread, it is a landscape with a definite feel of Greece.

While the foothills of the south face offered myth, the summit of the so-called Caucasus promised even greater rewards. Aristotle, who knew nothing of China and Far Asia, believed that the eastern edge of the world could be seen from the top of the Hindu Kush, and perhaps his former pupil remembered this, if anything, from any school hours spent in geography; the belief may have been common too among ordinary Greeks, and for a man aged twenty-six there could be no more momentous ambition. A short march eastwards, and he could survey the boundary of the world and see how the border lands of India merged with the eddying ocean. To an explorer such an ambition needs no further justification, while to an Achilles any fighting to attain it was so much more service in the cause of glory. From the top of the Khaiwak pass, Aristotle's geography would already seem suspect to anyone in the army who remembered it. Ridge upon ridge of mountains rose eastwards, but for the moment Bessus mattered more than the problem of the world's end, and the army was coaxed northwards in search of him down the far face of the Hindu Kush.

The descent lasted at most ten days; it was intolerable throughout. The snow, facing northwards, still lay heavily and masked the line of the pass; only a parallel can show what this might mean. In April 1398 Tamurlane crossed the same face of the Khaiwak, forcing himself and his Mongols to crawl its glaciers on hands and knees, drag their pack-animals by wooden sledge and swing across its open ravines on rope bridges lassoed round prominent rocks; more men were lost in the crossing than in the whole of the campaign year. Alexander's horses would have been fitted with the leather snowboots, which Greek generals found useful against deep or slippery drifts; nonetheless, they suffered severely, as their needs took second place to their riders'. The natives had stored their supplies in underground pits which were hard to find and harder to break open: famine, therefore, spread through the army, as the few available jars of wine and honey were sold at absurdly high prices. On the lower slopes, where herbs and the famous brown trout of the rivers filled out the soldiers' diet, the animals found no fodder and orders were soon given to slaughter them and use them as meat. The scrub bushes of prickly thrift, which served the natives as firewood, were still buried under the snow; in the absence of any other fuel, horse and pack-ass were seasoned with the juice of silphium and eaten raw.

The troops were saved by Bessus's incompetence and a coincidental victory near Herat. While Alexander struggled down from the Hindu Kush, a brisk cavalry charge could have disarrayed him, especially as Bessus had begun to burn the crops in the plains. Instead of following up this devastation, Bessus took fright, probably at bad news from Satibarzanes and the west, and galloped some two hundred miles northwards across the Oxus, only halting to burn his boats for good measure. It was very poor generalship and his 8,000 local Bactrian cavalry deserted in disgust, seeing little alternative but to join in the rapid surrender of their rich home province. Descending from the foothills in early June, Alexander made his untroubled way through Kunduz to the local capital of Balkh, mother of cities, and allowed his troops to refresh themselves in its relatively generous oasis. He also needed to wait for the rest of his baggage and siege equipment to catch up his advance.

Set on a stream of water, Balkh was far older than the Persians' empire and must have served as the centre for Bactria's earliest traders at least a thousand years before it fell to the Great King; 'flag-bearing', the Persians' sacred poems had called it, and besides the Persian flag its palace had been adorned with the image of Anahita, water goddess of the Oxus and very suitable for Balkh's oasis, where she was worshipped in her crown of stars and cloak of holy otter-hides.

To a man coming down from the Khaiwak pass, the province of Balkh, 'land of a thousand cities', lies stretched out like a fading carpet. It wears its place in history clearly on its surface: its plains alternate between gravel desert and pockets of fertility, the one a home for nomads, the other for settled villages, and the two landscapes have lived in continual mistrust. For those who controlled them, the province had rich resources: river-gold, superlative horses, mines of silver and rubies, and in the north-eastern hills of Badakshan, the Persian empire's only known source of lapis lazuli, whose blue fragments had been traded with Seistan and the south as a pleasure and a currency for the past 2,000 years. The villages conformed to the tensions of their landscape: they were built for self-defence behind the square of a mudbrick wall on whose inner face the village houses abutted, leaving room in the centre of the village for flocks to be stabled in case of invasion. Fortified turrets held each corner of the wall, while a watch-tower surveyed entry by the central gate: the pattern, like a toy fort, remains in the *qal'eh* villages of outer Iran, invented and maintained for refuge against nomads. Nomads, therefore, both within the province and to the north and north-west of its Oxus boundary, were the hazard which Alexander could deduce from the villages he saw around him.

In this strange and distant world the Persians had ruled through the local baronry, who lived secure in castles and rockbound fortresses, attended by troupes of retainers. Their satrap was often a blood-relation of the king, but he married into the Bactrian nobility and relied on his local in-laws to support him; Alexander, who recognized the easy virtues of Persian administration, did not wish to disturb the past, preferring to find an Iranian fit to continue it. Most opportunely the elderly Persian Artabazus arrived in Balkh in early June. As an experienced satrap in the west and a very old friend of the Macedonian royal family, he was also the nearest Alexander could come to a blood relation among the Iranians, for Artabazus was father of Barsine, the mistress whom Alexander had taken after Issus. It was good to see him again, especially as he had come with cheerful military news. He had been leading the cavalry against Satibarzanes' rebellion around Herat, and now reported that he and his three fellow-generals had routed Bessus's rebel associates in a fierce and distinguished cavalry charge and had lanced Satibarzanes himself to death. Presumably, it was this news which had caused Bessus to retreat with such

298

ill-advised rapidity. Alexander's mistaken trust in a rebel had at last been atoned for; he was now safe from the rear, and he could appoint the trusted Artabazus, father of his mistress, to govern his fellow-Iranians in Bactria. Local tradition was thus respected, and as the late June sun warmed up, the army left Balkh on Bessus's dwindling trail, a prospect tougher than they knew. They numbered scarcely 30,000, but they followed uncomplainingly, not the behaviour of men discontented with their leader's recent purge, his ambitions or his sparse adoption of a few Persian customs. He was still the Alexander they loved, for whose sake they had marched from Persepolis, looped through 3,000 miles of desert, starved, and crossed the snowbound barrier between two worlds in the course of a single year.

From Balkh, Bessus's trail stretched north to the Oxus through fifty miles of pebbled desert. The same troops and horses who had been freezing a month before now suffered dreadfully from the midsummer heat, unable to swallow the little water which their guides had advised them to carry. It was impossible to travel by day, when the heat-haze shimmered deceptively over the sand and even the lizards retired beneath the gravel; night was hardly kinder, though the more pious histories omitted all mention of the men's losses. Throughout, Alexander showed why he could ask so much of his army: when water was brought to him in a helmet, scooped from a small desert spring, he refused to accept the privilege, and tipped it away, sharing his soldiers' hardships. When the river Oxus was finally reached, the army was so scattered that fires had to be lit on a nearby hill to direct them into camp. Alexander 'stood by their route and refused to take food or drink or refresh himself in any way, until the entire army had passed him by'. The men took heart from his example, and late that night Alexander and his army slept in camp near Kilif, where the yellowing waters of the Oxus narrow and their current, slowed by reeds, floats by.

Before crossing on the morrow, the oldest Macedonians, the unfit and the few Thessalian horsemen who had volunteered at Hamadan were paid generously and sent back home with orders to father children, the soldiers of the future: they would rather have been spared their last fifty miles. The river Oxus is broad and lazy, and five days after their fellows' departure, the rest of the army were already on its far bank, helped by a well-known Oriental method of transport. Bessus had burnt the native boats and there was no local timber to build a bridge, so the troops stitched up their leather tentskins, as at the Danube, and stuffed them with hay to make floating rafts, to this day the time-honoured means of crossing a river in the east. Once beyond the Oxus, the army at once set foot in Sogdia, the north-eastern province of the Persian empire, from which one of the long-used routes branches off through the desert to China, the lifeline down which merchants of Sogdia would always travel, bringing anything from peaches and lotus to dances and radical religions into the homes of their Chinese clientele. To Alexander's army China was unknown and Sogdia no more than a sandy wasteland of stone and scrubby tamarisk, a site which only promised sickness, skirmishes with tribesmen, or more Alexandrias miles from the olive trees they knew at home. Only Bessus had ever lured them into it.

For the moment, pursuit continued to reward them. Bessus had been incompetent, and like Darius, he suffered from independent courtiers as a result; as the enemy crossed the Oxus, these henchmen seized him and agreed to hand him over. Ptolemy was sent to collect the traitor from a remote village and bring him naked, bound in a wooden collar. When he had been set on the right hand side of Alexander's road, Alexander passed by, stopped his chariot and asked why Bessus had murdered Darius, his lawful king and benefactor. Bessus blamed his helpers, but the excuse was not thought satisfactory: he was ordered to be scourged and proclaimed as an assassin before being taken to Balkh for further punishment. The incident says more for Alexander's shrewdness than his severity. Only a year before, Satibarzanes, another of Darius's murderers had surrendered and received a conspicuous pardon, but like Satibarzanes, Bessus had followed up treachery with rebellion, and rebels, in Alexander's ethic, could only expect the grimmest treatment. Bessus's crime was less that he had helped to kill Darius than that he had claimed to be the new king of Asia. And yet it was as a murderer that he was condemned: in summer 329, Alexander had Orientals serving in his army and he wished to convince them of his new position. He still fought to exact revenge, but not Greek revenge for Persian sacrilege so much as Persian revenge for Darius's murder. Bessus the royal pretender was stripped of his glamour under cover of Alexander's latest myth.

With Bessus safely in chains, the march northwards might have ended, had it not been natural to ride on to the nearby river Jaxartes and claim the north-east frontier of the Persian empire. Near Karshi, Alexander recruited the fine-blooded local horses to replace the many who had died in the desert; near Kungur-tao, the one hill in the sandy monotony of the landscape, his men were harassed by natives while looking, perhaps too desperately, for food. Reprisals are said to have killed some 20,000 natives, though they did manage to hit Alexander hard in the leg with an arrow and break his splint-bone, a danger in a desert climate which invited gangrene. The wound caused a quarrel, not a delay, for Alexander was determined to be carried on a stretcher to keep the expedition moving, and the choice of suitable bearers divided the army. Cavalry and infantry quarrelled for the privilege, a rift which would reopen six years later after Alexander's death. But in Sogdia Alexander was there to settle it and arrange that cavalry and infantry should take the job in turn. Loyalties were satisfied and within four days of desert marching, the army reached Samarkand, as yet a mere mud-walled summer palace of the ruling Iranians, watered by a river which the troops named Polytimetus, the Greek for 'very precious', no doubt a reference to the gold which was washed down its bed and is still remembered in its modern name Zarafshan or 'Scatterer of gold'. From here it was only 180 miles to the frontier river. Native villages were looted for food, burnt where resistant. Alexander, presumably, was still unable to walk.

The frontier was reached in July when humidity sinks as low as five per cent and the shade temperature rises to 43° C. At modern Kurkath, a few miles south of its main ford, the river was guarded by a Persian outpost which Cyrus had settled two hundred years before, and as in the Hindu Kush, Alexander ordered a new Alexandria to replace it: 'He thought that the city would be well sited and suitable for increase, especially as a guard against the tribesmen beyond, and he expected that it would become great both from the numbers of settlers merged into it and from the splendour of its name.' On the last point, he was mistaken; Alexandria-the-furthest was soon harassed by nomads and refounded by his successor as an Antioch, it then became known as modern Khojend, then, as other names seemed splendid, Stalinabad, then Leninabad.

The city's purpose was unmistakable: improved defence of a frontier which had loomed large in the Persians' past. By viewing Persia through the eyes of a western Greek, this anxiety has often been underestimated. To Persians of the future, it was not the defeats by the Greeks at Marathon which lived on as an uneasy memory so much as the fact that their great king Cyrus and their prophet Zoroaster had both died fighting against nomads of the northern steppes. The province of Sogdia was to Asia what Macedonia was to Greece: a buffer between a brittle civilization and the restless barbarians beyond, whether the Scyths of Alexander's day and later or the White Huns, Turks and Mongols who eventually poured south to wreck the thin veneer of Iranian society. In this barrier province, Alexander naturally followed his father's example and strengthened Sogdia, like Philip's Macedonia, with improved towns and military colonies to keep the Scyths where they belonged. Already envoys had crossed the Jaxartes river to talk to the Scythian king and spy out his peoples, the most expert horsemen known to east Iran. They were mobile and dangerous and the glorious art of their bridles, cups, carpets and tents is a reminder that the palace world of Asia and the city life of its Greeks were only brief punctuations in an older world of nomads, as light as dust but no less permanent, and never a society to be undervalued. It was an omen of the times that in a Persian love story, translated into Greek by Alexander's court usher, the villain of the piece had been changed since the mid-sixth century from a Bactrian aristocrat to a Scythian chieftain.

Before Alexandria-the-furthest could be begun, news arrived of rebellion, not among the Scyths, but in the rear. Since landing in Asia, Alexander had asked his men to march dreadfully hard, often without food, but he had never entangled them in a slow and self-sustaining struggle with guerrillas. Now for the first time his speed was to be halted. This Sogdian rebellion would exhaust his army's patience for eighteen unsatisfactory months, make new demands on his generalship and induce a mood of doubt among his entourage. The causes were simple; four of Bessus's henchmen still ranged free, led by Spitamenes the Persian whose name has a link with the Zoroastrian religion. All four now began to work on the native mistrust of the Macedonians. There was ample reason for it. Anxiously searching for food in the Sogdian desert, Alexander's army had plundered ricefields, looted flocks and requisitioned horses, punishing all resistance severely. His thirty thousand soldiers could not be fed from any other source, but it was a dangerous way to behave. Meanwhile, the natives saw garrisons installed in their main villages; Cyrus's old town was being changed into an Alexandria, and already, as in Bactria, Alexander had banned the exposure of dead corpses to vultures, because it repelled his Greek sensitivities. Like the British prohibition of suttee in India, his moral scruples cost him popularity, for Sogdians had not seen Persia overthrown only to suffer worse interference from her conquerors. It was time to be free of any empire, especially when a conference had been ordered at Balkh which the local baronry were expected to attend. If they went they might be held hostage. Bactrians, therefore, joined the resistance, the same Bactrians no doubt, whom Bessus had timorously abandoned, and from Balkh to the Jaxartes Alexander found his presence challenged.

Ignoring the nomad skirmishers who had gathered to rouse the south along the Oxus, Alexander turned against the nearest rebellious villagers. Here his garrisons had been murdered, so he repaid the compliment to the seven responsible settlements in a matter of three weeks. The mudbrick fortifications of the qal'ehs were treated contemptuously. Though siege towers had not yet been transported over the Hindu Kush, collapsible stone-throwers were ready to be assembled if necessary; they were not needed at the first three villages, which succumbed in two days to the old-fashioned tactics of scaling parties backed up by missiles; the next two were abandoned by natives who ran into a waiting cordon of cavalry, and in all five villages the fighting men were slaughtered, the survivors enslaved. The sixth, Cyrus's border garrison at Kurkath, was far the strongest, because of its high mound. Here, the mud walls were a fit target for the stone-throwers, but their performance was unimpressive, perhaps because there was a shortage of ammunition; stone is very scarce in the Turkestan desert and it cannot have been possible to transport many rounds of boulders across the Hindu Kush. However, Alexander noticed that the watercourse which still runs under Kurkath's walls had dried up in the heat and offered a surprise passage to troops on hands and knees. The usual covering fire was ordered and the king is said to have wormed his way with his troops along the river-bed, proof that his broken leg had mended remarkably quickly. The ruse was familiar in Greece, and once inside, the gates were flung open to the besiegers, though the natives continued to resist, and even concussed Alexander by stoning him on the neck. Eight thousand were killed and another 7,000 surrendered: Alexander's respect for his newfound ancestor Cyrus did not extend to rebellious villagers who wounded him, so Kurkath, town of Cyrus, was destroyed. The seventh and final village gave less trouble and its inhabitants were merely deported.

Seemingly unmoved by wounds and the August sun, Alexander left the Oxus rising and returned to plans for his new Alexandria. The only available materials for building were earth and mudbrick, hence the walls and main layout were completed in less than three weeks. Nor was there any shortage of settlers after the recent besieging and razing: survivors from Kurkath and other villages were merged with volunteer mercenaries and Macedonian veterans and were consigned to a life in the hottest single place along the river Jaxartes, where the sun rebounds at double heat from the steeply rising hills on the far bank. The houses were flat-roofed and built without windows for the sake of coolness, but of the comforts of life, of the temples and meeting-places, nothing can now be discovered. The new citizens were chosen from prisoners as well as volunteers, and given their freedom in return for garrison service: they would have to live with Greeks and veteran Macedonians, fiercely tenacious of their native customs and aware that they had been chosen as much for their unpopularity with their platoon commanders as for their physical disabilities. If the rebels further south had been unwisely forgotten in the first excitements of an Alexandria, it was not long before they forced themselves abruptly to the fore. The sack of seven nearby villages had done nothing for the true centre of revolt; Spitamenes and his nomad horsemen were still on the loose behind the lines, and during the building news arrived that they were besieging the thousand garrison troops of Samarkand. The message reached the Scyths on the frontier-river's far bank: they gathered in insolent formations, sensing that Alexander was under pressure to withdraw. This was a serious situation, for Alexander's troops stood at their lowest level of the whole campaign after the recent Alexandrias and detachments; caught between two enemies, he chose to deal with the nearer and detached a mere 2,000 mercenary troops to relieve Samarkand, leaving himself some 25,000, no more, to shock the Scyths. Two generals from the mercenary cavalry shared the command of the Samarkand detachment with a bilingual Oriental who served as interpreter and as staff officer. They were never to be seen again.

As the relief force rode south, Alexander stayed to teach the Scyths a lesson. At first he ignored their provocations and continued to build, 'sacrificing to the usual gods and then holding a cavalry and gymnastic contest' as a show of strength. But the Scyths cared little for Greek gods, less for the competitors, and started shouting rude remarks across the river; Alexander ordered the stuffed leather rafts to be made ready while he sacrificed again and considered the omen. But the omens were deemed unfavourable and Alexander's prophet refused to interpret them falsely: rebuffed by the gods, Alexander turned to his arrow-shooting catapults. These were set up on the river bank and aimed across the intervening river: the Scythians were so scared by the first recorded use of artillery in the field that they retreated when a chieftain was killed by one of its mysterious bolts. Alexander crossed the river, Shield Bearers guarding his men on inflated rafts, horses swimming beside them, archers and slingers keeping the Scyths at a distance.

On the far bank combat was brief but masterly. Scythian tactics relied on encirclement, whereby their horsemen, trousered and mostly unarmoured, would gallop round the enemy and shoot their arrows as they passed; others, perhaps, kept the foe at bay with lances. Alexander too had lancers, and he also had Scythian Mounted Archers who had been serving for a year in his army. He knew the tactics and dealt with them exactly as at Gaugamela; first, he lured the Scythians into battle with a deceptively weak advance force; then, as they tried to encircle, he moved up his main cavalary and light-armed infantry and charged on his own terms. For lancers, not bowmen, it was the only way to repulse nomad archers and the Scyths were jostled back with no room to manœuvre; after losing a thousand men, they fled away into the nearby hills, safe at a height of some 3,000 feet. Alexander pursued sharply for eight miles but stopped to drink the local water 'which was bad and caused him constant diarrhoea so that the rest of the Scyths escaped'. He was still suffering from his recent neck-wound which had also lost him his voice, and an upset stomach was a convenient excuse for giving up a hopeless chase, especially as his courtiers announced that he had already 'passed the limits set by the god Dionysus'. Like the cave of Prometheus, this mythical theme, important for the future, must not be treated too sceptically. In Cyrus's outpost, stormed by Alexander, altars had been found for Oriental cults which the Macedonians equated with the rites of their own Heracles and Dionysus. If Dionysus had not reached beyond Cyrus's outpost, furthest site of his equivalent Oriental cult, then Alexander could indeed be consoled for losing the Scythians. The omens had been justified by his sickness and failure.

Bursting the bounds of Dionysus was scant reward for what followed. While the Scythian king sent envoys to disown the attack as the work of unofficial skirmishers, Alexander heard a most unwelcome report from behind the lines. The 2,000 troops who had been sent back to Samarkand to deal with the rebel Spitamenes had arrived tired and short of food; their generals had begun to quarrel, when Spitamenes suddenly appeared and gave them a sharp lesson in fighting a mobile battle on horseback. Unlike Alexander, the lesser generals did not know how to deal with the fluid tactics of mounted Scythian archers, especially when they were outnumbered by more than two to one: their entire relief force had been trapped on an island in the river Zarafshan and killed to a man. The difference between frontline generals and reserves could hardly have been pointed more clearly, especially when Alexander had misjudged an enemy, not so much in numbers as in ability. Even if a larger force could have been spared from the scanty front line, Spitamenes's speed might still have destroyed it; what was needed was a first-class general in sole command, whereas Alexander had appointed three wrong men and left them to argue. The error was galling and nothing was spared to avenge it.

On the first news of the disaster, Alexander gathered some 7,000 Companions and light infantry and raced them through the 180 miles of desert to Samarkand in only three days and nights. Such speed through the early autumn heat is astonishing, but not impossible, yet Spitamenes easily escaped from another tired and thirsty enemy, disappearing westwards into the barren marches of his attendant nomads. There was nothing for it but to bury the 2,000 dead, punish such nearby villages as had joined the nomads in their victory and range the length of the Zarafshan river for any signs of rebels. The search was unrewarding and eventually even Alexander gave it up: recrossing the Oxus, he quartered for the winter at Balkh, where he could only ponder the most conspicuous mishap of the expedition and the decrease in his forces which were now close to a mere 25,000.

Two wounds, a continuing rebellion and shortage of men and food had made his past six months peculiarly frustrating. But just when his prospects seemed at the worst, hope for a new strategy was to arrive most opportunely in this winter camp. From Greece and the western satraps, 21,600 reinforcements, mostly hired Greeks, had at last made their way to, Bactria under the leadership of Asander, perhaps Parmenion's brother. and the faithful Nearchus who had given up his inglorious satrapy in Lycia to rejoin his friend in the front line. Far the largest draft as yet received, they allowed the army to be brought up to its old strength; they could be split into detachments, and at once Alexander's problems would be reduced. Sporadic raiders could be beaten off by independent units and the theatre of war would narrow accordingly. The rocks and castles of the east were fortunately untroubled; north beyond the Jaxartes one raid had so impressed the Scyths that they had sent envoys to offer their princess in marriage. In central Sogdia, 3,000 garrison-troops had been added to a region which had twice been punished; the new mercenaries could now hold Balkh and the Oxus, so that only the adjacent steppes to the west and north-west remained open to Spitamenes. Even here, his freedom was newly restricted.

To Balkh came envoys from the king of Khwarezm, not a hushed desert waste as poets suggested, but the most powerful known kingdom to the north-west of the Oxus, where the river broadens to join the Aral Sea. It had left little mark on written history until Russian excavations revealed it as a stable and centralized kingdom, defended by its own mailed horsemen, at least from the mid-seventh century B.C.: now, it hangs like a dimly discerned shadow over a thousand years of history in outer Iran. In art and writing, it shows the influence of the Persian Empire to which it had once been subject; it was a home for settled farmers, and its interests were not those of the nomads who surrounded it in the Red and Black Sand deserts. Spitamenes was using these deserts as his base, and safety inclined Khwarezm to Alexander's side. Its king even tried to divert the Macedonians against his own enemies, offering to lead them west in an expedition to the Black Sea. Alexander refused tactfully, though glad of a solid new ally: 'It did not suit him at that moment to march to the Black Sea, for India was his present concern.' It was the first hint of his future: 'When he held all Asia, he would return to Greece, and from there he would lead his entire fleet and army to the Hellespont and invade the Black Sea, as suggested.' Asia, then, was thought for the first time to include India, and not just the India of the Persian Empire. But polite refusals are no certain proof of his plans and it was easy to talk of the future in winter camp, the season when generals talk idly; it was only to hold back Spitamenes that the king of Khwarezm was wanted. Hopes in this direction had been raised for an early victory: the new reinforcements were brigaded and four Sogdian prisoners were conscripted into the Shield Bearers, because they were noticed by Alexander, going to their execution with unusual bravery. As winter passed, the traitor Bessus was sent to Hamadan, where the Medes and the Persians voted that his ears and nose should be cut off, the traditional treatment for an Oriental rebel.

CHAPTER TWENTY-TWO

Nothing says more for men's moods than how they interpret an omen, and as Alexander left Balkh in the spring of 328 for another year's fighting, he chanced on a very revealing one. When camp was pitched by the river Oxus two springs welled out of the ground near the royal tent, the one of water, the other of a liquid 'which gushed forth no different in smell or taste or brightness from olive oil, though the earth was unsuited to olive trees'. Missing their life among the oil lamps and cooking of the Mediterranean, the officers had explained petroleum by olive oil: Alexander sent for the royal prophet Aristander who pronounced the spring to be a sign of labours, but after the labours, victory. It was the first time that petroleum had been struck in Iran by westerners, and they used it to justify a patient hope for the best.

Their strategy, like the oil spring, promised victory after slow endeavour. In search of Spitamenes, the army had divided its new strength into six sections, two to remain and guard Bactria, three to cross the Oxus, and one to fortify the western oasis of Merv, long attached to the satrapy of Balkh. Though more than two hundred miles distant through wearying desert, Merv was a fertile and strategic pocket of civilization which could be strengthened to keep off Spitamenes if he tried to export his rebellion west towards the Caspian Sea. Craterus was ordered to found an Alexandria there and fortify lesser colonies inside the oasis. As it happened, his detachment would decide the war.

Across the Oxus, the objective, annoyingly, was once more the Sogdians. Their garrisons had not restrained them from a third revolt, and town after town had to be reconquered, punished by razing and resettled with loyalists. It made a hot summer's work and not until August did the sections at last unite near Samarkand. Spitamenes had still not been lured out from the western steppes, but while waiting for news of him, the officers indulged in hard-earned relaxation. Near Bazeira, there was a wooded game reserve, watered by natural springs and thickly planted with scrub: the Iranians had once built towers as stands for the hunters but the coverts had not been drawn for a hundred years. Alexander relished the chance for sport and profit and loosed his men into the woods with orders to kill on sight. The bag is said to have totalled 4,000 animals,

308

not so much a massacre as a necessary addition to a larder which had been short of meat for more than a year. In legend the hunt left a curious mark: a letter was invented in which Alexander described his Indian adventures to his tutor Aristotle and referred to a struggle with wild beasts which he called his Night of Terror. The story perhaps arose from this slaughter in Sogdia, but within weeks a true Night of Terror was to follow. It was hardly as Alexander's *Romance* suggested.

At Samarkand, a few evenings later, Alexander was banqueting with his Greek friends and army officers. It must be remembered how trying a moment it was in his career. For a whole year, Spitamenes had kept him from entering India, and as yet there was little prospect that he would be rapidly caught. The Macedonians' one brush with him had ended in disaster; ever since they had been wearily reconquering Sogdian villages in the midsummer sun, and the process was not yet completed. At dinner the local wine flowed very freely, more a sign of frayed nerves than of the new barbarism which historians later liked to detect in Alexander, for like Philip he had always enjoyed a drinking party and now, if ever, he had some excuse in his circumstances. Heavy drinking is the corollary of survival for a traveller in a Sogdian summer and the few lasting water-springs are naturally brackish and tainted with salt-petre. Wine is the one alternative to thirst, and it was taken in quantities which would appal a European: like the natives, the Macedonians drank it neat, a practice considered too strong for Greeks, who economized by mixing their wines with a third part of water. The surroundings may explain the drinking, but they cannot excuse the sequel. As Alexander drank and dined, an incident developed, so disgraceful that Ptolemy's memoirs seem to have suppressed it, while the eighty-year-old Aristobulus was reduced once more to special pleading.

When two contemporaries were secretive it is hard to be sure of what happened. Certainly, a quarrel blew up from the heavy drinking, when wine persuaded some men to boast and flatter, others to rebut what they did not like to hear. The most argumentative guest was Cleitus, Hipparch of the Companion Cavalry and probably in his late middle-age; his sister had nursed Alexander as a little boy. He and the king began to shout and provoke each other, made petulant by all that they had drunk and there is no saying which of them did more to fire the quarrel. Alexander's temper was the first to break and once it had broken, he lost all control. Nearby guests tried to hold him down, or so they later persuaded the historians, but Cleitus's taunts continued and Alexander struggled for whatever weapon lay to hand. He is said to have pelted Cleitus with an apple from the table; then, set on murder, he reached for his sword.

But a bodyguard, it is claimed, had prudently whisked it away. So Alexander bawled for his own Shield Bearers in Macedonian dialect, 'a source of especial alarm': he ordered his trumpeter to sound a note of warning and when the man refused, he punched him in the face. Cleitus's fate, meanwhile, was arguable. According to some, he was hustled out of the room by his friends and deposited beyond a ditch and a mud-wall. But he defied all restraint and found his own way back into the dining-room, staggering through the door just as Alexander, furious, was calling 'Cleitus'. 'Here's Cleitus, Alexander,' he replied, whereupon Alexander ran him through with a sarissa. Others, more plausibly, denied that Cleitus had ever left the room: Alexander merely seized a spear from a bodyguard and killed him on the spot. The tale of Cleitus's re-entry, which even claimed that only Cleitus was to blame, is a warning of the lengths to which courtly excuses would go.

Murder is said to have caused the king revulsion beyond telling. In horror, said the apologists, he leant the offending sarissa against the wall and planned to throw himself on to its point: at the last moment, his nerve failed and he took to his bed, as most are agreed, where he lay distraught for three whole days, repeating the words 'the murderer of my friends' in incoherent snatches between sobs and self-mortification. Three days passed before he would take food or drink, or care for his body, and only then was he brought to help himself by the long persuasions of his friends. The burden of shame was intolerable, the murderer's worst punisher was himself. Callisthenes and other wise courtiers cast round for an explanation which a deeply wounded sense of honour could use as a prop before the world. They were never slow to find one. The Macedonians had long held a yearly festival to Dionysus, Greek god of wine and life-giving forces: Alexander had not paid due sacrifice to the god of the season, but had made an offering to Castor and Pollux, sons of Zeus, instead. Dionysus, then, had been offended and had punished his neglecter through wine, his earthly agent. Historians, at least, enjoyed his lame defence; the army, who preferred their King to Cleitus, begged Alexander to forget his accident. Cleitus, they said, had deserved to be killed.

When such a quarrel breaks, it can light up the past like a flash of lightning and release thunder which has been long brooding in the air. But with Cleitus and Alexander there are several forks to the lightning, and the thunder has often been misunderstood. Far from the dining-room at Samarkand, Greeks were free to guess the quarrel's causes: they had no love for Alexander, and where historians had only seen a personal brawl, touched off by insults to the soldiers' reputations, they idealized the conflict and cast Alexander as a tyrant. Cleitus as the champion of freedom who persistently opposed all Oriental customs; he protested because he hated flattery and its fulsome parallels with Ammon, gods and heroes. 'The two friends who quarrelled were not really the two men; rather they were two different views of the world which exploded with elemental violence.' If this were correct, it would indicate a deep source of conflict in the court life of the past two years. But the evidence is fiction, the quarrellers were heavily drunk, and instead of high principles there were facts, ignored, in their background.

Days before the drinking-party, Cleitus had been given a new commission. He was to govern Bactria, a satrapy behind the lines. For a former Hipparch of the Companions, this was a poor reward: though Bactria would be staffed with some 15,000 Greek troops, an important responsibility, a soldier's life in its outbacks was notoriously grim, not helped by the knowledge that Alexander never appointed his closest friends to any satrapy away from court. Cleitus, therefore, was being downgraded: a fellow-officer, also commissioned for Bactria, had preferred to refuse and be executed rather than leave the centre of affairs. While his fellow Companions earned glory in India, Cleitus would live and grow old by the Oxus, where a man's one hope of distinction was the occasional repulse of unknown nomads. Retired against his will, he took to drinking, and heavy in his cups, he at last burst out into abuse.

His fall must have had a cause. After Philotas's plot he had been promoted to command the Companions with Hephaistion for reasons, perhaps, not all in Alexander's control. Cleitus was the most experienced cavalry leader. He also commanded the 6,000 Macedonians, then temporarily in Hamadan. They were crucial for Parmenion's removal, and they arrived to find a new Persian monarchy and the general's family purged. Their loyalty needed recognition, and perhaps Alexander trod carefully. Hephaistion sympathized with Persian customs; many Macedonians did not. The second Hipparch should be a staunch Macedonian, Philip's man. Cleitus was both, so he took the job. Even so, he had preferred his king to Parmenion and Alexander had not behaved more orientally since Seistan. Perhaps Cleitus would not have cared if he had: he would never have been retired to Bactria, the Iranian baronry's stronghold, if he seriously believed Iranians to be contemptible. Other staunch Macedonians continued to serve loyally. Cleitus's problems were more personal. He was ageing and had been ill; in the past year he had not held the highest field commands and when the reinforcements reached Balkh, six or more Hipparchs had probably been raised to replace him. Perhaps he had been wounded; perhaps he had been rude to Hephaistion, whom others too detested. His demotion may well have been personal: it certainly did not spring from a hatred of diadems and Persian ushers or a sudden passion for freedom, as philosophic Greeks implied. A temporary choice to steady Seistan's crisis, he had already been retired.

'Wine', said the Greeks, proverbially, 'is the mirror of the mind', and in a very drunken quarrel, its reflections should be especially clear; we only regret what we say in a moment of passion because we expose so much more of ourselves than of our victims. The gist of the taunts which caused Cleitus's murder can still be recovered, but their details remain obscure: they enflamed, like all chance remarks, because they caught on long latent obsessions, and reputation, not politics, was surely at the root of them. Alexander, some said, was listening to an after-dinner ballad which mocked the generals whom Spitamenes had destroyed a year before: such satire of delicate mishaps is known elsewhere in Alexander's circle, and it would be welcome light relief in a case where Alexander could secretly blame himself for the disaster. Others, less plausibly, said that Alexander was decrying his father Philip or approving flatterers who did the same. Certainly the past was mentioned, though Philip may not have been so bluntly insulted; soon Cleitus stood up to challenge the facts; he was a veteran and he had saved Alexander's life at the Granicus; he did not like to hear past glories belittled, so he championed the feats of the older men. Alexander's glory, he insisted, was Macedonian glory; the king took credit for what he had not done. After a year's hot and tiresome struggle against rebels, this old man's criticism was all the more enraging for being well-aimed; the rivalries with heroes, the flatteries of Callisthenes, are proof of Alexander's concern for his personal reputation, and at Samarkand in a year of little progress, it was easy to suggest that his pride in his generalship might yet be misplaced. A deep sensitivity had been affronted: young men and old began to shout, until they went wild with the threats to their own self-importance. No matter that their final jibes are unknown, for they were drunk and they had begun on each other's achievements. Sexual incompetence, Alexander's small stature, Cleitus's ageing courage, the failure to catch Spitamenes: they had plenty to bandy at each other, try though the older guests might to stop them. Cleitus, no doubt, made fun of father Ammon, and then suddenly he found himself speared with a sarissa, unable to take it all back.

Alexander's outburst was unforgivably horrific; as Aristotle would have taught him, 'the man who sins when drunk should be punished twice over, once for sinning, once for being drunk'. Yet it can be understood. Alexander's ideals were those of Homer's Achilles, devoted to glory and defended by personal achievement, however violent; in Homer's *Iliad*, even Patroclus, Achilles's lover, had first left his father's home for a murder committed in youth. To call Cleitus's murder Homeric is not to condone it, but it is to set the pattern for what followed. Alexander took to his bed, like Homer's Achilles on the death of Patroclus,

> And shed warm tears remembering the past,
>   lying now on his side, now, again, on his back,
> Now on his face;
>   then, he would stand upright
> And pace to and fro distraught,
>   by the shore of the boundless sea . . .

Worse than Achilles, he had not sent a Companion to his death in battle: he had murdered him before his guests at dinner. Apologists, perhaps, exaggerated his instant wish to die, but it is foreign to the few known threads of Alexander's character to belittle his three days' self-punishment or dismiss them as calculated play. He did not pretend to torture himself, as if to scare his soldiers and officers with the fear that he would never revive; the common foot-soldiers, understandably, had shown not the slightest distress at the accidental death of an ageing cavalryman, and if the officers had been likely to conspire, nothing could have been more foolish than to retire to bed for three whole days and leave them alone with their plans. It was not as if Cleitus had been spokesman of a principled opposition; no officer is known to have lost his job for a friendship with him, and as if to appease Alexander's conscience, Cleitus's own nephew continued in high favour among the king's friends for the rest of the reign. The murder was so painful precisely because it was a personal and accidental disgrace; Alexander suffered, as he lived, on the grandest scale, and a personal crisis drove him not to oriental tyranny, but to his Homeric attitude to life.

But that night of terror also revealed what every young man knows to be true: there is a deeper rift between old and young than between class and class, or creed and creed, and no successful son can be harangued on how much more his father's generation has achieved. It was not that veterans found Alexander changed for the worse: they continued to serve him and even to rise to high commands, but henceforward they would surely hesitate before overpraising their past with Philip to a man who felt, rightly, that he owed as much to his own initiative and to the guidance of Zeus Ammon as to any earthly father. Alexander did not disown Philip, any more than he had betrayed his father's ambitions; he merely excelled him. There is no reason to suppose that Philip too would not have been happy to overrun all Asia, wear the Persian diadem and stress his relationship with Zeus, but there is room for doubt that he ever had the necessary dash to do so. Whatever Cleitus said, Alexander had proved he could do it, and his astonishing success made an old man's comparisons all the more wounding for being untrue. There is no gainsaying the qualities of Philip's men, but they had achieved far more in five years with Alexander than they had in Philip's twenty: the months after Cleitus's murder show most pointedly why Alexander's sense of style still fascinated the classical world long after his father's energies had been forgotten.

With Cleitus dead, Alexander's misfortune began to wane. Remaining Sogdians were subdued and fortified in a matter of weeks, and their surrender at once cut Spitamenes off from his most promising source of support. As his 8,000 nomad horsemen were heavily outnumbered, he was reduced to raiding Balkh behind the lines, where he ambushed its few troops and invalids and killed most of them, including Aristonicus, harpist both to Philip and Alexander, who died 'fighting not as a musician might, but as a brave man'. The raid was a well-judged surprise, but it did little to advance his cause; as he tried to vanish westwards back into the desert, he was intercepted by Craterus, returning from the Merv oasis, who fiercely harried his Scyths in a cavalry charge. By now, Sogdians and Bactrians were serving in Alexander's army and Spitamenes seemed more of a bandit than a rebel-leader. He had little hope but to repeat his surprise raids behind the lines; at the first attempt he ran into Alexander's rear division and was routed completely despite his enlistment of 3,000 vagrant Scythians. Even these surviving desperadoes lost heart, and for the third time in two years Alexander's enemy was betrayed by associates. They cynically murdered their Persian leader and as autumn ended, Spitamenes's head was sent as proof to the Macedonian army.

Typically, Alexander was not yet satisfied. Three of Spitamenes's henchmen, all former minions of Bessus, were still at large in the area, while the eastern half of Sogdia had never submitted in the first place. Rebels had retreated there for safety, and so after a mere two months in their winter camp the army was set on an eastward trail, still discomforted by hunger as local supplies were long since dwindling. As they marched the snow lay thickly on the hillsides, and within three days a massive thunderstorm had driven them back under cover as thunderbolts flashed and hailstones bombarded their armour. Alexander took the lead and directed them to native huts where a fire could be kindled from the surrounding forest: he even gave up his royal chair by the fireside to a common soldier whom he saw shivering and exhausted. But 2,000 camp followers

314

had been lost, and 'it was said that victims could be seen still frozen on to the tree trunks against which they had been leaning'.

Near modern Hissar, on the Koh-i-nor mountains, a final cluster of Sogdian rebels were reported to have found refuge with the local baronry. Their natural fortress seemed impregnable to watchers who guessed that 'its height was more than three miles, its circumference at least fifteen', and when Alexander asked the leaders to a parley and offered them, through one of Artabazus's sons, a safe pass in return for surrender, they only laughed and told him to go and find troops with wings. Alexander hated to be mocked, let alone to be told what he could not do. If his men could not fly, they could at least climb; when the envoys had left, heralds invited mountaineers to stand forward from the ranks.

Their rewards were in keeping with the danger. The first to scale the rock would receive twelve talents, twelve times the bonus paid to the allied troops for four years' Asian service; the rest would be paid according to their position in the race to the summit. The three hundred experienced climbers who volunteered were told to equip themselves with flaxen ropes and iron tent-pegs, and that same winter's night, by the pale light of the stars, they moved round to a rock-face far too forbidding to be guarded.

They climbed with the patience of hardened alpinists. Every yard or so, they hammered tent-pegs into the crevices and frozen snow-drifts, lassoed them and hauled themselves up on the end of their ropes. On the way to the top, thirty of them slipped to their death and buried themselves beyond recovery in the snow beneath, but as the first streaks of dawn showed through the sky, the remaining 270 attained the summit. It was no time for celebration: smoke curling up from the funnels of rock beneath them showed that the Sogdians were already stirring. They had to be quick if they were not to be outnumbered; they had arranged to signal with linen flags to Alexander, who had been keeping watch all night at the foot of the rock-face. Bluffing, he sent heralds to invite the native pickets to look up and see his flying soldiers; they turned round and seeing the climbers high above them they surrendered, believing them to be an army. Baronial families who left their fortress were spared for the future, but search though the troops might, there were no large caches of food to be found.

A second rock was hardly less spectacular. Some fifty miles south-east of Leninabad, where the road to Boldzhuan crosses the Vachshi river stands the crag called Koh-i-nor, a common name in the area which says nothing for its extreme height and inaccessibility: 'about two miles high and six miles round', it was protected by a deep ravine whose only

315

bridge had been destroyed. It always took the challenge of a siege to bring the best out of Alexander's boldness. The troops were ordered to work in relays night and day until they had felled enough pine trees to span the abyss with a makeshift causeway. First, they climbed down the cliffs on ladders and drove stakes into the rock-faces at the ravine's narrowest point; then hurdles of willow-wood were laid on the network and surfaced with a thick layer of earth as a level road for the army and their weaponry. 'At first, the barbarians kept ridiculing the attempt as utterly hopeless', but like the people of Tyre, they soon began to see what a son of Zeus could do to the landscape. The bridge across the ravine was finished and arrows, perhaps from catapults, began to shoot into their lairs; their own shots in reply bounced idly off the Macedonian sheds and screens. Engineering had scared them, although their lair was still as inaccessible to troops, and it was only left to Oxyartes the baron, a prisoner from the first rock, to shout to their leader to surrender and save his skin: there was nothing, he called, which could not be captured by Alexander's army, something of a bluff as the rock was still impregnable although open now to shots from catapults. Sisimithres the leader agreed, and when Alexander brought 500 guards to inspect his fortress, he duly gave himself up. To please his captors, he also made mention of his larder, which was stored with corn, wine and dried meats, quite apart from the herds of livestock he stabled: there was enough, he boasted, to feed all Alexander's army for at least two years. He could have said nothing more opportune. After two hungry years the recurrent worry of stores for the camp had at last been resolved. There was no need to starve again, and Sisimithres, a baron who had married his own mother, perhaps because he was a Zoro-astrian, was gratefully restored to his rock by a king who had reason enough for his mildness.

On the high note of these successes, the struggle for outer Iran was ended, and after two years of bloodshed and arbitrary depopulation on a grand scale, it was time to return to Balkh and consider the future of provinces which the Persian kings, far distant in Susa, had tended to entrust to a member of their own family. Iranians were to retain the local aorts as Sogdian governors and the old Persian citadel beside the Oxus and the river Kokcha was to be rebuilt as a huge Alexandria with a palace and a formal street plan; Alexander had no responsible relations left alive, so he linked the Sogdian nobility to his own person in the time-honoured way. Among the captives from the first rock were the daughters of the Sogdian baron Oxyartes; one of them, Roxane, was said by those who saw her to be the most beautiful lady in all Asia, deserving her Iran-ian name of 'little star'. All were agreed that Alexander was entranced by her, some saying that he first met her eyes at a banquet and at once fell passionately in love. Nowadays, it is fashionable to explain away the passion and emphasize its politics, but that was not how contemporaries saw it. Marriage certainly made political sense but there were other Iranian ladies who would have served the purpose as well. Alexander may have followed his head but, aged twenty-nine, he was agreed to have chosen the only girl who fired his heart.

Rich in supplies, Alexander arranged a lavish wedding banquet on the summit of Sisimithres's sky-high fortress. His sense of style had not deserted him and the occasion had a decided touch of chivalry, for Alexander and Roxane symbolized their match before their guests by cutting a loaf of bread with a sword and each eating half as bride and groom. The sharing of the loaf was the Iranian custom which is still practised in Turkestan, though the sword was a military detail which could be Alexander's own. But the mood of the moment was best caught by the experienced and contemporary Greek painter Aetion: in his painting of Alexander's wedding, sadly lost, he depicted.

a very beautiful bedroom, with a wedding bed on which Roxane was sitting; she was an extraordinarily lovely girl but, modestly, she looked down at the ground, feeling shy before Alexander who stood beside her. Smiling cupids were in attendance: one stood behind and pulled back the veil from her face; another removed her shoe, while a third was tugging Alexander towards her by the cloak. Alexander, meanwhile, was offering her a garland, while Hephaistion assisted as best man, holding a blazing torch and leaning against a young boy, probably Hymenaios, the god of weddings. On the other side more Cupids were playing, this time among Alexander's armour; two heaved his spear, two dragged his shield by the hand-grips, on which sat a third, presumably their king; another had hidden under the breastplate, as if to ambush them.

So, through the baroque imagination of a Greek master, 'Alexander's Wedding to Roxane' won a prize at the festival games of Greek Olympia and survived through a Roman visitor's description to influence Sodoma and Botticelli.

Like Achilles, men said, Alexander had married a captive lady. But in politics, if not in personality, the new Achilles had come far since his pilgrimage to Troy. Nobody could have guessed that a pupil of Aristotle, who had once refused to take a wife, would fall passionately in love with a lady from outer Iran, marry her and use her as proof of goodwill to the conquered Iranian barony; his father-in-law, moreover, had been Bessus's close associate in a rebellion which had detained him for two awkward years. There was only one embarrassment. As father of Barsine, Alexander's first Persian mistress, Artabazus may have been disappointed by the decision to marry Roxane, especially as Barsine was known to be bearing her first child. However, he had already resigned his command in Bactria, pleading old age before the marriage was in view; the satrapy which had first been offered to Cleitus now went to another Macedonian with a suitably large force of hired Greeks. Artabazus would never be grandfather of Alexander's recognized heir, but he is not known to have borne any lasting resentment and his sons continued to be honoured. He was retired to the governorship of the first Sogdian rock in place of the baron Ariamazes who had been crucified. Ironically it was the rock on which Roxane had been captured.

Alexander's plans were already extending beyond marriage. At Balkh, he ordered 30,000 native boys to be chosen for military training; their weapons were to be Macedonian and their language Greek. It was the most determined attempt at a wide Hellenization of Iran to be made by any western king: like Philip's royal pages, not only would the boys be hostages against their fathers' misbehaviour, they would also become the dependent soldier class of the future, when the Macedonian veterans retired and the army could be filled with westernized Orientals. From a year of frustration, even of murder, a creative plan had at last taken shape; the Iranians, so far from being treated 'as plants and animals', would be called to share in the empire, obliged to Alexander alone and educated away from their tribal background. Whether the boys and their parents were grateful is another matter. At the same time, Alexander's courtiers too were to feel the change: while the cavalry officers were rearranged, Hephaistion had needed promotion in order to preserve his special dignity, and it was perhaps now that he became Alexander's official second-in-command. His title was Chiliarch, his job had military responsibilities. But both job and title had been created by the Persian kings.

To any such change, there were bound to be complications.

In my case, the efforts for these years to live in the dress of Arabs and to imitate their mental foundation quitted me of my English self . . .; at the same time, I could not sincerely take on the Arab skin: it was an affectation only. . . . Sometimes these selves would converse in the void, and then madness was very near, as I believe it would be near the man who could see things through the veils at once of two customs, two educations, two environments.

Though Lawrence of Arabia comes nearer to one side of Alexander than any man since, he theorized where Alexander only acted for the moment.

But with Alexander too there were now two veils to life, and the two selves did converse, if not in the void of madness, at least on an everyday level where tensions are no less real for being public. At Balkh in spring 327, with Roxane as bride and Hephaistion perhaps as Vizier, tension was to break into conflict and its victim would be a man whom the fighting of the past two years had so far left alone.

CHAPTER TWENTY-THREE

In Persian legend, Alexander was said to have soon sent Roxane away to Seistan, where he gave her its citadel as a wedding present to keep her safe when the men withdrew to the Punjab; this, however, is dubious, as Roxane did come to India and the walls of Seistan's capital probably belong to a later date. Presumably, she stayed in camp, where she would have assisted at one of the most misrepresented episodes in her husband's life. This cannot be understood without its Persian background, proof of the change in Alexander's plans. Once understood, it is a small but revealing glimpse of his mood: it turns on the matter of a courtly kiss.

Unlike the Chinese, who had no word for kissing, the kingdoms of the ancient east had long included a term for kissing gesture in their court vocabularies. This gesture was practised in Assyrian royal society, whence it was adopted first by the Medes, then by the Persians; its equivalent was known in Greece, probably as a borrowing from the East, and the Greeks described both their own and the Orientals' practice by one and the same word, *proskynesis*. The only descriptions of it were written under the Roman empire, but they fit well enough with early Greek and Persian sculpture: the payer of *proskynesis* would bring a hand, usually his right one, to his lips and kiss the tips of his fingers, perhaps blowing the kiss towards his king or god, though the blowing of kisses is only known for certain in Roman society. In the carvings at Persepolis, the nobles mounting the palace staircase or the attendants on King Artaxerxes's tomb can be seen in the middle of the gesture, while the Steward of the Royal household kisses his hand before the Great King, bending slightly forwards as he does so. These Persian pictures and the Greeks' own choice of words show that in Alexander's day, *proskynesis* could be conducted with the body upright, bowed or prostrate. The Romans believed that when Alexander asked for *proskynesis* from his closest friends, he expected them to grovel before him. But in Persia, as in Greece, it was only the suppliant or abject inferior who would go down on his hands and knees. Only if courtiers and aristocrats fell into disgrace or begged a favour would they prostrate themselves before the king. *Proskynesis* itself did not require it.

In Persia and Greece its social uses varied. In Greece it was a gesture reserved for the gods alone, but in Persia it was also paid to men: 'When the Persians meet one another in the street,' wrote Herodotus, with one of those deep insights into foreign customs which make him far the most congenial of Greek historians, 'in the following way, a man can tell whether they meet as social equals. If they are equal, they kiss each other on the mouth, instead of speaking a word of greeting; if one is slightly inferior to the other, he only kisses him on the cheek; if he is far less noble, he falls down and pays *proskynesis* to his superior.' There was another category, not to be seen in the street: a meeting with the Great King himself. Because the king was superhuman in his majesty, he received *proskynesis* from every-body; however, courtiers and royal Relations were noble enough to be spared the accompanying curtsey or prostration, and so they merely bowed. The Greeks noted this custom, and because they themselves paid *proskynesis* only to the gods, by a little sophistry some could suggest that the Persian king was considered to be a god himself. Intelligent Greeks knew this to be mistaken: in Persia *proskynesis* was also paid by the lower classes to the upper class, and not even in Persia was the entire upper class divine. It was a social gesture, but nonetheless a deeply traditional one.

At Balkh, Alexander decided to try out *proskynesis* among his Mace-donian friends. The decision was a bold one: *proskynesis* had caused trouble in the past when Greek met Persian, and it was open to misinterpretation, for whatever the Persians thought, it was not the way that a free Greek liked to greet a mortal. It had been left to the most radical of the Athenian dramatists, Euripides, to show *proskynesis* being paid on the stage to a man and even then he produced it as a foreign extravagance. At Persepolis, in the Treasury, the hands of officials paying *proskynesis* are the worst-damaged feature in sculptures which are otherwise well preserved: Alex-ander's army may have mutilated them on purpose, thinking this one gesture absurd. Greek ambassadors to the Persian court had been known on occasions to take an equally defiant stand: one had sent a letter in to the king, rather than pay *proskynesis* before him, and another was said to have dropped his signet ring, so that he could bow down to pick it up and seem respectful by his movement, though the true kissing gesture was missed in the course of bending forwards. Such stubborn refusals were less a matter of religion than of pride; if Greeks also came to Persia as prisoners or suppliants, at least in the eyes of the king, they were expected to go down on hands and knees as well as paying *proskynesis*, and the double disgrace had been known to prove too much for them. Aristotle had been told of an elephant trained to pay *proskynesis* to a king, no doubt by blowing the kiss with its trunk as Aristotle did not believe that elephants could bend both their front legs at once. But free Greeks were not brutes, and what befitted an elephant did not become a Hellene.

Nevertheless, Greeks like Themistocles and Alcibiades had been sensible enough to do as the Persians when in Persia, and it was in this spirit that Alexander broached the subject of *proskynesis* to his Companions. As Darius's heir, he would have been receiving such homage from his Iranians for the past three years: it came naturally to them, just as it did to Darius's queen when taken prisoner at Issus. Alexander had continued to attract more and more Iranians as hostages or helpers. Iranian brigades had been recruited to fight in India and at court the seven sons of elderly Artabazus had now been joined by Roxane's brothers and sisters, Spitamenes's daughter, many local barons and a grandson of the last King Artaxerxes; Alexander even had his own two Magi and a fugitive rajah from the Punjab. If these Orientals saw the Macedonians greeting him without first paying their respects, they might begin to wonder whether he was a proper king; this belief 'would have started among the servants and quickly spread everywhere', and at the end of a long and bloody native revolt, that was not a risk worth taking. New reinforcements and the recruiting of Greeks and Orientals meant that the Macedonians were now heavily outnumbered in the army; before invading India, the Macedonian courtiers should give way to their new supporters and take up their customs for the sake of social uniformity. But as in the case of Cleitus, later writers saw the tension differently; by ordering *proskynesis*, they insisted, Alexander was not considering court etiquette: he was intending to be worshipped as a god.

It is true that in Greece *proskynesis* was only paid to the gods, and that Alexander was doubtless aware of this. But in outer Iran, it was not Greek practice which was at issue. He was King of Asia, and his courtiers ought to tolerate an Asian social custom; in much the same way, he had been wearing the diadem, which among Greeks was a claim to represent Zeus, among Persians a claim to be king, but he had treated it entirely from a Persian point of view as heir of Darius, not rival of the gods. It was to be the same with *proskynesis*: his own Master of Ceremonies described the first attempt to introduce it and as the incident took place at a dinner party, he would have been present in the dining-room and able to see the result for himself. It was a far cry from Alexander the tyrant, seeking to become divine.

Alexander, said his servant, had ordered a banquet and was presiding over the after-dinner drinking: the guests had been carefully chosen and warned what was expected of them. A golden cup, filled with wine, was passed down from his seat and each guest stood up and drank from it, facing the hearth which perhaps stood behind the royal table; they either drank a toast or poured a libation, but so far all had happened in the manner of a normal Greek drinking-party. Then they went Oriental: they paid *proskynesis* to Alexander, kissing their hand and perhaps bowing slightly like the sculptured Persian officials. After this gesture, they walked up to the royal table and exchanged kisses with Alexander, perhaps on the mouth, more probably on the cheek. This unassuming little ceremony went the round of all the guests, each drinking, kissing his hand and being kissed in return by the king, until it came to Callisthenes, cousin of Aristotle. He drank from the cup, ignored the *proskynesis* and walked straight up to Alexander, hoping to receive a proper kiss. Alexander happened to be talking to Hephaistion and did not notice that his court historian had deceived him. But a Bodyguard leant across to point out the error and as Callisthenes had not complied, Alexander refused to kiss him. 'Very well,' said Callisthenes, 'I go away the poorer by a kiss.'

This after-dinner episode explains Alexander's intention beyond all doubt. Before enforcing *proskynesis*, he wished to experiment in private with a few selected friends: first, they were to pay him homage, just as the average Iranian had always paid it to his king, and then, because they were his Macedonians with whom he had shared so much, they were to be rewarded by a kiss which, among Persians, was only exchanged between social equals or between the king and his royal Relations. The kiss restored them to their former dignity and refuted any possible suggestions that Alexander sought *proskynesis* because he wished to seem divine: no god has ever destroyed his own illusion by giving his worshippers a privileged kiss. The plan could hardly have been tried more reasonably and despite the indignation of Romans, philosophers and others since who have missed its Persian background, Alexander came out of it all remarkably well. It was a social experiment, and for once a witness had described exactly what he was doing.

There remained the uncooperative Callisthenes. As a 'flatterer who had tried to make a god out of Alexander', he would have been the very last person at court to have spoken out against divine honours for a living man, but as a Greek who had worked with Aristotle, he saw this social custom as a different matter. To pay *proskynesis* to a man had long seemed slavish, at least to the Greeks, and whatever else, Callisthenes had been brought up to believe in the values of Greek culture; he knew and analysed the details of Greek myths; he agreed with the view that certain Egyptians were really descended from an Athenian: he even claimed that the name Phoenicia was derived from the Greek word for a palm tree (*phoinix*).

323

Like his kinsman and associate, Aristotle, he saw the barbarian world as the Greeks' inferior and so in an earlier part of his history, he seems to have described the waves of the Lycian sea as bowing to the king, as if doing *proskynesis* before him. That was fair enough for barbarian waves, but for a Greek, steeped in the Greek past, it was a gesture which smacked of slavishness. Educated Greeks should have no truck with oriental decadence: kissing the hand be damned, he would refuse, and trust to the consequences.

It is not easy to plot his recent relationship with Alexander, not least because Alexander's officers never referred to it in their histories. Six months before, said others, Callisthenes's comforts had counted for much as Alexander despaired of life after murdering Cleitus; fellow-Greeks and philosophers later disagreed, unwilling to believe that Aristotle's kinsman would ever have consoled a man whom they reviled as a tyrant. There was another Greek philosopher at court, Anaxarchus, who had come from a Thracian town and was known because of his opinions as the 'contented': it was he, said admirers of Aristotle, who had revived Alexander after the murder by teaching him the classic doctrine of an oriental tyrant, that whatever a king did was just and fair. 'Anaxarchus', wrote a later follower of Aristotle, 'only rose to a position of influence through the ignorance of his patrons: his wine would be poured out by a naked girl, chosen for her beauty, though all she in fact revealed was the lust of those whom she served.' Callisthenes, by contrast, was extolled for his austerity and self-sufficiency, as befitted Aristotle's kinsman; his fame as a wanton flatterer was conveniently overlooked. Not for the last time academic rivalries impinged on the writing of history, abusing Anaxarchus and idealizing his rival Callisthenes. But Anaxarchus would one day die a hero's death, owing nothing to Aristotle's schoolmen, while Callisthenes would be best remembered for hailing his patron as the new son of Zeus.

Since the comfortings which followed Cleitus's murder, there are signs, undated, that king and historian had been at variance elsewhere. Once at dinner, wrote Alexander's Master of Ceremonies, a cup of unmixed wine had come round to Callisthenes, who was nudged by a neighbour and asked why he would not drink. 'I do not wish,' he replied, 'to drink from Alexander and then need the god of medicine.' Like *proskynesis*, the drinking of undiluted wine was not a Greek practice and once again Callisthenes had refused to betray his Greek ideals. Philosophers told a second story, which Callisthenes was said to have confided to the slave who read aloud to him: during the after-dinner drinking, Callisthenes was once asked to speak in praise of the Macedonians, which he did so fulsomely that all the guests applauded and showered him with flowers. Alexander then asked him to denounce them no less fluently, and Callisthenes pitched into the subject and distressed his audience by his evident taste for it. If true, this unlikely story says much for Callisthenes's sophistry, and Aristotle was said to have remarked on hearing it that his cousin was a capable speaker but sadly lacking in common sense. If this incident followed the affair of the *proskynesis*, Alexander may also have played on his historian's defect in order to discredit him in public.

For it was the *proskynesis* affair, surely, which had first marked the parting of the ways between the two men. Hitherto, Callisthenes would hardly have earned much affection among the Macedonians, whose fun he spoilt at parties and whose individual heroics he described incorrectly though he never took to the battlefield himself. But now there were others who did not think very far: one of the older Macedonians had mocked a Persian for his *proskynesis* and told him to hit the ground harder with his chin, as he went down on hands and knees to pay the exaggerated respects of an abject inferior. The story was retold of several officers, and on each occasion Alexander was said to have lost his temper with the Macedonian concerned. That was fair enough. If Macedonians started to poke fun at oriental life, then the harmony at court to which Alexander was pledged would never come about: it was the older men, by and large, who found it hardest to adapt to oriental customs, though that did not stop several thousand veterans from continuing to serve contentedly or an officer like Craterus, fiercely tenacious of his Macedonian habits, from rising rapidly despite his principles. The issue was not an absolute division, and only if it had been mishandled could it have become very awkward. Grumble though the old men might, when it came to the choice a few weeks later, it was Callisthenes they saw unaided to his death, and though legend maintained that Callisthenes's one refusal deflated all plans for *proskynesis*, it is far from certain that the custom was ever dropped. Neither Ptolemy nor Aristobulus mentioned the attempt to introduce it, perhaps because they thought it insignificant. But their silence is more likely to have been deliberate, one more proof of the feelings which the affair could arouse in certain quarters. To a Greek public, a frank description would have put the sequel in a sinister light and neither historian wished to expose Alexander to the criticism of those who had not served with him.

Some time after the party and its related misadventures, perhaps days, perhaps months, the main army were quartered near a small Bactrian village. While four divisions fanned out to arrest the last of Spitamenes's accomplices on the edge of the Red Sand desert, a serious plot was uncovered in camp against the king's life: it could hardly have been more remote from the old and unadaptable. It broke among the Macedonian royal pages, boys of fifteen or so, who had been sent out to join the army three years before. According to the story, perhaps mere guesswork, one of them, son of a prominent cavalry commander, had blotted his record out hunting: a wild boar had been flushed out in Alexander's direction and before the king could take a shot at it the page had speared it to death. Alexander was annoyed that someone for once had been quicker than himself. He ordered the page to be whipped, while the other young boys looked on. He even took away his horse.

Here too, Persian customs may be relevant. On a Persian hunt it had always been agreed that the king should be allowed the first shot at game, whereas those who broke the rule had been known to be flogged: it is probable, however, that Macedonian kings had always treated insolent small boys in the same way as their oriental counterparts. Whether victim of a Persian outrage or not, the page felt he had a grievance, so he enrolled seven associates in a plot to murder the king. Now, the royal pages were very well placed to effect this. They served on night duty outside Alexander's tent and were in close daily access to his person, but as they numbered about fifty, the night guard would fall to one of the eight conspirators during the next fortnight. The night of Antipater, son of Asclepiodorus, was soon due and as only one page is likely to have stood guard at a time, he could easily admit his associates.

Eventually, Antipater's night came round. The plan was a simple one, to enter the royal bedroom and stab Alexander in his sleep. No mention is made of Roxane, probably because she was already sleeping in quarters of her own, perhaps away from the army altogether; but more worrying than a wife was Alexander's habit of not returning to bed before dawn, for at dawn the guard was changed. However, the risk was worth taking and when Alexander left in the early evening for the usual dinner with his friends the pages' hopes were high. But dinner proved very attractive and the king stayed drinking and watching entertainments: the conduct which led to the burning of Persepolis and the murder of Cleitus was, third time lucky, to save his life. Dawn found him still carousing with Companions a fact which so shocked the eighty-year-old Aristobulus that in his history he invented an excuse. Alexander, he wrote, did leave the table at a reasonable hour, but on his way to bed he met a Syrian prophetess. She had long been following the army and would wail words of warning, a habit which at first Alexander and his friends had thought amusing, but when all her warnings came true Alexander had taken her seriously and even allowed her to watch beside his bed while he slept. This time she implored him to go back to his drinking; he obeyed, not because he liked wine but because he trusted the woman, and so he grew more and more drunk against his will until dawn. This apology for his late-night habits is very remarkable: Alexander, Aristobulus maintained, would only sit over his wine for the sake of conversation, like a portly academic: facts were against him, but even after Alexander's death such apologies were felt to be needed by those who had known the man in person.

Drunk, not meekly superstitious, Alexander returned to his tent in daylight. A new page had replaced Antipater, and Alexander could go inside to bed, safer than he knew. Once again, his enemies could not keep a secret. In a matter of hours, one of the pages had told the plot to his current boyfriend, or so rumour believed: the boyfriend told the page's brother; the brother told two Bodyguards, one of them Ptolemy. At once the news was brought to Alexander who arrested all those named and put them to the torture. The informants were acquitted; the rest, said some, were tried before the soldiery and stoned to death. If true this punishment implies that the audience believed wholeheartedly in their crime. But a private execution is as likely.

The pages, though guilty beyond doubt, were in need of a motive; once again, posterity's guesses centred on politics, casting Alexander as the type of an eastern tyrant. In self-defence, their leader is said to have declaimed against tyranny, the wearing of Persian dress, the continuing practice of *proskynesis*, heavy drinking and the murders of Cleitus, Parmenion and all the rest: he and his friends were striking a blow for freedom and furthermore, said their Roman speechwriter, they would not stand for all the talk of Ammon any longer. But these speeches have no authority whatsoever, and there are facts, not fiction, which put the pages in a very different light. Their leader had been flogged degradingly, but he also had a father who had held a high command in the Companion cavalry ever since Alexander had come to the throne. A month or so before the plot, his father had been sent back to Macedonia, stripped of his position, 'in order to fetch reinforcements'; he never reappeared in camp. Another conspirator was son of the former satrap of Syria: he had recently left his province and joined Alexander with the last reinforcements, but he had not been returned to his governorship or given another command. In the two cases where anything is known of the pages' fathers, both can be shown to have changed their jobs in the past three months; a third was son of a Thracian, not a man to fuss about the betrayal of the Macedonians' traditions. But the informer, maybe, was an exception. As his brother was not in the plot, their family was not at stake. Hence, perhaps, his indiscretion. As with the deaths of Parmenion and Cleitus, the pages' plot probably turned in the end on the same old problem: the downgrading of officers who thought they deserved a longer or better service. Parmenion had been old, Cleitus, whatever the personal reason, had been falling out of favour; the pages' fathers were victims of unknown changes in the high command. Young boys of fifteen care more for themselves and their fathers' status than for the principles of Greek political thought: beyond that, their motives cannot be traced.

The plot itself was carried further. The mystery remained its background, for how could five young men have decided on murder and planned it carefully without considering the consequences? Perhaps they had only followed their emotions, rallying to an insulted friend and striking a blow for their fathers' reputations; perhaps, but it was also plausible to look for an elder statesman, and this time, the choice did not fall on a Macedonian: it was Callisthenes who was arrested, tortured and put to death. 'The pages admitted', wrote Aristobulus, 'that Callisthenes had urged them on to their act of daring', and Ptolemy wrote much the same. But others were more sceptical.

There is indeed a case to be made for the historian's arrest. He was condemned as an instigator, not a participant, and the leading page was said to have been his pupil, so that Greeks later maintained that it was his studies in liberal philosophy which had roused him to kill Alexander the tyrant. Their relationship is probably true, as Callisthenes would have finished his *Deeds of Alexander* down to the ending of the Greek allies' service, the natural place for the panegyric to stop, and as the pages had arrived in camp only shortly before the material for his book had ended, he would have been free to take charge of the young nobility's education. Disgusted by *proskynesis*, the drinking of unmixed wine and Alexander's oriental policy, he could have worked on the feelings of six young pupils who had reasons of their own for disaffection. But except for the word of Alexander's serving officers, there is nothing to prove his guilt, and as their word is not by itself enough, the truth remains uncertain.

It is conceivable that Alexander resented Callisthenes's opposition, that his retort 'the poorer by a kiss' had been too accurate to be forgotten and that the first opportunity was seized to rid the court of an enemy's presence; conceivable, maybe, but still unproven. Callisthenes's importance was easily exaggerated, and it is very doubtful whether his solitary show of stubbornness mattered enough to cause his unfounded murder. But the pages had conspired, and their plot made all the more sense if encouraged by their disgruntled tutor. Four hundred years later a letter could be quoted as if from Alexander, which, if genuine, would strongly

328

support the historian's innocence. It was addressed to three Commanders of the foot-phalanx, almost certainly out of camp at the moment of the plot: 'Under torture', it said, 'the pages have confessed that they alone had plotted and that nobody else knew of their plans.' It is, however, extremely improbable that private correspondence between Alexander and his officers survived for the use of historians, let alone a note whose contents were so dangerously frank. Forgeries abounded, and on the disputed death of Aristotle's kinsman, Greeks had every cause to invent a proof of his innocence. Alexander had no need to write to three generals a mere week or so away from base and implicitly accuse himself of murder. If there was a genuine letter of the moment, it was perhaps the one said to have been written to Antipater, who is known to have edited his own correspondence: in it, Alexander is made to accuse Callisthenes of plotting and affirm that he meant to punish 'those who had sent the sophist out in the first place', presumably a threat against Aristotle. The execution of Aristotle's kinsman cannot have helped relations between Alexander and his former tutor and as a first annoyed reaction, Alexander might indeed have vowed revenge. But Aristotle's son-in-law remained in high favour at court, and these threats never came to anything: on such a favourite topic of legend the menacing letter too may only be a later invention.

The last and only certain word went, fittingly, to Anaxarchus the contented. 'Much learning', he wrote, 'either helps a man greatly or harms him greatly: it helps the shrewd but harms the easy talker, who says whatever he pleases wherever he is. One must know the proper and appropriate measure of all things: that is the definition of wisdom.' The distrust of the academic had long been a feature of Greek thought and it is tempting to see it here as a topical allusion. Callisthenes, his rival, had been the clever man who could argue about earthquakes, derive place names from known Greek words and work out a date for the Fall of Troy; he died in the end for his indiscretion, opposing a policy which he thought to be barbaric, because he was stopped, like other Aristotelians, by a narrowly Greek outlook from seeing what was appropriate. His tale is a strange one: the flatterer who wrote up a crusade of Greek revenge in the most glowing terms, hailed its leader as the son of a god, slandered the Parmenion whom his patron had killed, and finally changed his mind when the Crusader became a king. It is for their early years that he and Alexander should be remembered, as king and Aristotelian scholar had made their way through Asia Minor, the king in rivalry with his beloved Achilles, the scholar improving his text of Homer and pointing out sites linked with Homer's poems. But patronage, as often, soured. 'Alexander and Alexander's actions', Callisthenes is said to have remarked, 'depend on me and my history: I have come not to win esteem from Alexander but to make him glorious in the sight of men.' When the historian died, not even those who knew the truth agreed on the manner of his death.

According to Ptolemy, Callisthenes was tortured and hanged, as a guilty conspirator deserved; according to Aristobulus, who involved Alexander less directly, Callisthenes was bound in fetters and taken round with the army until he eventually died, not on Alexander's orders but from disease. Chares the court Chamberlain disagreed: Callisthenes was 'kept in fetters for seven months so that he could be tried by the allied council in Greece in the presence of Aristotle', a careful retort, no doubt, to associates of Aristotle who were already complaining that Callisthenes had been murdered without a fair trial. Theophrastus, pupil of Aristotle, even wrote a pamphlet called *Callisthenes, or On Mourning*, in which he complained that Alexander was a 'man of the highest power and fortune, but did not know how to use his assets'. Not a bit of it, Chares the Chamberlain maintained: Callisthenes became 'excessively fat and ridden with lice', being flabby and lousy anyway, and died more than a year after his disgrace, before he could be tried in public. Apologetic tales of a lingering sickness were soon reversed: Callisthenes, said some, was mauled limb by limb: his ears, nose and lips were cut off: he was shut in a pit, or a cage, with a dog, or a lion, and only rescued by the high-minded Lysimachus, a future king in Europe, who slipped him a dose of poison.

When witnesses could make up such elaborate stories, the impact among Greek schoolmen of Callisthenes's death was neither shortlived nor insignificant; hence neither Ptolemy nor Aristobulus recorded his refusals of *proskynesis* in order to deny him the glamour of a hero. He had flourished in flattery, died in controversy, and there are few plainer insights into the hazards of a search for Alexander than that his own historian was said by informed contemporaries to have died in five different ways.

CHAPTER TWENTY-FOUR

The court disturbances near Balkh did not set the Macedonians against their king; the soldiery remained contented, the officers were not re-shuffled, and despite the rigours of the past two years Alexander felt safe enough to retrace his tracks for the grand adventure of his lifetime. He would cross the Hindu Kush and march east into India, a kingdom whose traders and spice plants had already been seen on the Oxus but whose way of life was known to the Greeks only through the fabulous tales of early romancers.

So far, Alexander's ambitions had been easily understood. He had first conquered Darius, then claimed his empire, marching out to its north-east frontier but going no farther. West Pakistan, which the ancients called India, had also been a part of the Persian empire, but the frontier which had once stretched into the Punjab had been lost for a hundred years, and if Alexander knew this fact of Persian history it is doubtful whether it influenced his Indian plans. In India he would soon go beyond the Persians' boundaries where there was no longer an empire to be reclaimed. His motives need a little imagination; they will never be certain, as historians can read a man's documents but never read his mind. Throughout history, armies have been drawn from Kabul into India as if by a continuing tide, and Alexander was anticipating Mongols and Moghuls, Bactrian Greeks, Kushans, White Huns and the others who have spilled into India for conquest from the Hindu Kush; he did not invade for a cause or an idea, but no successful invader ever has, and the slogans are only ambition's cloak before the simpleminded. 'You, Zeus, hold Olympus,' ran the verse on one of his official statues, 'I set the earth beneath me.' 'The truth', wrote an admiring officer, 'was that Alexander was always straining after more.' Except for Ammon's alleged assurance that he would conquer the world, which was surely the posthumous guess of his soldiers, there is no other evidence that Alexander had dreamt of world domination or was fighting to realize such a vague ideal. It is more to the point that he restored the rajahs whom he conquered; he did not inflict his own superiority on his subjects or work off a lasting sense of frustration at the expense of the vast majority of those who surrendered. Patriots and rebels were killed and enslaved by the thousand as always, but

331

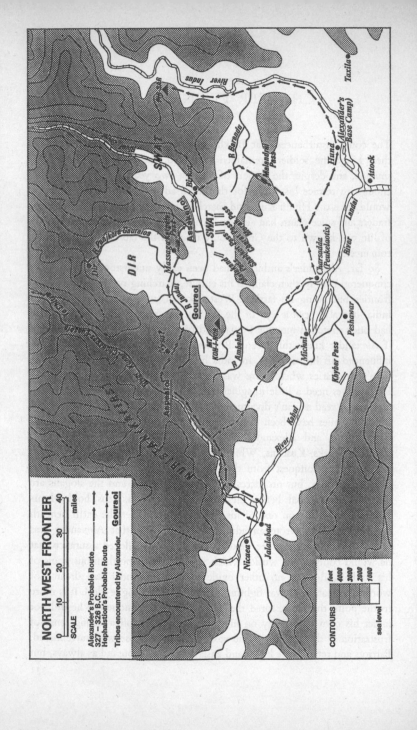

NORTH WEST FRONTIER

SCALE

0   10   20   30   40
miles

Alexander's Probable Route
327 – 326 B.C.

Hephaistion's Probable Route

Tribes encountered by Alexander.   Gouraoi

CONTOURS

feet
4000
3000
2000
1000

sea level

there is more of the explorer than the tyrant in the history of the campaign. For boredom is the force in life which histories always omit; Alexander was twenty-nine, invincible and on the edge of an unknown continent; to turn back would have been impossibly tame, for life in Asia could promise little more than hunting and the tedious tidying of rebellions and provincial decrees. Only in a speech to his troops is mention made of a march to the Eastern Ocean, edge of the world as the Greeks conceived it; though the speech is certainly not true to life it is tempting, not only because it is romantic, to believe that this detail is founded on fact. If the edge of the world was Alexander's ambition, it was a goal which appealed as much to his curiosity as to a longing for power.

To a curious mind this strange new world was irresistible, and of Alexander's curiosity there can be no doubt. 'His troops', said a contemporary, well placed to know, 'took a very hasty view of India, but Alexander himself was keen to be more exact and therefore arranged for the land to be described by those who knew it.' The Greek tales of India were part of any prince's education; his staff had heard the rumours of India's gold, said to be dug by gigantic ants or guarded by vigilant griffins: they would be keen to see the truth of the Sciapods, men who lay on their backs and shaded themselves from the sun with their one large foot. In India, men were said to live for two hundred years, making love in public, living according to caste and weaving their clothes from wool-bearing trees: there had been tales of falconry, fine purple, scents and silver: unicorns with red heads and blue eyes, pygmies and a sort of steel which could avert a storm. Like the first Christian missionaries to visit India, who explained the Hindus as descendants of St Thomas, the Greeks went east with their own myths and history and related what they saw to what they knew already. Nothing prepared them more than their own Herodotus; the flooding of the rivers, the Indians' dress and their wild plants were described in Herodotus's terms and as for his gold-digging ants, 'I did not see any myself', wrote Nearchus, Alexander's officer, 'but many of their pelts were brought into the Macedonian camp.' It took more than a personal visit to kill off the creatures of Greek fable; 'In a valley of the Himalayas', wrote one of Alexander's surveyors on his return, 'live a tribe whose feet are turned back to front. They run very fast, but because they cannot breathe in any other climate none of them could be brought to Alexander.' So begins the history of the Abominable Snowman.

The Punjab had already been visited by westerners, not only by the bravest man in early Greek history, Scylax the sailor from Caria, but also, as the troops were soon to believe, by the Greek gods Heracles and Dionysus in the very distant past. Six thousand and forty-two years, so the Indians claimed, divided Dionysus's invasion from Alexander's; there was stress on their self-government ever since, a theme which Alexander picked up, and there was no mention of the Persian empire. As for Heracles, he had come a little later, but the Macedonians were to see cattle in India branded with the sign of a club which their hero always carried. These parallels with the two divine ancestors of the Macedonian kings cannot be dismissed in the search for Alexander and within months of his invasion, they are to come into sharp perspective against a background of Indian myth. One son of Zeus was keen to rival another: it was in the spring before the invasion that Alexander's first Persian mistress Barsine gave birth to a son, believed, perhaps wrongly, to be Alexander's own. Aptly, the baby was named Heracles, after the royal hero of the moment, even if Alexander never recognized him with full honours after his marriage to Roxane.

Amid its myth and fable, India was a conqueror's chance for undying glory. The fighting would be tough, exactly what Alexander liked. The opponents were kings in their own right, his favourite class of enemy and as the Punjab was split between their independent tribes, many of whom had more of a link with Iran than India, they could as usual be set against each other. The Hindu religion had long centred in the plains, but it had not penetrated the wild mountain kingdoms; Buddhism was almost unknown, and there was no threat of a holy war. If Alexander succeeded his name would never be forgotten and even in their cups, men could no longer boast that Philip's achievements were superior: he would have conquered what had eluded all native kings, and he would have opened a whole new world to the West; Achilles's feats, by comparison, were very parochial.

As summer camp was broken in Bactria, the army he led eastwards showed the changes of the past two years. In size, it had grown but slightly. No new Macedonian troops had been received for the past four years. Fourteen thousand of the last year's Greek reinforcements had been left to supervise the two Oxus provinces; the Thracian and the Paeonian cavalry were absent, and most of the Thracian and other barbarian infantry were serving in the garrisons of Parthia and Hamadan. Some 50,000 men remained for India, scarcely more than at Guagamela, though a very sizeable force by the standards of classical warfare. But in style, they were different men, for only some 35,000 were westerners from Europe. The Foot Companions had abandoned the sarissa as too unwieldy for the mountainous ground and they never used it with Alexander again; the Mounted Lancers had done the same and been merged with the Companion Cavalry, whose numbers had now fallen to some 1,800 Macedonians in the absence of reinforcements from their homeland. Archers, in which India was strongest, numbered at least 3,000; on foot, strength was maintained by three brigades of the newer mercenaries, mainly Greeks from Europe and Asia, but now led by Macedonian noblemen. Iranian horsemen from Bactria and Sogdia swelled the cavalry, though kept in separate units from the Greeks and Macedonians: there were even a thousand horse-archers recruited from Spitamenes's nomads. As a whole, the army was lighter, more independent and better equipped with missiles. Iranians had given it balance, and the fluid tactics of their nomad horsemen along the Oxus had not been wasted on Alexander's officers.

But it was the pattern of command which wore the newest look. The Foot Companions had been rearmed and were still brigaded in seven battalions whose officers, where changed, were brothers of the previous barons; the commands of Alexander's highland infantry were very much a family affair. But through plots and depositions, the cavalry had lost all links with Philotas, Parmenion, Cleitus and the past. The diminished squadrons of the Companions had been spread for the last eighteen months into six or more Hipparchies, only one of whose known commanders had previously made his name as a leader of horsemen. The others were close friends, like Ptolemy or Hephaistion, or men like Perdiccas or Leonnatus, better known as royal Bodyguards; the Royal Squadron of Companions, once led by Cleitus, had been renamed and taken over by Alexander himself. Each had their friends and families, though their fickle currents of influence can no longer be usefully traced: an officer-class which had once been scattered with friends of Parmenion was now distinguished by future friends of Perdiccas, who would fight to keep the empire together after Alexander's death. Clearest was the case of the Royal Shield Bearers, now renamed the Silver Shields because of their smart new silver armour. Initially, this picked unit of veteran infantry had been responsible to a son of Parmenion, but shortly before his family's plot this son had died and now the Silver Shields looked to new officers, among them Seleucus, the future king of Asia, and Nearchus, Alexander's friend from childhood, soon to be admiral of the Indian fleet; their supreme commander was Neoptolemus, related to the Epirote royal family and so to Alexander's mother Olympias. By the summer of 327, a new group of marshals had emerged, not only in the royal Shield Bearers. These Hipparchs and trusted squadron-leaders now made it possible to divide the army more freely between different attacks at any one time, for long a principle of Alexander's siegecraft but not of his pitched warfare. Spitamenes had shown that second rate underlings were not equal to the task. Parmenion and Philotas had also shown that the cavalry, especially, could not be entrusted to any one man.

In the provinces, a similar pattern was emerging, less urgent for being remote. In June Alexander returned at a modest pace to the Hindu Kush and crossed it comfortably in ten days, presumably by the same road as he had used before, rather than by the treacherous road through modern Bamyan, future sanctuary of Buddha. The snows had melted and after the rich finds of food in the Sogdian fortresses there were no fears about a second starvation as the troops marched over the high grazing-grounds, among skylarks, buff hillsides and the pungent smells of wormwood and wild roses. Down near Begram, the new Alexandria-in-the-Caucasus was found to be giving trouble: its commander was deposed for insubordination, the eighth appointment to have proved a failure in the fourteen satrapies conquered since the year of Gaugamela, and although the replacement was another Oriental, he was the last Iranian, except for Roxane's father, to be given a governorship by Alexander. The experiment with the native satraps of the past four years had been convenient but risky, and by disappearing eastwards Alexander was inviting rebellion from those who still remained behind him; with only two exceptions, he was to reap a harvest of troubles on his return, 'I wish to go to India', Alexander was made to say in a fictitious letter, composed a thousand years later in Sassanid Persia, 'but I fear to leave alive my Persian nobles. It seems prudent to me to destroy them to a man, that I may carry out my purpose with untroubled mind.' To this, Aristotle was made to reply: 'If you destroy the people of Fars, you will have overthrown one of the greatest pillars of excellence in the world. When the noble among them are gone, you will of necessity promote the base to their rank and position; be assured that there is no wickedness or calamity, no unrest or plague in the world which corrupts so much as the ascending of the base to the station of the noble.' Nobody ever spoke more clearly for the views of a Persian gentleman than the Aristotle of Persian legend. But on returning from India the real Alexander would have more cause to question his advice.

The remaining summer months were spent peacefully in the Hindu Kush, a relaxation for the men who would otherwise have entered India in appalling heat, and a useful time for reconnaissance and the training of the new units. For the past two years the rajah Sasigupta had been maintained in camp, a man 'who had fled from India to Bessus, but now proved trustworthy to the Macedonians'. In the absence of any maps, he was an invaluable source of native information; in early autumn Alexander left Alexandria-in-the-Caucasus and came sharply down from the foothills of the Hindu Kush till he struck the river Laghman and could survey the panorama of the Punjab spread before him. On the far bank of the Laghman, he fortified a native village and gave it the confident name of Nicaea, city of Victory, the theme which he always emphasized. Then, sending a herald east down the long-used road by the river Kabul, he invited the rajahs of the valley to a conference, no doubt on Sasigupta's advice. It was early October before they arrived; meanwhile Alexander had declared the campaign open by a sacrifice, again to the goddess Athena of Victory.

His insistence on victory was not unfounded. He was bringing a professionally led army, complete with catapults, borers and siege-towers, into an independent world of border tribes, numerous but always at variance. Indian cavalry were not to be compared with squadrons of Companions and Iranians; the *yantras* of their epic heroes were only elementary slings and catapults. Their iron and steel and archery were famous, but they had none of the discipline of the Shield Bearers. The kings in the valleys still trusted in chariots, a force that meant little to the Macedonians of Gaugamela. There was one danger, and Alexander knew it to be very real: at the first news of invasion, Punjab rajahs would send for their mahouts, meaning to fight like their forefathers, trunk and tusk from the backs of the largest known animal species in the world. In India, Alexander was to be the first western general to do serious battle with *Elephas maximus*, 'nature's masterpiece, the only harmless great thing': catapults were as nothing to the menace of an elephant on *musth*.

The elephant so dominated the Indian imagination that in Hindu mythology, it was said to support the world on its shoulders. But within five years, Alexander had made it his own: elephants guarded his tent, and their images adorned his funeral chariot, while shortly after his death, his close friend Ptolemy depicted him on Egyptian coins as if dressed in a cap of elephant-skin. As a result the elephant became a symbol of grand pretensions in the west; Caesar would take one to Britain, Claudius would take two: Pompey would try to enter Rome in a triumphal chariot pulled by elephants, only to find that the city gate was too narrow and he had to dismount. Thanks to Alexander a more exact knowledge of the elephant first spread to the west: in his great works on natural history, Aristotle described one with an accuracy that could only have come from dissection, while he also knew how to cure its insomnia, wounds or upset stomach, and how much wheat or wine was needed to keep it in prime condition. But like Alexander's officers, he was inclined to believe that an elephant lived for two hundred years.

Through Alexander's army, the skills of elephant and native mahout first raced westwards back to Greece. The use of the howdah, or turreted seat on the elephant's back, became popular, and as neither art nor reliable literature mention it as native to India, the howdah may be an invention of Greek engineers. Within three years of Alexander's death his officers had made elephants fell trees, hold up a river's current and flatten a city wall. They were adorned, as in India, with bells and scarlet coverlets and again as in India, they served as executioners. And yet before him, they had never been seen in the uncongenial landscape of Greece. On the battle-field, their first shock proved decisive, though defenders soon learnt the value of planks of upturned nails against their tender feet: ditches were dug, and momentarily, the elephants halted, as they cannot jump. But when defences seemed to be winning, the Ptolemies shipped hunters to comb the forests of Ethiopia for new and braver recruits, while Carthage, gathering strength, began to explore her western marches for a suitable retort. Hannibal found them, and used them to terrify Italy; Rome, quick to learn, returned the compliment to Macedon and sent envoys east to the Syrian mud-parks of the Seleucids, with secret orders to hamstring every elephant in sight. Two years later, the Seleucid empire collapsed.

As enemies receded the Romans turned the elephant to show. They would dance, play the cymbals and walk a tight-rope in the circus, and for two hundred years, the audience loved what Alexander had first made possible. But it was the elephant who trumpeted last and loudest: in the mid-fourth century, as Persian power revived, hundreds of elephants tramped west through Asia in the dreaded name of Shapur, 'most mon-strous and horrific', wrote a Roman witness, 'of all war's units'.

With the fall of the Western Empire, the elephant vanished from Europe, except for occasional presents; for six hundred years it had symbolized the open frontier between East and West, a frontier which Alexander had been the first man to roll back. It was, perhaps, his most lasting con-tribution to classical life.

Without his Indian invasion, the elephant would surely never have been enrolled for Mediterranean military service. Its capture is hazardous and its disadvantages are serious. It dislikes winter cold and is happiest in warm mud; it must eat twice as much as it needs because of poor digestion, consuming 100 pounds of hay and up to fifty gallons of water daily: Aristotle knew of an elephant which would drink 140 gallons between dawn and dusk and then begin again at nightfall. Its hearing is superb but its sight dismally poor; it can swim but not jump, and its transport powers are unremarkable; it moves at a steady six miles an hour, charging rarely and then only for brief bursts at twenty m.p.h. It does not usually breed in captivity, though males spend awkward months on *musth*, exuding a

338

fluid from their temples which makes them too morose to be controlled. Worst of all, the elephant has no team spirit. Though it is deeply affectionate to its master and mild to small children, human wars mean nothing and it will run amok among friend and foe alike. The most notable elephant in Greek history, called Victor, had long served in Pyrrhus's army, but on seeing its mahout dead before the city walls, it rushed to retrieve him: hoisting him defiantly on his tusks, it took wild and indiscriminate revenge for the man it loved, trampling more of its supporters than its enemies in the process. In war, such devotion was a very mixed blessing.

Men, however, did their utmost to embolden it. In India, it was goaded, equipped with bells and fed on wine: in Ceylon, it was made to take opium. It was encouraged to whisk attackers in its trunk, at least until they wore the deterrent of spiked armour. Its tusks were strengthened with long steel daggers, tipped with poison; its body was protected in iron chain-mail, while seven or more warriors shot and speared from its saddled back, even without the protection of the howdah. Most important of all, though afraid of mice which would run up its trunk, it scared the wits out of horses: at Gaugamela, Alexander's Companion Cavalry had safely outflanked the few opposing elephants, but in the Punjab they would have to withstand hundreds, this time face to face. Alexander was extremely anxious.

His first news in India was that elephants were on his side, for by early October, rajahs from the Indus valley had followed his herald back to the frontier and they promised that their twenty-five specimens were at his disposal. Such a welcome caused Alexander to divide his troops. The main road ran along the banks of the Indus towards the distant town of Taxila, home of the rajah Ambhi who had come, as expected, to surrender. Hephaistion, the mercenaries and half the Companions were to follow him down through the plains of Peshawar and bridge the Indus at Hund where it bends back northwards. In the latter stages, Ambhi would guide and supply them, while on the way they could capture such cities as Pushkalavati, City of the Lotus, in its open fields of sugar-cane and sand; its governor, however, resisted them for a month behind his ditch and mudbrick ramparts, only to be put to death for the trouble. Alexander, meanwhile, had swung far north into the Swat highlands with some 22,000 troops to protect this main road's flank by tactics of terror: it was his lifeline back to Iran, and as a cautious tactician he could not leave northerly tribesmen to cut it when he still hoped for news and reinforcements from Asia. As the native kings had not surrendered, he decided to fight them, not bribe them. Choosing a road far up the river Alishang because it was reported to be the best supplied, he launched into an arduous six-month campaign with Sasigupta to guide him. The hill tribes were numerous, and they had determined to resist valiantly among mountains and fast-flowing rivers which were not to be bridged lightly, even in December. Failing their surrender, Alexander was not disposed to be any more kind to resistant patriots than usual: it boded ill for the style of the war that he was wounded at the first city and 'the Macedonians killed all prisoners, angry that they had pained their Alexander'.

But the grim business of war had its compensations. Up in the green valleys of the westerly Swat hills, perhaps near the peak of Koh-i-nor, camp had been pitched on a chilly December night and the men began to search for firewood at a height of some 5,000 feet. A bonfire was built and when timber ran short the troops smashed up square boxes of cedarwood which they found conveniently distributed over the hillside: they did not realize they were burning the natives' coffins. Before long the natives retaliated, but a brief attack rebuffed them and they preferred to surrender. Their envoys found Alexander in his tent 'still dusty from the march but fully armed, wearing a helmet and holding a spear; they were amazed at the sight of him and falling to the ground, they kept a long silence'. Through interpreters, terms were agreed: to Alexander's pleasure, the city was ruled by aristocrats, three hundred of whom were to serve in his cavalry while another hundred, after a brief argument, were left to keep the nobility in power. In the course of conversation, he became aware of a startling fact: these tribesmen had been settled by the god Dionysus, their town was the elusive sanctuary of Nysa and the mountain was therefore a holy place. In Greece the ecstatic followers of Dionysus wreathed their brows in ivy; on this Indian hill, alone of the ones they had visited, common ivy was growing in profusion. What better proof could the common soldier want? Dionysus had been this way before them.

Talk of Dionysus was spiriting to tired troopers and Alexander himself 'wanted the tales of the god's wandering to be true'. The cult of the god was old and fierce in his native Macedonia and no son of Olympias could underestimate it. He was keen as always to investigate, and the Companion Cavalry and Royal Squadron of Infantry were invited to join him in visiting the shady clumps of trees, the myrtle, box and laurel, symbols of the god and a blessing to eyes long wearied by rocky outcrop and dry salt desert. The place was a gardener's paradise, and the soldiers picked the common ivy and twined its acrid stems into wreaths. Crowned with ivy garlands, they sang hymns to the god on the hillside and addressed him by his many names, whereupon Alexander offered him a formal sacrifice: 'Many of the not unprominent officers around him garlanded themselves with ivy and – so several have written – were promptly possessed by the god and raised the call of Dionysus, running in his frantic rout.' *Ite Bacchai, ite Bacchai* ... – the words of the most memorable chorus in Greek drama, probably written in Macedonia itself, may have sounded on a Pakistani hillside.

This episode deserves to be believed, but its explanation is difficult. It is plausible to look first for an Indian background, and there are parallels which seem impressive. Alexander's officers named the hillside Meros, the Greek word for a thigh and a link with Dionysus who was believed to have been born from the thigh of Zeus. But the Indians may have led them to the name, for in early Hindu cosmology the world was believed to float like the four petals of a lotus around its central mountain Meru, which rose out of the surrounding waters to the peak of the easeful gods. Alexander might have heard the Indians in his camp talking of Meru and identified the word, as so often, with what he knew in Greek. As for the god himself, an Indian Dionysus was repeatedly mentioned by later Greek visitors to India and among the native pantheon none is more plausible than the Hindu god Shiva, who is worshipped by dancers and cymbalists, dressed like Greek Bacchants in the skins of wild animals. Ivy, Meru and Shiva might seem to have encouraged the Macedonians' fancy: scholars in Egyptian Alexandria later blamed the incident on Alexander's love of flattery, but they were men with dry minds. They had never seen the Swati highlands or shared the hazards of an Indian explorer.

But there are difficulties in this Indian explanation, for the people of Dionysus conspire in a stranger story which tends to discredit it. Alexander was in the modern region of Chitral, which adjoins Nuristan on the eastern border of Afghanistan, home of the people long known as the Kafirs, whose kinsmen lived in Chitral and the Swat highlands where they share the Kafirs' language and many of their stylish folk tales. The Kafirs are one of the least accessible and most enchanting peoples in Asia. Their skin is sometimes fair, their hair is occasionally blond. They have aquiline noses and noble foreheads and they wear a woollen headdress which has seemed to the imaginative to be like the broadbrimmed Kausia of the Macedonians. Ivy abounds in their well-treed mountains and the people, like Dionysus, are conspicuously fond of wine; their music and singing are famous, their architecture of carved wood is distinctive and often ornate. It was inevitable that these Kafirs should have attracted the attention of the Victorian British; in the nineteenth century the Kafirs did not yet practise as Hindus or Muslims, so some said they were early Christians, uncorrupted by the Catholic Church, others that they were Jews, while

341

others believed that they were Greek descendants of Alexander's garrisons, and hence had a European look, a story which was as old as Marco Polo and is still repeated; Kipling even paid these proto-Hellenes the honour of a story. But exploration proved that they neither spoke Greek nor cared for Jesus, and their origins soon lost popular appeal. But one strange fact had been noticed: alone of the tribes in the Hindu Kush the Kafirs expose their dead in wooden coffins, and so the Macedonians' search for firewood springs to mind: the troops had smashed up the coffins which lay to hand round their bivouacs and the custom is probably a link across thousands of years, so that the Kafirs of Nuristan are indeed descendants of the people whom Alexander met. This casts doubts on a link between Dionysus and Shiva, god of the Hindus.

Research has discovered that the Kafirs speak a language whose roots derive from the earliest Indo-European dialects; Kafirs, then, are descendants of the first invaders to sweep west from India to Europe several thousand years before Alexander; hence their European looks, a feature which also owes something to their attraction for enterprising British ladies on the north-west frontier. Their religion, before they were forced to become Muslim, contained no Indian god to be compared with Dionysus; they worshipped a sky god, whom the Greeks would have called Zeus Ombrios, and a demon god in the shape of a stone, but they were not Hindus with a knowledge of Shiva. However, they did have a lively cult of the ibex or mountain goat, as befitted the people of one of its most prolific haunts, and as the Greek Dionysus's worship included the killing and eating of a goat the parallel is very impressive. Possibly Alexander saw or heard of this equally ecstatic cult among the Kafirs, whose link with his own Dionysus seemed to be confirmed by their natural gardens and the western appearance of their spokesmen.

After Dionysus, it was time for Heracles. First, the rival son of Zeus made his laborious way across the waters of the Alishang and Kunar rivers, keeping far north and storming a strongly built citadel high on the Katgala pass: the ground was sheer, the walls protected by ditches and the defenders encouraged by 7,000 hired troops from farther east. In a preliminary skirmish Alexander was wounded in the ankle by an arrow from the city battlements and as his foot hung numb with pain, an Athenian all-in wrestler, who had long been applying his skills in the ranks, tried to atone for its bleeding by quoting the king a line of Homer: 'Ichor,' he remarked, 'such as flows from the veins of the immortal gods.' 'Nonsense,' Alexander retorted, 'it's not ichor: it's blood.' He had deserved divine honours by his prowess and he wished it to be known that he was specially

342

favoured by his father Zeus. But he had no illusions about his own mortality and he would never have claimed that he had himself turned into a god.

Wounded and repulsed, Alexander took thought for his machines. A mound was ordered, as at Gaza, from which the catapults and siege-towers could bring their barrage within range, but the natives had the pleasure of seeing their first drawbridge collapse beneath the weight of its Macedonians. The catapults were more formidable, and when one of the arrow-shooters killed the Indian chieftain, the tribesmen gave in to superior engineering. Their hired troops surrendered and were taken into Alexander's ranks, only to be massacred when they tried to escape on the following night. The rest were spared, including the chieftain's mother, who made up for the loss of her son to a catapult by sleeping with Alexander and conceiving a replacement.

It was now midwinter, and the storming of two more highland citadels kept the army busy well into the new year; the fighting continued to be strenuous and the weather chilly but food was no distress: only three months' earlier, a herd of 230,000 cattle had been captured, the finest of which had been chosen by Alexander who 'wished to send them back to Macedonia to work the land', a tribute to his keen eye for the agriculture on which all ancient economies depended; the rest sufficed to feed the army for several months on milk or meat, two rare luxuries in the diet of the classical world. Meanwhile the drift of the campaign was ever eastwards. Beyond the Swat hills, on the eastern side of the river Indus, lived a rajah whose people throughout history had always supported Alexander's present enemies on the near bank. Agitators and hired troops had already come to cause trouble and as Alexander sacked and resettled one city after another on the edge of the Indus, the survivors kept retreating towards this one source of help. By early March they had been penned up into the north-east highlands overlooking the Indus itself and had fled to a steep spur north of Attock which even the hero Heracles, men said in Alexander's army, had never been able to capture. At last, the scene was set for the climax to Alexander's career as the greatest besieger in history.

In 1926 the site of this spur called Aornos was fixed by the explorations of Sir Aurel Stein, and his remarkable search has since been confirmed by archaeologists. Aornos is indeed as impressive as Ptolemy's history suggested. Where the river Indus crooks westwards above the Nandihar valley, a complex of spurs and ridges are enclosed inside its bend. Among them is Pir-Sar, the 'peak of the holy man', a long flat-topped cliff which stands over a height of 7,000 feet, guarded on the east by the broad river

343

Indus to which it descends in a series of slippery gorges. Due north, the even higher spur of Bar Sar rises to a sharply conical point and meets Pir-Sar first by grass slopes, then by a particularly treacherous ravine, while to the west, sheer cliffs drop 2,000 feet to a strip of valley and thence rise straight to the highest peak of the whole range. To the south, Pir-Sar's terminal hillock breaks into three narrow branches, each more inaccessible than the next. As for Pir-Sar itself, its own flat summit commands a view dramatic enough to stir the most hardened Macedonian bodyguard, whether he looked away to the icebound eaves of the Upper Swat head-waters or south beyond the Indus to the metallic green of the plains round Peshawar. It was a site for mountaineers, but emphatically not for warriors.

From such a vantage point Alexander's looping march up the bank of the Indus was sure to be detected. On no side of the rock could his army hope for easy access, and they had to choose between a ridgeway or a ravine. As for starving out the enemy, that was impossible because Pir-Sar had its own water-springs and a summit wide enough to grow crops for its occupiers, as it still does for the local Gujars. The cliffs and gorges were far too sheer for the catapults to come within range: when the natives talked of their Hindu god Krishna, worshipped by men dressed in lion skins, it was only natural for the Macedonians to equate him with their own royal ancestor Heracles and spread the word that not even Heracles had been able to storm Pir-Sar. To Alexander, that was another reason for attempting it himself.

From the pass, he briefly visited the Indus to check on Hephaistion's bridge-building; he then approached Pir-Sar up river from the south. At the nearest base the heaviest troops and most of the cavalry were left to prepare supplies against a long siege, while the Horse-archers and all the crack skirmishing troops continued for a day and a half up the western bank until they met with a decisive stroke of luck: nearby tribesmen surrendered, offering to lead the army to the easiest point of assault. As usual, they were believed for lack of any alternative. Ptolemy and Alexander's secretary Eumenes were sent on a reconnaissance, and striking due north from the river they seized the spur of Little Una, due west of Pir-Sar itself, helped by its covering of pine-trees and wild rhododendrons. After putting up a stockade on the hilltop, they lit a fire signal as pre-arranged. Alexander saw it, but so did the defenders, and it took two days' skirmishing and the despatch of a native Indian messenger before king, secretary and historian were safely united on their advance ridge.

From Little Una, the outlook was very much more favourable. Pir-Sar, said the guides, was vulnerable on its hidden north face, so Alexander

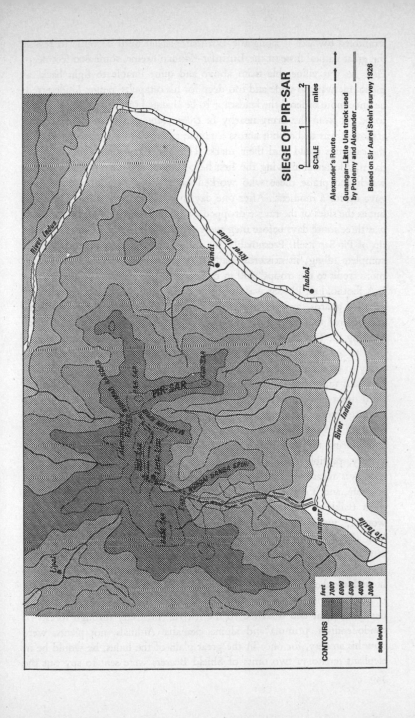

SIEGE OF PIR-SAR

→ Alexander's Route

▬▬ Gunangar–Little Una track used
by Ptolemy and Alexander

Based on Sir Aurel Stein's survey 1926

SCALE
0   1   2
miles

River Indus

River Indus

Dandi

Thakot

PIR-SAR

River Indus

Gunangar

to Taxila

CONTOURS

feet
7000
6000
5000
4000
3000
sea level

scrambled towards it along the Burimar plateau until he came to rest at the great natural fosse of the Burimar-Kandao ravine, some 800 feet deep. Here he was vulnerable from above and quite unable to fight back, as the ravine was too wide and too deep for his catapults' range. Undeterred, he once more ordered the landscape to be changed to suit him. Stakes were to be cut from the many nearby fir trees, some conveniently fallen, and a mound was to be built across a ravine as broad as a Punjab river until the catapults could find their mark. These amazing earthworks began at dawn, Alexander moving the first heap himself and then standing by 'to watch and praise those who worked eagerly but to punish those who gave up for a moment'. After one day, sixty yards were already finished, but as the sides of the ravine dropped away, the work slowed down and it was three more days before men were within fighting range of the nearest tip of Pir-Sar itself. Presumably the mound was more a platform than a complete filling; its crisscross pattern of stakes and brushwood was one more credit to the troops' skill in carpentry.

A foothold on Pir-Sar was not to be easily won. Alexander chose thirty advance guards, and 'at the sound of the trumpet, he turned to them and ordered them to follow him, for he would be the first up the rock'. Nearing the top ledge, he changed his mind and sent the guards ahead, only to see them crushed by boulders rolled down from above: he was lucky to escape with his life, and so he withdrew for the next two days. Day and night the Indians beat drums to celebrate the repulse, but the third night brought silence, a blaze of torchlight and their attempt at a surprise retreat. Hauling himself up the rockface by a rope, Alexander this time led his Shield Bearers up to the attack, killing several fugitives and clearing the summit for the building of altars to Athena goddess of victory, possible traces of which were discovered by Aurel Stein. The rock was measured by the surveyors, whose geometry was remarkably accurate, and it was then time to climb down, the last threat to the lines from Balkh to the Indus having been forcibly dispersed. 'I could only wonder,' wrote Stein, with the evidence of the landscape before him, 'that the story of Aornos should have escaped being treated altogether as a mythos. ... I had no victory to give thanks for, and yet I too felt tempted to offer a libation to Pallas Athene for the fulfilment of a scholar's hope, long cherished and long delayed.'

The last spring snows were melting along the Barandu valley as Alexander left Pir-Sar and marched to the natives' final city through forests of rhododendron, primula and alpine clematis. Animals, not plants, were now his anxiety, for once in the great plain of the Indus, he would be in elephant territory: two units of Shield Bearers were sent to spy out the land beyond, with special orders to interrogate captives about the numbers of elephants in the service of rajahs. Alexander encouraged the local mahouts to hunt out beasts for his own use, which they duly did, mounting them and bringing them into the ranks with the very briefest training, except for two rogue bulls who stampeded over a precipice. Mahouts and Macedonians then marched a hundred miles down the banks of the Indus towards its crossing point at Hund, which had long been bridged by the obedient Hephaistion.

At Hund the Indus is in lazy and expansive mood. Resting between the Himalayan foothills and the gorges of Attock, it spills across the plains to a width of six miles, inviting the traveller to take it at his leisure. Ambhi, rajah of Taxila, had been feeding Hephaistion's advance army with grain, another happy chance for the supply corps. He now sent presents in advance to the far bank, including 3,000 bulls, 10,000 sheep, many talents of silver and thirty elephants. Alexander first sacrificed the bulls 'to his usual gods', Ammon presumably among them, 'and held athletic games and a horse-show'. The sacrifices proved favourable, so he entrusted himself to Hephaistion's boats and bridge and perhaps to stuffed leather skins as well, and crossed the Indus to sacrifice again on the far bank, thankful that the rafts had not collapsed. Ambhi greeted him on the far side, 'his elephants appearing like castles between his troops', and as soon as they had established friendship, they marched into the plain north-west of Rawal-Pindi to a first true taste of Indian life.

In the shadow of the Murree hills, beside the Tamra-Nala river, the mudbrick town of Taxila lay open to the most outlandish visitors it had seen. Unlike the forts of Upper Swat, it stood at the meeting-point of three main roads, and had prospered accordingly. It was a seat of Hindu teachers and doctors, though probably not already of Buddhists too, whose founder the Greeks called Bouddhas, explaining him as the son of a fellow-soldier of Dionysus. But Taxila had none of the outward refinements of a university town. Its wide main street twisted through old and unplanned houses whose flat roofs caught the heat, each a different height from its neighbour, and whose walls of mud and rough-cut stone encroached on the passers-by; the simple rooms behind were floored with earth and let on their street side by the narrow slit of a single window. Only one public building stood in the town centre, a long and curving hall supported by wooden rafters; to left and right ran the narrow alleys of an Indian slum, where dirt and darkness were little improved by the presence of communal dustbins. While Alexander rode in to sacrifice, meet the local rajahs and hold a durbah in the city hall, his officers took closer note of their surroundings.

Physically, the Indians are slim [wrote Alexander's admiral Nearchus]. They are tall and much lighter in weight than other men. . . . They wear earrings of ivory (at least, the rich do), they dye their beards, some of the very whitest of white, others dark blue, red or purple or even green. Their clothes are of linen, either brighter than all other linen or made to seem so by the people's black skin: they dress in a tunic down to the mid-calf and throw an outer mantle round their shoulders: another is wound round their head. . . . They wear shoes of white leather, elaborately decorated, the soles of which are thickened to make them seem tall. And all except the very humblest carry parasols in summer.

Their hair, as Persian sculptures show, was gathered into a bun or top-knot and as for their customs:

Those who are too poor to give their daughters a dowry [wrote Aristobulus], put them up for sale in the market in their prime, summoning a crowd of buyers by the noise of shells and drums. When a customer steps forward, first, the girl's back is bared for inspection as far as the shoulders, then, the parts in front; if she pleases him and also allows herself to be persuaded, she lives with him on agreed terms.

Among other Indian tribes, impecunious virgins were bestowed as prizes in boxing-matches, where their lack of money did not matter, but the rich needed only to press their suit with the gift of an elephant to be sure of success. When the husband died, 'some people said that the wives would burn themselves on his pyre and that those who refused to do so were held in disgrace'. This, the custom of suttee, was accompanied by a practice which Alexander had already tried to ban in outer Iran: the exposure of dead bodies to dogs and vultures. For a happy after-life, nothing mattered more to Greeks than a proper burial, and Alexander could not bear to see his subjects ignore it.

Other discoveries were more delightful. Wise men were to be seen in the market-place where they anointed all passers-by with oil as a sign of their favour and chose whatever they wanted free of charge, whether figs, grapes or honey. Remarking on their two different sects, the one with long hair, the other with shaven heads, Alexander was keen to meet their leaders, and so he sent his Greek steersman of the Fleet, Onesicritus, to search them out. He had chosen his man carefully, for Onesicritus knew philosophy as well as the sea, having studied with the great Diogenes, master of the Greek Cynic school. Eastern and western wisdom met for polite discussion: fortunately, Onesicritus was also writing a history.

Two miles from Taxila he came on fifteen wise men, sitting or lying naked in various postures. One, whom the Greeks called Calanus, laughed aloud 'seeing that the visitor was wearing a cloak, a broad-brimmed Macedonian hat and knee-length boots'. Onesicritus was asked to take off his clothes and sit down if he wished to hear their teaching: 'But the heat of the sun', he later explained 'was so scorching that nobody could have borne to walk barefoot on the ground, especially at midday.' Less hardy than his master Diogenes, he hesitated in embarrassment, until the oldest and wisest guru, named Mandanis, excused him and began to talk. 'Mandanis,' he said, 'commended Alexander for his love of wisdom, even though he ruled so vast an Empire: he was the only philosopher in arms he had ever seen. ... He went on to ask about Socrates, Pythagoras and Diogenes, remarking that they seemed to be decent and easy men, though they paid too much attention to conventions and not enough to nature.' Three interpreters were needed for the conversation. 'Because my interpreters only understand the simplest language,' Mandanis was believed to have said, 'I cannot prove to you why philosophy is useful. It would be like asking pure water to flow through mud.' But Onesicritus filtered the dark wisdom of the gurus through his own Greek preconceptions: he could barely understand them, so 'steersman of fantasy, not of the fleet', he took them to be agreeing with his own philosophy. Hindus, therefore, vouched in his history for the truths of Diogenes the Cynic.

Even if misunderstood, two of these naked wise men did make their way down to occupied Taxila. There, they dined at Alexander's table and 'ate their food while standing ...: the younger and fitter of the two balanced on one leg and held up a wooden beam, about five feet long, with both of his hands; when the leg became tired, he shifted on to the other and stood there all the day long.' As proof of his self-control he left the camp and refused all inducements to return, as they would put him at Alexander's beck and call. The elder one, Calanus, had finished his thirty-seven years of prescribed asceticism and was free to adapt his way of life: for the next two years, he followed the army from Taxila to Susa and lectured to any officers who were interested. His death, aged seventy-nine, was to cause a remarkable stir.

Legend could hardly leave this meeting between East and West as it had happened. The theme was embellished with variations and for two thousand years, the name of the Gymnosophists, or Naked Philosophers, remained part of the common culture of lettered men. In India their meetings with Alexander passed through his *Romance* into the *Sayings of Milinda*, a classic Buddhist text; in the Mediterranean, they were prominent in the works and poems of scholars in Renaissance Florence; in England, after the death of Cromwell, Puritan gentlemen still pinned their revolutionary fervour on the Gymnosophists' ideal, praising the Indians in pam-

349

phlets for being Puritans before their time, and denouncing Alexander as the type of a monarch like Charles II. The Gymnosophists' fame had spread far beyond their town by the Murree hills, and all because a pupil of Aristotle had crossed the Hindu Kush in search of the eastern Ocean and a pupil of Diogenes had left the boats on his native island of Cos, joined the expedition and agreed, in India, to go out in the midday sun.

CHAPTER TWENTY-FIVE

Among the peculiarities of Taxila there was one which was to matter more to Alexander than any Gymnosophist or elephant: the first spring rains had begun to fall. But he paid no attention, though his Indian wise men were famed for their knowledge of the weather, and he turned to the task in hand. This was plain enough. The rajahs of the Punjab had their local animosities and, as usual, Alexander meant to play them off against each other. Ambhi of Taxila told of his neighbour Porus, who ruled to the south-east across the boundary river Jhelum: he had elephants and a large army and was likely to prove troublesome. Friendlier rajahs to the north were received and reinstated, as Alexander's thoughts had now turned eastwards, unwilling to interfere with native government provided his lines were assured: Ambhi was allowed to wear the royal diadem, happy in his reward of a thousand talents of booty, gold and silver tableware, Persian dress and thirty caparisoned horses, to the disgust of at least one Macedonian officer who could not see any merit in a decadent Indian.

In early May Alexander recruited 5,000 Indians and left Taxila, never to return to the Tamra-nala river and its province. His campaign in Swat had been no more immediately successful than any other attempt in history to exterminate mountain guerrillas. He had built walls, left Macedonian garrisons and restored the native chieftains wherever possible, but within three months, the tribesmen round Pir-Sar were to rise in revolt and murder his satrap. It needed harsher punishment to put them down for another eight years. As for Taxila, it too received a garrison and a settlement of invalided soldiers, but it was not for another two hundred years that the presence of Greeks in Iran and India forced it to break with its past. Then, had Alexander returned, he would have found a very different city, no longer the shambling disorder of an Indian slum but the neat rectangle of a Greek street plan, eventually to be defended by a stone-built wall whose twenty-foot width was buttressed with square towers.

North-west up the valley, Pushkalavati, City of the Lotus, was to wear a similar new look: its alleys would become broad boulevards, whose straight lines were edged with regular blocks of shops and town houses,

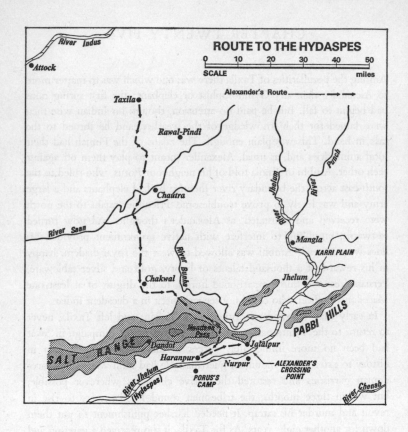

ROUTE TO THE HYDASPES

SCALE

0 10 20 30 40 50

miles

Alexander's Route

River Indus

Attock

Taxila

Rawal-Pindi

Chautra

River Saan

River Jhelum

River Punch

River Bunha

Mangla

KARRI PLAIN

Chakwal

Jhelum

SALT RANGE

Nandana Pass

Dandot

Haranpur

Nurpur

Jalalpur

ALEXANDER'S CROSSING POINT

PORUS'S CAMP

River Jhelum (Hydaspes)

PABBI HILLS

River Chenab

broken here and there by a Buddhist shrine. When Greek culture overtook the towns of the north-west Punjab, it did so decisively; some three hundred years after Alexander, the new town at Taxila was overlooked by a temple, perhaps for fire-worship, whose façade was distinguished by classic Ionic pillars. These changes were part of a different story, the conquests of the Greek kings who emerged in the province of Bactria a hundred years after Alexander, and of the later Scythian nomads who seem to have continued the Greek city plans which they saw on their way from Sogdia into India. Alexander had deposited in furthest Asia the great-grandfathers of Greeks who would one day alter city life in the plains near Rawal-Pindi, but he could take no credit for the change himself.

The road to the river Jhelum was short, flat and easy. An envoy had been sent to Porus, asking him to bring his tribute and meet Alexander at the river-frontier: Porus replied that he would come to a meeting, certainly, but his tribute would only be armed men. There was nothing for it but to fight. A march of 110 miles brought men and elephants to a suitable camp, probably near modern Haranpur, the crossing-point of the Jhelum for Sultan Mahmud 1,400 years later and nowadays the bridge-head for the British-built railway. Even without binoculars, scouts could hardly miss the outlines of Porus's army on the far bank three miles to the south: his cavalry seemed to number 5,000, his infantry more than 30,000, and as the Macedonians liked to exaggerate their enemies, there is little doubt that his forces were very much fewer than Alexander's. But his elephants brought to a head the anxieties of the past few months: two hundred, it seemed to the attackers, waited in harness for the signal to advance. In between the two armies, the river was rapidly rising, swollen by the prelude to the June monsoons. Alexander had neither the time nor the cover to ship elephants of his own to the far bank: Porus had the defender's advantage and only a tactical master-piece would show him that the defensive, at least on the battlefield, can be a very mixed blessing. Centuries later, when Alexander's histories were being read to Napoleon in Egypt, it was the forthcoming battle of the Jhelum that particularly caught his admirer's attention; not as grand as Gaugamela, it was subtler than anything seen in the field before.

At Haranpur, beneath the Salt Range mountains and west of the Pabbi hills, the Jhelum flows fast in its bed, about half a mile wide. As soon as Porus saw Alexander's encampment, he sent pickets further up the river bank and moved down to guard the nearest crossing in person. His planning was predictable, but it sufficed to block Alexander's path: 'The huge mass of his elephants stood along the bank and when carefully goaded, they wearied the ear with their hideous trumpeting.' Alexander could not cross a swollen river against animals who scared his horses so much that they would probably jump off their rafts in mid-stream and swim back to safety: he therefore took to a ruse, buying time for reconnaissance, while Porus saw no reason to make the first attack. Even the monsoon rains were soon to serve Alexander's purpose.

As at Gaugamela, he began his battle with a war of nerves. Boat parties and leather rafts ventured daily on to the river as if for an attack and sailed up and down out of bowshot, annoying the pickets on the far bank; the army was split into patrols and ordered to make such a noise that Porus would live on the alert. Even the Macedonians were kept under a false impression. Word had been spread in camp that it would not be possible to cross the Jhelum during the monsoons and therefore the men should prepare to bivouac until late autumn. Food was ostentatiously carted from the nearby country and stored where Porus's scouts could see it. Noting the supplies, the rajah presumed that Alexander meant delay.

And yet, even after a week or two he could not be certain. By night, he could hear the enemy cavalry cantering up and down their bank, and breaking the calm of the Punjab darkness with their *alalalalais*. As the din grew louder, his guards had to move to keep up with it; elephants were unloosed and hurred up the line, parallel with Alexander's own horsemen. Fortunately they are not animals who need more than three hours' sleep, so their tempers did not suffer. But for the men it was most exhausting. As soon as they had their enemy covered, the noise died away, only to begin again elsewhere. Night after night, these sham attacks continued, until Porus's guards would no longer play Alexander's game. They had seen their enemies' stores and they trusted in the coming monsoon; next time, they could stay at their posts and pass the night in peace.

Against an Alexander, peace is a dangerous ambition. During his scouting, a bend had been noticed in the river, some seventeen miles upstream from Haranpur. The banks were thickly treed and on Alexander's side the headland of Mangal Dev rose to a height of 1,000 feet; a mile-long ditch ran beside it into the main riverbed, which seemed to be very narrow, partly because it was divided by an island. Remote and well-hidden, it was exactly what Alexander had been wanting. He could take a select force, leaving others to cause a diversion, hide in the scrub near Mangal Dev and slip across the river under cover of night. His recent manœuvres had so lulled the Indians' suspicions that one more flurry would seem nothing unusual. Porus's guards were too few to stop him and by the time the

354

Rajah heard the news at base, his main force would be safely on dry land. This strategy would never have been considered had he not the highest confidence in his officers of staff. Some were to act as a decoy, others were to arrange the transport: all the while, the yellow waters of the Jhelum were rising and gathering speed.

On the night of the grand attack, fires were lit near Haranpur to suggest a permanent camp. The faithful Craterus, so often the second-in-command, was ordered to stay at base with more than a third of the army: he was briefed for each of two emergencies, depending on the conduct of the elephants.

If Porus fled, or took all his elephants up the bank towards Alexander's crossing-party, Craterus was to ford the river and attack the Indian camp opposite, however many troops had been left to guard it. But if Porus kept even a few of his elephants back where they now stood, Craterus was on no account to venture on to the river except in the case of a Macedonian victory.

There could be no more cautious tribute to the menace of an elephant in battle.

A few miles further up the bank, between Craterus at Haranpur and the crossing-point near Mangal Dev, the three mercenary commanders were posted with all their hired troops and ordered to brave the river only when the Indians were fully engaged. This engagement was to be the work of some 6,000 foot and 5,000 horse, chosen for their balance and experience. Shield Bearers, Agrianian javelin-men and archers would have little fear of the river and less of the elephants; their numbers imply that no Foot Companions were detailed to the front line. The cavalry, where Porus was weakest, were fundamental to the plan: the Royal Squadron and three brigades of the Companions would deliver their usual charge, thrusting-spears to the fore, while Scythians, mounted archers and the pick of the Iranian horse, probably armed with javelins, would first pin down the enemy at longer range. Alexander led the troops in person, accompanied by bodyguards and senior brigadiers: some said Ptolemy was left behind to raise a diversion, but Ptolemy himself insisted that he sailed with the leaders and fought as hard as the rest of them. It was not an adventure which a future Pharaoh would like to admit he had missed.

The preparations had been patient. Boats had been cut into sections and carted, presumably by night, to the chosen ford, where they were pieced together and hidden in the scrub, along with the usual rafts which were stitched from tent-skins and stuffed with hay. On the afternoon of the crossing, Alexander had looped back behind his lines as if in search of supplies, and led his troops by a roundabout route into the woodland near the Mangal Dev ford. There they were to wait and cross in the darkness. But nothing could be done to prepare the weather; in the early evening an electric summer storm broke overhead, thundering and hissing with rain so that even the Macedonian warcry would have been inaudible. The covering noise was not unwelcome, but the clouds blotted out any light from the stars and the men had to sit until the wind and rain subsided, whiling away the hours until dawn was perilously close. The river was racing faster than ever when Alexander launched out in a thirty-oared boat, showing his troops the way to what he believed to be dry land.

As he put in to the nearest bank he was sighted by Porus's pickets, who turned and galloped back across the seventeen miles of rough ground to their rajah at base. It seemed too simple to be true: they would not return for at least an hour and a half, by which time Alexander could have disembarked enough of his 11,000 men and 5,000 horses to repulse them. But in the aftermath of the storm, he had landed not on the far bank but on the island, deceptively placed in mid-stream. There was a ford across to dry land but the river had risen so fast that it was not easily detected, especially in a hurry: there was no time left to man the boats again and head for the shore. Alexander had to set his men an example. He urged Bucephalas down into the river and steadied the old horse as he felt for the reassuring clatter of a hard bed beneath and held his ground against water which now came up to his shoulder. Even when four or five have to clamber out of a river, it pays to be the first rider up the bank; when 5,000 horses are waiting their turn, latecomers can only dread the morass churned up by those in front. But they managed, even without stirrups, to steady themselves as the horses floundered. The infantry followed behind, up to their chests in water, all the more unpleasant for any who happened to be wearing breastplates.

Once on the far bank Alexander pressed ahead with his cavalry. This bold move was well planned. Any advance troops sent by Porus would be the very fastest in his army, no doubt the cavalry and chariots, for he would wish them to arrive before the Macedonians had crossed. In this aim they had failed, so the light Macedonian infantry were not needed to counter them. Alexander's horsemen outnumbered Porus's total cavalry, and chariots were no menace to veterans of Gaugamela, reinforced by mounted archers. If Porus decided to move his entire force at once, elephants included, it would be several hours before he appeared, and meanwhile the Macedonian infantry would have rejoined their king and the Companions, grateful for the cover they had been given.

Porus's retort, when it arrived, was variously described both in number and result. According to Ptolemy, who claimed to be present, 120 chariots and 2,000 horse came careering down the riverside only to run into a slanted wing of Companions and horse-archers, who attacked in squadrons and soon showed the Indians why they were the finest riders in the world. The chariots were of the fast four-horse variety, and they fell victim to muddy ground which the recent storm had made unusually slippery. Pelted by horse-archers, their teams careered with no respect for the reins, until the javelin-throwers on board found themselves struck in ditches off the beaten track. Those who could not reverse were wiped out, their general among them: some said he was Porus's son, others Porus's brother, but he died before revealing his identity. Alexander's cavalry had won a promising victory: they halted, the flanks of their horses still steaming from the rain, and when the infantry line overtook them, all 11,000 men could look forward to their next objective, Porus himself, some fifteen miles distant.

Porus's situation was unenviable but by no means hopeless. In mid-morning, he found himself threatened on two sides at once. Craterus was waiting to cross the river directly opposite, while Alexander had already crossed and was moving down the near bank, set on a pincer attack. Alexander, therefore, was his first priority, and he would do well to come far forward from base to meet him. Elephants and troops would have to be left to stop Craterus slipping across into the rear, but this division of his forces could ill be afforded. His cavalry was outnumbered, perhaps by three to one, and survivors of his advance party were talking dispiritedly of their defeat, for the Indians were practised horsemen, but in skills that now seemed irrelevant:

They carry two javelins and a small shield: their horses, however, are not padded and they do not use Greek bits, but they tie a noseband of stitched leather round the horse's lips and nose and fit it with spikes of bronze or iron: the rich however, use ivory. The spikes are not very sharp, but in the horse's mouth, they put an iron bar like a skewer, to which they attach the reins. When they pull on the reins, this bar masters the horse and the spikes prick into him, forcing him to obey.

Against the Companions, javelins and primitive curb-chains allowed neither a countercharge nor sharp manœuvre. As the advance party had already found, both were essential for victory.

The infantry, at least, had numbers on their side. Even after leaving guards for Craterus, Porus is said to have had some 30,000 foot-soldiers at his disposal. These outnumbered Alexander's infantry by five to one, as neither his mercenary troops nor any of the seven battalions of Foot Companions had crossed the river and there was no question of their fighting in packed formation with sarissas. The Indians' proper skill was archery:

Their bows are as tall as the archers themselves and to shoot them, they rest them on the ground and tread on them with their left foot, pulling the bow-string a long way back. Their arrows are about four feet long and no shield or breastplate, however strong, can keep them off. In their left hand, they hold a leather shield, narrower than themselves but not much shorter.

Others carried javelins, while 'all wear a broad sword, at least four and a half feet long: they wield this with both hands, so that its stroke may be more effective'. Despite these swords hand to hand fighting was a hazard they liked to avoid. Not so the Macedonians: Porus had no heavy infantry and nothing to compare at close quarters with Alexander's Shield Bearers.

Advancing up the bank to sandy ground he distributed his troops to the best advantage. The elephants were stationed fifty or a hundred feet apart, far in advance of the rest of the army: they stood like bastions, each with four men or more on their back, though they cannot have numbered two hundred, as Ptolemy perhaps implied, for their line would then have stretched between two and four miles wide. As it was not safe to put troops in the gaps between them, the infantry were drawn up behind, matching the intervals neatly and overlapping on each end; their wings were massed with cavalry and chariots, hoping for a clearer run. Drummers, meanwhile, were sounding the beat of battle, their rhythms pleasing the musical ear of the elephants 'who looked, at a distance, like towers, projecting from a wall of armed men'. Prominent among them rode Porus, dressed in a fine cuirass and a cotton Indian cloak; his hair was gathered into a top knot, as was the fashion, and he seemed to the Macedonians to be over seven foot tall.

Alexander, too, had halted for rearrangement. Outnumbered on foot, if not on horseback, he needed to use his brain, for each unit had its limitations; combined, they could still do what he wanted provided they were asked to do it in the right order. The Companions could charge down the Indian light infantry and outmanœuvre the fewer horsemen on each wing, but they could not attack the elephants without a panic. The Shield Bearers, archers, and Agrianians were equipped to deal with the elephants and come to close quarters with the Indian swordsmen, but they were vulnerable to a charge from enemy cavalry. The Mounted Archers could harass the chariots but not the elephants: the heavier arrows of the Indians would not have the range of Alexander's and the slippery ground might well hamper the methods of their bowmen. All these factors were balanced out until Alexander had resolved their contradictions. The plan was made ready: it had the added virtue of his ingenuity.

He decided to rely entirely on horsemen for a breakthrough. Because of the elephants, they were to leave the centre well alone and mass on the Indians' far left wing and as usual, their line was slanted. Alexander, the Mounted Archers, the Orientals and two squadrons of Companions, led by Hephaistion and Perdiccas, were furthest forward: the remaining two squadrons were sloped behind them at an angle and commanded by Coenus, the most trusted of the brigadiers. His orders were firm: while Alexander and the main body of cavalry rode far out to the Indian left, he was to detach his two rear units and swing wide behind the Indian right. This was not as risky as it sounded. Alexander's main charge to the left would cause the Indians to gather up all their cavalry from both wings and follow him for fear of being outflanked: they would hurriedly congregate against the main threat, taking their eye off the right, which they had not enough horsemen to defend. Coenus's encirclement would take them by surprise, and with any luck he would arrive in the Indians' rear just as Alexander was breaking through on the left. First, attract all the enemy cavalry on to one wing; then charge them from front and back at once and having routed them, loose the Shield Bearers against the elephants. The battle would be fought in well-defined stages, turning on the very cavalry movement which had proved decisive at Gaugamela.

The Indians took up the challenge as expected. When Alexander began to gallop far out to their left they moved all their cavalry on to one wing and struggled after him, disregarding Coenus on the other wing in their hurry. The Mounted Archers volleyed and charged: the Companions followed up with gusto: the Indians were still straggling in column and had no time to fan out into line. Before long, Coenus was careering round into their rear on their right, the last attack they can have expected. They tried to drop back a squadron or two to face him, but the shock of Alexander's charge on their left had so deranged them that they scattered into the centre and looked for safety among the elephants. Shield Bearers, archers and Agrianians now saw their chance. As the mahouts urged their beasts forward against any Companions who hoped to harass the retreating cavalry, the finest foot-brigades in Alexander's army swarmed among them, armed with a surprise weapon. While archers and Agrianian javelin-men aimed at the mahouts themselves, the 3,000 veterans of the Shield Bearers swung axes at the elephants' legs and daringly slashed at their trunks with curved scimitars. Alexander knew the weak points of an elephant and had equipped his men accordingly.

Hamstrung and trunkless, some fifty elephants were put out of action; the rest stampeded indignantly, tusking and trampling without respect for friend or foe. They were exposed to professional butchery and they hated it: 'It was particularly terrifying to watch them seize men and weapons in their trunks and dash them hard against the ground.' The battle, like its histories, became impossibly confused as the Companions charged down the fleeing Indian horsemen and Craterus at last began to cross the river, while the mercenary troops poured over from upstream. But the signal of defeat did not go unrecorded: 'When the elephants tired and no longer found strength to charge, they began to retreat step by step, emitting only a high-pitched whistle.' The Macedonians had witnessed an elephant's last resort: when too disgruntled to trumpet, they 'signify their apprehension by rapping at the end of their trunk smartly on the ground and emitting a current of air, hitherto retained, as if from a valve at high pressure'. The battle of the Jhelum began with the charge of cavalry and ended with the elephants' hoot of distress.

Porus was most unwilling to capitulate. He had fought in the thick of the battle and only when wounded in the right shoulder by an arrow had he goaded his elephant into retreat: 'Alexander had seen his might and gallantry and wished to save him. He therefore sent Ambhi the Indian to overtake him and give him a meassage. But when Porus saw his old enemy approaching, he turned his elephant and poised himself to throw a javelin.' Ambhi wheeled away in the nick of time, and an Indian prisoner less hurtful to the rajah was sent to try a different approach. Porus listened more kindly and even dismounted, feeling thirsty. 'His elephant,' said the more fanciful histories,

was of the very largest size and had shown remarkable intelligence and care for its king. While Porus was still active, it would vigorously repel his attackers, but when it saw he was flagging under his many wounds, afraid that he might fall off, it bent its knees and gently lowered itself to the ground; with its trunk, it tenderly took hold of each spear and drew them from his master's body.

Alexander and a few Companions came forward to meet their royal enemy; 'Alexander! my noble lord', the Persians' great epic poem, centuries later, made him say, 'Our two hosts have been shattered by the battle; The wild beasts feed on the brains of men; The horses' hooves are trampling on their bones. But both of us are heroes, brave and young. . . . Both noblemen of eloquence and brain; Why should slaughter be the soldier's fate? Or bare survival after the fray?' For once, legend had an excuse in history. As Porus approached, thin and remarkably tall, Alexander sent an interpreter to ask how he wished to be treated. 'Like a King', he replied, and won so much of Alexander's respect that he was reinstated as rajah and left with his kingdom intact: as Alexander advanced, seven new tribes and two thousand new cities would be added to Porus's dominions, a handsome reward for defeat. Chivalry suited the politics of balancing one Punjab rajah against another, but Indian historians have been unable to believe this intelligent generosity and still argue that if Porus received such honours, India's alleged defeat at the Jhelum can only be a western falsehood.

Victory, though resounding, did have one reservation. Alexander had gained a rajah and a new troop of elephants: he had also lost a life-long friend. In the opening skirmish with Porus's chariots, Bucephalas had been gravely wounded and within hours of the battle the old horse was reported dead; others, loyal to his invincibility, maintained that he had only collapsed of extreme old age. It was saddening news, but it could at least be honoured; Alexander had already decided to found two cities on the banks of the Jhelum, and the nearer of the two was a chance to pay his last respects. The easterly one on the battlefield he called Nicaea, City of Victory; the westerly one, near the site of Bucephalas's last river-crossing, he named Bucephala, in memory of a gallant horse. A funeral procession was organized, which Alexander led in person, and the horse's remains were presumably laid in a grave in his town; the site, soon to be damaged by floods, has never been located.

Bucephalas's fame could not be so easily washed away. In the art of Alexander's successors there recurs from Balkh to Egypt the novel theme of a horse with horns: at the eastern and western mints alike, it is to be found on the silver coins of Seleucus, his royal Successor in Asia: it also appears on a plaster plaque in the Egyptian kingdom of the Ptolemies. Now, Seleucus was to be famed for killing a bull with his bare hands, and hence it was said that his many portraits showed him wearing bull's horns: he was also to commemorate a horse which had once saved his life by a notable statue at Antioch. But these two motifs together do not wholly explain why his horse was shown horned as well, nor why the Egypt of the Ptolemies, his avowed opponents, had copied the same design. A theme which is shared by Seleucids and Ptolemies may be derived, most plausibly, from Alexander, their only common model. Bucephalas, said a late authority, 'did not as some believe, have horns of his own, but was adorned with golden horns, so they say, for battle', as the proper harness for charger whose name meant Ox-head. If true, this could be the meaning of the Successors' horned horses: they stressed their different links with Alexander but they also revived Bucephalas's memory, even on the side of their coins more usually reserved for a god. Such memories die hard. More than 250 years later, on his equestrian statue at Rome, Julius Caesar's horse was cast to suggest Bucephalas's features. A thousand years after that, the traveller Marco Polo was entertained in Balkh by stories of the rulers of Badakshan, between the Pamirs and the Oxus and close to the site of the most north-easterly Alexandria; their horses, they said, were descended from Bucephalas and so were born with a horn on their head, but jealousies in the royal family had caused the only stallion to be put to death, and so the line was now extinct. Men might never equal Alexander, but they could at least lay claim to his attributes, down to the very hooves and harness of the horse which had carried him for twenty years and died, an unforgotten hero, at the river Jhelum.

CHAPTER TWENTY-SIX

After winning the Jhelum and founding Bucephala, Alexander paid a sacrifice to the Sun. His choice of god was a symbol of his ambitions: his march was to take him eastwards, out towards the sunrise, and it would be helped by a sunny interval in the coming monsoon weather. 'In India,' a Greek had once written, safe at the Persian court, 'it never rains'; conversation with wise men and rajahs would have taught Alexander more of the truth. In the Hindu Kush he had defied the snow: his route to Siwah or Sogdia had made light of the desert. In India, when men talked of the summer rains, a sacrifice to the sun was all he felt he needed. The troops were encouraged with talk of treasure and presents of gold coin: Alexander would show them that a son of Zeus could not be deterred by the elements.

For a month, his disregard increased the danger, as he delayed in Porus's kingdom and enjoyed the supplies from the three hundred towns in its fertile country. He would have been better advised to hurry eastwards: three more rivers of the Punjab lay in his path and from mid-June onwards they would be dangerously swollen with the monsoon rains. But his mind had turned to a new and promising plan. He believed that he was near to a direct route home and when the day came to act on his belief, he would need a fleet. Men were sent up the Jhelum to the dense fir forests on the lower slopes of the Himalayas and ordered to fell timber to build ships, a familiar task to Macedonians, owners of the finest wood in the Balkans. Himalayan pine and deodar cedars, often twenty feet in girth, were a challenge to their skills of forestry; the men needed to be brave in these unfamiliar surroundings. Snakes of alarming size were seen slithering across the forest floor, and at a distance the chattering of apes was mistaken for the approach of an enemy. There were tigers, too, which the Indians said would attack an elephant, and also blue-green peacocks which so impressed Alexander that he forbade his men to kill them.

When crossing the Indus, two months before, Alexander had noticed crocodiles along the river: now, on marching east to the Chenab, third of the five Punjab rivers, he was much struck by the clumps of beans which grew on its banks. They reminded him of crops he had seen in Egypt five years ago and together with the crocodiles, they led him to a delightful theory: these upper waters of the Punjab must surely be the long-lost

363

source of the River Nile, as they shared its flora and fauna. The Chenab, he knew, joined the Indus: the Indus, he guessed, flowed south-west through the desert and curved round south of the Persian gulf into Upper Egypt where it changed its name to the Nile. His view of the world was compressed to fit the little he had seen of it. The Indian Ocean, the vast mass of Arabia and the Red Sea were obstacles of which he was as yet unaware and throughout his life he continued to underestimate the length of the Persian empire from north to south and the distance west from the Oxus to the Black Sea. 'Not long afterwards,' wrote his admiral Nearchus, 'he discovered his mistake about the Indus,' but when he first gave orders for ship-timber to be cut and seasoned, he was hoping eventually to explore the Indus and coast back home to Egypt and his Alexandria, having realized his aims in the east.

These aims seemed more plausible because of his faulty geography. India was believed to be bounded by the Eastern Ocean, a part of the waters which flowed round the Greeks' idea of the world, and though the facts were not yet certain, it did not sound as if the edge of India was impossibly far away. If the Eastern Sea was indeed Alexander's objective because it was the boundary of the world, then by playing each rajah off against his neighbour and crushing any resistance, Alexander could fight his way towards this thrilling end and crown his career with a sight which no Achilles had ever expected to see. 'You, Zeus, hold Olympus; I set the earth beneath my sway.' Even if he was only marching east to explore and conquer India, an aim to which the world's end was incidental, the narrowed view of India and the false view of the Nile were still a strong encouragement; for wherever he marched, home, down the Indus-Nile, was always within reach. His ambitions were those of an explorer as much as a conqueror and only to men who have never shared in a search and a struggle against nature do these seem madness. But for the first time since the battle at Issus, Alexander was living under a bad mistake, and from the Chenab onwards, things began to go wrong.

The natives were numerous, though their weapons were old-fashioned: on the border of the Chenab alone Alexander forced thirty-seven cities and at least as many villages to surrender and added their half million citizens to Porus's kingdom. It was nothing new to the Macedonians to be outnumbered, but there were hazards which needed a stronger nerve. 'In India,' wrote Theophrastus the botanist, who had heard the survivor's reports and is too astute to be disbelieved, 'the Macedonians ate a type of wheat which was so powerful that many actually burst apart.' Such insights into their hardships are all too few; the only convincing figures for casualties are on an occasion when Alexander was not present. But this one at least has the merit of being unforgettable. Others ate from a tree 'which was not particularly large but had pods like a bean, ten inches long and as sweet as honey'; this, the Greeks' first meeting with a banana or perhaps a mango, gave them such upset stomachs that Alexander forbade them to touch it, 'and you were unlikely to survive', wrote Aristobulus, 'if you ate one' against his orders. Other trees were safer, if no less alarming: by the river Chenab the troopers marvelled at the banyan, the wonder of Indian dendrologists. 'The shoots of a single tree spread out into a huge shaded arbour, like a tent with many pillars,' so wide that 'fifty horsemen could shelter from the midday sun beneath it.' Close inspection showed that each separate 'trunk' was a giant shoot from one and the same root system, while the fruits were small but deliciously juicy. Farther east, there were to be reports of a banyan which cast a shadow for half a mile, by no means an impossibility: the prize banyan of the Calcutta Botanic Garden resembles a huge wood, four acres big and a quarter of a mile in circumference.

Even a banyan was at the mercy of the weather. As the Chenab came in view, midsummer made way for the monsoon proper to begin, and at last the army understood why the local villages had been built on banks and mounds. As the rain teemed down, the river rose from its bed and came to life as if roused from a long and reluctant sleep. The nullahs began to flood and the ditches could no longer take their overflow. Camp had to be hastily moved as the current rose, ten feet, twenty feet, thirty feet, until it burst its banks in disdain for the invaders. The men retired to the villages and watched the water race across the plains, in places even deeper than the elephants, and as they watched, they became aware of a threat which could not be so easily avoided: the floods had caused their houses to be plagued with snakes.

'Their numbers and their ferocity,' wrote Nearchus, 'were very surprising: at the time of the rains, they retreat to the higher villages and the natives therefore build their beds well above the ground, though even then, they are often forced to abandon their homes by this overwhelming invasion.' Species of python as long as twenty-four feet came in search of a dry corner: others were too tiny to be noticed, but it was these smaller snakes, scorpions and cobras who brought the most discomfort. 'They hid in the tents, the cooking-pots, the hedges and the walls: those whom they bit bled from every pore and suffered agony, dying very rapidly unless help was found in the drugs and roots of the Indian snake-charmers,' whose skill, however, was remarkably effective. Medical supplies were summoned urgently from all quarters, while wherever possible the men hung hammocks between the trees and spent an anxious night above the ground. Only by crossing the Chenab could they hope for better things.

But the Chenab was foaming and roaring in its mile-and-a-half-wide channel. Though Alexander chose the broadest and smoothest stretch for the crossing, even Ptolemy admitted that many of those who crossed by boat, rather than by rafts of stuffed leather, were dashed against the rocks so that 'not a few were lost in the water'. Once on the far bank Hephaistion was sent to deal with Indians to the north, while Porus returned to recruit as many elephants as possible, a sign that Alexander was expecting heavy fighting. Supplies were to be convoyed eastwards as soon as the river allowed, and in the meantime, he would live off the land.

Marching eastwards he waded across the river Ravi with his lightest troops and received the surrender of its nearest tribesmen. They told him of a tribe called the Cathaioi in the plains near Lahore who were bellicose by nature; they were said to have planned resistance and inflamed the tribesmen south on the Indus. Alexander hurried down to their territory in three days' rapid marching, with only one day for rest, and arrived at Sangala, their largest fortress. The Cathaioi had drawn up a triple line of carts off which they could defend themselves; cavalry failed to provoke them down from their hill, so the infantry line pushed in amongst them and drove them back behind Sangala's solid brick wall. Alexander had no siege machinery and could only encircle the fort while tunnels were dug to undermine it; a night escape was anticipated and cost the Indians five hundred lives. Just when the tunnels were being completed, Porus arrived with 5,000 Indian volunteers and the siege engines, a credit to the transport section who had hauled them across the mud of a summer monsoon. The engines were not needed, as the sapper's job had already sufficed; the wall subsided into the tunnel, ladders were slung across the breaches and brave resistance did not save 17,000 Indians from being slaughtered, according to Ptolemy, and another 70,000 being captured. 'Less than a hundred of Alexander's troops died in the siege' but more than 1,200 were wounded, an unusually high proportion for Ptolemy to admit and one which included many officers. The wounded were another bad burden on morale, and all the while the thunder rumbled and the rain poured down on weary men.

Neighbouring tribesmen were pursued to the death if they ran away, pardoned if they surrendered; Alexander 'would not be harsh to them if they stayed and received him as a friend, any more than he had been harsh to other self-governing Indians who surrendered willingly'. The continued stress on their 'ancient self-government' was a thin, but revealing, cloak for the campaign; momentarily, matters improved when

366

the army reached Sopeithes's kingdom near Lahore and the river Beas.

When their engines of war drew near its capital city, out marched the native king, a tall figure dressed in gold and purple embroidery, golden sandals and bracelets and necklaces of pearl. He handed over his sceptre, studded with precious beryl, whereupon historians repaid his compliment:

Among these people, the strangest feature is their respect for beauty: they choose their most handsome man as king. When a baby is born, two months after its birth the royal council decides whether it is beautiful enough to deserve to live . . .: as for the adults, to improve their looks they dye their beards all sorts of bright colours. Oddly enough, their brides and bridegrooms even choose each other.

There were reasons for these friendly reminiscences: the ancient name of the country round Lahore meant 'prosperity' and for several days the army feasted in comfort, while the officers, at least, were housed away from the rain. The king entertained them with his famous breed of dogs, whose pedigree included the blood of tigers: four of them harassed a lion in public and refused to let go of his haunches even when the keepers were ordered to hack off one of their hind legs. The show appealed to Alexander's love of hunting and one of the dogs was given to him as a present; there were also reports of local veins of gold and silver, verified in the meantime by his Greek prospector-in-chief. The land of prosperity owned an enormous mound of salt: 'the Indians, however, have no experience of mining or casting metals', and 'are rather naive about what they own.'

East of Amritsar, only one more river of the Punjab remained to be crossed and there was no doubt now that Alexander meant to go beyond it. His staff needed little imagination to guess what he intended on the far side: for the past few weeks, they had been assembling as many elephants as they could find and they were now expecting the arrival of a batch of reinforcements from Greece and Asia far larger than any they had ever received before. Indians were joining in the march as well as any of the multitude of prisoners who had not been sold: the total strength of the army when reinforced was said to be 120,000, double its previous size and large enough for an expedition to the eastern ocean or for a view of the edge of the inhabited world. True, timber had been cut for a fleet on the Jhelum, but it would take time to season and even when ships had been built there was no need to use them immediately.

But Alexander was to pass from prosperity to disillusionment. The officers had heard stories of India and even knew the name and existence of Ceylon, but it was hard to connect these scraps of information with the brown and endless plain through which they were dragging their carts and sodden equipment, in mud which sucked the elephants down to a slow crawl. Alexander had talked of a four-month journey from Taxila and they had been prepared to believe him, but on the borders of the Beas the next king after Prosperity's lands gave the first clear warnings of what lay beyond. His knowledge may have been rough and ready, but its gist was unmistakable; beyond the Beas was a well-tilled land of peace and fertility, governed by aristocrats and well supplied with elephants. Beyond the Indus, if Alexander returned and marched down it, there came a twelve days' journey through deserted land; then the Ganges, some 'four miles wide', and deepest of all the Indian rivers, along whose lower course stretched the lands of Ksandrames the king, whose infantry was said to number 200,000, his horsemen as many again or more, while 2,000 chariots and 4,000 elephants would support them to the death. It was a dramatic piece of news. Like the Conquistador who first saw a boat from the un-known kingdom of the Incas, Alexander had been warned of a civilization which the western world had never known to exist. For the first time, he heard the name of Dhana Nanda, last of the nine great kings of Magadha, whose dynasty had ruled for the past two hundred years from their splendid palace at Palimbothra, where the Ganges runs down to the eastern sea.

It was hard to believe such a revelation. Alexander is said to have asked Porus to confirm it, which he duly did, adding that Ksandrames was a very common sort of man, who was only the son of a barber, raised to the throne by a family intrigue. That promised well for the invasion, while detailed inquiry gave a clear enough picture of the landscape, even down to such details as the turtles which swam in the Ganges. But wild surmise had quickly spread among the men and its dangers were obvious. Personally, Alexander relished the thought of a struggle with another Empire which was labouring, like Darius's, in its extreme old age. He would have to time his announcement carefully: unusual favours would help to prepare the audience, especially as the rains were showing signs of abating.

The troops, therefore, were given leave to plunder the nearby country, no mean privilege in a land where precious stones were theirs for the taking; in a river like the Chenab, jewels were washed to the surface, until no keen eye could miss the Indian beryls and diamonds, the onyxes, topaz and jasper and the clearest amethysts in the classical world. While the men were seeking their fortune, their women and children were called into camp and promised regular payments of corn and money. Such bribery was of no avail: when the soldiery returned from their plundering, they gathered in groups and sullenly discussed the rumours of their future. Their mood had not improved when Alexander summoned their commanders and at last explained his plans for what lay beyond.

His speech was better constructed than received. The officers heard him in silence and for a long while they were too embarrassed to take up his invitation to reply. At last, the veteran Coenus dared to put their feelings into words: the men would never agree to a march against such an enemy, and if Alexander still wished to go eastwards to the Ganges, he must go without his Macedonians. It was not so much a mutiny as the expression of a deep despair. The men had marched 11,250 miles in the past eight years, regardless of season or landscape; official figures were to claim that they had killed at least three-quarters of a million Asiatics. Twice they had starved, and their clothing was so tattered that most were dressed in Indian garments: the horses were footsore and the wagons were unusable in plains that had turned to a swamp. It was the weather which had finally broken their spirit. For the past three months, the rains had soused them through and through. Their buckles and belts were corroded and their rations were rotting as mildew ruined the grain: boots leaked, and no sooner had their weapons been polished than the damp turned them green with mould. And all the while the river Beas rolled on before them, defying them to cross it in search of a battle with elephants, not in their tens or hundreds but in thousand upon thousand. They had been told, rightly, that the elephants east of the Ganges were larger and fiercer, and there was even word of the heavier breed which lived on the island of Ceylon.

Their case could not have been put from a more respectable quarter. Coenus had served in the army for twenty years, latterly as a Hipparch in the Companion Cavalry, and Alexander would always choose him for the toughest missions. Lesser generals, therefore, felt free to approve his words: 'Many even shed tears as a further proof of their unwillingness to face the dangers ahead.' Alexander grew angry and blamed them for hanging back. When anger had made no impression, he sent them away and began to sulk. There is nothing harder for a man than when all he has planned is challenged, when he knows he can do it if only the others will think on his own bold terms.

The next morning, he called the officers back and told them that 'he would go on himself but he would not force a single one of his Macedonians to come with him; he would find the men to follow him willingly. As for those who wished to go home, they could go now and they could tell their friends that they had deserted their King in the middle of their enemy.'

But the officers had taken a stand and they were not to be shamed into surrender. They refused, and it was time for the King's last threat: Alexander retired in anger to his tent and refused to see his Companions for the whole of the next two days in the hope that his brooding would make them think again.

A profound silence fell on the camp. The men were annoyed with their king's loss of temper but they were not to be shifted from their ground. The hours passed, until they could even feel brave enough to despise him and boo if he kept up his anger any longer. Such stubbornness proved decisive, for Alexander realized that he was a beaten man. Like his hero Achilles, he could not stand the shame of a public humiliation: he sent for the priests and seers and told them he meant to offer sacrifice to see if he should cross the Beas or not. Animals were brought, 'but when he sacrificed, the offerings did not go in his favour'. Now that he could plead the gods' disapproval, he set aside his shame, and summoned his closest friends and elderly Companions to tell them that all seemed to point to a retreat. It was only three years since he had flouted the omens and crossed the Oxus in defiance of gods and prophets.

When the news was announced, a roar of relief went up from the ranks and many burst into tears that their wishes had come true. Amid such jubilation, respect for the gods was the one remaining solace for Alexander's sense of pride. The army was divided into twelve sections, each of which was ordered to build an altar for the twelve Greek gods of Olympus 'as thanks to those who had brought them victoriously so far and as a memorial of all they had been through together'. The altars were to be enormous, 'as high as the tallest towers and broader even than towers would be': Alexander did not wish to be remembered as the king whom the river Beas had humbled. Others said that he traced out a camp three times larger than the one he had used and surrounded it with a ditch fifty feet wide and forty feet deep. Inside, huts were to be built with beds nearly eight feet long and mangers twice the normal size; huge suits of armour and impossibly large bits and bridles were scattered on the ground 'to leave the native evidence that his men were big men, showing excessive physical strength'. Romance later claimed that the altars were inscribed to father Ammon, brother Apollo, the Sun and the Kabeiroi, wild gods who were favoured by his mother Olympias.

Only archaeology will ever settle how far these rumours are true and though several have searched, nobody has been lucky enough to find what could be one of the strangest memorials of the classical past. There is no doubting the altars, but until it is proved on the ground the megalomania

370

of the camp need only be posthumous gossip. What is certain is that Alexander had known his first defeat and that when he reached the Jhelum by the way he had come, he would find little joy in the sudden relaxation of the early autumn rain. Across to Amritsar, back to the river Ravi, and so to the river Chenab, less swollen than before: there, the retreat was briefly halted by a sudden loss in the high command. Coenus the Hipparch 'died of sickness and Alexander buried him as magnificently as circumstances allowed'. It was only a few weeks since his bold complaint had turned the army homewards.

'How often before, the Führer had removed an inconvenient associate not by dismissal, but by an allegation of illness, merely to preserve the German people's faith in the internal unity of the top leadership; even now, when all was almost over, he remained true to this habit of observing public decorum.' Parallels between Hitler and Alexander have been fashionable, but there is nothing to prove that they are valid. If Coenus had been a sick man, then his plea to return was all the more intelligible; it could have been dysentery, it might have been snakebite, but the man who had publicly thwarted a son of Zeus never lived to enjoy the results of his counsel.

The retreat he inspired has always seemed sympathetic. Alexander's eastern plans have not been well received by historians: many have argued that they never existed and some have maintained that all mentions of the Ganges, are best discarded as legend. Apart from the facts, these arguments assume that no sane man could have wished to go on; there are two sides to such a judgement, and only one finds its evidence in Greek accounts of the campaign. The kingdom of Magadha was powerful, certainly, but reports of its strength were no less fantastic than those of the legendary armies of Indian epic heroes, and however plentiful its elephants, it was passing through a painful old age. In native Jain tradition, Dhana Nanda, last of its kings, was long remembered as son of a common woman, born, therefore, outside the ruling caste and detested by many of his courtiers. In the epic book of Ceylon, he is said to have extorted heaps of gold from his subjects and hidden them, meanly, in the waters of the Ganges. Alexander, most remarkably, knew this perfectly well from his informants: Ksandrames, said Porus, was 'merely the son of a barber', and not only is a barber's son a common Indian idiom for a feeble and low-born king, but it is exactly echoed in later Indian histories as a judgement on Dhana Nanda himself. The last of the Nanda dynasty had no firm hold on himself or on Magadha's loyalties; like Cortes, Alexander had stood on the brink of an old civilization, rich but torn by internal discontent. The journey from the Beas to the Eastern Ocean would have lasted another three months down a royal road, and his officers knew it as clearly as he did. And yet they turned it down.

Only the future can prove what they missed. Within three years of Alexander's death, a pretender arose in northern India, Chandragupta the Mauryan, who marshalled an army and made Magadha his own. Dhana Nanda was deposed, and ten years later Chandragupta was even pressing on the Punjab frontier, perhaps drawing help from its seditious highland tribesmen. In return for five hundred elephants, Alexander's Asian successor Seleucus was forced to concede him the Indian provinces; Chandragupta returned to Palimbothra, where he heeded his minister Kautilya and ruled in state for another twenty years. Behind the wooden palisading of the palace he kept open court to Greek envoys, who would come by the royal road from Amritsar, admire his harem and stroll in gardens which seemed to have been his for a hundred years. When asked how he had done it, said the Greeks, Chandragupta would reply: 'I watched Alexander when I was still a young man; Alexander,' he explained, 'had been within an ace of seizing India, because its king was so hated and despised, both for his character and his low birth.'

If an Indian imitator could do it, so too could his master ten years before: Dhana Nanda's kingdom could have been set against itself and Alexander might yet have walked among Palimbothra's peacocks, improved its fencing and enjoyed the fish-ponds on which the Indian princes had always learnt to sail. But not far from its gates the Ganges spreads into an estuary and glides beneath palm-trees through the banks of the silt-brown fields: it asks to be followed, and Alexander need only have done so for another six hundred miles, until he saw the sea-shore opening before him and realized that at last he was near the edge of his world. The Eastern ocean was three months away, and the soldiers had refused it. The explorer's dream was gone, when he knew too well that it could have come true.

FOUR

Pyrrho of Elis began as an unknown and impecunious painter; he then joined Alexander and followed him everywhere. He met the magi and talked with Indian gurus and as a result his outlook changed. He founded scepticism, the most noble sort of philosophy, insisting that judgement should be suspended and that nothing could be said to be known. There is no one thing, he would say, which is fine or shocking, just or unjust; nothing really exists except for man's habits and conventions and these govern the way he behaves.

He lived out his life by these principles. He would avoid nothing and take no precautions against danger, whether from roads, cliffs or dogs; he ignored them all because he never trusted the evidence of his senses. He survived, but, men say, this was only due to his friends who walked and watched, always beside him.

DIOGENES LAERTIUS, Lives of the Philosophers, 9.61

CHAPTER TWENTY-SEVEN

The retreat from the Beas was a disappointment, not a danger. The men were not so much embittered as exhausted; as for the officers, none of them plotted to take advantage of their king's defeat. For defeat it was, and the disgrace would far outweigh the negligible fears in Alexander's mind. He would not easily live with such a rebuff to his sense of glory, the heart of his Homeric values. He reached the Jhelum, only to find that Bucephala had been washed away by the rains; worse, news came from the ladies' quarters that Roxane's first baby had miscarried.

Only Porus benefited from the new despair. The 'seven nations and two thousand towns' between the Jhelum and the Beas were added to his kingdom; they had lost their interest now that the march to the east had been cancelled. There was only one direction left which promised Alexander his required adventure. It would be ignominious to retrace his steps through the Hindu Kush; now, therefore, was the moment to put the ship timber to use and explore southwards down the Jhelum to the river Indus. It was not the safest route home, but as a link between the conquests in east and west, this waterway might prove invaluable. Though Alexander had at last discovered from the natives that the Indus would not bring him round into the Nile and Upper Egypt he may well have preferred to keep up this hope among his weary troopers.

Back on the Jhelum more than 35,000 fresh soldiers from the west were waiting, raising the army's strength to 120,000, a massive force by classical standards; they had also brought medical supplies and smart new suits of gold- and silver-plated armour. More important, they would raise morale. Eight hundred ships of various shapes and sizes were needed for the voyage down the Indus, but such was the energy of the newly equipped army that two months later the fleet was ready to be manned by the expert crews of Cypriots, Egyptians, Ionian Greeks and Phœnicians who had been following Alexander, as before they had followed the fortunes of the Persian kings. The journey downstream to the outer ocean could begin.

It is a commonplace of sermons and histories that powerful men are corrupted and pay for their licence by loneliness and growing insecurity. But in life, the wicked have a way of flourishing and not every despot ends more miserably than he began: power may turn a man's head, but only the virtuous or the uninvolved insist that it must always cost him his soul. Inevitably, with Alexander this moral problem begins to be raised: thwarted, did he lose his judgement and turn on the methods of a textbook tyrant in his isolation? Failure will often show in a general's style of leadership: he may no longer delegate his work, while refusing to take the blame for its consequences: he may be too exhausted to take a firm decision, too unsure to resist the meanest suspicions. It is only a legend that when Alexander heard from his philosopher Anaxarchus of the infinite number of possible worlds, he wept, reflected that he had not even conquered the one he knew. The need to justify a lost ambition can cause a man to over-reach; moralists, at least, might expect that Alexander's first rebuff from his army would mark the loosening of his grip on reality.

History does not confirm that this was so. As no officer describes the mood of the king in council, it is impossible, as always, to divide the credit for the army's actions between Alexander and his staff. Events, however, do not suggest autocracy or nervous indecision. Within two months, the entire fleet had been built from the felled timber, a tribute to the energy of officers and carpenters, and Alexander declared the enterprise open in characteristic style. After athletic games and musical competitions, he ordered animals for sacrifice to be given free to each platoon, and then

going on board, he stood at the bows and poured a libation into the river from a golden bowl, calling upon Poseidon and the sea-nymphs, the Chenab, the Jhelum and the Indus, and the Ocean into which they ran. Then, he poured a libation to his ancestor Heracles and to Ammon and to the other gods to whom he usually paid honour, Poseidon, Amphitrite and the sea-nymphs, and he ordered the trumpeter to sound the advance.

The sailors responded, cheered by the taste of free sacrificial meat and by the pomp and variety of their expedition. There were flat-bottomed boats for the horses, thirty-oared craft for the officers, three-banked triremes, circular tubs, and eighty huge grain-lighters for supplies. These, the famous zohruks still used on the river Indus, were now built for the first time to serve Greeks; each able to hold more than two hundred tons of grain, they were one of Alexander's most valuable borrowings from the East, and their shallow draught and huge single sail would soon prove themselves in strong currents against the usual Greek trireme.

In the hot sun, the men rowed naked. No ornament had been spared for their boats; for the first time, a Greek fleet's sails had been dyed deep purple, 'each officer competing with his rivals until even the banks looked on in amazement as the wind filled out their multi-coloured emblems'. Amid this luxury, their lines had been meticulously ordered: baggage-vessels, horse transports and warships were all to keep apart at the prescribed intervals and no ship was to break the line.

The plash of the oars was unprecedented, as was the shout of the coxes who gave orders for the rowers to take each stroke: the banks of the river were higher than the ships and enclosed the noise in a narrow space, so that it was magnified and re-echoed from one side to the other ... deserted clumps of trees on each bank helped to increase the effect.

There were also the celebrated songs of Sinde whose rhythms no traveller then or now can leave behind him. The shipment of the horses so surprised the native onlookers, that many of them

ran after the fleet, while others were attracted by the echoes and careered along the bank, singing wild songs of their own. The Indians are as fond of singing and dancing as any people on earth.

Alexander had been at pains to involve his officers in the enterprise. With a typical respect for the methods of Athenian government, he appointed thirty-two trierarchs, nineteen being Macedonians, ten Greeks, two Cypriots, and one being Bagoas his Persian favourite, who would take charge of individual warships, finance them and doubtless compete for efficiency of maintenance. Most of the baggage train would follow under escort by land. Its size can only be guessed by comparisons. By now, Alexander was said to be employing some 15,000 cavalry; in the same area in the nineteenth century, British armies would have allowed 400 camels to carry a single day's grain supply for his horses alone. Nearchus the sea captain gave the size of the expedition as 120,000 men and it is not very likely that this is wild exaggeration or flattery. When their families, concubines and traders are added for a probable nine months' journey, the scale of the quartermasters' duties begins to come to life. 'We need,' wrote a British colonel, at a time when only gunpowder, heavy boots and stirrups had increased a soldier's requirements,

an extraordinary assemblage of men, women and children, ponies, mules, asses and bullocks and carts laden with all sorts and kinds of conceivable and in-conceivable things: grain, salt, cloth, sweetmeats, shawls, slippers, tools for the turners, the carpenters and blacksmiths, goods for the tailors and cobblers, the perfumers, armourers, milk-girls and grass-cutters: moochees must work the leather, puckulias carry our water, while nagurchees will supervise the travelling canteen. What a sea of camels! What guttural gurgling groanings in the long throats of salacious and pugnacious males! What resounding of sticks, as some throw away their loads and run away, tired servants often getting slain or miserably losing the column, thousands of camels dying, not only from fatigue but from ill-usage and being always overloaded. Such is the picture of the baggage of an army in India; Smithfield market alone can rival it.

Protection and supply of the largest baggage train to be seen in the Punjab was one urgent reason for fighting any natives who threatened along the east bank. Another was that Alexander meant to retain any conquests and clear the river, like earlier Persian kings, as the natural frontier for his empire. Even before the retreat from the Beas, he had been warned of unrest among a local tribe called the Malloi. They had long resisted attacks from Porus and threatened to oppose all invaders. As it was not Alexander's practice to leave any such enemy unscathed, he first subdued their neighbours on the early stages down the Jhelum and then planned to search out the Malloi by disembarking where that river met the Chenab. So far, the boatmen had been coping bravely, showing no fear in surroundings as strange as the Zambesi to its first European crew. But the natives began to talk nervously of the current and at a sudden bend in the river the explorers became aware of what they meant. The Chenab was flowing in on their left; they 'heard the roar of rapids and stayed their oars ... even the coxes fell into frightened silence, amazed by the noise ahead'. There was no hope of stopping before the whirlpools caught the tublike transport vessels and spun them round, loaded with corn and horses; they were heavy enough to survive, but the lighter warships were smashed in collisions, so much so that Alexander himself was forced to leave the royal flagship and swim for his life. The prospect of repairs was one more strain on the men's morale.

Rather than risk a native attack in the meantime, Alexander left his broken boats and wisely divided his forces: Hephaistion and the remaining fleet were to sail ahead in order to cut off fugitives. Ptolemy, the baggage, and all the elephants were to follow slowly behind, while Alexander took his toughest troops to surprise the gathering Malloi with a mere 12,000 men. The plan was in Alexander's boldest style and left no scope for suspect loyalties. He was determined to catch his enemy unprepared and, with admirable decision, he took the roughest and most unexpected route: towns intervened, and unless they surrendered they were shown no more mercy than usual. First, the troops stocked up with water from the Ayek river, and then they hurried across forty mud-baked miles of the Chandra desert in a single night, arriving in time to storm the unsuspecting inhabitants of Kot Kamalia fortress and hound down fugitives from marsh-bound Harapur. Driving the tribesmen east across the river Ravi, they made light work of steep Tulamba, a town which later proved too much for Tamurlane, and 'pressed on boldly' until all the citizens had been enslaved. Then they hesitated and wondered what was the point of it all.

They could hardly be blamed. They were a select corps cut off from the fleet and many of their infantry were over sixty years old; their toughness was unique but had been strained by three days' forced marching through the desert, yet Alexander would not leave the Malloi alone. Their capital overlooked the river Ravi and they could use it to harass his approaching baggage; they had summoned troops against him and they could not expect a son of Zeus to turn away. He knew that he had to go on and this time, one of his famous harangues was all that the weary required. The men heard him talk, no doubt of gods and heroes, of Heracles, Dionysus and his own past fortune; emotion gave in to arguments they knew so well and 'never before was so eager a shout raised from the ranks, as they bade him lead on with the help of heaven'. Not for the first time, Alexander had been saved by his powers of oratory, a gift he had so often observed in his father Philip.

A speech urged the army forwards, but before the towers of the nearby fortress of Aturi, they again began to hang back. When walls had been undermined and ladders placed against the citadel it was left to Alexander to climb them and 'shame the Macedonians into following one by one'. After a brief rest, the peak of the march was reached: a huge troop of Indians, 'at least 50,000', had gathered near a ford across the Ravi. Here, at last, were the Malloi, but they were so harassed by 2,000 Macedonian cavalry that they retired across the river and shut themselves in their greatest city, the fortress of Multan.

Multan is a name engraved on the hearts of every mid-Victorian Englishman in India; only a familiarity with Captain Edwardes's siege of Moolraj the Sikh in 1848 can explain what Alexander faced at this fateful moment in his career. Like Edwardes he was outnumbered by more than ten to one; he approached across the river and cordoned off the outer wall with his horsemen until the infantry could catch him up. Multan, then as now, was a double city, ringed by a wall near the river bank, and by an inner rampart which marked off the steep city-fortress in its centre. Its position was commanding and its view stretched over a river plain of mangoes, dates and pomegranates. Lushness was not its distinctive quality. Multan, say the natives to this day, is famed for four features: graveyards, beggars, dust and heat. In the early months of 325, Alexander was attacking a fort which was cursed for its uncongeniality.

When the infantry arrived, he led them against one of the small gates whose descendants, centuries later, were to give access to Edwardes's Scottish sappers. The gate broke and the Macedonians poured in: further round the wall, wrote Ptolemy, scoring a point against his enemy, 'the troops under Perdiccas hung back'. The next attack gave historians even more of an incentive to disagree. The objective was the citadel itself, which was to defy Edwardes for a fortnight longer than the outer town. Alexander commissioned the diggers and tunnellers and sent for the men with ladders. They were slow to stand forward, so he seized the nearest ladder and scaled the battlements himself; three senior officers followed, one of them carrying the sacred shield of Achilles which Alexander had taken as spoils from the temple at Troy. Indian defenders were brushed away by a few sword-thrusts until the king stood pre-eminent, as at Tyre, his armour gleaming against the background of the sky.

Down below, the ladders had broken and no more bodyguards could climb the wall. Alexander was cut off, under attack from nearby towers. A cautious man would have jumped back among his friends, but caution had never caused Alexander to spare himself for the loss of glory, and so he jumped down into the city. It was a memorable feat, though most irresponsible. He happened to land on his feet beside a fig-tree which gave him slight protection from enemy spears and arrows, but soon the Indians were upon him and he took to vigorous self-defence. He slashed with his sword and hurled any stones which lay to hand: the Indians recoiled, as his three attendants leapt down to join him, carrying the sacred shield. But Indian skills of archery were his undoing; his helpers were wounded, and an arrow, three feet long, struck him through his corslet into his chest. When an Indian ran forward to finish him off, Alexander had strength enough to stab his attacker before he struck home; then he collapsed, spurting blood, beneath the cover of his Trojan shield.

Outside, his friends had smashed the ladders and hammered the pieces as footholds into the clay wall; others hauled themselves up on to willing shoulders and gained the top of the battlement, where at the sight of their king beneath, they threw themselves down to shield him. The Indians had missed their chance, and as their enemies broke down the bars on the gates, they fled for safety. Macedonians were pouring in to avenge a grievance and, like the British smarting under two civilian murders two thousand years later, they massacred the men of Multan, down to the last of the women and children.

Inspection showed that Alexander's wound was extremely serious and it was with little hope that the Macedonians carried him away on his shield. According to Ptolemy, who was not present, 'air, as well as blood, was breathed out of the cut'; this would be certain proof that the arrow had punctured the wall of Alexander's lung, were there not a complication in the medical theory of the Greeks. As the circulation of the blood was unknown and the heart was widely believed to be the seat of intelligence, it could be argued that the veins were filled with air or vital spirit and that in the case of a wound, the air came out first, making way for the blood to follow. Ptolemy may have meant no more than that vital spirit had escaped from the king's veins, and hence the speed with which he fainted. But if the arrow did indeed pierce Alexander's lung, as its length suggests, his wound is a fact of the first importance. He would never escape from it; it would hamper him for the rest of his life and make walking, let alone fighting, an act of extreme courage. Never again after Multan is he known to have exposed himself so bravely in battle. True, no more sieges are described in detail, but when Alexander is mentioned he is almost always travelling by horse, chariot or boat. The pain from his wound, perhaps the lesions from a punctured lung, are a hindrance with which he had to learn to live. So too did his courtiers, but typically no historian refers to their problems again.

For the moment, it seemed doubtful whether he would live at all. His Greek doctor from the Hippocratic school had excised the arrow, but the rumour quickly spread that Alexander was dead. Even Hephaistion and the advance camp heard it and when a letter was brought saying that he was about to come to them, they disregarded it as a fiction of the generals and bodyguard. Within a week Alexander was ready for what he knew he must do. He ordered his officers to carry him to the river Ravi and ship him downstream to the main army; the scene that followed was described by his admiral, and brings us very near to what it was like to be led by a son of Zeus.

As soon as the royal ship approached the camp where Hephaistion and the fleet were waiting,

the king ordered the awning to be removed from the stern so that he would be visible to them all. However, the troops still disbelieved, saying that it was only Alexander's corpse which was being brought for burial. But then, his ship put in to the bank and he held up his hand to the crowd. They raised a shout of joy, stretching their hands to heaven or towards Alexander himself; many even shed involuntary tears at this unexpected moment. Some of his Shield Bearers began to bring him a bed on which to carry him off the ship, but he told them no, they must bring a horse. And when he was seen again, mounted on his horse, rolls of applause broke through the entire army: the banks and the nearby woods re-echoed the noise. He then approached his tent and dismounted, so that he could be seen to walk too. The men thronged round him, some trying to touch his hands, other his knees, others his clothing; other just gazed on him from nearby and said a pious word, before turning away. Some showered him with ribbons, others with all such flowers as India bore at that time of year.

'His friends were angry with him for running such a risk in front of the army; they said it befitted a soldier, not a general.' The complaint betrays them; after Alexander's death, they never commanded such devotion. An elderly Greek came forward, noticing Alexander's annoyance: 'It is a man's job,' he said in his rough accent, 'to be brave' and he added a line of Greek tragedy: 'The man of action is the debtor to suffering and pain.' Alexander approved him and took him into closer friendship. He had spoken the very motto of an Homeric Achilles.

It was as if the wound had brought king and army together, for there were no more thoughts of mutiny, only an amazed relief. As for the local Indians, the slaughter at Multan induced them to send presents of surrender and plead for their 'ancient independence which they had enjoyed since Dionysus'. Their gifts were of linen, a thousand four-horsed chariots, Indian steel, huge lions and tigers, lizard skins and tortoise shells; they sufficed for them to be added into the satrapy of north-west India, for it is a point of some importance that Alexander still intended to rule what he had conquered. After a week or two of convalescence, distinguished by a lavish banquet for the Indian petty kings on a hundred golden sofas, Alexander ordered the fleet downstream to the bend where the Punjab rivers join the lazy current of the Indus; there, no doubt from his sick bed, he gave proof of his continuing plans for the future. First, he divided the satrapy of lower India between a Macedonian and Roxane's Iranian father; then, near Sirkot, he founded an Alexandria and stocked it with 10,000 troops, telling them to build dockyards 'in the hope that the city would become great and glorious'. A little lower down the Indus he did likewise, repeating the dockyards and the city walls. Though his many damaged ships needed rapid replacement, these two naval bases were more than a response to a present emergency. They could be lasting pivots in a scheme to develop the Indus river both as a frontier and as a line of communication: ships from the yards would patrol the river, while the northern plains round Taxila and Bucephala would be comfortably within their range.

Alexander was not contented with mere dockyards. Already, he had decided to explore a new route, and so his veterans, elephants and various infantry units were now detached to march home to Susa by the regular road, settling the troubles which had recently been reported among the Iranians south-west of the Hindu Kush. The hard core of the army would accompany him, despite his wound, down to the mouth of the Indus, from where they could strike west into the desert and make for home along the shore of the Persian gulf by a land route famed for its difficulty. A sizeable fleet would skirt it at the same time in order to test out the sea passage from the Indus to the Persian coast; the army's task was secondary, to keep the fleet supplied along the shore. It was a fateful plan which now found its first expression. If fleet and army could have struggled through to Babylonia and the mouth of the Euphrates river, they would have reopened a valuable link between Asia and India.

The aim, in outline, was worthwhile, the decision to pursue it intelligent; the route, under the Roman Empire, was to be the one fragile bond between India and the western world. But the past also puts the plan into perspective, for this sea-way was a passage of astonishing antiquity. Two thousand years before Alexander, trade from the Indus valley had flowed west to the Persian Gulf bringing copper, gems, iron and perhaps the peacock into the harbours near Susa. Heir to this long history of adventure, Darius I, king of Persia, had conquered the same frontier provinces of India and sent for Scylax the Carian explorer: he had told him to investigate the Indus and sail through the Indian Ocean to the Persian Gulf. Scylax had already sailed on the Caspian Sea: he had also rounded the tip of Arabia until he returned to the Persian Gulf and encouraged his patron's interest in the reopening of the Pharaohs' Suez Canal. He was an enterprising man, and the Indus had caused his little boat no trouble: he had written a Greek account of his voyage and dedicated it, fables and all, to Darius. There is no reason to suppose that Alexander had read it, but he did show possible acquaintance with the local Persian precedent: the first of his Alexandrias on the Indus was built on the site of an old Persian garrison, noted by Scylax and settled two hundred years before. Once again, the credit for the placing of an Alexandria belonged not to its namesake but to a long-forgotten Persian district commissioner, whose buildings provided materials for the town.

All such future developments depend on war to clear their way. Alexander's fleet had been on the river for some six months or more and spring 325 found them still a two-month journey from the ocean; they were in need of food and when they heard of a prosperous kingdom on the east bank whose king as yet had not sent envoys, they eagerly followed Alexander in a raid. Their approach was so fast that the Indians took fright and sent jewellery and elephants to buy them off, as well as an admission 'that they were in the wrong, which was the surest way with Alexander of being granted what one wanted'. Alexander admired his new conquest and left its king in command, supervised by another garrison fort:

Here, men live a long while, some of them reaching the age of a hundred and thirty ... they even use a system of soldiers' messes, like the Spartans, where men are fed at the state's expense. They have mines, but they do not use gold or silver; they do not study much science, except for medicine; some of the other sciences, such as military theory, are considered to be a criminal practice.

This attempt to explain a Brahmin community in Greek terms was belied by what followed. While the army moved east to burn and destroy rebellious towns on the border, the Brahmin king broke his word and allowed his subjects to revolt all the more bitterly for being encouraged, not by a military handbook, but by the preaching of the Brahmin sects. Their resistance became a holy vendetta, helped by their use of poisoned arrows; and it was only ended by hanging the learned instigators and destroying all troublesome communities. Suppliants were spared in the name of the gods, but 'over 80,000 Indians' were killed, according to the most exaggerated history, which thereby brought its total for native dead in the past six months to more than quarter of a million. The figures are not reliable, but they would have impressed, not appalled, the majority of their readers. Burning and massacring ill-equipped patriots, Alexander's style of warfare had not suddenly become more savage under the irritation of a failure and a wound; as at Thebes or Tyre or Gaza, in Swat no less than Sogdia, his treatment of rebels had never shown any mercy or given patriots reason to expect forgiveness. But to keep his men contented, he allowed them for once to plunder what they had subdued.

It was mid-July before the end of the river journey was in sight. The army was bivouacked near Pattala in the last of the petty kingdoms rich enough to keep them supplied; the natives had mostly run away and while they fortified villages and dug wells for water in the shale that edged the desert, Alexander arranged a wall for Pattala's citadel and another dockyard at the head of the Indus's estuary. The result, called the Wooden City, was built from timber, the only material to hand. When the work was to his satisfaction, he embarked with his friends on the swiftest ships and set the course for the nearby ocean. For a wounded man, the risk was considerable, as the natives had fled and there were no local pilots to be recruited. Alexander knew that he had to show the way, before asking his ships to follow: he had his reasons, but once again in the absence of local knowledge they were to be frustrated by the rise of the July monsoon.

The officers had grown accustomed to the summer heat of the great Thar desert which stretches east along the Indus's far bank. They were to describe it accurately in their histories and they had even observed the shrimps and smaller fishes in the river itself. But they had not been expecting wind and rain. No sooner had Alexander launched into the delta than a storm sank many of his stoutest ships, and although during the repairs, guides were at last captured from the nearby tribesmen, even their skill could not avoid the weather. Where the delta widened, the wind blew so strongly from the sea that the rowers missed their stroke and were forced to shelter in a backwater. After lying at anchor, they found they were high and dry: for the first time, Alexander's sailors had met a tide 'and it caused them considerable consternation, especially when the ebb-current changed in due course and the ships were floating back on the river'. Among Macedonian crews, this novelty led to more damage, and it was with a certain caution that Alexander sent out two of his heaviest flat-bottomed transports to inspect any further dangers before he advanced. They reported that an island stood conveniently in mid-stream; Alexander followed with a few of his bravest captains, until at last, the dash of the waves was heard against the royal trireme. He had reached the outer ocean, but it was not the Eastern Sea at which he had once aimed.

Success emboldened the crews. First Alexander 'offered sacrifice on the island at the river mouth to those gods which, he said, had been told him by Ammon'; on the following day he sailed to a further island and offered different sacrifices to different gods; 'these too were made in accordance with Ammon's prophecy'. Then, venturing right out on to the deep, 'he slaughtered bulls to the sea-god Poseidon and cast them into the sea; he poured libations, and threw their golden cup and golden bowls out into the waves'. On returning up river to his base camp, he searched out a westerly arm of the Indus estuary and explored it too, finding it more navigable because of the shelter of an inland lake. There, instead of sacrifices, he left plans for a boat-house and a garrison.

These sacrifices were not the thanksgivings of a romantic explorer; the outer ocean was only visited for a purpose, And Alexander had long revealed what this was to be. While the army marched west along the shoreline, the ships were to leave the mouth of the Indus, turn through the Indian Ocean and enter the Persian Gulf with the monsoon wind behind them; to a newly assembled fleet, the prospect was terrifying, and so Alexander had gone down to the ocean and made it his business to test the first stage in person with a proper show of piety. Only one gap remained in his plans: he himself would march by land, and he needed an officer to lead the naval expedition. Thinking through his friends, he chose, most happily, a Cretan who would also write a history.

'Alexander,' wrote Nearchus the Cretan, long domiciled in Macedonia and throughout his life a friend, longed passionately to sail the sea from India to Persia but he was fearful of the length of the voyage and of the possibility that the expedition might meet with a bare stretch of country or fail to find anchorage or run short of supplies and so be completely destroyed. If so, this would be no mean blot on his past achievements and would efface his entire good fortune. But even so, his desire to do something that was always new or strange triumped over his fears.

Only an explorer can understand the power of these feelings: Alexander discussed with Nearchus the possible choices of admiral 'but', wrote his friend, choosing his words artfully, 'as one after another was mentioned, Alexander raised an objection to them all; some, he said, were not tough enough, others were not willing to take a risk for him; others were longing for home'. And so the way was prepared for Nearchus: 'My lord,' he said, 'I am prepared to lead your expedition and may heaven help the enterprise.' Alexander demurred, 'unwilling to risk one of his own friends in such distress and danger'. Nearchus begged and besought him and at last was allowed to go.

The choice was perhaps less dramatic than its hero implied in his memoirs; Nearchus had been leading the fleet for the past ten months. The preparations, too, were awkward. Many of the triremes were waterlogged or in poor repair and as for the finances, the most mysterious aspect of Alexander's career, for once they are known to have been an added anxiety. The king's travelling treasury was empty, money to hire guides and buy supplies could only be raised by a levy among his friends. The decision was unpopular and several tried to evade it, not least of them Eumenes the royal secretary who is said to have refused two-thirds of his quota until Alexander ordered his tent to be set on fire to flush his true wealth into the open. Once obeyed, the levy did indeed force the officers to show concern for the preliminaries: 'The splendour of the equipment, the smartness of the ships and the patrons' conspicuous concern for the staff-officers and the crews encouraged even those who, a short while before, had been nervous about the undertaking.'

So it was that Alexander had defied the winds, his wound and the lack of pilots, in order to venture on to the outer ocean. 'What greatly contributed to the sailors' enthusiasm was the fact that Alexander had sailed down each of the mouths of the Indus in person and paid sacrifice to the gods of the sea. They had always believed in Alexander's extraordinary good fortune and now, they felt there was nothing that he would not risk and still achieve.' Hence, the trip to the ocean, for a wound in the lung had not altered Alexander's attitude to leading his men. But the next three months of marching were to alter the men's belief in their leader's fortune and infallibility.

386

CHAPTER TWENTY-EIGHT

The new expedition was to prove the most unpleasant in Alexander's career. It is also the most puzzling. Posterity has decked him out with many different virtues, each to suit its varying tastes; none has been more widespread or persistent than the idea of his invincibility. It set a pattern for Roman emperors; it kept its appeal a hundred and fifty years after his death for the kings and settlers in the Alexandrias of upper Iran. The last three months of 325 should have given the lie to the legend. Alexander the Invincible was to suffer an extremely grave defeat; worse, he seems at first sight to have invited it. To many this is so unthinkable that his route and his aims have been believed, against the facts, to have lain elsewhere, and even the landscape has been argued away to save his reputation.

While the fleet was detained by adverse winds at the mouth of the Indus, the land army set out through the barren and sandy plains which stretch to the north-west of modern Karachi. It was late August and water was in very short supply, but by the river Hab the Oreitan tribesmen, 'for long an independent people', were driven back in a skirmish. No quarter was shown; and near lake Siranda, the troops could briefly satisfy their thirst. They had already matched 150 miles in a temperature of more than 100° F and many were suffering from a skin irritation caused by the sand; they were still burning and slaughtering all local resistance, but they showed no signs of flinching from the task before them. The king's ambitions, therefore, deserve to be closely considered.

His admiral Nearchus, held up meanwhile at the Indus, has left a brief explanation.

It was not that Alexander was ignorant of the difficulties of the journey, but he had heard that nobody yet who had passed that way had come through safely with an army; Queen Semiramis, on her return from India, had only brought back twenty survivors, King Cyrus a mere seven. These rumours inspired Alexander with a wish to rival Cyrus and Semiramis: at the same time, he wished to be near to his fleet and keep it supplied with what it needed.

The desert tribes had sent envoys to surrender five years earlier and the difficulties of their land were indeed familiar. But no known legend already linked Semiramis, heroic queen of Babylon, with such a desert march. Her only local memorial was the 'hill of Semiramis' at the far end of the journey, where Alexander and Nearchus remet. By then the troops had suffered appallingly and any excuse was welcome. Semiramis's name greeted the survivors, so she could be said, for solace, to have gone through the desert too; 'only twenty', said the officers, had managed it, whereas Alexander had 'saved' thousands. Bagoas and other Persians could add a similar story of Cyrus. When he set out, neither precedent was needed nor suggested by the landscape. The adventure's difficulties attracted him and his men, as always. Mishaps of other kings were only invented at the end. But it was the fleet which kept him down on his fateful route.

As he founded another Alexandria on the river Maxates, site of one of the old trading towns on the Beluchistan desert, there were two available lines of advance to the west. Like Tamurlane or Babur after him, he could keep away from the shore of the Persian Gulf and head north-west where the river Porali waters the fertile Welpat pocket; he would reach the site of modern Bela, from where a rough road skirts the southern coastal hills and runs due west to Kirman through a countryside of cliff and sand, made tolerable by drifts of dates and grain-fields. A safe passage here would be rivalry enough of the legendary feats of Cyrus and Semiramis, but throughout, he would be blocked from the shore by a chain of mountains, and at a distance of a hundred miles, he could not liaise with the fleet or dig wells for its convenience. Hence he must have begun by intending to take the road to the south of the hills and seldom stray more than twenty miles from the sea until he reached Gwadar. His plan, after all, depended on linking the fleet and the army; the Gedrosians, people of Makran, had sent word of their surrender as far back as autumn 330, so resistance, at worst, would be tribal.

The plan itself was eminently worth while. Supported by land, the fleet would sail westwards from the Indus to the Persian Gulf and thence to the coast of Babylonia; a waterway was to the ancient world what a railway, relatively, was to nineteenth-century Europe, and if Alexander's fleet succeeded in its navigation, it would have reopened the fastest available route between Asia and India. Not that its speed would ever be predictable. With a following wind, the journey westwards took at least six weeks: a return to India would only be possible in spring, when the trade monsoon changed direction. But if its value for messages and strategy was limited, as a trade route it had risks and possibilities for the patient sailor. In India, Alexander had discovered luxuries and raw materials which the courts of Asia would gladly put to use, and throughout history it is luxuries which have driven merchants down their most spectacular routes. His prospectors had found gold and silver and mounds of salt; his troops had picked stones as precious as jasper and onyx from the rivers they had been asked to cross. There was ivory, horn, muslin and bales of cotton ready for the picking; Indian dogs and elephants were valuable cargo. Above all, there were the spices, the nards and cassia, cardamom, balsam and myrrh, sweet rush, resinous bdellium, and the putchuk which grew in the Punjab and the Indus delta.

The list of spices known to the Greeks after Alexander's death was five times more varied than before. For medicines and cooking, scents, fumigants and soaps, a wide range of spices was a rich man's delight, and though trade between India and Asia would be a hazardous and slow business, better left to foreign entrepreneurs, in spices alone there were imports enough to give it appeal. So much the cheaper if they could come by sea; only a priceless luxury has the value to reward a trader who runs such a risk over such a distance.

To this end, Alexander's plans were ambitious: he requested his admirals to keep close to the coastline and inspect every likely harbour, water-supply or stretch of fertile land; he had hopes of colonizing the shore and easing the journey for future sailors, but even here he had been anti-cipated; exploration of the Indian Ocean and the Persian Gulf was not the new idea that it seemed. For the past two thousand years, traders had been sailing west to Babylon from the Indian Ocean and towns had once flourished on the coastal rivers of Makran; the Persian kings had inherited the tradition and two hundred years before Alexander, Darius I had settled Greek and Carian sailors at the mouth of the Euphrates to expedite the naval routes which met there from the east. When the grand Persian palace was built at Susa, sissoo-wood had been shipped from the Punjab for its pillars, down the very sea route which Alexander now planned to investigate. As at the Indus, he was unaware that Scylax the sea captain had sailed two hundred years before and proved the truth of a long used tradeway to his enterprising Persian patron.

For the sake of an ancient sea route, therefore, he chose to march close to the shore. According to his admiral, 'he was not ignorant of the diffi-culty of the route'. Five years before, he had received ambassadors from the Gedrosians, men of Makran, who promised surrender, but this under-statement leaves the extent of his knowledge unclear. By marching by this southern road he was attempting the most abominable route in all Asia. No comparable army has ever tried it since and its few explorers have suffered so bitterly that they have doubted whether Alexander could ever have preceded them unless the Makran desert had been friendlier in his day than theirs. But his intended coastal march cannot be argued away. As for the desert, even though it had supported towns on its coastal rivers two thousand years before, geology suggests that it had never been mild. His officers described it as 'less fiery than India's heat' but they could give no such credit to its sand dunes or its sterility. 'Alexander was not ignorant of the difficulty. . . .' The march through Makran can only by understood by an explorer, for in the same mood, men have tried to climb the steepest face of Everest at the wrong season of the year or to conquer the North Pole in the inadequate care of a hot air balloon. There is a streak in man which drives him to dare what others have not thought possible, and Alexander had never believed in impossibilities anyway. Makran was the ambition of men who wished to set a record and had nothing left to conquer but a landscape which Persia had left alone. The route was not merely difficult; it was the most hellish march that Alexander could possibly have chosen. But nobody opposed it.

There are hints that he knew this more or less to be so. Some two months before, when approaching Pattala down the Indus, he had already detached all the Macedonian veterans whom he meant to discharge, probably some ten thousand in number, and had sent them together with two brigades of mercenaries and all the elephants west towards the foot of the Hindu Kush, from where they could follow the gentle lushness of the Helmand valley and reach the centre of the Empire without being troubled by desert. The Makran journey, therefore, was known to be a severe test, but for the rest of the army, there were consolations which may perhaps show local knowledge. They had been busied between Pattala and Karachi until early August; they would not toil over the sand-dunes of Makran until September, by which time the brief but regular rains could fairly be expected to fall in the hills and run down towards the coast. If Makran has a favourable season, it is perhaps late autumn; its coastline, for example, is a prolific home of the sweet-scented calotrope (*Calotropis procera*), which sheds its highly poisonous seeds from June to early September. The hot summer wind blows them into the face of summer travellers, who have suffered accordingly; by entering Makran in mid-September, Alexander would at least avoid disheartening wind and poison.

Supplies, however, are the proper point at which to assess his precautions, for they do not merely depend on Alexander's competence or otherwise, a topic which different fashions like to approach differently, however slender the facts. They also depend on his staff. For while the results must not be played down or excused, the march through Makran had been agreed and discussed by the same staff-officers who had transported more than 100,000 men down the Indus and equipped an army as far as the Beas. The troops had indeed gone hungry in the past, but that was one more reason for anticipating their needs in future. Makran was known to be a difficult desert, and yet the officers were confident that Alexander would bring them through; it is unthinkable that he had won this confidence without first explaining the sources of food. Had he tried to browbeat them by nothing more than talk of the mishaps of Cyrus and Semiramis and the challenge of difficult exploration, they would have been justified in deserting or poisoning a leader who had clearly lost his sense of the possible. They did neither, and in fact, there is proof that the march had been carefully considered. The region round Pattala was rich in grain and cattle and a huge heap of corn had been plundered: 'four months' supplies for the expedition' had been duly gathered near the base camp before the men set out for the river Hab, and four months, was the likely length of the desert march through the country of the Oreitans and Gedrosians.

The fate of these stores at Pattala is most mysterious. Wagons and pack-animals did follow the land army into the desert, together with children, women and traders. Clearly, Alexander was not aware of the full horror of Makran, and hoped that a part of the stores could be moved through its sand by pack and cart.

But he cannot have planned to convoy more than a small part of his store-heap in the army's train. Its volume was far too large, so the usual strategy would apply as in the years on the Mediterranean coast. The army's stores would be loaded into the huge grain-lighters which would thus supply the whole expedition from the sea. The histories imply only that Alexander was concerned to supply the fleet with water. There is no clear word of his own dependence on the ships. This may be a concealment of a plan which failed, or it may be one more example of their concentration on Alexander's own role. For the link with the fleet was surely planned to save Alexander, and for once his famous luck deserted him.

First, the monsoon winds blew up the Indus until mid October and detained the fleet for three months, stores and all. Alexander had not allowed for the seasonal weather. Then, the tribesmen struck a blow. Before entering Makran, Alexander had left several thousand troops, a Bodyguard and a satrap to round off the conquest of the Oreitans and to settle the new Alexandria on the old river-site; the satrap is said to have been given other firm orders, and they are easily deduced from the sequel. When the fleet finally reached the first depot in his territory, they took on ten days' supplies. Plainly, the satrap was to be Alexander's link with the fleet. He had been ordered to fill up its stores, direct it to suit the army's timing and detail its meeting-points with Alexander. These would have been specified from the Oreitans' local knowledge. But when Alexander marched west, the Oreitans round the new Alexandria united with their neighbours and harassed both the satrap and the fleet way back on the Indus. Perhaps they burnt a part of the store-heap. Certainly, they killed the satrap in a major battle. Meanwhile Alexander was far into Makran and daily despairing of contact with his fleet and his main supplies. It never occurred to him to blame their absence on a continuing wind. He could only think that his satrap had betrayed his orders, so he sent orders for his deposition as soon as the army had struggled out of the desert. He did not know that the man had died, still less that he had blamed a wrong, though plausible, culprit.

Alexander was leading a land army which was large, if not excessive: about half the Foot Companions and three-quarters of the Shield Bearers, many of them over sixty years old, had been sent home by the easier route, but his expedition still numbered some 30,000 fighting men, 8,000 of them Macedonians, though accuracy is impossible as the number of ships and sailors detached with the fleet is unknown. They might just have been fed sufficiently, had the satrap of the Oreitans in the rear fulfilled his orders and had Makran been no more fearsome than the desert which led to Siwah. But the fleet delayed, and the march through Makran was so indescribably unpleasant that neither of the two officers, who very probably had been through it could bring themselves to give a history which went beyond the sweeter-smelling kinds of desert flower and a trivial outline of anecdotes.

It was left to Nearchus, following by sea, to describe what the land troops had really suffered; he would have heard it plainly enough from Alexander and his officers when they eventually re-met. The beginning among the Oreitans was as nothing to the trials which followed; in Makran, land of the Gedrosians, their surroundings were hot, barren and hopeless. The men would only move by night, though even then the temperature would not have dropped below 35° C, and as the true nature of the desert became apparent, they would be forced across twelve or even fifteen miles at a stage. On solid gravel they had shown they could do it but Makran is not solid; it is a yielding morass of fine sand, blown into dunes and valleys, like waves on a turbulent sea.

In places, the dunes were so high that one had to climb steeply up and down quite apart from the difficulty of lifting one's legs out of the pit-like depths of the sand; when camp was pitched, it was kept often as much as a mile and a half away from any watering-places, to save men plunging in to satisfy their thirst. Many would throw themselves in, still wearing their armour, and drink like fish under water: then, as they swelled they would float up to the surface, having breathed their last, and they would foul the small expanse of available water.

The expected summer rains, which would run down from the mountains and 'fill the rivers and the water-holes and soak the plains' had not yet fallen along the coast; that was bad luck, but to crown it all, when the rains came, they fell out of sight in the hills and found the army bivouacked beneath near a small stream. Shortly before midnight, the stream began to swell with the spate of fresh water which was coursing down from its source in a flash-flood. 'It drowned most of the women and children who were still following the expedition and it swept away the entire royal equipment, including the remaining pack-animals. The men themselves only just managed to survive and even then, they lost many of their weapons.'

Hunger increased with despair. As long as the pack-animals survived, they could be slaughtered unofficially and eaten raw by the troops; many died of the drought or sunk into the sand 'as if into mud or untrodden snow', and these were fair game even for the officers. Dates and palm-tree hearts were available for those who were of a rank to sequester them, while sheep and ground flour were seized from the natives: it was the custom in Makran, in years when the harvest ripened without scorching, to store enough to last for the next three seasons. When the fleet first failed to join the army, Alexander had gambled. He had marched on by the most plausible route, eventually turning inland in desperation. Yet as soon as he found supplies he showed his greatness. Reasoning that the fleet, by now, must be starving too, he ordered part to be taken to the coast. This would signal the army's new route. As usual, he did not put himself first when marching. Not so his men, who ate the supplies when entrusted with their convoy to the coast.

The closer they kept to the coastline, the less their comfort from the Gedrosian natives. The men of Makran were 'inhospitable and thoroughly brutish. They allowed their nails to grow from birth to old age and they left their hair matted: their skin was scorched by the sun and they dressed in pelts of wild animals (or even of the larger fishes). They lived off the flesh of stranded whales'. They were a people still living in the Stone Age and they used their long nails instead of iron tools: the army named their neighbours the Fish-Eaters, because they caught fish in nets of palm bark and ate them raw. Their houses were built from oyster-shells and whale-bones, like Eskimos' in some warmer environment; a few sheep ranged on the edge of the sea, where the desert gives way to pebbles and salt cliffs; these were killed and eaten raw, but their flesh tasted horribly fishy. Dead fish had infected the whole district, and in the heat, which never moderates even on an autumn evening, it rotted and stank. It was as well that the army had picked the sweet nard grass which grew in the desert valleys, for they used it as bedding or roofing for their tents to dispel the smell of surrounding decay.

Other plants were less amenable. When the march began, Levantine traders who had followed the army were keenly collecting the desert spice plants among the Oreitans and around the new Alexandria and loading them on mules, sure of a market and a fortune if they could ever bring them home. But the mules had mostly died and plant-collecting was seen to be a risk, for spices were interspersed with a poisonous oleander whose juicy leaves, pointed and leathery like a laurel, caused any man or beast who ate them to foam at the mouth as if with epilepsy and die a painful death from convulsions. Mules and horses could not be allowed to graze, for there was also the danger of a prickly spurge, whose milky juice, used on poisoned arrows by pygmies, blinded any animal into whose eye it spurted. Its fruits were strewn invitingly over the ground.

Once again, it was the snakes who removed the men's last hopes of peace. They hid beneath the scrub on the hillsides and they killed every person they struck; if a man strayed far from camp, he put himself at serious risk, but the further the march went, the fewer there were who could not help straying. 'Some despaired of thirst and lay in the full sun in the middle of the road; others began to tremble and their legs and arms would jerk until they died, as if from cold or a fit of shivering. Others would desert and fall asleep and lose the convoy, usually with fatal results.' For those who survived, the unripe dates on the palm-trees proved too strong a food and many died from the sudden strain on their stomachs. To those who abandoned them they must have seemed happier dead; the stench, the sand flies, the ceaseless rise and fall of dunes which all looked the same, they ground men into the belief that they would never survive; then, near cape Ras Malan, some three hundred miles from their starting point, the native guides admitted they had lost their way. The sand-ridges carried no landmark; the sea was no longer in view. They had wandered too far inland, and they had made the last mistake they could afford.

In this crisis, they needed a man with a clear head to take charge and insist on the only calculation which could save them. How Alexander had been bearing the strain of Makran remains uncertain; there are stories of his self-sacrifice, but these probably belong on his earlier march to the Oxus, and as it was less than a year since his arrow-wound, the dust and the heat can only have exaggerated his pain. He knew that he could not be pampered and still continue to lead his troops, but he was no longer fit enough to go hungry or thirsty as an example. He did not walk, he rode;

and his horses would take the worst of the discomforts. True, he did not hang back, but in the desert it pays to be the first, and when the guides announced they had lost the way, he took charge with his usual sense and authority, and led a party of horsemen away to the south of the main army until they regained the coast. It was the decision of a sound leader, for with the help of the stars the sea was one landmark they were bound to find; the ride was exhausting, but less so than waiting to die of thirst in camp. Digging in the shale by the sea's edge, his helpers found drinking water and arranged for word to be sent to the army behind; Alexander, meanwhile stayed thankfully beside the waterhole. In a crisis, scouting has its rewards.

When the rest of the army arrived, they could only agree to follow the coastline and hope for the best. They were lost and starving, and for a week, they scrambled despairingly along the shingle. But suddenly, near Gwadar, the guides began to recognize the ground which rose on their right: it was the border of the one recognized track north up the valley. If so, they were close to the borders of Makran, and the fleet's well-being could now be forgotten. Risking their last strength for survival, they struck inland and to their relief, the landscape smoothed into a milder pattern: the scrub persisted, but here and there, the ground offered grazing to a few flocks, and the guides for once had been proved right. Another two hundred miles would bring them to the local capital at Pura and from there, it was an easy stage to their agreed meeting-point with fleet and reserves near Kirman. But heavy on Alexander's mind was the knowledge that his plans for supplies had failed and that the fleet was most unlikely to have survived.

In fact, the fleet had been slow in starting. The wind had been blowing up the Indus, not down it, and the natives had returned to attack most vigorously as soon as Alexander had marched west. It was the second week in October, perhaps 13 October, before the ships could set sail and even then, they were held up for nearly five weeks at the edge of the Indian Ocean by adverse breezes from the sea; the sailors varied their rations by hunting the mussels, razor-fish and oysters of unusually large size which frequented the sea pools. When the wind tacked round in mid-November, they at last began sailing westwards in earnest, all too aware that Alexander was now near the end of his nightmarish march. Many of the flat-bottomed grain-lighters were entrusted to the open waters of the Indian Ocean in order to carry supplies which remained at Pattala and to deposit the army's food heaps along the shore; several of the fleet were triremes, or three-banked men of war, and therefore unable to house sufficient water for more than two days' sailing, so that they, at least, depended on Alexander's plan to dig wells. Within the first week, they put in by the river Hab to collect ten days' rations from the depot he had left them near the new Alexandria; there, they heard the news that had escaped him, the major uprising of the Oreitans and their neighbours and the death of his official satrap. But all was quiet enough for them to continue; it was apparent that the plan for supplies had broken down and that even the army ahead was starving.

As they stopped nightly and found neither stores nor promised water they too began to run short of their food-cargo. Within two weeks, they had turned arrow-shooting catapults against a crowd of Fish-Eaters and driven them back from the beach in order to steal their flocks; here, a few goats; there, a store of dates, but nowhere the heaps of corn they had expected. A village was stormed for the sake of its powdered fish-meal; huts were raided in search of camels which were killed and eaten raw. There was no corn or firewood in a land encrusted with salt and sand, and the only excitement was the whales, which appeared for the first time to Greeks far out at sea, 'spouting water in such a way that the sailors were terrified and dropped the oars from their hands'. Nearchus, on native advice, replied by charging them boldly, trumpets blaring, oars splashing and sailors raising a full throated war-cry; naturally sharp of hearing, like their Arctic relations, the whales submerged in a hurry and only surfaced well behind the fleet where they continued spouting peacefully to rounds of applause from the crews. Not until two months later was a whale inspected at close quarters, when off the coast of Persia, one was found stranded 'more than a hundred and thirty feet long, with a thick skin coated in oysters, limpets and piles of seaweed'. There was nothing here to set hunger at rest, and Nearchus, like Europeans in the Arctic, never dreamt that whales could be speared and eaten for their blubber.

By now, some four hundred miles along the coast, interpreters and pilots had been recruited from the natives, and Nearchus would converse with them through Persian interpreters of his own. Their reports, when twice translated, caused alarm. Certain islands, they claimed, lay close to the coast of Makran and were haunted by evil spirits, whom the Greeks, reared on Homer's *Odyssey*, identified with the Sun and an unnamed sea nymph. Visitors to the Sun's island would vanish, while those who passed by the sea nymph would be lured to her rock, only to be turned into fish. The tale gained credit from the sudden disappearance of a warship and its Egyptian crew. The Sun, it was thought, had spirited them away, and as a metaphor, this was no doubt true. It was left to Nearchus to visit the island and refute the legend by surviving.

396

If the islands did not live up to their fame, it was not many days before the pilots pointed to something stranger than even they suspected. In the straits of Hormuz, where the Indian Ocean narrows against the coast of Arabia and runs into the Persian Gulf beyond, they indicated the Arabian promontory of Ras Mussendam on the starboard bow and explained that 'from this point, cinnamon and other spices were imported into Babylonia'. A new and unimagined perspective stretched far behind their words.

The report of this spice trade was true enough. It had been going on for more than a thousand years and it had already excited Alexander's curiosity. But among the spices, none was more rare or precious than this cinnamon, a plant whose natural home lies unbelievably far from the classical world. To the Greek historian Herodotus, cinnamon was a spice which grew beyond the sources of the Nile in a jungle protected by monstrous birds; the Romans, who bartered with the Arabs for as much as they could acquire, had a clearer idea of the facts behind the story, for they traced the cinnamon trade to the south-east coast of Africa and discovered that Madagascar island was involved. Rumour went further. Cinnamon, it was said, was shipped by raft across the eastern ocean on a journey which lasted five whole years, and for once, the rumours of ancient geography were justified. Cinnamon's natural home is not Arabia or even the African seaboard: it grows wild in the far-off valleys of Malaysia. In this one plant, the Greeks and Romans had reached unawares beyond their world. Once upon a time, it had been shipped across the Indian Ocean from Malaysia to Madagascar; from Madagascar, it had been attracted up the coast of Africa to Arabia and the Red Sea and so to the clientele of oriental palaces. By Alexander's day, the Arabs had naturalized it in their country, but the imports from the south's mysterious source continued; when Alexander's sailors were shown the cinnamon traderoute off Arabia, they were in contact with a product which had outtravelled their king. Cinnamon had once seen the truth which the munity on the Beas had saved Alexander from exploring. The world, it knew, went on beyond the Ganges.

For the moment, the sailors passed it by. They had been commissioned to explore the coast of the Persian Gulf and they were too short of supplies to linger over exotic reports. It was now early December and they had been on board for over ten weeks; they were hot, cramped and hungry but the wind was still propelling them, and when the end came, it came, as always, suddenly. Two days sailing into the Persian Gulf with a following breeze brought them at last to a friendly coastline: near Bander Abbas, they found corn and fruit-trees and knew they would no longer starve.

'All crops were born in abundance,' wrote their admiral, 'except for olives'—the deeply revealing complaint of a Greek who finds himself far from what he knows at home. But as a few of the sailors explored inland, they soon made up for this nostalgia: they met a man in Greek clothes who accosted them in Greek. It all seemed too marvellous to be true, and the sound of their native language brought tears to their eyes: tears turned to shouts of joy when they heard the man say he was a member of the army and Alexander himself was not far distant.

Since finding the inland route when the guides had failed on the borders of Makran, Alexander had not been idle. It was now only a matter of a few days before he and his survivors would be clear of the desert, and he knew he would need food immediately. Camel riders, therefore, were ordered to gallop north, north-east and north-west to as many provinces as they could reach, where they were to order baggage-animals and cooked food to be sent at once to the borders of Kirman. Such is the speed of a dromedary, especially over the salt waste of the Dasht-i-Kavir desert, that word even reached the satrap of Parthia near the Caspian Sea. The news caused commotion among men who had not expected to see Alexander alive, let alone returning from the ordeal of Makran. Three satraps, at least, obliged and when Alexander emerged from the desert in mid-November, he found supplies and baggage-animals waiting on the borders of Carmania. It was a sop to the repeated failures of the past eight weeks.

Kirman itself was scrubland, distinguished only for its wells and grazing and its mines of red gold, silver, bronze and yellow arsenic. Its people were not attractive and inevitably, they had been unruly, especially as Alexander had not passed that way before:

Because horses are scarce, most of the people there use donkeys even for war. The war-god is the only god they worship and they sacrifice a donkey to him too: they are an aggressive people. Nobody marries until he has cut off the head of an enemy and brought it to the King: the King then stores it in the palace, where he minces up its tongue, mixes it with flour and tastes it himself. He gives the remains to the warrior to eat with his family; the man who owns most heads is the most admired.

And yet this wretched corner of the empire had its blessings: the natives grew vines.

After sixty days in the desert, the survivors can hardly have dreamed that they would live to taste wine again. They had seen thousands die around them, perhaps half their fellow-soldiers and almost all the camp-followers. If 40,000 people had followed Alexander into the desert, only

15,000 may have survived to see Kirman. All such figures are guesses, but there is no mistaking the men's condition. 'Not even the sum total of all the army's sufferings in Asia,' it was agreed, 'deserved to be compared with the hardships in Makran.' The survivors were broken and bewildered men who needed to assert their common identity; it was some consolation when the veterans and elephants met them on the borders of Kirman, safe and happy in their detour down the Helmand valley, but even they brought news of unrest in the eastern satrapies. If anxiety could not be put away, it could at least be submerged in a show of relief, to nobody more welcome than to Alexander, who was racked by the growing conviction that he had launched his fleet to certain death. His close friends on the march were alive to a man, and that alone was a matter for thanks, if only by contrast with the fate of others: 'Sacrifices,' wrote Aristobulus, who saw them, 'were offered in gratitude for the victory over the Indians and for the army's survival for Makran.' There is a world of harsh experience left unsaid in those few words.

Men who have escaped from death by thirst and starvation are not so reticent about their celebrations, for when civilization is at last to hand it is hard for an explorer to respect it or to greet its petty rules. So while there were athletic games and a festival of the arts, there was, naturally, also a revel.

For seven days, they processed through Kirman; Alexander was carried slowly along by eight horses, while he feasted throughout the day and night with his Companions on a high and commanding dais, built in the shape of an oblong; dozens of wagons followed, some with canopies of purple and embroidery, others with roofs of branches kept fresh and green to shade off the sun. Inside, his friends and commanders lay garlanded and drinking wine. There was not a shield nor a helmet nor a sarissa to be seen, but all along the journey, the soldiers kept drawing wine in cups and drinking-horns and ornate bowls; as they walked or drove, they pledged a toast to one another. Pipes and flutes and stringed instruments played loudly and filled the countryside with their music; women raised the cry in honour of Dionysus and followed the procession in a route, as if the god were escorting them on their way.

The reports of this famous triumph were to influence the course of royal pomp for centuries. In the history of Greek kingship, the return of a triumphant king and the manifestation of a god to his worshippers are ceremonies which come closer together after Alexander's death: the theme of Dionysus was a favourite one not only with Alexander but also with his Macedonians, and its heartfelt celebration after eight weeks' suffering is very understandable. Dionysus too had returned after victories in India, though not through a desert or with a lung-wound which made it more comfortable to process in an eight-horsed chariot; Alexander's rivalry with Dionysus was no idle legend, but a fact which the customs of Hindu India had helped to confirm. His was the only Greek precedent for an Indian triumph and as ancestor of the Macedonian kings and god of the victory which Alexander stressed throughout his career, it was natural to turn to his example for this extraordinary procession. But what began on an impulse after disaster passed to the Ptolemies in Alexandria and so to the generals of Rome, to the triumphs of Marius and Antony, the new Dionysus, and to the emperor Caracalla who claimed in his triumphs to drink from the cups which Alexander had used in India.

Triumph though Alexander might, the fears for the fleet were overbearing. Again, communications were to blame, for as Alexander revelled his way through Kirman and tried to forget his worst suspicions, he could not know that a straggler from the army had already met the sailors down on the coast and that his worries were unfounded. Uninformed, the army still fretted anxiously in Kirman's capital, but not many miles away Nearchus was already blessing his good fortune and drawing up the ships to be repaired behind a double stockade and a stout mud wall. Suddenly, the message arrived in the army's camp; the governor near the coast had hurried inland with news which, he hoped, would earn him a rich reward, 'Nearchus,' he announced, 'is coming on his way from the ships.' Alexander wanted to believe him, but as the days went by and no Nearchus appeared, not even to the many search parties he had sent out, he began to despair, and even ordered the governor to be arrested for spreading a story which had only made the disappointment harsher. 'Both by his expression and his outlook, Alexander showed that he was greatly upset.'

Down by the coast, one search-party had at last been more fortunate. They had met a group of five or six men 'long-haired, dirty, covered in brine, wizened and pale from sleepless nights and other hardships'. They had thought no more, even when the wanderers asked where Alexander was waiting; they rode on by towards the sea presuming the men to be local vagabonds. But as they left, one of the wanderers turned to another and said: 'Nearchus, I expect those men were travelling the same way as us for no other reason than to find us, but we are in such poor shape that they cannot recognize us. Let's tell them who we are.' Nearchus agreed, and no sooner had he spoken than the search-party realized that in their dishevelled questioner they had found the admiral of the fleet.

Messengers ran ahead to Alexander, but in their excitement they could tell him no more than that Nearchus and five others had been found alive.

At once he presumed that only these few had survived from the entire expedition, and the news did little to lighten his mood, a despair which the sight of Nearchus, so long-haired and unkempt, did nothing to relieve. Giving his admiral his right hand, he led him aside and wept most bitterly: 'The fact that you, at least,' he said, 'and these others have come back to me is some consolation for the disaster; but how were the rest of the ships destroyed?' 'But, my lord,' Nearchus claimed to have replied, 'your ships are safe and sound and your army too; we have come with the news of their survival.' Alexander wept again, as his admiral told him they were being repaired at the river mouth. Then, in one of the rare insights into his way of thinking, 'he swore both by Zeus of the Greeks and Ammon of the Libyans that he was more pleased at this news than that he was returning, having conquered all Asia; his grief at the supposed loss of his fleet had outweighed all his other good fortune. In his extreme emotion, Zeus Ammon came naturally to the surface of his mind, and for once a friend recorded his words. But this 'conquest of all Asia' was a claim which could do little for the awful truth of Makran.

The governor who had first brought the news was released and a second sacrifice was decreed for the safety of the army, heralding games and a musical festival at which Nearchus was to be guest of honour. Fêted by his fellow-officers and showered with ribbons and flowers by the ranks, he took his seat of honour beside the king: 'I will not allow you,' said Alexander, 'to run such a risk again: someone else shall lead the fleet upshore to Susa.' But Nearchus objected: 'My lord, I will obey you always, as that is my duty, but the difficult and dangerous task was entrusted to me, so please do not take away the easy sequel whose glory is readily won and put it into another's hands.' Alexander complied, and the fleet was left to its brave commander to bring it down the final stage of the monsoon journey from India to the Persian palaces.

So they sat, king and admiral, and watched their festival games in the royal palace of Kirman. Flutes struck up a tune for the choral dance and actors prepared to compete with their plays and recitations. But however spiritedly they performed there were facts which all could see for themselves. The Companion Cavalry had been halved; the ranks of the Foot Companions were far below strength: the Shield Bearers only seemed numerous because so few had been detached into Makran. The highest officers were still alive and so was Alexander, but they had suffered a disgrace which was agonizingly irreversible. They had marched an army into the most murderous desert in Asia and had failed to meet the fleet for supplies as they had intended. Their errors and misfortunes can only be grasped in outline, and complexities remain which will never be understood; the men had followed for eight weeks, when even two days of Makran's desert should have been enough to make them rebel; when the convoy of supplies had failed to arrive at the first point, more prudent generals would surely have left a detachment to warn the fleet and then turned back to the river Hab as soon as their sufferings became apparent. Alexander had gone on and, amazingly, neither men nor officers had mutinied against him. The one truth, perhaps, was that prudence never swayed Alexander when a glorious plan had been laid in detail. Like Achilles, he put prowess before sound counsel and his staff felt the same; it was left to a desert to humble the mood which had helped to conquer Asia.

It was among these bitter truths that the acting stopped in Kirman's palace and the music and dancing died away. Prizes were awarded as usual, none more prominent than those to the Persian Bagoas, the eunuch who had served Darius and had risen as high in the new king's loving favour. Dressed in his garlands of honour, he 'passed through the theatre and took his seat, as a champion of the dance, by Alexander's side; the Macedonians saw and applauded and shouted to the king to kiss the victor, until at last, he threw his arms round Bagoas and kissed him again and again'. In a moment of elation, all had almost been forgotten. Almost, but not quite. The king might kiss his Persian favourite and reward him for a dance which only a man of the East had the skill to perform, but thousands of the men who had fought to punish Persia lay dead and buried in the Gedrosian sand. Alexander the Invincible, the new Dionysus triumphant, had sent his bravest supporters to their death, and if the Persian empire's history had one lesson to teach, it was that the news of royal disaster worked on men's disloyalties, and that failure was always followed by revolt.

CHAPTER TWENTY-NINE

To anxious watchers in Asia, the Makran disaster was less of a shock than the simple fact that Alexander had returned. Few of his satraps and fewer still of those in Greece and Europe had expected to see him again: in eastern Iran, unrest had been fostered by news of his wound. Incredibly, he had reappeared and the history of the next six months of his career turns on a problem which he had brushed aside by marching east: how to retain a vast and varied empire in the face of foreign language, heat and slow communications.

The problem has not gone short of answerers. 'The best course,' the Aristotle of Persian legend advised him once again, 'is to divide the realm of Iran among its princes and to bestow the throne on whomsoever you appoint to a province; give none ascendancy or authority over another, that each may be absolute on the throne of his own domain. ... Then will appear among them so much variance and disunity, so much presumption and haughtiness, rivalry about power, bragging about wealth, contention over degree and so much arguing over retainers that they will not seek vengeance or recall their past. When you are at the farthest bounds of the earth, each would menace his fellow with your dread, invoking your power and support.' This clear statement of a Persian gentleman's attitude would not have pleased Machiavelli. Rightly impressed by Asia's long obedience to Alexander's successors, he explained it as the surrender of a kingdom of servants, not of barons. Unlike barons, servants cannot be played against their masters, but once they fall, they fall for ever, finding no love among the people. Darius had ruled among servants and their defeat handed Alexander a kingdom with no resources for revolt.

Of the two philosophers, this Aristotle showed more grasp of Alexander's predicament, but he too had missed the Iranians' will to rebel. While Alexander sailed on the Indus, observers in Asia would only have agreed on one probability: his empire was likely to fall apart.

As he rested briefly in Kirman, fourteen of the twenty-three provinces of the empire were showing the marks of disturbance and revolt. The problem was not a new one, as it had troubled Alexander ever since the year of Gaugamela, and only one of his many governors, Antigonus the one-eyed, was to retain the same satrapy throughout his reign. The local causes varied. In Bactria, where the natives had been suppressed in two years' warfare, it was the hired Greek settlers who had rebelled. They had believed Alexander to be dead, they had elected an experienced Athenian as king and had seized Balkh in autumn 325. Then they had quarrelled, and by the time Alexander was returning, they had not escaped from the Alexandrias they detested. Mercenaries were also to blame in India. As soon as Alexander had turned for home, they had risen up and murdered Philip the satrap. The news only reached Alexander in Kirman, and at once he ordered the province to be shared between a Thracian and the rajah Ambhi. Bodyguards had already punished the ringleaders.

In the Hindu Kush it was different again. In spring 325 word had come through Roxane's father that the Iranian governor of its heartland was showing himself to be turbulent. It was not the first time that problems of independence had broken out among these mountain tribesmen; the man was deposed and Roxane's father took control of a province so important for the roads to Balkh and India. Meanwhile south of these roads, in the Helmand valley, chance had spurred on rebellion: the Macedonian satrap had died of sickness and before the request for a replacement could reach Alexander, Iranian chieftains had tried to seize power. But Alexander had the measure of them. When he had detached his veterans and elephants from the march into Makran, he had sent them by the Helmand valley to settle the trouble on their easy way home. This they did, and the Iranian culprits were brought to Kirman, chained and ready for execution.

Others soon arrived to join them. A pretender had set himself up among the Medes, 'wearing his tiara upright and giving himself out to be King of the Medes and Persians', but the local satrap, though Iranian, had reason to be loyal, so he had put him in chains together with his Iranian associates. The governor of neighbouring mountain tribes, also an Iranian, had repeatedly refused to answer orders and had fled from a final summons three years before: only now was he caught and sent to his king, to be ordered to an overdue death. In Kirman itself, home of the head-hunting tribesmen, the ruler was plausibly charged with insubordination, for Alexander had never conquered the country and its aggressive habits lent support to the suspicion. As Nearchus returned from the palace to the fleet, the new governor, he found, had still not pacified the tribesmen, who had seized the local strongholds and were continuing to prove as troublesome as their reputation suggested.

Westwards the outlook was similar. The Persians' own homeland had been seized by an aristocratic pretender; the province of Susa and its neighbouring tribes were held by two suspect Iranians who had formerly been servants of Darius and who were likely to find Alexander's absence tempting. To the north-west, in the highlands of Armenia and Cappadocia, Alexander's governors had never become established and power had passed back to Iranians and their refugees; in Phrygia by the sea, adjoining tribesmen had been unruly, probably killing the satrap, while in Europe Thracian tribes had overthrown much that Philip and Alexander had striven to retain by colonies and tribute for the past twenty years. They had been encouraged by an ambitious failure in Alexander's name; during the past year one of his generals had crossed with a large army from Europe against the nomads around the Black Sea, whom Alexander had mentioned to the king of Khwarezm as a possible target. Weather and native resistance had wiped out his army, a disaster which had encouraged a Thracian uprising and which many observers believed Alexander might now return to avenge. In the nine more peaceful provinces, such familiar figures as Ada the queen mother and Mazaeus had died, while the experiment with native governors in Egypt had not lasted long. The fight for the empire could not be said to have ended with Gaugamela.

The proof of an empire's strength lies in its powers of survival. On paper, Alexander's seems dangerously fragile, only held by some 40,000 provincial troops, two dozen or so Alexandrias and a high command which had included nine of Darius's former satraps. And yet none of the pretenders or turbulent satraps had managed to organize a popular revolt, except among pockets of hill tribesmen. It is a mistake to describe their rebellions as nationalist, as if Asia were nineteenth-century Europe. The Iranian peasant did not feel part of a nation whose boundaries were worth defining: he only knew that the greater part of his produce went to his distant masters, as three-quarters of it still does, and the identity of these masters was more or less a matter of indifference. The struggle, as Alexander returned unexpectedly, was not between nations or classes, but within the high command, where it centred on prominent Iranians. Six years had passed since Gaugamela and Darius's noblemen had not been as supine as Machiavelli suggested.

Such a crisis of loyalty can be viewed from two directions, from the provinces, where it originated, or from Alexander, where it was suppressed. It is true that Alexander had just left Makran and was living with the memory of conspicuous disaster; his nerves on first emerging had been delicate, and so he had arrested the first messenger of Nearchus's return because the man seemed to have brought him unjustified news of success. But the messenger had been released when proved right, and weeks of celebration had done much to improve the army's morale; to a new Achilles, by a twist of a hero's logic, the escape from Makran could begin to seem like a personal triumph, a survival where Semiramis had failed and a victory in the struggle against the grimmest forces of geography. 'I am more delighted at the news of your return than at the conquest of all Asia,' Nearchus remembered Alexander saying, and Asia had thus been narrowed to include no more than the army's march. Nowadays such self-defence seems thin and distasteful; nonetheless, it goes flatly against the pattern of all the evidence to blame the arrests which followed only on Alexander's presumed sense of insecurity or on a new and capricious mood of suspicion. Arrests were no new departure for the survivor of Parmenion, the pages or Philip's murder, let alone for any other Macedonian king, but not a single one of the courtiers, attendant Companions or staff-advisers is known to have lost his job or life during the coming year. If Makran had needed to be blamed on a scapegoat, it was among these assistants that a purge should first have been conducted. The arrests did not affect the court; they followed the fringes of the provincial high command, and it is from the provinces that their sequence must be interpreted. In each case, accusations were laid against the victims, and although such charges need not be truthful, there is often an independent background to make them entirely credible. Iranian revolt and satrapal turbulence were countered by gestures to the provincials' own sympathies, for against a pattern of Iranian rebellion, a union of satraps and subjects was a risk which Alexander could not afford.

As the rebel Iranians arrived to be sentenced in Kirman, the unlikelihood of any such union became obvious. Among the governors who came bringing the requested food and baggage animals, there appeared the Thracian and Macedonian generals from Hamadan, who had not seen their king for the past six years. Their last known dealings had concerned Parmenion's murder, when they had disposed of the elderly general in obedience to Alexander's letter: four of them had remained in Media ever since, at the central point of the empire's communications to upper Iran, where they must have received regular orders for forwarding men and equipment. Six thousand soldiers accompanied them from their garrison, but complaints were swiftly raised about their conduct. Native accusers insisted that the generals had allowed the plunder of temple properties, a particularly emotive offence against local opinion; evidently they were guilty, for when a Greek invasion entered Hamadan over a hundred years later they noticed how silver roof tiles and precious stones had been stripped from the temple by Alexander's men, a sacrilege which cannot belong with Alexander's own benign visits. His generals must have been responsible and they were also accused of the rape of respectable ladies, a crime which Alexander is always said in anecdotes to have detested. Their senior officer, brother of the same Coenus who had spoken up on the river Beas, 'had excelled them all in his mad passions, even to the point of assaulting an aristocratic virgin and giving her afterwards to his slave as a concubine'. These outbursts of violence were serious, but not surprising: two of the generals were commanders of Thracians, to whom such excesses had never been distasteful. When these blunt incriminations had been heard, 600 of the troops were put to death, a reprisal which could hardly have been conducted in the exempted presence of 5,000 of their fellows unless there had been grounds, and a distinction, to justify it. In a similar mood of inquiry and justice the four commanders were arrested and two of them executed on Alexander's orders. Complaints against a third did not seem convincing, and he was detained, although nobody had shown the slightest regret for the death of his fellow criminals. They had outraged the natives and they had given free rein to their ambitions at the pivot of the empire's roads. On both accounts, they were better out of the way, and the vast majority of their troops condoned their passing.

The misbehaviour of four generals and 600 soldiers would soon encourage a more audacious order: like the last successful king of Persia, he would 'order his satraps to disband their mercenary armies'. This briefly reported order is obscure and in need of qualification. Settlers in Alexandrias would be exempted because they were citizens, not mercenaries, and they are known to have stayed their ground until Alexander's death. It is not clear whether the provinces' standing armies were still mercenaries or whether they now served Alexander as part of his central army. Nor is the order clearly dated to any one of the next six months. News of the mercenary rising in India, the Greek revolt in Bactria and the purge of criminals from Hamadan must already have formed the idea in Alexander's mind; economy and the need to replenish his own royal army were also motives for centralizing troops. The idea has been criticized as ill-conceived, but he must have known there was no point in issuing an order from a distance unless it could be expected to be obeyed; 10,000 mercenaries, at most, would roam wild as a result of it, many of them natives, not Greeks. They would loot for a living, but their effects were mostly felt in Asia Minor, where larger hordes of vagrants were all too familiar. It was more important that no satrap would refuse the order, once issued: it only needed one more disturbance for Alexander to take the chance and issue it. With mercenaries on his mind Alexander took leave of Kirman, sent Nearchus back to the fleet and set out westwards by the long used road into Fars for the great Persian palaces in the centre of his empire. It was nearly seven years since he had last passed through them, and he can only have wondered what he would find; he was entering the second, most delicate, stage of his return.

The march from Kirman to the province of Persia is not a hard one, and in early spring 324, Alexander found himself already at Pasargadae, barely fifty miles from Persepolis. For once his steps can be followed exactly, for at Pasargadae he was to stand on the threshold of Cyrus's tomb, a building which his officers had already visited six years earlier and which still survives on its stone platform very much as he then saw it. Inside the narrow doorway of its pedimented entrance, he found unmistakable signs of vandalism. On their first visit, officers had talked of a golden sarcophagus with a bed beside it and a covering, carpets and purple hangings. The king's cape, his trousers, his blue-dyed tunics, his necklaces and scimitars and his jewelled earrings had all been lying on the bed and its table; now they had disappeared. The sarcophagus had been chipped and Cyrus's skeleton had been scattered carelessly on the floor.

As Alexander had long proclaimed himself to be Cyrus's heir, he was deeply perturbed at this disrespect. He tortured the Magi, who traditionally guarded the tomb for the fee of a sheep and a horse as a monthly sacrifice, but they named no culprits and the inquest was dropped. The historian Aristobulus was ordered to see to the repairs, replace the royal clothing and block the door with clay and stone, sealing it with the king's seal, and in the course of his work, he described the building accurately enough for explorers to recognize it two thousand years later: he even paraphrased King Cyrus's epitaph in Greek. And he understood the likely causes of the robbery: 'It was plainly not the work of the satrap,' he wrote, but of bandits, as they left behind whatever they could not easily carry away. It was one more example of the rebellious disturbances during Alexander's absence in Bactria and India.' A Macedonian was eventually put to death for the offence, perhaps with justice.

But the satrap's hour was soon to come. Of the very noblest Iranian family, he had taken command of Persia when Alexander's own nominee had died; his action was arbitrary, so he came to meet the army with huge presents of gold, coin, horses, furniture and jewelled tableware in order to excuse his self-promotion. He was received as he hoped, and from the hills near Pasargadae, he marched with the king to Persepolis, where he might have survived, had the natives and the buildings not served as evidence against him. He was found to have 'plundered the shrines and the royal tombs', which overlook the terrace of Persepolis, and to have 'murdered many Persians unjustly'. He had also been a usurper in Asia's one dangerously nationalist province, and the charges were enough to see him hanged, with Bagoas acting as interpreter and perhaps as accuser. He was replaced by Peucestas, the officer who had helped to save Alexander's life at Multan, and had since been made a personal Body-guard in recognition. The choice was tactful in a province where the Persians' traditions ran strongest, for Peucestas followed up his appointment by wearing oriental dress and learning the Persian language, much to the natives' satisfaction. In a continuing mood of reconciliation, Alexander distributed the traditional presents of money to the women of Persia as he passed through their province, a custom which recalled King Cyrus's history, but had been neglected by recent Persian kings. He also expressed regret that the royal palace of Persepolis had ever been set alight; it was too late to undo the effects of a woman and a banquet, but as his respect for the memory of Cyrus suggested, his myth had moved far since those early days of the invasion. When satraps were suspect, it paid, as with the Hamadan generals, to flatter their subjects' sense of propriety. A reigning Persian king had seldom been seen in Persia for the past thirty years.

While Nearchus brought the fleet to the far end of the Persian Gulf, Alexander arranged supplies for him and left Persepolis to march on westwards and meet him at Susa. Arriving in late March, he again fell foul of Iranian satraps. He was greeted by the local governor and his son, both of whom had served Darius at Gaugamela and had bought their reinstatement from Alexander afterwards. The son he put to death, some said by spearing him with his own sarissa, and the father he imprisoned, complaining that he had brought bribes of money, not supplies for the army, an oversight which was serious at any time, but never more so than after Makran when orders had been issued that all supply posts on the main roads should be filled by the governors for the army's passing. This and a suspicion of insubordination led to the man's execution, and at the same time the last of the four generals from Media was found guilty, perhaps fairly, of robbing Susa's sacred treasures. He was sent to a belated death.

With the Susa executions, the brief purge came to an end; there was nothing new about it. More officers had been sent to their death for suspected plotting in the three years before the invasion of India than were executed in the years after Makran. Since emerging from the desert, Alexander had removed four Iranian governors and four Iranian pretenders, together with their associates; he had caught up at last with a long-summoned Iranian offender, and disposed of four noted miscreants from Hamadan. The pattern had been important. Even before invading India, Alexander had been moving away from the use of Darius's Iranian satraps whom he had at first been pleased to receive and reinstate. But by summer 326, six had already been tried and found wanting, while another two had never established their rule in their satrapies; after his renewed executions, only four, excluding the Indian rajahs, continued to hold high provincial office. Of these, one was Roxane's father-in-law; another was Artabazus, father of Barsine, who was an old man, and confined to the command of one Sogdian fort; the third ruled the northern wilds of Media like an independent duchy and proved so memorable that his name, Atropates, passed into the province's new title of Azerbaijan; the fourth, Phrataphernes, was the conspicuous exception, the one satrap who had served Darius, yet still retained his satrapy of Parthia near the Caspian Sea, loyal enough to send cooked food and his two sons by camel to Carmania in answer to Alexander's pleas from Makran. Elsewhere, Europeans had taken the place of suspect Iranians, whose past with Darius could not be trusted when Alexander was absent. A Thracian ruled Indians; a Cypriot, most successfully, ruled the hardened tribesmen of the Arians' home province; Peucestas the Macedonian pleased the Persians by adopting their dress, their customs and language. During this time, Alexander is said to have become quicker to believe accusations and to punish 'even the lesser offenders heavily, because he felt that in the same state of mind, they would go on to commit more serious crimes'. In the circumstances, that was prudent and may well be true, though in the four years which followed Gaugamela, courtiers in plenty had already been put to death on mere suspicions. Twelve swift arrests sufficed to return the empire to a calm which lasted not only throughout Alexander's brief remaining lifetime but also throughout the forty selfish years of western struggle among his Macedonian Successors. The barons had had their day, and the empire thereafter behaved as if wrested from servants. In the eastern half of Asia the new appointments mostly remained in power for the next eight years and were praised as men who had governed well. The eastern purge, in short, had proved a signal success; it would be seventy years or more before Macedonian rule in Asia was shaken in so many provinces again, and then too the pattern and the provinces concerned were remarkably similar.

But in spring 324 the fate of the west was still in the balance. From Kirman, news of the king's return had sped dramatically towards the coast and at Babylon it can still be detected in its rapid passage: the city's garrison commander had come to meet Alexander near Susa, but 'seeing that he was punishing his satraps severely, sent back a letter to his brother in Babylon, who happened to be a prophet. He was frightened for his own safety and especially feared the king and Hephaistion.' The prophet, after asking for details, returned to his business and made ready a momentous answer. In the meantime, the news had passed beyond him and by early summer it had reached to the fastnesses of Cilicia and the fringe of the Aegean sea. Harpalus, a treasurer of the empire, heard it with dismay and retired to consider his own position in the private rooms of the castle at Tarsus. He had a guilty record, and he knew, as an officer in Hamadan when Parmenion was murdered, how a suspicion was treated in times of crisis.

Among Alexander's Macedonian officers, famed for their wrestling, their drinking and their silver-studded boots, none is more congenial than Harpalus the treasurer. Alexander had always liked him; they had grown up together, but as Harpalus was lame, he could not be used on active service. Nonetheless he had followed the army and shortly before Issus, he had travelled from Asia to Greece on a mysterious mission, probably as a royal spy. After Issus, he had rejoined the troops and at a time when Alexander was striking his first coins in Asia, he had become one of the army's treasurers. His responsibilities had increased with the booty, so much so that three years later he could be left in Hamadan to centralize the bullion of the Persian Empire. While Alexander had battled into India, Harpalus had gone about his leisurely life behind the lines. He would send books east for his king's light reading; he organized the hired reinforcements and supervised the despatch of smart new suits of armour to the Punjab. Much of his time was spent in the heat of Babylon, where he improved the Persians' palace by adding a gaily-plastered Greek portico to its inner courtyard. In a strange land, he had also found solace in gardening. At Alexander's request, Greek plants were to be naturalized in the terraces of Babylon's Hanging Gardens; Harpalus saw them into place, though the hot sandy soil was not to the liking of the ivies which refused to settle down.

A rich man, but lonely in his garden, he had felt the need for a female companion, and like Ptolemy, his tastes had inclined to the courtesans of Athens. Through friends in the city, he heard of the practised Pythionice; he sent her an invitation and, like Thais, she left the Piraeus to seek her fortune in the east. Harpalus spared nothing to impress her, he even shipped rare fish to Babylon from the distant Red Sea; and for two or three years they lived, Treasurer and slave-girl, in the Hanging Gardens until, despite his affairs with native women, Harpalus found he had fallen in love. Pythionice bore him a daughter, but at a time when Alexander was reported to be sailing on the Indus, she had died and left her lover to do justice to her memory. Harpalus was not the man to let her down, and in the process, he had involved himself in scandal.

It was inevitable that Alexander should have friends in the Greek cities of the empire and that these friends, often restored home by his favour, should prove articulate. On the Aegean island of Chios lived Theopompus the pamphleteer, a rich man who had travelled Greece in the name of history, only to write provocative slander about most of the facts he had seen or heard. Twenty years before, he had spent some time at Philip's court and had spared no abuse in describing the king and his courtiers; times soon changed, and Philip had become master of Greece, Alexander master of Asia and the Aegean; Theopompus found himself indebted to men who had been themes for his vituperation. So he wrote a panegyric on each of them and when Alexander returned from India, he sent him a stylized letter which respectfully discussed certain topics in the west. Among them was Harpalus's behaviour: Pythionice 'was a slave and a harlot three times over, but now that she has died, he has built two monuments for her at a cost of more than 200 talents. One stands in Babylon, the other in Athens', at the side of the Sacred Way from the city to Eleusis, framed by a distant prospect of the Acropolis: it was so much larger than any other, men said, that an innocent stranger would assume it honoured Pericles or a similar hero of the past. Her coffin had been escorted to the grave by a huge choir of famous musicians and lest she should be forgotten, 'this man, who pretended to be your friend, has dedicated a temple and a sacred enclosure to Pythionice Aphrodite, goddess of love, not only despising the vengeance of the gods but also making a mockery of the similar honours bestowed on you'. Harpalus, no less, had immortalized his mistress as a goddess at a time when others were already paying divine honours to his king. He had also set a fashion, as royal mistresses of the future would frequently be named Aphrodite and worshipped in similar style.

Even a goddess needed to be replaced. Applying once more to Athenian brothels, Harpalus had lured the well-known prostitute Glycera eastwards and left Babylon in order to meet her on the Asian coast; they had repaired to Tarsus, where 'Glycera was hailed as queen and received *proskynesis* from the people; it was forbidden to pay Harpalus a crown of honour without paying her one too. In a nearby town, he set up a bronze image to her, instead of to Alexander.' Romance kept him far from the treasury of Babylon, but as Tarsus was an important monetary centre, and there was a large local storeroom nearby, he could still give an air of attending to monetary duties. Proof of his irresponsibilities can still be seen in a rare series of silver coins, issued at Tarsus, which bear none of Alexander's types but return to the old Persian designs of the days when satraps were independent; when Alexander's governors had lost the right to issue their own silver money, such defiance meant open revolt. The longer he dallied with his lady, the closer his king had come to home. He would not stand for any 'king and queen' in Tarsus.

Whether or not Alexander received Theopompus's letter on returning to his Persian palaces is unimportant. Probably it arrived later, but even without it, Harpalus knew that such charges could be laid against him. When news of the purge in the east and the king's uncompromising mood reached Tarsus, he had every reason for alarm: he too had once been in Hamadan, where four generals and six hundred soldiers had now been executed for misconduct. He had two brothers, but one was no longer at court to plead for him, as he had been left to his death as satrap of western India; the other, leader of the archers, was either dead or busy on the borders of Makran. Worst of all, the king was approaching Babylon, where his absence, let alone his monument to Pythionice, were proof enough of his misbehaviour. Through his mistresses, he was well connected at Athens and he had donated a token present of grain to help the city in her time of persistent famine; he had been made an honorary citizen in return and it was not surprising when he decided to take his baby daughter, save what soldiers and money he could, and make for Athens across an early summer sea.

When the news reached Alexander, probably in May near Susa, it took him by surprise. Harpalus, said two messengers, had fled with 6,000 mercenary soldiers and as many talents of money and was heading for Athens, presumably with the intention of bribing the citizens to defend him. Alexander thought this incredible and put the messengers in chains. But confirmation earned them their release, and this latest menace from mercenaries finally caused him to order the dismissal of his other satraps' mercenary troops. Harpalus could not be treated so lightly. He knew too many Macedonian officers and he had enough money, unlike Agis or the Persian admirals; orders for his arrest were hastened to Athens both from Olympias the queen regent in Macedonia and from the senior governor on the coast of Asia. Athens, therefore, had reason to hesitate, and Alexander by now had his reasons for a closer interest in the affairs of Greece.

Together with news of Harpalus's flight, he happened to have received a European letter, not from the indignant Theopompus, but from the council of the allied Greek cities. In his absence, Greek politics are too obscure to be followed in detail, but Macedonian leadership had only served to aggravate the broader tendencies of their past two hundred years. Since Philip's conquest of Greece, there had been coups and counter-coups against a background of seven years' drought and famine; exiles and personal incrimination had not been stopped by Philip's allied council, least of all in the face of the revolts by Thebes and Sparta, for it suited the Macedonians to see their enemies expelled. Three years of Spartan discontent in southern Greece and the resulting battles in the year of Gaugamela had exposed the few Spartan allies to reprisals from Antipater and his generals, who had naturally tightened their hold by deposing former rebels and inserting juntas they felt they could trust. Unease, new governments and a major war had meant, as always, that the defeated parties found themselves in exile; they could expect no assistance from Antipater's generals, who had helped to drive them out, and despite the clauses of the 'common peace among allies', the delegates of Philip's Greek council either could not or would not intervene. More than 20,000 Greeks in all roamed homeless on the mainland, as so often in the past fifty years, and at a time of severe famine, their misery, though not a force for revolution, could well become a menace. The Council's letter presumably stressed the danger, and in reply Alexander intervened with the most misunderstood measure of his reign: he sent a proclamation which, among much else, ordered exiles from his allied Greek cities to be restored home.

This sudden order caused a stir which can still be sensed in the speeches of the Greek orators; each city was affected differently, and it is tempting to take the sharpest comments as the sum of its reception. The Exiles' Decree has thus been seen as the final outrage of a despot or as the effort of a frightened tyrant to restore a balance which he himself had upset. In fact, the problem was local and the decree was within legal limits; for the most part, it was welcomed. He did not issue a direct order to each city, but a general proclamation which left the governments free to carry it out according to their local laws. In practice, the distinction between order and proclamation was academic, as the king's word was backed by the sarissa. But the theory had been agreed by the Greek allies when they swore to obey Macedonians, and Alexander's successors would revive it when they wished to please Greek liberal opinion. For in theory a city was free to refuse the announcement, just as others obeyed 'according to their own decision and law'. Technically, their right to self-government had not been infringed by a proclamation whose contents were covered by Alexander's powers as leader of the Greeks. The allied council had a duty to prevent 'illegal deaths or exiles in member cities', but this ideal had scarcely been practicable in the face of Sparta's rebellion and the security measures of a Macedonian marshal and generals who were known to favour juntas. It was left to Alexander, as the allied leader, to intervene and uphold the oaths of his covenant, just as after the Persian war in the Aegean, he had formerly intervened in unsettled member islands. The firmness of his intervention reflects not on a new tyranny of method but on the powers of the sworn constitution of his Greek alliance; these, to be sure, were extreme, but fourteen years before their constitution had been the work not of Alexander but of his father Philip.

The decree was confined to allied cities and to exiles banished during the Greek peace's brief life: an accompanying request for the local Greek leagues to be broken up, though most advantageous to Alexander, was no less in keeping with the alliance's promise of local independence, a slogan which Philip had already used against Greece's leagues and empires.

In most cities, the decree was welcomed, but legality, as usual, had its quirks. Alexander did not wish to restore the Thebans to the city he had ruined, and as the allied council had ratified its ruin anyway, he felt no scruples about announcing their exemptions. His purpose, however, ran deeper than such convenient niceties. Many of the families he was restoring had formerly been his enemies, but they would mostly change their opinions in return for the most effective windfall which a politician could promise: the case of Theopompus, first a slanderer, then a panegyrist, was proof enough of that. Alexander could claim, correctly, that he had not been responsible for the exiles' banishment, for their cities had mostly caused it by their own decrees. At the same time he could take credit for their return, with the help of Antipater, to whom he had written with further instructions. Exiles had been restored often enough in Greek history, but never had a man been powerful enough to restore his past enemies and know he would benefit; such a sweeping gesture was sure to win favour, especially among the weaker cities. Its swift enforcement was complicated and obedience sometimes painful, but nobody could accuse Alexander of breaking his oath as allied leader: he chose an adopted son of his tutor Aristotle to take the proclamation to Greece and read it to the assembled exiles at the Olympic Games in early August. Six years as King of Asia had not made the Leader of the Greeks and the sacker of Thebes any more of a despot to his allies than before.

This massive decree was not connected with the dismissal of the satraps' mercenaries; many of them were not Greeks, very few were exiles, and none who ran free ever tried to return home on the strength of it. It belongs, rather, with the news of Harpalus. Some 20,000 vagrant Greeks, many exiled by Antipater's agents, were indeed better sent home before Harpalus could bribe them; the Decree, too, would scare Athens, his destination. For forty-one years, Athenians had enjoyed land and houses on Samos whose owners had been exiled from the island. Now, Alexander was talking openly of 'giving Samos to the Samians', and only diplomacy would deter him. The exiles had left the island before Philip's reign, so the Athenians could plead a special case. However, any support for Harpalus would ruin it. They might of course try to fight for the island, but most of Greece welcomed the new Decree and Alexander reasoned that Athens would not risk or afford a war alone. Events would prove he had judged the risk acutely. So, as he approached the palace of Susa in early summer, he felt safe enough to consider the harmony of his own ruling class, and after the confusion give scope to a creative design. Before he could reveal his plans, India, for the last time in his life, drew attention to herself.

Calanus, the Hindu Gymnosophist, had followed the army the whole way from the Punjab. He had never felt ill before, but the Persian climate had weakened him, and at the age of seventy-three he told Alexander that he preferred to die rather than be an invalid. Alexander argued with him, but the fakir insisted on a funeral pyre being built, a job which was entrusted to Ptolemy. At the head of a long procession, Calanus was borne in a litter to his deathbed, 'crowned with garlands in the Indian style and singing hymns in the Indian language'. Gold cups and blankets were strewn on the pyre to welcome him, but he gave them away to his followers: he climbed on to the pyre and reclined in full view of the army. Alexander 'did not like to see this happening to a friend', and the rest of the audience 'were amazed that he did not flinch at all in the flames'. Bugles sounded, as the pyre began to blaze; the army raised their war-cry and the elephants trumpeted shrilly as if for battle. 'Bodies you can move from one place to another,' Calanus was said to have written to Alexander, 'but souls you cannot compel, any more than you can force bricks and stones to talk.'

The sequel was conveniently forgotten: in Calanus's honour, Alexander held games and a musical festival and a 'drinking match in unmixed wine', said his master of ceremonies.

because the Indians were so fond of it. The money prizes were huge, but of the drinkers, thirty-five died immediately from a chill, while another six lingered briefly on in their tents. The winner downed three gallons, but even he died after four days.

This monstrous debauch, willingly supported by the drinkers, is a valuable reminder of life in Alexander's entourage: it was almost a prefiguration of the tragedies of the coming year.

One unfortunate festival did not deter Alexander from an even grander sequel. Since the desert, the amusements of court life had been rightly and properly increased; on entering Susa, word went round that there were to be midsummer weddings. In the absence of Macedonian noblewomen, the officers had not enjoyed such a family occasion for the past ten years, and details of the brides must have been eagerly awaited. When the announcement was made, there was cause for astonishment: the bridegrooms were Alexander himself and the Macedonian court Companions and the brides were well-born Iranian ladies.

Of all Alexander's many festivals, this was to be far the most remarkable. The man who had finally removed most of the Iranian males in his government was now to marry the females to more than ninety of his officers; the pomp would befit the palatial setting of Susa,

Ninety two bridal suites [wrote his master of ceremonies] were made ready in one and the same place; a hall was built with a hundred bedrooms and in each of them, the bed was decorated with wedding finery, to the cost of half a talent of silver: Alexander's own bed had legs of gold. All his personal friends were invited to the wedding reception and seated opposite himself and the other bridegrooms; the rest of the soldiers and sailors and foreign ambassadors were entertained in the courtyard outside. The hall was done up regardless of expense and equipped with sumptuous drapes and linen sheets and purple and scarlet rugs embroidered with gold. To hold up the tent, columns were built to a height of thirty feet, gilded and silvered and spangled with precious stones. Round the circuit of the whole hall, nearly half a mile in circumference, expensive curtains were hung, on gilt and silver curtain-rods; their material was woven with animal figures and gold thread. The banquets, as usual, were announced by the sound of the trumpet: the wedding was celebrated for five successive days. Entertainers, both foreign and Greek, gave of their services; conspicuous among them were the conjurers from India and celebrities from Syracuse, Tarentum and Lesbos. There were songs and recitations, and players of the lute, the flute and lyre; actors of Dionysus's company pleased the king with lavish presents, while tragedies and comedies were performed by his favourite Greek stars.

The bill for the wedding would not have disgraced a Shah, but flattery helped the accounts to balance, for 'the crowns which envoys sent him were worth some 15,000 talents'.

The weddings themselves were well considered, and were celebrated in the Persian fashion: 'Chairs were set out for the bridegrooms and after the drinking, the brides came in and each sat down next to their husbands, who took them by the hand and kissed them, Alexander being the first to do so. Never did he show more courtesy and consideration to his subjects and companions.' The matches had been arranged in proper precedence. Alexander took two new wives besides Roxane, the first the elder daughter of Darius, the second the youngest daughter of the previous king Artaxerxes III; Darius's daughter was made to change her maiden name, a common Macedonian practice, and take that of Stateira, the same as Darius's wife whom Alexander had respected as his captive until her death in childbirth. Politically, it was a sound decision to marry into the two royal houses of Persia at once and to continue a family name, but politics was also combined with sentiment; Hephaistion was married to Darius's younger daughter, sister of Alexander's new wife, 'because Alexander wanted Hephaistion's children to be his own nephews and nieces'. It is one rare and timely insight into the bond between the two men.

Other relationships were no less paradoxical. Many brides were probably mere girls, in accordance with Greek and Iranian practice, but they served a most intricate design. Ptolemy became brother-in-law of Eumenes, the Greek secretary whom he was soon to detest; both Eumenes and Nearchus, by marrying daughters of Alexander's first mistress Barsine, became the king's step-sons-in-law; these daughters were themselves half Greek and thus very suited to the purpose. Seleucus, commander of the Shield Bearers, married the daughter of Spitamenes, Alexander's rebel enemy, a union with far-reaching consequences. But these marital ironies did nothing to detract from Alexander's intention. After a time of grave uncertainty in his empire, he wished to attach the Greeks and the Macedonian nobility, from whom his governors were now mostly drawn, to the children of the native aristocracy they had finally supplanted. Just as the Persian courtiers had once married the Medes and Babylonians, so too the Macedonians would marry the daughters of loyal Persians for the sake of politics; it was at Susa that he had left Darius's family to learn Greek while he marched to Iran and India and his return visit satisfied him that they were fit to be married into his future. After two centuries of discord between Persia and Greece, this deliberate fusion was unprecedented. The weddings were celebrated publicly and arranged with Alexander's typical mixture of forethought and showmanship, and were also extended to the common soldiery. In the absence of Macedonian women, the troops had taken Asian mistresses during the campaign, and inquiry revealed that even after the march through Makran, these numbered 10,000.

418

Each of them, like the noble bridegrooms, now received a royal dowry in return for enrolling their names and having their Asian mistresses officially recognized as wives.

There were several consequences to such an order. The women would benefit most, for once they were full wives, their children would have to be recognized and their husbands could not so easily desert them or replace them with a woman of higher status. But Alexander did not spend an enormous sum in dowries simply to make his soldiers' children legitimate; it would have suited him more, as he soon showed, if the next generation were bastard children, with nobody to look to except their king. What mattered was that these were Asian women, just as his Companions' brides were Iranians: the weddings were an attempt to include his subjects in an empire whose satrapal offices had mostly been taken from them. Asians had been taken on as mistresses because there were no alternatives, but he was raising them to a status which Greek populations abroad had always resisted strenuously. In Greek cities in a foreign land, the children of barbarian mothers had not, in the only known cases, been recognized as citizens: after Alexander, in the military colonies where families held land from the king in return for service, Greeks and Macedonians can be shown to have married their sisters and granddaughters rather than share their property with a native wife. Only in the Asian countryside, where there was no alternative and less at stake, were mixed marriages common in the next generations of Alexander's successors. The point at issue was more one of status than racial prejudice, but it was none the less a strong one; Alexander knew he had to offer the bribe of the dowry in order to legitimize mixed marriages on a scale that was never attempted again. Among the officers, all were pleased at the honour, though a few were resentful that their brides were to be oriental. None of them dared to refuse.

It was a splendid moment of chivalry, but behind it lurked an awkwardness that might still break out to spoil it all. Ever since the previous summer, Alexander had decided to send his Macedonian veterans home and he had segregated them for that very purpose; they had returned from India by the Helmand valley and because they had avoided Makran, all 10,000 had survived to outnumber the Macedonian survivors by almost two to one. Age and fitness still advised they should be sent away, but at a moment when Alexander was marrying Iranians to Companions and approving the troops' mixed marriages, the dismissal of veterans would take on a new and painful air. But they must be coaxed to go home, for the years ahead no longer lay with sixty-year-old men who often resented the oriental policies of their king; there is nothing more dangerous than the frankness of old friends, especially when status is at issue. Only the next few weeks would show whether frankness would lead to conflicts, and whether Alexander's veteran troopers would succeed, where satraps, exiles and mercenaries had already failed to bring him down.

CHAPTER THIRTY

Fearing his veterans, Alexander once more prepared his way with generosity. It was his oldest tactic, and one which had nearly saved him on the river Beas. The Susa weddings had been the most prodigal display of his career and none of the guests could have failed to enjoy it, but the common soldiers still needed more reward than the dowries for their mistresses. As a balance to his officers' festivities Alexander announced that he was willing to pay off the debts of the entire army. Presumably, the soldiers were owed arrears of pay, as sufficient treasure could never have been carried in coin to keep them up to date in India, but it was not just the arrears that Alexander had in mind; they would also have lived on credit with the camp-traders, women and such quartermasters as were not paid in kind, and these debts remained to be paid to as many camp followers as survived to collect them. At first, the men suspected this astonishing offer as a means of prying into their debts, but when they were reassured that their names would not be taken, they presented themselves before the army accountants. 'A king,' Alexander is reported as saying, 'must never do otherwise than speak the truth to his subjects, and a subject must never suppose that a king does otherwise than tell the truth.' It was a revealing, but not a tactful, remark. Only one ancient monarchy ever stressed the virtues of telling the truth, and that was the Persians' own. Besides the dress of Cyrus's heirs, Alexander had openly picked up their ideals, and at a time when the Orient was too much in evidence, his veterans would not be pleased to hear his words.

The result of his promise was an enormous write-off of some 10,000 talents, or two-thirds of the annual treasure-income of the Persian empire in its prime. This largesse was accompanied by the usual rewards for competitive merit, for the value of medals was not lost on Alexander. Nearchus, now returned from the ocean, Peucestas and other bodyguards who had saved the king at Multan, Leonnatus who had routed the Oreitans, each were crowned with gold crowns as a public honour. The king was showing off his magnanimity; but then there arrived in camp a new crowd who at once undid his measured attempt at harmony.

From the Alexandrias and tribal villages of Iran, 30,000 young Iranians

421

appeared at Susa, dressed in Macedonian clothes and trained in the Macedonian style of warfare. It was more than three years since Alexander, near Balkh, had ordered them to be selected and trained, and they could not have arrived at a more explosive moment. When they began to show off their military drill outside the city, word quickly spread that Alexander had named them his Successors, and there were facts to support camp gossip. The Companion Cavalry had marched through Makran in near entirety and had suffered the loss of almost half its horsemen. No new Macedonians were yet available, so Alexander had filled up the ranks with picked Iranians who had hitherto been serving in separate units. After the disaster the Companions' newly mixed squadrons numbered four, and a fifth was now added, conspicuously oriental in its membership. Not even the king's own Battalion was exempted. The most esteemed Asiatics, men like Roxane's brother or Mazaeus's and Artabazus's sons, were enlisted into its exclusive ranks and equipped with Macedonian spears instead of their native javelins. Militarily, Iranian cavalry were more than equal to their king's demands, but it was not their competence which was at stake. They had been given a place in the most Macedonian clique of all; it was as if a British general had opened the ranks of the Grenadier Guards to Indian sepoys, and like most high-minded changes, it was unpopular from the start.

The ordinary soldier hated what he saw. He had lived with hints of it for a long while: Alexander's Persian dress, however moderate; his ushers; his Persian Companions and his *proskynesis*, at least from orientals, but as long as his own rank was assured, he did not mind these mild innovations enough to rebel against them; he enjoyed his Asian mistress, and whatever else, the East was a fabulous source of riches. But once he felt that he was being supplanted, all that the Orient stood for seemed dangerous and disgusting. His concubine had now become his legal wife; he did not like the look of the king's Persian marriages; he forgot all logic and resented Peucestas for pandering to Persian ways in Persia's home province as if they were something privileged. He began to grumble, fearing the Successors for the implications of their name; what did they know of starvation in the Hindu Kush, elephants in the Punjab or the sand-dunes of Makran?

For the moment, Alexander could escape a confrontation by moving westwards; his road, like the veterans', still led in the general direction of home, and reports from the last stage of Nearchus's voyage up the Persian Gulf, had aroused his interest in the river routes from Susa. He learnt he could sail down the river Pasitigris, venture on to the sea or a linking canal, and return up the mouth of the Tigris until he rejoined the

Royal Road; the idea appealed to him, so he detailed his new brother-in-law Hephaistion to bring the troops in attendance by land, and he embarked on the fleet to carry it out. The Pasitigris was pleasantly navigable and allowed him to inspect the irrigation methods of the area, but the Tigris had been blocked by weirs 'because the Persians, themselves poor sailors, had built them at regular intervals to prevent any ships sailing upstream and seizing their country'. Alexander 'said that such devices did not befit a victorious army and he proved them to be worthless by easily cutting through what the Persians had been so keen to preserve'.

At the mouth of the Tigris, he was able to lighten his load. Where the Dur-Ellil canal meets the eastern edge of the river estuary, the Persian kings had founded a royal garrison two hundred years before and stocked it with Carian settlers, fellow countrymen of Scylax the sea captain and thus well suited to naval work on the Persian Gulf. The garrison had fallen into disrepair and Alexander felt inclined to replace it; now that Nearchus had explored the Persian Gulf, a city at the mouth of the Tigris could resume the Carian sailors' duties and serve as the port for India's shipping and traders. The descendants of the Carians' garrison were recruited as settlers and combined with as many army veterans as could decently be shed. Once again, an Alexandria took its cue from an ancient oriental outpost, and again it would live up to its founder's hopes. The new Alexandria lasted barely a hundred years before being ruined by floods, but the site was twice restored by Greek and Parthian kings and became the main port for near-Asian trade with India, visited by the Roman Emperor Trajan and still maintained by the Arabs a thousand years after Alexander's foundation. Its neat parallelogram of streets and houses, designed as if it were a military camp, has recently been found by an English air survey. Alexandrias, as their founder recognized, were his surest claim on posterity.

Rid, therefore, of a few hundred veterans, Alexander left his new city to be built and sailed up the Tigris, removing weirs and allowing his surveyors to measure the length of the river. At Opis, on the river bend south of modern Baghdad, he paused to meet Hephaistion and the land army. He knew now that there was no escaping his problem. From this point onwards, his route and the veterans' would have to diverge, for it was impossible for boats to sail up the Tigris any further, and at Opis the road system offered an alternative; he could either strike west for Babylon or else follow the great eastern highway into Media and Hamadan. The late summer weather would make Babylon intolerably hot, so like the Persian kings, Alexander opted for a visit to Media and the cool of the hunting-lodges of Hulwan. But if the veterans followed him, they would be doubling back and veering away from home. They had to go west, and at Opis the issue was brought out publicly.

Ever since Susa and the sight of the Successors, the troops had been sullen and discontented. Now Alexander called them together and told them that the aged and infirm were to be discharged and returned to Macedonia; they would be handsomely rewarded 'both to the envy of their friends back home and to the emulation of those who stayed in service'. It was the least well-received suggestion he had ever made. The troops rioted and shouted him down. 'Go on campaigning,' they said are to have told him, 'in the company of your father,' meaning Ammon, not Philip, 'but if you dismiss the veterans, you must dismiss us all.' Other reports differed, as the taunts of mutineers are never recorded with accuracy, but whether or not men had referred to Ammon, their disobedience was curtly treated. Alexander jumped down from his platform attended by his closest officers, and pointed out the trouble-makers whom he wished them to arrest. Thirteen men were seized and marched away to their death: Alexander remounted the platform and launched into one of his powerful speeches. Then he strode away to the royal quarters, where he shut himself in, refusing to see any of his Companions or attend to his personal requirements. Only his intimates were allowed inside. None of his officers is known to have described the mutiny, but there is no mistaking the points at issue. Nobody complained that Alexander had lost his sense of proportion or his ability to rule the empire, yet many officers, even a Hipparch, had sided with the veterans, a rare split between Alexander's commanders and his close friends. They booed him, not because he had led them into Makran or because he was likely to lead them into further battles, but because he was trying to exclude them from the future they knew he still offered. It was not a mutiny of men who wished to go home, for after ten years in Asia, a home in the marches of Upper Macedonia had lost its very few attractions: former hill-shepherds had seen and plundered a vastly richer world and they meant to stay at the top of it. They did not intend to leave it to a corps of oriental Successors and a mixed brigade of Persian Companions, when there were perfectly good Macedonians, or so they felt, to carry on instead. It was a mutiny of men who wanted to stay firmly put; had they lost their faith in Alexander, they could have murdered him the moment he jumped off his platform, bodyguards and all. They did nothing, because they needed him.

But Alexander saw it differently. Many of the men he wished to disband were over sixty, or even seventy, years old; they were often unfit and generally resistant to change. Had he known how they were to return and dominate the battlefields after his death, he might have hesitated, but at

Opis, he was thinking of his own future and for that, old men were too short-term a liability. His ambitions would strain Macedonia's manpower, a source on which he had not been able to draw for the past seven years, and it made sense to call on his large oriental reserves to replenish an army which had been humbled by Makran. The province of Persia alone had more fighting men than his father had ever commanded in his new Macedonia, and by recruiting them, he could involve them in the profits and responsibilities of conquest. His weddings at Susa, his Iranian Companions and Successors were proof, to his great credit, that he knew where the loyal governing class of the future should be made to lie. He did not want a court which was recruited exclusively from Macedonians any more than he wanted the equality or the brotherhood of man; he wanted, rightly, to 'draw on the best recruits, whether Greek, Macedonian or barbarian'. There was no better guard against inflaming the national feelings of the peoples he had conquered than to invite their governors to share in his court.

The army had threatened him with what they believed he would never do, but being Alexander, it was not long before he announced that he would do it all the same. They had told him that if any veteran was dismissed they would all desert and leave him to his new Iranian friends; after an ominous silence from the royal tent, news came that the Iranians were his perfect and sufficient army of the future. There were to be Iranian Shield Bearers, Companions, Foot Companions and Royal Squadrons; the army commands were to be held by picked orientals, who would be treated as the king's equals and therefore allowed the traditional privilege of greeting him by a kiss. For two days after the announcement, Alexander remained in his tent, seen only by his Iranian officers, close Companions and Bodyguards. He was bluffing boldly, but if the troops had been stubborn, he would no doubt have carried on with his design.

With their leaders dead and their wages in danger, the troops hesitated, struck by Alexander's new announcement. It was a very different situation from the mutiny at the Beas. There too, Alexander had threatened to march on without them, but they had known they were indispensable. This time, they had challenged him to disband them and he had shown every sign of being prepared to do so. Many officers heard their rank was passing to Iranians, a hint that they too had sympathized with the mutiny. Alexander's close friends stood against them, and this they could not break. Threatened men, they took fright:

They ran to the royal quarters and threw down their weapons before the doors, as a fervent entreaty to their king; then they stood and began to shout to be allowed inside; they promised they would give up the instigators of the mutiny; they would not depart from the doors, day or night, until Alexander took pity on them.

Not for the last time in history, a group of agitators had led a majority where it wished it had never gone.

Alexander 'came out rapidly, and when he saw their imploring attitude and heard how many were crying and lamenting, he too began to shed tears'. An elderly Hipparch of the Companion Cavalry came forward to voice the men's entreaties. Persians, he said, had been made Alexander's Royal Kinsmen with the traditional right to kiss the King, but 'no Macedonian has yet sampled such an honour'. Alexander replied that from that day onwards, he called them all his kinsmen, widening a title to please them in the best tradition of the Macedonian kings, whereupon 'the Hipparch came forward to kiss him, as did any others who wished to do likewise. Then they took up their weapons, shouted and raised the song of victory on the way back to camp.' Master of the moment, Alexander followed up his success with a judicious festival: he offered sacrifice to the usual gods, Ammon, therefore, included, and announced a public banquet for the senior members of the court and army.

This banquet was planned with all Alexander's inimitable sense of style. A feast was laid out on the grass and around him sat his senior Macedonians; in a circle outside sat Iranians: outside again, sat distinguished representatives of other tribes in the empire. It was a scene of merriment and ritual on the grandest scale: Greek priests and magi led the ceremonies in their own distinctive manner and presided over the libations which Alexander and those around him poured together, ladling their wine from the same huge bowl. Those outside followed suit, until shared conviviality was rounded off with a common prayer. Alexander, in their midst, prayed for 'other blessings and for concord between the Macedonians and Persians and a sharing of the rule of the empire between them'. All the guests, to the number of 9,000, poured a common libation and accompanied it with a shout of triumph.

At this memorable moment the triumph was Alexander's.

Soon afterwards, all such Macedonians as were too old or disabled to fight departed from him, but now, as volunteers; they numbered more than 10,000. Alexander gave them their full pay not only for their past service but also for the length of their journey home; in addition, he presented them with a talent's bonus.

On reaching Macedonia, they would be rich enough on this alone to occupy a higher social position than they could ever have imagined possible ten years before; a talent's bonus meant more than fifteen years' combined wages for an ordinary soldier, and bonuses took no account of Indian plunder and oriental jewels. 'If they had any children by their Asian wives, they were to leave these with him so as not to import quarrels and strife into Macedonia between foreigners and foreign children and the native families and wives they had already left there.' These strays would be dependent entirely on Alexander as their mothers would no longer be recognized wives and by Greek law, children of unrecognized mothers were regarded as illegitimate. They had also been brought up to life in camp, where Alexander promised to see that they were educated in Macedonian fashion and trained especially for war; 'when they were grown up, he would bring them to Macedonia and hand them over to their fathers'. The promise of a Macedonian education was a careful sop to the veterans' feelings, but the arrival of several thousand bastard Asians in the life of long-neglected Macedonian women was one of the more unenviable meetings which history was spared through Alexander's death. Small wonder that 'his promise was vague and uncertain'.

But his handling of the mutiny had been masterly throughout. His speech, his rapid arrest of the leaders, his complete acceptance of his men's overhasty threats, his two days' silence and his banquet of reconciliation: no man could march an army through Makran and remain unchanged by the experience, but it is sequences like these which show that the change had not cost Alexander his astonishing flair for leading men. He showed none of the indecision or the meanness which attaches to the declining despots of fables and sermons; being a politician, he was of course ruthless, but being a great politician, he had the far rarer gift of making his purpose convincing. He could never have reduced his mutineers to abject pleading unless he had first been a man of extraordinary personality; the same blunt tactics from a mere tyrant would have ended in a war in the camp, or his execution by the bodyguards. His succeeding generals learnt that soon enough.

The banquet, however, was his master-stroke. He managed to seat Macedonians and Iranians together, the Macedonians around him in the position of honour, the Iranians in an outer circle, and he coaxed men who only two days before had been deriding any such pretensions to join with one accord in common libations and a prayer for concord and participation between their two peoples. Concord was a catchphrase of the time, but the emotions of the audience were brilliantly managed, and this effect was not forgotten: the form of the feast at Opis was to be copied eight years after Alexander's death by an officer who had witnessed it, again at a moment of friction and crisis. The gift of commanding a crowd can be a dangerous one, but at Opis it had been applied to the most commendable of ends; in the emotion of a common banquet, those who had refused to share their empire with its high oriental families and abundant soldiers were rightly and properly routed.

For, until these last years, Alexander had not fought to change but to take over. The royal scrolls of the Persian empire were still stored in the same files; the Royal Road still ran through the same post houses with the same immemorial threat of levies and requisitions. There were Honoured Friends at court, Royal Relations, Royal Fires, the royal harem, eunuchs, and a king who studiously wore the Persian diadem; gold brooches and purple robes were bestowed as marks of rank and even the daily outlay on the king's and Companions' dinners remained at the level long fixed by the Persian kings. In the provinces, there were satraps, Eyes of the King and treasurers under the same old Persian name: the Alexandrias were built, for the most part, on the sites of previous Persian outposts, however different their culture, street plans and constitutions. The one perceptible change in government, apart from minor alterations in the satrapal boundaries, was that satraps had gradually lost the right to issue their own silver coins. This continuity is not a criticism, for against the unalterable facts of time, distance and native tradition, deep change in the empire would have been either naive or irresponsible. But from a Greek point of view, such continuity was itself surprising; when taken to the lengths of Iranian brides and Successors, it broke completely with the slogans of the early invasion. To Greeks at home, Alexander's most memorable change had been to be conservative of what he conquered, but this conservatism had changed shape during the expedition. He had begun, mistakenly, by reappointing Darius's satraps; by the time he married Roxane, he was planning ahead, employing Iranians as separate army units and already thinking of younger Iranian recruits. Since coming out of Makran, he had shown an increasing keenness to treat all suitable orientals as equals in court and camp, if not in the satrapal commands; it is incorrect to explain this only in terms of replacing his heavy losses in the desert, as his 30,000 Iranian Successors had already been chosen three years before the attempt on Makran was considered. Like the Persian queen and her daughters, these new recruits were to be taught Greek and trained in Macedonian customs; the children of the Susa weddings, no less than the abandoned families of the returning veterans, were to be educated likewise, with the added asset of mixed parentage behind them.

Alexander's policy of fusion did not extend to a new way of life. For political reasons he wished to recruit from and marry into his oriental subjects but he was not acting from a racial faith in the half caste or a

428

belief in the mixed culture of new blood. All his courtiers and soldiers were to be given a Greek or Macedonian education, just as Barsine and her relations were brought up to Greek ways. The ideals of spreading Greek culture through cities and dignifying Asia with a Greek education were already much in the minds of Greek contemporaries; Alexander has been hailed as the founder of the brotherhood of man or criticized for betraying 'purity' of race, but it is as the first man to wish to westernize Asia that he ought to have been judged.

After the banquet, it was only natural that the disbanded veterans should be led home by the oldest and most conservative officers. Their command was entrusted to Craterus, a very close friend of Alexander, who was known for his doggedly Macedonian outlook: he was unwell, and so he received the seventy-year-old Polyperchon as his deputy. Polyperchon belonged to the royal family of the most backward hill-kingdom attached to Macedonia and as an officer who had once ridiculed the Persians' act of *proskynesis*, he would have little sympathy with Alexander's future government. The departure of their 10,000 men would thin the army of its Macedonians, nowhere more so than in the infantry battalions, where the three thousand Silver Shields, mostly veterans of Philip's corps of Shield Bearers, were leaving for home with their battle-scarred commanders. A mere 6,000, perhaps, of the 23,000 Macedonians recruited in the past ten years for Asia had survived or now remained in service in an army that wore an oriental look. Not that Alexander was unmoved to see their fellows go: 'He took his farewell of them all with tears in his eyes and they too cried as they left him.' Craterus, on arrival, was to take charge of Macedonia and 'the freedom of the Greeks', that specious slogan of Philip's Greek alliance, 'while Antipater was to bring out young Macedonians as replacements'. He had written to Antipater that the veterans and their families should enjoy seats of honour in the theatre for the rest of their lives; after ten years' absence, he naturally wished to see his ageing marshal, now over seventy, in person, but whether Craterus's appointment to Macedonia was to be temporary or permanent is uncertain. Camp gossip suggested that at last Antipater was to be supplanted after so much contention with Olympias the queen, but 'nothing open is reported to have been said or done by Alexander which would imply that Antipater was not as high in his affection as usual'. There was little point in inviting the marshal casually to Asia through the orders of a departing general, unless Antipater was more than likely to agree. And yet the last had by no means been heard of the marshal in Alexander's history.

As the veterans left Opis, many of them sick like Craterus and ill-suited to a rapid march home, Alexander was left to the diversions of his friends. After the high emotions of the past three months, it was a sudden and flattening moment and as for the first time there was not the prospect of immediate war, it is important to recognize who his friends would be. During the expedition, age, battles and conspiracy had accounted for half of his known officer class, or some fifty-five Companions and governors, but it is most remarkable how for the past three years his closest friends and camp-commanders had survived disasters almost to a man. Since the start of the Indian invasion, only two known generals had disappeared from court, one of whom was Coenus the Hipparch, a sick man; after Makran, the other great names still lived on, the same commanders of the Foot Companions, the Shield Bearers and five of the brigades of the Companion Cavalry. The seven royal Bodyguards remained unchanged, as close as ever to the man they protected, and they welcomed the favoured Peucestas as an eighth among them. Exclusively Macedonian, they were the nobles whom Alexander loved and trusted, whether tough like Leonnatus, famed for his gymnastics, or shrewd like Ptolemy, a friend from childhood; Hephaistion still predominated, faithfully inclining to the Iranian customs of his king and lover. Each had his family and favourites, none more so than the clique of Perdiccas, which included two of the leaders of the Foot Companions. Already, Alexander's eventual successor had founded his influence among the men who mattered, but they were not a divided group. Unless they had supported their king, he could never have won the Opis mutiny, for rulers never fall unless they are divided amongst themselves.

Bodyguards were not the only intimates. Ever since his childhood Alexander had been well disposed to Greeks from the outside world and enough of this earliest circle still lived to share the hopes and troubles of the day. Nearchus was safely and happily at court, a friend for life; the bilingual Laomedon, whose even dearer brother Erigyius had been buried in state six years before, was available to reminisce on all they had been through in the past decades. Eumenes, the Greek secretary, had first served Philip, then earned Alexander's closest confidence: his wiles had long worked in private and aroused both jealousies and firm allegiance, until his influence caused him to clash pettily and constantly with Hephaistion. Others of Philip's Greeks were loved for less menacing talents. Thettalus the tragic actor had always been a favourite of Alexander, a lifelong friendship which his prizes on the Athenian stage had done nothing to cool. He was still with the king at Opis, ready for a talk about Euripides or a recitation after dinner. The philosopher Anaxarchus offered civilized companionship and the Greek engineers could always be questioned

430

on their new machines of war. Architects and artists, musicians and poets of all kinds were keen for friendly patronage, while the Greek doctors and seers could claim high rank by their essential skills. Aristander the prophet was loved and alive, Philip the doctor and his associates still worked on, imperative friends for a king in a country of sicknesses and poisons. Pages and ball-boys were favoured, if more capriciously; Chares the Greek master of ceremonies was as appreciative as his high position demanded, while Greek aristocrats from Thessaly were always ready for a drink or a game of dice, and had prospered accordingly. Among Greeks alone, even if his officers had deserted him, the king had no cause to feel bereft of friends.

Officially, Alexander would dine among sixty or seventy Companions every day, and here, too, there were friends who deserved their courtesy title. The regiments were in impressively safe hands, especially now that eight of their oldest commanders had set out for Macedonia: men like Seleucus, future king of Asia, or Alcetas, brother of Perdiccas, sympathized with the plan of sharing their status with chosen Iranian nobles. They were easy to like for their opinions, while the Iranians themselves were a fresh source of conviviality, not only the favoured Bagoas, but also Roxane's family, the sons of Mazaeus and Darius's own brother, still a Companion: Darius's mother Sisygambis held Alexander in specially high regard. The 10,000 veterans had been replaced by 10,000 Iranian Immortal Guards from Susa, a thousand of whom served in their glorious embroidery beside the most intimate corps of the Macedonian Shield Bearers as a new Guard of Honour outside the king's tent. Harpalus, maybe, had let his friend Alexander down, but what with his new Iranian attendants and old Macedonian intimates, not to mention the copious concubines of the royal harem, three oriental wives, Bagoas and a mistress, it was not a lonely Alexander who reflected on his treasurer's brusque desertion. He lived among three groups of friends, Greek, Macedonian and oriental, where his worry was the jealousies and incompatibility of a varied company. Men who love a powerful or popular man do not therefore love each other, and it is no surprise that Craterus, for example, hated Hephaistion, Hephaistion hated Eumenes and Eumenes hated the leader of the Shield Bearers. Alexander, at the centre, did not spare himself in their interest. He had shown he would weep when taking his leave of veteran friends; now, he had more money than any man in the world and he was commendably willing to spend it. Emotionally and financially generous, he had the qualities to fête his court, never more so than with the desert behind him. In return, they gave him devotion and except for

Cleitus and the family of Parmenion, the court had preserved most of its prominent members throughout the past six years.

It was not, therefore, in crabbed seclusion that Alexander left Opis with his diminished army in August, and as if to stress the point, he indulged in a little sight-seeing on his way north-east to Hamadan. He travelled through the southern fringe of Hulwan, noting the descendants of a Greek community settled there by the Persians 150 years before; after a brief stay, he crossed the open plain of the main road north and made a detour to Bisutun, site of the famous inscription of King Darius on its cliff-face, 500 feet above the ground. 'According to righteousness have I walked: neither the weak nor the strong have I wronged': Alexander could not have read the old Persian lettering high above him but the sanctuary left its mark in Greek history as 'a place most suitable for the gods'. The name Bisutun means 'place of the gods': Alexander's officers had been impressed enough to ask their guides for a translation.

From Bisutun, the army made for Hamadan across the Nisaean Fields, celebrated pastures of the herds of royal horses, which ran to heavy bones on the lush Median lucerne. They had expected to find more than 150,000, but barely a third were now visible and the rest were said to have been removed by rustlers, an added proof of the vandalism among the Medes in Alexander's absence. This disappointment was put to rights by the satrap: he brought a hundred cavalry women, armed with axes and small shields, but 'Alexander sent them away from the army in case they should be abused by the Macedonians'. Inevitably, like the German females who tried to join the second Crusade, they were alleged to be Amazon tribeswomen: only through a myth could Greeks and medieval Europeans credit the sight of women in war. If true, this story suggests Alexander's respect for women, for he dismissed them, fearing the rape which he always detested.

Autumn was almost over by the time the army had at last made their leisurely progress to the turreted city of Hamadan, summer palace of the Persian kings and built for a circumference of one mile round a temple of silver, turquoise tiles and glittering jewels. The hot months of the year had passed in relaxation, the survivors' first taste of summer leisure in the last three campaign seasons; there were conjectures as to where war would take them next, but nothing firm had been revealed and there were still those who could argue that their next objective lay in Greece. By now, the Exiles' Decree had been read at Greece's Olympic Games and had been applauded by its audience of more than 20,000 exiles; after his first reception Harpalus's flight had failed, as the gates of Athens had finally been closed against him and he had fled with his mercenaries to think again on the island of Crete. Only a small part of his money had been left with Athens's politicians. But news of his failure would not have reached Hamadan by September; the camp would reason that Athens had always been their enemy and was now offended by part of the Exiles' Decree. She was still electing extremists as her yearly generals. There might also be new danger in the order to the Asian satraps to disband their mercenaries, for though it had nowhere caused rebellion, some 10,000 had run wild on the coast of Asia Minor and might seem tempting recruits to any Athenian who fancied war. There was talk, then, in Hamadan of a punitive march into Greece and a siege of Athens; others must have remembered how Alexander had always avoided any conflict with the city, and reasoned their march would lead elsewhere. The Black Sea, perhaps, against nomads who had destroyed a recent Macedonian army, or the Scyths around the Aral, as Alexander had once implied; and was the Caspian a lake or a gulf of ocean, and if a lake, who lived beyond? But Alexander gave nothing away, and as autumn broke in Hamadan, he kept up the mood of leisured festivity by ordering another week of athletic games and artists' competitions, sacrifices to the gods and free food and wine.

There is a penetrating sidelight on the entertainments which followed. The prologue of a comedy survives, probably performed for the first time at Hamadan, which was believed to have been written by Alexander. Perhaps he added a few lines; its main author was Python, either a playwright from southern Italy or a Greek sophist, known for his fatness, who had served with the Macedonians since the reign of Philip. There is no disputing the subject. The stage was set as if at the marshy entrance to the Greek underworld. On the right stood a mock mausoleum: a group of eastern magi appeared as the chorus and consoled the leading character by summoning up a spirit from the dead. Necromancy was nothing new on the Greek stage, but in this case it was topical: the mausoleum was meant to be Harpalus's monument to his mistress; the leading character was Harpalus himself, referred to by the nickname 'son of a phallus', and the ghost whom the magi summoned was none other than the Pythionice whom he had loved. The dialogue turned on suitably caustic remarks about Athens, Greek famine, Glycera and the rebellious treasurer: like the singers in Samarkand on the night of Cleitus's murder, dramatists knew they could amuse their patron by publicly ridiculing the friend who had let him down. And yet a year which had looked like emerging happily from disaster and revolt was to end in a tragedy which nobody expected.

In Hamadan, Harpalus was not the only friend to miss the festivals. The king and his Companions had been drinking at their usual parties, but Hephaistion had caught a fever and retired to bed; the games continued without him, and his doctor confined him to his room and put him on a strict diet. As it did not seem too serious, the doctor left to attend the theatre; equally untroubled, Hephaistion ignored his orders, ate a boiled chicken and washed it down with a flagon of wine. Disobedience aggravated the fever, perhaps because it had become typhoid and reacted to any sudden intake of food; the doctor returned to find his patient critical and for seven more days the illness showed no sign of abating. The games went on, however much Alexander worried; there were concerts and wrestling matches, but on the eighth day, when the crowds were watching the boys' races in the stadium, news arrived to the royal seats that Hephaistion had suffered a grave relapse. Alexander hurried to his bedside, but by the time he arrived it was too late. His Hephaistion had died without him, and it was on this cruel note that Alexander broke down for the second, and most serious, time in his life.

His grief was as uncontrolled as the rumours of it, the like of which had not been heard since the hours after Cleitus's murder; some said he lay day and night on the body, refusing to be torn away; others that he hanged the doctor for negligence and ordered a local temple to the god of healing to be destroyed in mourning. Certainly, he refused to eat or drink for three days after the event, whereupon envoys were sent to Ammon's distant oracle at Siwah to ask if it was proper to worship the dead man as a hero. At this moment of tragedy, the king was turning once more to his personal comforters, for it was said, probably truly, that he cut his own hair in Hephaistion's memory and clipped off the tails and manes of the horses in camp. The ritual has a Persian precedent but more tellingly, it also has a parallel in Homer's Greece: in the *Iliad*, Achilles had shorn his horses in honour of his dead and beloved Patroclus, and as Hephaistion had long been recognized as the new Patroculus to Alexander's Achilles, it is entirely appropriate that first Ammon, then Homer, came to the surface of Alexander's sorrow.

In his wild lamentation, Alexander was to show how much he minded about the one sure relationship of his life. For a week or more, he was in no state to take a decision; Bagoas, Roxane and the comforts of the Bodyguards ment nothing to him, and preparations for the funeral were left to be finalized at Ammon's bidding. The courtiers could only wait and suggest that Hephaistion needed a local memorial; it was a fortnight before Alexander had recovered enough to sanction it and decree that like other fallen Companions, Hephaistion should be honoured with a large stone carving of a lion: it still stands to this day, the Lion of Hamadan, more or less where Alexander ordered. Lion monuments were the one

Macedonian legacy to art, extending out to India from a kingdom where lions still abounded; centuries later, when Hephaistion had long been forgotten, the ladies of Hamadan would smear the nose of their lion with jam, hoping for children and easy childbirth. Hephaistion had ended his fame as a symbol of fertility.

There was no such perspective to comfort Alexander. He was a distraught man, stripped of all externals: he felt the loss of his love more bitterly than anything in his career and it did not seem as if time or renewed ambitions could ever reconcile him to sudden bereavement. Within the month, he braced himself to leave the Hamadan which he had come to hate, but a new and chilling feature had entered into the mood of the court, new but not entirely unexpected; Hephaistion was dead, Alexander almost despaired of living, and one man, at least, had been proved most curiously right. Five months before, when the rebellious satraps were being purged, the commander of Babylon had asked his brother, a prophet, to test the omens in the city; in due course, a sacrifice had been offered, first to consider the fate of Hephaistion. The victim's liver had been seen, surprisingly, to be without a lobe; hastily, the prophet had sent a letter to his brother, now in Hamadan, advising him that he need have no fears of Hephaistion as death was very near. Hephaistion had died, as predicted, the day after the letter had been opened in Hamadan; the commander was impressed by his brother and meanwhile, unknown, the brother had sacrificed again. This time, the offering was for Alexander and once more, the liver had no lobe; a letter was already on the road for Hamadan, predicting further doom. Only in a crisis do prophets detect bad omens: there was death in the air, and men were beginning to remember how Calanus the Indian had mounted his pyre and taken a cryptic farewell; he was said to have told the king he would be seeing him again in Babylon. It was all very strange: the liver had had no lobe, the Hindu sophist had talked, it seemed, of death and a Babylonian funeral, and now from Hamadan, a mere month later, Alexander was about to begin a roundabout march down through the hills of Luristan, south-west across Mesopotamia, and so to the very Babylon he had hitherto avoided. Nobody knew where the next year would lead them, whether to Greece or the Caspian, west to Carthage or south to the Arabs of the Hadramut valleys. The decision was Alexander's, but however firm he stood against Hephaistion's loss, the omens had implied he would never take it.

435

CHAPTER THIRTY-ONE

Nothing is harder than to appreciate Alexander after Hephaistion's death. He was a man living on a stupendous scale, but then he had the resources to support it and the years of achievement to justify it. Psychologically, there is no doubt that he had been shattered, but so have many others at the death of the person they love, even without the memory of a disastrous desert march a year before; it is a very different question how long the effects lasted. By the end of the year Roxane was pregnant, so one side of Alexander's life had not been interrupted and there was a comforting permanency in thoughts of a son and heir. He had changed over the years, inevitably, but the change is most apparent not so much in the unknowable recesses of his mind, where Ammon and Achilles still ranked prominently, as in the public and inarguable style of his life. This pomp is the focal point of Alexander's last days and deserves to be considered.

If a courtier had left us his memoirs, he would surely have commented on the past year that festival had followed festival as never before in Greek history. The tendency had always been present in Philip and Alexander's reigns, but Alexander was now bound for Babylon where such display could call on the full machinery of centralized despotism, which had long grown up round an economy of royal canals. The gangs of royal workers, the treasuries and, no doubt, the old bureaucracy would have survived Darius's fall. Since Makran, the army had lived for the grand occasion, the Susa weddings, the Opis banquet, the fateful games of Hamadan: Babylon's system could outdo them all in its last rites for Hephaistion. Three thousand athletes and artists were gathered for the games. A full funeral was to be celebrated at Babylon, by which time the envoys would have returned from Ammon with news of the proposed worship of Hephaistion as a hero. 10,000 talents were rumoured to be needed from king and subjects for the occasion; after Patroclus's death, it had been Achilles's prime concern to be seen to pay him fitting honour as much for his own public prestige as for the dead man's comfort. This same heroic attitude now came out in Alexander.

Though this expense was extraordinarily lavish, Alexander could well afford his share of it. His attitude to money was no different to that of

436

his father Philip or indeed of any well-to-do gentleman in the classical world; money in so far as it was used at all, existed to be spent, not saved, so that conspicuous consumption was an enduring feature of the life of ancient city aristocracies, whether Greek, Roman or Byzantine. For the men of antiquity, there was a judicious art in going bankrupt publicly, and Alexander was true to this attitude on the grandest possible scale. The only figures for his treasure reserves may well be unreliable, but of the 180,000 talents said to have been captured from the Persians' palaces, only 50,000 were said to have remained at his death. Embezzlement no doubt played its part, but as the few known expenses for the past six months totalled about 50,000 talents, some such capital outlay may not be too far from the truth, however dubious its source and statistics. Such resolute draining of reserves was nothing new to Greeks, especially in the absence of double entry accounting; Pericles, that over-praised Athenian politician, had followed a policy which would rapidly have bankrupted Athens of her deposits, had he not died in time. But the remaining 50,000 talents and a yearly tribute of another 12,000 or more still made Alexander far and away the most monied king in the world. Payments in kind mattered more than those in money and for these, there are no figures; he also received huge presents from envoys, and all the while, he could cut new coins from the raw metal ingots which the Persian kings had stored in their halls and bedrooms as decoration. Melting, engraving, stamping and the cutting of dies: these were the busy and essential processes which must have long been occupying Greek experts in the background of Alexander's empire. Thanks to their skills, not even Harpalus and his 6,000 stolen talents were mourned as a serious loss; the finances at Babylon were now entrusted to a Greek from the island of Rhodes who at once showed the typical shrewdness of his countrymen by initiating a scheme for fellow-officers to insure against the loss of their runaway slaves.

Private funerals at huge public expense were nothing new to the Persian empire, but at court Hephaistion's last rites had also opened up enticing possibilities. Hephaistion had died a Chiliarch, or Grand Vizier, with control over the Companion Cavalry and access to Alexander's private favour; in the event of campaigns in Arabia or the West, Alexander might well follow Persian precedent and designate a Royal Deputy to share an empire which, as his Successors soon found, was too burdensome for any one man. The office of Chiliarch was worth having, but it cannot have been a surprise when the royal-born Perdiccas was elevated to take it: his friends and relations already dominated the few high offices left at court, and he had long been loyal to Alexander and his oriental policies.

Perdiccas's cavalry command was given to Eumenes the secretary, a more controversial appointment. There were Macedonians who hated such an educated Greek outsider; they could, moreover, point to Eumenes's hatred of Hephaistion, which had caused them to quarrel constantly, even over such trifles as the housing of their slaves and the honours of a young Greek flute-player. But Eumenes had adapted himself to his king's oriental plans: he was a valuable man and a wily one. He therefore cleared his name by dedicating himself and his weapons to the dead Hephaistion, presumably acknowledging that he was now a divine hero. Other Companions felt obliged to follow suit: the secretary could not be allowed to steal a march.

Apart from the loss of Hephaistion, the courtiers looked out on very different surroundings. In the army, Macedonians were now outnumbered more than ten to one by orientals, and with this fundamental shift of power the new style of kingship which had developed since Darius's death was thrown into greater prominence. Alexander now did business from a golden throne and though dressed, as before, in the Persian diadem, girdle and striped tunic, he wielded a golden sceptre: his official tent was supported by golden pillars and roofed with a richly spangled baldachin, while inside, the five hundred remaining Shield Bearers kept guard over the silver-legged sofas, aided by a thousand oriental bowmen dressed in flame-scarlet, vermilion and royal blue. Five hundred Persian Immortals stood behind them, flaunting their glorious embroidery and their spear-butts, carved like a pomegranate; outside the tent, the Royal Squadron of elephants barred the path of unauthorized visitors, attended by 1,000 Macedonians, 10,000 lesser Persian Immortals and 500 privileged Wearers of the Purple. Magi, concubines, staff-bearers and bilingual ushers continued to play the prominent part they had earned in Persia for the past 200 years.

By this splendour, Alexander and his courtiers were involved in the old externals of a Persian monarchy. When they held audience in their park, reclining on ornate sofas, they were following a long-lived Persian precedent; the king's throne and audience tent had deep roots in the Persian past, as did the incense-burners which smoked by his side. Visitors would pay him their Persian *proskynesis*: he would ride in the privileged chariot, symbol of king and conqueror, and be drawn by the white team of heavy Median horses which had such sacred overtones for his followers. Like a Persian King, he celebrated two birthdays and was honoured by a personal Royal Fire; sacrifices were offered by oriental courtiers to his august spirit, while even his robust drinking habits had links with the necessary virtues of Persian kingship. To an unaccustomed Greek visitor these

Oriental privileges had nuances which are difficult to appreciate. If he had ever seen such pomp before, it would only have been on the stage, where Greek dramatists had presented it as Asiatic excess and conceit. There was a decided touch of the theatre in Alexander's new magnificence, but the conceit was politically excusable: he was wisely playing the Persian monarch to his fast-increasing ranks of orientals. They expected it: he, no doubt, enjoyed it, though the deeper religious overtones were sadly lost on him: Alexander never gave proof of understanding the god Ahura-Mazda, protector of the Persian kings. This ignorance had not cost him a superhuman aura. What he missed in his Persian background, were a king's majesty derived from the fact of his royalty, he received instead from Greeks; in grateful Greek cities of his empire, he was being freely acclaimed for his achievements as if he were a god.

Like the dead Pythionice, mistress of Harpalus, Alexander had already been receiving divine worship from Asian Greeks before he ever reached Hamadan. It was not a new solace, only demanded when Makran or Hephaistion's death had begun to make him feel inadequate. It was a free expression of tactful admiration: cities offered sacrifice in his name, especially on his birthday, or celebrated games called Alexandreia, or set aside a sacred precinct and an altar for his honour or carried his image in a procession of the other twelve gods of Greek Olympus. The city, not the private worshippers, set up this cult in return, or in hope, for Alexander's benefaction; to the plain man, it meant the pouring of libations at the altar outside his door on the days of the great processions when the king or his image was escorted through the streets. He would pour to the king from a flat bowl of cheap glazed pottery, stamped with the royal portrait; one such bowl to Alexander has come from Egypt's Alexandria, implying worship of the founder in his lifetime. Divine honours, as in primitive Rome, had long been paid to dead notables, where they merged with the similar cult of heroes, but Alexander was being worshipped in his lifetime, an honour whose origins and impact have been vigorously discussed, denounced or even explained away.

'It would be eccentric,' Aristotle had recently written, 'if a man were to say that he loved Zeus.' The love of god was not such an alien idea to the ordinary man, but the gods of fourth-century Greece cannot be approached with the hopes and attitudes of a modern Christian. If the boundary between gods and men could not be bridged by love, it was, in principle, an open frontier. 'Do not,' said a too-famous earlier Greek poem, 'seek to become Zeus'; becoming Zeus was not, therefore, an impossible aim, but, as the myths admonished, it was rash and inadvisable. And yet a truly superhuman show of excellence could still lead a man across the boundary; such excellence had been recognized long before Alexander, in two different quarters. There were the men of genius and mysticism, described, however loosely, as gods among men: Pythagoras and Empedocles, the two outstanding philosophers of the Greek West, had impressed their followers as divine, while at least one artist and a faith-healer had felt similarly about themselves, even if others had not agreed. More blatantly, because they were more popular, there were the men of achievement, none more extraordinary than Euthymus the boxer 150 years before Alexander. He too had come from south Italy, the Greek West, but he had punched his way to three victories in the Olympic Games, besides excelling against a mysterious adversary called the Hero of Temesa; his statues, both in Olympia and in his south Italian home-town, were believed to have been struck by lightning on one and the same day, and in recognition of this prowess, he was consecrated in his lifetime by the Delphic Oracle, who ordered sacrifice to be paid to him, as indeed it was, repeatedly: 'there was nothing special about this, except that the gods themselves had ordered it.' As befitted a god, Euthymus lived to an advanced old age, when it was believed that he escaped death by dis-appearing into his local river, which some had always suspected to be his father. Within months, the problem of how a god could die was to be faced by Alexander and his courtiers on remarkably similar terms.

But politicians, like athletes, were also men of power and achievement, and in certain outstanding cases, they too had been worshipped like gods. Again in the Greek West, Sicilian Greeks had feted Dion, their acknow-ledged Saviour of the moment; earlier in Greek Asia, similar honours had been paid to Lysander the Spartan general, by the exiles whom he had restored like Alexander, although these exiles were tyrants and oligarchs, favoured in the name of freedom. Not that this deification was confined to the extremes of the Greek world, to Sicily famed for its excess, or to the coast of Asia where worship of the Roman emperor later took such a deep and lasting hold: in Greek thought it was as old as Homer's epics and so, for example, it could be suggested of Spartan kings or of Pericles the Athenian. But for the most part, independent men of power had not arisen in the same way in the closed world of the cities of mainland Greece as in the kingships of Sicily and Asia. With the rise of Philip, the condi-tions had altered; Philip's father, King Amyntas, was worshipped with a shrine in a nearby Greek city, probably in his lifetime, while Philip himself had died pleasing the Greeks at a festival which enthroned him among the gods, and there can be little doubt that he would have been more freely worshipped in Greek cities had he survived. He had built a Philippeum at Olympia, in which statues of Olympias, Alexander and himself were displayed, and the round shape of this building and the gold and ivory of its statues perhaps imply that it was meant as a place of worship. 'The man who conquers Persia,' a Greek pamphleteer had told him, 'will have earned glory equal to the gods'; Aristotle suggested more cautiously that a man could only 'become a god' by a show of supreme excellence. He was not inclined to believe such excellence possible, but then his pupil Alexander went east, conquered Persia and displayed such extraordinary qualities from Babylon to the peaks of Pir-Sar that his reservations were agreed to be mistaken.

Against this background, worship of Alexander was neither unprecedented nor blasphemous. Even more than Dion and Lysander, he had freed Greek cities and restored Greek exiles; no returning democrat in Asia or restored exile in Greece would feel the slightest scruple about worshipping him for this godlike benefaction. Too much has been made, often by Romans, of the slavishness of classical ruler worship. It is more revealing that Greek cities almost always paid it in return for favours to their remaining liberties, while for the man in the street a public cult of Alexander meant another day's holiday, festive games, building-work and the chance to enjoy the rare luxury of eating meat, that most tangible blessing of a religious sacrifice in the ancient world. No cult of Alexander is yet known in his lifetime in a mainland Greek city, but Greek envoys soon came to him, some dressed as if on a delegation to a god; only one later anecdote referred to a letter from Alexander demanding this worship from the Greeks, but this story is both wildly unreliable and implausible. At Athens, the sole source of contemporary comment, Alexander's so-called divinity attracted the usual anecdotes and witty epigrams, attributed to his many Athenian enemies, but after much heated discussion it is possible that he was indeed paid public worship in the city at the end of his life. The evidence is not yet conclusive, but even a refusal would not have been a matter of high principle: when Alexander first marched into Greece, the Athenians had hastened to offer him 'even greater honours than they had bestowed on Philip', and it is hard to imagine what these could be apart from a temporary act of worship. Within twenty years, they hastened to offer every possible divine honour to a Macedonian who had freed them beyond any argument. In 324, especially, Alexander's benefits, past and future, to the city seemed disputable, and even if those who opposed his divine honours carried the day, they were not constrained by a demand from Alexander himself. His worship was spontaneous and scattered, a hopeful flattery where it was not genuine admiration.

Alexander himself would be pleased, naturally, to receive it. Throughout his life, he remained a scrupulously religious man who carefully sacrificed to the proper gods and consulted his oracles and seers before taking any momentous action; there are countless examples of this, but even in these last months, he was so impressed by the story of a Greek boy in a small Carian city who had been miraculously rescued and carried out to sea by a dolphin that he summoned him and appointed him to a priesthood of the sea-god Poseidon in Babylon. It is unthinkable that such a man would have dared to accept, let alone to demand, divine honours if they went against his own traditional religion. Deification had long been countenanced in Greek thought; he had seen his father's example, and he had studied with a tutor who saw nothing blasphemous in sacrifices, precincts or hymns to a living man: they were high honours, nothing more, as the ancient world did not draw distinctions between homage and worship. The only question was whether anybody in fact deserved them. Alexander's achievements put this beyond doubt: he seemed to be unbeatable, and so at Athens and presumably elsewhere it was suggested that he should be worshipped as an invincible god. The theme of invincibility which he had long encouraged thus found its final expression, despite the march through Makran.

These divine honours were more than an intelligible development from the past. With the single exception of Caesar, Alexander is the only man in ancient history whose divinity was ever to be widely accepted and believed. Here his unique career broke completely with his predecessors: he became a precedent himself, and after Alexander, the history of pomp and kingship could never be the same again. His royal Successors invoked his name, his guidance or his invincibility, copied his claim to be the son of a god as confirmed by an oracle, and even adopted the way he had held his head or worn his diadem. Among the Romans, his impression was even more vivid; here, his effects lived for more than five hundred years, first, in their establishment of a cult of the goddess Victory, probably on early news of his extraordinary successes, then in the continual imitations of their politicians and emperors, from Scipio to Caracalla, who laid claim to Alexander's cloak or breastplate, copied his shield and statues and even recalled the memory of his horse. Christian bishops in Antioch would still be troubled in the late fourth century to find that their congregations favoured Alexander's image on their seal-rings: for the classical world he had become the prototype of glory and superhuman excellence, and men were reluctant to forget him.

To project this back into his lifetime is difficult, but surely correct. For most of his worshippers, Alexander had the added aura of absence.

They had seen him once, at most, when he first freed them and they were left thereafter with a memory of a young man in full glory. If they came to court on his return, they would find evidence of divinity written large in his appearance: the Persian diadem suggested, wrongly, he was representing Zeus, his saffron shoes suggested Dionysus, and his *proskynesis*, if only from Persians, implied to the uncritical that he was himself divine. In art everywhere, these themes were prolific, and it is mistaken to try and date them all to the years after Alexander's death: by his favourite Apelles, he had already been painted holding a thunderbolt, just as later the same artist would show him between hemispheres, a symbol of Castor and Pollux, themselves divine, and of relevance to Alexander's supposed ascension into heaven. 'I hold the earth,' ran the inscription beneath his statue, 'you Zeus, hold Olympus,' and on a medallion, probably struck to commemorate his Indian campaign, this Zeus on earth was shown on horseback, attacking Porus's elephant and wielding the thunderbolt of Zeus in his hand. The theme recurs on an engraved gem, and in Egypt, after his death, small terra-cotta statues show him holding Zeus's aegis, or goat-skin mantle, over one arm. These humble monuments are proof, perhaps, of how the ordinary soldier remembered him, and presumably they derive from an original sculpture of his lifetime. As for his heroic ancestor Heracles, Alexander was shown wearing a helmet made from a lion's head on an otherwise lifelike series of sculptures carved soon after his death for the sarcophagus of the king of Sidon, his own Companion: the helmet was a symbol of Heracles, and no doubt Alexander wore it in real life. On coins, Heracles's standard Macedonian portrait had taken on Alexander's features: there were precedents for this, not least in the gold coin-portraits of Apollo issued by Philip but unmistakably influenced by Alexander's features; coins also showed Alexander in his lifetime wearing Ammon's ram's-horns, and this was a theme all his own. Both in art and literature, parallels were to be drawn between Alexander and Dionysus, but though there were decided similarities between his triumphal procession on leaving Makran and the epiphany, or manifestation of Dionysus and other gods, this is a theme which only arose after Alexander's death, especially when the Ptolemies began to derive their descent through Philip from Dionysus himself. By wearing oriental dress, Alexander had unintentionally assumed certain features of Dionysus's appearance, but the connection was incidental, and though Alexander might rival Dionysus, particularly in India, he never tried to represent the god directly.

To sceptics, it soon became fashionable to explain away Alexander's divinity as a trick designed to impress his subjects. Historians are too inclined to father their own incredulity on to figures of the past; they would do better to ask why the response they find incredible was felt to be needed by men, like themselves, in a human predicament. If Aristotle's writings reflect the mood of contemporaries, then there was already a feeling that the gods were indifferent to man's fate and content to live in disinterested ease. After Alexander this sense of a universe drained of divinity is more apparent. 'The other gods,' said an Athenian hymn to one of Alexander's Successors, twenty years later, 'are either far away, or have no ears, or do not exist, or pay us no attention. But you we see before us, not made of wood, or stone, but alive and real.' There was truth in this sophisticated tribute: Alexander, more than any Successor, was the dominant source of power on earth, and power had long been the distinguishing mark of the Greek gods. Like the gods, he was extraordinarily rich and royally born, and by a single order, he could change the history of men's lives: divine honours recognized this power won by achievement, exactly as Greek pamphlets had predicted they would, and the little that is known of Alexander's character suggests he would have accepted the comparison gratefully and seriously. As to how it affected him at the end of his life, only one description survives: it was written by a Greek pamphleteer, well aware of the details of the court, probably because he had been there. It is, by any standards, remarkable.

'Alexander,' wrote Ephippus of Olynthus, in a pamphlet on *The Deaths of Hephaistion and Alexander*,

would wear the sacred clothes of the gods at dinner-parties, sometimes the purple cloak, the slippers and horns of Ammon, sometimes the dress of the goddess Artemis, which he would often wear even on his chariot, where he dressed in Persian robes and showed a bow and a spear slung over his shoulders. Sometimes, he would also dress as Hermes, especially at parties when he would wear the winged sandals and the broad hat and hold a caduceus in his hand: often he carried a lion-skin and a club, like Heracles. . . . He would sprinkle the floors of his palace with precious perfume and sweet-smelling wines; myrrh and other incense was burnt for his enjoyment. But a hushed silence fell on all these present, as they were frightened: he was murderous and quite unbearable: he seemed, too, to be 'melancholic', that is, hot-tempered.

This is not only a clear statement that Alexander wore female dress like Artemis; it is also the only surviving character judgement by a contemporary on the last months of his reign. It is true that in modern cases of religious delusion, paranoiacs who call themselves God will dress up irrespective of sex in male or female costume to suggest their divinity, but since the rise of Christianity, all such modern psychiatric evidence is of very dubious relevance to Alexander's world; more important, Ephippus himself is hardly a witness beyond reproach. His home town, shared by Callisthenes and possibly by Aristobulus, had been destroyed by Philip's Macedonians, and Alexander had recently announced in Greece that he refused to rebuild it; the very little that survives of his work is either facetious or flagrantly prejudiced against the Macedonians. His own life history is uncertain: probably, he is the same Ephippus who was known as a comic dramatist, who had won prizes at Athens and whose plays poked fun at the alleged divine pretensions of other well-known Greeks, a common comic theme. He had even lampooned the philosopher Plato: certainly, he wrote maliciously and his judgements must be treated with extreme caution.

In their factual outline they make sense: dressing up as a god has a curious history, which helps to put Alexander's alleged behaviour into perspective. There were Greek myths which warned of its evil consequences, but in practice, rulers and outstandingly talented individuals had long thought otherwise. Some ninety years before Alexander, the painter Parrhasios had walked in the streets of Athens, dressed in a purple robe, a golden crown, a white ribbon and golden shoes, carrying a golden staff and claiming to be son of Apollo, god of the arts, and in close contact through dreams with the deified hero Heracles. Priests would occasionally wear divine robes, as would swearers of a sacred oath in Syracuse, who dressed in a goddess's clothes; in Greek Heracleia, on the Black Sea, the tyrant Clearchus, pupil of Plato and a man who modelled himself on the Sicilian kings, had already worn a purple robe, soft boots and a golden crown and been preceded by the image of Zeus's golden eagle. He dyed his face red to impersonate Zeus and suggest divine ichor, and named his son the Thunderbolt, a symbol which he often carried instead of a sceptre. But there was a stranger precedent, which may have meant more to Alexander, as he had probably seen it himself.

During Alexander's youth there lived in Syracuse, always a city of pomp, the famous faith-healer Menecrates. He cured various cases of epilepsy of which the doctors had despaired and as epilepsy was known as the sacred disease, its healer, who asked for no pay, could fairly claim to be divinely inspired: Menecrates thus called himself Zeus, dressed in the usual purples and golds and surrounded himself with a troupe of former patients, who also attired themselves as gods. One was a general from Argos, who had served in high favour with the Persians, and now called himself Heracles and dressed accordingly; another, a tyrant in a small Asian Greek city which Alexander had freed after the Granicus, wore Hermes's robes and wings and carried a caduceus; a third was dressed

445

as Apollo, a fourth as the god of medicine, while the fifth was none other than Alexarchus, son of Antipater and possibly the most extraordinary man of Alexander's generation; he called himself the Sun, and after Alexander's death, he would found an eccentric community, called City of the Heavens, on the top of Mount Athos.

Linked to Macedonia's viceroy, Menecrates's troupe is said very plausibly to have paid Philip's court a visit, where among much mirth, the new Zeus reclined at a gorgeous table, while his attendants burnt incense and poured libations in his honour. It was later suggested that Macedonian fellow-guests laughed so much at the sight that Menecrates fled the dining-room in embarrassment, but in view of Philip's own ambitions, Pella was not the place for men to ridicule an aspiring god. Alexander would surely have seen, or heard about, the doctor's divine arrival.

It is important that, like Menecrates, Alexander is only said to have dressed as the gods at dinner-parties. By ancient custom, the Greeks had long held banquets for the gods, at which an empty table and a portion of the food was left for the appropriate deity: in Athens, twelve fellow-diners, representing the twelve Olympian gods, were chosen to dine in the 'presence' of Heracles, and similar sacred feasts were known at Delphi and all across the Greek world. But Alexander was himself a god; he did not need an empty table, as he could reveal his presence in an epiphany, or moment of revelation, at such sacred dinners in his honour. The moment of epiphany of a living god would soon be freely celebrated for his Successors, and it is very credible that at a 'banquet of the gods' in his own honour, divine Alexander dressed as befitted his dignity. Ammon's horns and slippers were naturally his favourite choice, and remained without imitation, except for a later queen of the Ptolemies; Heracles's lion-skin was unexceptionable and more than forty Greek imitators of Heracles were known to Roman scholars; Hermes is more surprising but can be paralleled in Menecrates's troupe and in gems of Ptolemy II, showing his helmet adorned with Hermes's wings. As for Artemis, the background here is mainly Roman: the emperor Caligula is said to have preferred dressing as a goddess rather than a god, while Heliogabalus and Gallienus, neither beloved of the senators who wrote history, were reported to show themselves as Demeter and the Great Mother goddess respectively. Among Alexander's successors, Demetrius the Besieger appeared as Athena, but only because he was being worshipped by his own Athenians; a Cynic philosopher, however, is said to have dressed in grey as a female Fury, worn a crown of the twelve signs of the Zodiac and warned his pupils that he was sent from the underworld to judge them. Tales of royal trans-

446

vestism are most of them slander, and in Alexander's case, this is plainly so. Dressed as Artemis, he wore 'Persian dress and carried a bow and a lance', of a Macedonian variety especially favoured for hunting. Persian dress had long been derided as effeminate by intolerant Greeks; seeing Alexander wearing it in his chariot and armed unobjectionably for hunting, Ephippus had mockingly pretended that the new divine king who dressed effeminately was trying to look like the goddess of the chase. It was only a joke, and not a very good one.

The wearing of divine clothes, too, was a familiar libel. Enemies, for example, later maintained that the young Augustus had dressed as Apollo and held a sacred banquet among twelve friends dressed as the gods. But in Greece, not Rome, it did have intelligible roots, and despite Ephippus's bias, Alexander may well have adorned himself as his works of art repeatedly suggest. There were eastern precedents, too, for these fancy headdresses, while Bucephalas had probably worn horns, and Philip's image had been carried, no doubt with much decoration, among the twelve Olympian Gods. In outline, therefore, Ephippus may have been telling the truth, a truth, moreover, about Alexander's divinity among his friends. Whether he was also 'unbearable, murderous and evidently melancholic' cannot be decided from Ephippus alone; melancholia, in antiquity, meant a volatile and hasty nature more than a mood of listless ennui. There are no signs that Alexander was any quicker-tempered than at his accession. So far from cowing his courtiers into silence, he still hunted, diced, played ball, joked and banqueted freely with his Companions. Once again, not one of them is known to have lost his life or job in the coming months. As he had said, blood, not ichor, flowed in his veins.

But the fact remains that Hephaistion's death had unnerved him and that for a year, the Makran disaster had remained the last adventure of the 'conqueror of all Asia'. No doubt, too, there had been heavy drinking since the tragedy of Hamadan, though the only hint that Alexander had collapsed into extreme indulgence occurs in the Royal Diaries, a suspect witness whose purpose will soon emerge. The vast expense at court, the full play of pomp could be afforded, the divinity understood, yet they too raised the question whether the old genius was gone. But that inner genius can only be judged from events, for lack of other evidence. Their message remains crisp.

Within six weeks of Hephaistion's death, he had left Hamadan by the Royal Road to the south and briefly invaded the nomads who flanked its passes in the hills of Luristan. Attacking them in winter, he surprised and routed them in under six weeks: 'The men here had been independent

since the earliest times, and they live in caves, eating acorns and mush-
rooms and the smoked meat of wild animals.' The Persian kings had
always agreed to bribe them in return for use of the Royal Road, but
Alexander refused, and 'planned to settle these nomads into cities so that
they might become settled tillers of the fields'. When Greek city culture
first met nomads, it failed to understand them and tried, arrogantly, to fit
them into its own scheme of life. The plan, as Reza Shah was to find in
the 1930s, meant personal suffering to its victims and the destruction of a
way of life which uniquely fitted the landscape: Alexander could not even
promise better medicines or the spurious lure of richer employment. He
wanted to settle these free and proud wanderers into cities, simply because
they imperilled his highway. He failed, inevitably, and seven years later,
the same nomads were blocking the Royal Road with a vengeance against
his Successors.

Returning towards Babylon, winter residence of the Persian kings, he
was met by embassies from all over the world. Libyans, Ethiopians and
Carthaginians crowned him and pleaded friendship; Celts and Scyths
paid their respects, as did Iberians from Spain, only known previously
to the Greeks through the armies of Sicilian tyrants. From south Italy,
came envoys of the tribes with whom his brother-in-law had been recently
fighting; among them, some said, came ambassadors from Rome, a
city as yet of some 150,000 inhabitants, who had mastered their neighbouring Latins in the year that Philip had mastered Greece, but were
involved in war with the nearby Samnites. Alexander had already corresponded with Rome over the regulation of piracy in the Adriatic; his
brother-in-law had made a temporary treaty with her, and it was understandable that even in a crisis, she should send envoys to guard her
position abroad. The Romans who later preferred their own heroes to Alexander, did not take kindly to the suggestion of any such mission. Ptolemy
did not even single them out as especially noteworthy, while to Aristotle's
pupils Rome seemed nothing more than a Greek city.

These distant envoys at once raised the issue of what Alexander would
do next, an indication of his state of mind. If Carthage, Libya and Spain
promised friendship there was little to stop him marching west through
Egypt, along to the Pillars of Hercules, nowadays the Straits of Gibraltar,
and skirting up through Spain to Italy where his brother-in-law had
lost his life on an expedition. Rumour spread that western conquest was
his new ambition; some even suggested that he meant to sail completely
round Africa and enter the Mediterranean from the Atlantic. This extraordinary journey had already been made by a Carthaginian captain,
who took two years to complete it and suffered appalling hardship, well

known at court from Herodotus's history. It is just possible that Alexander had considered it, for the rumour of the plan may perhaps go back to Nearchus, with whom he had discussed plans at Kirman in the previous spring. Knowledge and rumours of Africa were abroad in the camp, but as explorers were being sent to sail round Arabia and up into the Red Sea, it is more likely that if Alexander had plans for the west, he would attack more directly through the Suez Canal and west through the Mediterranean. Possibilities are one thing, intentions another, and it is idle to guess what a man might eventually do with his life; more immediately, his plans were beyond all doubt. A Macedonian was ordered to take shipwrights north to Gurgan and fell timber from the thickly branched forests he had visited seven years before. Longboats were to be built to explore the Caspian, and see 'whether it united with the Black Sea or with the outer ocean which flowed round the world and bordered India'. In Babylonia cypresses were being cut for a mass of new warships: quinquiremes and quadriremes were already being dismantled and carted overland from the Lebanon and Cyprus, all in aid of an expedition at the opposite side of the outer ocean to Gurgan. There were even to be septriremes, which Alexander sponsored for the first time. After 'mastering all Asia', as he put it, Alexander had fixed his ambitions on the Arabs; with these preparations the court at last realized where their next year would be spent. Hot, sandy and remote, the deserts of southern Arabia were to claim them.

In a famous picture painted by Apelles, Alexander was shown in a chariot, followed by a prisoner with his hands bound behind his back; Romans of the age of Caesar interpreted this prisoner as War and Alexander, therefore, as the king who triumphed over fighting, an allegory, which Virgil took up and applied through the picture's details to Augustus as a prophecy that under his empire war would be no more. This Roman fancy had left its original very far behind: if there was one activity which Alexander could never have abandoned, it was fighting, and even at the end of his life he showed none of the signs of triumphing over his bellicosity. The Arabs had been friendly allies of several Persian kings, especially when Egypt had needed attention: on the tomb of Artaxerxes III, recent reconqueror of Egypt, an Arab was shown as one of the only two foreign dignitaries to wear the gold necklace and bracelet of high honour, perhaps because his tribe had assisted the Egyptian invasion. Alexander had 'heard that these Arabs only worshipped the sky and Dionysus, and he supposed that he would not be unworthy to be worshipped as their third god if he conquered them and gave them, like the Indians, their former and customary right of self-government'. He was not fighting in order to demand his own worship: he was observing, rightly, that if he succeeded, he would have deserved divine honours, just as his similar 'liberation' had deserved them in Asian Greek cities. But only by a distorted view of Persian and Arab history, which had already coloured his Indian expedition, could his purpose be described as the restoration of his victims' ancient independence.

His pretext, said his officer Aristobulus, was that the Arabs had never sent him an embassy, 'but in fact, he was insatiable for conquest, wishing to be master of everybody'. His armies had spilled into Italy and India, along the Black Sea and north to the Danube, and it is a frequent mistake to rationalize men's motives for war, as if they fought more for profit than glory. However, there was another side to the Arab expedition as well as mere universal conquest: in the Hadramut valley, spices grew so prolifically that the Arabs used them instead of firewood, sending a steady surplus north by camel and caravan, whose scent was such that the 'drivers become drowsy and only overcome their drowsiness by sniffing asphalt or the skin of goats'. By raft, these spices travelled to the mouth of the Euphrates, then up-stream to Babylon by rivercraft, and so on foot to the city itself: there were myrrh and frankincense, oases of cassia, bushes of naturalized cinnamon and fields of self-sown spikenard. To a man whose palace floor was strewn with sweet scent, these luxuries were irresistible. Alexander was also excited by the reports of harbours along the Arabs' coastline. New Alexandrias could be developed to guard the trade route round Arabia to the Red Sea and the Persian Gulf and grow rich and famous on its profits: a thousand talents annually of frankincense had once been paid by southern Arabia as tribute to the Persian kings, and although an old eastern proverb had said 'never show an Arab the sea or a Phoenician the desert', there was no reason why these spices could not be diverted from caravans to the fleet.

The plan had formed in his mind at least since his meeting with Nearchus in Kirman. There they had talked of the Persian Gulf's signs of a spice route, and four explorers had been sent one after another in thirty-oared craft to trace it back to its source. The first was one of Nearchus's fellow-captains who sailed south only as far as Bahrein; the second, son of an exiled Athenian general, was following him in the winter after Hephaistion's death and left a most observant account of Bahrein's natural history, down to the mangrove trees and orange groves which still distinguish it. He too went no farther. At the same time a third captain had set out on the reverse journey, from the Suez Canal, down the Red Sea and round Arabia into the Persian Gulf; heat and thirst defeated him and he turned back half way. The fourth explorer, a Cypriot, was bolder: he sailed as far as the Aden promontory, 'but despite orders to sail round to Egypt, he became afraid and returned, reporting that Arabia was even larger than India'. The route, however, had been sailed by local traders without fuss or fear for at least two thousand years.

Both the exploration of the Caspian and the conquest of Arabia were attainable ambitions and they speak for Alexander's continuing art of the possible. Neither was as original as it seemed to him: empires might rise and fall by sarissa and cataphract, but since the first dynasty of the Pharaohs, trade had been flowing from the Red Sea, Egypt and the kingdom of Punt, past Bahrein's island and up to the Persian Gulf. Scylax the sea-captain, everywhere a forerunner, had already found the secret of the Caspian's sources: he, too, had sailed round Arabia, beginning from the Red Sea and emerging into the Persian Gulf, ready to report on the need for repairing the Pharaoh's Suez Canal. Encouraged, his patron Darius I had cleared the canal and reopened the route from Persia, round Arabia, to the Mediterranean and this route had been used by ambassadors from the Aegean and traders from Phoenicia alike. At best, Alexander would regain the Persians' former knowledge of their empire's seas; at worst, he would have encouraged a trade route as old as history itself, for once more he came, unwittingly, to restore and to develop, not to change.

There were those in camp who had urged a more novel expedition: 'At a festival in Hamadan,' wrote Ephippus, 'Gorgo the royal munitions officer, a Greek from the island of Iasos, crowned Alexander son of Ammon with three thousand golden crowns and announced that when he besieged Athens, he would supply him with ten thousand suits of armour and as many catapults.' It was true that at Hamadan, an attack on Athens could well have been discussed by junior officers: Harpalus had fled there. and he had been received after a first refusal, while the city continued to elect as its yearly generals men who were known to be implacably opposed to the Macedonians, even choosing that same Thrasybulus who had caused Alexander such trouble at the siege of Halicarnassus ten years earlier. There was also the matter of Athens's tenancy of Samos which the decree to restore Greek exiles had suddenly endangered. Alexander had already announced in camp that he would 'give Samos to the Samians', but this may only have been a calculated threat on news of Harpalus's activities: however, the Athenian settlers on the island has served as a base to the Persian navy during the war in the Aegean, and the memory was not in their favour. Ephippus, as usual, knew how to rouse recent malice. Gorgo's name was loathsome to most Athenians, as he had had local contacts with the debate over Samos, and had vigorously pressed the Samian exiles' cause; thanks to men like Gorgo, the outlook for Athens's settlers was bad, and in autumn 324 the shrewder Athenians were already turning to flattery in order to save the island. Under the shadow of Samos they had been debating whether Athens should worship Alexander as a god: Demades had reminded his audience that 'they should not safeguard heaven, only to find they had lost the earth', while Demosthenes had commented that 'Alexander could be recognized as son of Zeus, for all he cared—and son of Poseidon too, if he really wanted', as long as this recognition seemed likely to save the Samian settlers. Alexander, as Athens agreed, was invincible, but he could at least be humoured with an offer of the worship which he was known to enjoy from Greeks elsewhere. Nobody objected to the principle of worshipping a living man, only to the fact that the man was their 'tyrant' Alexander. But diplomacy overcame disgust, and in the autumn of Hephaistion's death Athenian envoys set out with other Greeks to greet Alexander as a god, then put their case to him.

It is easily forgotten that the decision to restore the Samians had been received with delight by other Greek ambassadors. From Hamadan Alexander had no reason for besieging Athens into the bargain; Ephippus wrote gossip after his death and only put Gorgo's name to the proposal as a plausible touch of malice. As for his crowning as son of Ammon, the conceit seemed credible to contemporaries, and neither Ephippus nor hostile Athenians cared much for the truth; a letter was later invented, written as if to Athens about the ownership of Samos, in which Alexander was made to refer to Philip as merely his 'so-called father', and confirm, by implication, the Athenians' claim to the island. His true view of Ammon was less extreme, and in any case, it hardly befitted Athenians to mock the rumoured flatteries of Gorgo, when within twenty years, they themselves were hymning one of Alexander's Successors as a true 'child of the Sun and the goddess Aphrodite'.

Nonetheless, Alexander's threat had outraged Athens at a time when his position in Greece was not as secure as it often had been. Heavy new drafts of reinforcements were being summoned east from Macedonia to repair the gaps of Makran, and not only was the country's manpower strained by the demand, but Europe was also about to change its general. Antipater was aged over seventy and through letters and embassies, he had long been the subject of complaint, both from Olympias and Greek democrats; Alexander had maintained silence in the face of them, but he did once complain that his mother was punishing him hard for the mere nine months it had taken her to bear him. While Olympias was queen and Antipater mere general, there could never be peace between them. Now Craterus was approaching with orders to replace the general, perhaps temporarily while he visited Asia, perhaps for longer, as Alexander might wish to keep Antipater in Asia as second-in-command for all that gossip knew. It would be some months yet before Craterus returned, in poor health and with 10,000 veterans; his ageing troops were planning to winter in Asia, as Alexander had always allowed them, and for choice they would not leave the coast until summer, when sailing was easier; however, there were local disturbances in Cilicia which might delay them longer. They had only left for home after losing a mutiny, and they were not in any hurry; there was, however, a risk that Athens might abandon all reason and fight for the right to Samos before they returned. News of the recent rebellion in Thrace and the heavy Macedonian defeat on the Danube could only encourage their enterprise.

There was a man of the necessary recklessness. Leosthenes the Athenian had seen his father truckle to Macedonia, and in exile accept estates near Pella; himself, he did not agree, and so he had served as a mercenary captain and emerged in maturity as Macedonia's opponent. In July 324 he had been elected as one of Athens's ten generals for the year; when he took up office, Alexander had ordered his satraps to disband their mercenary armies, and in the autumn of 324 and the spring of 323 fugitive soldiers began to congregate along the Asian coast. The numbers were not large, no more than 8,000 or so, but Leosthenes saw them as an opportunity: Persian admirals and high officials, who had escaped Alexander's fleet nine years before, were still roaming free, prepared to accompany troops to Greece. Chares and Autophradates, both heroes of the war begun by Memnon in the Aegean, were waiting to take revenge, and Chares had used troops disbanded by satraps to good effect before. If he shipped them to the tip of southern Greece, a well-known mercenary base, Leosthenes could maintain them for Athens through his former professional contacts. Alexander was still in danger of the same piratical leaders as in the years when his invasion had begun.

The attempt was hazardous and not generally approved. Athens could call on a possible fleet of more than 300 ships, but she could never finance them, as Harpalus had already been turned from the city with his money and his troops before Leosthenes took up office: he was a lost hope, for news soon came that he had been murdered in Crete by a Spartan on his staff and that his troops were planning to raid North Africa rather than return. So Athens was left with little of the money she had long been needing, the prospect of some 8,000 mercenaries also needing pay, an unmanned fleet in dry dock, and a grievance in Samos which she dearly wished to settle. Leosthenes's plans to hire mercenaries had already been seen to fail the Spartan king Agis; even after Alexander's death they never added more than 5,000 troops to the city's resources. In Alexander's lifetime, the prospects were less enticing, for a huge Levantine fleet was at his disposal and all the while the Silver Shields and other Macedonian veterans were marching west from Opis, in slow stages, dangerously close to the coast and a fast boat home.

While Leosthenes was left to scheme in the background, one more embassy set out in autumn to plead for Samos to be exempted from its exiles' return; wisely, Athens's assembly had realized that she must try every outlet before risking a forlorn revolt. As the ambassadors travelled, Alexander was riding south by chariot from Luristan's nomads, down towards Babylon, habitual winter residence of the Persian kings and scene seven years before of the most triumphant welcome of his career. Then, in the first flush of victory, he had ordered its holy temple of E-sagila to be restored, along with the steep-stepped ziggurat of Etemenanki. But the priests of Babylon had preferred their own finances, for as long as the temples were incomplete, they could spend the income from sacred land on more congenial goods than sacrifice and silver-polish, and they had delayed the building plans to suit themselves. If Alexander entered the city, he would angrily hurry them and so they came towards the Tigris to stop him.

Well versed in astrology, they deterred him with a prophecy. Their god, they said, advised him on no account to enter Babylon from the west; some said Alexander scorned them, but Aristobulus, who was placed to know better, insisted that he made a careful detour of the Euphrates, trying to avoid the western quarters of the city, until he was halted by the local marshes. The priests, no doubt, had known this, and by warning him against the western approaches, had hoped to exclude him from the city altogether. While Alexander respected the warnings of the gods, he would not submit to the trick of their anxious ministers; he marched in defiance through the western gate, and within days earth was being moved for the temple's new foundations. Tithes were to be collected once more from temple properties, a useful addition to the royal treasury.

Inside Babylon, as winter took hold, Alexander continued in his mood of bold decision. Nearchus and the explorers reported on their discoveries in the Persian Gulf, including the islands of Bahrein and Failaka which Alexander named after the Greek hero Icarus, and told of prospects for the voyage against Arabia. Despite the explorers' failure to round Arabia, a harbour was ordered to be dug at Babylon with boat-houses for a thousand ships, far the largest fleet that had ever been countenanced in Alexander's world and a force which lent plausibility to rumours that after Arabia, it would be Africa or the West. This fleet was not all. While cypresses were felled in the countryside to meet this remarkable demand, recruiting officers went east to Syria and Phoenicia 'to hire or buy men used to the sea, for Alexander intended to colonize the shore of the Persian Gulf, as he thought it would be no less prosperous than Phoenicia itself'. Traders and messengers of the future would pass this new Phoenicia on their reopened route from India and put in for stores at these new harbour towns; the settlers too, would be sailors, able to follow the spring winds east to the Indus or strike out south for Arabia's spices and the newly conquered skeikdoms of the Hadramut. It was a far-sighted plan. Alexander's energy had all too plainly not deserted him, nor had the ruthlessness with which he and Philip had always transplanted settlements. But behind the order for the thousand ships lurked the officers' suspicion that Africa would follow Arabia and they would be made to sail round the south of the world.

When spring broke, he was quickly to work once more. Babylonian life had always depended on its intricate system of canals, and as Alexander sailed down the Euphrates to inspect the sites for his harbour and new settlements, he became aware that the irrigation was needlessly blocked, 'despite three months' work by ten thousand Assyrians to improve it'. Noticing a stretch of stony ground, he devised a simpler diversion for the river's overflow, and replaced the labours of 10,000 workmen by a single observation; then, sailing downstream, he explored the marshes at the mouth of the Euphrates and adorned, characteristically, the neglected tombs of its former kings and controllers. A site by the sea seemed to invite another Alexandria, so he ordered sufficient Greek mercenaries and disabled veterans to be selected as citizenry; but as he rowed back from his new creation, 'steering the boat in person', he suffered a slight misadventure: part of his fleet had lost the way, whereupon a sudden breeze blew off his royal hat, complete with diadem, and caught it in a clump of reeds. An unknown sailor swam away to retrieve it, and imprudently put the hat on his head as soon as he had disentangled it; his reward was a talent, but some said he was beheaded at the advice of the prophets before he could enjoy it, others, more plausibly, that he was scourged. All agreed he had sinned by assuming the diadem, already so powerful a symbol of royalty, and soon his rashness seemed itself to be an omen.

Back in Babylon, the flow of plans continued unabated and this time they touched on the army's final shape. Disbanded mercenaries from western Asia had arrived for service at the empire's centre, along with

20,000 native Persians and a group of nomads. The Persians were brought by Peucestas their satrap; all of them were archers and javelin-throwers, light-armed recruits, therefore, from the province with most cause to prove hostile in all Asia, but Alexander enrolled them into his Macedonian brigades, where their files were headed front and rear by highly paid Macedonian veterans. It was the climax of his integration in the army: apart from his Iranian Successors, Companions and cavalry, his Foot Companions were now to be doubled in strength, and Persians outnumbered Macedonians by three to one. For four years already the Foot Companions had fought in more open order without their sarissas; possibly, at the last the Macedonians in front and rear were returned to their famous weapon, while light-armed Persians were to shoot arrows or javelins over their heads. First, a long-range volley from the Iranians' composite bows of horn and leather in the centre; then, an advance with three rows of eighteen-foot spears, backed by a core of light-armed troops for impetus. There was sense, as well as magnanimity, in a mixed Perso-Macedonian phalanx, for it put the middle ranks to more varied use.

As the troops were drafted, discipline and training were not allowed to slacken: the ships were built, and 'Alexander exercised them constantly, causing the three-banked warships to compete again and again with the four-bankers, for the sake of crowns of victory'. For amusement, he even staged a mock battle on the river, whereby crew pelted crew with apples from the decks of the royal fleet; morale must be high for the Arabs, and he spared no favour in order to sustain it. Meanwhile, the embassies arrived from the Greeks, Athens included, and were heard in revealing order of their business's importance; first religion, then presents; then foreign disputes, internal problems and, last of all, the pleas for returning exiles. Some envoys had come wearing crowns, as if to honour a god, so these religious embassies which took priority even over presents must largely have concerned Alexander's own worship. Among these worshippers the great Greek sanctuaries took precedence; first Olympian Zeus, then Ammon of Siwah, 'according to the importance of their respective sanctuaries': for Alexander, Libyan Ammon remained a subordinate equivalent of the Zeus he knew in Greece. To most of the embassies, a generous answer was given in return for golden crowns, even if they had not come to worship him and thus came low on his list. But it is a rare glimpse of Alexander's last months that he put worship of himself and the gods above all other Greek business.

In late spring, this glimpse becomes more public in the final design for Hephaistion's monument. As the architects drew up their plans, Alexander breached a mile and a quarter of Babylon's walls and ordered the baked bricks to be collected. Then he marked out a square, whose sides were 200 yards long, and divided it into thirty sections; in each, the tomb's stories were to be supported by the trunks of palm trees. The outside walls were decorated, first with the golden prows of 240 quinquiremes, each equipped with two kneeling archers, six feet high, and armed warriors, taller still, between whom were stretched drapes of scarlet felt. On the next storey, 22-foot torches were wound with wreaths of gold and topped, amid their flames, with eagles, wings outstretched; serpents coiled around their bases. The third storey showed a hunting-scene, the fourth a battle of gold centaurs, the fifth a row of golden bulls and lions. The sixth showed Macedonian and Persian weaponry, while the top was crowned with hollow sirens, inside which a choir could be concealed to sing a lament for the dead man.

The whole was said to be some 200 feet high; the word 'pyra' described it, but a 'pyra' could be a monument. It did not have to be burnt.

These measurements may be nothing more than rumour. No trace of this monument has been found, probably because its patron died before it was far off the ground; the desire to complete it was publicized among Alexander's Last Plans, which his officers probably exaggerated to ensure their rejection. Hence, perhaps, the huge dimensions, though they would not be implausible anyway. For a less powerful man this monument would have been an impossible madness, but the show was in keeping with a hero's concern to be seen to pay the dead the most glorious honours possible and for Hephaistion Alexander would not drop his Homeric ideals. He had the treasure to finance it and the architects to carry it out. Pharaohs had long built pyramids, just as dukes would one day build palaces and bishops still build larger cathedrals, and only a parochial mind can uphold this new Pharoah's extravagance as a definite 'proof' of raving lunacy. The design was fantastic and obviously influenced by Babylonian architecture; aesthetically, it may have been hideous, but ugliness alone is not a proof that a man has lost his judgement, and there was always Harpalus's monument to his mistress in Babylon which asked to be excelled. Not every grand scheme was accepted. When Alexander's architect proposed to carve mount Athos's cliff face into his likeness, Alexander refused: megalomania strains for impossible grandeur, but in Babylon, heart of the centralized despotism which had passed to the Persian Kings with the system of royal canals, the vast royal work forces made vast royal buildings a tempting possibility.

Seeing a chance of favour, natives, generals, envoys and soldiers competed in gifts for the funeral celebrations and with their help the expense eventually totalled more than 10,000 talents. Gold and ivory images of

Hephaistion were carved in plenty; the provinces were ordered to quench the Royal Fire, until the ceremony had ended, a remarkable privilege which if Alexander understood its meaning, suggests that Hephaistion had been considered to be his successor and royal deputy, for the Royal Fires were only dowsed when a king died. A fortunate arrival gave profound meaning to the occasion: envoys returned from Siwah with news that Ammon had approved the worship of Hephaistion, if not as a god, at least as a hero. Such honours to the distinguished dead were nothing unusual in Greek tradition, but Alexander added his full enthusiasm to the new yearly cult. Ten thousand sacrificial animals were roasted and sacrificed as a first honour to its hero, and other cities in the empire would doubtless follow suit in the hope of reward. Probably, prominent Macedonians had already been worshipped locally as heroes after their death, just as Harpalus had worshipped his mistress; possibly even Athens now felt obliged, out of tact, to treat Hephaistion as his lover had publicly indicated.

But very properly, the cult had been delayed until approved by an oracle: Alexander, though divine, had lost none of his respect for the gods, especially when the god was Ammon. Through Hephaistion's funeral, Alexander too was to have his last dealings with Eygpt and his Alexandria: since his departure as Pharaoh, the Greek Cleomenes had risen from the rank of treasurer to satrap and had begun to show that same sense of a financial monopoly which later would be developed by the rule of the Ptolemies. In times of famine, he had dealt astutely in corn; as a result, he had amassed some 8,000 talents in Egypt's treasury and laid the foundations of its state economy. To this sharp financier Alexander now wrote a letter, requesting him to build Hephaistion two shrines in Alexandria and spare no expense in their design: Hephaistion's name, it was said, was now to be entered on all contracts between the city's merchants, an honour which was later paralleled under the Ptolemies. In return, reported Ptolemy himself, who was soon to have Cleomenes murdered, 'Cleomenes's past and future misdeeds would be pardoned'. Too much must not be made of this very suspect offer, especially in a letter rephrased and reported by a biased contemporary; the morality also had its precedent in the ancient East. 'I approve,' Herodotus had written, 'of the following custom: in Persia, the king will not kill a man, nor will the nobles punish a servant, for a single accusation. But instead, they think the matter through, and if they find that the man's misdoings are more or greater than his services, only then do they resort to revenge; otherwise, they let him off.' To Alexander, no service was now greater than a willing respect for the dead Hephaistion.

458

Among the challenging decisions of the past three months, this cardinal point could not be overlooked. For Hephaistion's memory, Alexander was stretching power to its limit. Elsewhere his plans were ambitious and plausible, but the loss of Hephaistion would have to be controlled if they were to be fulfilled. For Alexander had not lost his personal hold. The outlines of the Arabian campaign concerned him deeply and he intended to sail with the fleet in person: departure was scheduled for mid-June, the hottest season in the Persian Gulf. This timing did not invite a second Makran. If the fleet was ever to sail round Arabia and enter the Red Sea, as its explorers had tried but failed, it needed to reach the east tip of its Aden promontory by early October, when the monsoon winds tack round and blow ships north-west to the Suez Canal. The June departure, therefore, was well advised. But a land-army was also asked to follow as the fleet sailed from Failaka island to Bahrein and Aden. This was alarming. After Makran, it is amazing that troops would ever be detailed to a known sand desert in summer again. The order, whose reception is unknown, is a reminder that the daring explorer in Alexander still meant to triumph over natural hardship.

Such a plan was workable, but it relied on complete trust. The massive festival of the funeral was a dangerous background, and as it came to a head an omen occurred which spoke plainly for the mood behind the scenes. During the ceremonies, Alexander left his throne, some said to drink.

An unknown man, who some believed to be a prisoner, saw the throne empty and the silver-legged sofas vacated by the Companions: passing through the guard of eunuchs, he walked up to the throne and sat on it and began to put on royal dress. But the eunuchs tore their robes and beat their breasts and refused to drag him away, because of some eastern custom. Alexander ordered the man to be tortured, as he feared a plot, but the man would only say he had done it because it had suddenly come into his head. Whereupon, the seers prophesied that this implied even more disaster in store.

This curious incident is hard to interpret. The Babylonians had long celebrated an ancient festival, whereby a slave would dress as a king or master and hold sway for a single day, but this festival belonged in early autumn and cannot be relevant to Alexander's actions in late May. The New Year festival at Babylon is better timed, but then the king was not displaced; he merely went down on hands and knees before the statue of the god Bel. On only one occasion would the king make way for a commoner: when the astrological tables boded badly for his future. Then a substitute would take his place for up to a hundred days and assume the burden of the king's misfortune: if the king died in the meantime, the

459

substitute would become king, even if he was nothing more than the royal gardener. This substitution is last known to have been practised by the Assyrian kingdoms four hundred years earlier, but the Babylonian priesthood may have kept its memory alive and even applied it to Alexander. If the substitute had acted inadvertently, so much the worse, as the seers realized, for he would not have diverted the royal doom which the stars predicted. Perhaps the priests had instructed him, and he had been sent to take the throne because they feared for Alexander's future: so, at least, the eunuchs assumed, bewailing the sight of a royal scapegoat, and perhaps their lament was justified.

Within weeks, eunuchs and horoscopes were to be proved alarmingly right. An uneasy mood was still stirring in the byways of the court, amid its festivals and new ambitions: there was the omen of the liver without lobes, of the diadem lost on the river and now, of the substitute who had mysteriously taken the throne. Perhaps men feared that Alexander's energy could never last, that it was only a cover for a king who had lost his beloved Hephaistion. On the other hand the recent decisions were hardly those of a broken leader: Arabia, Carthage, Sicily, the Caspian, none was as wild an ambition as the first invasion of Asia with few ships, money or men. Richer than any other man alive, Alexander now united his empire in his person alone: 'In Egypt, a god and an autocrat; in Persia, an autocrat but not a god; among Greeks, a god but not a despot, and in Macedonia, neither god nor despot but a quasi-constitutional king.' The broad categories of history are always bloodless, never discerned by those who occupy them, and uneasiness persisted. Hephaistion's funeral had been huge. The plans for Arabia were huger. There was a rumour that Babylon would become the empire's centre, superbly placed for the sea route eastwards of which the troops had the grimmest memories. Above all, there were the rumours about Alexander himself. From Phaselis to Samarkand, on almost every occasion on which he is now seen at leisure by historians, he is flushed with wine of an evening. There are reports that Babylon had brought this drinking to nightly excess, scarcely slept off on the following day. Against the plans for Arabia, these reports became crucial. Alexander had been wounded in nine different places in the past twelve years, he was bereaved of his lover, and now the prophets had predicted a doom which his courtiers could not avert. The interesting question was the one which the stars could not answer: whether, at last, they had acted to put him out of the way.

CHAPTER THIRTY-TWO

After all his many mysteries, it would be improper if Alexander had died straightforwardly. Never simple, he did nothing of the sort. It was not that his death was forgettable. Quite the contrary: its memory was too dangerous to be freely discussed, and at first, his officers discouraged publication of the details; they knew how they stood to lose, if only from slander built on the facts. But then their secrecy itself bred rumours and soon they found they were quarrelling among themselves. Alexander's death became involved in their quarrels, and they used it as a crime to blame on each other without respect for the truth. The last days in Babylon tell as much of the Successors as of Alexander, a bias which does not bode well for the one important problem: what, at the age of thirty-two, caused Alexander to die?

Any answer must begin on 29 May. Amid omens and dark prophecies, Alexander had tried to avert bad fortune, if not by a substitute king, at least by a series of sacrifices; in apparently generous mood, he turned to amusements and festivities, setting aside Hephaistion's funeral and encouraging the court to the future. Nearchus was crowned as admiral of the campaign against Arabia, and preparations were to go ahead for the voyage to begin on 4 June. Leaving the crowd who had gathered to pay honour, he dined, drank far into the night and attended a late party given by Medius, a Companion from Thessaly: some said Medius had happened to waylay him; others, more cunningly, said that the party had long been arranged, as the day was the Thessalian festival in honour of the death of Heracles and Medius remained true to his home traditions. All are agreed that the drinking which followed was prolonged, but its pattern was vigorously disputed; on it, turns the truth of Alexander's death.

The earliest description which can be dated with any certainty is terse and unfriendly. Alexander, in the course of Medius's dinner.

demanded a three-quart cup of wine and pledged a toast to Proteas; in reply, Proteas took the cup, hymned the King fulsomely and drained the contents amid general applause. A little later, Proteas pledged a toast from the same cup to Alexander. Alexander took it, drank heartily, but could not stand the strain.

He fell back onto his cushion, where he dropped the cup from his hands. As a result of this he fell sick and during his sickness, he died.

His death occurred 'because of Dionysus's anger against him for besieging his native city of Thebes'. There was irony in this absurd explanation. Dionysus's anger had formerly been invoked to excuse the drunken murder of Cleitus: Proteas who helped drink Alexander to death was Cleitus's nephew.

While it is not impossible that Alexander died in part of drink it is improbable that this flippant account is true; its author, once more, was Ephippus, nothing more than a scurrilous spreader of gossip. Others saw the debauch differently. 'At the final dinner with Medius,' wrote an unknown author, later called Nicobule, 'Alexander recited an extract from Euripides's play *Andromeda*, which he had memorized; afterwards, he drank the health of all twenty guests in unmixed wine. They each pledged him to an equal amount, and when he left the party, it was not long afterwards that he began to go into a decline.' After toasting twenty guests, that is not surprising. At once, the question arises: apart from Medius the host, who were the other nineteen?

It is here that the story quickens and the two most curious documents in Alexander's career come into play. The first is a pamphlet, not to be found in any history. It is embedded in the largely fictitious Alexander *Romance*, a work of notorious imagination, most of which was compiled some five hundred years after Alexander's death. It survives in four varying texts, three of which end with a detailed account of Alexander's death. Their outline and personal information demonstrably belong within ten years of the event; it is as if new evidence on the death of Stalin were only to be found in a posthumous book of Russian nursery tales. Each text has been altered or expanded by a later hand and their manuscripts are often corrupt, but their outline goes back to the original pamphlet and deserves to be taken seriously. It gives what contemporaries, as it admits, had been afraid to publish: a complete list of the twenty guests at Medius's dinner and an explanation of their motives.

The twenty names are convincingly chosen, among them Ptolemy, Perdiccas, Eumenes the royal secretary, Philip the royal doctor, Philip the Greek engineer, Nearchus the admiral and Peucestas the persophile. All twenty men are known independently to have had reason to be at Babylon and most of them may have been at Medius's dinner. Fourteen of them, moreover, are said to have had the strongest possible reason for attending. That night, there was a devious plot to poison the king. They knew about it and they approved.

The plot itself is said to have been planned in Europe months before, where it centred on Antipater's family. As the pamphlet points out, motives for Antipater are not hard to imagine: the endless abuse of the reigning queen Olympias, the slow but menacing approach of Craterus and the veterans, the orders for his summons to Asia, the execution of old friends like Parmenion or relations like Alexander the Lyncestian, all these grievances might have urged him to self-defence. Two of his sons were already at Babylon and he had recently sent Cassander, the third and most forceful, to join them. He was equipped, said the pamphlet, with a small iron casket of poison, encased in the hoof of a mule, the only material which was strong enough to contain it. Many later believed that this poison was ice-cold water from the deadly river Styx, which flowed through the mountains of Arcadia before going down to the Underworld; but Arcadia was far from Antipater, and the modern Mavroneri falls, site of the ancient Styx, belie the ancients' belief in the power of its hellish water.

Cassander's arrival at Babylon in the last months of Alexander's life is a historical fact: it is true, too, that seven years later, he would show himself to be an implacable opponent of the king's memory and even murder Olympias, while gossip maintained that he could not look on Alexander's statue without feeling faint and uneasy. Once there, the pamphlet continued, he was to hand the poison to his brother Iollas and make ready his escape, as Iollas was butler to the king and could mix the poison into the royal wine without being noticed: all he needed was the occasion, none more convenient than Medius's banquet, as Medius, said the pamphlet, was in love with him. If the party was in honour of Heracles's death, there would be no risk of a change in Alexander's drinking habits. 'A cup of Heracles' was traditionally circulated and Alexander, rival and descendant of Heracles, was sure to be the first to drink from it. The poison's entry seemed assured.

The pamphlet mentions more accomplices than Medius and the butler. Of the twenty guests, only six are said to have been innocent: Ptolemy, Perdiccas, Eumenes and three others. The remaining fourteen, Nearchus and Philip the doctor included, were to keep up a suitable conversation while their Alexander drank doctored wine. They had all sworn oaths of secrecy and they hoped to profit personally from a change of king.

On the night of the banquet, said the pamphlet, all went as planned. Alexander drank from his cup and 'all of a sudden, he shouted with pain as if struck through the liver with an arrow'. After a few minutes, he could bear it no longer. He told the guests to continue drinking and he left for his bedroom, a doomed man. Amid all this sensational detail only one fact is certain: those who had been present at the banquet did

463

not wish their names to be published. They may have been guilty; they may only have feared the inevitable slander. The sequel alone can help to decide.

If Alexander had indeed been poisoned, the dose must have been enough to kill him beyond any doubt. There was no point in giving him half or doubtful measures, and even without cyanide the ancient world had enough herbal knowledge to produce an infallible poison. Strychnine, for instance, had long been extracted from nux vomica, known to Aristotle's school, and it would certainly have killed a young Macedonian. But its effects are more or less instantaneous, and here the timing of Alexander's death becomes important; fortunately, its published date is the one well-attested fact in the whole affair. From a contemporary Babylonian calendar, Alexander is known to have died on 10 June, whereas Medius's banquet, according to its only precise date, took place on 29 May; the king, therefore, had been reported ill for more than ten days, and whatever killed him, it cannot have been strychnine or any other instant poison. There are other possibilities, more remote, and there are confusions in ancient medicine which may be relevant, but in the absence of a ready poison, the alternative document deserves to be considered. It is nothing less than Alexander's Royal Diaries.

Round these Diaries, believed in antiquity to have been published by Eumenes the royal secretary and a certain Diodotus, there hangs an air of insoluble mystery. Quite suddenly, in the last days of the reign, the Diaries are quoted by later secondary sources for a day-by-day account of Alexander's business; to the frustration of historians, for whom only three long quotations now survive, they show him hunting birds and foxes, banqueting or playing dice, and all these activities seem to concentrate on his final month in Babylon. So, perhaps, did the whole work, but those who could read it in its entirety had noted how it kept referring to the king's recurrent drinking parties, even to his all-day sleeping in order to recover from a nocturnal debauch. This frankness is very remarkable. Alexander's drinking habits rapidly became a delicate subject, partly because of gossip, partly because the murderer of Cleitus had not always embraced sobriety: twenty-five years or so later, Aristobulus would plead, against the facts, that 'Alexander only sat long over his wine for the sake of conversation', like a portly country gentleman. And yet here, allegedly, was Eumenes the former secretary publishing a detailed diary of the king's continual carousing; our three brief extracts describe five debauches in the last month, each of which took thirty-six hours to sleep off before Alexander could begin to hunt, drink and dice again. The purpose of this strange publication can only be deduced from its contents.

464

These contents are insistent to the point of tedium. The month of the king's death began, it said, with a string of drinking-parties, one with Eumenes, another with Perdiccas, another at the 'house of Bagoas', not the eunuch but the former Vizier, whose country seat near Babylon was famous for rare date-palms and agreed to be royal property. It was eight years since Alexander had bestowed it on Parmenion as a reward. On each occasion Alexander spent the whole of the next day asleep, recovering his strength. On 29 May, after this series of nightly debauches, Alexander dined very late with his friends, drank still later with Medius, left the room unharmed, bathed, slept and returned the following day to 'drink once more far into the night'. This time, he left for the bath, ate a little but fell asleep in the bathroom, 'because he was already beginning to feel feverish'. Medius's party, so far from proving fatal, was followed by a repeat on the very next day and only then did Alexander sicken, not after a cup of poison, but after a bath, a sleep and a fever.

It is very hard not to sense a deliberate bias in the tone of such a Diary. Alexander, it seems to stress, did nothing unusual by drinking hard at Medius's banquet, for he had been drinking hard throughout the preceding month. Moreover, drink did not kill him, but an incidental sickness. The accounts of the following days are equally silent about poison. The next day, Alexander was carried out on a stretcher to sacrifice to his usual gods, Ammon no doubt among them, and he then lay in his bedroom instructing his officers in detail about the expedition to Arabia which he still intended to begin in four days' time. He was later carried by boat to the park on the far side of the Euphrates, probably the summer palace of Nebuchadnezzar in the cooler and northerly city-quarter; there, he continued to sacrifice, bath, talk to the officers and play dice with Medius, though his fever lasted all night. But the next day he took a marked turn for the worse and could not even manage to sacrifice. A move to the 'palace near the swimming-pool' did not improve him, though for the next two days, the Diaries still insist that he continued to instruct the officers about the voyage. At last, even the officers were ordered to wait outside in the courtyard and on 7 June a very sick king indeed was moved back by boat to the main palace where his fever had first broken out. When his officers came to see him he could no longer speak; on 8 and 9 June it was the same, and on the evening of the 9th, there occurred the only incident on which the Diaries and the pamphlet agreed: the common troopers rioted.

For the past ten days they had only seen the royal barge floating up and down the Euphrates. Their officers had told them that Alexander was ill but alive, and yet as the days passed without him, they were more and more inclined to disbelieve. They thought they were being deceived by the Bodyguards, so they gathered outside the palace doors and started to browbeat the officers of the watch. It was now two days since these lesser officers had last seen Alexander, and then only as a speechless invalid; they too might suspect a conspiracy of silence by their seniors, and so they let the troopers in. 'One by one, they all filed past Alexander's bed, dressed in their military tunics; he could no longer speak, but he made a sign to each of them, lifting his head with the greatest difficulty and gesturing to them with his eyes.' Quietly, they filed out through the far door. The next day, towards evening, it was announced, said the Diaries, that Alexander had died.

Except for the men's parade, which could hardly be denied, the Royal Diaries bear no resemblance to the pamphlet in their description of the days after Medius's banquet. In the pamphlet, there are no conversations with the officers, no games of dice with Medius and no sailing to and fro on the Euphrates: instead, there are scenes with Roxane and with Perdiccas. After his poisoning, said the pamphlet, Alexander had felt restless and unable to bear his friends and doctors: he wanted to vomit and, innocently, he asked the culprit Iollas to tickle his throat with a feather, which Iollas as a true son of Antipater had already coated in more poison. Alexander then sent his friends away, except for Perdiccas whom he designated his Successor; he passed a restless evening and at nightfall he set out on a memorable last exertion.

There was a door in the palace which led to the river Euphrates; this Alexander had ordered to be opened and left without its usual guard. When all his friends had departed and the hour of midnight was come, he rose from his bed, snuffed out the candle and crawled through the door on all fours, because he was too weak to walk. Gasping as he went, he made for the river, meaning to throw himself into it and disappear on its current. But when he drew near, he looked round and saw his wife Roxane running towards him.

She had found his room empty and guessed that he was gone to a farewell worthy of his courage; by following the sound of his groans, she had tracked him down to the river bank where she embraced him and begged him, through her tears, to desist. Complaining that she had impaired his glory, Alexander allowed himself to be led by his wife back to bed.

Whether or not this was true, it was relevant and influential. As the pamphlet realized, Alexander was believed to be a god, and gods do not do themselves credit by dying in public; in Rome, when Caesar died, his body remained for inspection, but it was not the least important of his claims to divinity that a comet soon appeared in the sky and allowed men to focus their belief in his immortal soul on this sudden new home for it. Just as Caesar had gone to heaven, so Alexander would go to the water: other new divinities were later thought to have done likewise, and such was the impact of Alexander's 'departure' that six hundred years later, Christian bishops could still be unnerved by suggestions that the Emperor Julian the Apostate had not really died but had disappeared like Alexander into the waters of the Tigris, whence he might one day resume his life's work of persecution.

Restored to bed, said the pamphlet, Alexander wrote his will and lingered for another nine days with the help of Roxane's drugs and poultices: eventually, having taken farewell of his soldiers among copious tears, he gave his ring to Perdiccas in the last hours and died on receipt of a third dose of poison: 'In the throes of death, he put Roxane's hand in Perdiccas's and commended him to her with a final nod: then, as his strength failed, Roxane closed his eyes and kissed his mouth to catch his departing soul.' So, in a manner fit for a Homeric hero, Alexander's soul left his body 'and the king left life to go to the gods'.

Conspicuously, therefore, the pamphlet and the Royal Diaries dispute both the cause and the course of Alexander's illness. Where they disagree, the authoritative name of Eumenes and the coherent detail of the Diaries have often seemed to carry more weight, and so from the Diaries alone the history of Alexander's last days is usually written. And yet neither the Diaries nor Eumenes and his helper Diodotus are authorities beyond reproach. The Diaries have certainly been altered since Eumenes's lifetime; on the night of Alexander's death, a group of his friends, they say, consulted the god Serapis in his Babylonian temple as to the wisest course of treatment. Serapis is not considered to have existed at the time, for he seems to have been created as a Greco-Egyptian god by Ptolemy some twenty-five years later. If Serapis had intruded into the Diaries, so perhaps has much else.

It is not convincing to dismiss all the Diaries as a later forgery by one of the several unknown writers credited with works of a similar title. Their detail is too life-like, even down to the geography of Babylon which does not conflict with the city's probable street plan in the year of Alexander's death. The falsity, rather, is one of tone. If the Diaries were issued by Eumenes, the former royal secretary, they must have been supported by Perdiccas, his master after Alexander's death; they both respected Alexander's memory as heirs to his empire and would never have issued such a compromising account of his final month of debauchery unless there had been some point in it. The Diaries seem pointless, except as an answer to gossip that the officers had poisoned Alexander; even here they are strangely

467

irrelevant. Having dwelt in detail on a month of heavy drinking they insist he only died of a fever; men concerned to uphold Alexander's name and rebut the charge of poisoning need only have chronicled the course of this serious illness, perhaps with a bulletin from the royal doctors. The drinking could be explained away as a consequence of the sick man's thirst, exactly the line which was followed forty years later by the ex-officer Aristobulus, defending his master's sobriety. The Diaries' month of debauchery suits neither Eumenes's attitude to Alexander nor the case against poison which he was presumably intending to plead.

There remains, however, the mysterious co-author Diodotus. He is said to have come from Erythrae, a Greek city in Asia Minor; only one Diodotus is known in the lives of Philip and Alexander, and he was remarkably appropriate. An able and educated Greek, he had served Greek dynasts in Asia Minor, whence he was recommended as an aide to Antipater; the Macedonians' closest Asian connection was the ruler of Erythrae, so it is very possible that this Diodotus first came to their notice through his home tyrant. It is a very attractive guess that he became a staff secretary, a Eumenes to the deputy Antipater. If so, his authorship of the Diaries falls into place. They were issued as if through the two Greek secretaries of Perdiccas and Antipater and would seem to belong within two years of Alexander's death. After that, Eumenes was busied away from court and Antipater and Perdiccas took to fighting each other. The Diaries, then, would seem to be a very early work. There are hints, but no proof, that rumours of poisoning reached Greece very quickly, and the Diaries may have been an immediate refutation.

Strong objections, however, tell against this. The Diaries' tone and contents are not those of an officer's self-defence; there is also the bias of the pamphlet. This pamphlet was obviously conceived by supporters of Perdiccas after they turned against Antipater; it stresses Perdiccas as Alexander's heir, even as his chosen husband for Roxane, and denounces Antipater's family as Alexander's poisoners. Perdiccas cannot, therefore, have recently published Diaries through his secretary which flatly disproved the subsequent slanders of his officers' pamphlet; the one would have made the other too unconvincing to be worthwhile. The Diaries, it seems, did not appear in his lifetime, a likelihood which is supported by a historian writing around 312 and giving alternative accounts which he had read of Alexander's death. He refers disbelievingly to the story of Antipater and the poison, which he would have read in the Perdiccan pamphlet, but he shows no knowledge, in so far as his history can be traced, of any of the Diaries' details. If the Diaries had already been published it would hardly have been possible to ignore their massive weight, among the alternative stories.

The Diaries were only necessary to refute the rumours of poison, so they must be tied to a man whom these rumours are known to have affected. If they do not belong to Antipater, slandered by Perdiccas, they might concern his son Cassander, who was fiercely accused of murder by Olympias seven years after Alexander's death; another nine years after that, prominent members of Aristotle's school, also associates of Cassander, were attacked as Alexander's poisoners by his veteran officer Antigonus the One-eyed, then ruler of Asia. The two lines meet in Cassander, the favourite candidate as Alexander's poisoner. Perhaps he first circulated the Diaries as his answer; he could claim to have found them among Diodotus's papers, especially if Diodotus had been his father's aide. Alone of the Successors, Cassander both opposed Alexander's memory and needed to rebut the charge of his murder; he would be happy to cast Alexander's final month as a long debauch, while maintaining that he died of fever, not of something he had drunk. His friends from Aristotle's circle had a similar interest. Many disliked Alexander, not least for murdering their fellow-philosopher Callisthenes, and although there was no truth in Antigonus's answering slander that Aristotle poisoned his royal pupil, its memory lived on for five hundred years and was even held against the Aristotelian school by the Roman emperor Caracalla. The philosophers too had an interest in an alternative account.

Among these Aristotelians none is more interesting than Cassander's associate Demetrius, who fled Athens under the slander from Antigonus that Aristotle had mixed the fateful poison. Demetrius was a prolific author; he fled to Egypt and wrote the earliest book on the new god Serapis, detailing the many cures which the god had brought about through dreams. Serapis's mention in the Diaries has always seemed an awkward intrusion; a man like Demetrius, acutely concerned with the detail of Alexander's last days, might have inserted the name of the new healing god whom he championed so fervently in place of an unfamiliar Babylonian deity. Moreover, three of the four officers who are said to have consulted Serapis about the best treatment for Alexander are famous victims or enemies of Antigonus, who encouraged the slander of poisoning against Demetrius and his master Aristotle; Cassander, too, had joined an alliance against Antigonus to defend or avenge these three high officers' maltreatment. Other details, the 'house of Bagoas', for instance, were known independently to Aristotelians in Cassander's circle. To remove the slander against themselves and Cassander, it is very possible that they published or elaborated Diaries in the name of the regents' secretaries. The Diaries' tone, dating and contents would fit their purpose neatly.

If the pamphlet began as Perdiccan propaganda and the Diaries were perhaps worked over by Cassander and his circle, the various causes of Alexander's death can only be judged on their merits, not on their authorities. Drink can be dismissed as the main cause, just as the ex-officer Aristobulus knew that it should; the Diaries are the only hint that Alexander drank more heavily before his death, and they were probably written by men who loathed him. It is probably irrelevant that one of his personal doctors wrote as an expert on drunkenness, though it is interesting that he believed in protecting against poison by the futile prescription of a regular diet of radishes. Fever seems far more plausible than drink. Alexander had been boating on the Babylonian canals where malaria had long been endemic and although his sudden decline after a week's sickness is not a common malarial pattern, the effects of his chest wound may have made themselves felt. He was, said Ephippus, 'melancholic'; it is an attractive, but mistaken, theory that the ancients' disease of melancholia was identical with malaria, whose symptoms it often shared, and Ephippus anyway meant by the word 'hot tempered'. This, rather, suggests poison, of a king who was 'unbearable and murderous'.

However, there is no evidence that the officers conspired among themselves or with Antipater before Alexander's death. True, the hot and demanding march to Arabia was only a week away; the pamphlet also refers, tantalizingly, to names of the guests at Medius's party 'whom Onesicritus the royal helmsman refused to cite for fear of their revenge'. Onesicritus published his book within two years of the event, but the pamphlet's words do not entail that he openly mentioned poison. He may well have begun the stranger story, repeated later by authors who used him, that Alexander drank from the cup of Heracles, cried as if struck by an arrow and then collapsed. Others believed this without even accepting the poisoning rumour; so too may Onesicritus, but he may not have dared to mention poison any more than the guests, and thus only dared to record that 'something dramatic happened at the party. He was an officer and contemporary, but a most unreliable witness; he is the one support for the possibility of poison and naturally, his word is not enough.

Conspirators apart, the poison itself is technically implausible. In an age which lacked any clear concept of disease or of the dangers of bad food and water, it was understandable that sudden illness should be blamed so often on slow-acting poison, a cause which was only identified after a chain of mysterious effects had been seen to their fatal conclusion. But unless slow poisons are sophisticated they cannot be guaranteed to be lethal: an acid, for example, could have caused Alexander to 'cry aloud as if struck by an arrow' and then worked slowly inside him until it eventually punctured his stomach or burnt his vocal chords to stop him speaking, but it is very doubtful whether ancient medicine was acquainted with an acid of the necessary powers. The poisons of herbalists were swift and irremediable, whether hemlocks, hellebores or belladonnas, and except as an explanation of mysterious illness, a slow poison met no need in the poison-chests of ancient Greece. If Alexander had been poisoned, he should surely have been given a massive dose which was absolutely certain to kill him at once. And yet Diaries, pamphlets and official calendars insist that twelve days elapsed between Medius's fateful banquet and the death of the king.

It is hardly possible to escape this. The Diaries' detailed narrative is not quite explicit that for the last five days of his life Alexander gave certain proof of being alive; however, on 9 June the troops processed past his bed and saw, allegedly a slight movement of his head and eyes while the king 'made a sign to them', in a Greek word which most naturally means a gesture of the right hand. He said nothing; he lay motionless in bed; but this sign implies he was still alive and that no poison had been given to him as long beforehand as 29 May. There have been too many allegations of poisoning in history before the nineteenth century for Alexander's to survive this damaging contradiction in the case.

Those who are accustomed to the deaths of powerful men will not be surprised that Alexander's is a mystery which is hard to solve beyond all dispute. History here has often been repeated, but of the attendant mood and circumstances, there is more to be usefully said: Alexander had died, a man 'generally agreed to be of a greater nature than is given to a mortal'; his divine dress would never be worn in entirety again, and watchers, though spared a march to Arabia, were left frightened and bewildered in a land very far from home. Outside the royal bedroom, nobody was sure what had happened; when the end was announced on 10 June, an ominous darkness fell on the battlements and broad streets of Babylon. Men strayed through the city, not daring to kindle a light: it was not that their invincible god had died, but he had, so they said, 'departed from life among men' and himself a sun-like deity, he had robbed them of light as his soul ascended to a home among the stars. His soul was immortal, but his body lay exposed in the desolate halls of Nebuchadnezzar's palace, and while the common soldiers fretted for their future, officers were already rumouring their divine king's last words. 'When they asked him to whom he had left his kingdom, he replied "to the strongest". He added that he foresaw that his prominent friends would stage a vast funeral contest in his honour ...' Whether through fever or poison, Alexander had died unable to speak, so that all such remarks can only be treated as legends. But he was watching, his men believed, from the heavens, and within a week, the second of his two alleged last sayings was already proving more true than the first. The funeral contest had begun, but many years would pass before the strongest could be seen to have emerged.

CHAPTER THIRTY-THREE

Men believed that Alexander had ascended to heaven, but for the next twelve years it must have seemed equally likely that all who had helped him were under a curse. The situation at Babylon was proof of the price that a king must pay for killing all rivals at his accession, a policy which strengthens the throne briefly, then delivers it into the hands of its barons. When Alexander died, Roxane was pregnant and her baby was not due for at least six weeks; it might anyway prove to be a girl. Alexander had also left a bastard son Heracles by his first Persian mistress Barsine, but the three-year-old boy had been ignored and no Macedonian took him seriously. Officers as prominent as Perdiccas, Leonnatus or the elderly Polyperchon claimed royal blood through their local dynasties in highland Macedonia; their claims were remote, had not Philip's bastard son Arrhidaeus been the only male alive in Alexander's royal family, an adult but also a half-wit. A choice had to be made, and as Alexander had bequeathed his ring to his Vizier Perdiccas, his was the first decision; disdaining the idiot Maccedonian, he encouraged the Bodyguards and cavalry to favour Roxane's unborn child. But the Foot Companions were roused by their brigadier Meleager to call for Arrhidaeus, a face they knew and for all his deficiencies, not of Oriental blood. The common man's hatred of Alexander's Oriental policy had not disappeared with his death. Meleager, too, had once complained of undue honours bestowed on conquered Indians.

The result was a quarrel which surprised even the officers. Perdiccas and Ptolemy fled with their friends to the chamber where Alexander was lying in state, only to find that the door was smashed in by Meleager's infantry who started to pelt them with spears; they were stopped, just, and Perdiccas withdrew with his cavalry to the fields outside Babylon where he began an insidious revenge. All food was blocked from reaching the city until Meleager and the infantry were starved into an agreement that Arrhidaeus should share the kingship if Roxane bore a son and that infant and half-wit should be guarded by Perdiccas and Meleager in partnership. According to custom, the army was then purified from the taint of Alexander's death by marching between the two halves of a disembowelled dog; when everyone was off their guard, Perdiccas had thirty of Meleager's faction seized and thrown to the elephants for execution. Meleager took his own life, seeing his cause was hopeless. All too plainly, order had broken down, although Alexander had only been dead for a week. This was indeed the 'age of paradox', for on the news of his death, the Greeks were roused to rebellion by Athens and her general Leosthenes, whereas the Persians shaved their heads and lamented the passing of a fair-minded king; Sisygambis, mother of Darius, fasted to death after only five days, mourning the man whose chivalry she had respected ever since her capture at Issus. It was the most telling tribute to Alexander's courteous way with women, and with the camp in disorder she could not be blamed for her gloomy view of the future.

Within a year the turbulence of Macedonia's baronry had burst over Asia and the Mediterranean. For many the empire was a unity, and should remain so; for a few, there were kingdoms to be carved out, whether in Egypt where Ptolemy first seized a satrapy and made it independent or in Maccedonia where Antipater's death raised hopes of a separate realm. For the next twenty years, separatism grew to overpower unity, until the world had been split into four: in Egypt, Ptolemy; in Asia, Seleucus, once leader of Alexander's Shield Bearers; in Thrace, Lysimachus, a former Bodyguard, and in Macedonia whichever king could raise and hold support. They were years of war and murder on the grand scale, and they swept men along with them; six years after Alexander's death, an army from the upper satrapies met an army from western Asia in the wild mountains of inner Media, perhaps near modern Kangavar, and began their massive battle in mid morning. When each side had routed one of the other's wings, night was already falling and they had strayed three miles from the battlefield. They rallied and by common consent drew up their lines again, elephants and all, to continue their fight by the light of the moon. Only at midnight did they stop to bury their dead; throughout there were Macedonian units slaughtering each other on either side.

The spell of disaster began at once among Alexander's associates. In Babylon Roxane sent for his second wife, now called Stateira, Darius's daughter, and poisoned her, with Perdiccas's approval. Roxane's baby turned out to be a son, Alexander IV, who was given Perdiccas as a guardian; within three years Perdiccas had been stabbed by his guards after asking them to cross the Nile against its crocodiles and sandbeds. Craterus, loved by the troops as a true Macedonian, was trampled to death in the same month, his horse having tripped in battle; his troops were conquered by Eumenes the secretary, who knifed a commander of the Shield Bearers in the course of victory. Already Ptolemy had murdered the financier Cleomenes and seized Egypt; he went on to murder Perdiccas's relations, various kings of Cyprus and Syria's satrap Laomedon, one of Alexander's oldest friends. Anaxarchus the contented refused to flatter a Cypriot king, was killed for his obstinacy and had his tongue pounded in a pestle and mortar; Peucestas was removed from Persia to the fury of the Persians who loved him; Porus was killed by a Thracian who coveted his elephants; the original Shield Bearers returned to the Asian battlefields at the age of sixty and more and fought with decisive ferocity, until one of their generals was thrown into a pit and burnt alive. The rest of the unit were dismissed to the satrap at Kandahar who was ordered to use them in twos and threes on particularly dangerous missions to be sure that they never combined and returned. Thais, meanwhile, saw her children prosper and her Ptolemy take political wives; Pyrrho the philosopher, who had accompanied Alexander, returned to Greece and founded the school of the sceptics who professed to know nothing for certain. Nobody referred to Bagoas again.

In Greece, the pattern was hardly brighter. Leosthenes of Athens died in battle and his rebellion collapsed; Demosthenes, in exile, took poison; Aristotle was driven from Athens because of his Macedonian past and ended his life in his mother's house on the island of Euboea, saying that he grew fonder of the myths in his loneliness; when Antipater died of senility, Olympias promptly clashed with his son Cassander. With the help of her Thracians she killed king Arrhidaeus and a hundred of Cassander's friends and family; to Eurydice, great niece of Philip, she sent hemlock, a noose and a sword and told her to choose; Eurydice hanged herself by her girdle, whereupon Cassander retorted. He besieged Olympias in the coast town of Pydna and reduced her to feeding her elephants on sawdust; she ate those that died, along with the corpses of her maids. After nine months she surrendered and went to a proud death; Cassander killed off her family and turned against Roxane who was visiting Greece with her son; they were murdered by his henchmen twelve months after their imprisonment. Most ruthless of Antipater's children, Cassander disgraced a brother and sister who had nothing to do with him; his brother founded a drop-out community on Mount Athos and his sister alone stood out in these savage times, defending the innocent and helping penniless couples to get married at her own expense.

While the world was ripped apart by feuding and ambition, Alexander was not allowed to rest in peace. At Babylon, Egyptians embalmed him for posterity and while his officers wondered who would befriend them, they put it about that his dying wish had been to be buried at Siwah, conveniently distant from all their rivals. Meanwhile, his last plans were produced from his official papers and put to the troops: Hephaistion's pyre was to be completed regardless of cost; a thousand warships, larger than triremes, were to be built in the Levant for a campaign against Carthage, along north Africa, up to the Straits of Gibraltar, back down the coast of Spain and so to Sicily; roads and docks were to be distributed along the north African coast; six temples were detailed for Greek and Macedonian religious centres at huge expense; the largest possible temple was to be set at Troy and Philip should have a tomb equal to the biggest Egyptian pyramid; last, but not least, 'cities should be merged and slaves and manpower should be exchanged between Asia and Europe, Europe and Asia in order to bring the greatest two continents to common concord and family friendship by mixed marriages and the ties of kith and kin.'

None of these plans is unlikely in spirit or outline. A harbour for a thousand ships had already been ordered at Babylon and after Arabia, the conquest of Carthage and the West was surely a reasonable plan, modest even, for a young man with time and money on his side and a record of victory which stretched as far as the Punjab. The opposition was not strong, and such was Carthage's low ebb that she had been raided and occupied by Sicilian adventurers within twelve years of his death. As for the buildings, if Alexander could afford anything he wanted, then six big temples and a gigantic one at Troy were intelligible ambitions, besides bringing welcome business to the workmen and citizenry of his chosen sites; a pyramid to Philip was not an inept idea for a son who may have been booed by his veterans for preferring his 'father' Zeus Ammon ever since his visit to the land of the Pharaohs. The merging of Europe and Asia is the plan which catches the attention; 'common concord' was a political catchphrase of the time, and therefore empty, but the plan of mixed marriage and forcible transfer of peoples befitted the man who had ordered the Levant to be drained of settlers for his new towns on the Persian Gulf, who had approved the oriental wives of his soldiers and who had forced Iranian brides on his Companions. It was a memorable plan, but not an impossible one; its announcement, however, was not above suspicion.

When the last plans were read to the soldiery, the officers had reason for wanting their cancellation. In the west, Antipater's intentions were not certain, and Craterus had already reached the Asian coast with Alexander's orders and the 10,000 veterans he was leading home; there was no reason yet to mistrust his ambitions, but he did hold the balance between Asia and Macedon if their very different courts could not cooperate. Meanwhile, it was a time of consolidation, until Roxane's baby arrived and the guardianship could be seen to work; rivals, however, might claim that Alexander had wished it otherwise. Craterus or Antipater were the danger, for they might publicize papers which Alexander had left them; it suited their fellow officers that all such documents should be aired first in Babylon and agreed to be impractical before anyone tried to invoke their authority. The plans were read by Perdiccas, friend and patron of Eumenes the royal secretary; what Eumenes may have done to the Diaries of Alexander's last days he may also have done to the plans, inflating their scale to ensure that the troops would reject their excesses. The 240-foot high pyre for Hephaistion, the cost of the temples and the size of Philip's pyramid are not unthinkable extravagances, nor are they proof that Alexander had lost all sense of the possible, for Pharaohs had built pyramids before him and colossal architecture was nothing new for kings who lived in Babylon or Susa. But in their political context, they perhaps owe more to Perdiccas's invention than to Alexander's wishes; the man who read them out did not intend to hear them approved, and 'mass transfers and marriages between Asia and Europe' were a powerful threat to troops who had just refused a son of Roxane as their sole Iranian heir. Possibly, Perdiccas made up the suggestion: 'They realized, despite their deep past respect for Alexander that these plans were excessive, and so they decided that none should be carried out.' But the plans had had to seem plausible to their announcers and audience; western conquest, honour for the Greek gods, a tribute to Philip that was perhaps too insistent to be sincere, and above all, the dreaded union and city-settlement of Asia and Europe on a huger scale than ever before, these were what friends and soldiers believed to have preoccupied their king at the end of his life. There is no surer evidence of how Alexander was eventually seen by his men than the spirit, if not the detail, of these final plans.

Men who turned his plans to their purpose could also make play with his remains. Possession of Alexander's corpse was a unique symbol of status, and until the west and Antipater seemed certain, no officer at Babylon was likely to let it go from Asia; there was talk of a Siwah burial to keep the soldiery quiet, and for two years, workmen were busied with elaborate plans for the funeral chariot. Meanwhile the situation in Macedonia was tested and found to be friendly, so much so that the corpse could at last be sent home. It was to lie among spices in a golden coffin with a golden lid, covered with purple embroidery on which rested Alexander's armour and famous Trojan shield; above it, a pillared canopy rose 36 feet high to a broad vault of gold and jewels, from which hung a curtain with rings and tassels and bells of warning; the cornice was carved with goats and stags and at each corner of the vault there were golden figures of Victory, the theme which Alexander had stressed from Athens across Asia and into the Punjab. Paintings were attached to mesh-netting down either side of the vault, Alexander with his sceptre and his Asian and Macedonian bodyguards, Alexander and his elephants, his cavalry, his warships; gold lions guarded the coffin and a purple banner embroidered with an olive wreath was spread above the canopy's roof. There were precedents for such a chariot, not least in Asia where it re-called the ritual chariot of the god Mithras, a divine nuance which was perhaps intended for Alexander's Persian admirers; the chariot was built in Persian style and its decoration of griffins, lions and a canopy recalled the throne ornament of the Persian kings. Sixty-four selected mules drew four separate yokes in Persian fashion; the ornate wheels and axles had been sprung against potholes, while engineers and roadmenders were to escort them on their way. When the whole was ready, Perdiccas its guard-ian was fighting the natives of Cappadocia, the one gap in Alexander's western empire; his back was turned, and Egypt's new satrap Ptolemy befriended the cortège's officer-in-command. Macedonia was not consulted; the chariot set out in secret for Egypt, where Ptolemy came to meet the spoils which would justify his independence. He had stolen a march on rivals who had talked too blandly of Siwah, and instead of sending the coffin into the desert, he displayed it first in Memphis, then finally in Alexandria, where it was still on show to the young Augustus when he visited Egypt three hundred years later. It will never be seen again. Despite fitful rumours, modern Alexandria has not revealed the site of its founder's remains; probably his corpse was last visited by Caracalla and was destroyed in the city riots of the late third century A.D.

Servant in death of Ptolemy's independence, Alexander had fought through ten years of his life for broader ends. Unlike Ptolemy, he had believed it possible for one power to rule from the Mediterranean to the far edge of India, by basing an empire on Macedonia and on the inex-haustible abundance of Babylon and her surrounding farmland. To this end and to ease the importing of Indian and Eastern luxuries, he had planned to reopen the old sea routes which had formerly met in the Persian Gulf. Once this was done, he had believed that the conquered Iranian nobility should share in their victors' court and government and that the army and the future of the empire depended on westernized native recruits and the children of soldiers' mixed marriages brought up in Macedonian style. Above all, he had believed that culture and government meant cities as all Greeks knew them, a belief to which the infinitely older and more adaptable style of the nomads was no exception. It has often been said that these three beliefs were sure to founder on the prejudice of his successors or the realities of any age that followed. Alexander was not such a shallow or unworldly judge.

Politically, his belief in one possible empire from the west Mediterranean to India was not refuted by the way that it failed within thirty years of his death. Those years were chaotic, but not once are the natives known to have risen seriously against Macedonian rule, except in the cities of mainland Greece which had never been firmly held anyway; there the uprising collapsed within a year. Egypt, a part of Iran and the Punjab were indeed lost to the court at Babylon, but Egypt was detached because its new satrap Ptolemy pursued his ambition of being an independent Pharaoh; some twenty years after Alexander's death, India, the Hindu Kush and probably the Helmand valley as far as Kandahar were abandoned for a price of 500 elephants to the new and ruthless empire of Chandragupta, admirer of Alexander and heir to the eastern kingdom of Magadha whose last ruler he had overthrown; if Alexander's men had not mutinied on the Beas, Magadha would have fallen to the west and Chandragupta's army would never have pressed so soon on the eastern frontier. Within eighty years of Alexander's death, Parthian tribesmen from the lower course of the Oxus had overrun new grazing-lands south and south-west of the river and cut off the one remaining land route to the rich upper satrapy of Balkh and Sogdia; there the Greek and Macedonian generals took the title of king, perhaps as much from helplessness as from sinister ambition. These Parthians, who later grew to rule Asia, were nomads and outsiders, men who would only have been forced into Alexander's satrapies by the uncontrollable pressures of weather and pasturage; as for the kings of Bactria, they were Greeks and Macedonians who wore the diadem like Alexander and went east to reclaim his Indian conquests in campaigns as surprising as they are obscure. Neither kings nor Parthians were native subjects; Alexander's empire was never challenged from beneath or within.

Secure from inside, his one kingdom could have been realized if only his high commanders could ever have agreed among themselves, for Ptolemy, Chandragupta and the Parthians only broke off their separate pieces at moments when the Asian Successors were absorbed elsewhere with struggles between themselves, their brothers and their wives. Reprisals came, but in each case too late and from kings who were pressed by rivals in western Asia; India and eastern Iran were not given up lightly as the huge price of 500 elephants was asked for them; it was proof of the kings' priorities that those elephants were promptly moved to the west, where they won the decisive battle that made Seleucus the king of Asia. Caught between west and east, the Successors put the west and its family struggles first; had Alexander lived, his personality would have towered over the Empire and held them together for the repulse of any nomads or Chandragupta. In another twenty years he could have schooled his sons to succeed him. As for the far west, the victories of Pyrrhus the Epirote and Agathocles the Sicilian in the next fifty years showed that the western plans which Alexander had begun through his brother-in-law and implied at the end of his life were not an impossibility. Both Pyrrhus and Agathocles linked themselves to Alexander's Mediterranean Successors; what was left to these two minor allies of his inheritance could surely have been achieved by Alexander himself and then entrusted to client kings. The 'frog-pond' of the Greeks would have extended from Sicily to the river Beas.

It was not, then, a grave lack of manpower or an outburst of native hatred which told against Alexander's aims; it was the older enemies of time and distance, combined against officers who fought amongst themselves through the accident of his early death. Because the Successors lost the east, they are often thought to have disdained it. This, however, is to pass improbable judgement on what is unknown. Alexander's belief that the court and army should include Iranians and a wide class of hellenized orientals has often been claimed as a victim of his officers' prejudices; again, the point is too complicated to go unqualified. By the third century the high court officials of the Successors' kingdoms were almost exclusively Greeks, attracted from the Aegean to a personal rank in royal service where neither class nor home were counted against them; even the Macedonians were relatively rare in administrative jobs outside the army. This open society did not extend beyond talented Greek immigrants. In the Ptolemies' Egypt, hellenized natives were very seldom admitted to high court rank; the name of Persian was confined to a privileged class of mixed settlers. There is hardly an Iranian satrap or servant known at the western court of the Seleucids; they are only known to have used Iranians in their army where they were too valuable to ignore. So much, it might seem, for Alexander's 'concord and partnership in the empire'. The heirs to his colonists resorted to tortuous inter-marriage to avoid taking native wives into their family property; there are very few Greeks in eastern cities who are known to have married wives with native names. It was the prejudice of the ruling class which finally won.

Their victory may not have been total or immediate. In Egypt Ptolemy began by employing certain natives in high posts and perhaps only hardened his policy later under the influence of philosophers from Aristotle's school.

In Asia, ninety-two Iranians had been married to Companions and only five are known in their new capacity. Three were deserted for western political wives, but of the other two one was Seleucus's wife, daughter of the rebel Spitamenes. When Seleucus rose to be king of Asia he did not divorce her; their son, Antiochus I, was sent to be regent of Iran among barons who remembered his grandfather's war of resistance. This was hardly the choice of a man lacking sympathy with the east or with the promotion of Iranians. In the upper satrapies Iranians and Greeks had reason to present a common front against the nomads, a tendency which Antiochus's origins must have encouraged. The Seleucids' method of rule there is still unknown, but the barons are likely to have rallied round this semi-Iranian king. The rejection of Alexander's 'concord' may only have set in gradually as his own generation died, taking its memory with them. In upper Iran it may never have died at all.

In Asia, therefore, the Successors lived in Alexander's shadow. They abandoned his plans for Arabia, but they may not have overturned his court policies at once and just as they rallied to a half-Iranian king, so they followed him in founding and renaming a host of Asian Greek cities. It had been Alexander's belief that the Greek city was worth planting all across Asia on the sites of old Persian citadels, and this one belief was his most lasting contribution to history. He had spent his youth in a palace-society, but he had watched his father Philip found cities as far east as the Black Sea; he had also learnt from his tutor, for Aristotle wrote his political theory round the web of the Greek cities which would last far longer than the empty succession of Asia's kings, flourishing on Asia's western coast for a thousand years, until the rise of the Arabs and Islam reduced their offspring to embattled forts. The thin crust of classical culture only formed in its cities, linked by rough roads and surrounded by alien country-tribes; though Alexander's conquests opened a vast new frontier to the east and south, this new sense of space meant as little as the Greeks' daily business as the manning of the moon has meant to the strident nationalism of the planet Earth. The age of kings did not kill the spirit of the city-states in Greece, for they fought and protested as much as in any Periclean age; politically, it was an age of new beginnings, of broader federations and closer unions, which were mostly handled by their Macedonian masters with a restrained disinterest. In Asia, the age of the Successor kings was no harsher to Greek city freedom and self-government than the empires of Athens, Sparta and Darius which had gone before. It was left to the Romans to stamp out the Greeks' democratic freedom and to lower their literature to a stale and academic toying with the past. Their loss of nerve cannot be laid to Alexander's charge; he had extended the cities' future not destroyed it.

East of the Euphrates and into the Punjab, some eighteen Alexandrias had been sited in the first shock of Alexander's conquests; seventy years ago their qualities could only be guessed, and the guesses were mostly pessimistic. Peopled with natives and Alexander's war wounded, their way of life had few intuitive admirers, until inscriptions and archaeology from Susa to the Oxus began to reveal its human face. The further a man is left from his home, the more fiercely tenacious he becomes of all it once meant to him. In Afghanistan, where the river Kokcha rushes down from the mountains and the blue mines of Badakshan to join the upper Oxus in sight of Russia and the corridor-road through the Pamirs to China, the huge Greek city of Ai Khanum has begun to be uncovered, probable site of the most north-easterly Alexandria, Alexandria-in-Sogdia, founded on a Persian frontier-fort in the months after the ending of Spitamenes's revolt. Three thousand miles from the Aegean, Greek, Macedonian and Thracian citizens enjoyed their temples, gymnasium and wrestling ring exactly as in a city of mainland Greece; the broad timbered roof of their enormous mud brick palace was guarded by a porch of delicate Corinthian columns and supported on capitals of carved Greek acanthus-leaves. Just as the radar-warning outposts of modern America try to create the home life of California on the northern coast of the Eskimos' Arctic under the blessing of the Pope, so this frontier town among Sogdian barons and buff-coloured desert had set up a perfect copy of the moral teaching of the Seven Sages as recorded at Delphi, holy centre of their home Greek world. 'In childhood, seemliness; in youth, self-control; in middle age, justice; in old age, wise counsel; in death, no pain'; the wording and lettering, like the marble sculptures found in the city, are as purely Greek as a fragment of distant Athens.

Alexandria-in-Sogdia is not alone in this. At Kandahar, Alexandria-in-Arachosia, Alexander had left veterans and 6,000 Greeks to settle with natives in a larger walled Alexandria round the old Persian fort; twenty years after his death, the city was given up to the Indian Chandragupta with an express provision that the Greek citizens could intermarry with Indians of any caste. But the Greeks' sons and grandsons had held so fast to their way of life that Chandragupta's grandson, Asoka the Buddhist king, could put up an edict of the Buddhist faith near Kandahar inscribed in clear Greek letters and phrased in impeccable philosophic Greek. He was writing for Alexander's heirs, for the Greek public of an Alexandria which was still described as a Greek city three hundred years later by a Greek geographer from the Persian Gulf. 'Those who praise themselves and criticize their neighbours are merely self-seekers, wishing to excel but only harming themselves. ...' Buddhist precepts fell elegantly into an idiom that Plato might have written, and were rounded off with the usual greeting of a worshipper at a Greek oracle. Kandahar was not a mere military outpost. It was a city with Greek philosophers, interpreters, stone-masons and teachers, where a man could read the classics or put on a Greek stage play; there was more discussed in Alexander's fortress than the charge of the Companions at Gaugamela or the merits of the Thracian hunting-sword.

In these Alexandrias, men from the Balkans were making a new start, and naturally they made it in the style of their past. Just as the English laid cricket pitches along the Yangste river, so Alexander's settlers built gymnasiums without respect for heat or landscape; every Greek city in the east required one, under the patronage of Heracles and the god Hermes, while on the 'island of Icarus' which Nearchus had discovered in the Persian Gulf, the athletic festivals of the Greek calendar were observed in a summer temperature which ought to have made exertion impossible. The tenacity of the Greek and Macedonian settlers was astonishing. At Dura, a military colony on the Euphrates, families with pure Macedonian names can be traced four hundred years after their foundation, still in close control of land allotments which they preserved by tight inter-marriage. When property was at stake, no native wife would be introduced lightly, for a colonist's farm was leased to him and his heirs; his reasons for keeping his family close were also reasons for clinging to his own Greek culture, irrespective of native outsiders. To that end, he would marry his sister, niece or granddaughter, rather than a foreigner.

In these cities, athletics and the gymnasium were part of every prominent citizen's education for he was not a slave to the will of the distant court. He served among magistrates and a citizen-body to whom the king addressed his respectful requests; decrees were passed in the ponderous style of Attic Greek; officials were not allowed to hold office twice running and were subjected to legal scrutiny, as in Athens, on giving up their public duties; Greek law ruled their private and public dealings and none of its clauses would have seemed foreign to a judge from the Aegean. Nor would the cities' entertainments, for all across Asia, Alexander had held Greek festivals of drama and the arts, and their literature did not fade away behind him; Sophocles was read in Susa; scenes from Euripides inspired Greek artists in Bactria; comic mimes were performed in Alexandria-in-the-Caucasus; Babylon had a Greek theatre and the tale of the Trojan horse was a favourite in Alexandria-in-Sogdia where men must have read it in early Greek epic poets; Homer, deservedly, reached

India and together with Plato and Aristotle, ended by being enjoyed in Ceylon. The settlers in Iran did not add to these classics, although a drab Greek hymn to Apollo was written by a settler at Susa; the company of expatriates does not encourage new writers unless they are novelists, and no Greek after Homer had shown a talent which could have produced the right kind of novel. The eastern cities had nothing to compare with the library and the posts for scholars in Egyptian Alexandria and so they never developed an academic school of poets from the literature they still enjoyed. When a man of letters was asked to stay in one of Mesopotamia's new Greek cities, a 'dish', he replied, 'cannot contain a dolphin'; these 'dishes' beyond the Euphrates have no creative writer to their credit.

But by their tenacity they had kept open the horizons of a wide and uniform Greek world, and this reached further than literary merit. 'The world my children ...', Asoka the Buddhist king proclaimed on the river-boundary of north-west India, and at a time when the struggles of the Successors in western Asia baffle the historians they now preoccupy, he wrote of his concern for each of the four Greek kings who ruled from Babylon as far west as Epirus and the Adriatic. This open horizon gave travellers a new freedom. Asoka's Buddhist monks set out on missionary journeys from India into Syria, where they may have encouraged the first monastic movements in the history of the Mediterranean; Greeks from Ionia helped to settle a city on the Persian Gulf and while the Successors warred, Greeks from Egypt travelled and settled south of the Caspian; Greek ambassadors passed from Kandahar by road to the Ganges and the Indian court at Palimbothra; the Delphic precepts of Alexandria-in-Sogdia were copied and brought to the city by the philosopher Clearchus, probably a pupil of Aristotle who walked the 3,000 miles from Delphi to the Oxus. He then wrote pamphlets which derived the wisdom of the Jews and the Brahmins from that of the Magi and described dialogues between Greek and Oriental philosophers to the marked advantage of the latter. In the generation after Alexander, this Aristotelian would have passed from one Alexandria to the next on his journey through Iran, visiting their new gymnasiums and talking with the men who shared his style of philosophic Greek; there was a comforting regularity about these new Greek cities, built over old Persian forts and citadels and set on a river-bank or wherever possible, on the meeting-point of two rivers; some were colonized from cities in western Asia, all used the same official dialect which Philip had first introduced to his court; they lived to a pattern, and their straight streets ran in the rectangular plan which signified the Greeks at home from the Punjab to southern

Italy. Only the olive-trees were missing, but the Macedonians in Babylonia were at least planting vines in their native manner.

This defiant network stands directly to Alexander's credit; it depended on him, and his death nearly undid it, for the Greek settlers in the upper satrapies rebelled at the news 'longing for their own Greek upbringing and way of life which they had only forfeited through fear of Alexander in his lifetime'. It took an army from Perdiccas at Babylon to turn them back and so save Greek Iran for history; some cities, those in the Merv oasis and Alexandria-the-furthest, were rapidly attacked by nomads and had to be rebuilt; those in India passed to Chandragupta; those in upper Iran were cut off after eighty years, and within two centuries every Greek city beyond the Euphrates had been overrun by Parthians and central Asian nomads. But politics are only one part of history and Greeks and Greek culture did not vanish with a change of masters; because years seem like minutes when they are so far distant, it is hard to remember that the Greek cities in Iran had lasted as long as the British Empire in India. Just as British cooking still disgraces the kitchens of the Caribbean and Shakespeare is still taught in Indian schools, so the prints of the Greeks can be traced for another seven hundred years, whether in the city-planning of their first nomad masters or in the shapes of small clay figures which were traded from Samarkand to China, in alphabets and central Asian scripts or in the astonishing funerary art of nomads beyond the Oxus. The one detailed book on the towns and routes of central Asia to be written by a westerner in the Roman Empire derived its facts from a Macedonian entrepreneur, whose father had left his colonial home in Syria and moved to Bactria, where he mastered the silk trade which ran from the Oxus to China.

Politically, this spreading of Greek culture had suited Alexander; in the process he forcibly rolled back the boundaries of the Mediterranean until the Greeks' own 'frog-pond' had threatened to reach to the outer ocean. This new horizon was extremely significant. Three centuries later, the frontier of his Roman successors came to rest on the river Euphrates, and even then the frontier was never absolute. A traveller from Roman Syria to the Parthians' Fertile Crescent had not passed into a different world of barbarity, for the Semitic peoples were a vigorous unity which forts and frontiers could not divide. Likewise, in the upper satrapies beyond them, Alexander's Mediterranean legacy had not altogether died. The common blood of Hellenism still survived in skills and settlers, while it also flowed from Egyptian Alexandria round Arabia and so to India by the great sea route which its founder had meant to realize. Beyond the

Roman frontier men were not barbarians; to a historian in senatorial Italy they 'had the deplorable quality of not being barbarian enough'. Greek culture had not been confined to Greek colonists; it was dominant and it had invited its subjects to surrender to it.

To an age which has seen the collapse of Iran to the ideals of western industry and the aping of America by a Japan which has lost its own nerve, this effect of Alexander's conquest is as fascinating as it is elusive. Every area responded differently, the broad divisions of Egypt, Asia Minor, the Semitic peoples and Iran, and within them every desert and valley, mountain and farmers' plainland; the thin veins of a road or the nearness of a royal estate and a westernized court could lift a tribe out of its past and link it with the skills and language of the Greeks, while neighbours inland continued their herding and grazing in the manner of their ancestors. The Syrians' Aramaic, the Iranian dialects and the country speech of Asia Minor's hinterland did not die before the new common Greek, but they certainly went underground. In Iran there was no native alphabet; in the west local dialects survived, but they seldom obtrude in the surviving evidence, apart from the names of native gods and the fact that a Phoenician under Greek rule wrote his people's prehistory in Aramaic prose.

As these dialects retreated before their rulers' Greek, the results of their westernization were varied and seldom edifying. The flowering of science and scholarship in the Ptolemies' third-century Egypt was mostly the work of Greek immigrants from the old Aegean world; it stood as a tailpiece to the history of classical Greece, owing very little to westernized Egyptians until the slow dilution of the Greek élite destroyed its vigour altogether. The special case of Egypt's Alexandria was mirrored in the fate of Babylon. The Successors favoured its temple communities in the manner of free Greek cities, and their tolerance limited hellenism to a few native governors and priests; Greek immigrants were scarcer and less of a distortion. Thus the Fertile Crescent did not lose its vigour; when the Parthians seized it two centuries after Alexander, it gave them a new and spiritual style of art and a flourishing architecture of vaults and arches. But these styles owed more to Semitic culture than to the upper layer of Greek taste which had never smothered the natives' unity.

The shining exception was Syria, always contested by the Successors' armies. Circumstances forced Seleucus to found four cities on undeveloped sites, diverting the caravan trade from the Persian Gulf through a backward patch of country. Hellenism surged through these cities and their nearby military colonies; Syrian philosophers and a school of Syrian poets sprang up, who wrote witty Greek epigrams and referred to their

486

homes as 'Assyria's Athens'. They left them soon enough, but it mattered more that Syria had joined the Greeks' common culture than that she could not contain her brightest children. This culture lasted and became the chain for the spread of Christianity. Without this common language of Greek, Christianity could never have spread beyond Judaea.

East of the Euphrates and among Iranians Hellenism has received less attention, partly because it has long been less known: few hellenized Persians are mentioned by name in surviving Greek literature, and the sense of an open frontier, where a man could speak Greek from Syria to the Oxus, can only be deduced from the horizons of Greek geographers and chance remarks in westerners' histories. Archaeology has recently added new evidence, a process which still has far to go: at a time of new beginnings the grandiose experiment of Alexander's eastern frontier deserves another thought.

First, the generalities. After Alexander, Greek became the culture of every Asian native who wished to succeed, and so it swept through the circles of Asia's governing classes; 'Let us make a covenant with the Gentiles', wrote the Jewish author of the only historical work which describes the conflicts of hellenizing the East, 'for since we have been different from them we have found many bad things. . . .' The urge to belong to the Greek world was the urge of successful men everywhere; it made no difference that much of Alexander's empire broke into local kingdoms within a hundred years. Just as the romanization of western Europe only took root through the efforts of local patron landowners four hundred years after Caesar's conquests, so the hellenization of the East was best served by these local kings, because they needed to work Greek culture down through their subjects and ensure secretaries, treasurers, generals and orators to plead their cause in the wide Greek world. Alexander had never controlled Cappadocia, mountainous refuge of many of Darius's followers, and under his Successors it became an independent kingdom with an Iranian aristocracy and line of kings. But two hundred years after Alexander, those kings patronized Greek actors and issued coins of pure Greek design; a Cappadocian man of letters was connected with Delphi, and an old Assyrian military colony in the Cappadocian plains had already turned itself into a Greek city which observed the law of Alexander's kingdom and passed decrees in perfectly balanced Greek. The neighbouring king of Armenia enjoyed Greek literature and wrote a play himself, though his kingdom had never acknowledged the Successors; the hellenizing families in Jerusalem were willing to buy from the Seleucid king the privilege of setting up a gymnasium to turn Jerusalem into a Greek city called Antioch, for they wished to belong to Alexander's legacy and their wish was all the stronger for being spontaneous.

It is not too remote to invoke Alexander's name in this. Apart from the ceaseless fighting, his years in the 'upper satrapies' beyond Hamadan had brought Greek into the lives of Iranians by deliberate and calculated stages, his persistent games, sacrifices and festivals in Greek style, his recruitment of 30,000 natives for Greek training, his mixed marriages and plans for their children, his Greek teachers for the Persian queen and her daughters, his Greek-speaking court, his use of Greek army commands in his integrated army and above all, the settling of more than 20,000 Greeks and veterans in rebuilt Alexandrias where they were mixed with a native citizenry and so spread their language through their wives, families and fellow-inhabitants. Each Alexandria was a full-blooded city where men had to vote on Greek decrees and agree to Greek law; citizenship was a privilege which did not extend to all the natives housed in these cities, nor was a city granted to every group of soldiers whom Alexander settled. A city was a distinct and special foundation. Just as the Persian kings had granted land to feudal tenants in return for military service, so Alexander manned military colonies in his own name, inheriting the Great King's colonists and adding settlers of his own. More than a dozen such settlements were left to guard against the nomads where the province of Media met their desert steppes; they were not full Alexandrias, but their farming soldiery grew to adopt the law and language of their western landlords, and it is from these 'second class citizens' that there come the most impressive tributes to the force of Greek culture among Iranians. None has yet been excavated in the upper satrapies, but at Dura on the Euphrates, an early colony of the Successors, every legal contract known for the next four hundred years conforms to Greek law, although the majority of colonists were Oriental natives and the colony had long passed to Parthian rule; in the Lydian plains on Asia's west coast, the Hyrcanian colonists whom Cyrus had settled came to be called Macedonian Hyrcanians and even under the Roman empire they retained their Macedonian military dress, while in the wild Kurdish mountains near Hamadan, where Alexander had barely trodden, native settlers were still drawing up the deeds of sale for their vineyards in passable Greek and clear Greek law a century after Greek rule in Asia had ended, the most compelling evidence so far for the spread of the language through inaccessible corners of Iran.

Through his court and his cities, Alexander had brought Greek speech and customs to some 100,000 Orientals from the upper satrapies alone; they would widen from one generation to the next, though the numbers of Alexander's first hellenizers are irrelevant, as Greek was the culture of the government and so it was bound to dominate. Within its limits, helenization had to be complete. These limits were not demanding; an Oriental became a recognized Greek simply by speaking the language and sharing the games and customs of a Greek court or community. He did not have to change his religion and his colour was irrelevant; the one bar was nudity, for the Greeks exercised naked in gymnasiums, a habit which Orientals found repugnant and embarrassing; and not the least of the worries of hellenizing Jews in their new Jerusalem was that they should be seen by fellow athletes to be circumcized. The names 'Greek' and 'Macedonian' were freely applied to Jews, Syrians, Egyptians or Persians provided that they spoke Greek and adopted Greek customs, if not Greek gods; to the first Christians, the word Hellene applied to every pagan, regardless of race or religion.

Because it excluded nobody, Greek culture could spread universally; to do so, it also had to seem impressive. Nowadays, the meek surrender of the East to western culture is a surrender to technology and industrial growth, helped by the by-ways of tourism, pop-songs and the drip-dry world of the businessman. In Alexander's empire, land transport was painfully slow and only the patient and hardy could travel; economically, the Greeks promised no miracle and although Cleomenes and the Ptolemies primed the royal economy of Egypt for the coins with which to hire their troops and sailors, it was the government who gained by this skilful change, not the vast mass of Egyptians. The founding of Egyptian Alexandria and the reopening of the sea route from India to the west were proof that Alexander had his father's awareness of the merits of trade, but the trade he inspired did not work deeply into the agricultural world of most of Asia. Alexandria's trade only flourished through the Greek middlemen of nearby Rhodes and through customer cities with the harbour or river to receive it, while the trade from India was the hazardous life of a minority, bringing luxuries west to the courts of the rich, not the villages of tribes and peasants. By opening a string of new mints from Sardis to Babylon, Alexander had encouraged a wide coinage on the same Athenian standard which had already prevailed in the satraps' mints on the Asian coast; more coins then circulated on a standard and a royal design which was generally used in Greece. and for the trading minority and the hired soldiery this was no doubt a useful convenience. But in this agricultural world where most men lived by a natural economy, the scattered finds of small everyday coins cannot support the sweeping theories of coinage which collectors of valuable gold and silver pieces have written into the classical past; Alexander has even been blamed for promoting inflation in the Aegean by coining too rapidly from Darius's vast treasures, as if the farming society of Greece would ever have been troubled by the fluctuations of his silver tetradrachms or this alleged glut of precious coin, sound proof of which has still to be discovered. As for Asia's nomads and country villagers, they had no need for a coinage which tended to circulate, if at all, in towns. The most notable find of Alexander's small-change coins in Iran are the bronze obols in the mouths of nomads' skeletons beyond the Oxus, presumably placed for the customary Greek offering to Charon the ferryman, who shipped the dead across the river of the Greek underworld.

If the Greeks promised no wide prosperity, like their western heirs they impressed the East with their technical skill. In places it was as if they were working on an underdeveloped 'third world': 'When the Indians saw sponges in use among the Macedonians,' wrote Nearchus, 'they imitated them by sewing hairs and string into a sort of wool; then they pressed the wool to make it like felt, carded it and dyed it different colours. Many of them, too, were quick to learn to make the "rubbers" which we used for massage and the flasks in which we carried our oil'. Technically the Indians could train elephants and cure the bite of their poisonous snakes, but it was probably a Greek engineer who first devised the howdah for the elephant's back, and Greek doctors were always used for the surgery of serious flesh wounds. 'The Indians here have huge resources of salt, but they are very naive about what they own ...' Alexander's Greek prospector reported critically on the minerals of each Asian province and though mining was an ancient art in Asia, the Greeks may have introduced the skill of splitting rocks by fire to tribesmen who formerly picked precious stones from the beds of their fast-flowing rivers. Greek surveyors paced out the first accurate distances through lands which had otherwise been measured by the variable stages of an hour's journey; irrigation had long been the basic skill of Iranian farmers, but two new Alexandrias show signs of an improved water system, probably due to their Greek inhabitants. The tools and calendar of agriculture are likely to have changed little, for local lore is always authoritative and its fertile results had impressed Greek observers. However, the spreading of Asia's precious trees and plants though the open frontiers of Greek Asia can be traced in the vigorous efforts of the Ptolemies to import new crops and spices into Egypt; minor kings in Greek Asia continued their botanical example. In their buildings Greek architects could manage a wider un-supported roof-span than the builders of Persepolis, while the simple rectangle of their city-planning was adopted in oases along the Oxus and continued by the nomads who finally burst on their cities; their towered walls and ditches were a necessary defence to their own new principles of siege-craft, powered by the torsion-spring which had so surprised the Oxus nomads. In Syria, the Greeks even dug new harbours from bays which had deterred Phoenician sailors.

This power of invention was all the more impressive for being a break with the Persian past. The Persians had borrowed their skills from their subjects, but the Greeks brought their own with them and then created more. The golden age of experimental Greek science under the patronage of the Ptolemies in Egyptian Alexandria is the purest tribute to the Greeks' gifted intellect, for no Persian ever calibrated a catapult, studied human anatomy, applied steam power to toys or divided the world into zones of climate. If Greek science was for too long the follower of Aristotle's dogmatism, always more theoretical than applied, it was nonetheless the symptom of a new mental liveliness. The financial exploitation of Egypt was a matter for Greeks, as the Pharaohs had already realized; under the Ptolemies in Alexandria, taxation, agriculture, improved canals, a coinage and commercial law helped to open a new economy to the Greek world. Visiting Greek doctors took the study of human anatomy far beyond Egyptian magic; the royal library encouraged the birth of classical philology and the deadening rise of textual scholarship. Whereas Babylon had been Asia's intellectual centre, the Greeks took the Babylonian records of astronomy and deduced the precession of the equinoxes which no compiler had ever detected; while a Babylonian wrote a book on the magical properties of stones, a Greek in the Successor's new Babylonian capital was arguing that the earth went round the sun and that the tides must be affected by the phases of the moon. Babylonians treated the particular, but the Greeks saw the general, and it was only to be expected that the liveliest political culture in the world should influence local government, the form of a Babylonian decree and the phrasing of a Jewish manifesto. The Greeks had an elegant mathematical theory and the power of abstract reasoning; a simple cell for electroplating silver on to copper has been found in Parthian Babylonia, and it is natural to credit its invention to a Greek.

To the tribes and villages of Iran, these skills must have appeared in the light of rifles and telescopes to their first Indian observers. The Greeks had more fundamental weapons, their art and their language, the two skills which still impress the classical past on an industrial world. To carve and to think in Greek was to work in a finer and more sensitive idiom, for it was well said by a Roman in the age of disputed theologies that if he started to discuss the Trinity in Latin, he could not avoid any one of three grave heresies. These new tools opened up a new world; there is no written history of the hellenization of the upper satrapies, but there are their arts and a few inscriptions and these are perhaps more revealing than mere events.

In Iran, Alexander had left Greek as the one written language. No Iranian dialect was literate and so the Persians' lame Aramaic was continued for native administration. With the annoying persistence of a pidgin jargon its script flourished far and long as a result, passing into Khwarezm beyond the Oxus where it served as the first native alphabet five hundred years after Alexander, and then as far as China where it was inscribed centuries later on the Heavenly Temple in Peking. It was no competitor for serious thought. Although the long tradition of the Iranian minstrel continued to flower in the professional *gosans* who sang at the Parthians' court, In Iran Greek was the only language for written poems and for the education of soldiers in each Alexandria; so the Greek classics appealed to the East with an impact which has only since been equalled by popular songs of the modern West. At the palace of Nisa, court of the Parthian kings on the lower Oxus, Greek plays were performed before an audience of former nomads, while among the palace documents directions have been found for the making of a mask for a tragic actor. In neighbouring Armenia, verses of Euripides were inscribed, perhaps as a school text, at a time when the province was ruled by an independent Iranian king; in Roman times, the tale of Castor and Pollux was known in the Swat highlands above the Indus; in the Punjab, five hundred years after Alexander, Indian Buddhists still carved the tale of the Trojan Horse alongside the life of their Buddha, a theme which is now known to have passed to them directly from Alexander's heirs in the neighbouring Greek kingdom of Bactria. Homer was always said to have been translated into an Indian language, and the extraordinary find of inscriptions in Ceylon which appear to discuss him together with Plato, Aristotle and Alexander in their Indian names more than five hundred years after Greek rule in Iran had ended should remove any doubts that the fate of Greek poetry in the East was brief or insignificant. When the Greek kingdoms fell, the Persian Gulf traders could still carry their legacy east by ship. The Persian kings had first settled Ionian Greeks as sailors in the ports near Susa, and their persistent Greek culture is the background to the Greek after-glow in western India.

The same is true of art. The coins and the silver trappings of the Greeks in Bactria are of the highest craftsmanship, and at the Parthians' palace of Nisa, their profound effect on Iranian neighbours can now be appreciated. Iranian drinking-cups were carved with the legend of Dionysus; Aphrodite, Heracles and Hera were sculpted in marble; the palace included a gymnasium and columns with acanthus leaves, a style which left its trace in the Punjab's art for another four hundred years. These kings were the sons of Iranian nomads, and yet they took to Greek art like Czarist Russians playing with French civilities; their taste had an astonishingly long history both among the nobles and the alternative culture of the nomads. Greek influence can be traced in the pattern of the oriental carpets found in central Asia of the same broad date as Nisa, again in the sculpture and architecture of an Iranian palace on the Oxus a century after nomads had seized Greek Bactria, in the coins placed for Charon in the mouths of the dead beyond Alexander's north-east frontier and in the clay figures made in Samarkand some seven hundred years after the last Greek Bactrian king. Through Alexander's planned sea route from Eygptian Alexandria along the Persian Gulf to the river Indus the Greek art of Alexandria reached to the Punjab and outer Iran for at least five hundred years; its designs may have helped the long life of Greek art in the area, and they certainly influenced the first carved Buddhist reliefs of north-west India. They had also come by the route which Alexander had determined to reopen.

And yet the hellenization of Iran was not deep or wide enough for permanent results. It was competing with an alternative, the Iranian nobility to whom a town was more the sum of its great families than a self-governing citizenry in an expanse of royal land. To these Iranians the family was life's one continuity, marked out by genealogies and rigid rule of precedence; a culture which spread through cities and administrators could not work down through their looser forms of rural government. Already at Nisa, the Parthians' documents were written in Aramaic, not Greek, and the courtiers' names were all Iranian, while the old words of rural Iranian government continued unchanged, the food-levy for the king's table, the land tax and the village commissioner, the satrapies and the baronial castles. 'Whosoever shall compel you to go with him a mile, go with him twain'; the word which Christ used for this requisitioning in hellenized Judaea was the Persians' old word for forced service on the stations of their Royal Road. In the country, Alexander had not come to change. His empire of vast spaces and wooded mountains could not be travelled swiftly or cheaply by centralized officials, so he chose to balance the old Persian forms. The new Greek cities were his chosen points of loyalty among tribesmen and desert-chieftains and once those cities fell to nomads or to the stronger pull of family allegiance, Iran had only the memories of Persian rule on which to feed; it was not by chance that the design of the throne of Achaemenid Persia lived on under Greek rule in the royal art of upper Iran. Persia, moreover, was still prepared to step back into her past, for Alexander's Successors had left the Persians' mountainous home province to Persian client-kings, and naturally, they had made no parade of hellenism. Five hundred years after Alexander, it was from this 'deep south' of Iranian feeling that the great Persian revival began, with a new line of kings, who at once brought back the titles of Darius's Empire. But this new Persia's triumphs were also inscribed on rock in an official Greek translation. Trapped between nomads and tribal barons, the heirs to Alexander's Greek cities had at last given way to a Persian court of country squires, but the embers of hellenism were still seen to glow in the brighter fire of Sassanid Persia.

During the centuries of their slow decline, the Greeks' own education by the East is a far more delicate subject. Although to western geographers, Alexander's conquests seemed to have opened a wider and more accurate knowledge of a far East where men spoke Greek, their own views of the East were not noticeably more correct. The one advancement may have been spiritual rather than scientific. Like western intellectuals who idealized Stalinist Russia, distant academics fathered utopian ideals on far eastern peoples whom they had not seen; this attitude was possible because they felt that the philosophy of the East had a claim to their respect. Though debates between Oriental wise men and Greek philosophers had already featured in Greek literature, under Greek rule the theme persisted that the East possessed the older and more venerable wisdom. So far from suppressing Oriental gods the Greeks identified them with their own and a certain attitude of deference shows through the art of the gods they combined. In portraits of Greco-Oriental deities, especially the many Eastern mother-goddesses, the oriental element tends to be dominant; it is easy to imagine how the diverse religion of the Olympians gave ground before the moral and spiritual faiths of Zoroaster and Buddha and the tenderer goddesses that characterized the obedient societies of the East, not the self-willed cities of free Greece. There are hints of this, even in the very limited evidence; there were Macedonians, probably in the colonies of Asia Minor, who followed the Magi and took to the Iranians' fire-worship, while in the Greek cities of western Asia, the influence of the Iranian families who held the city's priesthoods of the goddess Artemis, their own Anahita, cannot have been insignificant. When the kings of Greek Bactria put pagan Indian gods on their coinage, they may have intended more than a tactful appeal to the Indians in their kingdoms, while among the Greeks abandoned to Chandragupta and his Indian successors, a conversion to Buddhism is very likely, not least through their native marriages. An official in the restored Greek kingdoms of north-west India made a dedication to Buddha in Greek, while another,

494

perhaps a Macedonian, did likewise two hundred years after the ending of Greek rule; these wisps of evidence suggest Greek Buddhists were not uncommon. To those who see the wide appeal of eastern religion among the youth of the industrially dominant West there is nothing surprising about the Greeks' conversion.

If the Greeks were aware of a certain wisdom in the Orient, they still interpreted it in their own western terms. Unlike the British, who encouraged the study of native Indian culture, the Greeks took little interest in eastern tradition except where they could bend it to concepts of their own; they saw the East through eyes trained by Plato and Herodotus and their own culture determined the points which they chose to notice. Each eastern tribe and community was fitted into the Greeks' prehistory of myth and heroes without respect for their independent origins; Buddha became a fellow-soldier of Dionysus's Indian invasion, just as Thessalians in Alexander's army had already explained the Armenians as sons of their hero Jason, because they wore clothes of Thessalian style. No Greek writer is known to have spoken an Iranian dialect, and Orientals who wrote Greek books on their kingdoms' history tailored their narrative to concepts common to a Greek; a hellenized author could not distance himself from the Greek attitudes he chose to share. For Greeks, Zoroaster the prophet was described more as a magician than a religious reformer; it is only a worthless legend that Alexander arranged a Greek translation of the many Zoroastrian scriptures which he found at Persepolis.

When the history of the hellenized Orient is known more fully, it will still seem a story of missed opportunities, of new frontiers thrown away by the quarrels of Alexander's Successors. Alexander's own intentions will never be certain, but as he passed through the villages and tribal wastes beyond Hamadan, it must have been easy to feel that a Greek upbringing and Greek aspirations were a power from a superior world. The wide and absolute break with the past that came over the East after Alexander's conquest has so far seemed more obvious to historians of eastern art than to students of the written and scattered evidence. But art is a measure of society and the more that it known of it, the more Alexander deserves to be seen as decisive.

Most historians have had their own Alexander, and a view of him which is one-sided is bound to have missed the truth. There are features which cannot be disputed; the extraordinary toughness of a man who sustained nine wounds, breaking an ankle bone and receiving an arrow through his chest and the bolt of a catapult through his shoulder. He was twice struck on the head and neck by stones and once lost his sight from such a blow. The bravery which bordered on folly never failed him in the front line of battle, a position which few generals since have considered proper; he set out to show himself a hero, and from the Granicus to Multan he left a trail of heroics which has never been surpassed and is perhaps too easily assumed among all his achievements. There are two ways to lead men, either to delegate all authority and limit the leader's burden or to share every hardship and decision and be seen to take the toughest labour, prolonging it until every other man has finished. Alexander's method was the second, and only those who have suffered the first can appreciate why his men adored him; they will also remember how lightly men talk of a leader's example, but how much it costs both the will and the body to sustain it.

Alexander was not merely a man of toughness, resolution and no fear. A murderous fighter, he had wide interests outside war, his hunting, reading, his patronage of music and drama and his lifelong friendship with Greek artists, actors and architects; he minded about his food and took a daily interest in his meals, appreciating quails from Egypt or apples from western orchards; from the naphtha wells of Kirkuk to the Indian 'people of Dionysus' he showed the curiosity of a born explorer. He had an intelligent concern for agriculture and irrigation which he had learnt from his father; from Philip, too, came his constant favour for new cities and their law and formal design. He was famously generous and he loved to reward the same show of spirit which he asked of himself; he enjoyed the friendship of Iranian nobles and he had a courteous way, if he chose, with women. Just as the eastern experience of later crusaders first brought the idea of courtly love to the women's quarters of Europe, so Alexander's view of the East may have brought this courtesy home to him. It is extraordinary how Persian courtiers learnt to admire him, but the double sympathy with the lives of Greece and Persia was perhaps Alexander's most unusual characteristic. Equally he was impatient and often conceited; the same officers who worshipped him must often have found him impossible, and the murder of Cleitus was an atrocious reminder of how petulance could become blind rage. Though he drank as he lived, sparing nothing, his mind was not slurred by excessive indulgence; he was not a man to be crossed or to be told what he could not do, and he always had firm views on exactly what he wanted.

With a brusque manner went discipline, speed and shrewd political sense. He seldom gave a second chance, for they usually let him down; he had a bold grasp of affairs, whether in his insistence that his expedition was the Greeks' reverse of Persian sacrilege, though most Greeks opposed it, or in his brilliant realization that the ruling class of the Empire should draw on Iranians and Macedonians together, while the court and army should stand open to any subject who could serve it. He was generous, and he timed his generosity to suit his purpose; he knew better than to wait and be certain that conspirators were guilty. As a grand strategist, he took risks because he had to, but he always attempted to cover himself, whether by 'defeating' the Persian fleet on dry land or terrorizing the Swat highlands above his main road to the Indus: his delay till Darius could do pitched battle at Gaugamela was splendidly aggressive and his plan to open the sea route from India to the Red Sea was proof of what wider insight into economic realities to which his Alexandria in Egypt still bears witness. The same boldness encouraged the fatal march through Makran; he had tactical sense, whether on the Hydaspes or in the politics of Babylon and Egypt, but self-confidence could override it and luck would not always see self-confidence through. Here, it is very relevant that rational profit was no more the cause of his constant search for conquest than of most other wars in history. Through Zeus Ammon, Alexander believed he was specially favoured by heaven; through Homer, he had chosen the ideal of a hero, and for Homer's heroes there could be no turning back from the demands of honour. Each ideal, the divine and the heroic, pitched his life too high to last; each was the ideal of a romantic.

A romantic must not be romanticized, for he is seldom compassionate, always distant, but in Alexander it is tempting to see the romantic's complex nature for the first time in Greek history. There are the small details, his sudden response to a show of nobility, his respect for women, his appreciation of eastern customs, his extreme fondness for his dog and especially his horse; deliberately his court artists created a romantic style for his portrait and it was perhaps characteristic that from the sack of Thebes the one painting which he took for himself was of a captive woman, painted in the intensely emotional style which only a romantic would have appreciated. He had the romantic's sharpness and cruel in-difference to life; he was also a man of passionate ambitions, who saw the intense adventure of the unknown. He did not believe in impossibility; man could do anything, and he nearly proved it. Born in a half-world between Greece and Europe, he lived above all for the ideal of a distant past, striving to realize an age which he had been too late to share;

'My friend, if by deserting from the war before us
You and I would be destined to live for ever, knowing no old age,
We would do it; I would not fight among the first,
I would not send you to the battle which brings glory to men.
But now as things are, when the ministers of death stand by us
In their thousands, which no man born to die can escape or even evade,
Let us go.'

No man ever went as far as Alexander on those terms again. The rivalry of Homer's heroes died with him, fading only to the tombstones of late Roman gladiators, who called themselves by names from Homer, last heroic champions in an age when a hero's prospect had narrowed from the world to the arena and the circus.

Within five years of Alexander's death his Asian Successors gathered near Persia as if to discuss their differences; they could not be brought so much as to sit together, until the suggestion was made of Alexander's royal tent, where they could talk as equals before Alexander's sceptre, his royal robes and his empty throne. These men had been his officers, but they would not take common counsel without his unseen presence. A mood had gone out of the court with his death, and they knew it. Only a lover of Homer can sense what that mood must have been.

NOTES

For convenience throughout the book, I cite many quotations or opinions in the name of Alexander's original historians, Callisthenes, Ptolemy, Aristobulus, Nearchus and Onesicritus. I cannot stress too strongly that all these quotations and opinions are only known at second or third hand, as rephrased by other classical writers often four hundred years later, some of whom might be writing on banqueting, geography or grammar. No word or phrase can be assumed to have been retained from the original, especially as the Macedonian authors were known as poor stylists, but sometimes the secondary sources name their original authorities, and at others the original names can be restored, almost certainly, by comparison and cross-argument. In these rare cases, instead of writing 'said Aristobulus, as quoted by Strabo the Augustan geographer', I have just written 'said Aristobulus'. I only do so in cases where I regard the original's identity to be certain and I only imply that the general sense, not the wording, is authentic.

A brief introduction to the names behind the quotations: Callisthenes was born in Olynthus in north-east Greece, a town wrecked by Philip, and was a kinsman, probably a cousin, of Alexander's tutor Aristotle. He was employed as an already proven historian to write up Alexander's exploits in Asia, if not before. Ptolemy the Macedonian was Alexander's friend from boyhood and served as his officer. He wrote a history after Alexander's death, whose date of publication is unknown. He ruled Egypt after Alexander's death and founded the dynasty of the Ptolemies. Nearchus was a Cretan by birth who resided in the Greek town of Amphipolis which Philip had conquered and added to Macedonia; he too was a friend from boyhood and ended as Alexander's admiral, publishing a memoir of his service, again after Alexander's death. Onesicritus, from Astypalaea on the island of Cos, had studied under the philosopher Diogenes and ended by serving as a high officer in Alexander's fleet; his fanciful work was probably the first to appear after Alexander's death. Aristobulus is of unknown origin, though the name is known at Olynthus, home town of Callisthenes and close to his eventual residence in Cassandreia; he served Alexander, his only known task being to repair Cyrus's tomb at Pasargadae. Perhaps he was an architect and in view of the apologetic tone of his history, it is tempting to call him the Albert Speer of the Alexanderreich. He began writing at the age of eighty-four, at least twenty-three years after Alexander's death. One other historian matters: the little-known Cleitarchus, whose father had written a colourful history on Persia and who began life, probably, in the Ionian town of Colophon, a place with a long tradition of poets. He wrote in a lofty rhetorical style and was considered untrustworthy, though skilful. He is not known to have followed Alexander or witnessed his career, but he wrote by 310 B.C., within thirteen years of Alexander's death, and he read the published work of Callisthenes, Onesicritus and Nearchus. He is said to have settled in Egypt's Alexandria where he may have talked to Maccedonian officers and veterans, for his work ran into more than ten books and had access to accurate detail.

The main secondary authors are Arrian, a Greek from Bithynia (north-west Turkey) who rose to be a Roman consul under the emperor Hadrian and wrote his *Expedition of Alexander*, probably in later middle age, *c.* A.D. 150. He had read widely, but composed mainly from Ptolemy, Aristobulus and, for the last three books, Nearchus. Diodorus of Sicily lived perhaps *c.* 20 B.C. and produced a universal history by abbreviating original histories as casually as possible, confusing their datings and choosing incidents as much for their moral content and their proof of fortune's vicissitudes as for their historical value; in his Book 17, he dealt with Alexander simply by cutting down the work of Cleitarchus and adding a few of his own comments. Justin lived perhaps *c.* A.D. 150 and is a third-hand source, abbreviating the work of Trogus, an educated Gaul probably from the Augustan age (*c.* 10 B.C.) whose book has not survived; his sources often show traces of Cleitarchus, also of Aristobulus and Callisthenes, but as cut down by Justin, his narrative is very wild and cannot be usefully dissected. Perhaps Trogus used one of the many later composers who wrote between his own date and the original histories. The Roman Quintus Curtius wrote a history of Alexander whose Books 3–10 survive; like Diodorus, he makes full use of Cleitarchus, heavily rephrasing him in his own Roman manner, and he intertwines another source, close to one of Arrian's, perhaps Aristobulus more often, or rather, than Ptolemy. I believe he read and translated their originals from Greek. His date is unknown but there is a senator mentioned in Tacitus who would fit him neatly; if so, I guess he wrote *c.* A.D. 45 with a lively memory of the late emperor Caligula, whose favour for Alexander and alleged tase for oriental customs were much to the dislike of senatorial contemporaries and were sometimes recorded in words which match Curtius's own on Alexander. Other clues in his book support this; moreover, his account of the succession debates after Alexander's death can be interestingly compared with the crisis in A.D. 41 when Caligula died and Claudius (said to be feeble-minded, like Philip's bastard son Arrhidaeus) compelled the nobles to accept him.

Lastly there is Plutarch, the Greek from Chaeronea, whose *Life of Alexander* reflects his wide reading and memory of a full range of the original histories, rephrased in his own terms of the early 2nd century A.D. and sometimes marred by slips of detail. His biography was one of a series arranged in parallel pairs; Alexander paralleled Caesar. He also wrote rhetorical works defending Alexander against the charge that he was more lucky than talented.

It is always easy to blame the inadequacies of Alexander's contemporary historians, but we should remember that no Greek had previously recorded the exploits of a living king in a mood of accuracy, without moralizing or writing panegyric, and that there was never a king before or since with exploits as vast as Alexander's.

A NOTE ON THE NOTES

These selected notes do not pretend to be complete but I hope they will begin to explain all statements in the text which seem unusual or too curt. Bibliographies of modern research into Alexander have suddenly sprung into favour. N. J. Burich, *Alexander the Great: a bibliography* (1970) lists over a thousand items, many of them irrelevant; E. Badian discusses many items of the past twenty years in *Classical World* (1971), nos. 3 and 4. The very full survey by Jacob Seibert, *Alexander der Grosse* (1972) spans a wide field without marking the more obvious degrees of merit. Those who wish to sample the vast expanse of Alexander studies are referred to Badian and Seibert; I believe I have covered every article mentioned by them, except for four which were inaccessible, and here I refer only to those which add to our stock of knowledge. I omit those which attack each other or rely, in my opinion, on what we do not know, or else mistake the little we do. To list my reasons for rejecting so many opinions would have required a companion volume and would not have concerned the search for Alexander, the true historian's only business.

Those who like to multiply their ancient references to one broadly similar fact can profitably consult the very thorough noting of parallel passages in Konrat Ziegler's text of Plutarch's life (vol. II. 2 in the Teubner series, 1968); on the many background topics, where modern work is often vast, I have tried to single out the best or most recent study, leaving the reader to follow up the bibliography it cites. Apart from Arrian, Curtius, Plutarch, Justin and Diodorus, there are only two necessary books for Alexander scholarship, a cheering fact which the teeming bibliography must not conceal: Felix Jacoby's *Fragmente der Griechischen Historiker* (1929) 2B, no. 117ff., with a commentary in vol. 2 D that is perhaps the finest in the series so far, and H. Berve's *Das Alexanderreich auf prosopographische Grundlage*, vol. 1, pp. 147, 180–186, p. 276 (with chart) and all of the admirable vol. 2 (1926). I could never have written without these two great reference books, and my deep debt to them will be obvious to every fellow-researcher, all of whom depend on their help. Otherwise, the study of Alexander will only advance, if indeed it can, when historians make up their own minds and cut free of how others have made up theirs. A prime example is the fate of W. W. Tarn's *Alexander the Great*, 2 vols. (1950), the most influential work in English for both critics and admirers; the brief narrative of vol. 1 is explained in thirty-six appendixes in vol. 2, but as thirty-five of the thirty-six are persistently mistaken both in method and evidence, the work has been ignored throughout the writing of this book. But the industry of believing and refuting Tarn still continues apace.

Having prepared long appendixes on the army from 331 to 323, a detailed survey of the sources and detailed discussions of the evidence for the Granicus battle, Cleitus's murder and, above all, Alexander's death, I feel it is better to banish them to learned journals because their results are mostly negative and feed on alternative scholarly views.

Briefly, I single out from them the question of Alexander's relative scarcity of manpower from November 330 until winter 329/8. I believe seven hipparchies were introduced for strategic reasons in winter 329/8 when the massive reinforcements arrived. At the same time three new foot brigades, probably of half-trained non-Macedonian mercenaries, were added under Gorgias, Meleager and White Cleitus (soon replaced by Attalus Andromenous). These changes preceded Cleitus's murder; they may have helped that quarrel, but they did not reflect it.

The Companions had diminished to *c.* 1900, but Iranian horse, I believe, were not yet put in the inner hipparchies. 120,000 men, I argue, is indeed a plausible number for the start of the Indus voyage; at most 40,000 will have entered Makran, probably less, depending on the (considerable?) size of Nearchus's fleet. I suspect that here the fleet was larger than the land army. After Makran all numbers are impossible.

At the Granicus, I argue that DS's account has accurate detail that deserves respect and is supported by other sources and passages, proving it to be more than DS's own mistiming; I prefer it to A.-Ptol.-Aristob. and Plut., for several reasons, and in A. 1.14.8 it is Ptol., I suggest, who elaborated the theme of Parmenion the injudicious adviser. In QC (Cleitarchus?) Parmenion's advice tends almost always to be accepted; so, too, in Aristob. ap. P.21. But in A. (except for A.3.9.3–5, very probably due to Aristob. too), Parmenion is always rebutted. Just as (I believe) Callisth. may once have slighted Perdiccas, so he slighted Parmenion (e.g. P.33); Ptol., I suggest, elaborated the theme against Parmenion, as he evidently did against Perdiccas.

As for Cleitus, I feel the moderate account of QC and J. should be distinguished from the tyranny, philosophy, divinity and oriental decadence stressed by A. and P. (who does not use Chares as a main source). Contrast their two roles for Callisthenes and Anaxarchus and their various timings of the episode; like A., the prologue to DS 17 proves DS told the incident 'out of order'. I suspect this is DS's own moral bias, not Cleitarchus's. All sources are weak on the quarrel's cause. Ptol. omitted it.

On the sources, I believe that P. used a collection of Alexander's 'letters' throughout and if one is a forgery (as surely one is), then all are suspect. I do not agree they must be tested each on their own merit; such a test is anyway circular. I suggest there is more truth to Peripatetic hostility than is now assumed, though less than Tarn implied; I am convinced, too, against recent questioning, that Cleit. was the only source for DS 17 (the discrepancy between F1 and DS 17.14 can be explained) and QC's and DS's copious parallels are due to him (so far from overstating this case, E. Schwarz, R-E 4, 1873 ff. put it too mildly and vaguely). As for Ptol., I accept arguments of his personal bias in principle, but I disagree with some existing detail; I suggest his later relationship to Thais, Laomedon, Cleomenes, Cyrene, Cyprus's kings and fleet, Greek 'freedom', Perdiccas (applicable even more widely than has yet been shown), Syria and even Ammon (Paus. 9.16.1) have, all or some, left a mark in A.

As for Alexander's death, the acute account of A. B. Bosworth CQ (1971), pp. 112ff. raises many points I cannot accept, not least his supposed 'evidence' in DS 18 of a plot to remove Alexander. Other hypotheses can be framed for the Diaries and I mean to explore Cassander's influence (and, curiously, certain Peripatetics) as an alternative. Serapis, much of the Romance's pamphlet, the Aelian quotation from the Diaries, the probable roles of Ptol. and Aristob., all need a new look.

In the following notes I use these main abbreviations:

Ael.	Aelian
Aeschin.	Aeschines
Aeschyl.	Aeschylus
Amm. Marc.	Ammianus Marcellinus
A.P.	Anthologia Palatina
Aristob.	Aristobulus
Aristot.	Aristotle
A.	Arrian
Athen.	Athenaeus
B.E.	Yale Expedition to Babylon, volume and tablet number

Berve	H. Berve, Das Alexanderreich auf prosopographische Grundlage vol. 2 (1926). There every name has a number, which I cite where necessary; otherwise, 'Berve s.v.' means 'see the entry for the proper name involved in Berve, vol 2'.
Call.	Callisthenes
Cleit.	Cleitarchus
Dem.	Demosthenes
DL	Diogenes Laertius
DS	Diodorus Siculus; entries with chapter number only (e.g. DS 53) refer only to Book 17.
Eratosth.	Eratosthenes
HCPA	J. R. Hamilton, Hist. Comm. on Plutarch's Alexander (1968)
Hdt.	Herodotus
Hyper.	Hypereides
Isocr.	Isocrates
Jos.	Josephus
J.	Justin
Lys.	Lysias
Onesic.	Onesicritus
Paus.	Pausanias
Philostr.	Philostratus
Plin. NH	Pliny, Natural History
Pl.	Plutarch, Life of Alexander, when cited only with a numeral (e.g. P. 16). Other lives are cited in recognizable abbreviations.
P. Mor.	Plutarch, or Pseudo-Plutarch, 'Moralia'
Polyaen.	Polyaenus
Polyb.	Polybius
Ptol.	Ptolemy
QC	Quintus Curtius
S.	Strabo
Steph. Byz.	Stephanus the Byzantine
Suet.	Suetonius
Theophr.	Theophrastus
Thuc.	Thucydides
Tod GHI	M.N Tod, A Selection of Greek Historical Inscriptions, vol. 2
Val. Max.	Valerius Maximus
Xen	Xenophon

Other references are self-explanatory. Inscriptions and periodicals are cited in a form intelligible to scholars, who alone will use them. All fragments refer, unless specified otherwise, to numbers in F. Jacoby, Fragmente der Griech. Historiker (Ephipp. 126 F1, meaning fragment 1 of Ephippus, historian no. 126 in Jacoby's complex arrangement).

NOTES TO CHAPTER I (pp. 17-27)

Dating: A. 1.1.1 (archon 'Pythodemos', surely Pythodelos) implies July 336; cp. IG 2².1.240. Joseph. AJ. 19.93 is a strange misapprehension. *Niece-uncle marriage:* L.

Gernet, *Anthropologie de la Grèce antique* (1968) pp. 344ff. and the examples of this particular affinity which Dr J. K. Davies points out to me from his Ath. Propertied Familes (1970) nos 8792, 11672. *Philip the Leader*: Tod GHI, vol. 2, no. 177 with notes pp. 228–9. The fact that Philip was called the Leader implies to me that the notion of an alliance was inherent from the start, perhaps through the individual alliances sworn with many cities in 338/7 (C. Roebuck CP (1948) p. 73). A mere peace would not have a Leader but a president: cp. Sparta's Leadership of her Pel. *allies* (G. E. M. de Sainte Croix, Origins of the Pel. War (1972) pp. 303ff. and the suggestion by N. G. L. Hammond, Epirus (1967) pp. 538ff. of a similar hegemony by the Molossoi in Philip's Epirus). *Marriage to Cleopatra*: Berve s.v. Cleopatra nr 434. *Brawl*: J. 9.7.3. P. 9.6–10, Satyr. ap. Athen. 13.557D–E. The quip about illegitimacy was surely not aimed at Alex.'s lack of pure Mac. blood; Philip's own mother was Illyrian (S. 7.7.8) and the example, e.g., of Dionysius II suggests pure blood may not have mattered (but contrast Peisistratus's heir: Hdt. 1.61, 5.94, Thuc. 6.55.1) Either the remark refers to Olympias's divorced status or, its sources all being suspect, to the nonsense of the snake (P. 2.6, and esp. J. 9.5.9 where this must be Olympias's *stuprum*). *Cleopatra's children*: Caranus (despite Tarn) certainly existed and the *noverca* must, for logic in J. 9.7, be Cleopatra. If he was her son by a previous marriage – we do not know her age or home tribe – he would not have been the rival he was (J. 9.7.3, 11.2.3.). Cleopatra did have a daughter Europe by Philip (probably); Athen. 13.557E. But DS 17.2.3. does not specify the sex of the child born a few days before Philip's death; Paus. 8.7.7. (muddled by Berve) explicitly refers to a *son* of Cleopatra and it is not too serious that Satyrus as quoted by Athenaeus does not mention such a child (he only lived a very few days). The date of Philip's remarriage is entirely uncertain: it may well fall in early spring 337 and Eurydice-Cleopatra (a love-match, according to Satyr.) may have been pregnant by Philip already. She may have borne Europe in summer 337; DS 93.9 and P. 10.5 show she was married at the time of Pausanias's assault (Hamilton HCPA on P. 10.5 disbelieves this on no grounds except a wish to discredit the story) and if this was connected to an Illyrian campaign (Ds 93.6), the campaign may well fall in summer 337. Alex. will have fled for that summer, returned in autumn when the Pixodarus affair, a lengthy process of toing-and-froing, could fall either in the tail end of the sailing season of 337 or (as I prefer) in the sailing-season of 336. Caranus will have been conceived in October 337; his birth and the (recent?) exile of Alex's friends will have pressed on Alex. in July 336. Certainly Europe and Caranus are distinct (J. 9.7.3, 11.2.1 and the rhetorical plural of *fratres* in J. 12.6.14 as opposed to J. 9.7.12 and Athen. 557C) and it spoils the logic of J. 9.7 to assume an unknown son by, e.g., Phila the Elimiot (so Berve – he would then be older and it is odder still that Satyr.-Athen. mentions no such child). Given the chronology, Caranus is surely Cleopatra's baby son: his name too has a fine ring of Macedonian royalty (J. 7.7.7) which can only have scared Alex. more (cp. the name Europe?). The evidence of the Philippeum at Olympia is tantalizing (Paus. 5.20.9). It had statues of Philip's father, Alex., Olympias and Eurydice, probably commissioned by spring 337. Eurydice may of course be Philip's mother, but his new bride was called Eurydice before her marriage (A. 3.6) and Philip may have been so keen on her that he included her in the monument. If so, the marriage is confirmed to early 337. *Alexander of Epirus*: Berve nr 38. *Aigai*: Theophr. Peri Anemon 27 is decisive for a site on northern foothills of Mount Olympus; Theophrastus had lived in Macedonia and his precise local knowledge even of Thracian Philippi testifies to his travels (P. Collart, Phillippes (1937) pp. 185ff.). Edessa is a very modern name for the older Vodhena (if this derives from the Phrygian word *bedu*, or water, we should remember the tradition of Phyrgian occupation of Mt Bermion: Call. F54); it is perhaps not the ancient Edessa, which was anyway distinct from ancient Aigai, e.g. P. Pyrrh. 26.1. The Royal Tombs are always sited at Aigai, not Edessa: e.g. DS 22.12. In Sept. 1970 I noted Theophrastus's cloud-phenomenon at modern Vergina: for the burial grounds there cp. Balkan Studies (1961) pp. 85ff. and for the otherwise inexplicable palace: Vergina, Studies in Med. Archaeol. XII (Lund). Both are by M. Andronicos; despite a coin of Lysimachus in one foundation wall, the palace's dating is far from certain. See Addenda. *Sources for Philip's murder*: Aristot. Pol. 1311B is basic and may have helped to inspire DS 16.92ff. (from Diyllus the Athenian – DS 76.5 – and note the Athenian bias in perhaps 77.3 and 92.2; the theme of the sophist in 94 is very trite). J. 9.6–7 is of unknown source but not therefore worthless; simply because these sources are dramatic, their 'facts', not motives, are not necessarily untrue. *Persian background*: J. 10.3, DS 17.5.3, Ael V.H. 6.8. *Divine statue*: DS 16.92, Ael. VH.5.12, Athen. 6.251 B, Lucian Dial. de Mort. 1.3.2, Callixein. FGH 627 F2. OGIS 332.1.27. S. Weinstock HTR (1957) p. 235 n. 142–3 on probable use by Alex. Syll³ 589 lines 41ff. on the gay pomp of these moments. O. Weinreich, Lykien Zwolfgotterrelief, SB Heidel. (1913) pp. 1ff. is masterly. For Caesar, cp. Dio. 43.45.2, Cic. ad Att. 13.28.3. Was this honour invented by Philip? *His divine honours*: Tod 191, with which cp. Zeus Seleukeios and Aphrodite Stratonikis; the adjectival form probably means 'Zeus as patron of Philip' and is not a clear divinization of Philip, unlike, e.g. Juppiter Julius, Pythionice Aphrodite or Heracles Themison (FGH 80 F1). With A 1.17.10ff. cp. A. D. Nock IISCP (1930) p. 56 n. 2 whose doubts I do not share; more evidence in C. Habicht, Gottmenschtum u. die Gr. Stadte (1970) pp. 12f. Surely Philip was worshipped in his newly founded towns? DS 92.6, 93.1 show Philip's motives were not blasphemy and Suida s.v. Antipatros is irrelevant. Readers of J. Becker, De Suidae Excerptis Historicis (1915) will hesitate before accepting any entry in the Suida as historical, let alone their testimonies on blasphemy, when so much goes back to excerptors like the Christian monk George. *Pausanias's death*: DS 94.4 (abbreviated by DS?) implies on-the-spot murder; Pap. Oxyrrh. 1798. FGH 148 line 16 mentions *apotumpanismos* (here, *auton*, as restored, probably refers to Pausanias, not an accomplice). A. E. Keramopoullos's remarkable Ho Apotumpanismos (1923), with the full review by L. Gernet REG (1924) p. 261, and Aristoph. Thesmoph. 930–946, Aeschyl. Prometheus Bound 1ff. shows the plausibility of this; J. 9.7.10 latinizes the stake to a cross, but rightly notes that the body was buried. This fits *apotumpanismos* exactly, and in chains, Pausanias had days of hunger in which to talk. *Oracle*: DS 91.2, Paus. 8.7.6; cp. Ael. V.H. 3.45 (Trophonius). *Motive*: A. B. Bosworth CQ (1971) pp. 93ff. is unconvincing; does not explain timing of murder, a year or more after Philip's remarriage, or why Lyncestis (whose politics owed more to Illyrians) should not have felt equally 'excluded' by Epirote Olympias. Among many other objections, how do we know that Cleopatra was a plainswoman? She might have been Lyncestian too *Pausanias's grievance*: DS 93.8–9 shows it occurred after Philip's remarriage; no reason to backdate it to 344. 'Pleurias' may be Pleuratus or Glaucias (A. 1.5.6) and there are enough campaigns against Illyria of which nothing is known (e.g., QC 8.1.25, Frontin, 2.5.10, 3.4.5) for one to fit summer 337 or even 336. But Pausanias's status as Bodyguard (if precise) fits oddly with his youth (cp. J.9.6.5). *Aristotle's unreliability*: e.g., Politics 1304A, with R. Weil, Aristote et l'histoire (1960). *Orestids*: DS 93.3 with Hammond, Epirus pp. 528ff. *Horses*: J. 9.7.9, whose plural gives a role for accomplices. The revenge theme, applicable (in Aristot.) to Pausanias alone, and his instant death in DS 16 (mistaken?) do not rule out the purge of accomplices in DS 17.2.1., J. 11.2.1 (cp. A.125); others, e.g. Alex. of Lyncestis may have talked and Pausanias could use help in his getaway. It is wrong to talk of rival versions of the murder; they all dovetail, but no source is reliable. Pausanias was not murdered by two fellow-Orestids, for Leonnatus was a Lyncestid via Philip's mother (Berve s.v Leonnatus is wrong here, giving rise to the fantasy in C. B. Welles, Loeb Diodorus (1963) p. 101 n. 2: we do not know which Attalus this was, let alone whether the – middle-aged? – Perdiccas was already Alex.'s friend). *Alex.'s complicity*: only a belief in J. 9.7; P. 10.6 shows by the connecting *gar* that he has no more evidence than this witty quote from Euripides! J. 9.7.3. is right that Caranus's birth is grounds for a belief in Alex.'s possible guilt. But it is no proof, though P. Dem Poliorc. 3 is timely. Alex. had saved Philip's life (QC 8.1.24) and the vulgate's question at Siwah – e.g. DS 17.51.2 – is a reminder that it all remained a mystery. However, Alex.'s guilt is an old and sensational fancy – e.g. Niebuhr in the 1820s; there is no evidence, and E. Badian, Phoenix (1963) p. 244 has simply revived it with rhetoric and without Caranus. Either way, the 'silence' of Diodorus proves nothing about anybody's innocence. But for a similar role to Olympias's, the Seleucid Laodice and the murder of Antiochus III in 246 is a suggestive comparison: Appian Syr. 65. Phylarch. FGH 81 F24, Polyaen. 8.50 and J.27.1.1. Demosthenes's advance intelligence in 336 (P. Demosth. 22, Aeschn. 3.160) does not imply he was an accomplice (so Mary Renault, Fire From Heaven (1970)) but that the Athenian 'spies' in the north (Aeschn. 3.77) naturally brought the news to him first, and quickly.

See Bibliography for works on Macedonia. *Philip's new kingdom*: A. Momigliano, Filippo il Macedone (1934) passim. Note how the royal myth of Hdt. 8.137f. expands into Theopomp. F 393 to include Orestis in Caranus's legacy. Livy 45.18.3, 29.11 are fine proofs of how Macedon could best be unified. *Fen flooding*: Homer Iliad 21.157–8. *Fish*: e.g., Athen. 7.328; Dem. 19.229; Hdt. 5.16.4 for Paeonia. *Minerals*: useful maps in O. Davies, Rmn Mines in Europe (1935) and DS 16.8.6–7 (probably Peisistratus's old mining interests). Berve s.v. Gorgo with R. J. Hopper BSA (1953) pp. 200–254, (1968) pp. 293–326 for available skills; R. J. Forbes, Metallurgy in Antiquity (1953); R. Pleiner, Iron-work in ancient Greece (1969). *Drainage*: S. 9.2.18, Theophr. CP 5.14.6 and the inscription from Philippi in CRAI (1938) p. 251. *Forests*: Thuc. 2.100.2, Theophr. loc. cit, Hdt. 7.131 and G. Glotz REG (1916) p. 292; Theophr. H.P. 9.2.3 (vivid). *Hunting:* e.g. Hdt. 7.125–6, Xen. Kyneg. 11. *Trout*: Ael. Hist. Anim. 15.1. *Fruit*: e.g. Theop. 115 F 152. *Heraclion*: Ps.-Scylax 66f. on this whole coastline. *Dion*: S.7 F17, Livy 44.7.3. Arch. Delt. (1015) pp. 44ff. PAE (1931) pp. 47–55, PAE (1933) pp. 59ff., Arch D. (1966) pp. 346ff. *Orpheus*: Paus. 9.30.5, Orphic. Frag. (Kern) F342, Timoth. Persae 234–6. S. 7.17–18. *Coast-towns*: U. Kahrstedt, Hermes (1953) pp. 89ff. is unconvincing. *Rich cities*: Ps.Ar. Oec. 1350 A22. *City-land*: DS 16.8.5, 34.5. *Walls*: Polyaen. 4.2.15, DS 13.49.1. *Moments of freedom*: Dein 1.14, 1G4².94 for 360s. *Inland trade*: Meiggs and Lewis, Gk Inscr. 65 line 20f. *Law-courts*: Ps.–Dem. 7.12ff; A. R. W. Harrison CQ (1960) pp. 248ff. *Hoplites*: Thuc. 4.124. *Pella*: Ps.Scymm. 624–5. Strabo Epitome F20, 22. P. Mor. 603C. Ph. Petsas, Balkan Studies 4 (1960) pp. 157ff. (full bibliography). *Mosaics*: C. M. Robertson JHS (1965) pp. 71ff; again in C. Picard RA (1963) p. 205. *Lion Griffin*: the coins with this emblem from Asian mints on Antipater's arrival in Syria in 321/0 (G. F. Hill JHS (1923) pp. 160–1) perhaps imply it was his badge or regent's seal; the theme dies out in Macedon, to my knowledge, after his death. A. M. Bisi, Il Grifone (1965) is useful; Iranian carpet-patterns may be relevant (F. von Lorentz, Rom. Mitteil. (1937) p. 165), esp. in view of J. Boardman, Antiquity (1970) p. 143 for their influence on Macedonian tomb-paintings. *Paintings*: e.g. Ph. Petsas, Ho Taphos Tes Leukadias (1966); K. A. Romaios, Ho Taphos Tes Berginas (1951) and Dion drawings in PAE (1930) pp. 45ff. *Roses*: Theophr. HP 6.6.4, Hdt. 8.138.2, Caus. Plant 1.13.11 and Rosalia in HTR (1948) pp. 153ff. *Highlanders*: F. Papazoglou, Ziva Antika (1959) pp. 167ff. N. G. L. Hammond, Epirus (1967). J. B. Wace BSA (1911/2) pp. 167ff. *Titles*: e.g. Indica 18 or P. Perdrizet BCH (1897) pp. 112ff. *Hill-forts*: Thuc. 2.99ff; 4.125f. A. E. Keramopoullos PAE (1933) pp. 63ff., Arch. Ephem. (1932) pp. 48–133; Stud. Pres to Ed. Capps pp. 196ff. *Tymphiots*: S.7.7.9, Hesych. Deipaturos. Steph. Byz. Tymphe. Tzetz. on Lycophron Alex. 800 (Polyperchon) Berve s.v. Amyntas Andromenous and his brothers Attalus, Simmias, Polemon. Phillippos s. of Amyntas. *Orestai*: S 7.7.8, Hammond, Epirus p. 528 (very relevant, if correctly dated). Berve s.v. Perdiccas, Craterus, Amphoterus, Alcetas, Pausanias Kerastou. *Lyncestis*: S. 7.7.8, Thuc. 4.125f. Hdt. 5.92f. on Bacchiads. P. de lib. educ. 20, P. 40.1 = Phylarch. ap. Athen. 539f. *Highland dress*: Ziva Antika (1953) pp. 226, 234. Is it chance that the highest-priced slave in Meiggs and Lewis 79 and p. 347 (Hermocopid Lists) is a Macedonian woman? *Sheep*: A. 7.9.2 (suspect source). A. M. Woodward JHS (1913) p. 337 – splendid inscription. Note ox-drawn carts in Upper Macedonia: Thuc. 4.128.4. *Elimiot Policy*: Schol. on Thuc. 1.57.3. Aristot. Pol. 1311 B11 and note rich Elimiot graves in Arch. Eph. (1948/9) pp. 85ff. Berve s.v. Koinos, Kleandros and possibly the sons of Machatas, Harpalus, Tauron, Philip (and Calas Harpalou?). But a Machatas is known in Epirus (Polyb. 27.15 and another in S. G. Dial. Inschr. 1371) and the lowlands (IG 10.1032 – 3rd *c.* B.C.?; another in Syll. 1³.269 J); this is but one example of the extreme danger in reasoning about factions simply from the geographical hints of a man's father's name. The Elimiot faction, for intance, in E. Badian JHS (1961) p. 22 rests on such a guess, and nothing more. *Philip's new towns*: e.g. DS 16.71, S. 7.6.2, Plin. NH 4.41. Etym. Magn. s.v. Bine. Suida s.v. Doulon polis and Poneron polis. J. 8.5–6. *Feudalism*: A. 1.16.5, P. 15.3; SIG 332 gives land-holders freedom to sell their hereditary holdings. Double domiciles of Ptolemy Lagou, Aristonous, Perdiccas et. al. in Berve. *Clans*: for modern effects J. K. Campbell,

Honour, Family and Patronage: Institutions and Moral Values in a Gk. mountain community (1964). *Companions*: DS 17.16.4 (approx. nos.). J. Kalleris, Les Anciens Maced. (1954) s.v. Hetairideia and Peligan (a word also used in inscriptions in Macedonian colonies in Syria). *Titles*: W. W. Tarn, Alex. the Great vol. 2. pp. 138ff. Kalleris (e.g. 'edeatros') collects a few Macedonian court-officials, but the style of 4th C. Macedon's monarchy is unknown. *Blood-feud*: QC 6.11.20, DS 19.51. *Marriage*: Hdt. 5.92 on incestuous Bacchiads. For its general purpose, esp. the role of the dowry and kyrios, cp. W. K. Lacey, Family in Classical Greece (1968); also W. Erdmann, Die Ehe im alten Griechenland (1934). Livy 45.29 shows its importance in Macedonian power. *Trials*: QC 6.8.25 (the true Ms. reading is not what Germans make it) may well be Curtius's own guess; theories of Staatsrecht and clearly defined Army Assemblies are irrelevancies which I cannot refute here. Polyb. 5.27.6 is too vague to prove anything. *Spear clashings*: QC 10.7.14 and for its importance, G. E. M. de Sainte Croix, Orig. of Pel. War (1972) p. 348 (excellent). *Mass-marriage*: the discrepancy in numbers between Polyb-Callisth, F33 and A. 1.29.4 may be due to Polyb. including hundreds of bridegrooms married off in 334? QC 7.5.27 on Kings and birthrate. *Amyntas Perdikkou*: s.v. Berve, with Kynnane, Phil. Arrhidaeus (esp. P. 10.2, 77.7). *Carian affair*: must be during the sailing season in the Aegean, i.e. autumn 337 or, more probably in view of Philip's invasion, late spring 336; if so, almost a prelude to Philip's murder! P. 10 1–4, A. 3.6.5 cite it; cp. Isocr. Paneg. 162. *Succession*: Hdt. 8.139.2 with the stimulating parallels in M. Southwold's study of Buganda succession-patterns in Assoc. Soc. Anthrop. Monographs no. 7 (1968), esp. stressing the relevance of age. *Purges*: cp. Philip in J. 8.3.10; also Bk of Daniel 6.24; cp. Hdt. 3.119; J. 10.2.5; Amm. Marc. 23.6.81, 24.5.3, 17.9.5; Euseb. Praep. Evang. 8.14 and Southwold's Buganda parallels. *Alex. of Lyncestis*: A. 1.25 and Berve s.v.; DS 16.93f. is too brief to be dubbed 'incompatible' with the accomplices mentioned in DS 17.2, A. 1.23, 2.14. J. 9.6.9 gives them a possible role. *Aeropus*: Polyaen, 4.2.2; cp. the useful lists of Macedonian names in I.I. Russu, Ephemeris Dacoromana (1938) *Amyntas's friends*. J. R. Ellis JHS (1971) pp. 15–25 cites the necessary inscriptions; but his conclusions are almost all unacceptable. Reference should have been made to A. Aymard Études d'Hist. Anc. (1967) pp. 100–122, pp. 232–35 (important); I share the grave doubts of his p. 120. Note from the example of Doson and Philip (Aymard pp. 234–5) how a regent could be styled king; even if this Lebadeia inscription has been properly read (it is lost, now), who cut it, when, and how officially? We have no idea (IG I². 71, esp. lines 25ff., is tantalizing evidence for the existence of several kings at once in Macedon, and not only of highland tribes; possibly, Alex. I's kingdom was split between brothers, who each took the title; the parallel may be relevant to Philip and Amyntas IV). Berve s.v. Amyntas, Aristomedes (with the new inscription from Arch. Delt. (1966) A pp. 45ff. plausibly restored), Neoptolemus Arrhabaiou (surely the known Lyncestian Arrhabaios?). A. 1.5.4 dates Amyntas's death as nearly as we can. *Amyntas Arrhabaiou*: brother of Neoptolomos, nephew of Alex. the Lyncestian? J. 11.5.8 may refer to him, for the Mounted Scouts were in Asia (I agree with R. D. Milns JHS (1966) pp, 167–8) and he was their leader in 334 (A. 1.14.1). *Parmenion's links*: QC 6.9.17, 10.24. *Execution*: J. 11.2.2, 12.6.14. *Speech to army*: DS 17.2.2, J. 11.1.10 (A. 1.16.5 implies this tax-relief was temporary). *Philip's funeral*: DS 2.1 DS 19.52.5 Livy 40., Hesych. s.v. Xanthica. Similar festivals were known in Boeotia; cp. QC 10.9.11 for Alex.'s death. On 'Macedonian' style tombs, cp. Ph. Petsas, Atti de 7 Congr. Internaz. di Archeol. Classica (1961) pp. 401 ff. with vast bibliography. *Eurylochus's murder*: Berve s.v. with J. 12.5.14. *Attalus*: DS 17. 2.4–5 (orders to bring him back, if possible, alive). P. Dem 23.1. Berve s.v. *Hecataeus the Greek guide*: DS 17.2.5, with P. Eum. 3, DS 18.14.4 (such local knowledge of Cardia would be invaluable; perhaps already in 336 he was Antipater's friend? If so, he would be one reason for the enemity between Antipater and Eumenes, also from Cardia: P. Eum. 5.5). *Orestids*: Berve s.v. Craterus Perdiccas, Amphoterus, Alcetas, Atalante, Pausanias son of Kerastos. *Tymphiots*: Amyntas, Andromenous, Attalus his brother; Simmias, Polemon, Polyperchon, Philippos Amyntou. *Eordaia*: Ptolemy Lagou, Aristonous. *Elimea*: Cleander, Coenos and possibly (not certainly) Harpalus (note the many Machatai known outside Elimea) and if so, Tauron, Philippos Machatou. Possibly, too, Calas Harpalou, who ends up in charge of the advance force, 335/4. I cannot stress too strongly, despite the use which

I make of localities in this book, that these places of origin may be irrelevant (e.g. for Philip's pages rehoused in the lowlands), misleading (e.g. Harpalus) or just disputed. Take Peithon Crateuou, for instance; when, in 321/0 he helps his fellow-Eordaian Ptolemy to murder Perdiccas, it might look quite an impressive link. However Ptolemy is thought to have disliked Aristonous, also Eordaian, even to the point of a bias in his history; Eordoi had been expelled by Aigai's kings and their lands may have been settled with ethnic outsiders; Peithon's own home town is disputed. A.6.28.4 makes him Eordaian: Indica 18.6 (surely based on an official document) makes him a man of Alkomenai which, with S.7.326 and much else, has been identified beyond doubt by F. Papazoglou Klio (1970) p. 305 as in Lyncestis. This explains why J. 13.4.13 (based on Hieronym.) calls him Peitho Illyrius. Could a baron own lands in two or more highland areas, as Peitho may have done in Lyncestis and (Argead) Eordaia? Did their wives bring property with them? We do now know, and all attempts to construct Macedonian factions, even if valid in principle (I am sceptical), wear a big question mark in detail. For completeness, I note men with (possible) Epirote links or names or fathers: Neoptolemus the archihypaspist, Arybbas the bodyguard till 332, possibly Meleagros Neoptolemou. The differing fates of the differing Lyncestians in 336/3 is a warning to any such approach. *Alex.'s appearance*: Literary texts are collected in C. de Ujfalvy, Le Type Phys. d'Alex. (1902) and sifted by T. Schreiber, Studien uber das Bildnis Alex. (1903). The bibliography is vast (cp. J. Seibert, Alex. der Grosse (1972) pp. 51–61): best modern summaries in E. J. von Schwarzenberg Bonn. Jahrb. (1967) pp. 58ff. and T. Holscher, Ideal u. Wirklichk. in den Bildnissen Alex. (1971). H. P. L'Orange, Apotheosis. in Anc. Portraiture (1947) is intriguing; G. Kleiner in Jahr. der Deutsch. Inst. (1950/1) pp. 206–30 and Uber Lysipp, Festschr. B. Schweitzer (1954) pp. 227ff. are more valid than M. Bieber, Alex. in Gk and Romn Art (1964). *Official artists*: P.41–3 with J. P. Guepin, Bull. van Antik. Beschav. (1964) p. 129. *Shaving*: cp. Theopomp, F. 225 line 32. *Hair-style*: e.g. P. Pomp. 2, Ael. VH. 12.14 and every monument except the hunting scene on the Alex.-sarcophagus. It had heroic implications (Holscher pp. 27–8) and Leonine ones (Ps.-Ar. Physiogn 806 B – cp. E. Evans Trans. Am. Philos. Soc. (1969) for this neglected subject). The belief in Ephoros 70 F 217 is relevant; Ps.-Call. 1.13, Jul. Val. 1.13. Pella mosaic of lion hunt gives his hair-colour; cp. Ael. VH. 12.14. *Eyes*: P.4, P. Pomp. 2 and von Schwarzenberg p. 70f. The bi-coloured tradition in Ps. Call. 1.13, Jul. Val. 1.7, Tzetzes 11.368 8s surely worthless! *Scent*: Aristox. ap. P.4.41; the Byzantine Tzetzes in his Chiliad (cited by Ujfalvy p. 31) attributes this opinion to Theophrast. too, probably (not certainly) through misreading P. 4.4. *Height*: QC 5.2.13 (though Persian thrones were elevated). QC 7.8.9, 6.5.29, A. 2.12.6. Ps.-Call. 2.15 and esp. 3.4. I would not wish to wear the small Macedonian cavalry helmet in the Ashmolean Museum Oxford *Youthful achievement*: P. 9, with Tod 129 line 21 (restored) for an example of a deputy-king's sealing. QC 8.1.24–25 is tantalizing. There was nothing 'treasonable' about naming a city Alexandropolis in Philip's reign; nothing suggests it was a mere colony. J. 9.5.5 may be Alex.'s only visit to Athens.

NOTES TO CHAPTER 3 (pp. 43–67)

Childhood histories: Suida s.v. Marsyas. Diog. Laert 6.4.84 with Berve s.v. Onesicritus and Philiscus (his uncle or father?). *Birthday*: P. 3.5, A. 7.28.1, Ael. VH. 2.25 with W. Schmidt Geburtstag im Alterum (1908). Hdt. 1.131, 9.110; Plato 1 Alcib. 121 C, Genesis 40.20 (the Pharaoh), Esther passim. *Ephesus*: P. 3.6, 7 (magi are correct). *Birth Legends*: A. 4.10.1, P. 3.3 (Eratosthenes). *Olympias*: P. 2.2, QC 8.1.26, J. 7.6. 10–11, Athen. 557 B–C (chronological) with Samothrace vol. 2 part 1. The Inscriptions, (1960) p. 13 with Syll³ 372 lines 5–6. Her portraits: U. Scchilone, Enc. dell. arte antic. (5) p. 672 (too uncritical). *Coins*: W. Baege, De Macedonum Sacris (1913) p. 86, with Duris 76 F 52 and the (spurious?) letter of Athen. 14.659f. Cic. de Div. 2. 135; E. R. Dodds, Euripides's Bacchae (introduction, passim). Theophr. Peri Eusebeias F 8 (ed. Potscher) is very much to the point; cp. P. 2.2. *Dodona*: N. G. L. Hammond, Epirus p. 438 n. 5. *Atrocity*: J.9.7, Paus. 8.7.7, DS 19.11. *Vow to Health*: Hypereid. Pro Eux. 31. *Tutors*: Berve s.v. Leonidas; nrs 469, 470 may be the same man! P.5, P.24. The list in Ps.Call. 1.13 is corrupt and unverifiable; Menaichmus, pupil of Eudoxus, is also cited (correctly?) by Stobaeus; Anaximenes was indeed at court (Paus. 6.18.3). *First appearance*: Aeschin. 1.168. *Music*: Ael. VH 3.32. Suida s.v. Timotheus, Dio Chrys. Or. 2.26; also the coin in C. M. Kraay-Max Hirmer. Gk. Coins (1966) pl. 171.565, where Apollo wears Alex.'s looks! *Hunting*: Xen. On Hunt. 13.18, Hdt. 7.125–6, P.23. *Dogs*: P.61.3, Theophr. 115 F 340, DS 92. *Bucephalas*: Chares ap. Gell. NA 5.2, P.6 and A. R. Anderson AJP (1930) pp. 1–21 for his legend; Steph. Byz., Bucephala is interesting. The date (345/4?) is given by P. Timol. 21, DS 76.6 against Ps.-Call. 1.17. *Mounting*: QC 6.5.18 with Xen. Equ. 6.16, Pollux 1.213. *Macedonian patronage*: Hdt. 5.22, Thuc. 2.99.3, Hesiod F 3 (West), Pindar F 120–21 (Snell), Bacchyl. F 20 B (Snell), Suida s.v. Hippocrates and Melanippides, P. Mor. 1095D, Timotheus F 24 (Page). Ael. VH. 14.17. Athen. 8.345D, Ael. VH. 2.21. Euripid. F 232–246 (Nauck) with Hyginus Fabulae 219 and B. Snell, Griechische Papyri der Hamburg . . . (1954) pp. 1–14. Ael. VH 13.4.1 and the epigram of the Macedonion Addaeus A.P.7.51; Gellius NA 15.20.9 is nice (cp. Amm. Marc. 27.4.8). Eurip. Bacchae, esp. lines 556f. with Dodd's notes. *Immigrants*: Paus. 7.25.6, Theopomp. F 387, Dem. 50.46, 19.196. Isocr. Philipp. 18–19, Schol. ad Aesch. 2.21, Ps.-Aesch. Ep. 2.14. X. Hell. 5.2.13. *Emigrants*: Thuc. 6.7.3. Plut. Pelop. 26. *Xenophon*: Dem. 19.196; cp. QC 5.9.1, DS 16.52.3–4. *Painting*: the friendly junta at Sicyon with C. M. Robertson, Greek Painting (1955) and Berve I pp. 73–9. Contrast the Macedonian stele from Vergina in N. Andronicos BCH (1955) p. 87 and the rough grey 'Minyan' pottery found at 4th *c*. Pella, Kozani and Vergina; its primitive ancestors were classified by W. A. Heurtley, Prehistoric Macedonia (1939). *Campaspe*: Plin. NH. 35.86. Lucian Imagin. 7. Ael. VH. 12. 34. *Macedonians and Greek outsiders*: A. 210.7, 3.22, 5.26.6, 7.9.4 distinguishes Greeks and Macedonians. Indica 18.3 and 18.7 points the contrast particularly clearly; P. Eumen. 8 suggests a backlash. Before idealizing some stout Macedonian peasant-tradition, betrayed by Alex., we should remember the variety of Upper Macedonian tribes, each with traditions of their own, already 'betrayed' by Philip! When A. 2.14.4 identifies Greeks and Macedonians in a letter from Alex., this may reflect Alex.'s own style of writing (cp. Hdt. 5.20 for Argeads' urge to be Greek); equally, it may reflect Arrian's own beliefs, for by Roman times Macedonia seemed a 'part of Hellas'. Note that Indica 18.4–6 contrasts Nearch. and others with Greeks; Tod 182 implies differently, perhaps because it is an earlier document. 'Makedon', as under the Successors, is already a title of status, not racial purity. *Cosmopolitans*: e.g. Berve s.v. Eumenes, Critoboulos, Hippocrates, Xenocrates, Anaxarchus, Aristonicus, Polyeidus, Gorgo, Philonides and Aristander, with Lucian Philip. 21–22. Fools in Theophr. F 236. *Orientals*: Berve s.v. Sisines, Artabazus and Barsine, DS 16. 52.3–4 with P. Eumen. 1 and Aristob. ap. P. 21. She was royal though her mother Apame, daughter of Artaxerxes II; Tarn must be ignored! *Pages*: A. 4.13.1, Berve s.v. Perdiccas (A. Indic. 18.5–QC 10.7.8). Leonnatus (A. 6.28.4, Indic. 18.3, QC 10.7.8). Aristonous: A. Indic. 18.5 and A. 6.28.4. Ptolemy: ditto; cp. Berve 1 pp. 25ff. on bodyguards' identity. *Highlanders*: Menelaus in Tod GI II. 143, 148. Xen Hell. Suida s.v. Antipatros; Aeshcin. 2.43, 47. *Hephaistion*: cp. Aristotle's and Xenocrates' lists of titles of works. *Lysimachus*: A. 7.5.6, J. 15.3.6. *Harpalus*: Theophr. HP. 4.4.1. *Archaic goods*: see esp. Kallipolitis's finds of 5th–4th *c*. at Kozani in Elimea, well published in Arch. Eph. 1948/9 p. 85. *Jewellery*: H. Hofmann, P. F. Davidson Jewel. in Age of Alex. (1965). *Mistresses*: Berve s.v. Thais, Glycera, Pythionice. *Herodotus*: Ptol. F 2, Callisth, F 38, Nearch. F 8, 17, 18, 20 (though A. 6.28.8 implies his style was rough and its Herodotean flavour due solely to A.). Theopomp. F1–4 (prepared for Philip in Asia?). Alex. himself picks it up in P. 34.3. See now also O. Murray CQ (1972) pp 200f. *Alexarchus*: O. Weinreich, Menecrates Zeus (1933), p. 12ff. and 108ff. with full bibliography. *Alex.'s Tutor*: Letter of Speusippus (ed. Bickermann-Sykutris), passim. *Theopompus's panegyric*: F 255–6; he was a pupil of Isocrates's (hence, perhaps, Isocr.'s snide Ep. 5, written after his rejection for Aristotele). Philip's Platonic links were through Euphraeus, Xenocrates, the tyrants of Sicyon and Hermias and so forth. No reason to see Aristot.'s choice as political. M. Brocker, Aristotles als Alexanders Lehrer (1966) and W. Hertz, Gesammelte Abhandlungen (1905) pp. 1ff. are both excellent. *His father*: DL 5.1. *Stageira*: Brocker pp. 28ff. with the Ms. at DS 16.52.9 and the malice of Demochares ap. Euseb. Praep. Evang. 15.13–15. *His fee*: Athen. 9.398 E. Sen. Dial. 27.5. DL 5.12–16. Gellius NA. 3.17. Against Plin. NH 8.16, 44, cp. J. D'Arcy Thompson PCPS (1948) p. 7. *Riches*: DL

5.12–16 for his will, with the exaggerated Athen. 398 E, Gell. NA 3.17. *Wise man*: DL 5.31. *Mieza*: Ph. Petsas in Makedonika (1967) pp. 33ff. *Dating*: DL 5.2 and Philoch. ap. Philodemus, Index Acad. 6.28 on Aristot.'s absence in Macedonia in the year of Speusippus's death. *Writings for Alex.*: Brocker p. 30, all of them undatable and unknown. F 658 (Rose) may be spurious. *Philosopher in arms*: Onesicr. F 17A. *Aristotle and the young*: Rhetor. 1389 A, Polit. 1340 B 30. *Antipater's friendship*: Ael. VH. 14.1, Suida s.v. Antipatros, DL 5.9, Paus. 6.4.8. *Hephaistion*: DL 5.1.12. G. A. Gerhard, Phoinix v. Kolophon (1909) pp. 140ff., with Letter of Diogenes, Epist. 24 p. 241. (Teubner). His one possible bust is in the Istanbul museum, though identity is disputed. *Homosexuality*: G. Devereux. Symbol. Osl. (1965) pp. 68ff. is interesting, but not universally true; H. Licht, Sexual Life in Anc. Greece (1932) needs superseding; K. Bethe Rh. Mus. (1907) pp. 438ff. is only partly refuted by K. J. Dover BICS (1964) pp. 31ff.; Xen. Lac. Pol 2.12 with H. I. Marrou, Hist. of Educ. (1965) pp. 61ff.; Theopomp. F 225. *Alex and sex*: P. Mor. 717 F, 65 F and esp. P. 22.6 with Aristot. Nicom. Ethics 1102 B. P. 22, P. 40.2, 41.9. Theophrast. ap. Athen. 435A. *His sister*: P. Mor. 818 C. *Isocrates's letter*: Epist. 5, which I accept as authentic. *Ptol.'s parentage*: P. Mor. 458 B and de Nobil. 19. *Mieza*: Berve s.v. Peucestas. *Philip and Homer*: Ps.-Call. 1.35, in the recension quoted by Brocker p. 55. *Achilles*: P. 5.8, A. 1.12, P. 8.2, S.13.1.27, Plin. NH 7.108, Ath. 537C, Onesicr. F 38. P. 26.1–2 (from many sources). *Nicknames*: Pericles as Nestor (Plato Sympos. 221C): note Suet. J. Caes 50.1 for Pompey and Caesar. *Homer in Macedonia*: Athen. 620 (Cassander), DL 4.46 and P. Mor. 182 F. cp. the Megarian vase in Lyncestis, recorded in AJA (1934) p. 474; also SEG (15) nr. 473: a Hellenistic vase's inscription. *Philip*: DS 16.87.2; Isocr. Panathen. 74–80. Hdt. 1.2f. and the precedent of Agesilaus in Xen. Hellen. 3.4.3–4. *Margites*: Aeschin. 3.160, P. Dem 23.2, Marsyas 135 F 3; cp., perhaps, Hypereid. pro Lycoph. 6.21, Polyb. 12.4A. Schol. to Aesch. 3.160, Aristot. Ethics 1141A12, Plato Alcib. 2.147B, Suida s.v. Margites and esp. Eustathius 1669.41 (quoted in O.C.T. Homeri Opera vol. 5 p. 158); on the poem's authorship, Suidas s.v. Pigres the Carian (more or less of Philip's age) is interesting. Callisthenes: 124 T 10, F 10, F 14 line 18, F 32, F 53; cp. Aristob. F 6. L. Pearson, Lost Hist. of Alex (1960) pp. 36ff. sees the basic truth, but muddles its details. *Art*: T. Holscher, Ideal u. Wirklichkeit (1971) p. 28 and notes 80, 82, 183; von Schwarzenberg. BJ (1967), esp. p. 106 notes 65–6; C. Heyman, Antidor, Peremans (1968) p. 115, for coins. *Achilles's embassy*: A.3.6.2. *Homer's relevance*: Plato Ion, passim; Republic 1–3; Dem. speeches 18 and 19, Aristot. F 495–500. A. W. H. Adkins, Merit and Responsib. (1960); Morals and Values (1972); esp. relevant is J. G. Peristiany, ed; Honour and Shame: the Values of Mediterranean Society (1965): and cp. the splendid books of P. M. Leigh-Fermor, esp. Mani and Roumeli, passim. For *to philotimo*; cp. A. 7.14.4–5. *Macedonian customs*: Aristot. Pol. 1324B (date?), Ptol.-A.4.24.4 Athenae. 18A, P. Mor. 338D with the excellent note of E. Fraenkel, Aeschylus's Agamemnon, vol. 3. p. 754. *Hunting*: cp. the inscription in BSA (1911/2) p. 133 for Heracles the Hunter; the sport was essential for meat. *Toasts*: Ephipp. 126 F 1 and 2 with Nicobule 127 F 1; guest friends in Berve s.v. Iphicrates, Pindar; A. 2.5.9. *Companions*: C. A. Trypanis, Rhein. Mus. (1963) pp. 289 f. sees their contrast with kinship; cp. F. Carrata Thomas, Gli eteri dell Aless. Magno (1955) for a collection of their different names. The term *idioxenos* may have been applied to Philip's Greek courtiers and there may have been a growing class of (official) Friends; the terminology of Diodorus (despite K.M.T.-Atkinson Aegypt. (1952) pp. 204ff.) does not suffice to prove this. *Hetairideia*: Athen. 527D. *Philip and glory*: Speusippus's letter, published by E. J. Bickermann–J. Sykutris in Abhandl. der Sachs-Akad vol. 80 (Leipzig, 1928) is splendid evidence, together with much of Isocrat., e.g. Philipp. 114, 118–20, 132–145. Compare the similar fragments of Euripides's Archelaus, ed. Nauck: e.g. 236–240, 244 and 246. For Alex.; Demades, Peri Dodekaet. 12 is contemporary evidence. *Man's motives*: Thuc. 1.75–76, 3.82. *Alex.'s favourite Homeric line*: e.g. P. De Fort. A. 1.3 (the line varies in other sources). All these anecdotes in their various forms should be read with care, because of the Second Sophistic's taste for Homeric parallels, esp. on duties of kingship: cp. O. Murray JRS (1965) pp. 161ff., with copious notes. Cp. Lucian, Dial. Mort. 12. *Homeric dream*: P. 26.3; Steph. Byz. s.v. Alexandreia tells a similar story, referring it to Jason of Argos and making it suspect, unless Jason and Heracleides took it from a reliable prototype (as I suggest). The possibility that its teller

Heracleides, may have been the Alexandrian author says nothing for its truth; it is very simple-minded to trust local historians for local 'facts'. *Lowlanders from Crete*: S. 6.3.2, 6; S. 7 F 11. Aristot. F 443 (all refer to Bottiaea). *Mycenae*: Paus. 7.25.6.

NOTES TO CHAPTER 4 (pp. 68–80)

Thessaly: DS 17.4.1, J. 11.3, Polyaen. 4.3.23. *State of Greece*: note esp. P. A. Brunt CQ (1969) pp. 245ff.; the more open society can be gleaned at Athens from J. K. Davies, Ath. Prop. Families (1970) with S. Perlman, Athenae (1963) p. 327 and P. del P. (1967) p. 161; note, e.g., the origins of Lysander, Epaminondas, Iphicrates, and the internal arguments in mid 4th c. Sparta. *Arbitration*: Tod 179 and on the League U. Wilcken, Sitzb. Berl. Akad (1922), pp. 97ff., (1929) pp. 291ff. (fundamental, but to be read critically). *Garrisons*: P. Arat. 23.2, DS 16.87.3, 17.3.3, Ael VH. 6.1. *Freedom*: Polyb. 9.28 with 18.13–14; note SIG³ 317. *Sparta*: G. E. M. de Sainte Croix, Orig. of Pel. War (1972) cites the evidence; the alliances with Athens in the Peloponnese of the 340s should be viewed against Sparta's commitment elsewhere in S. Italy; when the Spartan king returns, Peloponnesian states promptly look to Macedon again. *Diogenes*: P. 14.2, A. 7.2.1, P. Mor. 331. *Invincible*: P. 14.6, DS 93.4, SIG 251 H with Tarn vol. 2 p. 338. Hyp. in Dem 32.4. S. Weinstock HTR (1957) pp. 211ff. (brilliant). *Philip's drill*: Polyaen. 4.2.1, 2.2, 2.15. Front. Strat. 4.1.6. *Servants*: Thuc. 3.17.3, 7.75.5, IG 2² 1751 (*therapontes* are servants), Theophr. Char. 25.4, Hdt. 7.229 and 9.29 (seven Helots per Spartiate!). *Supplies*: Front. Strat 4.1.6, Polyaen. 4.2.10, Polyb. 16.24.5, 9 (on figs). Dem. 18.157 on allies' responsibilities is very interesting (cp. Tod 183 and notes and for the principle, Thuc. 6.31.5, Xen. Cyrop. 6.2.38). *Philip's engineers*: E. W. Marsden, Gk and Rmn Artillery (1969–70) is the definitive work: Ath. Mech. W. 10.5f. Philon. Par. 83.7. *Right wing*: Polyaen. 5.16.2 (Pammenes) and so already in 359 known to Philip (DS 16.45). Contrast left wing at Leuctra: P. Pelop. 23.1. *Cavalry*: Theopomp. F 225 B (what date in lines 30?); DS 16.4.3 with 17.17.3–5. *Mares*: J.9.2. Contrast horses on coins of Alex. I with those on Philip's or in the Dion tomb-drawing of the late 4th c. (PAE (1930) p. 45) or on the Alex.-Sarcophagus. *Companions*: V. von Graeve, Der Alexandersarkophag (1970) pp. 88f.; A. Rumpf. Abh. Berl. Akad (1943) pp. 1ff. In art, e.g. Alcetas's tomb at Termessus. Elsewhere, I mean to survey the growing numbers of monuments showing Macedonian soldiers. *Cavalry tactics*: Hdt. 4.126–28, Thuc. 7.30, Xen. An. 6.3.7–8, Thuc. 7.78f., Xen. Cav. Comm. 7–8. *Macedonian horsemen*: Thuc. 2.100, cp. Xen. Hell. 5.2.41. Note the coins of Alex. I with horseman and two spears, one for lancing, the other for throwing. It is conceivable that the Companions copied this and that art only shows them with their second spear. *Cavalry spears*: A. 1.15.5, contrast Xen. Hell. 3.4.14 and Polyb. 6.25. *Sarissophoroi*: Berve vol. 1 p. 129. M. Rostovtzeff, Iranians and Greeks in South Russia (1922) plate 29; J. Baradez, Tipasa, ville antique (1952) p. 18 and perhaps the *kontophoroi* of Roman armies in the east: A. Tact. 4.3, S.10.1.12. Medieval Crusading cavalry were said to use lances up to 20 cubits long (Ibn Munqidh 1.131); cp. the seal of Pons of Tripoli in G. Schlumberger, Sigillographie de l'Orient (1943) plate 18. nr 5. *Prodromoi*: advised in Xen. Hipp. 1. For two-handed sarissa, cp. the example in F. Studnicza JDAI (1923–4) pp. 68–72. *Wedges*: Asclepiod. Tact 7.3; Migne Patrol. Graeca 36.61A; AA. 1.6.3, 3.14.2; A. Tech. Tact. 16.6. *Harness*: J. K. Anderson, Anc. Gk Horsemanship (1961) pp. 40–78, also I. Venedikov, Bull. de l'Inst. Arch. Bulgare (1957) pp. 153ff.; P. Vigneron, Le Cheval dans l'antiquite (1968) chap. 2 (excellent). *Foot Companions*: the word 'phalanx' in A. simply means an infantry line (e.g. A. 5.21.5), as elsewhere in Greek, and should not be applied to the sarissa-brigades only as a technical term. *Sarissa*: M. Andronicos BCH (1970) pp. 91ff.; also Theophr. HP 3.12.2 = Asclep. Tact. 5.1; Polyb. 18.29.2 (starting from Hellenistic lengths). Compare the Pangaeum stele in BCH (1931) p. 172 n.1. The 'short Macedonian cubit' is a fantasy: cp. Xen. Anab. 4.7.6 for a short Chalybian cubit! In early Egyptian chronicles there are references to enemies 'five cubits' high; there was no short Pharaonic cubit. The cornel trees would be *Cornus mas* and possibly *australis*. *Sanguinea* is too flimsy. *Philip's invention*: DS 16.3.2 (a long process) with Marsyas FGH 135 F 17. Spear-heads in D. M. Robinson, ed., Olynthus vol. X pp. 378–446 are perhaps sarissas, though not as long as Andronicos's finds at Vergina. Cp. those found in Lion of Chaeronea; Polyaen.

4.2.2 (mentioning *synaspismos*, a phalanx manœuvre) suggests the Foot-Companion formation fought at that battle, but all its accounts are vague and arguments from 'silence' of no weight. *Files and cloaks*: Callisth. in Polyb. 12.19.6; A. 1.6.1 for basic 8-depth, against the dekades of A. 7.23.3 and the Anaxim. fragment, FGH 72F4. Asclep. 6.2 and Arr. 15.2 imply 16 became the Hellenistic depth. Plut. Aem. Paul 18.3 (cp. Xen. Anab. 1.2.16) on cloaks. *Origins*: DS 15.44 (8½ feet to 13 feet?) Nep. Iphicr. 1.3–4, Chabr. 1; Xen. Anab. 1.8.9, Cyrop. 6.2.10; 7.1.33. Hdt. 7.8.1 (for the Egyptian precedent); Townley Schol. to Iliad 13.152 with Polyb. 18.29–30. Asclepiod. Tact. 4.3 (important); see now W. K. Pritchett, Anc. Gk. Milit. Practices vol. 1 (1971) pp. 144f. (more archaeological evidence now available than he uses for Macedonian shield and too dogmatic in assumptions). *Armour*: G. T. Griffith P.C. Phil. Soc. (1964) pp. 3ff. is unconvincing; breastplates may be costly (Aristoph. Peace 1210f. is not all absurd) but Philip had mines, could use leather (note the bonfire of spare armour in QC 9.3.22) and A. 1.20.10 implies Macedonians did all wear body-armour? cp. A. Hagemann, Griechische Panzerung (1919) for fuller archaeological evidence; cp. too the breastplated Ptolemaic footsoldier in Berytus (1964) pp. 71ff. Sometimes certain brigades of the Foot Companions are called 'the lightest' or 'most mobile': e.g. A. 3.23.2. Perhaps these were centre men without much body armour, a notion which helps with a frequent editorial blunder in the text of A. At A. 2.23.2, 4.23.1, 6.6.1 the one and only reliable Ms. (A) reads *astheteroi*, which must not be emended to *pezhetairoi*; A. 7.10.5 has the two terms together in the Ms. implying they are distinct! Some of these *astheteroi* were (partly) led by Coenus the Elimiot, then by his successor Peithon, and served in the centre of the 'phalanx', where one would expect lighter troops; Coenus's brigade was often chosen by Alex. to join the Shield Bearers on lighter raids (Amyntas's brigade in 330 may have been similar). The meaning of their name is obscure and A. 4.23.1f implies (wrongly?) that it covered all Foot Companions; there were not towns or citizens (*asthetairoi*?) in Elimea, for example. *Macedonian shield*: M. Launey's masterpiece, Recherches sur l'armée hellenist. (1949) pp. 346ff. P. Couissin, Institut. Milit. et navales (1932) pp. 76ff. R. Zahn. Festschr. für C. Schuchhardt p. 48; if the soldier with such a shield on King Patraos's Paeonian coins is a Paeonian (more prob. a Macedonian), this shield may have been another of Philip's borrowings. Cp. also the bucklers on the coins of many Macedonian military colonies in Asia minor: e.g. L. Robert, Villes d'Asie Mineure pp. 32–3. Asclepiod. Tact. 5.1 for size. *Daggers*: P. Aem. Paul. 20.5. *Cretans and slingers*: Olynthus X pp. 378–446. *Shield Bearers*: probably Philip's creation. Theopomp. ap. Schol. Dem Olynth. II (Dindorf p. 76) is too confused to be relevant. *Armour*: the Macedonian troops on the Alex. Sarcophagus are armed as I describe; despite von Graeve pp. 93–5, these cannot be Foot Companions, for their shields are too big to allow them to hold a sarissa. Shield Bearers surely carry a proper shield (hence, e.g., A. 1.1.9) and therefore no sarissa, as both hands are occupied. *Their lightness*: A. 2.4.3, and e.g. A. 3.18.1 and 3.18.5, 3.28.2–3 are decisive. Naturally they are called part of the 'phalanx', because phalanx means no more than infantry line (or units). *Slaves and harvest-armies*: A. W. Gomme, Hist. Comm. Thuc. vol. 1 pp. 14ff., Thuc 1.141.3: *Population*: the regaining and seizure of highland tribes (populous enough to provide all or most of Alex's. Foot Companions – Berve 1 p. 114 with DS 57.2, where I guess that Craterus the Orestid and Amyntas the Tymphiot led Orestids and Tymphiots, making two brigades from each of these two tribes which Philip first made part of 'the Macedonians') and the seizure of the new populous 'East Macedonia' are not allowed for in attempts to calculate a rising birth rate inside Macedonia from 359 to 320. Also, the possible recruitment of serfs as Macedonians could swell numbers. *Slaves*: e.g. Polyaen. 4.2.21, J. 9.7.15, Dem. 19.305, 19.139. P. Alex. 16.2 is explained by Etym. Magn. s.v. Daisois (harvest month); the festival Daisia (harvest?) is now known in an inscription from Lyncestis, c. 2nd c. B.C., F. Papazoglou, Klio (1970) pp. 305ff.

NOTES TO CHAPTER 5 (pp. 81–90)

J. 9.1–4 is the background (with QC 8.1.24?) to A.-Ptol. 1.1.4–1.4.8 and S.-Ptol. 7.3.8 (the quotations A. 1.4.7–8 and Ptol. F2 differ, but suggest Ptol. personally had read his Hdt.; cp. Hdt. 4.93). *Agrianians*: A. 1.5. *Dionysus*: Suet. Aug. 94.5, Macrob.

512

Sat. 1.18, with Aristot. Mirab. 122, Hdt. 6.125, and BCH (1961), pp. 812ff. for finds there; cp. the Dionysiac vase and papyrus in Arch. Deltion (1963) pp. 192ff. *Hounds*: Polyaen. 4.2.16, also Aen. Tact. 22.14. *Rafts*: Xen. Anab. 1.5.10; their history extends from Assyrian sculptures to the *utricularii* of the Roman army. Hdt. 4.72 (Scythian stuffed horses). *Illyrians*: N. G. L. Hammond BSA (1966) p. 239. *Olympias's murders*: J. 9.7.12, 12.6.14, Paus. 8.7.7. *Demosthenes*: Aesch. 3.239, Dein. 1.10.18. P. Dem. 20. *Theban background*: J. 9.4.6, Paus. 4.27.5, 9.1.3. Demades Perites dodekaetias 3f. *Returned boeotarchs*: A. 1.7.11. *Siege*: A.-Ptol. 1.7.7, 1.7.10–11, 1.8.5 stresses Alex.'s hesitation to attack (cp. P. 11.7, D.S. 9.2). A.-Ptol. 1.8 blames Perdiccas, Ptolemy's enemy; contrast DS 12.3 (surely correct). A.-Ptol. stresses Thebes' deeply divided opinion (1.8.11, cp. P. 11.12); Macedonians only enter the city through Theban apathy (1.8.5) and win easily (1.8.5f.), the lesser Boeotians excelling in the sack (A. 1.8.8. with DS 13.5, J. 11.3.8, P. 11.5). But DS 9.1 stresses Theban unanimity, enthusiasm (9.5, 10.2, 10.6, 11.4) and strong resistance; possibly the reserves in 12.1 are the force under Antipater mentioned in Polyaen. 4.3.12. All agree on the sally from the Cadmeia; only DS mentions Macedonian losses (DS 14.1). *Fate of city*: A.1.9.9 implies razing was referred only to the allies on the spot (mostly Boeotians). P. 11.11 is unspecific; DS 14 describes a decree of the full allied council, cp. J. 11.3.8, but the Theban sack became a favourite theme for rhetoric. The sequels at Athens etc. (A. 1.10) seem to me to fit better with an on the spot meeting. Given the Boeotians' part (stressed too by DS 13.5) the point is an academic one; an official ratification would eventually follow. *Sale of captives*: Cleit. F. 1 must be read in the context of Athen.'s speaker (4.146–8), concerned to minimize Greek wealth and probably not quoting directly but summarizing (unfairly) Cleit.'s description. Surely, Cleit. is the source of DS 14.4 too, where it is not entirely clear that this silver was raised solely from the sale of captives. The huge (unsold) plunder in 14.1 is not inconsistent with Cleit. F 1 (the second part of which probably is not Cleit.), given the tendency of Athen.'s quoting speaker to minimize Greek wealth. The 'whole wealth' means 'the whole wealth Alex. realized'. For price of slaves in smaller lots, cp. W. K. Pritchett Hesp. (1956) p. 277. Captives were sold as a block-bargain, e.g. Hellen. Oxyrr. 12.4, Thuc. 8.28.4 (20 drachs. a head!). *Theban losses*: D.S. 14.1 = P. 11.12. *Pindar's house*: P. 11.6 and A. 1.9.10 with Pindar F 106. Dio Chrys 2.33. W. Slater, Gk. Rmn. Byz. St. (1971) p. 141 is unconvincing. *Corn fleet*: does Ps.-Dem. 17, esp. 20, refer to autumn activities of Alex.'s Danube fleet in 335? Hence no mention of the Theban disaster (contrast G. L. Cawkwell Phoenix (1961) p. 74, dating the speech *c.* 332/1). But Macedonia already held Sestos and the Hellespont in 335 and the advance force needed food. *Athenian victims*: P. Dem. 23 (Aristob., despite Jacoby); DS 15.1, P.Phoc. 9, Suida s.v. Antipatros (10 victims); A. 1.10.4 (Ptol. not Aristob.?). *Festival*: DS 16, A. 1.11. *Marriage proposal*: DS 16.2, P. Dem. 23.5; Berve s.v. Balakros 200, Koinos 439. A. 1.24.1–2. *Parmenion's friends*: Philotas 802, Nicanor 554, Asandros 165, Koinos 439, Hegelochos 341, Amyntas 57, Attalus 181, Polyperchon 654, Simmias 704. *Italian invasion*: Aristot. F 614 (Rose). J. 12.2.1, 23.1.15, S. 6.280, Livy 8.24.4. *Alex and Rome*: S. 5.23.2 is plausible; Memnon FGH 434 F 18, 2 slightly less so (cp. the surprising parallel in Ps.-Callisth. A. 1.29–30). Also, W. Hoffman, Rom u. die Griech. Welt in 4 Jhdt. (1934) for a summary of the background.

NOTES TO CHAPTER 6 (pp. 91–105)

Antipater and Olympias: Berve s.v.; also Berve s.v. Cleopatra for their quarrels; Tod GHI 196 lines 10 and 21 prove Olympias to be queen-regent of Macedonia, Cleopatra of Epirus; their two kingdoms are missing from the grain list and their presence as the only two private individuals (with massive receipts) is otherwise absurd. *Greek invasion*: Philostr. VS. 1.9.4, Lys. 33, Xen.Hell. 6.1.12, Isocr. 5.119, Paus. 6.17.9, P. Mor 1126D. Isocr. Epist. 3.3 is important; cp. 5.18, Panath. 10–14, Philipp. 129–131. N. H. Baynes, Byz. Studies and Other Essays pp. 144–67 (excellent) and S. Perlman, Histor. (1957) pp. 306–17. *Peace among allies*: Tod GHI 177, 183, Ps.-Dem. 17 (very important), Tod 179, 192 and esp. A. Momigliano, Terzo Contrib. alla Storia (1966) pp. 406ff. *Athens*: the extraordinary inscription best discussed by M. Ostwald TAPA (1955) pp. 103–28. *Victory coins*: A. R. Bellinger Studies, pp. 12–13 misses the point.

H. A. Thompson, Ath. Stud. pres. W. S. Ferguson (1940) pp. 183ff. may be right; S. Perlman NC (1965) p. 57 is suggestive; note DS 18.26.6 for the *nike* theme. *Alex.'s view*: Onesic. F 19, DS 62.7. *Crusade*: not to the fore in Isocr. (but cp. 4.3.15); DS 16.89.2, J.9.4.6–10, A.2.14.4 with P. Pericl. 17 and Thuc. 1.96.1. Polyb. 3.6.12–14 is very interesting. *Athens*: Lycurg. in Leocrat.; Ps.-Dem. 17 passim; Hypereid. 3.29–32, cp. now F. W. Mitchel, Athens in the age of Lycurgus (1970). Polyb. 5.10 is misleading: 1G 2²1628.22 on Athens's ships (cp. DS 18.10.2). Also U. Kahrstedt Hermes (1936) pp. 120ff. on the Athenian contingent. A. (via Ptolemy, the eventual guarantor of Greek freedom?) does not bring out the full force of Greek and Athenian hostility to Macedonia, anyway a strange idea to him. *Thespians*: A.P. 6.344. *Sicily*: Berve s.v. Demaratus. *Use of satraps*: Isocr. Philip 103–4. *Callisthenes*: FGH 124 with F. Jacoby, R–E (Pauly) 10.2.1680, an excellent survey, though Call. is not known to have been pro-Theban or keen for a national regeneration! T2 is probable, but not certain evidence of his precise kinship to Aristotle; Chares F 15 proves their very intimate link, presumably as pupil and tutor (A. B. Bosworth Hist. (1970) pp. 407ff. is only a quibble and certainly does not damage a close link between Call. and many Peripatetics). Cp. T 23 with F 42, F 10 (Troy), F 23, 24, 29 (early poetry, F 19, F 38 (Hdt.). *Silliness*: T 5, P. 54, T 20 and esp. T 21 (the scholarly Philodemus is probably reliable); F 1 (heiress), F 50 (Sparta), F 43 with J. K. Davies, Ath. Propertied Families (1970) pp. 50–51; the myth of Socrates's two wives was so decisively refuted by E. Zeller, Die Philos, der Griechen (1963) vol. 2, 1.54 that it is surprising it should at once reappear in CQ (1970) p. 56; F 46. *Panegyric*: T 20, F 2. One should remember the shaky literary models open to Call. for his history of a king (Cyropaed., Theopomp. and so on). The reference to Dar.'s death in F 14 line 25 proves that this section was not published as a hot-line despatch and sent back to rebellious Greece in 331. *Athens and Egypt*: F 51 with Anaxim. 72 F 20 and Plato Timae. 23D. *Crusade*: Jacoby on F 28 is ingenious; F 10 may be relevant; F 36 proves nothing. *Homer*: T 10, perhaps T 6, F 10A, 12, 13, 14, 32, 33, 53. L. Pearson, Lost Hist. of Alex (1960) pp. 36ff. is right in principle but not in detail. *Persia*: see end bibliography for most of what follows. *Empire's fringes*: P. 65.6, a favourite story, cp. Hdt. 1.134.2. *Darius*: Berve. s.v., also s.v. Bistanes Ochou, cp. A. 2.14.5. *Communications*: P. 69.1 with the slow letter in L. Robert Hellenica vol. 7 p. 7 and A. Aymard R.E.A. (1949) p. 340. F. Oertel, Festschr. Braubach (1964) pp. 32ff. discusses Damastes FGH 5F 8 in terms of a journey by Suez Canal, for which cp. J. Breebart, Mnemosyne (1967) pp. 422ff. F. Lammert, R–E. 21.2. cols. 2438–42 rightly stresses the many floating boat bridges in the Empire. On fire-signals, a neglected topic, Aeschyl Agamem. 282 for the Persian word; Aristot. Meteor. is essential. On camels, I quote a Chinese Tang traveller to Bactria, as in E. H. Schafer's remarkable study in Sinologica (1950) pp. 165ff. *King's personal rule*: much earlier evidence, esp. Persep. Fort. Tabl. 6764; cp. Jos. A.J. 13.4.4, Hdt. 3.84 on brooches. The personal tradition lasted, hence the art of the royal handshake in Sassanid times. *Honoured equals*: Xen. Cyrop. 2.1.3, 7.5.7 and esp. DS 17.59 for a thousand Royal 'Relations' in army. *Bureaucracy*: for birth-rations, Persep. Fort. Tablets, ed. R. T. Hallock (1969) nr. 1219; Cp. Hdt. 1.136. The weights and measures in Aramaic evidence from Elephantine match those in the Persepolis tablets. *Supply-tickets*: Persep. Fort. 1351, 1358, 1404. *Persian weakness*: end to Xen. Cyrop., prob. genuine. Isocr. 4.140–9, 5.95–100. For her power, compare her fleet in 334/3 with the similar reports in the Egypt invasion of DS 15.42f. *Alex.'s surveyors*: note Tod. GHI 188 with SEG 14.376 and H. Bengtson Symb. Osl. (1956) pp. 35ff. on Philonides. *Supplies*: Xen. Cyrop. 6.2.25–40 is basic; in 396, Agesilaus's small army took food to Asia for 6 months (cf. Xen. Hell. 3.4.3), about the same volume as Alex. took. Xen. Anab. 1.10.18 is crucial (400 wagons for 10,000 men for a fortnight). Bakers are prescribed by Nicias for Sicily in Thuc. 6.22; prob. until Issus Alex.'s troops would do their own cooking (A 2.8.1; cp. Xen. Hellen. 7.2.22). There they captured Darius's cooks! Soldiers could also be paid money and left to serve themselves from a prearranged agora, so perhaps Alex.'s supplies were very decentralized. *Persian gardens*: P. Grimal, Les Jardins romains (1943) pp. 86ff. is outstanding; cp. Xen. Oecon. 4.13–14, 20; gardeners, of a sort, can perhaps be detected in Persep. Treas. Tabl. (ed. G. E. Cameron) nrs. 14 and 31. *Age of paradox*: Aeschin. 3.132. *Famine*: Tod GHI 196 line 3 with notes on pp. 275–6. *Fire temples*: K. Schippmann, Iran. Feuerheiligtumer (1968) on a tradition which, as excavations are now proving, extends back to Media., cp. the probable Achaemenid fire-temple found in Seistan and reported by Italians in East and West over the last ten years. *Long lease*: B.E. 9.48, from the 420s.

NOTES TO CHAPTER 7 (pp. 109–115)

Egypt revolt: F. Kienitz, Politische Gesch. Agyptens (1953) pp. 185ff. gives full space to the disputed figure of Khabash; that his revolt continued into 335/4 is still a possibility. *Approach*: A. 1.11.5f, DS 17.2 = J. 11.5.10 (Cleit., and so not a Roman anachronism). *The virgins*: A. Momigliano, CR (1945) pp. 49–53; also G. L. Huxley, Studies in hon. of V. Ehrenberg (1967) pp. 147ff.; E. Manni Miscell. Rostagnea (1963) pp. 166ff.; the dating is uncertain, but Lycophron's millennium may be Alexander's (see below). *Trojan sacrifices*: A. 1.12.1–3 (his word *legousin* does not exclude Ptol. and Aristob. as his sources). DS 17.3; J. 11.5.12; P. 15.8; Ael. V.H. 12.7; cp. Cic. Pro Arch. 24; Symm. Epist. 60.72, Jerome Vita Hilar. 1, Petrarch Africa 9.51–4 follow up the theme. Also Ps.-Call. 1.42.9–12. *Menoitios*: A. 1.12.1 and note the fickle Chares (QC 4.5.22). *Dicaearchus*: F. Wehrli, Die Schule des Aristot. (1967), vol. 1 pp. 13ff., esp. frag. 23. *Xerxes*: H. U. Instinsky, Alex. am Hellespont (1949) is unconvincing, not least because the details of Hdt. 7.43, 54–5 are different from A.; for the gold phiale, cp. A. 6.19.5, where Xerxes is not in question and for the heroic overtones of *phialai* (very relevant here) H. Luschey, R. E. s.v. Phiale, with cult evidence. *Thessalians*: Philostrat. Heroicos (ed. Teubner) p. 208, line 8f.; also Heliodor. Aethiopica 3.5; did the cavalry all stay with Parmenion (A. 1.11.6)? *Caracalla*: Dio 79.16.7, 18.2 and F. G. Millar, Studies in Cassius Dio (1964) pp. 214ff. I am grateful to Mr C. G. Hardie for drawing this to my attention. *Homeric road*: Hom. Il. 6.13–15. *Alex.'s favours for Troy*: S. 13.1.26–7, where he remits the tribute even before his victory.

NOTES TO CHAPTER 8 (pp. 116–125)

Troop-numbers: DS 17.3, with P. Mor. 327 D–E (A. 1.11.3 prefers Ptol. to Aristob.). P. 15.1, J. 11.6.2, Call. ap. Polyb. 12.19.1; on the squaring with Polyaen. 5.44, D.S. 7.10 (which names Macedonians in advance force), see e.g., P. A. Brunt JHS (1963) pp. 34ff., and R. D. Milns JHS (1966) pp. 167ff. All figures are speculative; the cavalry are esp. uncertain. *Cyzicus*: Polyaen. 5.44.5, DS 17.7. *Memmon's wages*: Ps.–Aristot. Oecon. 1359B. *Lampsacus*: the common source of Paus. 6.18.2, Val. Max. 7.3.4 and Suida s.v. Anaximenes is not likely to be good, but there may be one truth in this favourite sort of anecdote, that Alex. did at least visit the place. At A. 1.12.6 the only reliable MS. reads *prosaktios*, usually emended to the dubious River Praktios, with a curious twist in Alex.'s route as a result, up an impassable river gorge (W. F. Leaf, Strabo on the Troad (1923) pp. 71ff. has full geography). If we read something like *par' akten*, along the coast, Alex. would go naturally north to Lampsacus, a city of known abundance: cp. Xen. Hell. 2.1.19; note Ps.-Ar. Oec. 1351 for Persian minting there. *Persian plans*: A. 1.12.9 = DS 18.2 = Call. via a Persian captive, perhaps Barsine, Memnon's bilingual wife? *Tyrant at Zeleia*: SIG³ 279 with Berve s.v. Nikagoras are enough proof, to my mind. *Memmon's coins*: A. E. M. Johnston JHS (1967) p. 86. *Persian estates*: a vast subject. Xen. Hell. 3.1.25–7, 3.2.12, 4.1.15–16, 4.1.33. Xen. Anab. 4.4.2, 4.4.7, Oecon. 4.5, 4.20. P. Alcib. 24 and esp. Xen. An. 7.8, showing that 200 serfs were a mere handful! Who owned the eleven *choroi* at the source of the Granicus – Kaibel Epigr. Graec. nr 335? Persians, surely; cp. E. Benveniste, Paideuma (1960) p. 199 for Persian name for these domains. On *pyrgos – tyrsis – baris*, cp. L. Robert, Noms indigènes en Asie Mineure (1963) pp. 14–16, with bibliography. J. Keil-Premerstein, Dritte Reise, p. 102 gives the ground plan of one such 'tower'. *Daisios*: P. 16.2, Etym. Magn. s.v. Daisios. *Persian numbers*: A. 1.14.4, but DS 19.5 gives even fewer horse. *Persian armour*: Xen. An. 1.8.7, On Horsemanship 12; P. Bernard, Syria (1964) p. 195 is remarkable, amplifying J. K. Anderson JHS (1960) pp. 7–8, who cites an armoured Thessalian on a coin, perhaps relevant to Alex.'s cavalrymen? cp. E. Ebeling Zeits. Assyr. (1952) pp. 203ff. *Battle*: See my forthcoming study. P. 16 is similar to A. 1.13–16, despite additions and slips of memory; Aristob. ap. P. 16.15 = A. 1.16.4 but Aristob. certainly was not P's sole source or A.'s only authority. A. 1.13–16 must be agreed by Ptol. too.

DS 19–21 = Fragm. Sabbait. FGH 151 F 1 lines 3–4 (encamped); QC 8.1.20 = DS 20.6, against A. and P. Note the Hyrcanians in DS 19.4: exactly right: S. 13.629, Tac. Ann. 2.47, Pliny NH. 5.120; Head, BMC Lydia p. 122; A. Fontrier, Mouseion (1886) p. 11 for the site. I support DS-Cleit. against A.-Ptol.-Aristob.; note Xen. Anab. 3.4.35, QC 3.3.8 on Persian night habits, v. relevant to a dawn battle. *Hatred of Sparta*: e.g. Isocr. 5.74–5, Dem. 5.18, 6.9, 6.13–15; 19.10–11, 260–2, 303–6. See now G. E. M. de Sainte Croix, Origins of the Pel. War (1972) pp. 159ff. and esp. Appendix XXX. *Slogan*: A. 1.16.4, P. 16.18. Who drafted it? Callisthenes? *New Millennium*: Duris FGH 76 F. 41, and for possible Homeric overtones of the month (Thargelion = Daisios) Call. 124 F. 10A and B (important). *Nemesis*: Call. F. 28; cp. J. 11.6.10. For the Bactrians in the Lydian-Ionian force in DS 19.4, cp. the Bactrian names in Ionia in L. Robert, Noms indigènes and 'Orontes the Bactrian', leader of the satraps' revolt in 360s.

NOTES TO CHAPTER 9 (pp. 126–142)

Asia Minor: W. Judeich, Kleinasiat. Studien (1892), G. Glotz-Cohen, Hist. Grecque 4.1 pp. 21ff. Also M. Rostovtzeff in Studies pres. to Wm Ramsay (1923) pp. 366ff; on tyrants and Persian favourites, the lists in H. Berve, Tyrannis bei den Griechen (1967) p. 332–40 and vol. II pp. 690ff. are invaluable; an inscription, as yet unpublished, has been announced by J. Crampa which documents the Persian King's land-tax on Greek estate owners outside the *poleis* in Asia Minor. cp. Xen. Hell. 3.4.25–6 for Persian priorities here; tribute came first. *First moves*: J. 11.6.1, A. 1.17. *Troy*: S. 13.593. *Zeleia*: Berve s.v. Nikagoras with the (undatable) Syll. 1.297. *Sardis*: A. 1.17, with the copious evidence for interference by Persian judges and law in provincial matters: e.g. Hdt. 3.14, 3.31, 5.25, 7.194 and general statement in Dar. Bis. 1.21. Broad survey in E.B. Kraeling Brooklyn Aramaic Pap. (1953) pp. 36ff. In the Cowley papyri from Elephantine, there are Persian judges active in Memphis as well as the colony (16.7, 20.4, 27.9, 42.2 and 7: the *typt* in, e.g., Daniel 3.2 may be police-officers and the *frasaka*, an inquisitor: W. Eilers Iran. Beamtennamen pp. 5–43, Cowley 37 with Eilers p. 28); also in Babylonia passim – e.g. B.E. X. 97, King's canal-judges in B.E. X. 8, 92, judges of Parysatis's household, UM 133, judges of Gobryas's Satrapal Court – B.E. X. 84, 97, 128, judges of the Lands by the Sea – B.E. IX. 75. Also the circuit-trials of the King's Eyes: e.g. Cowley 27.9, Xen. Cyr. 8.6.16; also, garrison-commanders have judicial powers (Cowley 1.3, 25.2, Kraeling 8.2f.) and Sardis had a thousand-strong Iranian garrison and a mass of Hyrcanian colonists bivouacked nearby. Also, Persia persistently encouraged the coups of oligarchs in Greek cities; in view of this brief selection from the documents, the remarks of E. Badian Anc. Soc. and Institut (1966) p. 45 are unfortunate. The Jews are no counter argument, for if Ezra applied the Torah, he also had to apply the King's own law (Ezra 7.25f.). At Sardis, Alex. did bring change, as he announced. *Freedom and democracy*: A. H. M. Jones, Greek City (1940) p. 157, with OGI 222, 226, 229, 237. *Alex. and aristocrats*: A. 5.2.2. *New era*: C. Habicht Gottmenschtum (1970, 2nd ed.) p. 24. *Cult*: S. 14.640, P. Mor. 335A. Habicht pp. 18f. and 251. E.g. SEG 4. 521 for its persistence. *Precedent*: e.g. Lysander (Arch. Anz. (1965) p. 440 – decisive). *Syntaxis*: e.g. Tod 185. A. 1.17.7 implies it was also paid at Sardis, i.e. not confined to a Greek League. Whether the Asian Greeks belonged to the League of Corinth is a modern riddle whose importance escapes me (and, I imagine, Alex.) entirely; E. Badian Anc. Soc. and Inst. pp. 43–53 restates the view of A. H. M. Jones, Greek City p. 316 note 14 as follows: some Greek cities in Asia Minor paid a Contribution; members of the Second Athenian Confederacy paid Contributions; therefore all Greek cities in Asia were members of the League of Corinth. Apart from being a non sequitur, this does not allow for A. 1.17.7, implying (to my mind) that Sardis paid contributions too, without belonging to any league? *Alcimachus*: Berve s.v., with W. G. Forrest, Klio (1969) pp. 201–4. I believe him to be the Macedonian sent to Athens in 338. *Miletus*: A. 1.18.3f with DS 22 (different detail). Motives for fleet in 22.5 = A. 1.20 (mostly) = Call.? With 1.18.7 we should perhaps remember that Ptol. employed the Cypriot fleet himself after Alex.'s death. Is Ptol. or A. responsible for omitting the retained Athenians (DS 22.5)? Xen. Hell. 4.1.14 is relevant for merits of sea, as against land, transport in Asia Minor. The financing of ships by allied Chios in 332/1 (Tod 192.9) was probably not demanded of all allies in 334? *Miletus's magistracy*: Inschr. v. Milet 122. *Darius's son*: Berve Ariobarzanes, nr 116. *Caria*: SIG³ 45, 46, Head. Hist. Num. p. 617 (coins), Pammyes's elegiacs (SEG 4.191), J. M. Cook and G. E. Bean BSA (1955) pp. 143ff. G. Bockisch, Klio (1969) pp. 118ff. amasses a full history of Carian dynasts. *Ada*: S. 14.656, 635 and Berve s.v.; Alexandria by Latmos (Steph. Byz., Alexandria) is probably Alinda, for there is no alternative in that area, to my mind. *Halicarnassus*: G. E. Bean and J. M. Cook BSA (1955) pp. 85ff. is essential, pointing merits of DS 23.4–27. Again, A. omits hostility of Athenians (DS 25.6). Perdiccas's sortie (A. 1.21.1) cannot be a mere fiction of Ptol.'s malice as it also appears in DS 25.5 (DS-Cleit. did not use Ptol.); perhaps it was true, or in Call., and thus inspired Ptol. for his lies at Thebes. *Razing*: Vitruv. 2.8.10–14, Plin NH 35.172 against A. 1.24.6, DS 27.6. Ptol. had campaigned here himself in 309/8, perhaps relevant to his history? *New buildings in Asia*: J. M. Cook BSA (1958) p. 34; Plin. NH 5.117, S. 1.58 (Clazomenae); Erythrae (Plin. NH 5.116) Ilium (DS 18.4.5). *Priene*: Tod 184/5 (where the prefix *basileus* is not decisive for the date). *Land-gifts*: the wording of Tod 186.9–13 strongly recalls similar phrases in SIG 278 lines 9–11, OGIS 9, 10 where Successors also bestow land on Royal Favourites. K. M. T. Atkinson, Antichthon (1968) pp. 32ff. is a good survey, correcting Rostovtzeff's implausibilities. *New owners*: P. Eum. 8 only certain evidence, but satraps, too, should be added. Also Macedonian tyrants such as Eupolemus, Antipatrides (Polyaen. 5.35), Philetairos, Philomelos and the many others marshalled in Berve, Tyrannis (1967) vol. 1 p. 418 and notes to p. 718; they will not have stayed content with ordinary properties. Note, however, the possibility that despite Alex., the descendants of Procles and Damaratus continued their Aeolian estates (and tyranny?) undisturbed – T. Homolle BCH (1896) pp. 505ff. *Serfs*: G. Sventiskaya VDI (1967) pp. 85ff. cites very full evidence, with the proper Party bias. K. M. T. Atkinson pp. 37–41 is decisive against Rostovtzeff's view that serfs were freed. *Hyrcanians*: S. 13.629, Xen. Anab 7.8.15 (splendid evidence), DS 17.19.4 (Spithridates was also satrap of Lydia), the Pozzuoli pillar carved under Tib., Tacitean evidence and the inscriptions are admirably summarized by L. Robert Hellenica (6) pp. 19ff. We should always remember these colonies: cp. A. Keramopoullos Athena (1904) pp. 161ff.; also sites like Cambysene, Xerxene, Dareiou Kome, Cyroupedion. *Citizen-Iranians*: in need of study. The wise remarks of P. Bernard, Syria (1964) pp. 211ff. with full bibliography mark out a subject which I must elaborate elsewhere. *Anahita*: L. Robert, Hellenica (6) chaps. 2–4 is the best survey; the evidence for Asia Minor's Magi now stretches from the Dascylium reliefs to Pausanias, with a correspondingly vast bibliography. cf. P. Herrmann, Ergebnisse einer Reise in Nordost Lydien (1962) for more detail. *Iranian neokoroi*: Berve s.v. Megabyzus and the remarkable inscription (annoyingly unpublished) reported by L. Robert, CRAI (1953) pp. 410–11, also said to contain some 'beaux noms Cariens', confirming that the hellenization of the inland Carians was a matter of the 3rd c. B.C. Note the coins of Maiphernes the Iranian at Celainae (Noms indigènes p. 349) with Anahita as a symbol. Note too the Ephesus magi in P. Alex. 3.7 priests of Artemis-Anahita there.

NOTES TO CHAPTER 10 (pp. 143–151)

Lycian campaign: A. 1.24.5–29. Freya Stark JHS (1958) pp. 102ff. discusses the route, not the qualities of the evidence. *Omen*: P. 17.4, very interesting. *Theodectas*: P. 17.9, Onesic. F 22. *Alex. of Lyncestis*: A. 1.25. Aristob. F 2B, lines 8f., an unnoticed passage probably of some significance for the source-history of Alex.: Alex. of Lyncestis did lead Thracians in 335 (A. 1.25.1) and was certainly thought to be present at Thebes (A. 1.7.6). In this frag 2B, line 24, P. insists the culprit was a Macedonian; P. Alex. 12.3 says 'a Thracian', but this is merely a slip, caused by the fact that Alex. of Lyncestis led Thracians. Despite the frequency of the name Alexander, I am prepared to bet these two Alexanders are the same man and that (once again) Aristob. has (deliberately?) confused a suspect's demise. DS 32.1 has the true date; for Sisines, cp QC 3.7.11 very explicit and credible. *The Lyncestian's nephew*: Berve, s.v. Amyntas Arrhabaiou; A. 1.28.4 with his subsequent disappearance. *Alex. of Lyncestis's death*: DS 80.2, specifying a three-year imprisonment, i.e. an arrest in 333; cp QC 7.1.8 ('three whole years'). QC 8.8.6, 10.1.40 refer to 'two proofs' against the Lyncestian; probably this is an attempt

517

by QC or his source to conflate the two stories of the arrest. Obviously, QC knew both stories, for the absence of the arrest in Bk 3 means he told it in Bk 2, under 334, preferring A.'s version. But his preference is no proof of truths! Naturally, A. did not mark this (probable) discrepancy between Ptol. and Aristob.; under 334, Aristob. said nothing, having said it all in 335 in the Timocleia story, which A. omitted; so he just took Ptol.'s tale, the only one available. *Mount Climax*: Call. F 31; presumably Call. also mentioned divine aid, hence A. 1.26.2 and the general agreement on it by the Alex.-historians, well noticed by Jos. A.J. 2.2.348. *Phrygian march*: QC 3.1.1–8. *Gordian Knot*: A. 2.3, QC 3.1.14, J. 11.7.3, Ael. Nat. An. 13.1. *Macedon and Phrygia*: Call. F 54, Marsyas FGH 135 F 4. cp. E. A. Fredricksmeyer CP (1961) pp. 160f. *Telmissians*: A. 2.3.3. The important point is that Alex. waited till the very last day of his stay: cp. A. 2.4.1. 'on the next day'. Note that the Phrygian god was identified with Zeus the King (A. 2.3.6), particularly appropriate when Alex. was a king under increasingly evident protection of Zeus (e.g. rains at Sardis, eagle at Milet, Climax etc.). Greeks to return home: QC 3.1.9.

NOTES TO CHAPTER 11 (pp. 152–167)

Magi: Aristot. F 6, Theopomp. ap. P. Mor. 370 C, 115 F 65, with J. Bidez-F.Cumont, Les Mages hellenisés, vol. 2. 78. *Naval war*: DS 27.6 (Cos as base). A. 2.1 (note Alex.'s garrison at Mitylene – 2.1.4) and DS 29 belong mostly in May. DS 29.4 is vague, but 31.4 is perhaps too pessimistic (are these Greeks on mainland?). *Piracy*: A. 2.1.2. Alex.'s fleet: QC 3.1.9f. *Mitylene*: A. 2.1.4; presumably a peace was agreed afresh with each new Persian king. Possibly the admirals meant 'be our allies, free and independent as in 386' – but their wording and esp. A. 2.2.3 (Tenedos) imply that the islands had been obliged as allies since 386! This is not impossible, for Persian and satrapal interference in the Aegean, 386–334, needs a new study: cp. Tod GHI 138, 155, 165, Dem. 15.9, Polyaen. 5.44.3, Theopomp. F 121, Dem. 15.3.14 and the evidence, of course, for 336/3. *Alex. and Ancyra*: QC 3.1.22, Call. F 53. *Cappadocia*: S. 12.1.1.4 with Geogr. Graec. Min. (Muller) 2.86. Berve s.v. Sabictas, Abistamenes and the troops for Darius in A. 3.11.7. *Cilician Gates*: Xen. An. 1.2.20, QC 3.4 (QC 3.4.10 = Call. F 32, 33), A. 2.4.3. *Darius*: DS 30, QC 3.2–3; the parallels between Darius's dress and Caligula's alleged dress (Suet. Calig. 52) are one more point that incline me to favour a Claudian date for QC. For the sign of execution, cp. Xen. Anab. 1.6.10. *Naval war*: A. 2.2, QC 3.3.1. A. 2.2.2 shows Pharnabazus left 190 ships in Lycia. H. W. Parke, Greek Mercenary Soldiers (1933) p. 183 maps out the numbers nicely. *Cardaces*: S. 15.734 (this may not be their explanation – cp. the various passages in Stephanus's Thesaurus s.v. Kardax, col. 960 in vol. 5 of the 1841 edition, implying the name merely meant hired troops). *Babylonian colonists*: G. Cardascia, Les Archives de Murasu (1951) is fundamental; on king's estates cp. esp.W. Eilers OLZ (1934) p. 95 for Persian favourites; Cardascia pp. 82–83; fiefs: Cardascia p. 8, also Recueils de la Soc. Jean Bodin (1958) pp. 55ff. and M. Dandamayev, Festschrift Eilers (1967) pp. 37ff. (proving Median origin). *Taxes and collection*: Cardascia pp. 78ff. and esp. 98f. *Inalienable*: cp. San Nicolo, Ungnad: Neubab. Rechtsurk. 1, no. 10 and Hammurapi, Code 36–38. A creditor may seize the harvest but never the land; a woman cannot own it, either. Owner remains liable, despite lease; Ur Excavation Texts IV, nrs. 59, 60, 101, 106. *Continuity of fief in Seleucid times*: Moore, Neobab. Busin. and Admin Docs. (1935) p. 139. *Adopted Jew*: Cardascia pp. 180–1 with parallels. Cp. p. 29 n. 5 and B.E. X. 37 for family's holdings. Compare G. R. Driver, Aramaic Docum. (1957) – e.g. no. 1. On *the Jew's weapons*: E. Ebeling Zeit. Ass. (1952) pp. 203ff. As king drained silver into his own treasuries, silver for a soldier's own maintenance and *ilku* would become scarcer; where were Mesopotamia's silver mines? *Darius's dream*: P. 18.6, QC 3.3.2–5, DS 31.7. *His numbers*: Hamilton HCPA p. 48. *March*: QC 3.3.8 (I imagine this accurate account comes from Cleit. – DS 31 has a place for it. His father Deinon wrote a sound history of Persia). *Alex.'s illness*: DS 31.4 does not mention Parmenion's letter, but his silence (!) proves nothing QC 3.4.15 does not guarantee Parmenion stayed in Tarsus, any more than does A.2.5 (after a long interval). J.11.8.5 may be right; perhaps Parmenion had arrested a spy in Alex.'s rear? In view of Alex.'s sequel, I do not believe QC 3.5.10, DS 31.6. For Parmenion's 'guilt' cp. Ps.-Call. 2.8.25. The variants between P. 19, A. 2.4.7–11, J.

11.8.3–9, QC 3.5–7 are not significant. *Naval war*. A. 2.2 (Persian warships needed daily bases, hence delay in Cyclades). *Parmenion's mission*. A. 2.5.1, Xen. Anab. 1.4. *Anchialus*: A. 2.5.2–4 with Call. F 34, Aristob. F 9, Athen. 530 A, S. 14.5.9. *Soli*: A. 2.5.6, but with 7, cp. 2.13.4 (did Cos fall again?). *Alex. of Lyncestis*: DS 32.1. *Harpalus's flight*: A. 3.6.7, with Tauriscus who was *staleis* (suggesting officially). I guess Harpalus was a spy; if so, is this A.'s error or another example of Ptol.-Aristob.'s ignorance of motives in the inner sanctum? *March and geography*: Ps.-Scylax 102 puts Mallus on R. Pyramus (cp. S. 14.5.16) and Xen. Anab. 1.4.1–6 allows 25 parasangs (i.e. 25 hours' march) to the port of Myriandrus (five hours' march – i.e. on very rough road – from Syro-Cilician Gates, modern Pillar of Jonah). A. 2.6.2's two-day march to near (pros) Myriandrus is perfectly possible at, say, 12 normal hours a day: cp. M. Dieulafoy Mem. de l'Acad. Inscr. et Bell.-Lett. (1914) p. 58 for parallels. Also DS 18.44.2 for possible march-rate of 40 miles per day, 7 days running. *Parmenion's movements*: most interestingly, QC 3.7–8 has muddled the vulgate account and A.'s (ultimate) source into an incoherent whole; cp. Plin. Epist. 5.8.12 for this *onerosa collatio*! DS 32.2–33 does not know that Darius got round into Alex.'s rear (DS 32.4, last sentence is decisive): QC uses this dank preliminary, hence 3.7.5–10, esp. 10 ignores the 2-day march (3.7.5) and implies Alex. waited, on Parmenion's advice, at Issus; then, the Sisines story follows, unknown to A; QC 3.8.12 would fit DS 32.3, 31.2 but then (in defiance of 3.7.10) he picks up A.'s version: A. 2.7.1 = QC 3.8.13–17. Again, crazily, he returns to DS's version: that Alex. simply waited at Issus: 3.8.18 and esp. 19.3.8.20 is an effort to patch up his muddle; 3.8.22–23 = A. 2.8.1, then 2 (at dawn). Defying Call.'s 100 stades, he slips back to DS's 30 stades (3.8.24 = DS 33.1). 3.8.27–3.9 *passim* = A. 3.10.1 = DS 33.4; QC 3.10.4 = J. 11.9.3, 3.11.1–5 goes back to A.'s source; 3.11.7 fits DS again. This muddle (also detectable at Gaugamela) is Curtius at his worst. *Darius's tactics*: if Parmenion's activities in QC 3.7.7's muddle are true, would these barbarians have gone off to warn Darius? *The deserter's advice*: A. 2.6.3 = P. 20. The vulgate gives the same role earlier to Charidemus. C. L. Murison, Historia (1972) pp. 399ff. has now summarized the many old views of these preliminaries, with their refutations and a good map; I believe he has placed Issus too far south, while his pp. 420–1 make several unwarranted deductions which are not in any source (no agent would in fact have slipped out of Soli to warn Darius in Syria, because they probably, like Alex., had no idea he was there).

NOTES TO CHAPTER 12 (pp. 168–177)

Alex.'s speech: a very interesting problem. A. 2.7.3 may well not be A.'s own free composition; DS 33.1 = A. 2.7.3 on god's evident favour (perhaps not the most obvious comment in Alex.'s position?). J. 11.9.2–7 is strikingly close to QC 3.10 and surely due to Cleit. (QC 3.10.1–2, preceding it, = DS 33.4 = Cleit.). QC places his speech where A. puts his last-minute exhortation (A. 2.10.2), but even so they have parallels: e.g. A. picks up QC and J.'s theme of a different point to each unit (but he harps on Persian softness, not plunder) and also the prospect of conquering all Asia; A. 2.7.6 = QC 3.10.5 = J. 11.9.6 (*cumulus* picks up A.'s own favourite word *peras*). I would much like to know if Alex. did mention this vast prospect already (cp. A. 2.3.7); however, A. may have composed his speech from 'outside information' in Cleit and the vulgate, where the theme of world conquest was always present. At 2.7.8 the *legetai* (by whom? Ptolemy?) shows the Xen. ref. is not A.'s own. *Sacrifices*: Pap. Oxyrrh. FGH 148, 44 col. 2. *Battle-site*: A. Janke, Auf Alexanders des Grossen Pfaden (1904) p. 53 (accepted with bad arguments by F. W. Walbank, Hist. Comm. on Polyb. vol. 2, on Polyb. 12.17.3). W. Dittberner, Issos (1908) argued well for the Payas; the two decisive measurements are the 100 stades initially between Darius and Alex. (Polyb.-Call. 12.19.4: the northerly Deli requires this to be *c.* 160 stades) and esp. the 14-stade field width (Polyb.-Call. 12.17.4. Untrue of the wide Deli). *Persian scoutings*: A.2.8.5, QC 3.8.27–30. *Battle-sources*: Call. F 35 has strongly affected A. 2.7–11 (though Ptol. goes one wilder: A. 2.11.8–9 exceeds Polyb. 12.20.4; A. 2.10.3 implies Alex. was the first to launch into a charge – cp. A. 2.7.4, A. 2.10.1 for Persian cowardice; Polyb. 12.18.11 implies Persians began the charge on Alex.'s right, unless Polyb. has muddled Darius's right wing with Alex.'s. Call.-Polyb. agrees with A.'s flank-guard in Alex.'s line, the order of his approach march and its thinning, Darius's place in the centre and his 30,000 Greek mercs (A. 2.8.6 = QC 3.9.2 = Polyb.-Call 12.18.2) and his 30,000 front-line cavalry (A. 2.8.5 = Polyb.-Call. 12.18.2). Call.-Polyb. does not number the Cardaces, but A. gives 60,000 and QC 3.9.3, 5 give 40,000 + 20,000 foot on Darius's left and left centre. So presumably Call. gave 60,000 too. A. 2.8.6 calls them hoplites, not peltasts, but e.g., A. 1.1.8 (cp. Polyaen. 4.3.27, line 10, Teubner 1887 edit.) shows that to a Greco-Roman a hoplite meant an 'armed man'. It could even apply to a Foot-Companion. A. 2.10.3 puts Alex. on right, but does not clash with Polyb.-Call. 12.22.2, *Alex.'s wish to be 'opposite' Darius*; this need only refer to the angle of Alex.'s charge into the centre. QC continues to combine two sources – 3.9 = A. 2.8.5–7, 2.9, 3.11.1–3 = A. 2.9.2, 2.11.2; 3.11.4–9 = DS 33.6–34.4. The vulgate clashes openly with Call.: DS 33.1 = QC 3.8.23, giving 30 stades where Call. gave 100. *Alexander-Mosaic*: A. Rumpf AM (1962) pp. 229–41 seems to me more plausible than B. Andreae, Das Alexandermosaik (1967). *Spoils*: QC 3.11.16, 3.13, DS 36.5, P. 20.6–8. *Persian Queens and ladies*: DS 35.5 = QC 3.11.21–23 with similar stress on Fortune. Ptol.-Ar. – A. 2.12.3–5 = QC 3.12.1–12 = DS 37.3–4. But the stress on legality in A. 2.12.5 is from Ptol. and/or Aristob, an interesting insight. 2.12.6–8 = DS 37.5 = QC 3.12.13–23, ending with moralizing too, which implies this took its cue here from Cleit. P.20 follows A; he does not mention the Hephaistion story. The vulgate (rightly) plays on Alex. and Sisyg's friendship. *Alex.'s wound*: A. 2.12.1 = QC 3.12.2 = Chares F 6 (given by Darius) = DS 34.5 = J. 11.9.9 = Call. surely. *Parmenion's letter*: Athen. 13. 607F–608A – genuine? *Barsine*: Aristob. ap. P. 21, P. Eum 1 – decisive for her being Artabazus's daughter and so of royal blood by Apame, his mother. Married first to Mentor – QC 3.13.14, their children – then to Memnon. cp. J. 11.10.2. QC 3.13.12f. on other important captives; also, QC 3.12.26 = DS 38.2 on Darius's son. *Freedom of Greeks*: Theopomp. F 253 line 21. *Royal Mints*: Bellinger p. 50 summarizes.

CHAPTER 13 (pp. 178–193)

A. H. M. Jones, Cities of the East. Rmn Provs. (1971, 2nd ed.) and V. Tcherikover, Hellenistic Civiliz. of the Jews (English trans. 1961), esp. pp. 40–1 and 90ff. give a cultural outline; G. F. Hill, History of Cyprus (1940) vol. 1 pp. 125–56 and DS 16.42ff. (misdated) are essential. On siegecraft, Y. Yadin, Warfare in Biblical Lands (1963), the definitive work of E. W. Marsden, Greek and Rmn Siege Artillery (1969/70) to which I am heavily indebted, and the important text printed by R. Schneider in Akad. der Wissensch. Göttingen, Philol.-Hist. Kl Abhandl, XII (1912) pp. 1–87 explain the developments of machinery; for defences, cp. F. E. Winter, Greek Fortifications (1971). *Fire-ships*: cf. Thuc. 7.53.4. *Fire-pots*: Polyb. ap. Suida s.v. pyrphoros. *Ships*: L. Casson, Ships and Seamanship (1971) s.v. quinquireme. O. Leuze, Die Satrapieneinteilung in Syrien (1935) pp. 193ff. is for enthusiasts only, and pedantic throughout. *Sources*: at sea, A. 2.13.4–6, QC 4.1.34–39 (DS 48.5–6 = Cleit.), QC 4.5.13–22, A. 3.2.3–7 are crucial, but lack chronology. A. 2.13.3 = DS 48.2 = Call.-Cleit.? on burning of ships: pirates in A. 3.2.4, QC 4.7.18. The letter at A. 2.14 = outline of QC 4.1.10, and so is original, though rephrased (e.g. A.'s own word *achari*: 2.14.8). With 2.14.5, cp. Hdt. 3.2 and the survival of Bistanes son of Ochus (A. 3.19.5). G. T. Griffiths PCPS (1968) p. 33 sets out the evidence for Darius's embassies but draws ingenious conclusions from DS 39.2 which are far too subjective; DS 39.3 = QC 4.5.1 = J. 11.12.3 = Cleit. and so belongs with Tyre's siege, not with A. 2.14 (not implausibly arrogant letter!). The third embassy, DS 54.2 = QC 4.11 = J. 11.12.10 = Cleit. and is surely a misdated muddle, perhaps confused by Darius's wife's death; P. 30.1 attributes this to childbirth, i.e. surely to spring 332 (despite C. B. Welles Loeb DS p. 277!), and A. 4.20.1 may support the date (though she is still alive there – 4.20.2, perhaps an error). Surely this 'third' embassy is A.'s second one; QC and J. combine the sources and so list three embassies, but in fact Cleit. omitted the Marathus one and simply misdated the others! The Halys-offer is the only discrepancy which may conceivably reflect Alex's. dishonesty at Marathus or Tyre, but I doubt it. *Sidon*; Abdalonymus is known as a gardener to DS 47.4 = QC 4.1.16 = P. Moral. 340D = J. 11.10.9 = Cleit., possibly. S. Smith, Practice of kingship in early Semitic kingdoms, in

Myth. ritual and kingship (1958, ed. S. H. Hooke) esp. pp. 58–9 is relevant, with H. E. Hirsch, Archiv. der Orientforschung (1963) p. 5. The thorough work of V. von Graeve, Der Alexandersarkophag (1970) is important, esp. pp. 125–32; A.'s silence may possibly be due to Ptol.'s own experiences in Sidon (against Abdalonymus?) in 312. *Siege of Tyre*: cp. J. 9.2.10ff.; for the 'cause', Polyb. ap. DS 30.18 on laws of war. QC 4.2ff. is mostly very close to DS-Cleit.; he stresses the difficulties (4.3.7 = DS 42.5; 4.2.12 and 4.3.25–26 = DS 44; 4.41 = DS 45.7). Arr.-Ptol.? omits the crucifixions (QC 4.1.17 = DS 46.4 = J. 18.3.18 = Cleit.); A. 2.20.4 omits Perdiccas (QC 4.3.1), perhaps through Ptol.'s bias? The (agreed) heroism of Admetus must be agreed via Call. Chares F 7 ap. P. 24.14 is valuable. *Siege of Gaza*: QC gives Alex. three wounds (rightly?); A. only one. Batis in QC 4.6.29 = Cleit.; also cp. Heges. FGH 142 F 5 with Aristot. F 495–500. E. Rohde, Psyche (1923) pp. 582ff. is suggestive. *Resettlement*: J. 18.3.19 (for Tyre, with siege of Antigonus); Joseph. AJ 13.150f. (for Gaza). *Kings' coinage*: Bellinger, Essays, pp. 50–6 is proof of impossibility of generalizations. The Attic standard, also, was used in Cilicia and Phoenicia before Alex. (cf. A. Reifenberg, Jewish Coins (1947) pp. 8ff.), and perhaps by Azemilk of Tyre (F. Cross, Biblical Archeol. (1963) pp. 110ff. – possibly, however, a coin of 332/1). Kings also issue own coins after Alex.; rarely, but cf BMC Catal. Phoenicia, pp. 19–20, p. 66. *Alex. and Cyprus*: Berve Pnytagoras, with Duris F 12; Pumiathon ruled Citium, the least hellenized port on the island, and so his penalty here would not be surprising. For the great Euagoras's capture of Tyre, cp. Isocr. 9.62, stressing it was taken by force.

NOTES TO CHAPTER 14 (pp. 194–218)

Barathra: DS 16.46, 20.73. Berve s.v. Amyntas, Sabaces. *Egyptian philosophy*: DL proem. 2. *Pers. rule*: G. Posener, La première domination perse en Egypte (1936); E. Seidl, Aegyptische Rechtgeschichte (1956); F. K. Kientiz, Politische Geschichte Aegyptens (1953) cover most of the scanty evidence; the introduction to E. B. Kraeling, Brooklyn Aramaic Papyri (1963) is the best survey of the Aramaic documents. For state monopolies, J. M. Wickersham, BASP (1970) p. 45 usefully points out Hdt. 2.94, as opposed to Ptolemaic practice. Papyr. Rylands 9.7.10 (cp. Seidl pp. 30f.) is evidence for the long tradition of oppressing Egypt's countrymen, no new innovation by Persia, or Cleomenes or Ptolemy. Hdt. 2.149, 3.89, 4.166 gives Persian tribute; W. Spiegelberg, Die sogennante demotische chronik (1914) is an invaluable text, but written strictly from a priest's view. *Temple land*: Kienitz pp. 125–6, citing the Edfu temple's estate. For the garrisons' evidence, see end bibliography on Persia. *Semtutefnakte*: H. Schaefer, Festschr für G. Ebers pp. 92ff. *Priest's power*: Plato Polit. 290 D with J. Gwyn Griffiths CR (1965) pp. 150ff.; cp. O. Murray JEA (1970), p. 141, an excellent inquiry. *Artaxerxes and Apis*: Deinon, ap. P. Mor. 363 C, 355 C, Ael. N.A. 10.28. *Coronation*: only in Ps.-Call. 1.34.2, perhaps confirmed by the official titles in temples; cp. the bust of Alex. in the Pharaoh's crown, in T. Schreiber, Studien über das Bildn. Alex (1903) p. 149. *Pharaoh's divinity*: G. Posener, De la divinité du Pharaon (1960) is not convincing, but marshals the evidence; the best account is still A. Moret, Caract. Relig. de la roy. phar. (1902). *Ethiopia*: QC 4.8.3 with the Nectanebo myth in O. Weinreich, Der Trug Nektanebos (1911); *Callisthenes and Nile*: F 12, not implausible, even in the extreme form of 12 A; J. Partsch Abh. Leipz. Akad (1909) p. 551 is not conclusive against its truth, any more than the circular argument of P. Bolchert Neu. Jahrb. der Kl. Alt. (1911) p. 150. *Alexandria*: A. 3.1.5–3.2. With P. 26.5 compare Ps.-Call. 1.32.4 and Steph. Byz. s.v. Alexandria; QC 4.8.6. *Rhacotis*: S. 17.792, with S.-Eratosth 17.802. G. Jondet, Les Ports submergés de l'ancienne île de Pharos (1916) suggests an earlier harbour. *Motives*: P. 26.2, A. 3.1.5f. cite fame; Vitruv. 2. pref. 4. plumps for commerce. V. Ehrenberg, Alex. u. Ägypten (1926) pp. 23f. stresses the harbour's fine site. I can see no evidence, apart from relative silence, for the view of J. G. Milne JEA (1939) pp. 177ff. that Greek trade with Egypt had dried up; Dem. 56 and perhaps the Naucratis Stele (cp. U. Wilcken AZ (1900) p. 133) imply the opposite. On *Alexandrian trade*: S. 17.793 is most illuminating; on Rhodes' role, see the survey and bibliography of E. Will, Hist. Polit. du monde hellenist. (1966) vol. 1 pp. 133.–86 and the very interesting evidence for the koina of Rhodian merchants, discussed by G. Pugliese Carratelli, Annuario (1939–40) pp. 147ff., only one of which is tentatively dated even to the 3rd c. B.C.! Early Ptolemaic trade was certainly slow to organize itself, however high it ranked in the kings' priorities; cp. E. Ziebarth, Beitr. zur Gesch. Seeraubs u. Seehandels in alt. Griech. (1929) pp. 90ff. for comparative evidence elsewhere. *Naval war*: QC 4.5.13–22 is essential; A. 3.2.3–7 records it, as usual, when announced to Alex. cp. QC 4.8.11. Tod 191 lines 30–2 is very demonstrative; Tod 192 is too imprecise to guarantee that Alex.'s behaviour in A. 3.2.7 flouted its line 15. It may only have been issued after the ringleaders had been sentenced by Alex.; he could say, line 14, that they were to be arrested according to the allies' decree, but like the Spartan ringleaders in 331/0) they had to be tried by him personally, perhaps as his allied oaths specified in dangerous cases. Also, if in line 20 *mechri an* means 'until', not 'as long as' (nothing is decisive for this), then the inscription may belong in an earlier context? Certainly, the comments of U. Wilcken, Alex. the Great p. 120 are too dogmatic. *Visit to Ammon*: C. B. Welles Histor. (1962) p. 271 must be ignored as mistaken throughout; his argument that the foundation date of 25 Tybi means an April date is easily refuted by the likelihood that Ps.-Call. used the Roman calendar, mistakenly, rather than the Ptolemaic calendar, as Welles assumes *Ammon and legend*: A. R. Anderson, HSCP (1928) pp. 7ff. *Motives*: Call. F 14 (I stress that this only survives in S.'s quotation and rearrangement). Note, however, that S.'s wording implies part, at least, of the Alex.-histories was worthy of belief. The mention of Darius's death, as predicted by oracles sent to Memphis, dates Call.'s final version to 330 at the earliest. *Perseus*: in Egypt, Hdt. 2.91.2.15 and A. B. Lloyd, JHS (1969) p. 79; evidence for Perseus in Libya is late (schol. Pind. 10.47; Apoll. Rhod. 4.1513, Ovid Metam. 4.617) and before Alex., he is not said to have consulted Siwah. For his integration, Hdt. 6.53–4, 7.61, 7.150; E. Babelon, Catal. des monn. grecques: Les rois de Syrie, Arménie et Commagène p. 29f., pl. 8.1, p. 38; cp. Malalas p. 199 (ed. Bonn) for the Seleucids and the similar coin types of Mithridates's dynasty; cp. F. Cumont, RA (1905) p.180 and the excellent survey by G. Glotz, Dictionn. Antiqu. s.v. Perseus. As an Argive hero, Perseus would appeal to Alex. the Argead King (cp. Philip V); as a Greek-Persian link, to Alex. the new Persian king. *Arrian's motive*: A. 3.3.1–2 I will discuss in a study elsewhere; I stress again that none of the explanatory clauses (or any other part) can be referred to Ptol. or Aristob. in particular; A. 3.3.6 proves A.'s wide reading and even if Ptol. was responsible, this certainly would not make the motive true, in view of the talking snakes, his own role as Pharaoh and favour for Ammon (Paus. 9.16.1). Not one word of A. 3.3.1–2 can be pinned on any one source and the alleged parallel with QC 4.7.8 does not impress me. *Ammon's origins*: A. Fakhry, The Siwa Oasis (1944) supersedes earlier discussions; J. Grafton Milne, Miscell. Gregoriana (1941) p. 145 draws attention to a possible Libyan original; C. J. Classen, Histor. (1959) pp. 349ff. is incomplete. Amasis was deciphered by Fakhry p. 73; *Cyrene*: F. Chamoux, Cyrène sous les Battiades (1953), dating the Zeus Ammon temple c. 500. *Amasis's mistress*: Hdt. 2.181. Amasis's link with Ammon helps to explain his friend Croesus's consultation there (Hdt. 1.46). *Spread in Sparta*: Paus. 3.18.3, 21.8, DS 14.13.6 (family link). Paus. 5.15.11 for Olympia, with F. Chamoux, Études 2 (1959) p. 31 and the new Siwah papyrus (c. 150 B.C.?) for Parammon; this trio may reflect Egyptian practice. Pindar: Pyth. 4.5.9, esp. 4 line 17; Fragm. 17. Paus. 9.16. Vita Pindari 1.29 (Westermann) Suida s.v. Pindaros. *Lysander* P. Lys 20.4, Paus 3.18.3 Steph. Byz. s.v. Aphute. DS 14.13. *Cimon*: P. Cimon 18.7 (some truth here). P. Nicias 13, 14.7. *Athens*: A. M. Woodward BSA (1962) p. 5, S. Dow HTR (1937) p 184. A. Dain Inscr. grecques du Mus. du Bardo (1936) no. 1 (Zeus Ammon at Athens). IG 2² 1496 line 95, 1GZ² 338 Eurip. Alcestis 112f.; Aristoph. Birds 618. Hipponicus son of Callias had the nickname Ammon (whatever the reason, or merit, of the story). *Ammon in Aegean*: cp. Head, Hist. Numm. under Melos, Mitylene, Lampsacus; also coins of Lycian dynasts in 5th and 4th c. and the most easterly reflection, the hoard of Mesopotamian seal-impressions (from Greek coins), in E. Porada Iraq (1960) pp. 220ff. *Nectanebo*: Fakhry pp. 77–9; his Libyan origin, as argued by Kientiz, Polit. Geschichte Ägyptens (1953), may match up with this building interest. *Curiosity*: A. 3.3.1–2 has the word *pothos* where QC 4.7.8 has an *ingens cupido*; too much must not be made of their particular choice of words, but the theme of 'a strong urge' took root from Call. who (in S.'s quotation) mentioned *philodoxia*. *Aristotle's example*: Aristot. Constit. Cyrene F 531 (Rose) and esp. F 103; cp. Athen. 2.44D. *Cyrene*: DS 49.2, QC 4.7.9. Oddly, A.

7.9.8, in a speech compiled by A. refers to Cyrene's submission; I therefore suspect Ptol. suppressed it under 332/1, for Ptol. was more than a mere 'friend and ally' of Cyrene! *Alex.'s route*: Bayle St John, Adventures in the Libyan Desert (1849) is the finest account; G. Steindorff, Dürch die Libysche Wüste zur Ammonsoase (1904) is also a useful survey, though his description of the site in Z. fur Äg. Sprache u. Altert. (1933) p. 1 (with H. Ricke and H. Aubin) is superseded by Fakhry and marred by mistakes. Of the sources, QC 4.7.10 = DS 49.3 = Cleit., evidently much influenced by Call. (rain, guiding crows, though not the winds). P. 27.2 quotes Call., 29 27.1 may perhaps be his in outline too; the most important comment is in A. 3.3.6, on the multiplicity of stories. Aristob. agreed with crows of Call.; with Ptol's snakes, cp. Theophr. HP. 4.3 and Aristot. Hist Anim. 8.29. What purpose (whether religious or merely marvellous) these snake-guides served in Ptol.'s mind, I do not pretend to know. QC 4.7.30 mentions camels; the description in DS 49.6 and 50 is confirmed in detail by St John and presumably stood in Call. too (who accompanied Alex.?). Eratosth. ap. S. 1.3.4 and 15 is interesting; is the 3000-stade road the direct return route from Siwah to Memphis, for the Paraetonium road is only *c.* 200 miles (1700 stades)? If so, the measurement may be a bematist's. *Oasis*: we must hope for great things from the excavation begun by Ahmed Fakhry and reported in Beitr. zur Ägyp. Bauf. u. Alertumsk. (1971) pp. 17–33 and Zeit. für Papyr. u. Epig. (1972) p. 68, its first find of importance. *Spring of the Sun*: Hdt. 4.181, Aristot. F 153 and esp. Chares F 8, muddled in its geography (the fault of its quoter? cp. F 15) but surely relevant to Siwah. *Bribes*: J. 11.11.6; cp. his story of Alex.'s friends asking if they should worship him as a god (11.11.11), unacceptable on J.'s word alone as he is so bad here. *Alex.'s privileged welcome*: Call. F. 14. *Greeting*: I stand firmly by the views of U. Wilcken Sitzb. Preuss. Akad (1928) p. 576, (1930) p. 159, (1938) p. 101; true, S., quoting Call., cites the other flatteries as *ta hexes*, implying he is narrating them in order. But at *touto mentoi* he breaks off the ordered list, in my opinion, and rounds off the list with the prime flattery of all, the 'express remark' (*rhetos* never meant 'in so many words' in ancient Greek!) that Alex. was son of Zeus. Wilcken's acute reasons for seeing this as the priest's greeting are decisive. Call.-S.'s words 'the priest *hypokrinamenou ton Dia*' show decisively that Call. (and Alex., therefore) identified Zeus and Ammon; cp. Pindar F 17 and, beyond all argument, the Athenian inscription of the 360s, recording offerings to Zeus Ammon: A. Dain, Inscr. Grecques du Bardo (1936) no. 1. For a similar identification of Amun Ra as Zeus Thebaios, cp. BMI inscriptions no 1088 (also late 4th c. B.C.). F. Taeger, Charisma (1959) vol. I, pp. 193–4 n. 17 lists Ammon and Zeus in their interchangeable guises, noting how Greek usage preferred the name Zeus. *Oracle procedure*: J. Cerny BIFAO (1930) p. 491, (1936) p. 40 and esp. in Brown Egyptological Studies vol. 4 (1962) p. 35 with full illustrations; these are all fundamental to DS 50.6–51.2. cp. Lucian De Dea Syria 7. *Inner sanctum*: Fahkry, Siwah Oasis pp. 72–3. *Order of ceremony*: greatly disputed and prob. insoluble. The size of the temple court, at least as visible nowadays, does not leave much room for a full procession as described by DS 50.6 but S.-Call.'s word *themisteia* and the 'nods and signs' (or do *symbola* mean tokens, as Cerny cites for Egypt?) surely guarantees that a procession took place. R. Laqueur, Hermes (1931) p. 467 argues well that *themisteia* entails a procession, so S.-Call. is indeed saying that the Egyptian ritual took place and Alex.'s friends could not hear the boat properly. *Hypokrinomenos ton Dia* means 'playing the role of Zeus' only in the sense of 'speaking his part'. I guess this took place in the sanctum after the procession, however the 'maidens' were crammed into the small court. Certainly I do not think DS 50.6 is a conventional description based on Egyptian practice elsewhere; it definitely picks up Call. and is true for Siwah. Beyond all doubt, as Wilcken stressed, friends did not hear the oracle's message; this was a secret, and remained so. *Pleasing response*: A. 3.4.5. *Sacrifice*: A. 6.19.4–5. Indica 18.11 may be relevant; Indic. 36.3 is not. Xen. Anab. 3.1.6. *Legend's questions*: QC 4.7.26 = DS 51.2 = J. 11.11.9 = P. 27.4 = Cleit, and perhaps many others; P. 27.5, though I doubt if these included Call. (the responses reported at Memphis in F 14 would be an anti-climax if these Siwah questions had been reported by Call.; however, anti-climax was an inevitable part of the truth and perhaps artistically satisfactory for an episode which centred on Siwah). I am impressed by the two sacrifices made according to Ammon's *epithespismos* on the Indus in A. 6.19.4–5, each to different gods in a different way. This perhaps implies a detailed talk at Siwah, unless Alex. was invoking Ammon's name lightly in 325. *Among friends*: P. 47.11–12, also in India. *Usual sacrifice*: A. 6.3.2, where the libation (no less of an honour) is made to Heracles his ancestor and to Ammon and to *the* other gods, such as were his custom. *Tois* allois is decisive, for the sense, that Ammon and Heracles were also part of the 'customary gods'; the text must not be emended (Tarn at his worst), and if anything follows from the mention of Heracles as propator, it is that as next in sequence, Ammon is *pater*, certainly not that he is nothing special at all! Nearchus cp. Ind. 35.8, where the *te* proves the close identification of *Zeus kai Ammon* in Alex.'s mind. *Hephaistion's death*: A. 7.14, P. 72.3, DS 115.6. *Siwah burial*: DS 18.3.5, QC 10.5.4, J. 12.15.7. *Ptolemy's coins*: H. Kricheldorf, Munzen u. Medaillen Sammler (1969) p. 641; O. H. Zervos Amer. Num. Soc. Mus. N. (1967) pp. 1ff. *Local coins*: J. F. Healey NC (1962) p. 65. *Callisthenes's stress*: T 21, F 14 line 19 and 24, F 36; Megasthenes (see my note ad.loc.) in A. 7.2.3; S. 15.1.9. *Seleucus*: J. 15.4.3, DS 19.90.4, Sokolowski, Lois sacrées (1955) nr 24. OGIS 212 line 13, 219 line 26. *Paidios*: P. 27.9 (who were these *enioi*?). Only the new papyrus published in Z. für Papyrol u. Epigr. (1972) p. 68 testifies as yet to Greek at Siwah, and it belongs *c.* 150 B.C. But Greek must have been known since *c.* 500 and Cyrene's visits; the ruler's name of Etearchus, as hellenized in Hdt. 2.32, may tell more of Hdt. than of Siwah's early hellenism. *Egyptian background*: neat summary in M. Gyles, Pharaonic Policies (1956) pp. 48ff.; cp. J. H. Breasted, Anc. Rec. of Egypt 4.942, Hdt. 3.2–4. But Siwah was not a mere puppet of Egypt and though her ritual was Egyptian, she would not necessarily have greeted Alex. by a Pharaoh's title. Did the Memphis 'coronation', if true, precede or follow Siwah? *Opis boos*: A. 7.8.3; J. 12.11.6; neither unimpeachable. *Makedon*: Hesiod (West) F 3, *Spartan kings*: Thuc. 5.16.2, Hdt. 6.57–8, X.Lac.Pol. 15.9, Hell. 3.3. *Hermes ancestry*: Hellanic. 323 F 24A, C. *Plato*: DL 3.1.2, cp. Pythagoras: Porphyr. In Pythag. 2. *Genesis*: the two examples of mere descent quoted by L. and S., genesis, are irrelevant; Hdt. 2.146, Soph. Trachin. 380. Both mean paternity: cp. Call. F 14 line 24, surely not just S.'s word; A. 3.3.2, 7.29.3. This is a stronger claim than, e.g. that made by Ptol. Philadelphus in OGIS 54, who is called Zeus's *apogonos*. *Homeric heroes*– Iliad 24.55, 66. Cp. Hesiod, Theog. 96; U. Wilamowitz, Glaube der Hellenen vol. 1 p. 332ff. for Zeus's fatherhood. *Dionysius*: P. Mor. 338B. *Aegis*: Polyb. 12.12.B (Call. T. 20) and the statuettes in P. Perdrizet's Mon. Piot (1910) p. 598. *Envoys in 324*: DS 113.4. *Lion on womb*: Ephor. 70 F 217 (prob. Ephor. was dead by 330, or at least had written his work). *Thunderbolt*: P. 2.3. *Letter* (*suspect*, *esp. as not in the majority tradition*): P. 27.8, as opposed to *hoi pleistoi*. *Callisthenes*: A. 4.10.2: could be a later anecdote, but A. 4.10.1 may only show A. had not read Call.'s history. Eratosthen. ap. P. 3.3. (Eratosthen may have disbelieved Olympias's rumour, but he certainly believed she spread it! P. M. Fraser PBA (1970) p. 198 note 2 has missed this distinction.) Anthol. Graec. 13.725 is an interesting comparison. *Margites*: Scholion to Aeschin. 3.160, Tzetzes Chiliads 4.867, 6.592 (important), Suida s.v. Margites, Eustathius 1669.41 in OCT Homeri opera, vol. 5 p. 158. Note how later inscriptions call Alex. son of Zeus or *ho ek Dios*: cp. IG 10.275, 276, 278. Kaibel Griech. Inschr. 1088; IG 2⁴4260; all are witness to the theme's long life. *Dionysius I's heirs*: P. Dion. 2, implying rivalry between wives; Dion. 6, Theopomp. ap. Athen. 425, DS 16.6. Dionysius II, like Alex., was the older son. *Disowning Philip*: P. 50.11, with QC 8.1.42. But it was so natural to a Roman to overstress this, in search of something for speakers to say (e.g. QC 6.9.18, 6.10.26–27, 6.11.5, 8.5.5, 8.10.29 – a revealing misquote of Aristob. F 47 – QC 8.7.13. The theme attached to Philotas probably because of his alleged plot in Egypt, A. 3.26, otherwise inexplicable to QC's mind!). QC 8.1.23 is a different matter to disowning Philip. Alex. was already enraged anyway at Opis and Samarkand, so the mention of Ammon did not by itself infuriate him: A. 7.9.2 (though A.'s fiction) suggests A. himself did not believe the 'disowning' story. DS 18.4.5 is the best evidence of contemporaries' beliefs. *Athenian letter*: P. 28.2. Hamilton's arguments, where positive, are circular and prove nothing; the wording, esp. the mildly surprising word *polis*, for a landed cleruchy, fits the inscriptions of the Samians returning to Samos but that is no guarantee of the letter's truth. One more letter from the forged collection, surely. *Nectanebo*: Onesic. F 39 may not be a slip for Ps.-Call.; cp. O. Weinreich, Der Trug Nektanebos (1911). *Scipio*: Livy 26.19.7. *Octavian*: Epigramm. Bobiensia 39 with Asclepiad. 617

524

F 2; cp. Paus. 4.14.7–8 on the Messenian hero Aristomenes. The most interesting parallel is that of Arsinoe II, favoured for comparisons with a host of Egyptian gods and even called 'child of Ammon', perhaps by reference to Alex., more probably by reference to Egyptian Pharaonic titles. Cp. J. G. Milne, Studies pres. to F. U. Griffith (1932) pp. 32ff.; note how Roman emperors, e.g. Vespasian (Acts of Pagan Martyrs (ed. Musurillo (1954) nr. 5B pp. 15ff.) were also called 'son of Ammon', again, surely, by a Greek interpretation of the Egyptian ruler's title. But by then, Egypt was hellenized and more of an open book to outsiders; I do not believe this interpretation was likely, let alone so significant, for Alex. and his staff in 331. At the very least, it fed on a strong wish, for Greek reasons, to believe it. *Best of men*: P. 27.11, possibly a true remark once made by Alex. It is certainly independent of P.'s preceding anecdote. *Alex.'s return route*: so far from being 'impossible', it was last described by W. Jennings-Bramley in Geogr. Journ. (1896) pp. 597ff. *Justinian*: Procop. De Aedibus 6.2. The sacrifice to Zeus Basileus at Memphis need have nothing to do with Amun-Ra; Alex. was King, and favoured by Zeus, and so the title (which appears late in Greek history, frequently in Boeotia) was as natural as at Gordium, where Zeus's thunder approved the King's cutting of the knot.

NOTES TO CHAPTER 15 (pp. 219–232)

Erythrae: Paus. 2.1.5, Plin. NH 5.116 (probably never completed); Syll. 1014 (cult *c.* 270 B.C.); DS 3.34.7 (probably Agatharchides) on sailing times. *Egypt administration*: A. 3.5.2 with QC 4.8.4 (muddled and brief; so much for QC as a precise source for officialdom). None of this administration was new. See esp. G. R. Driver, Aram. Docs. (1957), the most instructive source for Persian rule in Egypt, though I consider it misdated (Arsam, I believe, is the king's son active in the 460–450s; 5.7, despite Driver's note, can indeed read as Inaros, the Libyan rebel, thus dating the revolt; also, Arsam's officers Artavanta, Artahanta, Artachaya, Artarahya can all be identified with characters in Hdt. known at this earlier date). *Upper and Lower Egypt*: Driver 2.2, 5.6; and the disputed area 'Tshetres' (Cowley papyr., e.g. 24.39, 27.9) or Pathros (Pap. Ryland 7.13) which probably (despite J. Leibovitch, Bull. Inst. Egyp. (1934/5) p. 69) means Upper Egypt. *Nomarchs*: A. E. Samuel, Essays in hon. of C. B. Welles (1966) p. 213 stresses the Greek term's vagueness; however, note the old Pharaonic title of 'Governor of the South' in J. H. Breasted, Anc. Records of Egypt 1. 320, 364 and the frataraka (the Foremost) who is based at Elephantine (Cowl. 27) and is more than a mere general (note esp. the title's probable use on the coins of the Persepolis dynasts of 3rd c. B.C.). If Elephantine is the administrative seat for all Tshetres or Upper Egypt, then Cowl. 16.7, 20 and 30 give Persia's nomarchs, 490–410. Doloaspis has the Iranian-sounding 'aspa' in his name. For Petisis's, cp. the important evidence of Psamtik I's Petisis, Papyr. Ryland vol. 3, 9.5, esp lines 13f., with Griffith's notes pp. 71ff. and 106ff., written also by a Petisis, a priest of the later 6th century B.C. The link of Alex.'s Petisis is strongly suggested to me by the known adherence of Semtutefnakte (summarized in F. K. Kienitz, Polit. Gesch. Ägypt. p. 111), whose origin at Heracleopolis is probable and whose eponymous ancestor (I imagine) was also, like Petisis, highly prominent under Psamtik and thereafter. For similar continuity, cp. J. Vercoutter BIFAO (1950) p. 86. *Generals and admirals*: cp. the Saite practice in the useful table in M. Gyles, Pharaonic Policics and Admin. (1959) p. 76. Note how officials could hold masses of titles (cp. Kienitz p. 42). *Garrisons*: Aram. *rab hayla* (Cowley 1.3, 16.17 etc.). The overseer may be a King's Eye – C.27.9. The secretary is prob. the scribe: Hdt. 3.128.3, Cowl. 17.1, Pap. Ryl. no. 17.2. *Treasurers*: no exact parallel to Cleomenes, but Cowl. 26 refers to accountants of the treasury. Berve s.v., with his coins in B. Emmons, Amer. Num. Soc. Mus. Notes (1964) p. 69. E. Will REA (1960) pp. 254ff. puts him in context; cp. B. A. van Groningen's commentary on Ps.-Aristot. Oeconom. Bk. 2 (1933). Lucian, Rhetor. Didask. 5 may refer to his rise to power. *Persian methods*: Driver 7 and 12 are interesting; would Cleomenes use nothing but Egyptian agents? *Temples*: A. T. Olmstead, Hist. of Pers. Emp. (1948) p. 512 for references. *Nectanebo*: O. Weinreich, Der Trug Nektanebos (1911) is excellent. *Sesostris*: H. Kees, RE 2.2 (1923) 1861f. with F. Pfister, Stud. zum Alexanderroman, Wurzb. Jahrb. für die Altertumwissensch. (1946) pp. 56ff. *Hector*: Berve s.v., with Jul.

Epist. 50 (Loeb) 446A, to be read in context of a letter to a man called Nilus. A. 3.26.1 may be relevant. *Samaria*: QC 4.8.9 with F. M. Cross, Biblic. Archaelog. (1963) pp. 110ff., justifying the unfairly disputed Sanballats in Jos. A.J. 11.311.25. J. 36.3 supports Curtius; F. M. Cross, HTR (1966) pp. 201ff. supports land-grants mentioned in Jos. A.J. 11.344. This major event is omitted by Ptol. (A.), I suspect because of Perdiccas's role in this area later so sensitive to the Successors. Steph. Byz s.v. Gerasa (with Henri Seyrig Syria (1965) p. 25; also in Syria (1961) p. 75; also Euseb. 2.116 and Syncell. p. 496 (Bonn) for Samarian towns; cp. Steph. Byz. s.v. Dion. *Agis*: A. 3.6.7 (whose past tense is one decisive blow against delaying the revolt till 330; QC 6.1.21 is another). QC 4.1.39 on Crete: the discrepancy between the naval orders in A. and QC is not serious: both date them at Tyre (QC 4.8.16) and each gives half the orders. *Reinforcements*: DS 49.1 = QC 4.6.30, QC 5.1.40–1. I cannot agree with the conjecture of G. Wirth, Historia (1971) p. 629 that these men fought Agis, then were shipped across a winter sea to Syria! *Islanders*: QC 4.7.12. *Achilles*: A. 3.6.2. *Ammonias*: Ath. Pol. 61.7 with Dein, F 14.2. This is the first example of the subsequent practice of naming a ship after a god: I believe it was a careful flattery, made in the months after Agis and news of Gaugamela. *Mytilene*: J. R. Healey N.C. (1962) p. 65 where the dating depends on the plausible assumption that Alex.'s own coin-types and standards grew to exclude any new Mitylenean issues in the latter half of his life and that this issue is Mytilene's own last electrum type. Cp. Tod 201 lines 45–7 (I agree with Welles and Bickerman on a 332/0 date); we should remember Erigyius, Laomedon and Chares, all highly honoured Mytilenaens with Alex. *Army quarrel*: Eratosth. in P. 31.1–5; very remarkable. *Cypriots*: P. 29 with Berve, Stasanor, Nicocreon, Pasicrates. *Numbers*: A. 3.12.5. *Supplies*: QC 4.9.12's 11 days cannot be for the whole stage from Tyre to Thapsacus; only a partial measure like most in the sources. A. 3.6.8 shows the problem; Xen. Anab. 1.10.18 the scale. DS 19.58.2–3, 20,75.3 for parallels. *Darius's alleged third peace-offer*: QC 4.11, DS 54, J. 11.12.7–16, P. 29.7 and the story of Tireus (A. 4.20.1–4) which belongs in 332, if anywhere. *Two routes*: E. W. Marsden, Campaign of Gaugamela (1964) p. 12, an entertaining book but frequently mistaken. Xen. Anab. 1.4–6 with R. D. Barnett JHS (1963) pp. 1ff. *Julian's camp*: Amm. Marc. 24.1f. *Mazaeus*: A. 3.7, DS 16.42 and J.P. Six, Num. Chron. (1884) pp. 97ff. DS 55.1–2 and QC 4.9.12 muddle the Euphrates and the Tigris and the two different operations, one on each river: (1) Mazaeus with 3000 (A. 3.7) or 6000 (QC 4.9.7 and 12) horsemen to bar the Euphrates and probably burn its south route: (2) Satropates and 1000 men to burn granaries on the Tigris's far bank. QC 4.9.7, 14 (where Mazaeus may be an error). Some 6 weeks divided these two tasks. *Thapsacus*: I share the doubts of Barnett p. 3 n. 8 over the new northerly site suggested by W. J. Farrell JHS (1961) pp. 153ff. Note too, it was only 7 stages by river from Babylon: Aristob. F 56.11 line 18. *Alex.'s route*:A. 3.7.3; S. 11.9.1 on gold mines; Erat. in S. 2.1.38 on the distance. *Tigris*: A. 3.7.5 with DS 55.3 = QC 4.9.15–21. Compare DS 19.17.3; also Liban. Orat. 17.262–3, Amm. Marc. 24.8.5, 24.6–7 for Julian's predicament here. Marsden's chronology p. 75 is wrong; his conjectures for Persian battle-numbers make too many unjustified assumptions. *Darius's advance force*: A. 3.8.1, QC 4.9.24 = 4.10.10 (Satropat. and 1000 men in QC 4.7.9). Ariston's heroics in P. 39.1 belong here. *Panic*: Polyaen. 4.3.26, QC 4.12.14–17, P. 31.5. *Daybreak attack*: A. 3.9.2–3. *Alex.'s retort*: P. 31.11 = A. 3.10.1 = QC 4.13.3 = Call, surely (A.'s *legousi* can include Ptol. and Aristob.).

NOTES TO CHAPTER 16 (pp. 233–243)

Alex. asleep: P. 32, DS 56, QC 4.13.17–25, J. 11.13.1–3. *New weapons*: QC 4.9.3–5, DS 53.1–2. *Stakes*: QC 4.13.36, 4.15.1, Polyaen. 4.3.17 (Marsden pp. 41ff. is not convincing). *Alex.'s battle-order*: DS 57 = QC 4.13.26–31 = A. 3.12 (except for the new leader of Amyntas's battalion) = Call., surely. *Amphistome taxis*: Polyb. 2.28.6, Arr. Tact. 29.1, Asclep. Tact 3.5. *Reserves*: Thuc. 5.9.8, Xen. Anab. 6.5.9, Xen.-Hell. 6.4.12. *Caesar's example*: Dio 41.34.1. *Diothen gegonos*: cp. Isocr. Euagoras 13–14, 9.3. *Persian battle-order*: Aristob.-A. 3.11.3 = QC 4.12.6f. (who fills Aristob.'s gaps) = Call., surely. A. 3.8.3 gives the commanders, not their battle order, and so is not a doublet of 3.12 or obviously drawn from Ptol. *Curtius's two sources*: 4.13.17–34 = DS 57; 4.14.8 = DS 59.2 4.15.1–11 = DS 59.5–8; 4.15.12–15, 18–19 fit A. 3.13.3, 14.1–2.

526

Alex.'s own heroics: A. 3.14.3, DS 60.1, QC 4.15.19. *Persian flight*: A. 3.14.3–6 remains very puzzling: as at Issus, A. is harsher on Darius's own conduct than either DS or QC (note 4.16.9 – from a Persian captive?) *Parmenion's message*: contrast Call. ap. P. 33.10 (how much of this quote is Call.'s own?) with DS 60.8, A. 3.15.1 and QC 4.16.2, 19 claim the message was obeyed; DS 60.7 (Alex. was too far away to be reached) picks up QC 4.16.3; probably QC again combined two different stories and hence the clumsiness of 4.16.16–19. P. does likewise; P. 32.5–7 may be DS's story (cp. Polyaen. 4.3.6), whereas 33.9 matches A. Hamilton HCPA p. 83 defends the "structure' of these chapters without explaining the absurd tenses used in 37.8. *The wounded around Alex.*: QC 4.16.32 = DS 61.3 = A. 3.15.2 = Call.? *Alex.'s letter to Greeks*: P. 34.2. *South Italy*: P. 34.3 with Hdt. 8.47; proof that Alex. (and his staff) knew Hdt.'s works? *Mount of Victory*: S. 16. 1.4, 15.1.9, Dio 36.50.3, Suet. Aug. 18.2 Cp. Zoroaster F 12 with J. Bidez-F. Cumont, Les Mages hellenisés vol. 2.119.

NOTES TO CHAPTER 17 (pp. 244–257)

Motives: DS 65.5 = QC 5.2.8 = Cleit. A. 3.19.1 may be comparable (ultimately Call. via a Persian captive?). *Enioi* in DS 85.5 is v. interesting. I imagine this is not DS's wide reading, but a reflection of different stories related by Cleit. side by side. *March south*: DS 64.3 = QC 5.1.11, perhaps explained by Amm. Marc. 23.6.16–17. *Persian Babylonia*; G. Cardascia, Les Archives des Murasu (1951) is fundamental and an outstanding study; G. Driver, Aramaic Documents (esp. nos. 2 and 5 with notes) is relevant. *Fertility*: Hdt. 1.192, 3.92–94, esp. Hdt. 1.193. Theophr. HP 3.3.5, Xen. Anab. 1.6f. *Palm-trees*: E. Benveniste J.As. (1930) pp. 193–225. *Foreign soldiers*: Cardascia pp. 6–7, B.E. 9.28, 10. pp. 8ff. *Parysatis*: Xen. Anab. 2.4.27 (slaves), UM 50, 60, 75 and esp. 133. Xen. Anab. 1.4.9 Ctesias F 89, Plato Alcib. 1. 123B. *Bagoas's estate*: Theophr. 2.6.2 Ephemerides 117 F 2. *Named estates*: Cardascia pp. 82–3 for 4 Iranian squires. *Arsames's leases*: Driver passim, usefully summarizing the nine documents on pp. 88f., cf. I. M. Diakonoff VDI (1959) p. 70. *Favourites*: W. Eilers, Iran. Beamtennamen p. 52, 90 on a eunuch from Paphlagonia. *Guarantee*: VS 6.171. *King's land*: B.E. 9.7, UM 2.16, 73.5, 58, 59 and crop-yields in Cardascia p. 160. UM 133, vol. 2. 1.63 (chickens). *Canal-leases*: Cardascia pp. 77, 130, B.E. 10.84, 123. 10.54 is a fishing lease. *Welcome*: QC 5.1.17f. (important, and cf. F. Pfister, R–E Supp. 4.277. s.v. Epiphaneia for religious parallels). *Inflation*: W. Dubberstein AJSL (1939) p. 20 collects scraps of evidence and generalizes wildly regardless of the sold goods' quality the scanty information and so forth. *Interest rates*: Cardascia p. 5: $13\frac{1}{2}\%$ under Nebuchadnezzar becomes 40–50% for Murasu (B.E. IX 6, 66, 68 – their lending was higher risk, however, and their capital overheads were larger). Cp. G. R. Driver and J. C. Miles, The Babylon: Laws I pp. 173ff. (c. 20% in Assyrian and Babylonia Old periods). Cowley Pap. 10 and 11 are fine parallels: c. 60% rate for silver. Kraeling Pap. 11.3 shows the far higher rate (50% a month) paid for grain: throughout, special factors must be considered. But 6–8% was common in Roman Egypt and the Achaemenids were draining silver out of the provinces into Susa. *Slaves*: the *garda* on Babylonian estates – B.E. X. 92, 127, 128, 95, 118 – are probably Royal Workers – W. Eilers, Iranische Beamtennam, pp. 63–7. Their exact status is uncertain; Russians assume they are slaves, and stress the clauses against slaves' escape (no new feature in Babylonian – or any other – law – cp. for Alex., Ps.-Aristot., Oecon. 1353A). M. A. Dandamayev, Palestin. Sbornik (1965) p. 84 discusses detailed lists of fugitive slaves most interestingly. *Callisthenes*: Jacoby T 3 with Theon. Alex. Comm. on Almagest. 3.1 and B. L. van der Waerden, Archiv für Orientforsch. (1963) p. 98. *Bel and priesthood*: A. 3.16.4–5 with I. M. Diakonoff in Festschrift B. Landsberger (1963) pp. 343ff.; G. H. Sarkisian VDI (1952) pp. 68ff. and A. Aymard REA (1938) pp. 1–42, an outstanding survey. The King and the temples I must discuss elsewhere; cp. M. Dandamayev VDI (1966) pp. 17–39 (excellent) and Festschrift Franz Altheim pp. 82ff. (tithes). But note Ps.-Arist. Oec. 1352B for their return in 323 B.C. *Favours*: G. H. Sarkisian V.D.I. (1953) pp. 59–73 with S. Smith Babyl. Hist. Texts (1924) pp. 150–9; also Eos (1957) pp. 29–44. *Alex.'s governors*: A. 3.16.4 with QC 5.1.43, DS 64.6. The lion-staters in Bellinger pp. 62–5 are not nearly so certainly dated as many imply; their Attic standard had been in use for years in Phoenicia and despite the hint of their

527

four mint-marks (for each of Mazaeus's four years in Alex.'s Babylon?) they could belong to the late 340's or 334-1. For a possible link with Babylon, Berve s.v. Antibelos, Brochubelos or Artiboles. But the name Mazday-Mazaeus is derived from Ahura-Mazda. *Babylon's sights*: F. Wetzel–E. Schmidt–A. Mallwitz, Das Babylon der Spätzeit (1957); F. E. Ravn, Herodotus's Description of Babylon (1942) – very useful. R. Koldewey, Das Wideresthende Bab. (1925) and esp. Die Königsburgen von Babylon (1931/2, two parts); cp. now the good survey in F. Schachermeyer, Alex. in Babylon (1970) pp. 49ff. *Hanging gardens*: P. 38.15, Mor. 648 C, Theophr. HP 4.4.1 (is the failure of the ivy a sly hit at Alex.'s parallels with Dionysus? cp. the preceding sceptical reference to Meros and Dionysus). *Pay*: QC 5.1.45 = DS 64.6. This could total over 2000 talents at a stroke. *Reinforcements*: DS 65.1 = QC 5.1.39–42, as opposed to A. 3.17.10 (A. is v. thin through all this phase). *Agris's revolt*: dated by QC 6.1.21 (against DS, never a source for chronology). DS 73.5 = QC 6.1 (admitting he recounts it out of place); DS 62 is better placed; 63.1 is important. *Susa treasures*: QC 5.2.8, P. 36. *Demaratus*: P. 37.7, P. Ages 15.4, Mor. 329 D, DS 66.3 with QC 5.2.13–15 (note the broad correspondence between them, even in their reported speech, though DS adds stress on the changes and chances of Fortune). A. Alfoldi, La Nouvelle Clio (1950) p. 357 is not decisive; theories such as H. Montgomery. Opusc. Athen. (1969) pp. 1ff. (that the eunuch's wailing was ritual) are absurd. *Greek festivals*: A. 3.17.6, QC 5.2.17 = DS 67.1. *Nomads*: DS 67.4 = QC 5.2.3. A. agrees on the alternative route (A. 3.17.2), but not on the repulse (QC 5.3.9) or Tauron's attack. Ptol. ap. A. 3.17.6 matches QC 5.3.12 but not 5.3.15; I do not pretend to understand how Ptol. and Cleit. (?) could partially agree, without Aristob. (and so not via Call.?). *Persian Gates*: Aurel Stein, Geogr. Journ. (1938) pp. 314ff., E. Herzfeld, Peterm. Mitteil. (1907) map 2 with Ur tablet 292 for Keys of Ansan (Persian *kleides*) and the Arab Hamdallah nuzhat 129. *Battle*: DS 68 = QC 5.3.4 = Cleit. A. 3.18.2 exaggerates the numbers given in DS 68.1 = QC 5.3.17; A. 3.18.3 is as reticent about defeat, as usual. QC 5.4.20 and 30 mistakes role of Coenus's brigades – A. 3.18.6. The hill-march was fearfully quick: A. 18.6 says *dromoi*, and proves the lightness of the hypaspists. A. 3.18.9 does not specify this Ptol. as Ptol. Lagou. P. 37.2 = QC 5.4.10 = Polyaen. 4.3.27 on Lycian guide. QC 5.4.14 might be a corruption for archers *and* cavalry (cf. A. 3.18.4); Polyaen 4.3.27 gives Meleager's role to Hephaistion and Philotas. '*Most hateful city*': DS 70.1 = QC 5.6.1. *Greek prisoners*: J. 11.14.11–12, DS 69.2 = QC 5.5 (4000, not 800 Greeks but DS 69.8 = QC 5.5.24).

NOTES TO CHAPTER 18 (pp. 258–264)

Persepolis: E. F. Schmidt, Persepolis (1953–7) vols. 1 and 2; G. Walser, Die Volkerschaften aus der Persepolis Reliefs (1966); the astronomical speculations of W. Lentz, W. Schlosser ZDMG (1969) p. 957 seem to me to be irrelevant. *Most hateful city*: QC 5.6.1 = DS 70.1 = Cleit. *Slaughter*: DS 70.2 = QC 5.6.6 = P. 37.3 (referring to Persepolis, after a presumed gap in the Mss.). *Camels*: DS 71.2 = QC 5.6.9. *Pasargadai*: QC 5.6.10, A. 3.18.10; the *prote epidemia* in Aristob. F 51B line 22 is distinct from the restoration in 324, despite the slightly vague order of events in lines 15–25. *Persian campaign*: QC 5.6.12–19 (30 days). *Dating*: QC 5.6.12, where the Mss. are corrupt and the *sub* anyway imprecise. The heavy snow suggests a mid-March campaign; DS 73.1 has inverted the sequence. Alex. prob. reached Persepolis in mid-Jan 330 and left (P. 37.6) in mid or late May; the confusions expressed in C. A. Robinson AJP (1930) pp. 22ff. are one more example of the failure of scholars to realize how fast an army, esp. Alex.'s army when smaller and hungry, can march through mid-Iran's bare steppes (cf. R. D. Milns Hist. (1966) p. 256 for another instance of this). S. 15.2.10 means what it says: Nov. 330, a possible date, as my text shows. *Appointments*: A. 3.18.11, with Berve s.v. Rheomithres QC 5.6.11. *The burning*: A. 3.18.11–12 (Ptol.?), if S. 15.3.6 is indeed from Aristob. who omits (thanks to S.'s quotation ?) Parmenion's advice. But surely here, of all places, if Ptol. had disagreed with Aristob, A. would have given his alternative. *Alex.'s regrets*: P. 38.8 (agreed, and immediate); QC 5.7.11 ('agreed', and immediate). A. 6.30.1 (six years later). Whether Alex. regretted it on the spot and ordered instant extinguishing is far more dubious (A., QC 5.7.6–8, DS do not mention or imply this), so too much must not be built on P. 38.8's airy remark.

528

Even if ordered, archaeology proves extinguishing did not succeed. *Thais*: Cleitarch. F. 11, hence QC 5.7.1f (stresses wine), P. 38 (is 38.7 a guess ?); DS 72 is Dryden's source, stressing the madness and the Dionysiac revel. It is important that all versions alike stress the theme of revenge; that, at least, may be due to Call.? *Thais and Ptolemy* P. 38.2. Athen. 13.576D. SIG 314; certainly DS and QC play up the heroic role of women (Sisygambis, the Amazon, Spitamenes's wife etc.) and their source stresses Ptol. perhaps even more than Ptol.'s history (DS 103.6 = QC 9.8.22, DS 104.5 = QC 9.10.6 = Cleitarchus who after all, was an Alexandrian), but I doubt if these two tendencies could combine to invent his mistress as a pyromaniac. QC 5.7.10 for what it is worth, sees through the A. story, firmly dismissing it as mere cover.

NOTES TO CHAPTER 19 (pp. 267–278)

Pursuit of Darius: G. Radet, Mélanges Glotz vol. 2 (1932) p. 765; also A. von Stahl, Geogr Journ. (1924) p. 312 for the end. *Reinforcements*: QC 5.7.12, muddling Socrates the Macedonian with Plato the Athenian! Probably these troops brought the news of Agis's revolt: whether P. Agesil. 15 bears any relation to the truth (who would record it, in Media?) I cannot say. *Darius's plans*: QC 5.8.1 = A. 3.19.1, 5.8.2 = DS 73.2 = A. 3.19.3 for the second one. *Isfahan*: Tabae in QC 5.13.2–3 shd be Gabai, for it was on the Media-Paraitacene border (A. 3.19.4) and a palace at Gabai is named there by S. 11.1.18, DS 19.26.1, 34.7. Persepolis to Hamadan is a rugged 450 miles, taking about 6 weeks. *Crusade ends*: A. 3.19.5, against QC 6.2.17 = DS 94.3 (Cleit.). At Gaugamela, Erigyios led the allied horse, but at 3.20.1, in Hamadan, he leads mercenary horse; evidently his allied unit had broken up. Cleit. did not serve as a Greek ally, then, for he did not know when the allies were sent home. DS 74.3–4 (QC 6.2.17) explains the 'volunteers' in A. 3.20.6. *Parmenion's orders*: A. 3.20.7, an inexplicable passage, as he seems to have disobeyed it; the only purpose in going to Hyrcania would be to meet Alex. But he never did. At 20.8, Cleitus is the Black, the future Hipparch. *Finance*: A. 3.20.7 probably refers only to a part of Persian treasure, as much was being convoyed to Susa (DS 71.2); DS 80.3 contradicts this, wrongly? We do not know if there was a Head Treasurer, still less if Harpalus was such a chief. Readers of A. R. Bellinger, Essays p. 48ff., A. Andreades, Annales d.'histoire économ. (1929) pp. 321ff., R. Knapowski in Geschichte Mittelasiens im Altertum (1970, ed. F. Altheim–R. Stiehl) will recognize that we cannot usefully plot Alex.'s finances at all, apart from remembering the problem. Knapowski's detailed sums are the most positive attempt, but are full of unargued assumptions; I stress that we know next to nothing of payment in kind, sharing of booty (apart from the baggage-burning), Alex.'s weight-system (what was a talent to him?), his army pay (DS 64.6 is not necessarily the pay for Macedonian troops for 2 months; Tod 183 proves nothing; A. 7.23.3 is the one landmark, but only for 324, and are we sure the stater is an Attic stater?); only a simple faith in Ms. figures could suggest that J. 12.1.3 (190,000 T at Hamadan) and DS 80.3, S. 15.3.9 (180,000 T with Parmenion in Hamadan) mean that 10,000 T were taken east by Alex. himself! For evidence of bullion with Alex., 330–25, cp. QC 8.12.15; gold would be more precious in relation to weight. Travelling mints in Iran are known (e.g. the coins of Gotarzes the Parthian stamped *kata ten strateian*(but if a barcurrency were in use in Iran anyway (cp. A. D. H. Bivar, Iran (1971) p. 97 for this liklehood) minting would not be necessary. All in all, an insoluble problem and one which the fearfully tedious classification of Alex.'s coinage cannot advance, except further to weaken any lingering generalizations. The implication of DS 74.5 = QC 6.2.10 (if this is not mistakenly applied to Alex.'s own officers) are far reaching. *Posthouses*: cp. Persep. Fortif. Tabl. 1351, 1358, 1555. Driver 6. Ps.-Ar. Oecon. 1353A. *Alex.'s route*: note he has divided his forces at Hamadan for speed and easier supplies. QC 5.13 is hopelessly confused, ignoring his stay at Hamadan. For 9-day caravanjourney to Rhagae, cp. the comparative figures in J. Marquart Philolog., Supplem. 10 (1907) pp. 19ff.; A. 3.20.2 prob. applies to all 11 of Alex.'s days, implying he made a detour. *Darius's arrest*: QC 5.8.6–12.20 is rhetoric and not due to any mercenary source (though Bagoas and others must have discussed the affair later). Its few details are mostly known to A. (21.1, 4–5, 10); the numbers are too high (A. 16.2, 19.5). Barsaentes is omitted; Darius is made to 'know' Greek (QC 5.11.5 – actually believed by Marsden Gaugam. p. 6!) so that he can make a speech proving how a Greek had saved him (QC 5.11.9); in fact he needed an interpreter (QC 5.13.7) whose capture coincided with A. 3.21.4; possibly he was the source of enemy details in 21.4–6? *Pursuit*: von Stahl pp. 312f. ends it near Damghan, to my mind more plausibly than Radet's more distant Shahroud. In the last 18 hours, Alex. does between 45–50 miles; as Damghan was about 200 miles away and he took 6 days, he may have spent a day foraging before setting out? J. 11.15.1 calls the village of the arrest Thara, surely Chavar (Pliny NH 6.17.2 – Choarene). *Darius's death*: A. 3.21.10 (22.2 has the usual poor view of Darius, perhaps A.'s own as much as his sources, though it is a recurring theme, not shared by QC–DS). A.'s account does not rule out P. 43.3–4, though much adorned (cp. P. 30.12, A. 4.20.3); cp. J. 11.15, QC 5.13.24. One wonders who gave the alternative version in DS 73.4; is this known to DS from his own reading, or had Cleit. mentioned it from, e.g., Onesicritus? *Alex.'s behaviour*: P. 43.5, Mor. 322F. QC 6.2.7 (this Hystaspes is a very important figure in Alex.'s life: cp. A. 7.6.5). *Gifts*: P. 74.5. QC 6.2.10, both to be referred back to Hamadan. DS 78.1. *Persian borrowings*: Hdt. 1.135.2 *Medes' legacy*: I. M. Diakonov, Istoriya Midii (1956) is a remarkable study, followed by a brilliant paper in W. B. Henning, Memorial Vol. (1968) pp. 98ff. on Median as source of Old Persian; M. Mayrhofer Anzeig. der Österr. Akadem. (1968) pp. 1ff. is an adventurous attempt at reconstructing the Medes' lost language; the excavations at Nush-i-Jan (Iran, 1968ff.), Takht-i-Suleiman (ed. H. H. von der Osten, 1962) and other sites listed in W. G. Culican, Medes and Persians (1965), a book better on Medes than Persians anyway, all add to a growing study. For their tribes, cp. H. von Gall, Arch. Mitt. Iran (1972) pp. 261ff. *Their court life*: the outstanding chapter by W. Hinz, Iran. funde u. Forschungen (1968), pp. 63ff. has put this in a new light; Hdt. 1.99, the first two books of the Cyropaedia, Hdt. 1.135, 7.6.1f. are but a few of the classical sources which fit his observations from Persepolis's reliefs. *Babylon*: cp. D. J. Wiseman, Iraq (1966) p. 155, A. J. Sachs, Iraq (1953) p. 167, G. Widengren, Anc. Near East Relig. (1951) pp. 20ff. 'King of Kings' is a title known in Urartu; if the Persians borrowed this symbolism, did they ever take these elements seriously? Their own nomad rituals are a different matter. Persep. Fortif. Tablets nos. 1807, 1810, 1821–2, 1828, 1830. *Greeks and others*: G. Goossens, La Nouv. Clio (1949) pp. 32ff. is still useful. It is odd that R. T. Hallock did not identify his official 'Yauna' (PF 1800, 1810) as a Yona, i.e. a Greek, prob. an interpreter, or his Karkis (PF 878, 882) as, surely, a Carian, whose compatriots were settled as sailors by Darius I on the Persian Gulf. *Intermarriage*: G. Cardascia, Murasu pp. 6–7, Rec. de Soc. J. Bodin (1958) pp. 115ff. Clay-Hilprecht B.E. 9. pp. 27–8, 10 pp. 8–9, 88. Kohler and Ungnad, Hundert ausgewahlte Rechtsurk. (1911) p. 73. Kohler-Peiser Aus dem babyl. Rechtsleben (1898) vol. 4 p. 5 is p particularly nice example. *Whipbearers and Medes*: W. Hinz, Iranische Funde, pp. 63ff. *Bureaucracy*: Fortific. Tablet 6764 quotes the King's own words, an apt reminder that Persian rule was personal, despite the hordes of workmen and supply officers now revealed in R. T. Hallock's Fortification Tablets: PF 1940, 1957, 1997 are cited for backlog of work, but it must be stressed that the translation of these documents is mostly an act of faith. *Seclusion*: Hdt. 1.99, 3.84. Xen. Cyr. 8.4.2, 8.3.10, Hdt. 7.16, Chares F 4. – *Dinners*: Esther 1 and 5, Heracleid. 689 F 2. Deinon ap. Athen. 146C, DS 11.69.1, Poseidon. F 68 (exaggerated?). *Food-offerings*: Theopomp. F 124, an intriguing complement to Corp. Inscr. Graec. 2693B, possibly of the 5th c B.C., though these sacrifices were presumably offered to men like Mausolus too. G. Widengren Numen, Supplem. 4 (1959) p. 242 makes interesting suggestions, not all valid. *Royal dress*: P. Themist. 16.2, Artax. 24.6, Xen. Cyrop. 1.3 and 8.3; also G. Thompson Iran (1965) p. 121. Anne Roes, Iran. Antiqu. (1964) p. 133 and Bibl. Or. (1951) p. 137 with full bibliographies. The exact nature of the tiara can be disputed by invoking late lexicographers and the problem of the kidaris; I believe the Persepolis reliefs show the king in the 'upright' tiara and kidaris, and written evidence is too late or confused to realize the two terms refer to one style. *Liongriffin*: G. F. Hill JHS (1923) p. 156. *Accession ritual*: P. Artax. 2, Nicol. Damasc. 90 F66 with the brilliant analysis by A. Alfoldi, Schweiz. Archiv für Volkskunde (1951) pp. 77ff. There is no evidence that Alex. knew the Cyropaedia or indeed had to, once bilingual courtiers had joined him to talk of Cyrus. *Alex.'s legendary proclamation*: Ps.-Call. 2.21. *Elburz campaign*: A. 3.23–24; DS 75–76 = QC 6.2–6.5 very closely, differing from A. and giving an

530

accurate landscape. *Bagoas*: Indica 18.9 (despite Berve) is the neatest proof of his existence and high favour; it may be right to identify his father with Pharnouches the Lycian in A. 4.3.7 (perhaps a Greek-speaker?). Bagoas's house at Babylon (Diaries Fl; misplaced in P.39.6) was not the eunuch's (Plin. NH 13.41) DS 5.3–6 is a bit suspicious on Bagoas the elder's manner of death, but age and looks probably disqualify this one from being the same man, and Nabarzanes his fellow surrenderer was anyway the new Chiliarch in the old Bagoas's place. *Caspian*: Aristot. Meteor. 2.1.10, S. 11.7.4–5 say nothing of Alex.'s own view. J. R. Hamilton CQ (1971) pp. 106ff. needs rearguing, not least with the knowledge that the water of the south Caspian is famously sweet (e.g. Camb. Hist. Iran vol. 1 p. 48). *Amazon*: P. 46, Cleit. F. 16 (via Onesic.?) with J. 12.3.5, DS 77.1f., QC 6.5.24 and M. Rostovtzeff, Iran. and Greeks in S. Russia (1928) for matriarchy *Persian friends*: Berve s.v. Artabazus, Phrataphernes, Nabarzanes, Bagoas, Autophradates; note QC 6.2.9 on their numbers; the 'conquest' of the forest tribes (cp. Baeton F 1 for their habits) will have impressed these Iranian nobles, whose descendants would later prefer the Arab invader to the threat of the mountain peoples. *Alex.'s dress*: Eratosth. ap. P. Mor. 330 A and the negative evidence of art (on the Alex. medallion, Alex. wears his two-plumed helmet, as on the Mitylene coins, not the King's tiara), together with Cleit. DS 77.5 refute the excesses and inaccuracies of P. 45.1–2, A. 4.7.4, 8.4, 9.9, QC 6.6.4 and J. 12.3.8f. *Wearers of purple*: DS 77.4–5 with Xen. Anab. 1.2.10; the splendid Macedonian horseman in P. Couissin, Instit. mil. et naval. (1932) plate 1; P. Eum. 8. QC's *purpurati* have a precise background, though loosely applied. *Honoured Friends*: e.g. A. 2.11.8 and 9, with 1.17.4 (is *en time* a precise phrase?). Indica 27.8 (same phrase, in Ionic). Cp. Welles, Royal Correspondence nr 44 line 2, 45 for Hellenistic continuity. *Concubines*: DS 77.6, QC 6.6.8. *Diadem*: Livy 24.5.4 for Sicily: H. W. Ritter, Diadem und Königsherrschaft (1965); H. Brandenburg Stud. zur Mitra (1966). *Caesar*: Dio 44.11.2, 44.15.3. For nuances to the kandys, or sleeved cloak, which Alex. rejected, cp. A. Alfoldi, Stud. in Hon. of A. M. Friend (1955) pp. 40ff. *Letter forms*: Chares F 10, QC 6.6.6, '*Spoils of victory*': QC 6.6.5. *Brother-in-law*: Berve s.v. Alexander of Epirus. J. 12.1.4. *Hecatompylos*: DS 75.1, QC 6.2.15, name omitted at A. 3.23.1, though A. wrote a book on Parthians. Site found by J. R. Hansman JRAS (1968) pp. 111ff.; Eratosth. in S. 11.8.9 gives a distance which does not suit this site, but Eratosth.'s figures are not reliable or uncorrupt: e.g. the absurd distances given in S. 15.3.1. Parthian measurements in S. 11.9.1 do fit Hansman's site (his short stade is a needless muddle, as the number of stades is only given roundly); von Stahl Geogr. Journ. (1924) pp. 312ff. had ended the pursuit of Darius anyway on Hansman's site; the rock Stiboetes (QC 6.4.3, DS 75.2) fits it well: P. Pedech REA (1958) p. 67. *Speech and answer*: DS 74.3, J. 12.3.2–3, P. 47, QC 6.2.15, 4.1 agree broadly on an incident A. omits – because it reflects poorly on the men's loyalty?

NOTES TO CHAPTER 20 (pp. 279–291)

Aria: A. 3.25.5 does not entail Alex. went south to Herat, then up the rough Hari-Rud valley, a long detour; the troops in A. 3.25.2 need only have guarded the fringe of Aria, while Alex. set off by the shorter road to Merv. *Baggage*: QC 6.6.15 dates this better (the roads to Balkh are all bad!) than P. 57.1, Polyaen. 4.3.10. *Herat*: Avesta Vindev. 1.9, Mithra Yasht 10.14; R. N. Frye, Heritage of Persia (1963) pp. 23ff. S. 11.514, Pliny NH 6.61. 6.93 (important). *Reinforcements*: QC 6.6.35. *Parmenion's troops*: a major problem, for where were the 6000 Macedonians of A. 3.19.7, left with Cleitus the Black? The appointment of Cleitus as Hipparch in Seistan implies that he and these 4 phalanx-brigades had joined Alex. by then; before, though, or after the plot? A. 3.25.4 says 'having all his troops now together', implying Cleitus joined Alex. again in Parthia. But A. does not record the reinforcements of QC 6.6.35, who arrived at this point, and this may have confused him; they alone may have united with Alex. QC 7.3.4 definitely implies Parmenion still had the 6000 Maced, or at best that they were en route for Alex. The army commands support this: the 3 brigades of Coenus, Craterus and Amyntas were with Alex. from Hamadan onwards and these three are prominent not only in A.'s narrative but in QC's account of the trial; Perdiccas also features once in QC and although he had led an infantry brigade, now left with

Cleitus, he is there called *armiger* (QC 6.8.17), suggesting he had given up his command to Alcetas his brother, later known to have held it. If so, his presence in Seistan does not imply the presence of Cleitus's troops. This explains the few Macedonians who gather to hear the trial in QC 6.8.23; as for Parmenion, his orders to move east (A. 3.19.7) had probably been changed, for if he was flouting them, this surely would have been recorded to explain his murder. Certainly he had the other troops in A. 3.19.7; Berve s.v. Cleander, Agathon, Sitalces, Heracon, Menidas and perhaps Koiranos. *Sources*: A.-Ptol. 3.26.2–3 is basic (note *ischuros* in 2!), but I feel it is too brief for 26.2's wording to prove that the only real evidence was Philotas's silence; other charges were 'not unclear', and though A. omits them, 26.3 and 4 refer confidently to Philotas's 'epiboule'. DS 79.3 is less sure (but note the 'confession' in 80.2). The structure of QC 6.8–1.11 is suggestive: 6.8.15 is neatly picked up again at 6.11.10 (6.11.8 is very clumsy: why postpone Philotas's death?). Implies QC elaborated 2 sources: (1) Ptol.-A. that Philotas was accused in public; 6.8.25 is prob. only QC's guess, and its true Ms. text is interesting. Typically, QC built speeches from a few past facts (e.g. 9.17, the Egyptian 'plot'). (2) P. 49.11: Philotas was tortured privately: excuse for more speeches in QC. This would explain the double sentencing (6.11.8, 11.38), did not DS-Cleit. (surely QC's main source) mention *both* the public trial *and* the confession by torture (80.1–2). Did Ptol. omit the torture or did Cleit. invent it as an excuse? On stoning: R. Hirzel, Die Strafe der Steinigung, Abhandl. Leipzig Akad. (1909) p. 25. *Macedonian language*: 6.19.34–5, 11.4 (apt reference to Phrygians, old rulers of Macedonia). *Alex. the Lyncestian*: DS 80.2, QC 7.1.7; not in Ptol.-A., nor are the Disorderlies (QC 7.2.35–38 = DS 80.4 = J. 12.4.4–8 = Cleit.). Only DS 79 = QC 6.7 = Cleit. has the preliminaries, and these are too similar to the Pages' plot. *Suspects*: QC 6.7.15 is an unhelpful list, misdating Demetrius (A. 3.27.6). *Persons in plot*: Berve s.v. Antigone, Philotas (esp. P. 40.1, 48.4, DS 67.7 and the cavalry reforms in A. 3.16.11). *Purge*: QC 6.11.20, where the 'law' is QC's own way of phrasing a custom; cp. 8.6.28, not refuted by 8.8.18. This family fear is not refuted, either, by the survival of Coenus, Parmenion's son-in-law; he disowned Parmenion all the more vigorously (QC 6.9.30) because he had to clear his own life. Cleander the murderer was Coenus's brother. On the other hand, Berve nr. 165, Asandros (Parmenion's brother, possibly) arrived, ignorantly, in camp in 329 (A. 4.7.2), and is probably never mentioned again. Philip Menelaou, leader of Thessalians under Parmenion, also disappears after Sept. 330. Was Parmenion the cause, or mere chance, the Thessalians being disbanded in 329 anyway? Erigyios, who had led the allies on the left wing under Parmenion, actually denounced his c.-in-c. vigorously: QC 6.8.17f. So much for solid army factions. One wonders, of course, whether references to Asander in 323 (all listed under Berve nr 164) might in part refer to Parmenion's possible brother (nr 165). Maybe he survived too; it is impossible to prove the ruin of Parmenion's 'faction', let alone the 'extermination' of his family which is conjectured so often nowadays. *Prophthasia*: P. Mor. 328 F, Steph. Byz. s.v. Phrada. Only a miscalculation by Droysen has concealed the fact that this is modern Farah, a point about 180 miles distant from Herat and so within a mile or two of fitting the bematists' figures of 1500–1600 stades, given uncritically and rounded down in S. 11.8.9.

NOTES TO CHAPTER 21 (pp. 292–307)

Alex.'s route to Kandahar: K. Fischer BJ (1967) p. 136 discusses the whole area with great thoroughness, but granted that Alex. begins from Farah, there is no reason for his wide loop south past the Vanishing Lake, except possibly for supplies, as Seistan was a famous granary even in Arab times. *Arimaspoi*: F. W. Thomas JRAS (1906) pp. 180ff.; Ctesias, ap. Photius, had already referred to *Skythes amyrgioi* in Sakastane, cp. Hellanicus F 171 on this Scythian plain. I wonder if an influx of these Scyths ended the city-culture of Seistan, as reported yearly by its Italian excavators in East and West. Arachosia = Hetumati (in the Avesta) = Etymandros in Plin. NH 6.92. Bisitun inscript. 40f. on its satrap Vivana's loyalty in 521; also the evidence in the Ritual Texts and the Fortificat. tablets from Persepolis for contacts with Persepolis and Arachosia as seat of a haoma cult. *Satraps*: Berve s.v. Menon, with the admirable chart in his vol. 1 p. 276. *Kandahar*: K. Fischer, as above: cp. A. Fussmann Arts Asiatiques (1966) p.

33. The Asoka inscriptions show Kandahar as a lively area of hellenism, finally refuting Tarn's plea that this Alexandria was at Ghazni. Kandahar's derivation from Iskander is correct. *Elephants*: ivory from Harahvatis in Darius's Susa inscription and the wise remarks of A. J. Toynbee, Between Oxus and Jumna (1961) pp. 71ff. on Lashkari Bazar. *Alex.'s route*: A. Foucher, La vieille route de Bactres à l'Inde (1947) is the best account of the possibilities, esp. vol. 1 pp. 209ff. on the links between India and Arachosia. *Scenery and supplies*: A. 3.28.1, 28.9 is improved by QC 7.3.6 = DS 82–3 (scenically correct), cp. QC 7.4.22–5 and S. 15.621. I quote from Emil Trinkler, Through the Heart of Afghanistan (1928). For the whole of the next two years, F. von Schwarz Alex. Feldzuge in Turkestan (1893) is an indispensable guide to geography, based on 12 years' military service in Sogdia (though he wrongly differentiates Balkh from Zariaspa; to the bematists, as in S. and Plin., they were identical). *Alex. in the Caucasus*: A. 3.28.4, 4.22.4–5; DS 83 surely corrects the text of QC 7.3.23. Note Plin. NH 6.92 on Cyrus and Capisa; cp. R. Ghirshman in Mem. Del. Arch. Fr. en Afghan. (1946). DS 83 implies other nearby cities; cp. Ptol. Geogr. 6.18.4 one of which may be Kabul. We do not know whether Greeks and natives enjoyed equal civic status. *For Prometheus*: DS 83.1 = QC 7.3.22 = Cleit (via Onesic.?) Eratosth.'s doubts: S. 11.5.5; A. 5.3.1–4; *uparisena* and Persian background in E. Herzfeld, Persian Empire (1968) pp. 336–7. Aristot. and Hindu Kush: Aristot. Meteor. 350A. *Supplies*: QC 7.4.22f., and for prices cp. W. K. Pritchett Hesperia (1956) pp. 182ff. *Balkh*: Avesta, Vendidad 1.7, Yasht 5 (Anahita). For its walls, Monum. Preislam. d'Afghan. (DAFA vol. 19, 1964). For villages, S. P. Tolstov, Drevnei Chorezmskoi Tsivil. (1948, Germ. trans. 1953) pp. 122–33. *Resources*: W. W. Tarn, Gks. in Bactria and India (1951) pp. 78ff. Lapis in R. J. Gettens, Alumni (Rev. du cercle des Alumni des fondations scientifiques, 1950) pp. 342ff. G. Herrmann Iraq (1968) p. 21. *Persian administration*: Smerdis son of Cyrus, Hystaspes brother of Xerxes, Masistes are examples of King's family as satraps; there was a brief revolt, according to Ctesias, in Bacteria under Artaxerxes II. *Bactrian desert*: QC 7.5 = prologue to DS Book 17 = Cleit. (scenically correct). A. omits the hardship! *Alex.'s endurance*: QC 7.3.17, 7.5.9 (more plausible here than in Makran), 7.5.16. *Bessus*: A. 3.30.4, 25.8 with A. 3.23.4. *Branchidae*: QC 7.5.28 = 5.11.11.4 = Callisth. (despite F 14 line 22) is unlikely to have extended his history so far. Onesic. (used by S. and Cleit.) is perhaps responsible (cp. P. 60.3 for his spurious crusading) and it is impossible to be sure his story is true. Not, however, a point of much importance. *Sogdian independence*: QC 6.3.9, with their lack of satrap and their command, together with the independent Indians, by Bessus at Gaugamela (A. 3.8.3). *Alex.'s bearers*: QC 7.6.7f. *Cyropolis*: E. Benveniste, Journ. As. (1943–5) pp. 163ff. *Alexandria-Eschate*: A. 4.1.3, 4.1. *Nomads*: cp. K. Jettmar, Die Fruhen Steppenvolker (1969); M. Rostovtzeff, Iranians and Greeks in South Russia (1928); E. D. Phillips, Brit. Journ. of Aesthetics (1969) pp. 4–18 is a good introduction to their art; Aristot. Pol. 1256 A saw their point. *Love-story*: Chares F. 5 with Jacoby's commentary. *Spitamenes*: S. 11.8.8 calls him a Persian, not a Sogdian or Bactrian. Spitam. was a kinsman of Zoraster. *Prohibition*: Onesic. frag. 5. Machines in A. 4.2.2 must be catapults, as trench would stop towers; stone-throwers too, as they pound the walls (A. 4.3.1). Razing of Cyropolis (QC 7.6.21) omitted by A. and (hence?) calls natives in 4.4.1 'volunteers'. QC 7.6.27 = J. 12.5.4 say prisoners, rightly. A. omits Meleager and Perdiccas (QC 7.6.19); were they suppressed by Ptol.? New towns/settlements in Sogdia and Bactria: A. 4.16.3, QC 8.1.1, J. 12.5.13, S. 12.517 (includes the 7 razed cities). *Bounds of Bacchus*: QC 7.9.15, Plin. NH 6.92; presumably a haoma-cult on the frontier. Casualties in QC 7.9.16 are omitted and losses in 7.7.39 minimized by A.; he also omits numbers of reinforcements at 4.7.2. *Khwarezm*: S. P. Tolstov, Drevnei Chorezmskoi Tsivil. (1948, German trans. 1953); cp. M. M. Diakonov's fine account in Po Sledam Drevnikh Kultur (1954) pp. 328ff.; B. Rubin Historia (1955) pp. 264ff. discusses the early cavalry; Khwarezm horsemen can also be seen in the widespread terracottas found in western palaces (M. Rostovtzeff-Yale Class. Stud. (1935) p. 188. pl. 7) where they evidently served as garrisons, a point now proved by the reliefs in S. P. Tolstov, Po drevnim deltam Oksi (1962) from Koi-Kilgan-Kala. In the Persepolis inscription of Artaxerxes II or III, Uvarazmis (Khwarezm) occurs as a subject area; this does not mean it still was one. QC 7.4.5, A. 4.15.4 show its independence in Alex.'s day; the architectural influence of Achaemenid styles in Khwarezm

noted in S. P. Tolstov (1962), pp. 112, 114, 128, may or may not imply membership of the Empire. *Army numbers and Hipparchies*: see my forthcoming study.

Omen: P. 57.5, A. 4.15.7–8 (stressing Ptol.'s role): QC 7.10.13–14. *Merv:* Plin. NH 6.47 implies an Alexandria there, and Plin.'s evidence is good on these cities; QC 7.10.15 supports him and from a splendidly ingenious deduction, F. Schachermeyer Alex. der Grosse (1949) pp. 515–16, note 187 adduces Craterus as the officer in charge in Merv. *Bazeira:* QC 8.1.10–19 with R. Merkelbach, Die Quellen der Alexanderroman (1954) pp. 48, 252; cp. the prologue to DS 27, i.e. Cleit. *Sources for Cleitus:* see my forthcoming study. His relegation: QC 8.1.20. *His nephew:* Berve s.v. Proteas. *Spitamenes's death:* A. 4.17.7 gives no support to QC 8.3.1–15, typically romantic. *Sogdian rocks:* QC 8.4 = DS prol. = Cleit. on the snowstorm. *Alex.'s throne:* QC 8.4.15, Val. Max. 5.5.1. Front. Strat. 4.6.3. *Geography:* F. von Schwarz, Alex. in Turkestan pp. 75ff., esp. on the second rock's impregnability. QC 7.11, though 28–29 is vivid, puts the first rock in winter 328; so too does the prologue to DS 17, one more excellent proof of their close adherence to their source Cleit. A. 4.18.4 (Ptol., probably) omits the crucifixion of Ariamazes but puts it, surely rightly, in early 327. Sisimithres's rock (QC 8.2.19) bore also the regional name of Rock of Choriene (A. 4.21): only QC 8.2.20 mentions, correctly, the river in its ravine. *Roxane's marriage:* A. 4.19.5f. is not chronologically precise; S. 11.517 dates the wedding to Sisimithres's rock; QC 8.4.21 a while after that; Sisim.'s food (QC 8.4.18f.) is the essential prelude to this wedding banquet! QC 8.4.21 (emending the Ms. to Oxyartes) implies a return visit to Oxyartes; the wedding probably belongs there (after A. 4.21.10). P. 47.2 and QC 8.4.23 specify love at a banquet; A. 4.19.5 (citing Ptol. and Aristob. and contemporary opinion) insist on the love; P. and A. approve Alex.'s temperance (a theme of Aristob.?). QC does not explain that Roxane had already been a captive; A. muddles the timing, so that love at first sight seems even more plausible: *Wedding custom:* M. Renard and J. Servais, Antiqu. Class (1955) p. 29 bring no worthwhile argument against the observation of this custom by von Schwarz in Turkestan; QC 8.4.27 is merely QC's ignorant guess. *Painting:* Lucian Imagin. 7; Plin. NH 35.34 for Aetion's contemporary date, so that the amorous style of his picture reflects the love story of Alex.'s own officers. *Oxyartes and Artabazus:* A. 3.28.10 (Oxyartes and Bessus). A. 4.17.3 and QC 8.1.10 (Cleitus's appointment) date Artabazus's resignation some months before Roxane's marriage, so the two are unlikely to be related; however, Barsine had conceived Heracles by the time of Alex.'s wedding, so the Roxane affair must have been a snub (DS 20.20.1 for the child's birth-date); note, though, that Berve s.v. Cophen served contentedly, so a rift with Artabazus is not in any evidence. *Successors or Epigonoi:* P. 47.6, QC 8.5.1 (important). *Possible Chiliarch:* I reason this as follows: Hephaistion and Cleitus had been joint Hipparchs in 330; in winter 329/8, I believe, more hipparchs were appointed, while Cleitus was offered Bactria as his province. Hephaistion needed some new status, for he too had been a hipparch already; in 327, Alex.'s orientalizing took its first and last turn between 330 and 324; I suggest Hephaistion became Chiliarch then, esp. when Alex. was marrying a wife and therefore risking the spite of his oldest lover. For the office, which existed in various forms, none clearly distinguished by the Gk. term, let alone by later lexicographers and sources as bad as Ael. VH. 1.21, cp. A. 3.23.3, Nepos Conon. 2 for it in its highest form, though lesser army and court officials could also be called 'Commander of a 1000': A. 1.22.7.

Proskynesis: J. Horst, Proskynein (1932) collects the Greek evidence; Feodora, Prinzessin von Sachsen-Meiningen discusses it outstandingly well in Geschichte der Hunnen (1963, ed. Franz Altheim) vol. II pp. 125ff.; however, her linguistic argument fails in view of Call. F 31, for waves cannot blow kisses and evidently by Call.'s time (or his quoter's) the word *proskynein* could also be used in a wider sense. The Audience Scene at Persepolis has been explained by Herzfeld and others as the Median usher sheltering his breath from the Sacred Fire; this is absurd, as the burners beside him may be for incense, not holiness, and nobles on Artaxerxes's tomb pay the same gesture nowhere near a burner. The more plausible view, that the hand indicates the Mede is talking, is challenged by the very curious reproduction of the scene on the inside of a shield on the Alex. sarcophagus, revealed by the photography in V. von Graeve's excellent Alexandersarkophag (1970) pl. 70. The hand here definitely is paying *proskynesis*; cp. the horseman on the Pazyryk carpet now in the Hermitage (5th c. B.C.). E. J. Bickermann Parola del Passato (1963) pp. 2141ff. is another fine study; Hamilton HCPA pp. 150–1 has missed its point and is unaware of the work cited above; for background, B. Meissner, Berlin Akad (1934) pp. 2ff. and for Sassanid differences: W. Sundermann Mitt. der Inst. für Orientfor. (1964) p. 275. J. P. V. D. Balsdon Histor (1950) pp. 363ff. is also valuable, though his note 48 on Alex.'s curious father-complex quotes bad evidence. That the Greeks believed the Persians paid *proskynesis* to their king because he was a god (cp. 'Xerxes the Persians' Zeus' in the extravagant Gorgias, ap. Longinus 3.2) is implied in Isocr. Panegyr. 151 and asserted in QC 8.5.11, both of them highly unreliable. Xen. Anab. 3.2.13 proves nothing; Aristot. De Mundo p. 398, 22 ed. Bekker is worthless; Greeks complained *proskynesis* was slavish (Xen. Hell. 4.1.35, P. Them 27.4), not blasphemous: cp. R. W. Frye Iran. Ant. (1972) p. 102 for the custom's continuity. *Greek ambassadors*: Hdt. 7.136, P. Themist. 27–28. Nepos Conon 3.3 and esp. P. Artax 22.8 (where *kupsas* rules out prostration) are not evidence that grovelling was standard practice, only that the King thought Greek envoys so abject that sometimes when they came as prisoners or pleaders, he made them go right down. The joke in A. 4.12.2 was that the Persian was overdoing it! *Elephant*: Aristot. Hist. Anim. 498 A 9, improving on others' views: cp. De Incess. An. 709 A 10; Hist. An. 630B and Ael. Nat. An. 13.22.1. *Persian queen*: A. 2.12.6. *Sources*: A. 4.10.5f is completely worthless and unlikely even to derive from a peripatetic (not that that would say much for it?). A. 4.14.2 is very different from Aristot.'s own view in Rhet. 1361 A 36 (a barbaric honour, no more, no less). QC 8.5.13f. shares the same broad structure: a speech for, a speech against by Call., a veto on the practice, a mocking of Persians. However the opinions and style are not similar to A.'s: A. 4.10.3, 14.3–4 are proof of A.'s wide reading here and he may even have composed the speeches largely himself (A. 4.11.9 drags in Xenophon!). Certainly, the nearest parallels are Imperial Roman: Ps.-Call. 2.22, Claudius's letter to the Alexandrians and Cyme's proposal for Labeo; cp M. Charlesworth PBSR (1939) pp. 1ff. Chares in P. 54.4 and A. 4.12.3 has the truth, to which add L. R. Farnell JHS (1929) pp. 79ff.; it is true that an *eschara* is known to have held the Sacred Fire in processions (Xen. Cyrop. 8.3.12) but it is a German fancy to see such fire in the mention of the *hestia* here. Call.'s attitude: F 23, 24, 42, 50 for his hellenism; T 21 is important, cp T 20; F 31 is prob. near enough to his own words. J. 12.6.17, QC 8.8.22 (as comforter). *Anaxarchus*: Berve. with full evidence. Against the bias of Clearchus ap. Ath. 548B (important), cp. Ael. VH 9.37 Timon F 58. Philodem. De Vitiis 4.5.6 is very interesting; cp. perhaps A. 4.10.6–7 for the sentiment; with 4.11.6 cp. 4.9.7. *Call.'s wine*: T 12. *His speech*: Hermipp. ap. P. 54.1 (dubious, as Hermippus was quite close to peripatetic). *Mocking of Persian*: A. 4.12.2, QC 8.5.22, P. 74, each of a different officer. Only QC 8.5.20 and P. 53.1 single out the elder men as esp. hostile, but both passages are tendentious. *Craterus's tenacity*: cp. P. Eumen 6.2. *Dropping of proskynesis*: Only in A.'s false version, J. 12.7 and QC 8.5.21 is *proskynesis* stated to have been dropped; A. 4.14.2 (though false) implies a different tradition. Chares's story says nothing either way. DS 18.61.1 shows the Macedonians paid it posthumously to Alex. as a god; conceivably, Ptol. and Aristob. said nothing, because the incident was insignificant, except to fans of Call. But their silence (hence A. does not refer to them) may have been a carefully considered one. *Pages' plot*: A. 4.12.7, 13.5, 14.1 show A.'s wide reading here. However, the close and exact similarity of A. 4.13 to QC 8.6.1–23 suggests they used a common source; A. 4.13.4, 13.7 differs trivially from QC 8.6.9, 6.20. In view of A. 4.13.5 = 8.6.16, this source may well be Aristob., throughout. QC 8.6.11 is the only clue to the date after the *proskynesis*: S. 11.11.4 names the village as Cariatae, a name traceable near the Oxus. *Persian hunting-custom*: Ctes. 688 F 40, Xen. Cyrop. 1.4.14, P. Mor. 173 D. *Protests*: QC 8.7f. picks up the false A. 14.2. At 8.7.2, Sopolis had in fact gone home! (A. 4.18.3). *Fathers*: Sopolis (A. 4.18.3)

Asclepiodorus (A. 4.7.2 with the past participle in 4.13.4). Charicles may be son of the loyal satrap of Lydia, but for another Menander see P. 57.3. *Callisthenes's role*: A. 4.12.7 implies two separate points, Call. as accomplice, Call. as instigator. Ptol. and Aristob. are not known to have asserted Call.'s complicity (A. 4.14.1; cp. QC 8.6.24, P. 554); this was a variant story (A. 4.12.7). QC 8.8.20 claims Call. was altogether guiltless (cp. 'some' in A. 4.14.1), though he suggests mild involvement as instigator (8.6.24). *Alex.'s letter*: if Hamilton can deduce the recipients' absence from A. 4.22 with QC 8.5.2 and 22 in 1961, a third century forger could have done so far more easily with the original histories, not A.'s choppy narrative, in front of him. I cannot see how such a letter would survive nor why Alex. should ever write so frankly. P. 55.6 says 'nobody knew the pages' plans'; that is not inconsistent with instigation by Call.? *Anaxarchus's comment*: Diels Vorsokr. 2. p. 239 (from his On Kingship). *Letter to Antipater*: P. 55.7, as if in Call's lifetime, only fits the delayed-action of Call.'s death (apologetic and therefore false?). *His death*: A. 4.14.3, Chares ap. P. 55.9 (*Malloi Oxydrakai* may be P.'s own slip?) J. 15.3.3-7.

NOTES TO CHAPTER 24 (pp. 331-350)

India's traders: Aristob. F 20 and cp. the bdellium trade Theophr. HP 9.1.2 with Plin. NH 12.35. *Indian legends*: J. W. McCrindle Invasion of India by Alex. (1896) is a good sourcebook; Ctesias 688 F 45; Nearch. F 8, 11, 17-20 and Baeton 119 F 4; E. J. Bickermann CP (1952) pp. 65ff. is outstanding; cp. now O. Murray CQ (1972) pp. 200f. *Heracles and Dionysus*: A. Dahlquist Megasthenes and Ind. Relig. (1962) collects much evidence and draws wrong conclusions. The 'date' in Magasth. ap. Ind. 9.9. The constant stress on India's 'ancient independence' and the lack of any mention of the Persian precedent is interesting. *Heracles*: Berve nr 353, despite Tarn's will to disbelieve. *Alex. and kings*: P. Alex. 4. *Army*: see my forthcoming study. *Satraps*: A. 4.22.5 and Berve I p. 276 (chart of satraps). *Sasigupta*: Berve Sisikottos nr 707. *Nicaea*: A. Foucher CRAI (1939) pp. 435f. *Indian army*: e.g. B. K. Majumdar Milit. Syst. in Anc. India (1960). *Elephants*: P. Armandi, Hist. Mil. des Éléph. (1843); H. Bonitz, Index Aristotelicus (1961) s.v. Elephas; H. F. Osborn, Proboscoidea (1936-42) vols. 1-2 and R. Carrington, Elephants (1958); a vast subject, and now, P. Goukowsky BCH (1972) pp. 473ff. on howdahs. *Alex.'s route*: S. 15.1.26 for its logic; O. Caroe, The Pathans (1958) pp. 45ff. improves on Stein's views. The Swat excavations by Italians, reported in East and West, cannot be tied to place or date. *Peucelaotis*: M. Wheeler, Charsada (1962), guessing a link with Alex. *Nysa*: A. 5.1-2, QC 8.10.7 = DS prologue = Cleit., P. 58.6. *Kafirs*: E. T. Schuyler-Jones, Annotated Bibliog. of Nuristan (1966) is full of interest; G. Robertson, Kafirs of the Hindu Kush (1896); Eric Newby, A Short Walk in the Hindu Kush (1972, 2nd ed.) is the most delightful book referred to in these notes; K. Jettmar Proc. Amer. Philos. Soc. (1961) pp. 79ff. discusses ibex worship and ecstatic dancing of females (Bacchants?); cp. Robertson p. 384. G. M. Grierson JRAS (1900) pp. 501ff. on Kafir's language; F. Maraini, Where Four Worlds Meet (1964) for Kafir religion. *Meru*: Polyaen. 1.1.2, QC 8.10.12, A. 5.1.6. Cp. D. C. Sircar, Ind. Stud. Past and Pres. (1967) pp. 233f.; *Coffins*: QC 8.10.8. *Pir Sar*: A. Stein, On Alexander's Track to the Indus (1929), esp. pp. 100-59, is a masterpiece; cp. R. Fazy, Mélanges Ch. Gilliard (1944) pp. 7ff. *Heracles myth*: said to urge on Alex. (A. 4.28.4) despite Arr's. own uncertainties as to its truth (28.2) QC 8.11.5 credits Eumenes (Ptol's enemy) with heroics which A.-Ptol. 4.29.1 confines to Ptol. *Taxila*: Sir John Marshall, Taxila vols. 1-3 (1951) with M. Wheeler, Flames over Persepolis pp. 112-15; cp. the Aramaic inscription found there, of uncertain date (Seleucid?), by Cowley and Barnett JRAS (1915) p. 340. *Indian customs*: Nearch. F 11, 28. Aristob. F 42. Onesic. F 5. *Gymnosophists*: Onesic. F 17, Aristob. F 41, Nearch. F 23; A. 7.2.2f. is based on Megasthenes, not Onesic. (cp. 5.15.1). P. 65.3 proves the chapter is a patchwork (against Hamiltion HCPA p. 180). Only Megasthen. mentions the theme 'son of Zeus', not the contemporary Onesic.; the drastic emendation of J. Enoch Powell (JHS 1939 p. 238) for P. 65.2 is neither sense nor necessary. U. Wilcken Sitzb. Berl. Akad. (1923) pp. 161ff. wrongly argues that Aristob. F 23 refutes Onesic.'s entire story. *Their legend*: A. 7.1.5f., with the new papyrus of V. Martin and P. Photiades, Rhein. Mus. (1959) pp. 77-139; despite J. D. M. Derrett, Class. et Med. (1960) pp.

64ff., I do not believe it to be a lost work of Arrian. F. Pfister Hermes (1941) pp. 143ff on the Gymnosophist legend; cp. J. D. M. Derrett, Zeitschr. für Relig. u. Geistesgesch (1967) pp. 33ff., best account so far of the Milindapanha and its link with the Alex Romance.

NOTES TO CHAPTER 25 (pp. 351–362)

Porus's reward: QC 8.12.18; S. 15.1.28. *New cities*: M. Wheeler, Flames over Perse-polis (1968) pp. 98–118 with new evidence. *Battle site*: uncertain, but I prefer A. Stein, Arch. Reconn. in N.W. India (1937) pp. 1–36. *Battle*: A. 5.9–19, QC 8.13–14, DS 87–89 (weak), P. 60 citing Alex.'s own letter which I deeply suspect; P. 60.2 does time the battle (cp. QX 8.14.28) but all the letter's other details match A.'s except for the absurdity of the thunderstruck Macedonians (P. 60.2) which, despite Hamilton HCPA pp. 163ff., surely condemns it. Ptol. is left behind in QC 8.13.27, 23; not so in A. (and cp. QC 8.14.15)! QC 8.14.5 names Perdiccas; Ptol.-A. 5.15.1 omits him – deliberately? In my opinion, Ptol.-A. never mentions the Foot Companions in battle (contra DS 88.2, QC 8.14.16 on their sarissas against elephants). At A. 5.12.2 I believe Cleitus's and Coenus's brigades to be Hipparchies (cp. A. 5.16.3; and soon after, A. 5.22.6) and I suspect A. has muddled these 2 former Foot-commanders with their former units; A. 5.13.4 mentions no Foot Companions in the infantry line (phalanx merely means 'battle-line' here, as often); A. 5.14.1 names 6000 infantry (cp. 5.18.3), and 3000 hypaspists, 1000 Agrianians and 2000–3000 archers makes this up alone (A. 5.12.2; cp. their 3 commanders in 5.16.3); A. 5.13.4 implies Alex. had more than the 3 Hipparchies of 5.12.2 to choose from. I suggest he took Cleitus's and Coenus's too, and that they were no longer phalanx-leaders, though A. confused them under the neutral word *taxis*. *Coenus's charge*: Against the enemy right (A. 5.16.3); QC 8.14.18 is muddled. *Elephant-weapons*: QC 8.14.29. For Porus, s.v. Berve nr 683. *Bucephalas*: Seal-stone in A. D. H. Bivar, Journ. Num. Soc. Ind. (1961) pp. 314–16, with O. Rubensohn, Hellenistisches Silbergerät in antiken gipsabgussen (1911) pp. 45–6 and pl. 6. E. T. Newell, Seleucid Mints (1938) esp. p. 239 and pl. 51, E. Babelon, Les monn. des Rois de Syrie (1890), introd. pp. 18–25; Appain Syr. 56, Malalas p. 202 (ed. Bonn). Suidas s.v. Bucephalas (emended text). *Marco Polo*: A. Ricci, Travels of Marco Polo (1939²) p. 57. *Alex. Medallion*: cp. also W. B. Kaiser, JDAI (1962) pp. 227ff. *Caesar*: Dio 37.54.2, Plin. NH 8.155 and now S. Weinstock, Divus Julius (1972) pp. 86–7.

NOTES TO CHAPTER 26 (pp. 363–372)

F. Schachermeyer Innsbruck. Beitr. zur Kulturgesch. (1955) pp. 123–35 (reprinted in G. T. Griffith, Main Problems) is properly indulgent to Alex.'s aims. *Sacrifices*: QC 9.1.1; DS 89.3. *Weather*: Ctesias F 45: contrast A. 5.10.1, for Alex.'s knowledge. *Timber*: DS 89.4 = QC 9.1.4 = S. 15.1.29 = Cleit. Onesic. *Plans*: Nearch. (ap. Str.) F 20; A. 6.1.2f.; their quotes disagree. Theophr.: HP 8.4.5 (surely these unknown Pissatoi are Indians?) Banyan: Onesic. and Aristob. in S. 15.21–24: Theophr. HP 4.4.4–5. Ael. Hist. An. 5.21 on Alex.'s peacocks (QC 9.1) is very nice. *Rains*: Aristob. and Nearch. in S. 15.1.17–18: cp. Indica 6.5. *Snakes*: Nearch. F 10B, Indica 15.11, Aristob. F 38; Onesic. F 16, 22. A.'s Anabasis is unforgivably flat, omitting all these details on principle. *Chenab*: Ptol. ap. A. 5.20.8. *Porus's mission*: A. 5.21.2. *Indian casualties*: A. 5.24.5. *Prosperity's Kingdom*: S. Levi, Journ. As. (1890) pp. 234–40. Onesic. F 21. *Dogs*: Aristob. F 38, 40 (cp. S. 15.1.31). *Reinforcements*: DS 95.3; QC 9.3.21. *Ceylon*: Onesic. F 12,13. *Phegeus*: DS 93.2 = QC 9.2.1–7, P. 62. Magadha: e.g. Camb. Hist. Ind. pp. 279ff. K. A. N. Sastri, A Hist. of S. India from Prehist. Times . . . (Oxford, 1966) pp. 82ff. *Ksandrames*: against Camb. Hist. Ind., the name is better derived from Augrasainya, son of Ugrasena (B. Prakash, Stud. in Ind. Hist. and Civ. (1962) pp. 104ff. shows the link with Magadha's dynasty, anyway attested in Buddhist sources). *Landscape*: A. 5.25.1 knows of a fertile land beyond the Beas (cp. Ael. Hist. An. 15.7!); DS 93.2 (QC 9.2) refers to a deserted land 'beyond the Indus river'; i.e. the Thar desert. D. Kienast Hist. (1965) pp. 184ff. wishes to emend this 'Indus' also to the Beas, and so criticize Cleit.'s geography. But Alex. may indeed have asked about the Indus too; cp. S. 15.1.26, 32, for his (initial) knowledge of the Thar desert, perhaps acquired from Phegeus on this occasion. As Alex. may have been further south on the Beas than Kienast believes (S. 15.1.32 does not exclude this), the Thar desert may in fact have been near to the south (the rivers and steppe-geography of the area are not known for 326 B.C.). Certainly, Cleit. the Alexandrian (who wrote *c.* 25 years before Megasthenes) did not dream up such a precise reference to Ksandrames, and whether or not his geography is a slip, Alex.'s staff knew the truth beyond the Beas (cp. A. 5.25.1). *Ganges:* Polycleit. F 10; A. 5.26.2, DS 18.6.2 are not to be discounted, esp. as a Royal Road with milestones ran from Taxila to Palimbothra (Plin. NH 6.61f.). *River-Jewels:* Plin. NH 37.1–77. *Bribery:* DS 94.3, J. 12.4.12–11; again omitted by A! DS 94 1–3 is excellent. *Mutiny:* A. 5.28–29 (again, Alex. sulks 'for two days') DS 95 = QC 9.3.19 = P. 62.7 = J. 12.8.16, and I doubt if it is mere legend. Philostr. Vita Apoll. 2.43 is interesting. *Dhana Nanda:* F. F. Schwarz Die Griechen u. die Maurya-Dynastie, in F. Altheim, Geschichte Mittelasiens im Altertum (1970) pp. 267ff. *Barber's son:* B. Prakash, Studies in Ind. Hist. pp. 114ff. and the Jain Hermacandras Parisistaparvan 6.232, 8.2–3; his rule, e. g. the Visnupurana 4.24. *On numbers:* B. K. Majumdar, Milit. Syst. in Anc. India (1960) with epic parallels; cp. S. Digby, Warhorse and Elephant in the Delhi Sultanate (1971) pp. 55ff. for comparable numbers. *Chandragupta:* P. Alex. 62.9, Mor. 542D B. Prakash, Studies, passim. On Kautilya, studies are countless; e.g. U.N. Goshal, Hist. of Ind. Pol. (1966); H. Scharfe, Unters. zur Staatsrechtl. des K. (1968); Megasthenes needs study; R. C. Majumdar Class. Accounts of India (1960) and JAOS (1958) p. 273, (1960) p. 248 are moves in a better direction than O. Stein, Megasthenes u. Kautil. (S–B, Wien 1921). *Palimbothra:* L. A. Waddell, Report on Excav. at Patna (1903), M. Wheeler Flames over Persepolis (1968); Megasth. FGH 715 F 18, 19, 32; Ael. Hist. An. 13.18.

NOTES TO CHAPTER 27 (pp. 375–386)

Roxane's miscarriage: Epit. Mett. 70. *Fleet:* contrast Ind. 19–20 with the different details and numbers of A. 62.3–4. Nearch. puts the fleet lower than Ptol. and for his figure of 120,000 men see my forthcoming study. *Qurqurrus:* S. Casson, Ships and Seamanship (1971) p. 163. Horse-transport by sea is itself a skill, which, for example, the Normans only learnt from the Arabs and so managed to ship cavalry across the channel: Diction. des Antiquit. s.v. Hippagogoi for evidence. One wonders how Sassanid Persians brought horses from India by sea to Persia! *Baggage-train:* I quote from Mooltan by J. Dunlop, M.D. (1849). *Purple sails:* Plin. NH 19.22. *Malloi:* A. 5.22.2 is important for prior enmity. *Style of the campaign;* A. 6.14.2, 6.20.1–2, cp 6.15.1, 6.6.1 and esp. 6.15.7 and Aristob. ap. A. 7.20.1–2: restoration of freedom and *autonomia.* Implies that memories of Persian rule on lower Indus were short (A.6. 14.2 – but note the startling QC 9.7.14, which in view of links with Arachosia discussed by A. Foucher, La vieille Route (1947) vol. 1 p. 209f. may not be wrong; the more we know of Arachosia, the more is mattered). *Atrocities:* A. 5.24.3–5 for their existence before the mutiny. Surrenders were treated mildly (DS 96.2.3, A. 6.4.2; DS 102. QC 9.8.4–7) but resistance was savaged: DS 96.3, QC 9.4.5–6, A. 6.6.3, 6.6.5–6.7, 6.11.1 with DS 99.4. *Alex.'s aims:* M. E. L. Mallowan, Iran (1965) p. 1; W. F. Leemans, For. Trade in Old Bab. Period (1958) pp. 159ff. put them in perspective. For Alex. – Opiane, cp. Steph. Byz and A. 6.15.2 with Steph. s.v. Opiai, quoting Hecataeus (F 299) and (ultimately) Scylax; DS 102.4, QC 9.8.8 probably refer to this Alexandria too, whose location (under a wrong ancient name) is discussed by Maj.-Gen. A. Cunningham, Ancient Geography of India, vol. 1 (1871) pp. 170ff. *Mutinous doubts:* A. 6.7.6, QC 9.4.16. *Multan:* A. 6.8.4 (the 'greatest city') and its topography support the site (P. Mor. 327B, 344C are mere rhetoric). *Alex.'s rescuers:* omission by A. of Aristonous (QC 9.5.15) is less likely to be Ptol.'s bias than is the vilification of Perdiccas in A. 6.9, which recurs nowhere else. But it fits ill with views of Ptol.'s 'personal' history that he denied Cleit.'s story of his glorious presence; the denial does not prove which of them wrote first. *Previous audacities:* e.g. A. 4.3.3, 26.6; QC 4.4.10. *Medical theory:* e.g. Galen 4. 708–9; F. Steckerl, Fragms. of Praxagoras (1958) pp. 17ff. F. Lammert, Gymnas. (1953) pp. 1–7 on the wound. *Alex.'s recovery:* A. 6.12–13. *Peace offerings:* QC 9.7.15, 9.8.1. *Building plans:* A. 6.16.7, 6.17.1, 17.4, 18.1, 18.7, 20.1; 6.20.5, is surely Xylinepolis, the Wooden City, of Onesic. and Nearch. F 13.

Brahmins: DS 102.5 is briefer and darker than the credible A. 6.15.6f., proof of why severity was needed; cp. the '80,000' killed in Sambus's kingdom, QC 9.8.15 = DS 102.6 = Cleit., where A. 6.16.4f. is subtler and more realistic. A.-Ptol. omits (Cleit.'s?) flattering affair of Ptol.'s cure: QC 9.8.25, DS 103.6, 5.15.2.7. *Detachment of Craterus*: A. 6.15.5, picked up again at A. 6.17.3 (despite Craterus's job at 6.15.7). Conceivably, the massacre of the Brahmins was omitted by Ptol. or Aristob. (or both) and A. flicked to a new source for it, returning to Craterus (cp. J. 12.10.1) where he left off. But the slip may simply be stylistic, like many of mine. *Sacrifices at Pattala*: A. 6.19.4–5, both to Ammon's (differing) order. For the tide, cp. Periplous of Red Sea 37–40. *Nearchus*: Indica 20, esp. 20.2 (near to pothos) and 20.11. *Financing*: P. Eumen. 2.

NOTES TO CHAPTER 28 (pp. 387–402)

The Makran march has been brilliantly discussed in the one outstanding modern article on Alexander: H. Strasburger Hermes (1952) pp. 456ff. and his note in Hermes (1954) p. 251. I agree that A. 6.23 = Ptol.; A. 6.24–25 = S. 15.2.6–7.1 = Theophr. HP. 4.4.13 = Nearch. But *polloi* in A. 6.24.1 implies Nearchus was not the only (original?) source to give a frank account. *Gedrosians' embassy in 330*: A. 3.28.1, one important source of A.'s 'knowledge'. *Geography*: the coastline is now known to have receded greatly (cp. the most recent inspection by the Pennsylv. Mus. team, reported in their bulletin 'Expedition' for 1962). The 3rd millenn. towns perhaps imply a kinder prehistory than Strasburger (and Sven Hedin) believe: cp. Antiquity (1962) p. 86, (1964) p. 307 for reports. But R. H. Raikes and E. Dyson in Americ. Anthropologist (1961), (1963) argue from study that this early settlement did not presuppose a milder climate; note, however, S. 15.2.3 where Makran is 'less fiery' than India. Mere heat was not its basic horror. *Alexandria-Rhambaceia*: A. 6.21.5, 22.3 for its founding; DS 104.8 places it 'near' the sea; Periplous of the Red Sea 37 knows of a capital town 7 days inland, on a river. Steph. Byz. s.v. Alexandria names an Alexandria-in-Makarene (Makran), on the river Maxates; probably it was near Coccala (Ind. 23.5 for Leonnatus's meeting with the fleet) perhaps on the modern river Purali and doubtless on an ancient site. How far the spice trade mattered (A. 6.22.4) rather than the surrounds (Peripl. 37) I do not pretend to know. The settling of the town with Arachosii (QC 9.10.7) is not an error; under Persian administration (e.g. Darius Bisitun 47, and the absence of any province called Gedrosia), Makran was part of Arachosia (hence A. 3.28.1), an arrangement that Alex. returned to when his satraps died. *Skirmishings*: the stress on Ptol. in DS 104.5 = QC 9.10.7 = Cleit. is omitted from Ptol.-A. cp. the very interesting DS 103.6 = QC 9.8.21–28 = 5.15.2.7, prob Cleit.; cp. now P. Goukowsky REA (1969) p. 320 (unconvincing). One should remember too the 'pro-Ptolemaic' source (Cleit. ?) in DS 18. *Motives for the march*: Nearch. in A. 6.24.2–4 (too often mistranslated), S. 15.2.5 (note 'they say' - Nearch. and Cleit.?). Indica 20.1; 32.10 (important). *Semiramis*: QC 7.6.20, 9.6.23 and W. Eilers, Semiramis (1971) for her legend. *Sea-trade*: H. Schiwek Bonn. Jahrb. (1962) pp. 43–86; ponderous, but much bibliogr. on Nearchus's route. N. Pigulewskaya, Byzanz auf den Wegen nach Indien (1969) is worth comparing. *Spices*: J. I. Miller Spice Trade of the Rmn. Emp. (1969) cites much evidence, to be used critically. *Persian sea-trade*: Dar. Susa inscrip. 30–5. *Alex. and Staff*: A.'s *autoi ge* at A. 6.23.1 is the only hint of disagreement. *Supplies*: A. 6.20.5 with QC 9.8.29; not for the garrison but the *stratia* (expedition, but in A. 6.21.3 = land army, not fleet). Some of these supplies may have been eaten by Nearch. during adverse winds (first 2 months), but Ind. 21.13 implies men were going hungry very soon. *Satrap's death*: Ind. 23.5, A. 6.17.1; to call him an innocent scapegoat is sheer fantasy. *His troops' victory*: DS 106.8 garbles QC 9.10.19, whose source and order he is following; Ind. 23.5 (cp. A. 7.5.5) is Nearch.'s own report and obviously correct (R. D. Milns Alex. the Great (1968) p. 235 is absurd). *Sources for the march*: Strasb. p. 478–86 is excellent. *Nearchus's voyage*: Indic.21–35. *His grain-ships*: *kerkouroi* in 31.3.23.3. *Cinnamon*: J. I. Miller, Spice Trade, pp. 154f. *Alex.'s rescue-camels*: DS 105.6, QC 9.10.17, P. 66.3, A. 6.27.3 (C. B. Welles's note in his Loeb Diodorus pp. 426–7 is another of his blunders). *Kirman*: S. 15.2.14, Onesic. F 32. *Revel-triumph*: A. 6.28.2; doubts are important (unlike 5.1.2, they did not have gods to allay them – cp. the revel at A. 5.2.7, incredible to A.) but he probably had not read Cleit, who sponsored the story first. DS 106.1 = QC 9.10.22 = P. 67.1–3. = Cleit.; though an Alexandrian (Jacoby T 12). Cleit. perhaps wrote before the Dionysus myth had been fully adopted by Ptolemies. *Results*: cp. A. Alfoldi, Rom. Mitt. (1954) pp. 88ff., F. Pfister, Real-Encycl. supplem. 4. 177ff., s.v. Epiphaneia (very thorough); Kallix. FGH 627 F 2; Val. Max. 3.6.6, Plin. NH 33.150; Dio 77.7.1. Ptol. and Aristob.'s silence is without weight: could all this have begun from mere literary legend? *Nearchus's return*: Ind. 33–36, esp. 35.8. *Bagoas*: Dicaearch. ap Athen 13. 603 A–B *Numbers of losses*: Uncertain, but Strasburger pp. 486–7 is wrong.

NOTES TO CHAPTER 29 (p. 403–420)

Aristotle's advice: Mary Boyce, trans. Letter of Tansar (1968) pp. 27ff. Machiavelli The Prince, chap. 4. *Provincial unrest*: the chart in Berve vol. 1 p. 276 is invaluable. *Bactria*: QC 9.7 where I suspect Berve nrs 27 and 29 are the same man. The election of a king is not compatible with the move to go home, perhaps a minority attempt (QC 9.7.11 is vague). *Iranian revolts*: Berve s.v. Tyriaspis (cp. Proxees), A. 6.27.2 (India); Menon (with A. 6.27.3); A. 6.29.3 (how many associates?) Berve s.v. Autophradates (summoned yet again in winter 328/7: A. 4.18.2, AC 8.3.17 and eluded arrest; *regnum affectasse suspectus* he was at last brought to Susa in 325/4 and deservedly killed; QC 10.1.40–42 is a good warning against QC's own rhetoric; Berve s.v. Astaspes (cp. Indica 36.8 – the cause or the effect of his arrest? P. 68.6 suggests it was the cause; Berve s.v. Orontes and Sabictas; Zopyrion (a very interesting march: J. 12.2.16, 37.3.2 on its scale; Marob. Sat. 1.11.33 on its direction, recalling Alex.'s objectives in A. 4.15.6; note how Olbia was an ally of 'free' Miletus, Tod 195). *Alleged reign of terror*: E. Badian in JHS (1961) pp. 16ff. has inspired whole books for the general reader by his trenchant comments; unfortunately, not only his opinions but at many vital points his evidence are mistaken. A thorough refutation is long overdue. In his list of victims, Apollophanes (no scapegoat, but explicable simply in terms of a native revolt and the East's bad roads), Autophradates (summoned earlier), Antipater (uncertain) and perhaps Agathon should be removed, leaving 8 certain depositions, 5 of them Iranian, 4 of them governors under Darius. The statistics for 331–328, when arrests were made at court, are far more impressive; by then, Alex. had not been thwarted on the Beas. (We can omit Mazaeus, Phrasaortes and others between 331 and 327 who 'died in time'). Badian's list of detentions ignores geography (in Atropates's case), evidence (Stasanor: A. 6.29.1; Peucestas: arrived on the eve of Alex's death), possible slander in the pamphlet of Alex.'s last banquet (were the 20 officers present, or only accused of being present?) and, incidentally, the evidence for absentee satraps who often lived at court in Persian times (e.g. a vast subject, Driver, Aramaic Documents passim on Arsames, and esp. Xen. Cyrop. 8.6.4–5). *Alex.'s increasing harshness*: Indic. 36.1–2 is interesting; A. 6.27.4 proves nothing; 6.27.5 is A.'s own comment; 7.4.3 picks up 6.17.4 and is relevant (but who said so – *legetai*?) Aristob. in 7.18.1 is the best evidence, but again Alex. was punishing, not venting his own frustration! DS 106.2 (note his term *misoponeria*; was this idea present in Cleit.?) thinks it all justified; there is no objective original source with which to 'tear away' any 'veil of unreality', for even Cleit. wrote a eulogy and all other decent sources were courtiers. There is only the silly rhetoric of Curtius himself; cp. his twisting of the arrests of Astaspes (deliberately misdated: QC 9.10.21 and 30), Autophradates (misinterpreted) and Orxines (muddled, see below). I would like to know more of P. 68.7, Alex.'s own spearing of a satrap, but note P. 68.3, vindicating Alex.'s purge. Personally, I cannot see that he was any harsher than at his accession (though sources later liked to stress his change, Roman style, for the worse). QC 10.9.18, DS 18.37.2, 19.51, put this brief purge into perspective! *Median generals*: Berve s.v. Cleander, Sitalces the Thracian, Agathon (once i/c Thracians) and Heracon. It is most odd that Badian does not list the mass killing of 600 mercenaries, but then he does not refer to the charges laid against their leaders either. *Temple plunder*: Polyb. 10.27 is very relevant; for the offence cp. the death of Antiochus III in Persia, DS 28.5. *Rape*: cp. the anecdotes in P. 22, 41 and Moral 333A, *Disbanding of mercenaries*: cp. Schol. on Dem. 1.19 for precedent. DS 106.2–3, though geographically in Kirman (Jan.–Feb. 324?) suggests this order belonged after (because of?)

540

Harpalus's flight (for who else had gathered money to escape?). Harpalus fled from Tarsus (Theopomp. F 253-4), not Babylon, absurdly far to lug so much treasure. He must have reached Athens by 22 July 324; he was admitted by Philocles whose generalship (as described in Deinarch 3.1) is known to have been held by another man in 324/3 (IG 2² 1631). Badian p. 42 reaches the same view for the wrong reason and adds an impossibly vague argument from Timocles's Delius. I would guess Harpalus arrived in July, as did Nicanor; he will have fled Tarsus in June, with his 6000 mercenaries. If so, the mercenary order belongs c. mid-simmer 324; men in Alexandrias were apparently unaffected (DS 18.7.1f – were these mercenaries too or citizens of the realm?) and I wonder if, e.g., Cleomenes had to give up his troops? Certainly, many would not be Greeks, let alone Exiles! *Pasargadai*: Aristob. ap. A. 6.29, S. 15.3.7. F 51. The 'first visit' in line 22 was in early 330; the repair order was given on the second visit. P . 69.3 names Polymachus as the culprit. Aristob. F 51 B line 27 insists it was not the work of the satrap; QC 10.1.27f. is thus claptrap, for if the satrap had been accused of rifling Pasargadai, the apologetic Aristob. would not have refuted the charge. In fact, Orxines was hanged at Persepolis for robbing royal tombs (H. Strasburger Gnomon (1937) p. 492 asks 'which royal tombs, then?' Answer: those all round Persepolis's terrace, still on view today). A. 6.30.1 does not exclude Bagoas from among the accusers. QC 10.1.37f. is merely Roman colouring! *Susa*: Aboulites and Oxathres, Berve s.v. Ps.-Aristot Oec. 1353A is valuable background; cp. Indica 38.9. *Loyal Iranians*: Berve s.v. Atropates, Phraphernes, Artabazus, Oxyartes. We certainly do not know their replacements were 'nonentities'. They may have been princes, every one of them: DS 19.48.1-2 is very relevant to their merits; for Archon, satrap of Babylon cp. his prestigious inscript. in BCH (1959) pp. 158-66, dated by J. Bosquet to refer to a victory in the games before 334. *Babylon prophet*: Aristob. ap. A. 7.18. *Harpalus*: Berve s.v., with all the evidence. *Babylon portico*: F. Wetzel-E. Schmidt, Das Babyl. der Spätzeit (1957) pp. 24ff. Theopomp. 115 F 255-7; 253-4, esp. 253 lines 25f., a vital comment. Berve lists all the precious evidence of comic poets too. DS 108.4: we do not know whether Harpalus was head treasurer or only one among many. For Pythionice Aphrodite cp. Athen 254A, 588C, 587B and P. de Amat. 9 (Belestiche) and the mass of evidence for Arsinoe Aphrodite. *Tarsus coins*: E. T. Newell Tarsos under Alex., pp. 16-22, surely a trace of Harpalus. H. von Aulock J. für Num. u. Geldg. (1964) p. 79 does not affect this. The nearby treasury at Cynda is discussed by R. H. Simpson Histor. (1957) p. 503. *Harpalus's brothers*: Berve s.v. Tauron, possibly Philip and Calas Harpalou may be relevant; we simply do not know that Harpalus's father Machatas was Elimiot (see my counter-examples on Chap. 2) or that this link with Cleander the Elimiot would have mattered, any more than, say, Ptolemy favoured Aristonous, his fellow Eordean, or Craterus favoured Perdiccas, also Orestid, in the not so dissimilar chaos when Alex. actually had died. Old neighbours can hate each other more violently than strangers. *Arrest of messengers*. if Harpalus's first 'flight' was planned (as I believe) for spying, P. 41.8 must refer to the second one. *Letter from Greece*: QC 10.1.43, where *Coeni* is surely a silly Ms. or Curtian slip for *tou koinou* in the Greek original. *Exiles*: DS 18.56.3, and esp. 4-5 are a fine reminder that exiles did not cease being exiled in 336-4. Arcadia, from which the one certain inscription referring to the Exiles Decree has come (Tod 202), had supported Agis in 332/1 and opposed Alex. in 336/5. In each case, men will have been exiled; cp. DS 18.56.4, implying many exiles had been banished since 334 inside Greece. P. A. Brunt CQ (1969) pp. 241ff. makes the 20,000 a wholly plausible number: DS 18.8.5 is quite explicit that *all* the exiles had gathered, numbering over 20,000 (no reason to 'add in their wives and families', with Badian!). *Exiles Decree*: not relevant to Alex.'s deification or to his mercenaries! If Alex. primarily wanted his roaming mercenaries to go home, he would have issued a Mercenaries Decree; in fact, there is no hint that these mercenaries were mostly exiles, rather than starving vagrants; still less are they known to have been Greeks. Badian pp. 25-40 muddles the whole issue; here, I only note that even by late 323 a mere 8000 were waiting at Taenaron and long after the Exiles Decree, showed not the slightest sign of returning 'home' (DS 18.9.1; 18.21.1 is probably their remnants); that there were most certainly not 'more mercenaries in the Persian service than those at Issus' (the reference to Hammond, Hist. of Gr. p. 665 is empty); that only at the Granicus (where Alex. slaughtered most Greek mercenaries available to Darius) were any Greek mercenaries branded as traitors and these were sent back to Macedonia's mines, not punished with exile (A. 1.16.6); that the few Greek mercenaries left after the Granicus massacre and the Issus dispersion either died at Gaugamela or were mopped up in 330, on terms, when known, which turned not one of them into an exile (A. 3.24.5). One could elaborate, but mercenaries and exiles are not the same problem at all; I imagine the Exiles Decree applied only to the Greek League (DS 111, hardly a 'grim and vivid description', does not gainsay this, any more than it specifies that the men involved were Greek exiles, not Carians, Egyptians etc. Like 106.2. I imagine this is mere hyperbole, DS 18.8.5 is decisive for the numbers involved – not more than those lured by Agis!) If the disbanding order does belong after Harpalus's flight, the Exiles Decree may have been sent back to Greece before any mercenaries were on the roam at all. Tod 202 lines 9–16 shows that in Tegea at least, many returning exiles had been extremely well off. Arcadia was famed for mercenaries, but at Tegea, site of the most solid evidence for the exiles' return, we also know of upheavals after Agis (QC 6.1.20), a more relevant point. Throughout we must allow for flocks of exiles who were driven out even before 338. *The Decree*: E. Bickermann REA (1940) pp. 25ff. is the one outstanding discussion, pointing out its legality (in theory) and the tactful revival of *diagrammas* in 319 (DS 18.56.1 with 56.3). I have nothing to add to an article which should have settled the matter. *Bearer of decree*: Berve s.v. Nicanor nr 557. *Date*: R. Sealey CR (1960) p. 185. *Calanus*: P. 69.6–70.2 (the debauch), A. 7.3, 18.6, DS 106. S. 15.717–8. Athen. 437A. Ael. VH 2.41. Cic. de Div. 1.47. Val. Max. 1.8 ext. 10. Suida s.v. Calanus. *Weddings*: Chares F 4 with A. 7.4.4–8. On the points of status cp., e.g., W. K. Lacey, Family in Class. Greece (1968). The Dura marriage – evidence is remarkable: F. Cumont, Fouilles de Dura (1926) chapter 6, nos 62–67 and pp. 344–5. S. 14.5.25 is correct, culturally; cp. S. 17.1.12 where *migades* surely only means Greeks of mixed Greek origin, not Greco-Eyptians.

NOTES TO CHAPTER 30 (pp. 421–435)

Debts: A. 7.5, where 7.5.2 does not, to my mind, read like A.'s own invention (despite A. Prol. 2) but a straight report of Alex.'s (alleged?) words. Only the Persian monarchy made a parade of truth as a virtue of a ruler. A. 7.5.3 agrees, interestingly, with J. 12.11.2–3 for the amount; the precise P. 70.3 with QC 10.2.9–11 (cp. DS 109.2) seems preferable. A. stresses it was debts (*chrea*) in excess of pay (A. 7.5.1); conceivably, the soldiers were owed money for their *trophe*, which they may have borrowed money to buy, instead of being given money officially during the Indian campaign. But Indians did not use easily equatable coinage and Greek accounting was feeble. *Epigonoi*: A. 7.6, P. 71, omitted by QC. *Companions' losses*: 7 or more Hipparchies seem to have shrunk to 4 by 324 (A. 7.6.4); true, Hephaistion is named in autumn 324 as a chiliarch leading a cavalry chiliarchy, but this need not have been 1000 men, any more than a Macedonian dekas was 10 men or a Roman century 100. Anyway, the unit is so called only after the replenishment at Susa: I do not believe the hipparchies' number had been halved, because the strength of each had been raised to 1000, before the name chiliarchy occurs. I cannot solve the text of 7.6.4, if indeed it is corrupt; cp. 7.8.3 for similar use of *alla gar*: I discuss the hipparchies elsewhere. *Pasitigris*: A. 7.7 with S. 16.1.9. Cp. the maps in G. B. Le Rider, Suse (1965). *Alexandria*: Plin. NH 6.138–9 with J. Hansman, Iran, Antiqua (1967) pp. 21–58 (not all cogent); E. Herzfeld, Pers. Emp. (1968) p. 9, a brilliant point; cp. Isaiah 22.5. The Arab name Karkh Maisan could mean 'fortress' as well as Carians. *Opis meeting*: a subtle affair, wasted on QC 10.2.12 who has not even reported the arrival of Epigonoi: we do not know if Ptol. or Aristob. recorded this; broad features are agreed, perhaps all through Cleit.; Alex.'s enraged speech (DS 109.2, QC 10.2.14, P. 71.4, A. 7.9, J. 12.11.7; of course the actual speech in A. is A.'s own construct from scraps of wide reading and of no independent value, any more than QC's), arrest of ringleaders (A. 7.8.3, J. 12.11.8, QC 10.2.30 agree on thirteen), two days' sulk (A. 7.11.1, P. 71.7; very suspect, after similar wait on the Beas and after Cleit.'s murder!). *Persian appointments*: DS 109.3, P. 71.4, QC 10.2.5, J. 12.12.3 and A. 7.11.3, the decisive text for the existence of both *asthetarioi* and *pezhetairoi*. *Weeping surrender*: DS 109.3, J. 12.12.6, QC 10.3.5, P. 71.6–8, A. 7.11.4.

Quip about Ammon: P. 71.3 has a variant, which perhaps discredits A. 7.8.3 = J. 12.11.6. *Site of the mutiny*: QC is too fragmentary to be specific; so is DS (despite 110.3) and J.; P. 71 gives no location, except between Susa (70) and Hamadan (72). No doubt the grumbling began at Susa. *Banquet*: A. 7.11.8–9 with P. 70.3 (in muddled order, but giving the very interesting detail of the gift of a gold cup). P. knows the logos in A. 7.11.9. *Homonoia*: Dem. 14.36, Isocr. Philipp. 39–40, Panegyr. 173–4 etc. Cp. E. Skard, Zwei religios. polit. Begriffe (1932), a most useful study, esp. of the virtues of Heracles as befitting Alex. DS 18.4.4–5 and Tod 201 line 30 show A. 7.11.9 is not just A.'s rewording: the word *homonoia*, though pretty empty, was definitely in the air. *Promise to children*: A. 7.12.2; cp. 7.8.1 with P. 71.10. *Ethelontai ede* in A. 7.12.1 says much: the veterans' departure had been planned since A. 6.17.3; at Opis, their fellow-Macedonians were protesting that if any Macedonians were sent home, then they'd all walk out (A. 7.8.3, P. 71.3, J. 12.11.5; QC 10.2.12 misses the nuance of Persian replacements) *Imitation of Alex.'s banquet*: DS 19.22. *Alex. and Persian methods*: e.g. S. 2.69 (*gazophylax*); S. 2.1.6 (royal files). *Episkopoi* in e.g. 3.22.1, 28.4 are presumably the old King's Eyes. Wearers of Purple in P. Eum 8.7. *Origins of Greek culture*: not an anachronistic ideal to see in Alex.; cp. Isoc. 5.154 (perhaps as limited by S. Perlman, Histor. (1967) p. 338) and DS 1.28.9 (using Hecataeus of Abdera, writing under Ptolemy I: O. Murray JEA (1970) pp. 141ff., esp. p. 152 for the date and relevance). A. Diller, Race-mixture among the Greeks before Alexander (1937) is a useful background to Alex.'s dilution of his Hellenic ruling class and for the tenacity of Greek civic bodies abroad (it may have been different in the countryside, for such Greeks as lived there). Outside Egypt's chora, note the rarity of mixed marriages in the (admittedly scarce) evidence for Greek 'citizens' in Egypt; W. Peremans, Vreemdelingen en Egyptenaren (1937) is still the fullest survey, with the judicious views of V. Martin, Actes du 8th Congrès Int. de Papyrol. (1955) pp. 85–90, which further decrease the numbers. F. Chamoux, Cyrène sous les Battiades pp. 215–25 underlines this. S. 14.5.25 firmly rules out any Greco-barbarian culture; note the famous case of the Macedonian who married an Arab and brought his children up as Greeks (to judge by their names): DS 32.10. This fits A. 7.12.2; note the ready favour for Artabazus's bilingual children (e.g. 7.4.6); Darius's daughters were only married when they had learnt Greek (DS 67.1) Peucestas was the one exception (A. 7.6.3 only makes sense if he was something unique); Alex., despite Bagoas, Magi and diadems, stood first for a hellenized culture and class. *Elderly veterans*: A. 7.12.6 (their condition); J. 12.12.8 (valuable); for Polyperchon, cp. QC 8.5.22; Antigenes was Philip's man (P. 70.5); Craterus (P. Eum 6, P. 47, DS 18.4.1). *Antipater*: note that orders were still addressed to him (P. 71.8 and DS 18.8.4). A. 7.12.7 (based on A.'s own wide reading?) is decisive that all sinister guesses about Antipater's future were guesses then, and still are. P. 49.14 lacks any date or precision (no reason to date it to 324/3 rather than 330 or any other year); Antipater may have bought off the Aetolians with a treaty in 332/0, in order to be free for Agis; cp. DS 18.25.5 for a similar false treaty with them. There is no other sign (least of all after 323!) of any close friendship between Aetolia and Antipater. *Returning veterans*: Antigenes's presence and the points adduced by F. Schachermeyer, Alex. in Bab. (1970) pp. 14 n 10 and 160 n 147 imply the elderly Silver Shields left for home in entirety; DS 18.12, A. 7.12.1, DS 109.1, J. 12.12.7 all put their numbers at 10–11,000. The numbers in DS 18.16.4 are for Alex.'s own veterans and for Craterus's 'recruits on the march' (i.e. in 323/2). *Dead generals*: only Demetrius (apparently) and Coenus the Hipparchs. *Bodyguard*: Berve 1 p. 27. *Perdiccas's clique*: Alcetas and Attalus Andromenous, with family: only 2 of the 4(?) remaining Foot Companion brigadiers. F. Schacherm. Alex. in Bab. pp. 13ff. characterizes the court allegiances in 323, but deduces too much from men's behaviour after Alex.'s death, which changed everything, not least personal loyalties. *Aristander*: Ael. VH 12.64 (omitted by Berve). *Alex.'s dinners*: Ephippus 126, F 2. *Hatreds*: P. 47, A. 7.12.7, P. Eum. 10 and 55 (Antipater). *Bisitun*: DS 110.5. The route in 110.3–4 is not without logic, once it is realized that it refers to his journey from Susa to Spasinou Charax (the Carian Villages), then through Sittacene (cp. S. 16.1.17); Sambana goes back to Kampanda (the old Persian name for the district of Bisitun); then, to the Celones (site of exiled Eretrians, Hdt. 6.119, not Boeotians!), then to Bisitun. The days' intervals are incomplete and the list is in a muddled order, but this itinerary certainly goes back to an eye-witness. *Nisaean Fields*: DS 110.6, rounded down in A. 7.13.1. *Amazons*: A. 7.13.2 with S. Runciman, Hist. of Crusades vol. 2 (Peregrine ed.) p. 262 n 1; also Xen. Anab. 4.4.17. *Hamadan*: DS 110.6 (influenced by Hdt.'s fabulous city? or by Deinon, via his son Cleit.) is refuted by the clear Polyb. 10.27. *Harpalus's comedy*: Athen. 586 D, 595E – 596B with B. Snell Scenes from Greek Drama (1964) pp. 99f. and H. Lloyd Jones, Gnomon (1966) pp. 16ff. *Hephaistion*: A. 7.14, based on wide reading; a very fair critique (note that the story given in his abbreviation of Epictetus, 2.22.17, is repeated here disbelievingly). A. 7.14.8 omits the role of Perdiccas (DS 110.8) but here, this must be due to A.'s shortening, not Ptol.'s malice. P. Pelop. 34.2 and Ael. VH 7.8 have the dismantled battlements; Polyb. 10.27 refers to Hamadan as a 'wall-less city', which may be relevant. *Hair cutting*: cp. P. 72.3 with Hdt. 9.24. Cp. too P. Eum 2, 9.10. Polyaen. 4.3.31 (with P. 72.5's comment). *Lion of Hamadan*: al Masudi, Les Prairies d'Or 9.21 (French transl. 1865),'the probability of which has been well stated by Prof, Luschey in a lecture in Tehran, still unpublished; the Lion of Chaeronea, the Lion of Amphipolis (for Nearchus) and even perhaps the Lions on the Asoka columns suggest this style was introduced and diffused by Macedonians (who lived among mountain-lions). *Omen*: Aristob. in A. 7.18; preferable to P. 73.3–5.

NOTES TO CHAPTER 31 (pp. 436–460)

Alex.'s finances: DS 114.4 (contribution to funeral from subjects) with P. Artax. 23.5; P. Eum. 2.5 (another personal contrib.). F. Altheim–R. Stiehl, Die Aram. Sprache unter den Achaimen. (1963) vol. 1 pp. 109ff. discusses the evidence fully; J. 13.1.9 is the crucial text, a measure of the whole subject's impossibility. If 30,000 talents seems an absurd sum for yearly tribute (and it does) then we simply cannot emend it and at the same time hold to the 50,000 figure for reserves! *Alex.'s generosity*: e.g. P. 39 with Xen. Cyrop. 8.2.7 on traditional generosity of Persian King: cp. P. 69.1. Also Theopomp. F 224 (biased?) for Philip's attitude. *Antimenes the treasurer*: Berve s.v. with Ps.-Ar. Oec. 1352B, 1353A. A. Andreades BCH (1929) pp. 10–18. *Chiliarch*: J. Marquart, Philolog. Supplem. (1907) pp. 222ff.; P. J. Junge Klio (1940) p. 13; E. Benveniste, Titres et noms propres en Iranien (1966) pp. 68ff.; W. Hinz, Iran. Funde (1968) pp. 63ff., the most plausible view; F. Schachermeyer, Alex. in Bab. pp. 31ff. *Eumenes*: P. Eum. 2.4. *Pomp*: DS 18.60.5 (throne and sceptre – 18.27.1). Phylarch 81 F (cp. DS 17.17.4, QC 9.7.15). Polyaen. 4.3.24. Duris 76 F 49 with Chares 125 F 4 (the audience tent served for weddings too). *Persian parallels*: cp. A. Alfoldi, La Nouvelle Clio (1950) pp. 537f.; also Studies in Hon. of A. M. Friend (1955) p. 50 for theatrical element and the precedent of Dionysus. *Deification*: Theopomp. F 253 lines 27f. are decisive for divine honours being paid by Greeks, somewhere, before 324 B.C. (the *timai* must be the same as those offered to Pythionice, for the sense of the sentence; for *time* as a divine honour cp., e.g., P. Mor. 804B). *Honours*: Tod 201 lines 45f. (plausibly restored). I agree with Welles and Bickermann in dating this to 332; one should remember the Ammon coins in NC (1962) p. 65 from Mitylene F. Salviat BCH (1958) pp. 193ff. has birthday games in Thasos *c.* 300 B.C. C. Habicht Gottmenschtum (1970, 2nd ed.) lists later evidence on pp. 17ff. S. Weinstock HTR (1957) p. 234 argues cogently for Alex.'s statue in divine procession. I feel it needs no qualification to assume all this during Alex.'s lifetime in, e.g., Greek Asia; that was what Theopomp. F 253 meant. *Aristotle*: Magna Mor. 1208B, not refuted by K. Latte, Klein. Schr. p. 51 on fondness for local deities. *Becoming Zeus*: Pindar Isthm. 5.14, Olymp. 5.56, cp. the (late) evidence for the Salmoneus myth; Apollod. 1.89, Hyginus Fables 61. *Pythagoras and Empedocles*: Ael VH. 2.26, 4.17, 12.32, 13.19. Empedocles 31B, 112n, 4f. (Diels) *Euthymus*: Plin. NH 7.152, citing Callimachus; Paus. 6.6.4–12. Ael. V.H. 8.18, S. 6.1.5. Inschr. von Olymp. Nr 144, cp. the Thasian athlete in J. Pouilloux, Thasos vol. 1 pp. 62ff. *Dion and Lysander*: Habicht pp. 1–16, with the decisive new evidence in Archaeol. Anz. (1965) p. 440. *Philippeum*: Paus. 5.20.9 with K. Scott TAPA (1931) pp. 101ff., a valuable point not wholly refuted by P. Herrmann, Istanb. Mitteil. (1965) p. 87 n 49. cp. the Amynteion in Pydna (Schol. to Dem. Olynth. 1.5, Aristid. 1.715D). Also the Timoleonteion (P. Tim. 34, DS 19.6.4); was the Mausoleum posthumous? *Pamphlet's advice*: Isocr. Philipp. 132, 137, 145 and esp. Epist. 3.5; cp. Hesiod Theogony 96, Isocr. to Nicocles 3.26. Aristot. Politics 1288 A 15 with Ethics 1145 A 23, Rhet. 1361 A.

Freedom and divine kings: Habicht pp. 160ff. and A. D. Nock, Papers pres. to F. C. Grant (1951) pp. 127ff. *Alex. and Athens*: E. Bickermann, Athenae (1963) p. 70 with the full evidence on this insoluble topic. Hyper. Epitaph. 21 is in too highflown a context to begin to be decisive; we do not know what Hyper. meant by *ananke*! The tomb for Harpalus's mistress on the Sacred Way could be relevant to the quip about 'servants as heroes'. But Demades's prosecution suggests, to my mind, that some honours had gone through in 324/3 (Ael. VH. 5.12, Athen. 251B). A. 1.1.3 must be pondered; A. 7.23.2 proves nothing. For Athens' later attitude cp. P. Demetr. 10.1 and DS 20.46. *Alex.'s alleged 'demand'*: Ael. VH. 2.19, P. Mor. 219E share the one surviving source for this and, like Hogarth (cp. J.P.V.D. Balsdon, Histor. 1950 pp. 383ff.) I think it is 'a statement so worthless that it does not deserve a place in the creed of any responsible historian'. The wearing of crowns by the envoys (as by *theoroi*) in A. 7.14.6 (where *dethen* is A.'s own irony, not necessarily implying the comparison was false) may imply Greek worship, but says nothing for Alex.'s demands. *His religiosity*: Lucian Slips of the Tongue 8 (note Eumenes's letter!); Val. Max. 7.3 ext. 1 (cp. Suet. Aug. 96.2). *Dolphin*; Duris ap. Athen. 13.606, Ael. Hist. An. 6.15, Plin. NH 9.8, Pollux 9.84, proved to my mind by the coin in Head Hist. Num. 528. *His credibility*: A. Heuss, Antike U. Abendland (1954) p. 65 (excellent). L. C. Ruggini Athenaeum (1965) p. 3; D. Michel Latomus (1967) p. 139. M. Simon, Rech. d'hist. judéo. chrétienne (1962) DS 18.60,61 is basic. *Saffron shoes* A. Alfoldi, Studies for A. M. Friend (1955) pp. 60ff.; M. Bieber Archaeol. Jahrb. (1917) p. 21. *Thunderbolt*: Plin. NH 35.92, P. Alex. 4 and the Porus Medallion. *Castor and Pollux*: Plin. NH 35.93 with F. Cumont, Le Symbolisme funér. des rom. (1942) pp. 64ff. *Neisos gem*: Furtwangler Antik. Gemm. plate 32.11. *Egyptian statues*: P. Perdrizet Monum. Piot (1913): pp. 59ff.; J. Bernouilli Erhalt. Darstell. des Alex (1905) p. 112. The portrait in faience depicted in Bull. van der Antik. Besch. (1965) p. 80 suggests a cult-bowl, like those used in Ptolemaic ruler-cult. *Apollo coins*: Kraay–Hirmer plate 171. cp. Mausolus and Artemisia as Heracles and Demeter on coins. *Alex. and Dionysus*: A. D. Nock, JHS (1928) pp. 21ff. remains definitive, though at times a little too logical. *Distant gods*: P. Merlan, Zeitschr. für Philos, Forschung (1967) p. 485 is important; cp. the Demetrius Hymn (Duris F 14). *Ephippus*: 126 F 5. He has nothing whatsoever to do with the Ephippus in A. 3.5.2 whose patronymic must not be emended to an ethnic! Kock CAF vol. 2 pp. 250ff. seems to me to be the same man (probably); his victory at Athens in the 360s (IG 2²23 25.145) puts his birth *c*. 390 and even if his F 3 and 5 have been too hastily ascribed to Alex.'s doings in 335, F 14 (against Plato) and F 17 are suggestive. Athen., admittedly, does not specify him as 'Chalcideus' when he quotes him; I readily suppose, though, that Ephippus 'comicus' would also write in prose. *Divine dress*: O. Weinreich: Menekrates Zeus u. Salmoneus (1933) is a brilliant study, with wide-ranging notes. *Parrhasios*: Ael. VH. 9.11, Plin. NH 35.71; J. M. Edmonds, Elegy and iambus nr 3. *Clearchus*: J. 16.5.8, Suida s.v., Isocr. Epist. 7.12, Memnon 434 F 11; M. Wallisch, Philolog. (1955) p. 250. *Menecrates*: Athan. 289 C, Weinreich passim and esp. pp. 92ff. for sources in full Isocr. To Nicocles 32 is valuable on the overtones of royal excess in dress. *Divine pretensions in Macedon*: I do not believe that Macedonians found these cults nationally repugnant; inscriptions are simply too scarce as yet to prove their basis, or otherwise, in Macedon, where there were few towns, anyway, in most areas. P. Perdrizet BCH (18) p. 417 is a good prelude; readers of J. Bekker, De Suidae Excerpt. Histor. (1916) will not set much store by Antipater's alleged shock in the entry in the Suida, a work partly excerpted by a Byzantine monk from an epitome of Virtues and Vices. *Sacred feasts*: Diodor. Comicus ap. Athen. 239B; P. Demetr. 12, Antony 24. W. Herzog, Heilig. Gesetze von Kos nr 10 (Ab. Berl Ak. 1928). More in A. B. Cook, Zeus 2. 1168f., A. D. Nock HTR (1944) pp. 150ff. F. Herter Wien. Stud. (1966) p. 556 on DS 18.61; cp. Theocrit. 17.18. The Zalmoxis banquet in Thrace should be compared; Theopomp. F 31 with F. Pfister in Studies pres. to D. M. Robinson pp. 1,112ff. It is these practices which explain the quips in Chariton, Chaereas and Callirhoe 6.17.2; the finest Roman example is the Gytheum inscription for Augustus; Ehrenberg and Jones nr 102. On epiphanies, cp. F. Pfister R. E. Supplem. 4 vol. 301ff. *Alex.'s dress*: E. Neuffer, Das Kostum Alex. (1929) is still useful; J. P. Tondriau, Rev. de Philol. (1949) p. 41 is an invaluable complement. *Hermes*: Athen. 289C with Furtwangler, Antike Gemmen. pl. 31.24, vol. II.

158.24. *Heracles*: Varro in Servius ap. Virgil. Aene. 8.564. Full list in R.E. 3.1109. Also A. R. Anderson HSCP (1928) pp. 8ff.; *Artemis*: Philip's statue in Ephesus's temple of Artemis is probably irrelevant. DS 18.4.5 is Alex.'s link with her. *Roman parallels*: In the Gytheum inscription, Drusus is linked with Aphrodite; Caligula in Dio 69.26.6, Suet. Cal. 52; Philo. Emb. to Gaius 78f. omits the goddess bit. H. Delbruck Antike und Abendl. (1932) p. 21. Histor. Aug., Heliog. 28; P. Demetr. 23f. DL 6.102 (Menedemus the Cynic). As Artemis, Ephipp. refers to Alex.'s *sibune*: for its Macedonian meaning, cp. Hesych. s.v. Sibune, DS 18.27.2; Papyr. Cairo Zenon 59362 lines 34f. *For the attitudes to divine dress*: Suet. Aug.. 70 (a smear story). But note Suet. Aug. 94.6. Weinreich pp. 82ff. deals well with Salmoneus. More Roman parallels in H. G. Niemayer, Stud. zur Statuar. Darstell. der Rom. Kais. (1968) p. 198; the sealstones in E. Porada Iraq (1960) pp. 220ff. esp. pl. 31.3, 9 are a very curious parallel, possibly all depicting gods and goddesses. Note too R. Merkelbach Quellen des Alexanderroman pp. 252–3. *Alex. as melancholic*: Ephippus F 5 line 34; (see Addenda) *Drinking*: the Diaries are the lynch pin for A.'s 'increasing alcoholism' and they are suspect;. Aristob. F59, 62 may be apologetic, but one only apologizes when one thinks one has a case worth defending. *Nomads*: A. 7.15.1, DS 111.4–6, Indic. 40. 7–8 (important). P. 72.4 (P.'s own comment). S. 11.13.6. DS 19.19.3. *Embassies*: A. 7.15, DS 113.2, J. 12.13.1. Cleit. F 31 specified Romans, a trivial point to invent *c.* 310 B.C.; the silence of Ptol. and Aristob. (A. 7.15.6) can be explained by disinterest or by inclusion of Rome in the Tyrrhenians. A. 7.15.5 cites two obscure historians, not necessarily because A. had not read Cleit., but because only these two had the prophecy by Alex. of Rome's future eminence (naturally omitted by Cleit.). DS's silence proves nothing, though it may be due to DS's own milieu rather than his negligence. S. Weinstock HTR (1957) p. 247 tends to support this Roman embassy; so do the events of 334–29 in southern Italy. A. 7.15.5 has an interesting stress on world mastery – cp. *legousin*, which includes Ptol.-Aristob; cp. 'kingship of Asia' in 15.4. Dionysius I in fact had introduced Greeks to Celts and Iberians. *New plans*: Carthage's embassy is important: J. 21.6.1, Frontin. 1.2.3. Oros. 4.6.21. QC 10.1.17 (following dealings with Nearch. drawn ultimately from the Indica) may just conceivably go back to Nearch. too, via Cleitarchus. A. 7.1.2 refs. to 'some historians' for a plan which the word *eiso* after Gadeira proves to be the circumnavigation of all Africa: cp. P. 68.1 (source unknown). Hdt. 4.42–3 puts the plan in perspective. A. 5.26.1 need only derive from this rumour; it is untrue that the 'geography is not Alex.'s' for we do not know Alex.'s own opinions, still less what he would say to encourage his men. A. 7.16.2 suggests he thought the Caspian might be Ocean. How could he know the truth? He certainly did not know minor works of Aristotle by heart. *Apelles and War*: Pliny NH 35.93–4. Virg. Aen. I. 294f. R–E 8A col. 2526f. *Arabs*: A. 7.20 (a *logos*, but in fact Aristob. F 56: the S. quote does not suggest that Aristob. himself reported this as only a logos). P. A. Brunt, Greece and Rome (1965) p. 211 cites this passage as supporting evidence for Alex.'s 'demand' for worship; in fact there is no word of any demand here. In A. 7.20.1 he 'did not think it unfit that he should be so worshipped'; in the S. passage, 'he supposed he would be so honoured'. In view of his honours in Greek Asia this was a fair (and dry) comment. On Arabs cp. F. Altheim–R. Stiehl, Die Araber in der alt. Welt (1964) vol. I. Unfortunately S. and A. differ in their quotes; S. in Jacoby line 22 says Alex. was 'aiming to be master of everyone'; Arr. 7.19.6 (quoting this, unacknowledged, as adapted to his own view, as elsewhere) that he was insatiable (A. 7.1.4 suggests S. may be nearer the original). S. 785C says Alex. wished to make his *basileion* in Arabia. *Spices*: A. 7.20.2, Aristob. F 57. S. 16.4.19, Periplous of Red Sea 29. *Explorers*: A. 7.20.7, S. 16.765–6, Berve s.v. Hieron, Archias, and Androsthenes s. of Callistratos, I would guess son of the famous Athenian who went to Thasos in exile: Dem. 50.52, Scylax 67. This fits nicely with the pro-Macedonian conduct of their relation Callimedon, Ps.-Aesch. Ep. 12.8. *Gorgo*: Ephippus F 5; SIG 312. Berve s.v. He may well be the same man as the metal-prospector. *Samos*: SIG 312, DS 18.8.7, notes to Tod 190. Note in SIG 312, DS 18.8.6 how popular this decision was with other Greeks. *Samos in 334*: A. 1.19.8. F. W. Mitchel, Athens in the Age of Lycurgus (1970) is useful for background, *Thrasyoulus*: CIA 2. 808A, 39. *Attack on Athens*: J. 13.5.1 and QC 10.2.2 are mere gossip; cp. Athen. 59 E for more camp background, all made plausible by Harpalus. When Harpalus's failure was known, this gossip collapsed. *Deification*: Ael. VH 5.12, Val. Max. 7.2.13. Gnom. Vatic. 236 (Sternbach). Timae. ap. Polyb. 12.12.3; Dein. in Dem. 94. Hyper. in Dem. 31, 15f. *Alex.'s letter*: P. 28.2 (to be rejected in the absence of proof). *Athens's attitude*: Duris 76 F 13. *Craterus's march*: nothing sinister in the time it took! They were sick men (A. 7.12.14); they missed the sailing season of 324; there had been troubles in Cilicia (DS 18.22.1), possibly in 324/3. They would rest in winter. *Leosthenes*: chronology very difficult. Badian JHS (1961) p. 27 antedates it wrongly. DS 17.111 (our only guide, together with 18.9) is quite explicit; first, Alex. disbanded his mercenaries (order given in summer 324, probably received and obeyed by July?); mercenaries ran wild (better not to confuse the issue with QC 9.7.11, a very garbled passage); 'afterwards' (*meta tauta*) they flocked to Taenarum. 'Finally' (*to teleutaion*) they chose Leosthenes as leader. They were a mere 8000 (DS 18.9); they paid no attention to the Exiles decree, because it had nothing to do with most of them (cp. another – or remaining? – 2500, still at Taenarum in DS 18.21). DS 18.9.4 suggests Leosthenes's negotiations took place in spring-early summer 323, when he was general (cp. Berve). 50 talents (111.3) would not pay much of a force; note the scanty Athenian help in 323 July (DS 18.11.3). Paus. 8.52.5 is worthless (for the number, cp. QC 5.11.5, anyway excessive; Alex. had killed most of these and the rest came to grief with Agis or Amyntas in Egypt; the suggestion of E. Lepore, Parol. del Pass. (1955) p. 169 that Paus, copied the figure from a votive inscription is absurd). Paus. 1.25.3 is equally chaotic, though implies this took place in A.'s life. I am inclined to believe Leosthenes never went to Asia, ran no 'ferry service' and just met the men at Taenaron (DS 111.2–3 confirms). Harpalus's men had fled to Africa, taking money (and another 1000 mercenaries?) with them: (DS 18.19.2 with 17.108.6; contrast the 6000 men given by Arrian 156 F 9. 16f.). In spring 323 Leosthenes's prospects were even worse than Agis's (note Athens's guarded support throughout); even after Alex.'s death his effort failed, perhaps only hiring 5500 mercenaries (DS 18.9 less DS 18.21). *His father*: Schol. on Aeschin. 2.21, implying he fled to Macedon after his exile following the defeat by Alex. of Thessaly. *Persian admirals*: the answer to Badian p. 28 is men like Autophradates (never caught or retained in 331) and Chares (likewise, P. Mor. 848E). After 331, Pharnabazus had joined Alex. and his kinswoman Barsine (P. Eumen. 7.1). *Babylonian prophets*: Aristob. ap. A. 7.16.5f. (cp. Appian B.C. 2.153) explains Alex.'s entry into Babylon as only made after a sincere attempt to obey the priests – is this apology? J. 12.13.3 (specifying Borsippa), DS 17.112, P. 73 (surely specifying Nearch. as ultimate source) make the priests warn him away from Babylon altogether. In DS, Anaxarchus persuades him to go in. The massive authority of Nearch. and Aristob. guarantees that Alex. did try to take these warnings (whatever their nature) seriously. *Plans for fleet*: A. 7.19.3 = Aristob. F 56, garbled (intelligibly, though) in QC 10.1.19, P. 68.2. Plin. NH 7.208 (important), DS 18.4.4. *Canals*: A. 7.21.1 with Aristob. F 56 line 12 (Arabia his motive). Geography here is very vexed: cp. R. D. Barnett JHS (1963) pp. 1ff. and G. B. Le Rider, Suse (Mem. de la mission archéol. en Iran. 1965), esp. maps. Presumably the city was on a former outpost, perhaps the Diridotis of Indica 41.6. *Diadem*: Aristob. in A. 7.22, cp. App. Syr. 64, with the brief DS 116.5 (out of chronological order). Aristob. (against DS) insists that it was the rest of the fleet who were lost, not Alex.'s and that the man was not killed! Cp. J. 15.3.11 for the theme of the story. *Army*: A. 7.23, where 23.3–4 imply that at most there were *c.* 6700 Macedonians in camp, if all 20,000 Pers. were enrolled in the new 'phalanx'. The Carian reinforcements may include disbanded mercs. *Festivals*: Chares F 9 with A. 7.23.5. *Embassies*: A. 7.23.2, DS 113.3,–4 (revealing). *Hephaistion's pyre*: DS 115 (for the cost cp. A. 7.14.8. not mentioning Perdiccas's role: DS 110.8). A. and DS both specify it was to be a pyre (cp. DS 18.4.2); J. 12.12.12 has tumulus, P. 72.5 a *taphos* and much else. I am quite prepared to believe that Alex. planned an inflammable pyre; DS 115.2 has the imperfect, *perietithei*, and nothing suggests this pyre was ever finished (cp. 18.4.2 – evidently still incomplete). Hamilton p. 188 says 'we know the memorial was certainly completed'. We do not, anywhere. The measurements may be inflated by rumour simply because they never were finished; cp. the Last Plans. At Babylon, Harpalus's precedent of a tomb to his dead mistress should not be forgotten. Apart from the cube-shape of a ziggurat, the Greekness of the design is stressed by C. Picard, Manuel d'art grecque vol. 4, p. 1182. *Mt Athos*: P. 72.7, Mor.

335C. S. 14.641. Lucian pro Imagin. 9. Vitruv. 2.2.3. *Funeral*: DS 114.4–115.1. *Cult*: A.7.14.7, 23.6 with P. 72.4 (heroic *enagismos*!). DS 115.6 with Lucian Calumn. 17 are mistaken but explained by E. Bickermann Athen. (1963) pp. 81ff. Hyper. Epitaph. 21 is too vague and obscure to guarantee that Alex. actually *demanded* Hephaistion's worship by subject cities, and the plural *anankazometha* may refer to all Greece, not just Athens. *Cleomenes*: Berve s.v. Ps.-Ar. Oecon. 1352 A should be read with van Groningen's sensible commentary and with the similar moves made by Chabrias under Tachos (E. Will REA (1960) p. 254). Dem. 56.7f. is simply a complaint from an Athenian view; famine in Egypt itself (Aristot. Oecon. 1352B 14–20) is the background to Cleomenes's sharp practice. Despite the rhetoric of E. Badian JHS (1961) p. 19, A. (probably Ptol.!) 7.23.6 is still the best evidence for Cleomenes's 'sins'; otherwise, he ruled like any other shrewd official in occupied Egypt, suiting Alex.'s needs and showing the skill of many modern financiers on a commodity exchange (which no 'philanthropic' Socialism has ever tried to curb). The letter in A. is not original; note its Herodotean *achari* (cp. A. 156 F 130). I suspect Ptol. interfered here, anyway. For the contracts, cp. Papyr. Hibeh 199 lines 11f. for an early Ptolemaic parallel; also Welles RC 36; possibly a priest of Hephaistion would seem to have been presupposed by such an order and hence Cleitarchus, an Alexandrian, wrongly believed from contracts that Hephaistion was a full god. *Stranger on throne*: A.-Aristob. 7.24.1–3 (the best account, which in 24.3 mentions torture by Alex.; unlike DS and P., Aristob. does not say the man was killed. Cp. his account of the retrieved diadem!). DS 116.2–4 (picking up the alternative in A. 24.2); P. 73.7–74.1, the worst version (condemned by anachronistic mention of Serapis). R. Labat, Le Caractère religieux de la royauté assyro-babylonienne (1939) pp. 95–110 is a good background. Berossos 680 F 2 gives the Sacaea's date, thereby ruling it out here; the description in S. 11.8.4–5 would not fit this affair, either. Dio Chrys. 4.1.26 may merely be guesswork based on this passage. For Babylon's New Year Festival cp. Labat p. 103, also irrelevant here. *Substitute kings*: R. Labat, Rev. d'Assyr (1945/6) pp. 123–42, W. G. Lambert, Archiv für Orientf. (1957/8) pp. 109–12. (1959/60) p. 119, S. Smith in Myth, ritual and Kingship (ed. S. Hook 1958) pp. 58–9. Most recently, Parpola's commentary in LESEA (1971) pp. 54–65, a reference I owe to Prof. O. R. Gurney. For the Persian custom, which the eunuchs mistakenly invoked, cp. QC 8.4.15. It is very relevant that the Chaldeaans had warned Alex. away from Babylon; Theophrast.'s great respect for their predictions of death (recorded by Proclus, Plato Timae 3. p. 151, ed. Diehl) may derive from the way Alex.'s doom was 'foretold'. '*In Egypt, a god*': I quote from Tarn, Alex. vol. 1, p. 138. Alex.'s mistake was to kill off his scapegoat-substitute, instead of letting him bear the doom.

NOTES TO CHAPTER 32 (pp. 461–472)

Throughout, A. B. Bosworth CQ (1971) pp. 112ff. is the sharpest account; see, however, my forthcoming study. *Successors' resistance*: Onesic. F 37, DS 118.2, QC 10.10.18, J. 12.13.10. *Ephippus*: F 3 cp. Nicobule 127 F 1 and 2 but note the doubts in F 1 of her identity. *Pamphlet*: most conveniently set out and discussed in R. Merkelbach, Die Quellen des Alexanderromans (1954) pp. 220ff., building on A. Ausfeld, Rhein. Mus. (1895) p. 339, (1901) p. 517; cp. P. Ruggini, Athenae. (1961) p. 285. I discuss its problems, together with the Diaries in a forthcoming study. *Antipater*: DS 118, QC 10.10.14, A. 7.27. J. 12.14.1, P. 77 with the Stygian water in Paus. 8.17.6, Plin. NH 30.149. Theophrast. ap Antig. Caryst. Mir. 158 is misleadingly cited by Hamilton HCPA p. 215; Theophr. mentions the marvel of the poisonous water, not its use by Antipater. Possibly, Aristot. first commented on it and so it got into the story of Alex.'s death (Aristot. would naturally be said to poison him by a deadly Aristotelian method!) *Cassander's later fear of Alex.*: P. 74, Mor. 180 F, both undatable stories. *Poisons*: cp. J. Berendes, Die Pharmacologie bei den alt. Culturvolkern (1891). When R. D. Milns, Alexander (1968) p. 257 cites strychnine as a poison which ancients mixed in wine, he is muddling the soporific *Withania somnifera* with the murderous *Datura strymonium*; Theophr. HP 7.15.4, also 9.11.5 distinguishes them clearly. Only the former was used in wine; it is not lethal. Strychnine, anyway, kills instantaneously, never after 10 days. *Diaries*: U. Wilcken, Alex. the Great (new ed., 1968) p. 236 first

saw their point as propaganda. A. E. Samuel, Histor. (1965) pp. 1ff. adduces a Babylonian parallel which is irrelevant and anyway false, no such Diary being known (or
possible) in Babylonian kingdoms. Much depends on the dating of F2A, for if *Diou
menos* is read, Dios, on the correct equation, should be Octob.–November. See my
article. *The topography of Alex.'s illness*. F. Schachermeyer, Alex. in Babylon (1971)
pp. 65ff. *Immersion in Euphrates*: H. Pease HSCP (1942) pp. 10ff. with DL 8.69, Suet.
de Gramn. 26 and C. Honn, Stud. zur Gesch. der Himmelfahrt in Altertum (1928).
Aristobulus: F 59, contrast Diaries F 3 lines 24–5. *Decree for Iollas*: Moral. 849 (I am very
sceptical of this). *Eye-witnesses in Athens*: DS 18.9.4. *Poisoning in history*: David
Douglas, William the Conqueror (1964) pp. 408ff. is a useful comparison; for Con-
stantine, cp. Julian 277D, Liban Or, 18.42 Amm Marc. 16.2.8. *Aristotle and Caracalla*:
Dio 77.7.3. Alex. 'more than mortal': Polyb. 12.23.5. *Darkness*: QC 10.5.15–16. I
cannot see that this has anything to do with Schachermeyer's beloved Royal Fire
(Alex. in Bab. p. 47). *Alex.'s ascension*: DS 18.4.1, 18.56.1 and IG 12.2.645. *Alex. and
Stars*: F. Salviat RA (1966) pp. 33ff. for Thasos; Plin. NH 35.93; W. Wirgin, Hist. of
Coins and Symb. in Anc. Israel (1958) plates 6–7. *Last words*: omitted by Ptol. and
Aristob. – cp. A. 7.26.3 where *porro* means 'beyond', as usual, for we know that
Aristob. (F 59) said things 'different from' the Diaries. DS 117.4, 18.1.4, QC 10.5.5
(with a Roman comment on deification!) J. 12.15.6, A. 7.26.3, Ps.-Call. 3.33.26. The
date of Alex.'s death is settled by D. M. Lewis CR (1969) p. 272; the legend of Aristotle's involvement is traced by Plutarch, through a certain Hagnothemis, to Antigonus. This implies it sprang up *c.* 308–6, when Antigonus was hostile to Cassander
and his 'peripatetic' henchmen, esp. Demetrius of Phalerum who eventually fled to
Egypt out of fear for Antigonus; when Theophrastus, Cassander's aide, was writing
(why?) about the poison of 'Stygian water', the legend was a gift to Antigonus's
propaganda! I must, finally, stress Eumenes's co-author Diodotus; Isocr. Letter 4 refers
to the only Diodotus known in Macedonian circles between 360 and 320 and the man,
an educated ex-pupil, is to be employed by Antipater (4.9). The Diaries' author came
from Erythrae: Isocr.'s pupil had worked for 'Asian dynasts' (4.7), fitting this allusion
splendidly. If Diodotus worked on Antipater's staff, the Diaries may indeed have been
published as if by Antipater and Perdiccas, in the name of their respective secretaries.
Who the authors really were is another matter; I suspect retouching by Cassander's
circle, possibly, too, by Demetrius of Phaleron who wrote books on the cures of
Serapis. DS 19.56.1 may help to explain some of the names cited favourably in
A.7.26.2.

NOTES TO CHAPTER 33 (pp. 473–498)

The fate of the officers can be followed in QC 10.5 (Hieronymus?), J. 13.1f. and DS 18
and 19; E. Will, Histoire Politique du monde hellenistique vol. 1 (1966) is the best
survey of the struggle's logic, giving full bibliographics on dates and events. In the
description of Alex.'s funeral-chariot (DS 18.26.3), we must note its name as a *har-
mamaxa*, a specifically Persian vehicle, and apply the Mithras precedents in A. Alfoldi,
Rom. Mitteil. (1935) pp. 127ff., with full bibliography. Alex.'s plans have been put
into a telling perspective by E. Badian, HSCP (1968) pp. 183ff.; A. B. Bosworth CQ
(1971) pp. 112ff. has settled the problem of Perdiccas and Craterus. R. M. Errington
JHS (1970) pp. 49ff. takes the Successors' quarrel inch by inch, down to 321/0, but we
should read Curtius (see F. Schachermeyer, Alex. in Babylon (1970) pp. 81ff. for the
less plausible view that his source was Cleit.) with the succession crisis of 41, not 14
A.D., firmly in mind. However, J. 13.1f. is a good support. The vast subject of the
spread of hellenism can only be covered here in the bibliography; one of the few
hellenized Persians known by name is 'Boxos' in Geographi Graeci minores vol.
p. 111f., 2–4, based on Agatharchides; there is also the nameless Persian whose Greek
epitaph in Alexandria is known in A.P. 7162 Note, men like Mithridates (DS 19.39.2)
and Orontobates the Mede (DS 19.46.5) who appear in the Successors' armies briefly;
at the Seleucids' court and in their administration, Iranians remain very rare indeed.
The inscriptions of Greek Asia and nearby Aegean islands are the richest source of
hellenized Iranians, naturally enough, ranging from descendants of Median family
names to hellenized Bactrians making dedications at Delphi.

ADDENDA

p. 19. I am pleased to see that the suggestion that ancient Aigai was modern Vergina has been supported with other more solid arguments by N.G.L. Hammond in his remarkable History of Macedonia vol 1, which replaces all earlier work on the historical geography and prehistory of the country. He adds the exciting guess that the fourth-century throne found in one of Vergina's vaulted tombs may actually be Philip's; one can only hope this will be followed up on the site.

p. 104. An excellent account of the continuity of water worship (Anahita) in Iran, with modern ritual, is given by M. Boyce JRAS (1966) p. 110.

p. 202. I must stress that even if the drift of motive in A. 3.2-3.3 for Alex.'s visit to Siwah was derived from Ptolemy, that does not make it true. Ptol. certainly was not 'out of sympathy' with Alex.'s ideas about Ammon; apart from his coins showing Alex wearing the ram's horn on the elephant cap, he dedicated an altar at Siwah (Paus. 9.16.1). The word *pothos*, of course, cannot possibly be traced back to Alex., through Aristotle or any contemporary. Call. as quoted by S., used the word *philodoxia*, hence the themes of the *ingens cupido* or *pothos* urging him to Siwah, as agreed in A. and QC. The use of *pothos* perhaps is a Herodotean idiom (as argued by H. Montgomery, Gedanke und Tat) and A. allows Herodotean words to mar the purity of his anyway cumbersome Attic style in the Anabasis (e.g. *acharis, atrekes*). Montgomery lists the many uses of the word in historians of the late Hellenistic age; this puts A.'s practice into perspective, with the one reservation that these earlier uses are limited to a *pothos* to found a city, be king of Asia and so forth, which are *pothoi* that suit Alex.'s career. It would thus be possible, though unnecessary, to argue that a historian of Alex. established the word; for many reasons I refuse to believe this.

Chaps. 21-24. Peter Levi, Light Garden of the Angel King (1972) is a perceptive and elegant account of Afghanistan, based on six months' travel and a study of possible Greek sites.

p. 414. I feel it needs no proof (there is no sound evidence either way) that the Exiles Decree was sent to the League of Corinth. The Council, as in the 302 revival, met at the major Greek festivals, and Alex.'s Decree was surely reserved for the Olympic Games in order to coincide with a Council meeting. It was upheld by Polyperchon in 319 when 'freeing' the Greeks by an edict which strongly recalls Alex.'s own (DS 18.56, esp. last clauses). Despite the doubts of E. Will (Hist. pol du monde hellen. I p. 43f.). I still incline to Larsen's view that in 319, Polyperchon revived Philip's League. If so, Alex.'s edict on exiles, which he also revived, is likely to have gone through the same unit.

The Samians may suggest otherwise, as they had been exiled before the League existed, yet were restored in 324. However, Philip had arguably stretched a point against them in 338 and against his own League Charter by leaving the Athenians in possession of their island. Like the small Boeotian cities, Samos had a right to be 'free and autonomous', a clause which the Athenian cleruchy, arguably, infringed. Alex.'s decision was popular with other Greeks, and could have corrected Philip's on these 'legal' grounds (cp. his dissolution of the Arcadian League, also in 324). If he had merely been issuing a completely arbitrary edict, Philip's precedent would not have been relevant, or worth raising. The Athenians thought it was, although it failed. So, on balance, I do not think the Samians are the exception which disproves my view.

The use of an edict, certainly, was no new tyranny. We do not know when, or how, Philip and Alex. were 'entitled' to issue *diagrammata* to Greek cities, but plainly Philip did (DS 18.56), and Alex. issued one to Eresos in 332, usually assumed to be a League member (Tod 191, lines 35, 60, 129, 142 where 'diagrapha' is a *diagramma*, though the 'laws' are Eresos's own, a point proved by line 132f. Philip III's brisk résumé in 99–100 ignores the point that the tyrants are condemned off Eresos's own bat: cp. line 60). The copy of Alex.'s ruling to Chios (also by *diagramma*?) may be abbreviated, but it has a brusqueness, already in the 330s, which had not been seen in Greek inscriptions since the hey-day of democratic Athens's Empire. The *diagramma* of 324 was no new approach. It may even have been more politely phrased than its predecessors.

The details are tricky. The edict in DS 18.8 is at best an excerpt, and was followed by the full *diagramma* ruled on complex inheritance (line 57) and house-ownership (10), a reminder that we should not yet underestimate Alex's chancellery. However, Philip's League, as revived in 302, also passed rubrics on inheritance (I.G.IV. 1^2.28 line 50 (34): *kleronomoi*), so Alex.'s edict may only have ordered these to apply to the returning exiles in 324.

Other royal clauses are hinted at by agreements between the Tegea text and other texts restoring exiles throughout Alex.'s reign. Both at Mytilene (Tod 201. line 31) and Tegea (line 57), an oath of amnesty is sworn: Alex may have enjoined this from. above, perhaps as at Ephesus in 334 (A. 1.17.12). At Tegea and Calymna (Michel, nr. 417) there were boards of foreign judges, by order of the *diagramma* (Michel, line 44). At Mytilene (line 21–23) the judges were exiles and citizens, a divergence which strengthens the view that this law belongs in 332, not 324. If so, Alex.'s rulings on exiles developed (wisely) between 332 and 324. For this foreign arbitration, at least between states, cp. Tod 170, as prescribed by the League. Again, the League charter may be the source for a ruling in the *diagramma* of 324.

These clauses, common to Tegea and Calymna, do persuade me that the Exiles' *diagramma* was circulated through one centralized unit, not just through the distant night of Antipater. Philip's League forbade exiling and changes of government; perhaps where these 'evils' happened despite the Council, a clause *entitled* the king to intervene by *diagramma* (hence Tod 191; also the submission of Spartan rebels to Alex.'s will in 330). That does not make the Exiles' Decree any less stringent, but it does mean that in 324, Alex. was not necessarily acting on some new despotic whim or despising all formalities.

p. 434. H. Luschey's lecture on the Lion of Hamadan now appears in Archaeologische Mitteilungen aus Iran (1968) p. 115.

Chap. 32. W.H.S. Jones, Malaria in Ancient Greek History once equated the symptoms of 'melancholia' with those of the nervous hysteria which he had observed in cases of malaria. I doubt this, and 'melancholia' could anyway be used more widely; hence Aristotle says all great poets and philosophers have a streak of melancholia, a word frequently occurring with *oxutes* or sharpness. This volatility or nervous quickness is what Ephippus alleged of Alexander.

Chap. 33. The theme of 'universal conquest' is certainly not the invention of modern Germans as a motive for Alex. A.7.15.5 (where the *legousi* can include Ptol. and Aristob.) the (contemporary, in my opinion) inscription on Lysippus's Alexander with the Spear, and above all, Aristob. F56 line 23 imply it was in the minds of contemporaries. The 'vulgate's' questions at Siwah are at least evidence for the subsequent gossip, and one must consider how far the later aspirations of Demetrius the Besieger, painted at Athens as master of the globe, were due to his own wild ambition or a play on Alex.'s own aspirations. The latter is at least plausible: S. Weinstock, Divus Julius (1972) traces the effects of this, and much else, in extraordinary detail.

p. 280. Isidore, Stathmoi 15 and 5.11.10.1 prove that Artacoana and the new Alexandria were distinct. If Alexandria is Herat, they must have been far apart.

p. 357. Alexander's initial route through Makran remains uncertain. Stein's proposal (Geogr. Journal, 1943) is too easy a road and founders on S.15.2.4–6's insistence that the march 'repeatedly' touched the coast (unless this is S's own phrasing, and worthless). Also, it entails that Alex. abandoned his coastal route as soon as the fleet did not meet him near his Alexandria. I doubt this. Strasburger's proposal (Hermes, 1954) is difficult, too; if Alex. sent Thoas to inspect the shore early on, and found it desert, he surely would have avoided a march along it. I suspect the truth lies between Stein and Strasburger, with several loops as the guides went wrong. The coastline has certainly altered since 324 B.C.

SELECT BIBLIOGRAPHY

A. SOURCES

Despite frequent and ineffective challenge, the fullest and soundest discussions are still to be found in the articles in Pauly-Wissowa, *Realen-encyclopädie der Altertumswissenschaft*, by F. Jacoby (articles on Callisthenes and Cleitarchus) and E. Schwartz (Arrian-Aristobulus, Curtius and Diodorus). Disagreements are mostly minor, except for the theory that Ptolemy used the Royal Diaries, now admitted to be irrelevant. P.M. Fraser, *Opuscula Atheniensia* (1967), pp. 27ff. remains an essential background to these Diaries' problems; H. Strasburger, *Ptolemaios und Alexander* (1934), is of much scholarly value but errs on the side of optimism (when A.B. Bosworth's commentary on Arrian is complete, it will no doubt be impossible to neglect Arrian's own phrasing any more) and overvalues Ptolemy's own impartiality.

As for the coinage, A.R. Bellinger, *Essays on the Coinage of Alexander the Great* (1963) can only be used critically; E. Pegan, *Jahrb. für Numism. u. Geldgeschichte* (1969) p. 99, corrects one point, the dating of Alexander's gold issues, but there is more to be refuted. Perhaps this will be the achievement of G.B. Le Rider, whose surveys of this field in *Annuaire de l'École Pratique*, 1968/9, 1969/70 have unfortunately been unavailable to me. On the role of coinage in antiquity, Dr M.H. Crawford, JRS (1970), p. 40 has some especially interesting comments.

B. MACEDONIA

i. GENERAL BACKGROUND

S. Casson, *Macedonia, Thrace and Illyria* (1926)
M. Delacoulonche, *Mèmoire sur le berceau de la puissance macédonienne* (1858)
M. Dimitsas, *He Makedonia en lithois phthengomenois* (1896)
N.G.L. Hammond, *Epirus* (1967)
L.A. Heuzey and L. Daumet, *Le Mont Olympe et l'Acarnanie* (1860)
—— *Mission Archéologique en Macédoine* (1876)
Colonel W.M. Leake, *Travels in Northern Greece* (1835)
A. Struck, *Makedonische Fahrten, I and II: Zur Kunde der Balkan Halbinsel. Reise und Beobachtungen*, nos. 4, 7 (1907/8)

ii. EVIDENCE

Inscriptiones Graecae, vol. x, covering inscriptions found in Macedonia, although stones found in ports like Thessalonica may have arrived from elsewhere
J.N. Kalleris, *Les anciens macédoniens* (1954): a dictionary of Macedonian words
I.I. Russou, *Ephemeris Dacoromana* (1938): a collection of Macedonian names
Arnold Toynbee: *Some Problems in Greek History* (1969): conjectural account of early Macedonian history

iii. ARCHAEOLOGICAL STUDIES

A vast bibliography of most excavations this century can be consulted in the periodical

Makedonika (1966/7), pp. 277ff., followed up in subsequent issues. The equally useful annual *Balkan Studies* is a good introduction, its volume for 1962 containing a survey of the field. Here I single out a few articles of special interest; we are not yet able to trace the origins of Macedonia's material culture (though the tradition of a Phrygian invasion may be one clue: the so-called 'Macedonian' tombs have parallels at Gordium, the Phrygian capital), nor can we single out Macedonian features, if any, in the spread of hellenism through Asia (though the main building at Ai Khanum already shows some interesting similarities to the palace at Vergina). D.M. Robinson, *Excavations at Olynthus*, especially vols. ii and x, remains the essential comparison.

M. Andronicos, *Bergina* (1969)
—— BCH (1955), p. 87: funeral stelai from Vergina
C.F. Edson, CP (1951), p. 1: route of the Via Egnatia
    Hesperia (1949), p. 78: tomb of Olympias, with inscriptions
B. Kallipolitis, *Arch. Ephem.* (1948/9), pp. 85ff.: late fifth-century finds at Kozani
A.E. Keramopoullos, *Arch. Ephem.* (1932), p. 32: finds in Upper Macedonia
—— PAE (1940), stilt village at Kastoria
G.P. Oikonomos, *Ath. Mitt.* (1926), pp. 80ff.; bronzes from Pella
P. Perdrizet, BCH (1898), pp. 335ff.: Macedonian tombs
Ph. Petsas, *Balkan Studies* (1963), pp. 150ff.: Pella

Of the brief notices of finds given yearly in the BCH *Chronique des fouilles* and the *Archaeologikon Deltion*, the following are of interest: BCH (1965), pp. 808–10 (bronze bowl, papyrus and armour at Derveni), (1966), p. 864 (walls of Dion), p. 867 (Mieza), p. 871 (Pella). *Archaeol. Deltion* 16 (1960), pp. 72ff. discusses Pella, 1957–60; 21 (1966), Chronik, p. 344 notes fourth-century tombs at Edessa, not however of a size to suit the royal graves at Aigai, misplaced there.

C. PERSIA

i. GENERAL BACKGROUND

Gertrude Bell, *Persian Pictures* (1894)
Cambridge History of Iran, vol. i (1968): geographical
G.N. Curzon, *Persia and the Persian Question* (1892)
R.N. Frye, *The Heritage of Persia* (1963)
Anne Lambton, *Landlord and Peasant in Persia* (1953)
A.T. Olmstead, *History of the Persian Empire* (1948)
G. Rawlinson, *The Fifth Oriental Monarchy* (1876)
E.H. Schafer, *The Golden Peaches of Samarkand* (1963)
Lt J. Wood, *A Journey to the Sources of the River Oxus* (1872)

ii. NATIVE DOCUMENTS

(a) In Old Persian, a language probably inherited from the Medes and used only for the official inscriptions of the kings until *c.* 460; Alexander's court would speak Middle Persian. J. Duchesne-Guillemin surveys all but the most recent work here in *Kratylos* (1963), pp. 1ff.
W. Brandenstein, *Wiener Zeitschr. für die Kunde Süd-und Ostasiens* (1964), p. 43: old Persian in Aristophanes
W. Eilers, *Beitr. zur Namenforschung* (1964), p. 180: study of the name Cyrus
W. Hinz, ZDMG (1963), p. 231; *Orientalia* (1967), p. 327; improvements in Bisitun text
R.G. Kent, *Old Persian Grammar, Texts and Lexicon* (2nd edn, 1953)
R. Schmitt, ZDMG. (1967), p. 27: Median and Persian in Herodotus

(b) Babylonian

G. Cardascia, *Les Archives des Murasu* (1951): full supporting bibliography

(c) Elamite

G.G. Cameron, *Persepolis Treasury Tablets* (1948)

—— JNES (1958). p. 161, (1965), p. 167: more treasury evidence

R.T. Hallock, *Persepolis Fortification Tablets* (1969): vital, but sparse, new sources

W. Hinz, ZDMG (1960), p. 236: another survey

(d) Aramaic: a small selection

R.A. Bowman, *Aramaic Ritual Texts from Persepolis* (1970)

E. Bresciani, 'Le lettere aramaiche di Hermopoli, *Atti del. Acc. Naz. dei Lincei* (1966), p. 357

A.E. Cowley, *Aramaic Papyri of the Fifth Century* B.C. (1923)

G.R. Driver, *Aramaic Documents* (2nd edn, 1957)

E. Kraeling, *Brooklyn Aramaic Papyri* (1953)

iii. SPECIAL STUDIES

L.T. Altbaum, B. Brentjes, *Die Wachter des Goldes* (1972)

F. Bergman, *Archaeological Researches in Sinkiang (Sino-Swedish Expedition,* 7), p. 120: an Iranian bow

P. Bernard, *Syria* (1964), p. 195, (1965), p. 272: horsemen and harness

M. Boyce, JRAS (1957), p. 10; Persian minstrelsy

—— JRAS (1966), p. 100, BSOAS (1969), p. 10, (1970), p. 22: Zoroaster

P.R.L. Brown, *The World of Late Antiquity* (1971), pp. 160ff.

M.A. Dandamayev, *Iran pri pervykh Akhemenidakh* (1963)

M. Echtecham, *L'Iran sous les Achéménides* (1946)

I. Gershevitch, BSOAS (1957), p. 317: wood at Susa

R. Ghirshman, *Un Village perse—achéménide* (1954)

G. Gropp, *Archaeol. Mitt. Iran* (1969), p. 147: fire-temples

E. Herzfeld, *The Persian Empire* (1968)

W. Hinz, ZDMG (1960), p. 236: stability of prices

S.V. Kisselev, *Artibus Asiae* (1951), p. 169: cavalry

B. Laufer, *Sino-Iranica*, with special reference to plants (1919)

—— *Felt How it was made and used* (1937)

R. Lyddeker, *Wild Oxen Sheep and Goats of All Lands* (1898)

M. Nicol, *Iran* (1967), pp. 137–8: advance report on survey of the Royal Road

B.B. Porten, *Archives from Elephantine* (1968)

J.P. Roux, *Central Asiatic Journal* (1959), p. 27: the camel

E.H. Schafer, Iranian Merchants in Tang Dynasty Tales, in *Semitic and Oriental Studies Presented to William Popper* (1951), p. 403

K. Schippmann, *Iranischer Feuerheiligtumer* (1968)

D. Schlumberger, *L'Argent grec dans l'empire achéménide* (1953)

M.L. West, *Early Greek Philosophy and the Orient* (1971)

G. Widengren, *Festchr. L. Brandt* (1968), p. 323: feudalism

F. Willmann, *Rocznik.* (1951/2, 1953), p. 250: Anahita

Hellenism in Asia, especially among Iranians: the artistic remains are discussed with full bibliography in D. Schlumberger's excellent *L'Orient hellénisé* (1969). The Soviet excavations are most accessible to those who cannot read Russian in C.A. Frumkin's *Soviet Excavations in Central Asia* (1970) and his general survey in the Central Asian Review (1969); M.A.R. Colledge, *The Parthians* (1967) lists most of the literature for Parthian documents and Asian art in the Parthian period. M.I. Rostovtzeff, *Social and Economic History of the Hellenistic World* (1953) remains the outstanding sketch of the age; the briefer essay of A.H.M. Jones, *Past and Present* (1963), p. 1 is equally provocative. I only list here a few specialized studies, mostly not covered in these general works.

B. PALESTINE AND SYRIA

M. Avi-Yonah, *Oriental Art in Roman Palestine* (1961)
Comte du Mesnil du Buisson, *Études sur les dieux phoeniciens* (1970)
M. Hengel, *Judentum und Hellenismus* (1969)
B. Lifschitz, *Euphrosyne* (1970) p. 113: the spread of Greek in Palestine, a subject also discussed and, to my mind, exaggerated by M. Sevenster, *Do You Know Greek?* (1968).
H. Seyrig, *Syria* (1970), pp. 290ff.: a brilliant survey of certain effects of Seleucid rule.
J.B. Ward-Perkins, *Proc. Brit. Acad.* (1965), p. 175: so-called 'Parthian' art of Mesopotamia
C.B. Welles and others report on Dura Europos, the Excavations (1929 onwards) and
C.B. Welles summarizes one crucial point in The Population of Roman Dura, in Studies Presented to A.C. Johnson (1951), p. 251

B. BABYLON

A. Al-Hail, *Sumer* (1964), p. 103: the chemical cell
A. Aymard, *Une Ville seleucide de la Babylonie*, reprinted in his *Études d'hist. ancienne* (1967): a brilliant survey
R.A. Bowman, *Amer. Journ. Semit. Lang.* (1939), p. 235
G. Sarkisian, *Vestnik dreyney istorii* (1952), p. 68; (1953), p. 59. *Eos* (1956), p. 29
E. Unger, *Babylon, Die Heilige Stadt* (1931), esp. pp. 318–19 on Greek style in Babylon's decrees
The best study of Berossus and Greek and Babylonian astronomy is to be found in *Trans. Amer. Philosoph. Soc* for 1963; the most provocative study of hellenistic science is the essay by C. Préaux, in *Studies presented to C. B. Welles* (1966)

C. WESTERN IRANIANS

A.J. Festugière, *Symb. Oslo.* (1950), p. 89; Greek hymn at Susa
C. Habicht, *Hermes* (1953), p. 251: school text of Euripides in Armenia
G.B. Le Rider, *Suse sous les Seleucides et Parthes* (1965)
E.H. Minns, *JHS* (1915), p. 22: Greek documents from Avroman
H.S. Nyberg, *Le Monde oriental* (1923), p. 182: same documents
L. Robert, *Noms indigènes en Asie Mineure* (1963), esp. pp. 457ff. on hellenized Cappadocia
—— *Epistemonike Epeteris of the Philos. School at Athens* (1962), p. 520: Greeks at Susa
J. and L. Robert's, *Bulletin Épigraphique* (REG 1961), nr 819: Greek gymnastics. L. Robert, *Hellenica*, vol. 7, p. 7, vol. xi–xii, p. 8: Greek inscriptions in Iran

D. UPPER SATRAPIES

R.D. Barnett, *Iran. Antiqua* (p. 1968), 34: Oxus treasure
P. Bernard, *Syria* (1968), p. 111: Corinthian capitals at Ai-Khanum
—— *Syria* (1970), p. 327: ivory Achaemenid style thrones
E.J. Bickermann, *CP* (1952), p. 65: brilliant sketch of Greek approach to the east
A.D.H. Bivar, *JRAS* (1970), p. 65: Parthian ostraca in Iran
M. Boyce, *JRAS* (1957), p. 10: Iranian minstrelsy and the Parthians
M. Bussagli, *Riv. dell' Instit. naz. d'Archeol.* (1953), p. 171: Greek art in Central Asia
M.L. Chaumont, *Journ. As.* (1968), p. 16: Parthian ostraca

I.M. Diakonov, V.A. Livshitz, *Dokumenty iz Nisy* (1960)

I.M. Diakonov, V.A. Livshitz, *Sbornik I.A. Orbel* (1960): Iranian names at Nisa

—— *Materialy i issledovaniva po arkheolog. SSSR* (1950), p. 161: Charon's coins and Oxus nomads

R. Ghirshman, *Persian Art, the Parthians and Sassanids* (1962)

—— *Begram* (1946), esp. on the walls and water, for which cp. H. Fischer *Gnomon* (1966), p. 282

W.B. Henning, *Bull SAOS* (1960), p. 47; 'Mitteliranisch', in *Handbuch der Orientalistik* (ed. B. Spuler), 1958, p. 22: use of Aramaic in Seleucid Iran; cp. the Taxila inscription, the Chorasmian alphabet of the third century A.D. and Chinese evidence mentioned in A.J. Toynbee, *Between the Oxus and the Jumna* (1961)

E. Herzfeld, *Archaeological History of Iran* (1935)

—— *Iran in the Ancient East* (1941)

Sir John Marshall, *Taxila* (1951)

M.E. Masson, *VDI* (1951), p. 89; Greek city in Merv oasis; *VDI* (1954), p. 159: Greek seal-stones at Nisa; *VDI* (1955), p. 42: lack of small-change coinage in finds in Iran before the second century A.D.

M.E. Masson, G.A. Pugachenkova: *Parfansky ritony Nisy* (1965)

E.H. Minns, *JHS* (1943), p. 123: review of K.V. Trever, as below

A.L. Mongait, *Archaeology in the USSR* (1961, pelican ed.), esp. pp. 239ff. on nomads statuettes

G.A. Pugachenkova, *VDI* (1952), p. 26: Merv

G.A. Pugachenkova, *VDI* (1951), p. 128: vase from Termez

—— *Iran. Antiqua* (1965): Greek art at Khaltchayan

B. Rowland, *The Art Quarterly* (1955), p. 174: Hellenistic sculpture in Iran

W.W. Tarn, *Greeks in Bactria and India* (1951): to be used extremely critically

S.P. Tolstov, *Iran. Antiqua* (1961): report on Khwarezm in French

—— *Po drevnim deltam Oksa: Jakarta* (1962), esp. pp. 125ff.: nomads' ossuaries

K.V. Trever, *Pamyatniki greko-baktribskovo iskusstva* (1940)

L. van den Berghe, *Archéol. de l'Iran ancien* (1959)

K. Weitzmann, *The Art Bulletin* (1943), p. 289: Euripides on Bactrian silver

M. Wheeler, *Flames over Persepolis* (1968): Indo-Greek material

Far the most important evidence are the Asoka inscriptions, first discussed by L. Robert and others in *Journ. Asiat.* (1958), pp. 1ff. and the finds at Ai Khanum, regularly reported in *Compte Rendu de l'Acad. des Inscript. et Belles Lettres*, from 1964 onwards. The reports by P. Bernard and D. Schlumberger in *BCH* (1965) and by P. Bernard in *Proc. Brit. Acad.* (1967) are important; the finest study, however, is by L. Robert, *CRAI* (1968), 'Des Delphes à l'Oxus', p. 416 citing the whole range of Greek inscriptional evidence. The theme of the Trojan horse has now turned up at Ai Khanum, explaining its presence in Gandharan art; there are hints of the knowledge of Greek myth in the Swat highlands in the many Italian finds there, reported in *East and West* from 1960 onwards. The Ceylon inscriptions naming Homer and Greek sages are discussed by S. Paranavitana, *The Greeks and the Mauryas* (1971).

We must hope for great things from Ai Khanum; its site on the south bank of the Oxus does not rule it out as Alexandria-in-Sogdia; Darius I's great Susa building inscription refers to lapis lazuli from Sogdia, not Bactria. The lapis mines were on the Kokcha river, like Ai Khanum, which stood, therefore, in Sogdia too.

INDEX

Abdalonymus, King, 180
Abu Dhahir, 228
Achilles, 44, 59–62, 64–7, 112–15, 122, 155, 168, 193, 215, 216, 313
Achilles the Athenian, 223
Ada, Queen of Caria, 135, 136, 139, 176, 405
Admetus, 190
Adriatic Sea, 17, 84, 90
Aegean Sea, 26, 102, 134, 178, 189, 198
Aeolia, 129, 130
Aeropus, 37
Aeschines, ambassador, 46
Aeschylus, 48, 94
Aetion, painter, 317
Afghanistan, 50, 63, 101, 200, 267, 279, 292, 314, 482
Africa, 75
Agamemnon, King, 60, 63, 64, 65
Agathocles, 480
Agathon, dramatist, 48
Aghurmi, 207
Agis, King of Sparta, 185, 199, 223–4, 226, 252, 454
Ahriman, 152
Ahura Mazda, 99, 152, 213, 229, 257, 273
Aigai 19, 20, 26, 30, 31, 36, 39, 68
Aisopus, R., 119
Ajax, 112, 114
Albania, 34
Alcetas, 431
Alcibiades, 322
Alexander the Great: early life, 18, 20, 22–8, 31–66; and army, 68–73, 75, 77, 79–80; in Thrace, 81–90; background to Persian campaign, 91–6, 98–104; Troy, 109, 111–15; battle at Granicus, 116–24; frees Asian cities, 126–36; siege of Halicarnassus, 137–42; at Phaselis and Gordium, 143–51; moves against Darius, 152–6, 158, 160–7; battle at Issus, 168–77; at

Tyre and Gaza, 178, 180–93; to Egypt, 194–218; seeks out Darius, 219–32; battle at Gaugamela, 233–42; at Babylon and Susa, 244–56; Persepolis, 258–64; heir to Darius's empire, 267–78; conspiracy with Parmenion and Philotas, 279–91; at Balkh, 292–307; and Cleitus, 308–314; marriage to Roxane, 315–19; and Callisthenes, 320–30; invades India, 331–49; battle against Porus, 351–62; retreat, 363–72; siege of Multan, 375–380; plans new expedition, 381–6; Makran and Kirman, 387–402; Susa, 403–20; Hamadan, 421–35; deification, 436–60; death, 461–72; aftermath, 473–98
Alexander IV, s. of Alexander, 474
Alexander, King of Epirus, 20, 90, 164, 278
Alexander, Prince of Lyncestis, 36, 37, 40, 86, 145, 146, 164, 285, 288, 463
Alexandretta, 177
Alexandria, 66, 182, 198, 199, 200, 204, 205, 212, 213, 221
Alexandropolis, 42
Alexarchus, 446
Alinda, 136
Amasis, Pharaoh, 202
Ambhi, rajah, 339, 347, 351, 360, 404
Ammon, god, 200–8, 210, 211, 214, 216, 217, 219, 222, 224, 376, 385, 401, 443, 444, 446, 451–2, 456, 458, 476
Amphoterus, 153
Amritsar, 371, 372
Amun, god, 197, 201–4, 208–9, 212, 213, 221
Amyntas III, 38, 165, 166, 175, 194, 195, 284
Amyntas III, King of Macedonia, 53, 440

561